Occult Encyclopedia

of Magic Squares

Planetary Angels and Spirits
of Ceremonial Magick

Ishtar Publishing
Vancouver
www.ishtarpublishing.com

OCCULT ENCYCLOPEDIA OF MAGIC SQUARES:
PLANETARY ANGELS AND SPIRITS OF CEREMONIAL MAGICK
AN ISHTAR PUBLISHING BOOK:
978-1-926667-09-6

PRINTING HISTORY
Ishtar Publishing edition published 2009

1 3 5 7 9 10 8 6 4 2

CONTENTS   PAGES

PREFACE

You are probably wondering what you could possibly do with a book that consists of hundreds of magic squares. How would you use such knowledge in your life today to bring about tangible benefits? The short answer is to use them like private phone calling cards to attract immense spiritual power into your life. What this book will give you that no other English book has given you before is the precise numbers to dial.

Let me explain…

As far as secular science is concerned, magic squares are nothing more than mathematical curiosity. They just are with no deeper meaning or cosmic aim. They are patterns that occur and serve no purpose besides stimulating our minds with their simplicity and ingenuity. Kind of like an ancient form of Sudoku.

Those who adhere to an esoteric belief system rooted in antiquity believe otherwise. Ancient sages influenced by the teachings of the like of Pythagoras of Samos believed that numbers and geometry hold within them the keys to nature. They are expressions of a Divine mind, a Universal Architect or Geometer. Numbers contain deep mystical meanings and powers that we can awaken and reawaken. In this cosmic view, magic squares are numerical illustrations of deep cosmic principles. They are magnets to spiritual forces.

You will find magic squares part of any serious book on talismanic magic dating back centuries. Most of those books will give you the same patterned squares and often no more than seven.

There is only one problem with this. If that is all you have, then you have a phone without a number to dial. The basic patterns are powerful in their own right, but using them is more like dialing an operator without having a party in mind.

This is what makes this book so unique. You now have specific numbers and extensions to enable you to connect with more than one hundred and sixty distinct spiritual beings that rule over the astrological tides. By using these magic squares in magical rituals, you can enlist the aid of these beings to help you along your spiritual evolution. For example:

- You do not have to be at the mercy of bad communications when Mercury goes retrograde. This could mean the difference between keeping your job and losing it.
- You can overcome difficulties in finding stable relationships due to afflictions of Saturn in the seventh house.
- You can improve your own intuitive connections or even strengthen any latent psychic powers.
- Your strengthened spiritual connections with angelic beings will guide you and open you to higher states of spiritual well being and inner peace.

I do not expect you to take my word for it. Just consider this: If I am right, can we agree on the tremendous potential available? I hope so. I hope you benefit from this gift and it becomes a valuable asset in your spiritual kit.

I have a confession to make before we go on.

I did not set out to write this book as a practical workbook filled with magical formulas. I know there is a drought of books on the practical applications of magic squares. I intend for the practical magic aspect to be a book in its own right.

What I did set out to do in this series, was to create a sourcebook for practitioners of the sacred magical arts, kabbalists, Hermetics and scholars of the mysteries. What you are holding in your hands is an occult encyclopedia in the true sense. It contains exhaustive magic square listings filled with all the association, aspects, correspondence you may need in your cosmic connections.

In this first volume, I have focused on the angels and spirits of the planets and Zodiacal signs. I am familiar with more than one classical system of correspondences. For this book, I have chosen to use the one familiar to the students of the Golden Dawn system and its offshoots, due to its widespread familiarity in modern occult circles. I hope to provide the same treatment for classical systems rooted in Arabic and Hebrew grimoires in the next volumes.

Enjoy...

QUICK GUIDE TO MAGIC SQUARES

Kamea is the word most commonly used in Western occult circles to refer to magic squares. It is a Hebrew word, which means talisman or amulet. The Arabic word used to describe magic squares is al-Wifeq, which carries a similar meaning.

The typical magic square consists of a grid that forms at minimum three columns and three rows for a total of nine cell squares. The values in those cell squares, if added vertically, horizontally, or diagonally, must match for it to be a correct magic square.

There are four main types of magic squares:

- NUMERICAL: consists only of a sequence of numbers
- ALPHABETICAL NUMERICAL: consists of digits represented by their equivalent letters
- ALPHABETICAL: consists only of letters and of different type than alphabetical numerical
- ALPHANUMERICAL: combines both numbers and letters.

Each of the aforementioned variations of magic squares has its own application in magic. Numbers are to letters as souls are to bodies. Numerical and alphabetical numerical magic squares are effective for evoking the corresponding force in the material world. Numerical, alphabetical, and alphanumerical squares are very useful when working with angelic or celestial beings. We will be focusing on the numerical, alphabetical, and alphanumerical squares in this book, since we are working with angelic and spiritual forces.

Here is an example of both basic numerical and alphabetical numerical magic squares:

ד	ט	ב
ג	ה	ז
ה	א	ו

4	9	2
3	5	7
8	1	6

In this example, the Hebrew letters on the right have the same numerological values as their corresponding cell squares on the left. By addition of numbers, you can see that each column, row, and diagonal direction adds up to fifteen.

15	15	15	15
15	4	9	2
15	3	5	7
15	8	1	6
15			

The same is true if we replace the letters with their corresponding numerological range values. In the Hebrew alphabet, the first letter or Aleph (א) has the value of one, as it is the first letter of the alphabet just like one is the first number. The second letter has value of two and so forth. Once you reach the eleventh letter, the values progress in units of ten and then hundreds. The first nine letters of the Hebrew alphabet correspond to the nine numerical digits.

15	15	15	15
15	ד (4)	ט (9)	ב (2)
15	ג (3)	ה (5)	ז (7)
15	ח (8)	א (1)	ו (6)
15			

Quick Guide To Magic Squares

Hebrew Letter	Large Range Values
א	1
ב	2
ג	3
ד	4
ה	5
ו	6
י	7
ח	8
ט	9
י	10
כ	20
ל	30
מ	40
נ	50
ס	60
ע	70
פ	80
צ	90
ק	100
ר	200
ש	300
ת	400

Now, here is an example of both alphabetical and alphanumerical magic squares:

ל	א	י	ג	ד
י	ג	ד	ל	א
ד	ל	א	י	ג
א	י	ג	ד	ל
ג	ד	ל	א	י

אל	י	ג	ד
3	51	13	28
12	29	2	52
49	5	30	11

The alphabetical magic square consists of permutations of a word or phrase to form a pattern similar to the properties of the numeric magic squares. You will find that the same letters used in the word are in different order but without repetition or subtraction in each column, row, and diagonal line.

I inserted the digits one to five in the grid to make it easier to follow the permutation of the letters from row to row. The sequence starts at the right side, because we write Hebrew from right to left.

5ל	4א	3י	2ג	1ד
3י	2ג	1ד	5ל	4א
1ד	5ל	4א	3י	2ג
4א	3י	2ג	1ד	5ל
2ג	1ד	5ל	4א	3י

The alphabetical magic square has limitations. Some magic squares sizes do not work. In those cases, even if you get the horizontal and vertical permutations to work, the diagonal lines repeat some of the letters twice. We know there is no square for a size 3 by 3. It is also still unknown if it is possible to create a square sized 9 by 9. It would take a computer program on a multi-processor server hundreds of millions of tries to run through every possible computation, before any conclusion was possible.

The alphanumeric square tries to combine the previous kinds of squares into one. I have rarely seen larger grid sizes in old manuscripts. Some of the oldest references to it are in the writing of the 12th century master occultist al-Buni. It is rarely used in practical occultism and what uses I have seen were in association with Divine names.

The first row in the alphanumerical square consists of letters that spell out a particular name, often angelic or Divine. You can group the letters of the name together or keep them separated. These letters count as numbers even if written in letter format. The rest of the numbers consist of additions and subtractions to the numerical values of the first row as in the following example:

95	95	95	95	95	95
95	31 אל	10 י	50 נ	4 ר	
95	(4-1) 3	(50+1) 51	(10+3) 13	(31-3) 28	
95	(10+2) 12	(31-2) 29	(4-2) 2	(50+2) 52	
95	(50-1) 49	(4+1) 5	(31-1) 30	(10+1) 11	

Going through the various types, you will probably conclude that numerical squares are the most popular in the modern Western world. This stems from reliance on European sources such as the early 16th century Agrippa's Three Books of Occult Philosophy versus much older texts found in the Near East, in which various magic squares played a prominent role.

It is my hope that we will begin to see a wider utilization of alternate structures of magic squares with the introduction of these ancient teachings into modern occult vernacular.

General and Specific Squares

Imagine for a moment that you have managed to gain entry into one of the established occult lodges in the West. You are sitting across from a figure with the title of an adept. You go on politely about wanting to create a talisman for the intelligence of Saturn, Agial, and searching for a magic square most suited for the job.

I am betting you will end up with the following square as that adept's recommendation:

4	9	2
3	5	7
8	1	6

You ask again about the proper square to use for the spirit of Saturn, Arathron.

I would bet on the following square as the answer that you would receive:

4	9	2
3	5	7
8	1	6

You will most likely get the same answer repeatedly, as long as you keep asking about anything remotely associated with Saturn. Many modern Western mystery schools provide their initiates with only seven squares. These are widely familiar due to their association with the seven classical planets used in occultism.

Now, let us take a trip back in a time machine and sit down with a classical wizard of the ancient world. You ask politely about the creation of a talisman for the intelligence of Saturn, Agial.

I believe you would get the following square as being most suited for the job:

14	19	12
13	15	17
18	11	16

Quick Guide To Magic Squares

You ask again about the proper square to use for the spirit of Saturn, Arathron.

I would bet on the following square as the answer that you would receive:

287	282	289
288	286	284
283	290	285

You might notice a few things right away, so my apologies if I am pointing out the obvious. You will see that both squares are 3 by 3 in size and that both squares follow the traditional pattern presented earlier in this chapter. Quick math will show that the first square the classical magician presented would add up to the value 45, which happens to be the numerological value of the word Agial. The second square the ancient adept presented adds to the value 858, which is the numerological value of Arathron.

The general pattern squares familiar to modern occultists are raw plates. They are primordial in form. They are something you would want to use when working the essence of the planets and their corresponding spiritual forces. You need to make that square very specific when you want to work with specific spiritual beings or have a specific purpose in mind or would like to channel this energy to a particular person.

I find it disheartening that very few modern magicians seem cognizant of this classical principle of the art. Think of the general pattern square as the area code of a country. You get hold of an operator when you use it. You will still need to know the actual number you are dialing or make the effort to ask the operator to connect you. For hundreds of years people in the West have kept dialing the area code, while their Near Eastern colleagues dialed individual numbers.

Most modern magicians would argue for the effectiveness of their approach, because general patterns are raw magnets. They are also relying heavily on either the power of belief or their own personal energy to charge the square. That may be so, but imagine if that raw force was laser-focused. Imagine how stronger your belief becomes when it is specific versus being general in nature.

All the squares provided to you in this book are specific in nature. This will save you a tremendous amount of time in calculating ones you may need for your occult working.

It is stated in the Emerald Tablet of Hermes that things found in the above and things found in the below are parallel. The author of this sublime piece of Hermetic literature was hinting at astrology. The astral plane of the ancients is the realm of the planets and stars. It is the Mazloth of the Kabbalah or the heavenly sphere of the Zodiac. The Emerald Tablet is one of the oldest documents outlining the ancient belief in astrological correspondence.

The most basic of all astrological correspondences are those between the planets and the geometrical shapes and numbers. For example, I mentioned earlier how the magic square of 3 by 3 corresponds to Saturn in modern and classical occult teachings. Saturn corresponds to the third emanation in the cosmic diagram used in the Kabbalah known as the Tree of Life. It is the first planet used in the ancient Near Eastern order that originated in Babylon. The three by three square is the first magic square.

Planet	Size
Saturn	3 x 3
Jupiter	4 x 4
Mars	5 x 5
Sun	6 x 6
Venus	7 x 7
Mercury	8 x 8
Moon	9 x 9

Today, modern astrologers recognize the newly discovered planets. This has led modern occult thinkers to extend their associations of magic squares to new planets. Initially, it seems to make sense since Western occultism primarily focuses on only seven magic squares. This leaves many larger squares available for new associations. In actuality, these squares are not free of associations, as the ancients simply restarted the cycle. Applying them to different planets would require a re-evaluation of classical thinking. Here is a brief list of associations between the planets and some of the larger squares:

Quick Guide To Magic Squares

Planet	Size
Saturn	3x3, 10x10, 17x17, 24x24, 31x31, 38x38, 45x45, 52x52, 59x59, 66x66, 73x73, 80x80, 87x87, 94x94
Jupiter	4x4, 11x11, 18x18, 25x25, 32x32, 39x39, 46x46, 53x53, 60x60, 67x67, 74x74, 81x81, 88x88, 95x95
Mars	5x5, 12x12, 19x19, 26x26, 33x33, 40x40, 47x47, 54x54, 61x61, 68x68, 75x75, 82x82, 89x89, 96x96
Sun	6x6, 13x13, 20x20, 27x27, 34x34, 41x41, 48x48, 55x55, 62x62, 69x69, 76x76, 83x83, 90x90, 97x97
Venus	7x7, 14x14, 21x21, 28x28, 35x35, 42x42, 49x49, 56x56, 63x63, 70x70, 77x77, 84x84, 91x91, 98x98
Mercury	8x8, 15x15, 22x22, 29x29, 36x36, 43x43, 50x50, 57x57, 64x64, 71x71, 78x78, 85x85, 92x92, 99x99
Moon	9x9, 16x16, 23x23, 30x30, 37x37, 44x44, 51x51, 58x58, 65x65, 72x72, 79x79, 86x86, 93x93, 100x100

In this table, I stopped at 100 x 100, but I could go on indefinitely. You will find that, based on this system of association, a 49 x 49 square corresponds with Venus, as it should. You will also find that the ultimate magic square, which I covered in Magic Squares and the Tree of Life, sized 100 x 100, corresponds with the Moon, as it should. Adding the extra planets into this mix and rearranging the structure, as some modern authors champion, would throw the whole system off.

You probably will use very few of the larger squares in your occult practice, even though some of them possess unique ability. Still, there is one particular case where they are extremely useful. There are numbers that you cannot insert without fractions into some of the smaller squares such as the square 3x3, as we did with Agial and Arathron. In those cases, I would use one of the larger squares, such as 10x10, that share the same planetary correspondence as the smaller square. I have done this several times in this book. I have not exceeded the 10x10 size due to the space limitations in a book of this kind, not to mention the limited surface on most magicians' tools.

You will also find some numbers that are too small to fit into a 10x10 or larger square and cannot fit into a square such as a 3x3. In a case like this, you can work with a square size whose planet is harmonious to your planet of focus such as 5x5 (Mars), as Mars is a friend of Saturn, or 8x8 (Mercury), as Mercury can take on multiple natures, being malefic with a malefic and benefic with a benefic.

In all honesty, you do not have to limit yourself to only one size per name. You can have multiple squares, possibly even all of the seven planetary ones for a given number. This opens the door for working with very focused energies of a given spiritual being, including angels associated with the planets and signs of the Zodiac. This would be a case of sub-planetary focus. As we have Earth of Air, we can have Mercury of Venus.

We have done exactly that in this book. You will find all possible squares from 3x3 up to 10x10 calculated and provided for all entries listed. This way you can work any sub-planetary force for any name and given purpose.

To sum it up:

- There are infinite numbers of magic squares for each of the seven ancient planets.
- The smallest size square is the best choice for general working.
- You can use larger squares for their own unique properties. Some of those properties were passed down via old manuscripts, but most we have to discover on our own.
- You can use one of the larger squares to replace one of the smaller squares of the same planetary correspondence.
- You can have all the planetary squares for a single entity or purpose. This is just like how the seven planets appear and influence a person in their astrological chart, regardless of that person's dominant Sun sign or Ascendant.

Magic Squares – Elemental Attributes

Anomalies! Anomalies! One modern occult author referred to magic squares arranged differently from the ones listed in the Three Books of Occult Philosophy as anomalies because, in her opinion, they are unorthodox. In actuality, they are very orthodox, as long as you accept that the knowledge and history of magic squares date back much further than the 16th century Agrippa. Why am I bringing this up? I am doing so because dismissing these variations can inadvertently lead to dismissing an important principle in classical teachings on magic squares. One of the key reasons for the variation in the numbering sequence of magic squares has to do with their correspondence to the four Elements. I have included two samples from the same manuscript showcasing the antiquity of the correspondence between the Elements and the magic squares.

ادخال الكسر فيه و وجدت ذلك مرسوماً و يرفع عن شيخنا
العالم الفقيه عبد الله بن هداد النزي رحمه الله ● وهذه
صفته الثلاثي على الطبايع الاربع و الروح الاثني عشر وخواصه

غزرائل			جبرائل			ميكائل		وهو اسافل	
٤	٩	٢	٦	٧	٢	٢	٧	٦	٨ ١ ٦
٣	٥	٧	١	٥	٩	٩	٥	١	٣ ٥ ٧
٨	١	٦	٨	٣	٤	٤	٣	٨	٤ ٩ ٣

ناري شرقي حار يابس	هوائي غربي حار رطب	مائي جنوبي بارد رطب	ترابي شمالي بارد يابس
للقبول والوجه	للتسخين والجلب	لاستجلاب الرزق	للتفريق والعداوة والسجن
الحمل ذكر	الجوزاء ذكر	السرطان انثى	الغور انثى
الاسد ذكر	الميزان ذكر	العقرب انثى	السنبلة انثى
القوس ذكر	الدلو ذكر	الحوت انثى	الجدي انثى

والعزيمة التي تتلى عند وضع الحروف في بيت كل حرف تتلى عليه
اسماؤه سبع مرات و يكون البخور على النار وهو اللبنك
الجاوي او ما شاء الله من الطيب ● فعند وضع الواحد تقول
الوهيم الوهيم آة آة آة ايه ايه افشال اظرشا ● وعند
وضع الباء تقول بقطريال قطريال بدهيال دهيال
بشهروش ● وعند وضع الجيم جليش جليش جه جه
جمر وشح ● وعند وضع الدال دهيال دهيال دلو لا
دلو لا دهمر وشد ● وعند وضع الهاء هططوش

وتسير في باقي البيوت بزيادة واحد الى ان يتم الوفق
وهي هذه

رباحي				ترابي				مائي				ناري			
١	١٤	١١	٨	١٥	٤	٩	١٠	١٠	٥	٤	١٤	٨	١١	١٤	١
١٢	٧	٢	١٣	٦	٩	٥	٣	٣	١٦	٩	٦	١٣	٢	٧	١٥
٦	٩	١٦	٣	١٢	٧	٣	١٣	١٣	٣	٧	١٢	٣	١٦	٩	٦
١٥	٤	٥	١٠	١	١٤	١١	٨	٨	١١	١٤	١	١٠	٥	٤	١٥

يضرب في شرف عطارد او يومه وساعته في الفضة او في
الرصاص لرفع الجدري وغيرذلك من الامراض والشرح وطرق
اخرى وما ذكرناه كفاية ۞ القول على الوفق الخامس وهو من
اقسام الزهرة وشكلها والعمل ان تكون الزهرة في بيتها او
شرفها ويومها وساعتها مسعودة بنظر السعود من التسديس
او التثليث والتسديس اولى ولحسن ذلك ان تكون في نظر
المشتري والشمس من تسديس او تثليث وعدده لح ع وضعه
بتقوان يكون اسم الله ديان او اسم مكة وغايت الكرسيه
اربعة فاذاكانت الكرسيه واحدا فيكون في بين
الحادي والعشرين واذاكانت اثنين فيكون في
بيت السادس عشر واذاكانت ثلاثة ففي الحادي عشر
واذاكانت اربعة ففي بيت السادس وهذه صورته

Quick Guide To Magic Squares

It would have been inconceivable to lock the Elements out of the art of magic squares, considering their importance in classical occultism. The four Elements are Fire (hot and dry), Air (hot and moist), Water (cold and moist) and Earth (cold and dry). Just as the size of the grid determines the association between a magic square and one of the seven classical planets, the direction of its internal numbering determines its association with the four Elements.

The table in the first manuscript page translates as follows:

Azrael	Michael	Israfel	Gabriel
4 9 2 3 5 7 8 1 6	6 7 2 1 5 9 8 3 4	2 7 6 9 5 1 4 3 8	8 1 6 3 5 7 4 9 2
Earthly, Northern, Cold and Dry	Watery, Southern, Cold and Moist	Aerial, Western, Hot and Moist	Fiery, Eastern, Hot and Dry
Separation, Betrayal, and Imprisonment	Bringing of Prosperity	Arousing of Passion and Attraction	Being well received and respected
Taurus Female	Cancer Female	Gemini Male	Aries Male
Virgo Female	Scorpio Female	Libra Male	Leo Male
Capricorn Female	Pisces Female	Aquarius Male	Sagittarius Male

The second manuscript page contains the following table:

Aerial				Earthy				Watery				Fiery			
1	14	11	8	15	4	5	10	10	5	4	15	8	11	14	1
12	7	2	13	6	9	16	3	3	16	9	6	13	2	7	12
6	9	16	3	12	7	2	13	13	2	7	12	3	12	9	6
15	4	5	10	1	14	11	8	8	11	14	1	10	5	4	15

You will note a discrepancy between the two tables when it comes to association between numbering direction and the Elements. For those unfamiliar with ancient manuscripts or for those who take such ancient writing as sacred relics, they will find this confusing and may even end up with a bruised head or a self-inflicted bald spot.

The truth of the matter is that handwritten manuscripts do regularly contain some errors and, more often than not, authors bound by secrecy switched information around to hide their secrets from those without a teacher. This is why it is critical not to follow the instructions of any grimoire verbatim, without due analysis and comparison with other texts. Aware of their intentional omissions, many old writers advocated finding a teacher who could help the novice fill in the blanks.

Let me help decode the discrepancy of the two tables. You will notice the first table is more comprehensive than the second is. The author has provided you with important aspects of the attribution linking the square with the Elements and the Zodiacal signs. The astrological information is correct. Classical texts use the Elemental sequence Fire-Air-Water-Earth, based on the alchemical weight of the Elements.

Notice the location of the number one in each of those four squares. The first square has number one in the center of the top row and corresponds to Fire. The second square has number one on the right and corresponds to Air. It appears the author is moving in a clockwise direction, so in the next square we would expect the number one to be at the bottom. The author does not do this; instead it is on the left, with the next one on the bottom.

The second table contains the Elemental sequence Fire-Water-Earth-Air, which is rarely if ever used in classical occultism. Yet, the sequence of the number one as you move through the squares is clockwise. The discrepancy is the author's way of leaving us a clue. Replace the Elemental sequence of the second table with that of the first table and the magic squares of the first table with that of the second table. We will now have the correct tables:

Quick Guide To Magic Squares

Azrael	Michael	Israfel	Gabriel
4 9 2 3 5 7 8 1 6	4 9 2 3 5 7 8 1 6	2 7 6 9 5 1 4 3 8	8 1 6 3 5 7 4 9 2
Earthly, Northern, Cold and Dry	Watery, Southern, Cold and Moist	Aerial, Western, Hot and Moist	Fiery, Eastern, Hot and Dry
Separation, Betrayal, and Imprisonment	Bringing of Prosperity	Arousing of Passion and Attraction	Being well received and respected
Taurus Female	Cancer Female	Gemini Male	Aries Male
Virgo Female	Scorpio Female	Libra Male	Leo Male
Capricorn Female	Pisces Female	Aquarius Male	Sagittarius Male

Earthly				Watery				Aerial				Fiery			
1	14	11	8	15	4	5	10	10	5	4	15	8	11	14	1
12	7	2	13	6	9	16	3	3	16	9	6	13	2	7	12
6	9	16	3	12	7	2	13	13	2	7	12	3	12	9	6
15	4	5	10	1	14	11	8	8	11	14	1	10	5	4	15

Astrologers reading this book may be wondering why we are using Fire-Air-Water-Earth when there is a profound link between magic squares and the planets. In astrology, the Elemental sequence is as follows: Fire-Earth-Air-Water. I believe the reason for this boils down to personal preference. In classical magic, I have seen the alchemical weight and the natural astrological sequence used interchangeably in classical magic for many techniques.

Personally, I am in favor of using the astrological arrangement. I like to keep things harmonious and simple. I have used this arrangement throughout the book. You will notice a header like this: Fire-Saturn over a square to indicate its connection with the Element and the Planet. Should you desire to use the alchemical arrangement listed in the quoted manuscript, simply switch the correspondence in your mind. The squares themselves remain valid. However, I would urge you to try the classical astrological elemental correspondences, for I have found them more effective.

We can achieve powerful results by focusing on a particular Elemental version of a square. This is true even when working with a planetary energy. For example, the Earth of Jupiter might be more suited for your next prosperity talisman than Water of Jupiter, especially if your business involves agriculture.

MAGIC SQUARES AND MYSTICISM OF NUMBERS

Magic squares are, in the end, a collection of numbers. Our understanding of magic squares will never be complete without deeper awareness of the metaphysical nature of numbers. All numbers consist of the first nine digits, so the ancients wove them into their cosmology.

ONE: This number represents the beginning of all things. In effect, all numbers are manifestations of one. Some ancients even argued against counting one as a number, as it is the source of numbers. It is the initial impulse and the sum of all things. It is unity of the Godhead made manifest and the symbol of wisdom.

TWO: The number two represents polarity and duality. By the power of the duad, the deep was created as a mirror to the heaven above. It symbolized ignorance, but the Pythagoreans also called it the mother of wisdom.

THREE: It is the first equilibrium of unities. It represents peace, prudence, temperance, friendship and it is the cause of wisdom and understanding. The ancients considered the triad sacred, because it contains the monad and the duad in perfect balance and harmony.

FOUR: It represents the root of all things, the fountain of nature, and connects all things in nature.

FIVE: It is the sacred symbol of light, vitality and health. It symbolizes the fifth element ether. Sometimes we refer to it as the Hierophant or the priest of the mysteries, due to its spiritual connection.

Quick Guide To Magic Squares

SIX: Considered the perfection of all parts, the ancients called it the form of forms, the articulation of the universe, and the maker of the soul.

SEVEN: The number seven is one of the most sacred of numbers and, for the Pythagoreans, it was called 'worthy of veneration'. They connected it with religion and called it the number of life. It represents fortune, custody, dreams and visions, and all that leads things to their end. It is also the number of the Divine law.

EIGHT: This number represents love, counsel, law, and convenience. It was the number associated with the Eleusinian mysteries.

NINE: It is the number of human beings, because of their nine-month embryonic gestation. In effect, it is the end and termination of the nine digits. Among its keywords are horizon and ocean, because of the belief that they were without end. Likewise, all the cycles that come after the number containing the previous digits are boundless and limitless.

Let's look at some of the basic numbers derived from constructing the first sixteen magic squares.

Planet	Size	Total Number of Cells	Sum of Any Line	Sum of Entire Square: Esoteric Number
Saturn	3 x 3	9	15	45
Jupiter	4 x 4	16	34	136
Mars	5 x 5	25	65	325
Sun	6 x 6	36	111	666
Venus	7 x 7	49	175	1225
Mercury	8 x 8	64	260	2080
Moon	9 x 9	81	369	3321
Saturn	10 x 10	100	505	5050
Jupiter	11 x 11	121	671	7381
Mars	12 x 12	144	870	10440
Sun	13 x 13	169	1105	14365
Venus	14 x 14	196	1379	19306
Mercury	15 x 15	225	1695	25425
Moon	16 x 16	256	2056	32896

Let us apply Pythagorean reduction to the esoteric numbers listed in the earlier table. Pythagorean reduction is about returning all numbers to the first nine digits by adding their compositions together. For example, 666 = 6+6+6 = 18 = 1+8 = 9

Sum of Any Line	Sum of Any Line Pythagorean reduction	Esoteric Number	Esoteric Number Pythagorean Reduction
15	(1+5) = 6	45	(4+5) = 9
34	(3+4) = 7	136	(1+3+6) = (1+0) = 1
65	(6+5) = (1+1) = 2	325	(3+2+5) = (1+0) = 1
111	(1+1+1) = 3	666	(6+6+6) = (1+8) = 9
175	(1+7+5)= (1+3) = 4	1225	(1+2+2+5) = (1+0) = 1
260	(2+6+0) = 8	2080	(2+0+8+0) = (1+0) = 1
369	(3+6+9) = (1+8) = 9	3321	(3+3+2+1) = 9
505	(5+0+5) = (1+0) = 1	5050	(5+0+5+0) = (1+0) = 1
671	(6+7+1) = (1+4) = 5	7381	(7+3+8+1) = (1+9) = (1+0) = 1
870	(8+7+0) = (1+5) = 6	10440	(1+0+4+4+0) = 9
1105	(1+1+0+5) = 7	14365	(1+4+3+6+5) = (1+9) = (1+0) = 1
1379	(1+3+7+9) = (2+0) = 2	19306	(1+9+3+0+6) = (1+9)=(1+0)=1
1695	(1+6+9+5) = (2+1)=3	25425	(2+5+4+2+5) = (1+8) = 9
2056	(2+0+5+6) = (1+3) = 4	32896	(3+2+8+9+6) = (2+8) = (1+0)=1

The first thing we discover is that the esoteric numbers of all magic squares reduce to the numbers one and nine. The number nine represents the end of things. It is the last number in the single digit sequence, after which a new sequence starts. The number one represents the beginning of all things. It is often associated with the Godhead.

Sages of the past believed that magic squares mathematically represented divine order and harmony. They were right, for each square holds within its body the energy of the Alpha and Omega. Some squares are Alpha squares and some are Omega squares. If we start with the first mathematically possible magic square, the number pattern found within the squares is 911. If we assume that the squares sized 1x1 and 2x2 do exist on some metaphysical level, the sequence is 119. Either way, this pattern repeats itself through the squares until infinity.

Quick Guide To Magic Squares

The metaphysical existence of the potential 1x1 and 2x2 shouldn't be dismissed solely due to impossibility of its calculation in our reality. Let's look at the pattern of Pythagorean reduced values of the sums of any line. Starting with the 3x3 you will notice a pattern that consists of non-repeating first nine digits in a different sequence from their natural one: 6-7-2-3-4-8-9-1-5. Once you reach five, you start again with the number 6 and the pattern continues until infinity.

If we were to assume the existence of the hypothetical 1x1 and 2x2, the actual sequence would start at one. It would be like this: 1-5-6-7-2-3-4-8-9. This sequence would begin with the Alpha and end with the Omega with the digits in between constituting the remaining seven numbers, but in a difference sequence from that with which we are familiar.

The numbers 1-5 in the sequence are not initially manifest. The number 15 was associated with one of the oldest Divinities in human history, the ancient Goddess of the Near East. Actually, the cuneiform for the number and the name of the Goddess was interchangeable. The first number of manifestation is the perfect number six. The biblical narrative tells us that God created the world in six days.

This number first appears in connection with the 3x3 square. The sum of any line in this square is 15, which is the numerological value of Eve in Arabic. The total sum of the entire square is 45, which is the numerological value of Adam in Arabic and Hebrew. This gives a completely new meaning to Eve's creation from Adam's rib.

Let us look again at how the primal 3x3 square is constructed. This time we will keep in mind that Pythagorean numerology considered odd numbers masculine and even numbers feminine.

4	9	2
3	5	7
8	1	6

The even numbers (feminine) appear in the corners, containing the odd numbers (masculine). This is a mathematical symbol of the act of sacred union or marriage. The male cross is contained by and united in the female womb.

Where does the number 119 fit in all this? The number 119 is the result of multiplication of seven by seventeen. The sacred and revered number seven has an extended association with the Goddess, especially in the Lady of Love aspect. It is the number of Venus of Nature. According to the Romans, the number seventeen represented death and misfortune. Thus, we are seeing a combination of life and death in the number 119. Jabir Ibn Hayyan (Geber), the famed medieval scholar and alchemist, considered all that is in the universe as governed by the number 17. Some modern thinkers, such as Henry Blanquart, argue that it is the junction between the spiritual and material worlds.

Number 119 has other meanings. Astrologically, the 119th degree of the Zodiac is the 28th degree of Cancer. The Moon rules over Cancer and completes its cycle in 28 days. It embodies the full power of the moon and femininity. This degree is the fall of Mars, the destroyer. The 29th degree of the Cancer that follows it is the critical degree and partakes of the energies of Leo (Sun) and Cancer (Moon). The union of Sun and Moon also represents the concept of Divine marriage or sacred union.

ANGELS AND JINN OF THE MAGIC SQUARES

What do Agial, Yophial, Graphiel, Nachiel, Kadmael, Tirial, and Chasmodai all have in common?

They are all planetary spirits whose names' numerological values we find naturally occurring in magic squares.

Spirit	Numerological Value	Magic Square	Sum of a Row in Magic Square	Total Sum of Magic Square
Agial	45	3x3	N/A	45
Yophial	136	4x4	N/A	136
Graphiel	325	5x5	N/A	325
Nachiel	111	6x6	111	N/A
Kadmael	175	7x7	175	N/a
Tirial	260	8x8	260	N/A
Chasmodai	369	9x9	369	N/A

It is an open secret that there is a relationship between numbers connected to magic squares and planetary spirits and intelligences. I believe this to be a Western adoption of a more complex system of associating the numbers of a magic square with angels and jinn. They used this system in the ancient Near East as revealed in Arabic manuscripts. I have given glimpses of this system in my earlier work, Magic That Works, which I co-authored with Frances Harrison. I will be revealing it again here and in future work, because I am a firm believer of its importance in practical occult workings.

The underlying principle of this system is very simple. Just as we can turn letters to numbers, so can we turn numbers to letters. Numbers are to letters as the soul is to the body. Key and essential numbers, related to its construction and thus existence, are inherent in a magic square. If you can convert those numbers into letters, i.e. give the energy form, then you have the means of further activating and awakening the spiritual forced contained in the magic square.

Eight angelic beings made of light and eight jinn beings made of smokeless fire are associated with every single magic square. Ancient magicians would use the angels for constructive purposes and the jinn for destructive. You can also evoke the angels and the jinn together for material manifestation, with the angels commanding the jinn.

Please, keep in mind that we can only directly link those names to the magic square. As an example, if your square is for the angel Gabriel, those sixteen beings are associated with that particular square of the angel Gabriel and not with the angel Gabriel directly. Since the connection between the angel Gabriel and the square is directly related to numerological match, multiple names could share the same square.

Number Found in the Square	Title of Corresponding Angel or Jinn
First Number in the Square	Usurper
Last Number in the Square	Guide
First Number + Last Number	Mystery
Total Sum of a Row	Adjuster
Total Value of All Rows	Leader
Total Sum of a Row + Total Sum of All Rows	Regulator
(Total Sum of a Row + Total Sum of All Rows) X 2	General Governor
((Total Sum of a Row + Total Sum of All Rows) X 2) X Last Number in the Square	High Overseer

Let us look at these values as they apply to the primary seven magic squares.

3X3 MAGIC SQUARE

Title of Corresponding Angel or Jinn	Number
Usurper	1
Guide	9
Mystery	10
Adjuster	15
Leader	45
Regulator	60
General Governor	120
High Overseer	1080

4X4 MAGIC SQUARE

Title of Corresponding Angel or Jinn	Number
Usurper	1
Guide	16
Mystery	17
Adjuster	34
Leader	136
Regulator	170
General Governor	340
High Overseer	5440

5X5 MAGIC SQUARE

Title of Corresponding Angel or Jinn	Number
Usurper	1
Guide	25
Mystery	26
Adjuster	65
Leader	325
Regulator	390
General Governor	780
High Overseer	19500

Quick Guide To Magic Squares

6x6 Magic Square

Title of Corresponding Angel or Jinn	Number
Usurper	1
Guide	36
Mystery	37
Adjuster	111
Leader	666
Regulator	777
General Governor	1554
High Overseer	55944

7x7 Magic Square

Title of Corresponding Angel or Jinn	Number
Usurper	1
Guide	49
Mystery	50
Adjuster	175
Leader	1125
Regulator	1300
General Governor	2600
High Overseer	127400

8x8 Magic Square

Title of Corresponding Angel or Jinn	Number
Usurper	1
Guide	64
Mystery	65
Adjuster	260
Leader	2080
Regulator	2340
General Governor	4680
High Overseer	299520

Occult Encyclopedia of Magic Squares

9x9 Magic Square

Title of Corresponding Angel or Jinn	Number
Usurper	1
Guide	81
Mystery	82
Adjuster	369
Leader	3321
Regulator	3690
General Governor	7380
High Overseer	597780

Converting those numbers into letters requires a basic familiarity with either Arabic or Hebrew alphabets. I believe the conversion is easier in Arabic than in Hebrew, as Arabic naturally has a letter that represents the value of 1,000.

Large Range Values	Hebrew Letter	Name	English Equivalent	Arabic Letter	Name	English Equivalent
1	א	Aleph	A		Alef	A
2	ב	Beth	B, V		Ba	B
3	ג	Gimel	G, J		Jeem	J
4	ד	Daleth	D		Dal	D
5	ה	Heh	H		Ha'	H
6	ו	Waw	V, U, W		Waw	W, U
7	ז	Zayin	Z		Zai	Z
8	ח	Heth	Ch, H		Ha	H
9	ט	Teth	T		Toa	T
10	י	Yod	Y		Ya	Y, I
20	כ	Kaf	K		Kaf	K

Quick Guide To Magic Squares

Large Range Values	Hebrew Letter	Name	English Equivalent	Arabic Letter	Name	English Equivalent
30	ל	Lamed	L		Lam	L
40	מ	Mem	M		Meem	M
50	נ	Nun	N		Nun	N
60	ס	Samekh	S		Seen	S
70	ע	Ayin	O, A		'ayin	'a
80	פ	Pe	Ph, F		Fa	F
90	צ	Tsadi	Ts		Sad	Ts
100	ק	Qof	Q		Qaf	Q
200	ר	Resh	R		Ra	R
300	ש	Shin	Sh		Sheen	Sh
400	ת	Tav	T, Th		Ta	T
500	ת ק				Tha	Th
600	ת ר				Kha	Kh, Ch
700	ת ש				Dhal	Dh, Tz
800	ת ת				Dad	D
900	ק ת ת				Zhoa	Zh, Z
1000	א				Ghain	Gh, G

The majority of angels have the suffix 'AL' at the end. El is an ancient Semitic word for God, pronounced differently based on Semitic language and dialect. The two most common pronunciations are El in Hebrew and Il in Canaanite, from the Akkadian Ilu. El (אל) in Hebrew has the value 31, but in Arabic, we write Il phonetically Aeel (ايل) with the value of 41.

We calculate Jinn suffixes based on subtraction of the angelic suffix from the number of degrees in a circle. If we subtract 41 from 360, our remainder will be 319. Converting numbers into Arabic letters we would have 300 (Sheen), 10 (Ya), 9 (Toa). Starting first with the smallest, we will end up with To-Ya-Sha or Teesh. Since the Hebrew angelic suffix has different numerological value form the Arabic, we will need to extract a different value for the jinn suffix in Hebrew. It will be 360-31 = 329. Converting 329 into Hebrew would be 300 (Shin), 20 (Kaph), 9 (Teth) or Takesh.

How this works in practice is simple. Let us as use the number 136, which is the total sum of the 4x4 square. We want to use Hebrew, so we subtract 31 from 136, which leave us with 105. We subtract the suffix first because otherwise it will increase the original number. We want the total value of the name, including the suffix, to equal the desired value. The only way to ensure that is to subtract the suffix first. Converting 105 to Hebrew letters starts by actually pronouncing the number. Pronouncing it gives us a clue as to the order of the letters. In this case, it is one hundred and five thus 100 (Qoph) and 5 (Heh). The complete name of the angel, including the suffix, is QHAL (Qahael).

What happens if we are dealing with a large number such as 1030? The same thing applies. First, we subtract the suffix (31) then we convert the remainder (999) from numbers into letters. Many magicians in the West are familiar with the idea of final values for some of the letters. This principle hasn't always been in use in ancient Kabbalah. Furthermore, it can't be used when the name needs to end with a suffix like El. Luckily, the Hebrew numeration system exists for larger numbers. Here is how we do it:

999 is broken down to

900
90
9

There is no direct corresponding letter to the number 900 (finals not counted). Therefore, we have to break it down using the value of the last letter of the Hebrew alphabet. It is broken down like this:

900 = 400+400+100

We reformulate the whole number thus:

400
400
100
90
9

or

ל א ט צ ק ת ת

The English equivalent is Th-Th-Q-Ts-T-A-L pronounced: Thathaqetstael

When dealing with values like 20000 we numerate them like this:

ר ת ת כ

Here is where Arabic makes this process easier. Arabic shares the same exact letters with the Hebrew alphabet in the same sequence. However, in addition, it also includes six letters bringing the numerological range to 1,000. Let us say we have the resulting value of 351,123; that would be pronounced as three hundred (Sheen) and one (Alef) fifty (Nun) thousand (Ghyin) and one hundred (Qaf) and three (Jeem) twenty (Kaf) three. In Arabic, they don't say twenty-one, but instead one-twenty even though it is written the same. The resulting values are ShANGhQJK (Shanghaqajek) + suffix.

You may have noticed that some values are less than the suffix value. This makes it impossible to subtract without incurring a negative value. I have seen the following workaround in old manuscripts. You begin by actually adding the number of degrees in a circle, 360, to the original value; then you subtract the suffix and proceed as normal.

I realize most of my readers will find this process challenging, as most English speakers are unfamiliar with either Hebrew or Arabic. There is no way around this, as angelic names were traditionally in Semitic languages. However, through practice and gradual familiarity, this system will become a cinch to use. Remember, you don't need to learn the language, but merely get to know the alphabet in question. I hope you make the effort for, in my experience, the benefits are worthwhile.

Yes, the process of constructing talismans with magic squares is more complicated than most people have been lead to believe by modern occult writers – that is if you want to get the same results the ancients did. Most occultists these days use magic squares as a last-step decorative element in a cornucopia of sigils on a talismanic implement. Truth be told, if created and empowered properly, a magic square is the only talisman you actually need to get wicked results.

I will be covering the complete process in depth in a book dedicated purely to this topic. In this book, I will provide you with an overview of some of these benefits. I will be dividing the benefits based on planets and the Zodiacal signs.

I have used a basic keyword structure for generic correspondences. These keywords represent how the planetary and Zodiacal influences materialize. You can then create talismans in harmony with those influences. For example, you want a talisman to help you deliver a spiritual lecture. You would then call on the angels of Sagittarius, Jupiter, and Mercury using their corresponding magic squares. If you want to treat a disease then look at the planet associated with that body part. If you want to develop a specific personal trait, then again look at the corresponding influence.

SATURN:

Obstructions, Delays, Defects, Fatalities, Losses, Sorrows, Poverty, Decay, Long Illnesses, Long Relationships.

Teeth, Ligaments, Skin, Skeleton, Gall Bladder, Auditory Organs, Knees, Sigmoid Fexture, and Left Ear

Conservative Business, Real Estate, Mining, Undertakers, Jailers, Farmers, Masons and Bricklayers.

Analytical, Tactful, Responsible, Punctual, Studious, Faithful, and Chaste.

JUPITER:

Honors, Long Journeys, Legal Affairs, Protection, Religious Affiliations, Successes, and Friendships.

Quick Guide To Magic Squares

Liver, Glycogen, Thighs, Hips, Right Ear, Viscera, Arterial System, and Upper Forehead.

Lawyers, Ministers, Financers, Insurance, Charity Workers, General Physicians, Restaurant Workers, Philanthropists, Merchants, Clothiers, and Philosophers.

Benevolence, Honor, Joviality, Patience, Wisdom, Justness, Popularity, Piety, Compassion, and Well-Respected.

MARS:

Muscular Tissues, Bile, Nose, Motor Nerves, Red Blood, External Generative Organs.

Strife and Conflicts, Wounds, Burns, Poisoning, Fires, Sudden Death, Impetuous Actions, Adventures, Enthusiasms.

Military, Chemists, Metal Workers, Dentists, Engineers, Barbers, Butchers, Firefighters, Competitive Sports and Surgeons.

Bravery, Expertise, High Energy, Strength, Independence, High Mindedness, and Impulsiveness

SUN:

Fame, Health, Powerful Friends, Public Office, Fortunate Circumstances, Elevation to High Positions, and Success in Public Enterprises.

Heart, Vital Fluids, and Blood Circulation

Executive Positions, Jewelers, Goldsmiths, Judges, Public Servants, Acting, Monarchs and Leaders.

Vitality, Ambition, Dignity, Versatility, Education, and Good Character.

Venus:

Love Affairs, Beautiful Environments, Friendship of Women, Pleasure, Marriage, Desires of All Kinds.

Kidneys, Throat, Oral Ducts, Mouth, Cheeks, Thymus Gland, Ovaries, and Internal Reproductive System.

Singers, Actors, Musicians, Designers, Botanists, Painters, Dancers, Poets, and Fashion Creators.

Artistic Temperment, Diplomatic Nature, Affection, Attractiveness, Poetic Ability, Artistic Ability, Love, Harmony, Luck and Increase in Love and Social Circle.

Mercury:

Quick Travel, Commerce, Sudden Changes, Scattered Thoughts, Worries, and Communication Challenges.

General Nervous System, Tongue, Senses, Thyroid Gland, Nerve Fluid, Vocal Cord, Hearing and Sight, and Intestines.

Accountants, Broadcasters, Advertising Agents, Jesters, Debaters, Orators, Journalists, Writers, Inventors, Booksellers, Publishers, Clerks, and Civil Engineers.

Dexterity, Subtlety, Brilliance, Industriousness, Retention, Wit, Literacy, Strong Intellect, Fluency, and Impressionability.

Moon:

Water Travel, Popularity, Idealism, Visions, Popularity, Emotionalism, and Rapid Changes.

Stomach, Breasts, Lymphatics, Tear Ducts, Nerve Sheaths, Mucous Membranes, and Brain Matter.

Sailor, Psychologists, Childcare Providers, Cooks, Fishery, Nutrition, Psychic

Work, Spy Work, Nurses, and Healers.

Positive Psychic Development, Imagination, Peaceful Temperament, Personal Magnetism, Emotional Strength

ARIES:

Pioneering, Enterprising, Confident, Explorative, Independent, Precise, Expedient, Aggressive, Competitive, Dictatorial, Scientific, and Ingenious.

Same professions as Mars

The Will to Accomplish, the Power from Adversity, Cosmic Urge, and Consciousness.

TAURUS:

Persistent, Steadfast, Patient, Determined, Stubborn, Materialistic, Emotionally Driven, Conservative, and Retentive.

Same professions as Venus

Ebb and Flow of the Cosmos, Attraction and Repulsion, Universal Motion and Celestial Rhythm.

GEMINI:

Inventive, Versatile, Superficial Thinker, Analytical, Tricky, Dextrous, Adaptable, Self-Expressive, and Curious.

Same professions as Mercury

Mirror of the Spirit, Power of Imagination, Universal Substance, and the Vision of Relationships.

CANCER:

Self-Sacrificing, Veneration for Tradition, Cautious, Reserved, Brooding, Negative, and Receptive.

Same professions as the Moon

Physical Life Principle, Sustaining Energy, Power of Receptivity, and the Sacred Breath.

LEO:

Ambitious, Optimistic, Magnanimous, Opposed to Secrecy, Challenging, Bold, Autocratic, and Generous.

Same professions as the Sun

Will to Illuminate, Faith, Will to Rule, and Life Principle.

VIRGO:

Witty, Studious, Versatile, Methodical, Skeptical, Critical, Ingenious, Fear of Disease and Poverty, Indifferent of Appearance, Scheming, and Scientific.

Same professions as Mercury

Form in Bondage, Desire to Serve, Feeling Pity, and Shadow of the Spirit.

LIBRA:

Imitative, Tactful, Undecided, Persuasive, Fond of Show, Materialistic, and Intriguing.

Same professions as Venus

Power of Sex, Consciousness of Judgment, Order of Creation, and the Symbol of the Fall.

Quick Guide To Magic Squares

SCORPIO:

Penetrating, Temperamental, Sarcastic, Vindictive, Altruistic, Executive, Intellectual, Scientific, Explorative, and Anarchistic.

Same professions as Mars

Spiritual Power in the Mundane, Fashioner, Desire Impulse, and Spiritual Memory

SAGITTARIUS:

Jovial, Philosophical, Frank, Eclectic, Intrepid, Prophetic, Extremely Ambitious, Progressive, and Financially Inclined.

Same professions as Jupiter

Seat of Intuition, Cosmic Thinker, Patron of Conscious Evolution, and Esoteric Understanding.

CAPRICORN:

Laborious, Economical, Conservative, Scrupulous, Detailed Thinker, Fatalistic, Stubborn, Domineering, Egotistic, Brooding and Cautious.

Same professions as Saturn

Individuality, Separateness, Competitive Spirit, and Lack of Connection with Spiritual Reality.

AQUARIUS:

Inventive, Creative, Independent, Discreet, Humanitarian, Optimistic, Superficial, Unforseeing, Tolerant, Reasonable and Diplomatic.

Same professions as Saturn

Soul and Seat of Perceiving Power

PISCES:

Intuitive, Abstract, Introspective, Religious, Clairvoyant, Impractical, Procrastinating, Fatalistic, Insecure and Compassionate.

Same professions as Jupiter

Meditation on the Source and the Will to Renounce.

These make up a general overview. You need to look at your specific situation to be truly successful in your talismanic work. For example, it is easy to pick, let's say, Jupiter as a general planet associated with growth and do a prosperity talisman. However, step back for a second and look at what you actually do for a living. You may need something different. If you are a CEO and looking to impress your board with your new proposal, you may want a Mercury talisman to gain new funding or a Sun talisman to gain more respect and obedience. If you are in the military and hoping to rise in rank, you may want either a Saturn or Sun magic square. If you are a real estate agent, you may want to use the Moon as it deals with one's abode.

You will need to compliment those talismans with squares of angels and various spirits associated with the astrological forces you intend to channel. You will find yourself returning to this book more than once to get those extra squares to supercharge your talisman.

I would like to end my introduction with a small gift. I will provide you with one of my personal magic squares for generating endless opportunities for income growth. I felt it would be the most suitable of gifts to my loyal readers in this time of economical challenge. I would love to hear from you after you put it to use and walk out of the bank grinning. Let's get started:

TIMING: Moon is in the 8th degree of Virgo. There should be no negative aspect to the Moon, Mercury and Jupiter.

INCENSE: Frankincense, Saffron, and Amber

CONSTRUCTION: You will need to construct your talisman on a natural surface. Please, avoid using synthetic materials and under no circumstances laminate a printer-produced talisman. You need to make this by hand and you will be carrying it with you in your wallet or handbag. You can use natural paper, leather, or cloth.

You will be using two squares in the talisman. The first consists of an 8x8 square consisting only of the letter Cheth to represent the number eight. The other is the words Aobel (אובל) Ha (ה) Gazzah (גזה) Dehab (זהב), which translate to "Bring The Golden Fleece". Surrounding both squares is a large 8 either upright or on its side to represent the infinity symbol.

Start first by drawing the large infinity symbol to cover the bulk of the page. When drawing this symbol chant repeatedly: Nathan Sha'al Aosher Kabowd Aiysh Melek Yowm. You can also say the same sentence in English: "And I have also given thee that which thou has not asked, both riches and honor, so that there shall not be any among the kings like unto thee all thy days."

In the right (or top) loop draw the following square:

ח	ח	ח	ח	ח	ח	ח	ח
ח	ח	ח	ח	ח	ח	ח	ח
ח	ח	ח	ח	ח	ח	ח	ח
ח	ח	ח	ח	ח	ח	ח	ח
ח	ח	ח	ח	ח	ח	ח	ח
ח	ח	ח	ח	ח	ח	ח	ח
ח	ח	ח	ח	ח	ח	ח	ח
ח	ח	ח	ח	ח	ח	ח	ח

The total value of this square is 512 = 5+1+2=8

After you draw each letter, put your finger over it. Recite the following eight times with your mouth near your finger: Chesed (Mercy), Chamal (Compassion), Chai (Living). Breathe on the letter with your finger on it eight times saying with your breath: Chartom (Magician), Chen (Charm), Chayil (Wealth). Visualize the letters glowing with a white hue filled with golden sparkles.

In the left (bottom) loop draw the following square:

זהב	גוה	ה	אובל	זהב	גוה	ה	אובל
גוה	ה	אובל	זהב	אובל	זהב	גוה	ה
ה	אובל	זהב	אובל	ה	גוה	זהב	גוה
גוה	זהב	אובל	ה	אובל	ה	גוה	זהב
אובל	זהב	גוה	ה	גוה	ה	אובל	זהב
ה	גוה	זהב	גוה	ה	אובל	זהב	אובל
אובל	ה	גוה	זהב	גוה	זהב	אובל	ה
זהב	אובל	ה	גוה	זהב	אובל	ה	גוה

Make sure you pronounce the words audibly as you are writing them. You should be doing the inscription right to left.

Once you are done, wrap this talisman with a white cloth and put it in your wallet. I would recommend you pull it out every time the moon re-enters the 8th degree of Virgo and retrace the inscription with your fingers, coupled with the chanting.

In the remaining pages of the book, you will find the pre-calculated squares for the angels and spirits of the Zodiac according to the modern Western Mystery Tradition. In the next volumes of this series, I will be presenting classical materials directly from Hebrew and Arabic sources. The book Magic Squares and Tree of Life was intended to be a bonus chapter of this series, but it has since became a book unto itself. It will provide advanced students with additional important information, and beginners with more depth to their theoretical body of knowledge. In the end, these are how-to manuals and resources, begging people looking to improve their lives whether spiritually or materially or both to use them. Let the magic happen…

ARIES

SIGN ARIES: TALEH (44)

Hebrew Squares Not Available

Fire - Jupiter

3	14	8	19
18	9	11	6
13	4	20	7
10	17	5	12

Air - Jupiter

12	5	17	10
7	20	4	13
6	11	9	18
19	8	14	3

Earth - Jupiter

10	13	18	3
17	4	9	14
5	20	11	8
12	7	6	19

Water - Jupiter

19	6	7	12
8	11	20	5
14	9	4	17
3	18	13	10

	Number	Angel Value (Arabic)	Angel Value (Hebrew)	Jinn Value (Arabic)	Jinn Value (Hebrew)
Usurper	3	322	332	44	34
Guide	20	339	349	61	51
Mystery	23	342	352	64	54
Adjuster	352	311	321	33	23
Leader	1056	1015	1025	737	727
Regulator	1408	1367	1377	1089	1079
General Governor	2816	2775	2785	2497	2487
High Overseer	56320	56279	56289	56001	55991

ARCHANGEL OF ARIES: MALKIDIEL (135)

אל	די	ב	מל
69	21	17	28
16	29	68	22
19	71	30	15

Fire - Saturn

46	41	48
47	45	43
42	49	44

Earth - Saturn

42	47	46
49	45	41
44	43	48

Air - Saturn

44	49	42
43	45	47
48	41	46

Water - Saturn

48	43	44
41	45	49
46	47	42

	Number	Angel Value (Arabic)	Angel Value (Hebrew)	Jinn Value (Arabic)	Jinn Value (Hebrew)
Usurper	41	360	10	82	72
Guide	49	8	18	90	80
Mystery	90	49	59	131	121
Adjuster	135	94	104	176	166
Leader	405	364	374	86	76
Regulator	540	499	509	221	211
General Governor	1080	1039	1049	761	751
High Overseer	52920	52879	52889	52601	52591

Fire - Jupiter

26	37	31	41
40	32	34	29
36	27	42	30
33	39	28	35

Air - Jupiter

35	28	39	33
30	42	27	36
29	34	32	40
41	31	37	26

Earth - Jupiter

33	36	40	26
39	27	32	37
28	42	34	31
35	30	29	41

Water - Jupiter

41	29	30	35
31	34	42	28
37	32	27	39
26	40	36	33

	Number	Angel Value (Arabic)	Angel Value (Hebrew)	Jinn Value (Arabic)	Jinn Value (Hebrew)
Usurper	26	345	355	67	57
Guide	42	1	11	83	73
Mystery	68	27	37	109	99
Adjuster	1080	1039	1049	761	751
Leader	3240	3199	3209	2921	2911
Regulator	4320	4279	4289	4001	3991
General Governor	8640	8599	8609	8321	8311
High Overseer	362880	362839	362849	362561	362551

3

Occult Encyclopedia of Magic Squares

Fire - Mars

15	39	33	27	21
28	22	16	35	34
36	30	29	23	17
24	18	37	31	25
32	26	20	19	38

Air - Mars

32	24	36	28	15
26	18	30	22	39
20	37	29	16	33
19	31	23	35	27
38	25	17	34	21

Earth - Mars

38	19	20	26	32
25	31	37	18	24
17	23	29	30	36
34	35	16	22	28
21	27	33	39	15

Water - Mars

21	34	17	25	38
27	35	23	31	19
33	16	29	37	20
39	22	30	18	26
15	28	36	24	32

	Number	Angel Value (Arabic)	Angel Value (Hebrew)	Jinn Value (Arabic)	Jinn Value (Hebrew)
Usurper	15	334	344	56	46
Guide	39	358	8	80	70
Mystery	54	13	23	95	85
Adjuster	135	94	104	176	166
Leader	405	364	374	86	76
Regulator	540	499	509	221	211
General Governor	1080	1039	1049	761	751
High Overseer	42120	42079	42089	41801	41791

Occult Encyclopedia of Magic Squares

Fire - Sun

5	16	36	22	26	30
11	21	32	35	9	27
17	39	25	15	31	8
28	7	18	33	12	37
34	23	14	6	38	20
40	29	10	24	19	13

Air - Sun

13	19	24	10	29	40
20	38	6	14	23	34
37	12	33	18	7	28
8	31	15	25	39	17
27	9	35	32	21	11
30	26	22	36	16	5

Earth - Sun

40	34	28	17	11	5
29	23	7	39	21	16
10	14	18	25	32	36
24	6	33	15	35	22
19	38	12	31	9	26
13	20	37	8	27	30

Water - Sun

30	27	8	37	20	13
26	9	31	12	38	19
22	35	15	33	6	24
36	32	25	18	14	10
16	21	39	7	23	29
5	11	17	28	34	40

	Number	Angel Value (Arabic)	Angel Value (Hebrew)	Jinn Value (Arabic)	Jinn Value (Hebrew)
Usurper	5	324	334	46	36
Guide	40	359	9	81	71
Mystery	45	4	14	86	76
Adjuster	135	94	104	176	166
Leader	405	364	374	86	76
Regulator	540	499	509	221	211
General Governor	1080	1039	1049	761	751
High Overseer	43200	43159	43169	42881	42871

ANGEL OF ARIES: SHARHIEL (546)

אל	הי	ר	ש
299	201	18	28
17	29	298	202
199	301	30	16

ל	א	י	ה	ר	ש
ר	ה	ל	ש	י	א
י	ש	א	ר	ל	ה
ש	ר	ה	י	א	ל
ה	ל	ר	א	ש	י
א	י	ש	ל	ה	ר

Fire - Saturn

183	178	185
184	182	180
179	186	181

Earth - Saturn

179	184	183
186	182	178
181	180	185

Air - Saturn

181	186	179
180	182	184
185	178	183

Water - Saturn

185	180	181
178	182	186
183	184	179

	Number	Angel Value (Arabic)	Angel Value (Hebrew)	Jinn Value (Arabic)	Jinn Value (Hebrew)
Usurper	178	137	147	219	209
Guide	186	145	155	227	217
Mystery	364	323	333	45	35
Adjuster	546	505	515	227	217
Leader	1638	1597	1607	1319	1309
Regulator	2184	2143	2153	1865	1855
General Governor	4368	4327	4337	4049	4039
High Overseer	812448	812407	812417	812129	812119

Fire - Jupiter

129	140	134	143
142	135	137	132
139	130	144	133
136	141	131	138

Air - Jupiter

138	131	141	136
133	144	130	139
132	137	135	142
143	134	140	129

Earth - Jupiter

136	139	142	129
141	130	135	140
131	144	137	134
138	133	132	143

Water - Jupiter

143	132	133	138
134	137	144	131
140	135	130	141
129	142	139	136

	Number	Angel Value (Arabic)	Angel Value (Hebrew)	Jinn Value (Arabic)	Jinn Value (Hebrew)
Usurper	129	88	98	170	160
Guide	144	103	113	185	175
Mystery	273	232	242	314	304
Adjuster	4368	4327	4337	4049	4039
Leader	13104	13063	13073	12785	12775
Regulator	17472	17431	17441	17153	17143
General Governor	34944	34903	34913	34625	34615
High Overseer	5031936	5031895	5031905	5031617	5031607

Occult Encyclopedia of Magic Squares

Fire - Mars

97	122	115	109	103
110	104	98	118	116
119	112	111	105	99
106	100	120	113	107
114	108	102	101	121

Air - Mars

114	106	119	110	97
108	100	112	104	122
102	120	111	98	115
101	113	105	118	109
121	107	99	116	103

Earth - Mars

121	101	102	108	114
107	113	120	100	106
99	105	111	112	119
116	118	98	104	110
103	109	115	122	97

Water - Mars

103	116	99	107	121
109	118	105	113	101
115	98	111	120	102
122	104	112	100	108
97	110	119	106	114

	Number	Angel Value (Arabic)	Angel Value (Hebrew)	Jinn Value (Arabic)	Jinn Value (Hebrew)
Usurper	97	56	66	138	128
Guide	122	81	91	163	153
Mystery	219	178	188	260	250
Adjuster	546	505	515	227	217
Leader	1638	1597	1607	1319	1309
Regulator	2184	2143	2153	1865	1855
General Governor	4368	4327	4337	4049	4039
High Overseer	532896	532855	532865	532577	532567

Fire - Sun

73	84	107	90	94	98
79	89	100	106	77	95
85	110	93	83	99	76
96	75	86	101	80	108
102	91	82	74	109	88
111	97	78	92	87	81

Earth - Sun

111	102	96	85	79	73
97	91	75	110	89	84
78	82	86	93	100	107
92	74	101	83	106	90
87	109	80	99	77	94
81	88	108	76	95	98

Occult Encyclopedia of Magic Squares

Air - Sun

81	87	92	78	97	111
88	109	74	82	91	102
108	80	101	86	75	96
76	99	83	93	110	85
95	77	106	100	89	79
98	94	90	107	84	73

Water - Sun

98	95	76	108	88	81
94	77	99	80	109	87
90	106	83	101	74	92
107	100	93	86	82	78
84	89	110	75	91	97
73	79	85	96	102	111

	Number	Angel Value (Arabic)	Angel Value (Hebrew)	Jinn Value (Arabic)	Jinn Value (Hebrew)
Usurper	73	32	42	114	104
Guide	111	70	80	152	142
Mystery	184	143	153	225	215
Adjuster	546	505	515	227	217
Leader	1638	1597	1607	1319	1309
Regulator	2184	2143	2153	1865	1855
General Governor	4368	4327	4337	4049	4039
High Overseer	484848	484807	484817	484529	484519

9

Fire - Venus

54	95	80	65	85	98	69
99	70	55	89	81	66	86
67	87	100	71	56	90	75
91	76	61	88	101	72	57
73	58	92	77	62	82	102
83	96	74	59	93	78	63
79	64	84	97	68	60	94

Earth - Venus

79	83	73	91	67	99	54
64	96	58	76	87	70	95
84	74	92	61	100	55	80
97	59	77	88	71	89	65
68	93	62	101	56	81	85
60	78	82	72	90	66	98
94	63	102	57	75	86	69

Air - Venus

94	60	68	97	84	64	79
63	78	93	59	74	96	83
102	82	62	77	92	58	73
57	72	101	88	61	76	91
75	90	56	71	100	87	67
86	66	81	89	55	70	99
69	98	85	65	80	95	54

Water - Venus

69	86	75	57	102	63	94
98	66	90	72	82	78	60
85	81	56	101	62	93	68
65	89	71	88	77	59	97
80	55	100	61	92	74	84
95	70	87	76	58	96	64
54	99	67	91	73	83	79

	Number	Angel Value (Arabic)	Angel Value (Hebrew)	Jinn Value (Arabic)	Jinn Value (Hebrew)
Usurper	54	13	23	95	85
Guide	102	61	71	143	133
Mystery	156	115	125	197	187
Adjuster	546	505	515	227	217
Leader	1638	1597	1607	1319	1309
Regulator	2184	2143	2153	1865	1855
General Governor	4368	4327	4337	4049	4039
High Overseer	445536	445495	445505	445217	445207

Fire - Mercury

36	52	103	81	70	86	67	51
44	60	89	73	78	100	59	43
87	71	50	66	53	37	80	102
101	79	42	58	61	45	72	88
65	49	68	84	105	83	38	54
57	41	76	98	91	75	46	62
82	104	55	39	48	64	85	69
74	90	63	47	40	56	99	77

Earth - Mercury

74	82	57	65	101	87	44	36
90	104	41	49	79	71	60	52
63	55	76	68	42	50	89	103
47	39	98	84	58	66	73	81
40	48	91	105	61	53	78	70
56	64	75	83	45	37	100	86
99	85	46	38	72	80	59	67
77	69	62	54	88	102	43	51

Occult Encyclopedia of Magic Squares

Air - Mercury

77	99	56	40	47	63	90	74
69	85	64	48	39	55	104	82
62	46	75	91	98	76	41	57
54	38	83	105	84	68	49	65
88	72	45	61	58	42	79	101
102	80	37	53	66	50	71	87
43	59	100	78	73	89	60	44
51	67	86	70	81	103	52	36

Water - Mercury

51	43	102	88	54	62	69	77
67	59	80	72	38	46	85	99
86	100	37	45	83	75	64	56
70	78	53	61	105	91	48	40
81	73	66	58	84	98	39	47
103	89	50	42	68	76	55	63
52	60	71	79	49	41	104	90
36	44	87	101	65	57	82	74

	Number	Angel Value (Arabic)	Angel Value (Hebrew)	Jinn Value (Arabic)	Jinn Value (Hebrew)
Usurper	36	355	5	77	67
Guide	105	64	74	146	136
Mystery	141	100	110	182	172
Adjuster	546	505	515	227	217
Leader	1638	1597	1607	1319	1309
Regulator	2184	2143	2153	1865	1855
General Governor	4368	4327	4337	4049	4039
High Overseer	458640	458599	458609	458321	458311

Occult Encyclopedia of Magic Squares

Fire - Moon

64	77	39	48	106	32	68	84	28
24	67	89	44	60	76	31	53	102
98	36	52	88	20	72	81	43	56
91	23	66	75	46	59	101	30	55
51	100	35	71	87	22	58	80	42
38	63	79	34	47	105	27	70	83
37	50	99	21	73	86	41	57	82
78	40	62	104	33	49	85	26	69
65	90	25	61	74	45	54	103	29

Earth - Moon

28	102	56	55	42	83	82	69	29
84	53	43	30	80	70	57	26	103
68	31	81	101	58	27	41	85	54
32	76	72	59	22	105	86	49	45
106	60	20	46	87	47	73	33	74
48	44	88	75	71	34	21	104	61
39	89	52	66	35	79	99	62	25
77	67	36	23	100	63	50	40	90
64	24	98	91	51	38	37	78	65

Air - Moon

29	103	54	45	74	61	25	90	65
69	26	85	49	33	104	62	40	78
82	57	41	86	73	21	99	50	37
83	70	27	105	47	34	79	63	38
42	80	58	22	87	71	35	100	51
55	30	101	59	46	75	66	23	91
56	43	81	72	20	88	52	36	98
102	53	31	76	60	44	89	67	24
28	84	68	32	106	48	39	77	64

Water - Moon

65	78	37	38	51	91	98	24	64
90	40	50	63	100	23	36	67	77
25	62	99	79	35	66	52	89	39
61	104	21	34	71	75	88	44	48
74	33	73	47	87	46	20	60	106
45	49	86	105	22	59	72	76	32
54	85	41	27	58	101	81	31	68
103	26	57	70	80	30	43	53	84
29	69	82	83	42	55	56	102	28

	Number	Angel Value (Arabic)	Angel Value (Hebrew)	Jinn Value (Arabic)	Jinn Value (Hebrew)
Usurper	20	339	349	61	51
Guide	106	65	75	147	137
Mystery	126	85	95	167	157
Adjuster	546	505	515	227	217
Leader	1638	1597	1607	1319	1309
Regulator	2184	2143	2153	1865	1855
General Governor	4368	4327	4337	4049	4039
High Overseer	463008	462967	462977	462689	462679

Fire - Saturn

5	23	30	68	59	98	52	44	76	91
16	80	73	64	100	89	7	49	35	33
31	36	60	99	90	75	24	12	53	66
37	62	97	92	25	71	79	20	9	54
50	96	94	29	40	63	67	77	22	8
57	14	15	82	70	46	42	32	87	101
69	51	11	18	84	39	27	88	104	55
83	72	47	6	17	34	85	103	58	41
93	26	38	45	13	21	102	56	74	78
105	86	81	43	48	10	61	65	28	19

Occult Encyclopedia of Magic Squares

Earth - Saturn

105	93	83	69	57	50	37	31	16	5
86	26	72	51	14	96	62	36	80	23
81	38	47	11	15	94	97	60	73	30
43	45	6	18	82	29	92	99	64	68
48	13	17	84	70	40	25	90	100	59
10	21	34	39	46	63	71	75	89	98
61	102	85	27	42	67	79	24	7	52
65	56	103	88	32	77	20	12	49	44
28	74	58	104	87	22	9	53	35	76
19	78	41	55	101	8	54	66	33	91

Air - Saturn

19	28	65	61	10	48	43	81	86	105
78	74	56	102	21	13	45	38	26	93
41	58	103	85	34	17	6	47	72	83
55	104	88	27	39	84	18	11	51	69
101	87	32	42	46	70	82	15	14	57
8	22	77	67	63	40	29	94	96	50
54	9	20	79	71	25	92	97	62	37
66	53	12	24	75	90	99	60	36	31
33	35	49	7	89	100	64	73	80	16
91	76	44	52	98	59	68	30	23	5

Water - Saturn

91	33	66	54	8	101	55	41	78	19
76	35	53	9	22	87	104	58	74	28
44	49	12	20	77	32	88	103	56	65
52	**7**	24	79	67	42	27	85	102	61
98	89	75	71	63	46	39	34	21	10
59	100	90	25	40	70	84	17	13	48
68	64	99	92	29	82	18	6	45	43
30	73	60	97	94	15	11	47	38	81
23	80	36	62	96	14	51	72	26	86
5	16	31	37	50	57	69	83	93	105

Occult Encyclopedia of Magic Squares

	Number	Angel Value (Arabic)	Angel Value (Hebrew)	Jinn Value (Arabic)	Jinn Value (Hebrew)
Usurper	5	324	334	46	36
Guide	105	64	74	146	136
Mystery	110	69	79	151	141
Adjuster	546	505	515	227	217
Leader	1638	1597	1607	1319	1309
Regulator	2184	2143	2153	1865	1855
General Governor	4368	4327	4337	4049	4039
High Overseer	458640	458599	458609	458321	458311

LORD OF TRIPLICITY BY DAY: SATERATON (398)

נ	עש	שר	ס
59	210	82	47
81	48	58	211
208	61	49	80

נ	ש	ע	ר	ש	ס
ש	ר	נ	ס	ע	ש
ע	ס	ש	ש	נ	ר
ס	ש	ר	ע	ש	נ
ר	נ	ש	ש	ס	ע
ש	ע	ס	נ	ר	ש

Fire - Jupiter

92	103	97	106
105	98	100	95
102	93	107	96
99	104	94	101

Air - Jupiter

101	94	104	99
96	107	93	102
95	100	98	105
106	97	103	92

Earth - Jupiter

99	102	105	92
104	93	98	103
94	107	100	97
101	96	95	106

Water - Jupiter

106	95	96	101
97	100	107	94
103	98	93	104
92	105	102	99

	Number	Angel Value (Arabic)	Angel Value (Hebrew)	Jinn Value (Arabic)	Jinn Value (Hebrew)
Usurper	92	51	61	133	123
Guide	107	66	76	148	138
Mystery	199	158	168	240	230
Adjuster	3184	3143	3153	2865	2855
Leader	9552	9511	9521	9233	9223
Regulator	12736	12695	12705	12417	12407
General Governor	25472	25431	25441	25153	25143
High Overseer	2725504	2725463	2725473	2725185	2725175

Occult Encyclopedia of Magic Squares

Fire - Mars

67	94	85	79	73
80	74	68	90	86
91	82	81	75	69
76	70	92	83	77
84	78	72	71	93

Air - Mars

84	76	91	80	67
78	70	82	74	94
72	92	81	68	85
71	83	75	90	79
93	77	69	86	73

Earth - Mars

93	71	72	78	84
77	83	92	70	76
69	75	81	82	91
86	90	68	74	80
73	79	85	94	67

Water - Mars

73	86	69	77	93
79	90	75	83	71
85	68	81	92	72
94	74	82	70	78
67	80	91	76	84

	Number	Angel Value (Arabic)	Angel Value (Hebrew)	Jinn Value (Arabic)	Jinn Value (Hebrew)
Usurper	67	26	36	108	98
Guide	94	53	63	135	125
Mystery	161	120	130	202	192
Adjuster	398	357	367	79	69
Leader	1194	1153	1163	875	865
Regulator	1592	1551	1561	1273	1263
General Governor	3184	3143	3153	2865	2855
High Overseer	299296	299255	299265	298977	298967

Occult Encyclopedia of Magic Squares

Fire - Sun

48	59	84	65	69	73
54	64	75	83	52	70
60	87	68	58	74	51
71	50	61	76	55	85
77	66	57	49	86	63
88	72	53	67	62	56

Air - Sun

56	62	67	53	72	88
63	86	49	57	66	77
85	55	76	61	50	71
51	74	58	68	87	60
70	52	83	75	64	54
73	69	65	84	59	48

Earth - Sun

88	77	71	60	54	48
72	66	50	87	64	59
53	57	61	68	75	84
67	49	76	58	83	65
62	86	55	74	52	69
56	63	85	51	70	73

Water - Sun

73	70	51	85	63	56
69	52	74	55	86	62
65	83	58	76	49	67
84	75	68	61	57	53
59	64	87	50	66	72
48	54	60	71	77	88

	Number	Angel Value (Arabic)	Angel Value (Hebrew)	Jinn Value (Arabic)	Jinn Value (Hebrew)
Usurper	48	7	17	89	79
Guide	88	47	57	129	119
Mystery	136	95	105	177	167
Adjuster	398	357	367	79	69
Leader	1194	1153	1163	875	865
Regulator	1592	1551	1561	1273	1263
General Governor	3184	3143	3153	2865	2855
High Overseer	280192	280151	280161	279873	279863

Fire - Venus

32	73	58	43	63	82	47
83	48	33	67	59	44	64
45	65	84	49	34	68	53
69	54	39	66	85	50	35
51	36	70	55	40	60	86
61	80	52	37	71	56	41
57	42	62	81	46	38	72

Earth - Venus

57	61	51	69	45	83	32
42	80	36	54	65	48	73
62	52	70	39	84	33	58
81	37	55	66	49	67	43
46	71	40	85	34	59	63
38	56	60	50	68	44	82
72	41	86	35	53	64	47

Air - Venus

72	38	46	81	62	42	57
41	56	71	37	52	80	61
86	60	40	55	70	36	51
35	50	85	66	39	54	69
53	68	34	49	84	65	45
64	44	59	67	33	48	83
47	82	63	43	58	73	32

Water - Venus

47	64	53	35	86	41	72
82	44	68	50	60	56	38
63	59	34	85	40	71	46
43	67	49	66	55	37	81
58	33	84	39	70	52	62
73	48	65	54	36	80	42
32	83	45	69	51	61	57

Occult Encyclopedia of Magic Squares

	Number	Angel Value (Arabic)	Angel Value (Hebrew)	Jinn Value (Arabic)	Jinn Value (Hebrew)
Usurper	32	351	1	73	63
Guide	86	45	55	127	117
Mystery	118	77	87	159	149
Adjuster	398	357	367	79	69
Leader	1194	1153	1163	875	865
Regulator	1592	1551	1561	1273	1263
General Governor	3184	3143	3153	2865	2855
High Overseer	273824	273783	273793	273505	273495

Fire - Mercury

18	34	81	63	52	68	49	33
26	42	71	55	60	78	41	25
69	53	32	48	35	19	62	80
79	61	24	40	43	27	54	70
47	31	50	66	83	65	20	36
39	23	58	76	73	57	28	44
64	82	37	21	30	46	67	51
56	72	45	29	22	38	77	59

Earth - Mercury

56	64	39	47	79	69	26	18
72	82	23	31	61	53	42	34
45	37	58	50	24	32	71	81
29	21	76	66	40	48	55	63
22	30	73	83	43	35	60	52
38	46	57	65	27	19	78	68
77	67	28	20	54	62	41	49
59	51	44	36	70	80	25	33

Air - Mercury

59	77	38	22	29	45	72	56
51	67	46	30	21	37	82	64
44	28	57	73	76	58	23	39
36	20	65	83	66	50	31	47
70	54	27	43	40	24	61	79
80	62	19	35	48	32	53	69
25	41	78	60	55	71	42	26
33	49	68	52	63	81	34	18

Water - Mercury

33	25	80	70	36	44	51	59
49	41	62	54	20	28	67	77
68	78	19	27	65	57	46	38
52	60	35	43	83	73	30	22
63	55	48	40	66	76	21	29
81	71	32	24	50	58	37	45
34	42	53	61	31	23	82	72
18	26	69	79	47	39	64	56

	Number	Angel Value (Arabic)	Angel Value (Hebrew)	Jinn Value (Arabic)	Jinn Value (Hebrew)
Usurper	18	337	347	59	49
Guide	83	42	52	124	114
Mystery	101	60	70	142	132
Adjuster	398	357	367	79	69
Leader	1194	1153	1163	875	865
Regulator	1592	1551	1561	1273	1263
General Governor	3184	3143	3153	2865	2855
High Overseer	264272	264231	264241	263953	263943

Fire - Moon

48	61	23	32	86	16	52	68	12
8	51	73	28	44	60	15	37	82
78	20	36	72	4	56	65	27	40
75	7	50	59	30	43	81	14	39
35	80	19	55	71	6	42	64	26
22	47	63	18	31	85	11	54	67
21	34	79	5	57	70	25	41	66
62	24	46	84	17	33	69	10	53
49	74	9	45	58	29	38	83	13

Earth - Moon

12	82	40	39	26	67	66	53	13
68	37	27	14	64	54	41	10	83
52	15	65	81	42	11	25	69	38
16	60	56	43	6	85	70	33	29
86	44	4	30	71	31	57	17	58
32	28	72	59	55	18	5	84	45
23	73	36	50	19	63	79	46	9
61	51	20	7	80	47	34	24	74
48	8	78	75	35	22	21	62	49

Air - Moon

13	83	38	29	58	45	9	74	49
53	10	69	33	17	84	46	24	62
66	41	25	70	57	5	79	34	21
67	54	11	85	31	18	63	47	22
26	64	42	6	71	55	19	80	35
39	14	81	43	30	59	50	7	75
40	27	65	56	4	72	36	20	78
82	37	15	60	44	28	73	51	8
12	68	52	16	86	32	23	61	48

Water - Moon

49	62	21	22	35	75	78	8	48
74	24	34	47	80	7	20	51	61
9	46	79	63	19	50	36	73	23
45	84	5	18	55	59	72	28	32
58	17	57	31	71	30	4	44	86
29	33	70	85	6	43	56	60	16
38	69	25	11	42	81	65	15	52
83	10	41	54	64	14	27	37	68
13	53	66	67	26	39	40	82	12

	Number	Angel Value (Arabic)	Angel Value (Hebrew)	Jinn Value (Arabic)	Jinn Value (Hebrew)
Usurper	4	323	333	45	35
Guide	86	45	55	127	117
Mystery	90	49	59	131	121
Adjuster	398	357	367	79	69
Leader	1194	1153	1163	875	865
Regulator	1592	1551	1561	1273	1263
General Governor	3184	3143	3153	2865	2855
High Overseer	273824	273783	273793	273505	273495

LORD OF TRIPLICITY BY NIGHT: SAPATAVI (236)

י	א	עָ	טַט
139	80	10	7
9	8	138	81
78	141	9	8

י	ו	א	ט	ע	פ	ס
א	ט	ע	פ	ס	י	ו
ע	פ	ס	י	ו	א	ט
ס	י	ו	א	ט	ע	פ
ו	א	ט	ע	פ	ס	י
ט	ע	פ	ס	י	ו	א
פ	ס	י	ו	א	ט	ע

Fire - Jupiter

51	62	56	67
66	57	59	54
61	52	68	55
58	65	53	60

Air - Jupiter

60	53	65	58
55	68	52	61
54	59	57	66
67	56	62	51

Earth - Jupiter

58	61	66	51
65	52	57	62
53	68	59	56
60	55	54	67

Water - Jupiter

67	54	55	60
56	59	68	53
62	57	52	65
51	66	61	58

	Number	Angel Value (Arabic)	Angel Value (Hebrew)	Jinn Value (Arabic)	Jinn Value (Hebrew)
Usurper	51	10	20	92	82
Guide	68	27	37	109	99
Mystery	119	78	88	160	150
Adjuster	1888	1847	1857	1569	1559
Leader	5664	5623	5633	5345	5335
Regulator	7552	7511	7521	7233	7223
General Governor	15104	15063	15073	14785	14775
High Overseer	1027072	1027031	1027041	1026753	1026743

Occult Encyclopedia of Magic Squares

Fire - Mars

35	60	53	47	41
48	42	36	56	54
57	50	49	43	37
44	38	58	51	45
52	46	40	39	59

Air - Mars

52	44	57	48	35
46	38	50	42	60
40	58	49	36	53
39	51	43	56	47
59	45	37	54	41

Earth -Mars

59	39	40	46	52
45	51	58	38	44
37	43	49	50	57
54	56	36	42	48
41	47	53	60	35

Water - Mars

41	54	37	45	59
47	56	43	51	39
53	36	49	58	40
60	42	50	38	46
35	48	57	44	52

	Number	Angel Value (Arabic)	Angel Value (Hebrew)	Jinn Value (Arabic)	Jinn Value (Hebrew)
Usurper	35	354	4	76	66
Guide	60	19	29	101	91
Mystery	95	54	64	136	126
Adjuster	236	195	205	277	267
Leader	708	667	677	389	379
Regulator	944	903	913	625	615
General Governor	1888	1847	1857	1569	1559
High Overseer	113280	113239	113249	112961	112951

Fire - Sun

21	32	57	38	42	46
27	37	48	56	25	43
33	60	41	31	47	24
44	23	34	49	28	58
50	39	30	22	59	36
61	45	26	40	35	29

Earth - Sun

61	50	44	33	27	21
45	39	23	60	37	32
26	30	34	41	48	57
40	22	49	31	56	38
35	59	28	47	25	42
29	36	58	24	43	46

Occult Encyclopedia of Magic Squares

Air - Sun

29	35	40	26	45	61
36	59	22	30	39	50
58	28	49	34	23	44
24	47	31	41	60	33
43	25	56	48	37	27
46	42	38	57	32	21

Water - Sun

46	43	24	58	36	29
42	25	47	28	59	35
38	56	31	49	22	40
57	48	41	34	30	26
32	37	60	23	39	45
21	27	33	44	50	61

	Number	Angel Value (Arabic)	Angel Value (Hebrew)	Jinn Value (Arabic)	Jinn Value (Hebrew)
Usurper	21	340	350	62	52
Guide	61	20	30	102	92
Mystery	82	41	51	123	113
Adjuster	236	195	205	277	267
Leader	708	667	677	389	379
Regulator	944	903	913	625	615
General Governor	1888	1847	1857	1569	1559
High Overseer	115168	115127	115137	114849	114839

Fire - Venus

9	50	35	20	40	58	24
59	25	10	44	36	21	41
22	42	60	26	11	45	30
46	31	16	43	61	27	12
28	13	47	32	17	37	62
38	56	29	14	48	33	18
34	19	39	57	23	15	49

Earth - Venus

34	38	28	46	22	59	9
19	56	13	31	42	25	50
39	29	47	16	60	10	35
57	14	32	43	26	44	20
23	48	17	61	11	36	40
15	33	37	27	45	21	58
49	18	62	12	30	41	24

Occult Encyclopedia of Magic Squares

Air - Venus

49	15	23	57	39	19	34
18	33	48	14	29	56	38
62	37	17	32	47	13	28
12	27	61	43	16	31	46
30	45	11	26	60	42	22
41	21	36	44	10	25	59
24	58	40	20	35	50	9

Water - Venus

24	41	30	12	62	18	49
58	21	45	27	37	33	15
40	36	11	61	17	48	23
20	44	26	43	32	14	57
35	10	60	16	47	29	39
50	25	42	31	13	56	19
9	59	22	46	28	38	34

	Number	Angel Value (Arabic)	Angel Value (Hebrew)	Jinn Value (Arabic)	Jinn Value (Hebrew)
Usurper	9	328	338	50	40
Guide	62	21	31	103	93
Mystery	71	30	40	112	102
Adjuster	236	195	205	277	267
Leader	708	667	677	389	379
Regulator	944	903	913	625	615
General Governor	1888	1847	1857	1569	1559
High Overseer	117056	117015	117025	116737	116727

ANGEL RULING 1ST HOUSE: AYEL (42)

This Hebrew Squares Not Available

Fire - Saturn

15	10	17
16	14	12
11	18	13

Earth - Saturn

11	16	15
18	14	10
13	12	17

Air - Saturn

13	18	11
12	14	16
17	10	15

Water - Saturn

17	12	13
10	14	18
15	16	11

	Number	Angel Value (Arabic)	Angel Value (Hebrew)	Jinn Value (Arabic)	Jinn Value (Hebrew)
Usurper	10	329	339	51	41
Guide	18	337	347	59	49
Mystery	28	347	357	69	59
Adjuster	42	1	11	83	73
Leader	126	85	95	167	157
Regulator	168	127	137	209	199
General Governor	336	295	305	17	7
High Overseer	6048	6007	6017	5729	5719

Fire - Jupiter

3	14	8	17
16	9	11	6
13	4	18	7
10	15	5	12

Air - Jupiter

12	5	15	10
7	18	4	13
6	11	9	16
17	8	14	3

Earth - Jupiter

10	13	16	3
15	4	9	14
5	18	11	8
12	7	6	17

Water - Jupiter

17	6	7	12
8	11	18	5
14	9	4	15
3	16	13	10

	Number	Angel Value (Arabic)	Angel Value (Hebrew)	Jinn Value (Arabic)	Jinn Value (Hebrew)
Usurper	3	322	332	44	34
Guide	18	337	347	59	49
Mystery	21	340	350	62	52
Adjuster	336	295	305	17	7
Leader	1008	967	977	689	679
Regulator	1344	1303	1313	1025	1015
General Governor	2688	2647	2657	2369	2359
High Overseer	48384	48343	48353	48065	48055

ANGEL OF FIRST DECANATE: ZAZER (214)

Hebrew Squares Not Available

Fire - Jupiter

46	57	51	60
59	52	54	49
56	47	61	50
53	58	48	55

Air - Jupiter

55	48	58	53
50	61	47	56
49	54	52	59
60	51	57	46

Earth - Jupiter

53	56	59	46
58	47	52	57
48	61	54	51
55	50	49	60

Water - Jupiter

60	49	50	55
51	54	61	48
57	52	47	58
46	59	56	53

	Number	Angel Value (Arabic)	Angel Value (Hebrew)	Jinn Value (Arabic)	Jinn Value (Hebrew)
Usurper	46	5	15	87	77
Guide	61	20	30	102	92
Mystery	107	66	76	148	138
Adjuster	1712	1671	1681	1393	1383
Leader	5136	5095	5105	4817	4807
Regulator	6848	6807	6817	6529	6519
General Governor	13696	13655	13665	13377	13367
High Overseer	835456	835415	835425	835137	835127

Occult Encyclopedia of Magic Squares

Fire - Mars

30	58	48	42	36
43	37	31	54	49
55	45	44	38	32
39	33	56	46	40
47	41	35	34	57

Air - Mars

47	39	55	43	30
41	33	45	37	58
35	56	44	31	48
34	46	38	54	42
57	40	32	49	36

Earth - Mars

57	34	35	41	47
40	46	56	33	39
32	38	44	45	55
49	54	31	37	43
36	42	48	58	30

Water - Mars

36	49	32	40	57
42	54	38	46	34
48	31	44	56	35
58	37	45	33	41
30	43	55	39	47

	Number	Angel Value (Arabic)	Angel Value (Hebrew)	Jinn Value (Arabic)	Jinn Value (Hebrew)
Usurper	30	349	359	71	61
Guide	58	17	27	99	89
Mystery	88	47	57	129	119
Adjuster	214	173	183	255	245
Leader	642	601	611	323	313
Regulator	856	815	825	537	527
General Governor	1712	1671	1681	1393	1383
High Overseer	99296	99255	99265	98977	98967

Occult Encyclopedia of Magic Squares

Fire - Sun

18	29	50	35	39	43
24	34	45	49	22	40
30	53	38	28	44	21
41	20	31	46	25	51
47	36	27	19	52	33
54	42	23	37	32	26

Air - Sun

26	32	37	23	42	54
33	52	19	27	36	47
51	25	46	31	20	41
21	44	28	38	53	30
40	22	49	45	34	24
43	39	35	50	29	18

Earth - Sun

54	47	41	30	24	18
42	36	20	53	34	29
23	27	31	38	45	50
37	19	46	28	49	35
32	52	25	44	22	39
26	33	51	21	40	43

Water - Sun

43	40	21	51	33	26
39	22	44	25	52	32
35	49	28	46	19	37
50	45	38	31	27	23
29	34	53	20	36	42
18	24	30	41	47	54

	Number	Angel Value (Arabic)	Angel Value (Hebrew)	Jinn Value (Arabic)	Jinn Value (Hebrew)
Usurper	18	337	347	59	49
Guide	54	13	23	95	85
Mystery	72	31	41	113	103
Adjuster	214	173	183	255	245
Leader	642	601	611	323	313
Regulator	856	815	825	537	527
General Governor	1712	1671	1681	1393	1383
High Overseer	92448	92407	92417	92129	92119

Fire - Venus

6	47	32	17	37	54	21
55	22	7	41	33	18	38
19	39	56	23	8	42	27
43	28	13	40	57	24	9
25	10	44	29	14	34	58
35	52	26	11	45	30	15
31	16	36	53	20	12	46

Air - Venus

46	12	20	53	36	16	31
15	30	45	11	26	52	35
58	34	14	29	44	10	25
9	24	57	40	13	28	43
27	42	8	23	56	39	19
38	18	33	41	7	22	55
21	54	37	17	32	47	6

Earth - Venus

31	35	25	43	19	55	6
16	52	10	28	39	22	47
36	26	44	13	56	7	32
53	11	29	40	23	41	17
20	45	14	57	8	33	37
12	30	34	24	42	18	54
46	15	58	9	27	38	21

Water - Venus

21	38	27	9	58	15	46
54	18	42	24	34	30	12
37	33	8	57	14	45	20
17	41	23	40	29	11	53
32	7	56	13	44	26	36
47	22	39	28	10	52	16
6	55	19	43	25	35	31

	Number	Angel Value (Arabic)	Angel Value (Hebrew)	Jinn Value (Arabic)	Jinn Value (Hebrew)
Usurper	6	325	335	47	37
Guide	58	17	27	99	89
Mystery	64	23	33	105	95
Adjuster	214	173	183	255	245
Leader	642	601	611	323	313
Regulator	856	815	825	537	527
General Governor	1712	1671	1681	1393	1383
High Overseer	99296	99255	99265	98977	98967

ANGEL OF FIRST QUINANCE: VEHUEL (48)

אל	ו	ה	י
5	6	9	28
8	29	4	7
4	7	30	7

ל	א	ו	ה	י
ו	ה	ו	ל	א
ו	ל	א	ו	ה
א	ו	ה	ו	ל
ה	ו	ל	א	ו

Fire - Saturn

17	12	19
18	16	14
13	20	15

Earth - Saturn

13	18	17
20	16	12
15	14	19

Air - Saturn

15	20	13
14	16	18
19	12	17

Water - Saturn

19	14	15
12	16	20
17	18	13

	Number	Angel Value (Arabic)	Angel Value (Hebrew)	Jinn Value (Arabic)	Jinn Value (Hebrew)
Usurper	41	360	10	82	72
Guide	49	8	18	90	80
Mystery	90	49	59	131	121
Adjuster	135	94	104	176	166
Leader	405	364	374	86	76
Regulator	540	499	509	221	211
General Governor	1080	1039	1049	761	751
High Overseer	52920	52879	52889	52601	52591

Fire - Jupiter

4	15	9	20
19	10	12	7
14	5	21	8
11	18	6	13

Earth - Jupiter

11	14	19	4
18	5	10	15
6	21	12	9
13	8	7	20

Air - Jupiter

13	6	18	11
8	21	5	14
7	12	10	19
20	9	15	4

Water - Jupiter

20	7	8	13
9	12	21	6
15	10	5	18
4	19	14	11

	Number	Angel Value (Arabic)	Angel Value (Hebrew)	Jinn Value (Arabic)	Jinn Value (Hebrew)
Usurper	4	323	333	45	35
Guide	21	340	350	62	52
Mystery	25	344	354	66	56
Adjuster	384	343	353	65	55
Leader	1152	1111	1121	833	823
Regulator	1536	1495	1505	1217	1207
General Governor	3072	3031	3041	2753	2743
High Overseer	64512	64471	64481	64193	64183

ANGEL OF SECOND QUINANCE: DANIEL (95)

אל	י	נ	ד
3	51	13	28
12	29	2	52
49	5	30	11

ל	א	י	נ	ד
י	נ	ד	ל	א
ד	ל	א	י	נ
א	י	נ	ד	ל
נ	ד	ל	א	י

Fire - Saturn

33	28	35
34	32	30
29	36	31

Earth - Saturn

29	34	33
36	32	28
31	30	35

Air - Saturn

31	36	29
30	32	34
35	28	33

Water - Saturn

35	30	31
28	32	36
33	34	29

Occult Encyclopedia of Magic Squares

	Number	Angel Value (Arabic)	Angel Value (Hebrew)	Jinn Value (Arabic)	Jinn Value (Hebrew)
Usurper	28	347	357	69	59
Guide	36	355	5	77	67
Mystery	64	23	33	105	95
Adjuster	96	55	65	137	127
Leader	288	247	257	329	319
Regulator	384	343	353	65	55
General Governor	768	727	737	449	439
High Overseer	27648	27607	27617	27329	27319

Fire - Jupiter

16	27	21	32
31	22	24	19
26	17	33	20
23	30	18	25

Earth - Jupiter

23	26	31	16
30	17	22	27
18	33	24	21
25	20	19	32

Air - Jupiter

25	18	30	23
20	33	17	26
19	24	22	31
32	21	27	16

Water - Jupiter

32	19	20	25
21	24	33	18
27	22	17	30
16	31	26	23

	Number	Angel Value (Arabic)	Angel Value (Hebrew)	Jinn Value (Arabic)	Jinn Value (Hebrew)
Usurper	16	335	345	57	47
Guide	33	352	2	74	64
Mystery	49	8	18	90	80
Adjuster	768	727	737	449	439
Leader	2304	2263	2273	1985	1975
Regulator	3072	3031	3041	2753	2743
General Governor	6144	6103	6113	5825	5815
High Overseer	202752	202711	202721	202433	202423

Occult Encyclopedia of Magic Squares

Fire - Mars

7	32	25	19	13
20	14	8	28	26
29	22	21	15	9
16	10	30	23	17
24	18	12	11	31

Air - Mars

24	16	29	20	7
18	10	22	14	32
12	30	21	8	25
11	23	15	28	19
31	17	9	26	13

Earth - Mars

31	11	12	18	24
17	23	30	10	16
9	15	21	22	29
26	28	8	14	20
13	19	25	32	7

Water - Mars

13	26	9	17	31
19	28	15	23	11
25	8	21	30	12
32	14	22	10	18
7	20	29	16	24

	Number	Angel Value (Arabic)	Angel Value (Hebrew)	Jinn Value (Arabic)	Jinn Value (Hebrew)
Usurper	7	326	336	48	38
Guide	32	351	1	73	63
Mystery	39	358	8	80	70
Adjuster	96	55	65	137	127
Leader	288	247	257	329	319
Regulator	384	343	353	65	55
General Governor	768	727	737	449	439
High Overseer	24576	24535	24545	24257	24247

ANGEL OF SECOND DECANATE: BEHAHEMI (62)

י	מ	ה	בה
6	6	43	7
42	8	5	7
4	8	9	41

י	מ	ה	ה	ב
ה	ה	ב	י	מ
ב	י	מ	ה	ה
מ	ה	ה	ב	י
ה	ב	י	מ	ה

Fire - Jupiter

8	19	13	22
21	14	16	11
18	9	23	12
15	20	10	17

Air - Jupiter

17	10	20	15
12	23	9	18
11	16	14	21
22	13	19	8

Earth - Jupiter

15	18	21	8
20	9	14	19
10	23	16	13
17	12	11	22

Water - Jupiter

22	11	12	17
13	16	23	10
19	14	9	20
8	21	18	15

	Number	Angel Value (Arabic)	Angel Value (Hebrew)	Jinn Value (Arabic)	Jinn Value (Hebrew)
Usurper	8	327	337	49	39
Guide	23	342	352	64	54
Mystery	31	350	360	72	62
Adjuster	496	455	465	177	167
Leader	1488	1447	1457	1169	1159
Regulator	1984	1943	1953	1665	1655
General Governor	3968	3927	3937	3649	3639
High Overseer	91264	91223	91233	90945	90935

ANGEL OF THIRD QUINANCE: HECHASHIAH (328)

יה	ש	ח	ח
4	9	303	12
302	13	3	10
7	6	14	301

ה	י	ש	ח	ה
ש	ח	ה	ה	י
ה	ה	י	ש	ח
י	ש	ה	ה	ה
ה	ה	ה	י	ש

Fire - Jupiter

74	85	79	90
89	80	82	77
84	75	91	78
81	88	76	83

Air - Jupiter

83	76	88	81
78	91	75	84
77	82	80	89
90	79	85	74

Earth - Jupiter

81	84	89	74
88	75	80	85
76	91	82	79
83	78	77	90

Water - Jupiter

90	77	78	83
79	82	91	76
85	80	75	88
74	89	84	81

	Number	Angel Value (Arabic)	Angel Value (Hebrew)	Jinn Value (Arabic)	Jinn Value (Hebrew)
Usurper	74	33	43	115	105
Guide	91	50	60	132	122
Mystery	165	124	134	206	196
Adjuster	2624	2583	2593	2305	2295
Leader	7872	7831	7841	7553	7543
Regulator	10496	10455	10465	10177	10167
General Governor	20992	20951	20961	20673	20663
High Overseer	1910272	1910231	1910241	1909953	1909943

Occult Encyclopedia of Magic Squares

Fire - Mars

53	80	71	65	59
66	60	54	76	72
77	68	67	61	55
62	56	78	69	63
70	64	58	57	79

Air - Mars

70	62	77	66	53
64	56	68	60	80
58	78	67	54	71
57	69	61	76	65
79	63	55	72	59

Earth - Mars

79	57	58	64	70
63	69	78	56	62
55	61	67	68	77
72	76	54	60	66
59	65	71	80	53

Water - Mars

59	72	55	63	79
65	76	61	69	57
71	54	67	78	58
80	60	68	56	64
53	66	77	62	70

	Number	Angel Value (Arabic)	Angel Value (Hebrew)	Jinn Value (Arabic)	Jinn Value (Hebrew)
Usurper	53	12	22	94	84
Guide	80	39	49	121	111
Mystery	133	92	102	174	164
Adjuster	328	287	297	9	359
Leader	984	943	953	665	655
Regulator	1312	1271	1281	993	983
General Governor	2624	2583	2593	2305	2295
High Overseer	209920	209879	209889	209601	209591

Fire - Sun

37	48	69	54	58	62
43	53	64	68	41	59
49	72	57	47	63	40
60	39	50	65	44	70
66	55	46	38	71	52
73	61	42	56	51	45

Earth - Sun

73	66	60	49	43	37
61	55	39	72	53	48
42	46	50	57	64	69
56	38	65	47	68	54
51	71	44	63	41	58
45	52	70	40	59	62

Occult Encyclopedia of Magic Squares

Air - Sun

45	51	56	42	61	73
52	71	38	46	55	66
70	44	65	50	39	60
40	63	47	57	72	49
59	41	68	64	53	43
62	58	54	69	48	37

Water - Sun

62	59	40	70	52	45
58	41	63	44	71	51
54	68	47	65	38	56
69	64	57	50	46	42
48	53	72	39	55	61
37	43	49	60	66	73

	Number	Angel Value (Arabic)	Angel Value (Hebrew)	Jinn Value (Arabic)	Jinn Value (Hebrew)
Usurper	37	356	6	78	68
Guide	73	32	42	114	104
Mystery	110	69	79	151	141
Adjuster	328	287	297	9	359
Leader	984	943	953	665	655
Regulator	1312	1271	1281	993	983
General Governor	2624	2583	2593	2305	2295
High Overseer	191552	191511	191521	191233	191223

Fire - Venus

22	63	48	33	53	72	37
73	38	23	57	49	34	54
35	55	74	39	24	58	43
59	44	29	56	75	40	25
41	26	60	45	30	50	76
51	70	42	27	61	46	31
47	32	52	71	36	28	62

Earth - Venus

47	51	41	59	35	73	22
32	70	26	44	55	38	63
52	42	60	29	74	23	48
71	27	45	56	39	57	33
36	61	30	75	24	49	53
28	46	50	40	58	34	72
62	31	76	25	43	54	37

Occult Encyclopedia of Magic Squares

Air - Venus

62	28	36	71	52	32	47
31	46	61	27	42	70	51
76	50	30	45	60	26	41
25	40	75	56	29	44	59
43	58	24	39	74	55	35
54	34	49	57	23	38	73
37	72	53	33	48	63	22

Water - Venus

37	54	43	25	76	31	62
72	34	58	40	50	46	28
53	49	24	75	30	61	36
33	57	39	56	45	27	71
48	23	74	29	60	42	52
63	38	55	44	26	70	32
22	73	35	59	41	51	47

	Number	Angel Value (Arabic)	Angel Value (Hebrew)	Jinn Value (Arabic)	Jinn Value (Hebrew)
Usurper	22	341	351	63	53
Guide	76	35	45	117	107
Mystery	98	57	67	139	129
Adjuster	328	287	297	9	359
Leader	984	943	953	665	655
Regulator	1312	1271	1281	993	983
General Governor	2624	2583	2593	2305	2295
High Overseer	199424	199383	199393	199105	199095

Fire - Mercury

9	25	74	54	43	59	40	24
17	33	62	46	51	71	32	16
60	44	23	39	26	10	53	73
72	52	15	31	34	18	45	61
38	22	41	57	76	56	11	27
30	14	49	69	64	48	19	35
55	75	28	12	21	37	58	42
47	63	36	20	13	29	70	50

Occult Encyclopedia of Magic Squares

Earth - Mercury

47	55	30	38	72	60	17	9
63	75	14	22	52	44	33	25
36	28	49	41	15	23	62	74
20	12	69	57	31	39	46	54
13	21	64	76	34	26	51	43
29	37	48	56	18	10	71	59
70	58	19	11	45	53	32	40
50	42	35	27	61	73	16	24

Air - Mercury

50	70	29	13	20	36	63	47
42	58	37	21	12	28	75	55
35	19	48	64	69	49	14	30
27	11	56	76	57	41	22	38
61	45	18	34	31	15	52	72
73	53	10	26	39	23	44	60
16	32	71	51	46	62	33	17
24	40	59	43	54	74	25	9

Water - Mercury

24	16	73	61	27	35	42	50
40	32	53	45	11	19	58	70
59	71	10	18	56	48	37	29
43	51	26	34	76	64	21	13
54	46	39	31	57	69	12	20
74	62	23	15	41	49	28	36
25	33	44	52	22	14	75	63
9	17	60	72	38	30	55	47

	Number	Angel Value (Arabic)	Angel Value (Hebrew)	Jinn Value (Arabic)	Jinn Value (Hebrew)
Usurper	9	328	338	50	40
Guide	76	35	45	117	107
Mystery	85	44	54	126	116
Adjuster	328	287	297	9	359
Leader	984	943	953	665	655
Regulator	1312	1271	1281	993	983
General Governor	2624	2583	2593	2305	2295
High Overseer	199424	199383	199393	199105	199095

ANGEL OF FOURTH QUINANCE: AMAMIAH (165)

ה	מ	מ	ע
69	41	43	12
42	13	68	42
39	71	14	41

ה	י	מ	מ	ע
מ	מ	ע	ה	י
ע	ה	י	מ	מ
י	מ	מ	ע	ה
מ	ע	ה	י	מ

Fire - Saturn

56	51	58
57	55	53
52	59	54

Air - Saturn

54	59	52
53	55	57
58	51	56

Earth - Saturn

52	57	56
59	55	51
54	53	58

Water - Saturn

58	53	54
51	55	59
56	57	52

Occult Encyclopedia of Magic Squares

	Number	Angel Value (Arabic)	Angel Value (Hebrew)	Jinn Value (Arabic)	Jinn Value (Hebrew)
Usurper	51	10	20	92	82
Guide	59	18	28	100	90
Mystery	110	69	79	151	141
Adjuster	165	124	134	206	196
Leader	495	454	464	176	166
Regulator	660	619	629	341	331
General Governor	1320	1279	1289	1001	991
High Overseer	77880	77839	77849	77561	77551

Fire - Jupiter

33	44	38	50
49	39	41	36
43	34	51	37
40	48	35	42

Air - Jupiter

42	35	48	40
37	51	34	43
36	41	39	49
50	38	44	33

Earth - Jupiter

40	43	49	33
48	34	39	44
35	51	41	38
42	37	36	50

Water - Jupiter

50	36	37	42
38	41	51	35
44	39	34	48
33	49	43	40

	Number	Angel Value (Arabic)	Angel Value (Hebrew)	Jinn Value (Arabic)	Jinn Value (Hebrew)
Usurper	33	352	2	74	64
Guide	51	10	20	92	82
Mystery	84	43	53	125	115
Adjuster	1320	1279	1289	1001	991
Leader	3960	3919	3929	3641	3631
Regulator	5280	5239	5249	4961	4951
General Governor	10560	10519	10529	10241	10231
High Overseer	538560	538519	538529	538241	538231

Occult Encyclopedia of Magic Squares

Fire - Mars

21	45	39	33	27
34	28	22	41	40
42	36	35	29	23
30	24	43	37	31
38	32	26	25	44

Air - Mars

38	30	42	34	21
32	24	36	28	45
26	43	35	22	39
25	37	29	41	33
44	31	23	40	27

Earth - Mars

44	25	26	32	38
31	37	43	24	30
23	29	35	36	42
40	41	22	28	34
27	33	39	45	21

Water - Mars

27	40	23	31	44
33	41	29	37	25
39	22	35	43	26
45	28	36	24	32
21	34	42	30	38

	Number	Angel Value (Arabic)	Angel Value (Hebrew)	Jinn Value (Arabic)	Jinn Value (Hebrew)
Usurper	21	340	350	62	52
Guide	45	4	14	86	76
Mystery	66	25	35	107	97
Adjuster	165	124	134	206	196
Leader	495	454	464	176	166
Regulator	660	619	629	341	331
General Governor	1320	1279	1289	1001	991
High Overseer	59400	59359	59369	59081	59071

Fire - Sun

10	21	41	27	31	35
16	26	37	40	14	32
22	44	30	20	36	13
33	12	23	38	17	42
39	28	19	11	43	25
45	34	15	29	24	18

Earth - Sun

45	39	33	22	16	10
34	28	12	44	26	21
15	19	23	30	37	41
29	11	38	20	40	27
24	43	17	36	14	31
18	25	42	13	32	35

Air - Sun

18	24	29	15	34	45
25	43	11	19	28	39
42	17	38	23	12	33
13	36	20	30	44	22
32	14	40	37	26	16
35	31	27	41	21	10

Water - Sun

35	32	13	42	25	18
31	14	36	17	43	24
27	40	20	38	11	29
41	37	30	23	19	15
21	26	44	12	28	34
10	16	22	33	39	45

	Number	Angel Value (Arabic)	Angel Value (Hebrew)	Jinn Value (Arabic)	Jinn Value (Hebrew)
Usurper	10	329	339	51	41
Guide	45	4	14	86	76
Mystery	55	14	24	96	86
Adjuster	165	124	134	206	196
Leader	495	454	464	176	166
Regulator	660	619	629	341	331
General Governor	1320	1279	1289	1001	991
High Overseer	59400	59359	59369	59081	59071

ANGEL OF THIRD DECANATE: SATANDER (323)

ר	ד	נ	סט
68	51	7	197
6	198	67	52
49	70	199	5

ר	ד	נ	ט	ס
נ	ט	ס	ר	ד
ס	ר	ד	נ	ט
ד	נ	ט	ס	ר
ט	ס	ר	ד	נ

Occult Encyclopedia of Magic Squares

Fire - Jupiter

73	84	78	88
87	79	81	76
83	74	89	77
80	86	75	82

Air - Jupiter

82	75	86	80
77	89	74	83
76	81	79	87
88	78	84	73

Earth - Jupiter

80	83	87	73
86	74	79	84
75	89	81	78
82	77	76	88

Water - Jupiter

88	76	77	82
78	81	89	75
84	79	74	86
73	87	83	80

	Number	Angel Value (Arabic)	Angel Value (Hebrew)	Jinn Value (Arabic)	Jinn Value (Hebrew)
Usurper	73	32	42	114	104
Guide	89	48	58	130	120
Mystery	162	121	131	203	193
Adjuster	2584	2543	2553	2265	2255
Leader	7752	7711	7721	7433	7423
Regulator	10336	10295	10305	10017	10007
General Governor	20672	20631	20641	20353	20343
High Overseer	1839808	1839767	1839777	1839489	1839479

Fire - Mars

52	79	70	64	58
65	59	53	75	71
76	67	66	60	54
61	55	77	68	62
69	63	57	56	78

Air - Mars

69	61	76	65	52
63	55	67	59	79
57	77	66	53	70
56	68	60	75	64
78	62	54	71	58

Earth - Mars

78	56	57	63	69
62	68	77	55	61
54	60	66	67	76
71	75	53	59	65
58	64	70	79	52

Water - Mars

58	71	54	62	78
64	75	60	68	56
70	53	66	77	57
79	59	67	55	63
52	65	76	61	69

Occult Encyclopedia of Magic Squares

	Number	Angel Value (Arabic)	Angel Value (Hebrew)	Jinn Value (Arabic)	Jinn Value (Hebrew)
Usurper	52	11	21	93	83
Guide	79	38	48	120	110
Mystery	131	90	100	172	162
Adjuster	323	282	292	4	354
Leader	969	928	938	650	640
Regulator	1292	1251	1261	973	963
General Governor	2584	2543	2553	2265	2255
High Overseer	204136	204095	204105	203817	203807

Fire - Sun

36	47	69	53	57	61
42	52	63	68	40	58
48	72	56	46	62	39
59	38	49	64	43	70
65	54	45	37	71	51
73	60	41	55	50	44

Air - Sun

44	50	55	41	60	73
51	71	37	45	54	65
70	43	64	49	38	59
39	62	46	56	72	48
58	40	68	63	52	42
61	57	53	69	47	36

Earth - Sun

73	65	59	48	42	36
60	54	38	72	52	47
41	45	49	56	63	69
55	37	64	46	68	53
50	71	43	62	40	57
44	51	70	39	58	61

Water - Sun

61	58	39	70	51	44
57	40	62	43	71	50
53	68	46	64	37	55
69	63	56	49	45	41
47	52	72	38	54	60
36	42	48	59	65	73

Occult Encyclopedia of Magic Squares

	Number	Angel Value (Arabic)	Angel Value (Hebrew)	Jinn Value (Arabic)	Jinn Value (Hebrew)
Usurper	36	355	5	77	67
Guide	73	32	42	114	104
Mystery	109	68	78	150	140
Adjuster	323	282	292	4	354
Leader	969	928	938	650	640
Regulator	1292	1251	1261	973	963
General Governor	2584	2543	2553	2265	2255
High Overseer	188632	188591	188601	188313	188303

Fire - Venus

22	63	48	33	53	67	37
68	38	23	57	49	34	54
35	55	69	39	24	58	43
59	44	29	56	70	40	25
41	26	60	45	30	50	71
51	65	42	27	61	46	31
47	32	52	66	36	28	62

Air - Venus

62	28	36	66	52	32	47
31	46	61	27	42	65	51
71	50	30	45	60	26	41
25	40	70	56	29	44	59
43	58	24	39	69	55	35
54	34	49	57	23	38	68
37	67	53	33	48	63	22

Earth - Venus

47	51	41	59	35	68	22
32	65	26	44	55	38	63
52	42	60	29	69	23	48
66	27	45	56	39	57	33
36	61	30	70	24	49	53
28	46	50	40	58	34	67
62	31	71	25	43	54	37

Water - Venus

37	54	43	25	71	31	62
67	34	58	40	50	46	28
53	49	24	70	30	61	36
33	57	39	56	45	27	66
48	23	69	29	60	42	52
63	38	55	44	26	65	32
22	68	35	59	41	51	47

Occult Encyclopedia of Magic Squares

	Number	Angel Value (Arabic)	Angel Value (Hebrew)	Jinn Value (Arabic)	Jinn Value (Hebrew)
Usurper	22	341	351	63	53
Guide	71	30	40	112	102
Mystery	93	52	62	134	124
Adjuster	323	282	292	4	354
Leader	969	928	938	650	640
Regulator	1292	1251	1261	973	963
General Governor	2584	2543	2553	2265	2255
High Overseer	183464	183423	183433	183145	183135

Fire - Mercury

8	24	76	53	42	58	39	23
16	32	61	45	50	73	31	15
59	43	22	38	25	9	52	75
74	51	14	30	33	17	44	60
37	21	40	56	78	55	10	26
29	13	48	71	63	47	18	34
54	77	27	11	20	36	57	41
46	62	35	19	12	28	72	49

Earth - Mercury

46	54	29	37	74	59	16	8
62	77	13	21	51	43	32	24
35	27	48	40	14	22	61	76
19	11	71	56	30	38	45	53
12	20	63	78	33	25	50	42
28	36	47	55	17	9	73	58
72	57	18	10	44	52	31	39
49	41	34	26	60	75	15	23

Occult Encyclopedia of Magic Squares

Air - Mercury

49	72	28	12	19	35	62	46
41	57	36	20	11	27	77	54
34	18	47	63	71	48	13	29
26	10	55	78	56	40	21	37
60	44	17	33	30	14	51	74
75	52	9	25	38	22	43	59
15	31	73	50	45	61	32	16
23	39	58	42	53	76	24	8

Water - Mercury

23	15	75	60	26	34	41	49
39	31	52	44	10	18	57	72
58	73	9	17	55	47	36	28
42	50	25	33	78	63	20	12
53	45	38	30	56	71	11	19
76	61	22	14	40	48	27	35
24	32	43	51	21	13	77	62
8	16	59	74	37	29	54	46

	Number	Angel Value (Arabic)	Angel Value (Hebrew)	Jinn Value (Arabic)	Jinn Value (Hebrew)
Usurper	8	327	337	49	39
Guide	78	37	47	119	109
Mystery	86	45	55	127	117
Adjuster	323	282	292	4	354
Leader	969	928	938	650	640
Regulator	1292	1251	1261	973	963
General Governor	2584	2543	2553	2265	2255
High Overseer	201552	201511	201521	201233	201223

ANGEL OF FIFTH QUINANCE: NANAEL (132)

אל	א	נ	נ
29	31	4	28
3	29	28	32
29	31	30	2

ל	א	א	נ	נ
א	נ	נ	ל	א
נ	ל	א	א	נ
א	א	נ	נ	ל
נ	נ	ל	א	א

Fire - Saturn

45	40	47
46	44	42
41	48	43

Air - Saturn

43	48	41
42	44	46
47	40	45

Earth - Saturn

41	46	45
48	44	40
43	42	47

Water - Saturn

47	42	43
40	44	48
45	46	41

	Number	Angel Value (Arabic)	Angel Value (Hebrew)	Jinn Value (Arabic)	Jinn Value (Hebrew)
Usurper	40	359	9	81	71
Guide	48	7	17	89	79
Mystery	88	47	57	129	119
Adjuster	132	91	101	173	163
Leader	396	355	365	77	67
Regulator	528	487	497	209	199
General Governor	1056	1015	1025	737	727
High Overseer	50688	50647	50657	50369	50359

Occult Encyclopedia of Magic Squares

Fire - Jupiter

25	36	30	41
40	31	33	28
35	26	42	29
32	39	27	34

Air - Jupiter

34	27	39	32
29	42	26	35
28	33	31	40
41	30	36	25

Earth - Jupiter

32	35	40	25
39	26	31	36
27	42	33	30
34	29	28	41

Water - Jupiter

41	28	29	34
30	33	42	27
36	31	26	39
25	40	35	32

	Number	Angel Value (Arabic)	Angel Value (Hebrew)	Jinn Value (Arabic)	Jinn Value (Hebrew)
Usurper	25	344	354	66	56
Guide	42	1	11	83	73
Mystery	67	26	36	108	98
Adjuster	1056	1015	1025	737	727
Leader	3168	3127	3137	2849	2839
Regulator	4224	4183	4193	3905	3895
General Governor	8448	8407	8417	8129	8119
High Overseer	354816	354775	354785	354497	354487

Fire - Mars

14	40	32	26	20
27	21	15	36	33
37	29	28	22	16
23	17	38	30	24
31	25	19	18	39

Air - Mars

31	23	37	27	14
25	17	29	21	40
19	38	28	15	32
18	30	22	36	26
39	24	16	33	20

Earth - Mars

39	18	19	25	31
24	30	38	17	23
16	22	28	29	37
33	36	15	21	27
20	26	32	40	14

Water - Mars

20	33	16	24	39
26	36	22	30	18
32	15	28	38	19
40	21	29	17	25
14	27	37	23	31

	Number	Angel Value (Arabic)	Angel Value (Hebrew)	Jinn Value (Arabic)	Jinn Value (Hebrew)
Usurper	14	333	343	55	45
Guide	40	359	9	81	71
Mystery	54	13	23	95	85
Adjuster	132	91	101	173	163
Leader	396	355	365	77	67
Regulator	528	487	497	209	199
General Governor	1056	1015	1025	737	727
High Overseer	42240	42199	42209	41921	41911

Fire - Sun

4	15	38	21	25	29
10	20	31	37	8	26
16	41	24	14	30	7
27	6	17	32	11	39
33	22	13	5	40	19
42	28	9	23	18	12

Air - Sun

12	18	23	9	28	42
19	40	5	13	22	33
39	11	32	17	6	27
7	30	14	24	41	16
26	8	37	31	20	10
29	25	21	38	15	4

Earth - Sun

42	33	27	16	10	4
28	22	6	41	20	15
9	13	17	24	31	38
23	5	32	14	37	21
18	40	11	30	8	25
12	19	39	7	26	29

Water - Sun

29	26	7	39	19	12
25	8	30	11	40	18
21	37	14	32	5	23
38	31	24	17	13	9
15	20	41	6	22	28
4	10	16	27	33	42

	Number	Angel Value (Arabic)	Angel Value (Hebrew)	Jinn Value (Arabic)	Jinn Value (Hebrew)
Usurper	4	323	333	45	35
Guide	42	1	11	83	73
Mystery	46	5	15	87	77
Adjuster	132	91	101	173	163
Leader	396	355	365	77	67
Regulator	528	487	497	209	199
General Governor	1056	1015	1025	737	727
High Overseer	44352	44311	44321	44033	44023

ANGEL OF SIX QUINANCE: NITHAEL (132)

אל	ת	י	נ
49	11	403	28
402	29	48	12
9	51	30	401

ל	א	ת	י	נ
ת	י	נ	ל	א
נ	ל	א	ת	י
א	ת	י	נ	ל
י	נ	ל	א	ת

Fire - Jupiter

115	126	120	130
129	121	123	118
125	116	131	119
122	128	117	124

Air - Jupiter

124	117	128	122
119	131	116	125
118	123	121	129
130	120	126	115

Earth - Jupiter

122	125	129	115
128	116	121	126
117	131	123	120
124	119	118	130

Water - Jupiter

130	118	119	124
120	123	131	117
126	121	116	128
115	129	125	122

	Number	Angel Value (Arabic)	Angel Value (Hebrew)	Jinn Value (Arabic)	Jinn Value (Hebrew)
Usurper	115	74	84	156	146
Guide	131	90	100	172	162
Mystery	246	205	215	287	277
Adjuster	3928	3887	3897	3609	3599
Leader	11784	11743	11753	11465	11455
Regulator	15712	15671	15681	15393	15383
General Governor	31424	31383	31393	31105	31095
High Overseer	4116544	4116503	4116513	4116225	4116215

Occult Encyclopedia of Magic Squares

Fire - Mars

86	111	104	98	92
99	93	87	107	105
108	101	100	94	88
95	89	109	102	96
103	97	91	90	110

Air - Mars

103	95	108	99	86
97	89	101	93	111
91	109	100	87	104
90	102	94	107	98
110	96	88	105	92

Earth - Mars

110	90	91	97	103
96	102	109	89	95
88	94	100	101	108
105	107	87	93	99
92	98	104	111	86

Water - Mars

92	105	88	96	110
98	107	94	102	90
104	87	100	109	91
111	93	101	89	97
86	99	108	95	103

	Number	Angel Value (Arabic)	Angel Value (Hebrew)	Jinn Value (Arabic)	Jinn Value (Hebrew)
Usurper	86	45	55	127	117
Guide	111	70	80	152	142
Mystery	197	156	166	238	228
Adjuster	491	450	460	172	162
Leader	1473	1432	1442	1154	1144
Regulator	1964	1923	1933	1645	1635
General Governor	3928	3887	3897	3609	3599
High Overseer	436008	435967	435977	435689	435679

Fire - Sun

64	75	97	81	85	89
70	80	91	96	68	86
76	100	84	74	90	67
87	66	77	92	71	98
93	82	73	65	99	79
101	88	69	83	78	72

Earth - Sun

101	93	87	76	70	64
88	82	66	100	80	75
69	73	77	84	91	97
83	65	92	74	96	81
78	99	71	90	68	85
72	79	98	67	86	89

Occult Encyclopedia of Magic Squares

Air - Sun

72	78	83	69	88	101
79	99	65	73	82	93
98	71	92	77	66	87
67	90	74	84	100	76
86	68	96	91	80	70
89	85	81	97	75	64

Water - Sun

89	86	67	98	79	72
85	68	90	71	99	78
81	96	74	92	65	83
97	91	84	77	73	69
75	80	100	66	82	88
64	70	76	87	93	101

	Number	Angel Value (Arabic)	Angel Value (Hebrew)	Jinn Value (Arabic)	Jinn Value (Hebrew)
Usurper	64	23	33	105	95
Guide	101	60	70	142	132
Mystery	165	124	134	206	196
Adjuster	491	450	460	172	162
Leader	1473	1432	1442	1154	1144
Regulator	1964	1923	1933	1645	1635
General Governor	3928	3887	3897	3609	3599
High Overseer	396728	396687	396697	396409	396399

Fire - Venus

46	87	72	57	77	91	61
92	62	47	81	73	58	78
59	79	93	63	48	82	67
83	68	53	80	94	64	49
65	50	84	69	54	74	95
75	89	66	51	85	70	55
71	56	76	90	60	52	86

Air - Venus

86	52	60	90	76	56	71
55	70	85	51	66	89	75
95	74	54	69	84	50	65
49	64	94	80	53	68	83
67	82	48	63	93	79	59
78	58	73	81	47	62	92
61	91	77	57	72	87	46

Earth - Venus

71	75	65	83	59	92	46
56	89	50	68	79	62	87
76	66	84	53	93	47	72
90	51	69	80	63	81	57
60	85	54	94	48	73	77
52	70	74	64	82	58	91
86	55	95	49	67	78	61

Water - Venus

61	78	67	49	95	55	86
91	58	82	64	74	70	52
77	73	48	94	54	85	60
57	81	63	80	69	51	90
72	47	93	53	84	66	76
87	62	79	68	50	89	56
46	92	59	83	65	75	71

Occult Encyclopedia of Magic Squares

	Number	Angel Value (Arabic)	Angel Value (Hebrew)	Jinn Value (Arabic)	Jinn Value (Hebrew)
Usurper	46	5	15	87	77
Guide	95	54	64	136	126
Mystery	141	100	110	182	172
Adjuster	491	450	460	172	162
Leader	1473	1432	1442	1154	1144
Regulator	1964	1923	1933	1645	1635
General Governor	3928	3887	3897	3609	3599
High Overseer	373160	373119	373129	372841	372831

Fire - Mercury

29	45	97	74	63	79	60	44
37	53	82	66	71	94	52	36
80	64	43	59	46	30	73	96
95	72	35	51	54	38	65	81
58	42	61	77	99	76	31	47
50	34	69	92	84	68	39	55
75	98	48	32	41	57	78	62
67	83	56	40	33	49	93	70

Earth - Mercury

67	75	50	58	95	80	37	29
83	98	34	42	72	64	53	45
56	48	69	61	35	43	82	97
40	32	92	77	51	59	66	74
33	41	84	99	54	46	71	63
49	57	68	76	38	30	94	79
93	78	39	31	65	73	52	60
70	62	55	47	81	96	36	44

Occult Encyclopedia of Magic Squares

Air - Mercury

70	93	49	33	40	56	83	67
62	78	57	41	32	48	98	75
55	39	68	84	92	69	34	50
47	31	76	99	77	61	42	58
81	65	38	54	51	35	72	95
96	73	30	46	59	43	64	80
36	52	94	71	66	82	53	37
44	60	79	63	74	97	45	29

Water - Mercury

44	36	96	81	47	55	62	70
60	52	73	65	31	39	78	93
79	94	30	38	76	68	57	49
63	71	46	54	99	84	41	33
74	66	59	51	77	92	32	40
97	82	43	35	61	69	48	56
45	53	64	72	42	34	98	83
29	37	80	95	58	50	75	67

	Number	Angel Value (Arabic)	Angel Value (Hebrew)	Jinn Value (Arabic)	Jinn Value (Hebrew)
Usurper	29	348	358	70	60
Guide	99	58	68	140	130
Mystery	128	87	97	169	159
Adjuster	491	450	460	172	162
Leader	1473	1432	1442	1154	1144
Regulator	1964	1923	1933	1645	1635
General Governor	3928	3887	3897	3609	3599
High Overseer	388872	388831	388841	388553	388543

Fire - Moon

58	71	33	42	99	26	62	78	22
18	61	83	38	54	70	25	47	95
91	30	46	82	14	66	75	37	50
85	17	60	69	40	53	94	24	49
45	93	29	65	81	16	52	74	36
32	57	73	28	41	98	21	64	77
31	44	92	15	67	80	35	51	76
72	34	56	97	27	43	79	20	63
59	84	19	55	68	39	48	96	23

Earth - Moon

22	95	50	49	36	77	76	63	23
78	47	37	24	74	64	51	20	96
62	25	75	94	52	21	35	79	48
26	70	66	53	16	98	80	43	39
99	54	14	40	81	41	67	27	68
42	38	82	69	65	28	15	97	55
33	83	46	60	29	73	92	56	19
71	61	30	17	93	57	44	34	84
58	18	91	85	45	32	31	72	59

Air - Moon

23	96	48	39	68	55	19	84	59
63	20	79	43	27	97	56	34	72
76	51	35	80	67	15	92	44	31
77	64	21	98	41	28	73	57	32
36	74	52	16	81	65	29	93	45
49	24	94	53	40	69	60	17	85
50	37	75	66	14	82	46	30	91
95	47	25	70	54	38	83	61	18
22	78	62	26	99	42	33	71	58

Occult Encyclopedia of Magic Squares

Water - Moon

59	72	31	32	45	85	91	18	58
84	34	44	57	93	17	30	61	71
19	56	92	73	29	60	46	83	33
55	97	15	28	65	69	82	38	42
68	27	67	41	81	40	14	54	99
39	43	80	98	16	53	66	70	26
48	79	35	21	52	94	75	25	62
96	20	51	64	74	24	37	47	78
23	63	76	77	36	49	50	95	22

	Number	Angel Value (Arabic)	Angel Value (Hebrew)	Jinn Value (Arabic)	Jinn Value (Hebrew)
Usurper	14	333	343	55	45
Guide	99	58	68	140	130
Mystery	113	72	82	154	144
Adjuster	491	450	460	172	162
Leader	1473	1432	1442	1154	1144
Regulator	1964	1923	1933	1645	1635
General Governor	3928	3887	3897	3609	3599
High Overseer	388872	388831	388841	388553	388543

TAURUS

SIGN TAURUS: SHOR (506)

No Hebrew Squares Available

Fire - Jupiter

119	130	124	133
132	125	127	122
129	120	134	123
126	131	121	128

Air - Jupiter

128	121	131	126
123	134	120	129
122	127	125	132
133	124	130	119

Earth - Jupiter

126	129	132	119
131	120	125	130
121	134	127	124
128	123	122	133

Water - Jupiter

133	122	123	128
124	127	134	121
130	125	120	131
119	132	129	126

	Number	Angel Value (Arabic)	Angel Value (Hebrew)	Jinn Value (Arabic)	Jinn Value (Hebrew)
Usurper	119	78	88	160	150
Guide	134	93	103	175	165
Mystery	253	212	222	294	284
Adjuster	4048	4007	4017	3729	3719
Leader	12144	12103	12113	11825	11815
Regulator	16192	16151	16161	15873	15863
General Governor	32384	32343	32353	32065	32055
High Overseer	4339456	4339415	4339425	4339137	4339127

Occult Encyclopedia of Magic Squares

Fire - Mars

89	114	107	101	95
102	96	90	110	108
111	104	103	97	91
98	92	112	105	99
106	100	94	93	113

Air - Mars

106	98	111	102	89
100	92	104	96	114
94	112	103	90	107
93	105	97	110	101
113	99	91	108	95

Earth - Mars

113	93	94	100	106
99	105	112	92	98
91	97	103	104	111
108	110	90	96	102
95	101	107	114	89

Water - Mars

95	108	91	99	113
101	110	97	105	93
107	90	103	112	94
114	96	104	92	100
89	102	111	98	106

	Number	Angel Value (Arabic)	Angel Value (Hebrew)	Jinn Value (Arabic)	Jinn Value (Hebrew)
Usurper	89	48	58	130	120
Guide	114	73	83	155	145
Mystery	203	162	172	244	234
Adjuster	506	465	475	187	177
Leader	1518	1477	1487	1199	1189
Regulator	2024	1983	1993	1705	1695
General Governor	4048	4007	4017	3729	3719
High Overseer	461472	461431	461441	461153	461143

Fire - Sun

66	77	102	83	87	91
72	82	93	101	70	88
78	105	86	76	92	69
89	68	79	94	73	103
95	84	75	67	104	81
106	90	71	85	80	74

Earth - Sun

106	95	89	78	72	66
90	84	68	105	82	77
71	75	79	86	93	102
85	67	94	76	101	83
80	104	73	92	70	87
74	81	103	69	88	91

Occult Encyclopedia of Magic Squares

Air - Sun

74	80	85	71	90	106
81	104	67	75	84	95
103	73	94	79	68	89
69	92	76	86	105	78
88	70	101	93	82	72
91	87	83	102	77	66

Water - Sun

91	88	69	103	81	74
87	70	92	73	104	80
83	101	76	94	67	85
102	93	86	79	75	71
77	82	105	68	84	90
66	72	78	89	95	106

	Number	Angel Value (Arabic)	Angel Value (Hebrew)	Jinn Value (Arabic)	Jinn Value (Hebrew)
Usurper	66	25	35	107	97
Guide	106	65	75	147	137
Mystery	172	131	141	213	203
Adjuster	506	465	475	187	177
Leader	1518	1477	1487	1199	1189
Regulator	2024	1983	1993	1705	1695
General Governor	4048	4007	4017	3729	3719
High Overseer	429088	429047	429057	428769	428759

Fire - Venus

48	89	74	59	79	94	63
95	64	49	83	75	60	80
61	81	96	65	50	84	69
85	70	55	82	97	66	51
67	52	86	71	56	76	98
77	92	68	53	87	72	57
73	58	78	93	62	54	88

Air - Venus

88	54	62	93	78	58	73
57	72	87	53	68	92	77
98	76	56	71	86	52	67
51	66	97	82	55	70	85
69	84	50	65	96	81	61
80	60	75	83	49	64	95
63	94	79	59	74	89	48

Earth - Venus

73	77	67	85	61	95	48
58	92	52	70	81	64	89
78	68	86	55	96	49	74
93	53	71	82	65	83	59
62	87	56	97	50	75	79
54	72	76	66	84	60	94
88	57	98	51	69	80	63

Water - Venus

63	80	69	51	98	57	88
94	60	84	66	76	72	54
79	75	50	97	56	87	62
59	83	65	82	71	53	93
74	49	96	55	86	68	78
89	64	81	70	52	92	58
48	95	61	85	67	77	73

Occult Encyclopedia of Magic Squares

	Number	Angel Value (Arabic)	Angel Value (Hebrew)	Jinn Value (Arabic)	Jinn Value (Hebrew)
Usurper	48	7	17	89	79
Guide	98	57	67	139	129
Mystery	146	105	115	187	177
Adjuster	506	465	475	187	177
Leader	1518	1477	1487	1199	1189
Regulator	2024	1983	1993	1705	1695
General Governor	4048	4007	4017	3729	3719
High Overseer	396704	396663	396673	396385	396375

Fire - Mercury

31	47	98	76	65	81	62	46
39	55	84	68	73	95	54	38
82	66	45	61	48	32	75	97
96	74	37	53	56	40	67	83
60	44	63	79	100	78	33	49
52	36	71	93	86	70	41	57
77	99	50	34	43	59	80	64
69	85	58	42	35	51	94	72

Earth - Mercury

69	77	52	60	96	82	39	31
85	99	36	44	74	66	55	47
58	50	71	63	37	45	84	98
42	34	93	79	53	61	68	76
35	43	86	100	56	48	73	65
51	59	70	78	40	32	95	81
94	80	41	33	67	75	54	62
72	64	57	49	83	97	38	46

Occult Encyclopedia of Magic Squares

Air - Mercury

72	94	51	35	42	58	85	69
64	80	59	43	34	50	99	77
57	41	70	86	93	71	36	52
49	33	78	100	79	63	44	60
83	67	40	56	53	37	74	96
97	75	32	48	61	45	66	82
38	54	95	73	68	84	55	39
46	62	81	65	76	98	47	31

Water - Mercury

46	38	97	83	49	57	64	72
62	54	75	67	33	41	80	94
81	95	32	40	78	70	59	51
65	73	48	56	100	86	43	35
76	68	61	53	79	93	34	42
98	84	45	37	63	71	50	58
47	55	66	74	44	36	99	85
31	39	82	96	60	52	77	69

	Number	Angel Value (Arabic)	Angel Value (Hebrew)	Jinn Value (Arabic)	Jinn Value (Hebrew)
Usurper	31	350	360	72	62
Guide	100	59	69	141	131
Mystery	131	90	100	172	162
Adjuster	506	465	475	187	177
Leader	1518	1477	1487	1199	1189
Regulator	2024	1983	1993	1705	1695
General Governor	4048	4007	4017	3729	3719
High Overseer	404800	404759	404769	404481	404471

Fire - Moon

60	73	35	44	98	28	64	80	24
20	63	85	40	56	72	27	49	94
90	32	48	84	16	68	77	39	52
87	19	62	71	42	55	93	26	51
47	92	31	67	83	18	54	76	38
34	59	75	30	43	97	23	66	79
33	46	91	17	69	82	37	53	78
74	36	58	96	29	45	81	22	65
61	86	21	57	70	41	50	95	25

Earth - Moon

24	94	52	51	38	79	78	65	25
80	49	39	26	76	66	53	22	95
64	27	77	93	54	23	37	81	50
28	72	68	55	18	97	82	45	41
98	56	16	42	83	43	69	29	70
44	40	84	71	67	30	17	96	57
35	85	48	62	31	75	91	58	21
73	63	32	19	92	59	46	36	86
60	20	90	87	47	34	33	74	61

Air - Moon

25	95	50	41	70	57	21	86	61
65	22	81	45	29	96	58	36	74
78	53	37	82	69	17	91	46	33
79	66	23	97	43	30	75	59	34
38	76	54	18	83	67	31	92	47
51	26	93	55	42	71	62	19	87
52	39	77	68	16	84	48	32	90
94	49	27	72	56	40	85	63	20
24	80	64	28	98	44	35	73	60

Water - Moon

61	74	33	34	47	87	90	20	60
86	36	46	59	92	19	32	63	73
21	58	91	75	31	62	48	85	35
57	96	17	30	67	71	84	40	44
70	29	69	43	83	42	16	56	98
41	45	82	97	18	55	68	72	28
50	81	37	23	54	93	77	27	64
95	22	53	66	76	26	39	49	80
25	65	78	79	38	51	52	94	24

	Number	Angel Value (Arabic)	Angel Value (Hebrew)	Jinn Value (Arabic)	Jinn Value (Hebrew)
Usurper	16	335	345	57	47
Guide	98	57	67	139	129
Mystery	114	73	83	155	145
Adjuster	506	465	475	187	177
Leader	1518	1477	1487	1199	1189
Regulator	2024	1983	1993	1705	1695
General Governor	4048	4007	4017	3729	3719
High Overseer	396704	396663	396673	396385	396375

Fire - Saturn

1	19	26	64	55	94	48	40	72	87
12	76	69	60	96	85	3	45	31	29
27	32	56	95	86	71	20	8	49	62
33	58	93	88	21	67	75	16	5	50
46	92	90	25	36	59	63	73	18	4
53	10	11	78	66	42	38	28	83	97
65	47	7	14	80	35	23	84	100	51
79	68	43	2	13	30	81	99	54	37
89	22	34	41	9	17	98	52	70	74
101	82	77	39	44	6	57	61	24	15

Occult Encyclopedia of Magic Squares

Earth - Saturn

101	89	79	65	53	46	33	27	12	1
82	22	68	47	10	92	58	32	76	19
77	34	43	7	11	90	93	56	69	26
39	41	2	14	78	25	88	95	60	64
44	9	13	80	66	36	21	86	96	55
6	17	30	35	42	59	67	71	85	94
57	98	81	23	38	63	75	20	3	48
61	52	99	84	28	73	16	8	45	40
24	70	54	100	83	18	5	49	31	72
15	74	37	51	97	4	50	62	29	87

Air - Saturn

15	24	61	57	6	44	39	77	82	101
74	70	52	98	17	9	41	34	22	89
37	54	99	81	30	13	2	43	68	79
51	100	84	23	35	80	14	7	47	65
97	83	28	38	42	66	78	11	10	53
4	18	73	63	59	36	25	90	92	46
50	5	16	75	67	21	88	93	58	33
62	49	8	20	71	86	95	56	32	27
29	31	45	3	85	96	60	69	76	12
87	72	40	48	94	55	64	26	19	1

Water - Saturn

87	29	62	50	4	97	51	37	74	15
72	31	49	5	18	83	100	54	70	24
40	45	8	16	73	28	84	99	52	61
48	**3**	20	75	63	38	23	81	98	57
94	85	71	67	59	42	35	30	17	6
55	96	86	21	36	66	80	13	9	44
64	60	95	88	25	78	14	2	41	39
26	69	56	93	90	11	7	43	34	77
19	76	32	58	92	10	47	68	22	82
1	12	27	33	46	53	65	79	89	101

	Number	Angel Value (Arabic)	Angel Value (Hebrew)	Jinn Value (Arabic)	Jinn Value (Hebrew)
Usurper	1	320	330	42	32
Guide	101	60	70	142	132
Mystery	102	61	71	143	133
Adjuster	506	465	475	187	177
Leader	1518	1477	1487	1199	1189
Regulator	2024	1983	1993	1705	1695
General Governor	4048	4007	4017	3729	3719
High Overseer	408848	408807	408817	408529	408519

ARCHANGEL OF TAURUS: ASMODEL (142)

אל	וד	מ	אם
60	41	13	28
12	29	59	42
39	62	30	11

ל	א	ד	ו	מ	ס	א
ד	ו	מ	ס	א	ל	א
מ	ס	א	ל	א	ד	ו
א	ל	א	ד	ו	מ	ס
א	ד	ו	מ	ס	א	ל
ו	מ	ס	א	ל	א	ד
ס	א	ל	א	ד	ו	מ

Fire - Jupiter

28	39	33	42
41	34	36	31
38	29	43	32
35	40	30	37

Air - Jupiter

37	30	40	35
32	43	29	38
31	36	34	41
42	33	39	28

Earth - Jupiter

35	38	41	28
40	29	34	39
30	43	36	33
37	32	31	42

Water - Jupiter

42	31	32	37
33	36	43	30
39	34	29	40
28	41	38	35

Occult Encyclopedia of Magic Squares

	Number	Angel Value (Arabic)	Angel Value (Hebrew)	Jinn Value (Arabic)	Jinn Value (Hebrew)
Usurper	28	347	357	69	59
Guide	43	2	12	84	74
Mystery	71	30	40	112	102
Adjuster	1136	1095	1105	817	807
Leader	3408	3367	3377	3089	3079
Regulator	4544	4503	4513	4225	4215
General Governor	9088	9047	9057	8769	8759
High Overseer	390784	390743	390753	390465	390455

Fire - Mars

16	42	34	28	22
29	23	17	38	35
39	31	30	24	18
25	19	40	32	26
33	27	21	20	41

Air - Mars

33	25	39	29	16
27	19	31	23	42
21	40	30	17	34
20	32	24	38	28
41	26	18	35	22

Earth - Mars

41	20	21	27	33
26	32	40	19	25
18	24	30	31	39
35	38	17	23	29
22	28	34	42	16

Water - Mars

22	35	18	26	41
28	38	24	32	20
34	17	30	40	21
42	23	31	19	27
16	29	39	25	33

	Number	Angel Value (Arabic)	Angel Value (Hebrew)	Jinn Value (Arabic)	Jinn Value (Hebrew)
Usurper	16	335	345	57	47
Guide	42	1	11	83	73
Mystery	58	17	27	99	89
Adjuster	142	101	111	183	173
Leader	426	385	395	107	97
Regulator	568	527	537	249	239
General Governor	1136	1095	1105	817	807
High Overseer	47712	47671	47681	47393	47383

Fire - Sun

6	17	38	23	27	31
12	22	33	37	10	28
18	41	26	16	32	9
29	8	19	34	13	39
35	24	15	7	40	21
42	30	11	25	20	14

Air - Sun

14	20	25	11	30	42
21	40	7	15	24	35
39	13	34	19	8	29
9	32	16	26	41	18
28	10	37	33	22	12
31	27	23	38	17	6

Earth - Sun

42	35	29	18	12	6
30	24	8	41	22	17
11	15	19	26	33	38
25	7	34	16	37	23
20	40	13	32	10	27
14	21	39	9	28	31

Water - Sun

31	28	9	39	21	14
27	10	32	13	40	20
23	37	16	34	7	25
38	33	26	19	15	11
17	22	41	8	24	30
6	12	18	29	35	42

	Number	Angel Value (Arabic)	Angel Value (Hebrew)	Jinn Value (Arabic)	Jinn Value (Hebrew)
Usurper	6	325	335	47	37
Guide	42	1	11	83	73
Mystery	48	7	17	89	79
Adjuster	142	101	111	183	173
Leader	426	385	395	107	97
Regulator	568	527	537	249	239
General Governor	1136	1095	1105	817	807
High Overseer	47712	47671	47681	47393	47383

ANGEL OF TAURUS: ARAZIEL (249)

אל	'	ז	אר
200	8	13	28
12	29	199	9
6	202	30	11

ל	א	'	ז	ר	א
ר	ז	ל	א	'	א
'	א	א	ר	ל	ז
א	ר	ז	'	א	ל
ז	ל	ר	א	א	'
א	'	א	ל	ז	ר

Fire - Saturn

84	79	86
85	83	81
80	87	82

Earth - Saturn

80	85	84
87	83	79
82	81	86

Air - Saturn

82	87	80
81	83	85
86	79	84

Water - Saturn

86	81	82
79	83	87
84	85	80

	Number	Angel Value (Arabic)	Angel Value (Hebrew)	Jinn Value (Arabic)	Jinn Value (Hebrew)
Usurper	79	38	48	120	110
Guide	87	46	56	128	118
Mystery	166	125	135	207	197
Adjuster	249	208	218	290	280
Leader	747	706	716	428	418
Regulator	996	955	965	677	667
General Governor	1992	1951	1961	1673	1663
High Overseer	173304	173263	173273	172985	172975

Fire - Jupiter

54	65	59	71
70	60	62	57
64	55	72	58
61	69	56	63

Earth - Jupiter

61	64	70	54
69	55	60	65
56	72	62	59
63	58	57	71

Occult Encyclopedia of Magic Squares

Air - Jupiter

63	56	69	61
58	72	55	64
57	62	60	70
71	59	65	54

Water - Jupiter

71	57	58	63
59	62	72	56
65	60	55	69
54	70	64	61

	Number	Angel Value (Arabic)	Angel Value (Hebrew)	Jinn Value (Arabic)	Jinn Value (Hebrew)
Usurper	54	13	23	95	85
Guide	72	31	41	113	103
Mystery	126	85	95	167	157
Adjuster	1992	1951	1961	1673	1663
Leader	5976	5935	5945	5657	5647
Regulator	7968	7927	7937	7649	7639
General Governor	15936	15895	15905	15617	15607
High Overseer	1147392	1147351	1147361	1147073	1147063

Fire - Mars

37	65	55	49	43
50	44	38	61	56
62	52	51	45	39
46	40	63	53	47
54	48	42	41	64

Air - Mars

54	46	62	50	37
48	40	52	44	65
42	63	51	38	55
41	53	45	61	49
64	47	39	56	43

Earth - Mars

64	41	42	48	54
47	53	63	40	46
39	45	51	52	62
56	61	38	44	50
43	49	55	65	37

Water - Mars

43	56	39	47	64
49	61	45	53	41
55	38	51	63	42
65	44	52	40	48
37	50	62	46	54

Occult Encyclopedia of Magic Squares

	Number	Angel Value (Arabic)	Angel Value (Hebrew)	Jinn Value (Arabic)	Jinn Value (Hebrew)
Usurper	37	356	6	78	68
Guide	65	24	34	106	96
Mystery	102	61	71	143	133
Adjuster	249	208	218	290	280
Leader	747	706	716	428	418
Regulator	996	955	965	677	667
General Governor	1992	1951	1961	1673	1663
High Overseer	129480	129439	129449	129161	129151

Fire - Sun

24	35	55	41	45	49
30	40	51	54	28	46
36	58	44	34	50	27
47	26	37	52	31	56
53	42	33	25	57	39
59	48	29	43	38	32

Air - Sun

32	38	43	29	48	59
39	57	25	33	42	53
56	31	52	37	26	47
27	50	34	44	58	36
46	28	54	51	40	30
49	45	41	55	35	24

Earth - Sun

59	53	47	36	30	24
48	42	26	58	40	35
29	33	37	44	51	55
43	25	52	34	54	41
38	57	31	50	28	45
32	39	56	27	46	49

Water - Sun

49	46	27	56	39	32
45	28	50	31	57	38
41	54	34	52	25	43
55	51	44	37	33	29
35	40	58	26	42	48
24	30	36	47	53	59

	Number	Angel Value (Arabic)	Angel Value (Hebrew)	Jinn Value (Arabic)	Jinn Value (Hebrew)
Usurper	24	343	353	65	55
Guide	59	18	28	100	90
Mystery	83	42	52	124	114
Adjuster	249	208	218	290	280
Leader	747	706	716	428	418
Regulator	996	955	965	677	667
General Governor	1992	1951	1961	1673	1663
High Overseer	117528	117487	117497	117209	117199

Fire - Venus

11	52	37	22	42	59	26
60	27	12	46	38	23	43
24	44	61	28	13	47	32
48	33	18	45	62	29	14
30	15	49	34	19	39	63
40	57	31	16	50	35	20
36	21	41	58	25	17	51

Air - Venus

51	17	25	58	41	21	36
20	35	50	16	31	57	40
63	39	19	34	49	15	30
14	29	62	45	18	33	48
32	47	13	28	61	44	24
43	23	38	46	12	27	60
26	59	42	22	37	52	11

Earth - Venus

36	40	30	48	24	60	11
21	57	15	33	44	27	52
41	31	49	18	61	12	37
58	16	34	45	28	46	22
25	50	19	62	13	38	42
17	35	39	29	47	23	59
51	20	63	14	32	43	26

Water - Venus

26	43	32	14	63	20	51
59	23	47	29	39	35	17
42	38	13	62	19	50	25
22	46	28	45	34	16	58
37	12	61	18	49	31	41
52	27	44	33	15	57	21
11	60	24	48	30	40	36

	Number	Angel Value (Arabic)	Angel Value (Hebrew)	Jinn Value (Arabic)	Jinn Value (Hebrew)
Usurper	11	330	340	52	42
Guide	63	22	32	104	94
Mystery	74	33	43	115	105
Adjuster	249	208	218	290	280
Leader	747	706	716	428	418
Regulator	996	955	965	677	667
General Governor	1992	1951	1961	1673	1663
High Overseer	125496	125455	125465	125177	125167

LORD OF TRIPLICITY BY DAY: RAYDEL (246)

לא	ד	י	רא
200	11	7	28
6	29	199	12
9	202	30	5

ל	א	ד	י	א	ר
א	י	ל	ר	ד	א
ד	ר	א	א	ל	י
ר	א	י	ד	א	ל
י	ל	א	א	ר	ד
א	ר	ר	ל	י	א

Fire - Saturn

83	78	85
84	82	80
79	86	81

Air - Saturn

81	86	79
80	82	84
85	78	83

Earth - Saturn

79	84	83
86	82	78
81	80	85

Water - Saturn

85	80	81
78	82	86
83	84	79

Occult Encyclopedia of Magic Squares

	Number	Angel Value (Arabic)	Angel Value (Hebrew)	Jinn Value (Arabic)	Jinn Value (Hebrew)
Usurper	78	37	47	119	109
Guide	86	45	55	127	117
Mystery	164	123	133	205	195
Adjuster	246	205	215	287	277
Leader	738	697	707	419	409
Regulator	984	943	953	665	655
General Governor	1968	1927	1937	1649	1639
High Overseer	169248	169207	169217	168929	168919

Fire - Jupiter

54	65	59	68
67	60	62	57
64	55	69	58
61	66	56	63

Air - Jupiter

63	56	66	61
58	69	55	64
57	62	60	67
68	59	65	54

Earth - Jupiter

61	64	67	54
66	55	60	65
56	69	62	59
63	58	57	68

Water - Jupiter

68	57	58	63
59	62	69	56
65	60	55	66
54	67	64	61

	Number	Angel Value (Arabic)	Angel Value (Hebrew)	Jinn Value (Arabic)	Jinn Value (Hebrew)
Usurper	54	13	23	95	85
Guide	69	28	38	110	100
Mystery	123	82	92	164	154
Adjuster	1968	1927	1937	1649	1639
Leader	5904	5863	5873	5585	5575
Regulator	7872	7831	7841	7553	7543
General Governor	15744	15703	15713	15425	15415
High Overseer	1086336	1086295	1086305	1086017	1086007

Occult Encyclopedia of Magic Squares

Fire - Mars

37	62	55	49	43
50	44	38	58	56
59	52	51	45	39
46	40	60	53	47
54	48	42	41	61

Air - Mars

54	46	59	50	37
48	40	52	44	62
42	60	51	38	55
41	53	45	58	49
61	47	39	56	43

Earth - Mars

61	41	42	48	54
47	53	60	40	46
39	45	51	52	59
56	58	38	44	50
43	49	55	62	37

Water - Mars

43	56	39	47	61
49	58	45	53	41
55	38	51	60	42
62	44	52	40	48
37	50	59	46	54

	Number	Angel Value (Arabic)	Angel Value (Hebrew)	Jinn Value (Arabic)	Jinn Value (Hebrew)
Usurper	37	356	6	78	68
Guide	62	21	31	103	93
Mystery	99	58	68	140	130
Adjuster	246	205	215	287	277
Leader	738	697	707	419	409
Regulator	984	943	953	665	655
General Governor	1968	1927	1937	1649	1639
High Overseer	122016	121975	121985	121697	121687

Fire - Sun

23	34	57	40	44	48
29	39	50	56	27	45
35	60	43	33	49	26
46	25	36	51	30	58
52	41	32	24	59	38
61	47	28	42	37	31

Earth - Sun

61	52	46	35	29	23
47	41	25	60	39	34
28	32	36	43	50	57
42	24	51	33	56	40
37	59	30	49	27	44
31	38	58	26	45	48

Occult Encyclopedia of Magic Squares

Air - Sun

31	37	42	28	47	61
38	59	24	32	41	52
58	30	51	36	25	46
26	49	33	43	60	35
45	27	56	50	39	29
48	44	40	57	34	23

Water - Sun

48	45	26	58	38	31
44	27	49	30	59	37
40	56	33	51	24	42
57	50	43	36	32	28
34	39	60	25	41	47
23	29	35	46	52	61

	Number	Angel Value (Arabic)	Angel Value (Hebrew)	Jinn Value (Arabic)	Jinn Value (Hebrew)
Usurper	23	342	352	64	54
Guide	61	20	30	102	92
Mystery	84	43	53	125	115
Adjuster	246	205	215	287	277
Leader	738	697	707	419	409
Regulator	984	943	953	665	655
General Governor	1968	1927	1937	1649	1639
High Overseer	120048	120007	120017	119729	119719

Fire - Venus

11	52	37	22	42	56	26
57	27	12	46	38	23	43
24	44	58	28	13	47	32
48	33	18	45	59	29	14
30	15	49	34	19	39	60
40	54	31	16	50	35	20
36	21	41	55	25	17	51

Air - Venus

51	17	25	55	41	21	36
20	35	50	16	31	54	40
60	39	19	34	49	15	30
14	29	59	45	18	33	48
32	47	13	28	58	44	24
43	23	38	46	12	27	57
26	56	42	22	37	52	11

Earth - Venus

36	40	30	48	24	57	11
21	54	15	33	44	27	52
41	31	49	18	58	12	37
55	16	34	45	28	46	22
25	50	19	59	13	38	42
17	35	39	29	47	23	56
51	20	60	14	32	43	26

Water - Venus

26	43	32	14	60	20	51
56	23	47	29	39	35	17
42	38	13	59	19	50	25
22	46	28	45	34	16	55
37	12	58	18	49	31	41
52	27	44	33	15	54	21
11	57	24	48	30	40	36

	Number	Angel Value (Arabic)	Angel Value (Hebrew)	Jinn Value (Arabic)	Jinn Value (Hebrew)
Usurper	11	330	340	52	42
Guide	60	19	29	101	91
Mystery	71	30	40	112	102
Adjuster	246	205	215	287	277
Leader	738	697	707	419	409
Regulator	984	943	953	665	655
General Governor	1968	1927	1937	1649	1639
High Overseer	118080	118039	118049	117761	117751

LORD OF TRIPLICITY BY NIGHT: TOTATH (424)

ת	ט	ו	ט
8	7	12	397
11	398	7	8
5	10	399	10

ת	ט	ו	ט
ט	ו	ט	ת
ט	ת	ט	ו
ו	ט	ת	ט

Fire - Jupiter

98	109	103	114
113	104	106	101
108	99	115	102
105	112	100	107

Air - Jupiter

107	100	112	105
102	115	99	108
101	106	104	113
114	103	109	98

Earth - Jupiter

105	108	113	98
112	99	104	109
100	115	106	103
107	102	101	114

Water - Jupiter

114	101	102	107
103	106	115	100
109	104	99	112
98	113	108	105

	Number	Angel Value (Arabic)	Angel Value (Hebrew)	Jinn Value (Arabic)	Jinn Value (Hebrew)
Usurper	98	57	67	139	129
Guide	115	74	84	156	146
Mystery	213	172	182	254	244
Adjuster	3392	3351	3361	3073	3063
Leader	10176	10135	10145	9857	9847
Regulator	13568	13527	13537	13249	13239
General Governor	27136	27095	27105	26817	26807
High Overseer	3120640	3120599	3120609	3120321	3120311

Fire - Mars

72	100	90	84	78
85	79	73	96	91
97	87	86	80	74
81	75	98	88	82
89	83	77	76	99

Air - Mars

89	81	97	85	72
83	75	87	79	100
77	98	86	73	90
76	88	80	96	84
99	82	74	91	78

Earth - Mars

99	76	77	83	89
82	88	98	75	81
74	80	86	87	97
91	96	73	79	85
78	84	90	100	72

Water - Mars

78	91	74	82	99
84	96	80	88	76
90	73	86	98	77
100	79	87	75	83
72	85	97	81	89

	Number	Angel Value (Arabic)	Angel Value (Hebrew)	Jinn Value (Arabic)	Jinn Value (Hebrew)
Usurper	72	31	41	113	103
Guide	100	59	69	141	131
Mystery	172	131	141	213	203
Adjuster	424	383	393	105	95
Leader	1272	1231	1241	953	943
Regulator	1696	1655	1665	1377	1367
General Governor	3392	3351	3361	3073	3063
High Overseer	339200	339159	339169	338881	338871

Occult Encyclopedia of Magic Squares

Fire - Sun

53	64	85	70	74	78
59	69	80	84	57	75
65	88	73	63	79	56
76	55	66	81	60	86
82	71	62	54	87	68
89	77	58	72	67	61

Air - Sun

61	67	72	58	77	89
68	87	54	62	71	82
86	60	81	66	55	76
56	79	63	73	88	65
75	57	84	80	69	59
78	74	70	85	64	53

Earth - Sun

89	82	76	65	59	53
77	71	55	88	69	64
58	62	66	73	80	85
72	54	81	63	84	70
67	87	60	79	57	74
61	68	86	56	75	78

Water - Sun

78	75	56	86	68	61
74	57	79	60	87	67
70	84	63	81	54	72
85	80	73	66	62	58
64	69	88	55	71	77
53	59	65	76	82	89

	Number	Angel Value (Arabic)	Angel Value (Hebrew)	Jinn Value (Arabic)	Jinn Value (Hebrew)
Usurper	53	12	22	94	84
Guide	89	48	58	130	120
Mystery	142	101	111	183	173
Adjuster	424	383	393	105	95
Leader	1272	1231	1241	953	943
Regulator	1696	1655	1665	1377	1367
General Governor	3392	3351	3361	3073	3063
High Overseer	301888	301847	301857	301569	301559

Fire - Venus

36	77	62	47	67	84	51
85	52	37	71	63	48	68
49	69	86	53	38	72	57
73	58	43	70	87	54	39
55	40	74	59	44	64	88
65	82	56	41	75	60	45
61	46	66	83	50	42	76

Earth - Venus

61	65	55	73	49	85	36
46	82	40	58	69	52	77
66	56	74	43	86	37	62
83	41	59	70	53	71	47
50	75	44	87	38	63	67
42	60	64	54	72	48	84
76	45	88	39	57	68	51

Occult Encyclopedia of Magic Squares

Air - Venus

76	42	50	83	66	46	61
45	60	75	41	56	82	65
88	64	44	59	74	40	55
39	54	87	70	43	58	73
57	72	38	53	86	69	49
68	48	63	71	37	52	85
51	84	67	47	62	77	36

Water - Venus

51	68	57	39	88	45	76
84	48	72	54	64	60	42
67	63	38	87	44	75	50
47	71	53	70	59	41	83
62	37	86	43	74	56	66
77	52	69	58	40	82	46
36	85	49	73	55	65	61

	Number	Angel Value (Arabic)	Angel Value (Hebrew)	Jinn Value (Arabic)	Jinn Value (Hebrew)
Usurper	36	355	5	77	67
Guide	88	47	57	129	119
Mystery	124	83	93	165	155
Adjuster	424	383	393	105	95
Leader	1272	1231	1241	953	943
Regulator	1696	1655	1665	1377	1367
General Governor	3392	3351	3361	3073	3063
High Overseer	298496	298455	298465	298177	298167

Fire - Mercury

21	37	86	66	55	71	52	36
29	45	74	58	63	83	44	28
72	56	35	51	38	22	65	85
84	64	27	43	46	30	57	73
50	34	53	69	88	68	23	39
42	26	61	81	76	60	31	47
67	87	40	24	33	49	70	54
59	75	48	32	25	41	82	62

Occult Encyclopedia of Magic Squares

Earth - Mercury

59	67	42	50	84	72	29	21
75	87	26	34	64	56	45	37
48	40	61	53	27	35	74	86
32	24	81	69	43	51	58	66
25	33	76	88	46	38	63	55
41	49	60	68	30	22	83	71
82	70	31	23	57	65	44	52
62	54	47	39	73	85	28	36

Air - Mercury

62	82	41	25	32	48	75	59
54	70	49	33	24	40	87	67
47	31	60	76	81	61	26	42
39	23	68	88	69	53	34	50
73	57	30	46	43	27	64	84
85	65	22	38	51	35	56	72
28	44	83	63	58	74	45	29
36	52	71	55	66	86	37	21

Water - Mercury

36	28	85	73	39	47	54	62
52	44	65	57	23	31	70	82
71	83	22	30	68	60	49	41
55	63	38	46	88	76	33	25
66	58	51	43	69	81	24	32
86	74	35	27	53	61	40	48
37	45	56	64	34	26	87	75
21	29	72	84	50	42	67	59

	Number	Angel Value (Arabic)	Angel Value (Hebrew)	Jinn Value (Arabic)	Jinn Value (Hebrew)
Usurper	21	340	350	62	52
Guide	88	47	57	129	119
Mystery	109	68	78	150	140
Adjuster	424	383	393	105	95
Leader	1272	1231	1241	953	943
Regulator	1696	1655	1665	1377	1367
General Governor	3392	3351	3361	3073	3063
High Overseer	298496	298455	298465	298177	298167

Fire - Moon

51	64	26	35	88	19	55	71	15
11	54	76	31	47	63	18	40	84
80	23	39	75	7	59	68	30	43
78	10	53	62	33	46	83	17	42
38	82	22	58	74	9	45	67	29
25	50	66	21	34	87	14	57	70
24	37	81	8	60	73	28	44	69
65	27	49	86	20	36	72	13	56
52	77	12	48	61	32	41	85	16

Earth - Moon

15	84	43	42	29	70	69	56	16
71	40	30	17	67	57	44	13	85
55	18	68	83	45	14	28	72	41
19	63	59	46	9	87	73	36	32
88	47	7	33	74	34	60	20	61
35	31	75	62	58	21	8	86	48
26	76	39	53	22	66	81	49	12
64	54	23	10	82	50	37	27	77
51	11	80	78	38	25	24	65	52

Occult Encyclopedia of Magic Squares

Air - Moon

16	85	41	32	61	48	12	77	52
56	13	72	36	20	86	49	27	65
69	44	28	73	60	8	81	37	24
70	57	14	87	34	21	66	50	25
29	67	45	9	74	58	22	82	38
42	17	83	46	33	62	53	10	78
43	30	68	59	7	75	39	23	80
84	40	18	63	47	31	76	54	11
15	71	55	19	88	35	26	64	51

Water - Moon

52	65	24	25	38	78	80	11	51
77	27	37	50	82	10	23	54	64
12	49	81	66	22	53	39	76	26
48	86	8	21	58	62	75	31	35
61	20	60	34	74	33	7	47	88
32	36	73	87	9	46	59	63	19
41	72	28	14	45	83	68	18	55
85	13	44	57	67	17	30	40	71
16	56	69	70	29	42	43	84	15

	Number	Angel Value (Arabic)	Angel Value (Hebrew)	Jinn Value (Arabic)	Jinn Value (Hebrew)
Usurper	7	326	336	48	38
Guide	88	47	57	129	119
Mystery	95	54	64	136	126
Adjuster	424	383	393	105	95
Leader	1272	1231	1241	953	943
Regulator	1696	1655	1665	1377	1367
General Governor	3392	3351	3361	3073	3063
High Overseer	298496	298455	298465	298177	298167

	Number	Angel Value (Arabic)	Angel Value (Hebrew)	Jinn Value (Arabic)	Jinn Value (Hebrew)
Usurper	7	326	336	48	38
Guide	88	47	57	129	119
Mystery	95	54	64	136	126
Adjuster	424	383	393	105	95
Leader	1272	1231	1241	953	943
Regulator	1696	1655	1665	1377	1367
General Governor	3392	3351	3361	3073	3063
High Overseer	298496	298455	298465	298177	298167

ANGEL RULING 2ND HOUSE: TOEL (46)

ל	ﬡ	ﬁ	ﬢ
8	7	4	27
3	28	7	8
5	10	29	2

ל	ﬡ	ﬁ	ﬢ
ﬢ	ﬁ	ﬡ	ל
ﬡ	ל	ﬢ	ﬁ
ﬁ	ﬢ	ל	ﬡ

Fire - Jupiter

4	15	9	18
17	10	12	7
14	5	19	8
11	16	6	13

Air - Jupiter

13	6	16	11
8	19	5	14
7	12	10	17
18	9	15	4

Earth - Jupiter

11	14	17	4
16	5	10	15
6	19	12	9
13	8	7	18

Water - Jupiter

18	7	8	13
9	12	19	6
15	10	5	16
4	17	14	11

	Number	Angel Value (Arabic)	Angel Value (Hebrew)	Jinn Value (Arabic)	Jinn Value (Hebrew)
Usurper	4	323	333	45	35
Guide	19	338	348	60	50
Mystery	23	342	352	64	54
Adjuster	368	327	337	49	39
Leader	1104	1063	1073	785	775
Regulator	1472	1431	1441	1153	1143
General Governor	2944	2903	2913	2625	2615
High Overseer	55936	55895	55905	55617	55607

ANGEL OF FIRST DECANATE: KEDAMIDI (78)

י	ד	מ	כד
23	41	7	7
6	8	22	42
39	25	9	5

י	ד	מ	ד	ב
מ	ד	ב	י	ד
ב	י	ד	מ	ד
ד	מ	ד	ב	י
ד	ב	י	ד	מ

Fire - Saturn

27	22	29
28	26	24
23	30	25

Air - Saturn

25	30	23
24	26	28
29	22	27

Earth - Saturn

23	28	27
30	26	22
25	24	29

Water - Saturn

29	24	25
22	26	30
27	28	23

Occult Encyclopedia of Magic Squares

	Number	Angel Value (Arabic)	Angel Value (Hebrew)	Jinn Value (Arabic)	Jinn Value (Hebrew)
Usurper	22	341	351	63	53
Guide	30	349	359	71	61
Mystery	52	11	21	93	83
Adjuster	78	37	47	119	109
Leader	234	193	203	275	265
Regulator	312	271	281	353	343
General Governor	624	583	593	305	295
High Overseer	18720	18679	18689	18401	18391

Fire - Jupiter

12	23	17	26
25	18	20	15
22	13	27	16
19	24	14	21

Air - Jupiter

21	14	24	19
16	27	13	22
15	20	18	25
26	17	23	12

Earth - Jupiter

19	22	25	12
24	13	18	23
14	27	20	17
21	16	15	26

Water - Jupiter

26	15	16	21
17	20	27	14
23	18	13	24
12	25	22	19

	Number	Angel Value (Arabic)	Angel Value (Hebrew)	Jinn Value (Arabic)	Jinn Value (Hebrew)
Usurper	12	331	341	53	43
Guide	27	346	356	68	58
Mystery	39	358	8	80	70
Adjuster	624	583	593	305	295
Leader	1872	1831	1841	1553	1543
Regulator	2496	2455	2465	2177	2167
General Governor	4992	4951	4961	4673	4663
High Overseer	134784	134743	134753	134465	134455

Fire - Mars

3	30	21	15	9
16	10	4	26	22
27	18	17	11	5
12	6	28	19	13
20	14	8	7	29

Air - Mars

20	12	27	16	3
14	6	18	10	30
8	28	17	4	21
7	19	11	26	15
29	13	5	22	9

Earth - Mars

29	7	8	14	20
13	19	28	6	12
5	11	17	18	27
22	26	4	10	16
9	15	21	30	3

Water - Mars

9	22	5	13	29
15	26	11	19	7
21	4	17	28	8
30	10	18	6	14
3	16	27	12	20

	Number	Angel Value (Arabic)	Angel Value (Hebrew)	Jinn Value (Arabic)	Jinn Value (Hebrew)
Usurper	3	322	332	44	34
Guide	30	349	359	71	61
Mystery	33	352	2	74	64
Adjuster	78	37	47	119	109
Leader	234	193	203	275	265
Regulator	312	271	281	353	343
General Governor	624	583	593	305	295
High Overseer	18720	18679	18689	18401	18391

ANGEL OF FIRST QUINANCE: MEBAHIAH (62)

יה	ה	ב	מ
39	3	8	12
7	13	38	4
1	41	14	6

ה	י	ה	ב	מ
ה	ב	מ	ה	י
מ	ה	י	ה	ב
י	ה	ב	מ	ה
ב	מ	ה	י	ה

Numerical Squares See Page: 39

ANGEL OF SECOND QUINANCE: POYEL (127)

אל	י	ו	ם
79	7	13	28
12	29	78	8
5	81	30	11

ל	א	י	ו	ם
י	ו	ם	ל	א
ם	ל	א	י	ו
א	י	ו	ם	ל
ו	ם	ל	א	י

Fire - Jupiter

24	35	29	39
38	30	32	27
34	25	40	28
31	37	26	33

Air - Jupiter

33	26	37	31
28	40	25	34
27	32	30	38
39	29	35	24

Earth - Jupiter

31	34	38	24
37	25	30	35
26	40	32	29
33	28	27	39

Water - Jupiter

39	27	28	33
29	32	40	26
35	30	25	37
24	38	34	31

	Number	Angel Value (Arabic)	Angel Value (Hebrew)	Jinn Value (Arabic)	Jinn Value (Hebrew)
Usurper	24	343	353	65	55
Guide	40	359	9	81	71
Mystery	64	23	33	105	95
Adjuster	1016	975	985	697	687
Leader	3048	3007	3017	2729	2719
Regulator	4064	4023	4033	3745	3735
General Governor	8128	8087	8097	7809	7799
High Overseer	325120	325079	325089	324801	324791

Occult Encyclopedia of Magic Squares

Fire - Mars

13	39	31	25	19
26	20	14	35	32
36	28	27	21	15
22	16	37	29	23
30	24	18	17	38

Air - Mars

30	22	36	26	13
24	16	28	20	39
18	37	27	14	31
17	29	21	35	25
38	23	15	32	19

Earth - Mars

38	17	18	24	30
23	29	37	16	22
15	21	27	28	36
32	35	14	20	26
19	25	31	39	13

Water - Mars

19	32	15	23	38
25	35	21	29	17
31	14	27	37	18
39	20	28	16	24
13	26	36	22	30

Fire - Sun

3	14	38	20	24	28
9	19	30	37	7	25
15	41	23	13	29	6
26	5	16	31	10	39
32	21	12	4	40	18
42	27	8	22	17	11

Air - Sun

11	17	22	8	27	42
18	40	4	12	21	32
39	10	31	16	5	26
6	29	13	23	41	15
25	7	37	30	19	9
28	24	20	38	14	3

Earth - Sun

42	32	26	15	9	3
27	21	5	41	19	14
8	12	16	23	30	38
22	4	31	13	37	20
17	40	10	29	7	24
11	18	39	6	25	28

Water - Sun

28	25	6	39	18	11
24	7	29	10	40	17
20	37	13	31	4	22
38	30	23	16	12	8
14	19	41	5	21	27
3	9	15	26	32	42

	Number	Angel Value (Arabic)	Angel Value (Hebrew)	Jinn Value (Arabic)	Jinn Value (Hebrew)
Usurper	3	322	332	44	34
Guide	42	1	11	83	73
Mystery	45	4	14	86	76
Adjuster	127	86	96	168	158
Leader	381	340	350	62	52
Regulator	508	467	477	189	179
General Governor	1016	975	985	697	687
High Overseer	42672	42631	42641	42353	42343

ANGEL OF SECOND DECANATE: MINACHARAI (315)

אי	ר	ח	מנ
89	9	203	8
202	9	88	10
7	91	10	201

י	א	ר	ח	נ	מ
נ	ח	י	מ	ר	א
ר	מ	א	נ	י	ח
מ	נ	ח	ר	א	י
ח	י	נ	א	מ	ר
א	ר	מ	י	ח	נ

Fire - Saturn

104	99	106
105	103	101
100	107	102

Air - Saturn

102	107	100
101	103	105
106	99	104

Earth - Saturn

100	105	104
107	103	99
102	101	106

Water - Saturn

106	101	102
99	103	107
104	105	100

Occult Encyclopedia of Magic Squares

	Number	Angel Value (Arabic)	Angel Value (Hebrew)	Jinn Value (Arabic)	Jinn Value (Hebrew)
Usurper	99	58	68	140	130
Guide	107	66	76	148	138
Mystery	206	165	175	247	237
Adjuster	309	268	278	350	340
Leader	927	886	896	608	598
Regulator	1236	1195	1205	917	907
General Governor	2472	2431	2441	2153	2143
High Overseer	264504	264463	264473	264185	264175

Fire - Jupiter

69	80	74	86
85	75	77	72
79	70	87	73
76	84	71	78

Air - Jupiter

78	71	84	76
73	87	70	79
72	77	75	85
86	74	80	69

Earth - Jupiter

76	79	85	69
84	70	75	80
71	87	77	74
78	73	72	86

Water - Jupiter

86	72	73	78
74	77	87	71
80	75	70	84
69	85	79	76

	Number	Angel Value (Arabic)	Angel Value (Hebrew)	Jinn Value (Arabic)	Jinn Value (Hebrew)
Usurper	69	28	38	110	100
Guide	87	46	56	128	118
Mystery	156	115	125	197	187
Adjuster	2472	2431	2441	2153	2143
Leader	7416	7375	7385	7097	7087
Regulator	9888	9847	9857	9569	9559
General Governor	19776	19735	19745	19457	19447
High Overseer	1720512	1720471	1720481	1720193	1720183

Fire - Mars

49	77	67	61	55
62	56	50	73	68
74	64	63	57	51
58	52	75	65	59
66	60	54	53	76

Air - Mars

66	58	74	62	49
60	52	64	56	77
54	75	63	50	67
53	65	57	73	61
76	59	51	68	55

Earth - Mars

76	53	54	60	66
59	65	75	52	58
51	57	63	64	74
68	73	50	56	62
55	61	67	77	49

Water - Mars

55	68	51	59	76
61	73	57	65	53
67	50	63	75	54
77	56	64	52	60
49	62	74	58	66

	Number	Angel Value (Arabic)	Angel Value (Hebrew)	Jinn Value (Arabic)	Jinn Value (Hebrew)
Usurper	49	8	18	90	80
Guide	77	36	46	118	108
Mystery	126	85	95	167	157
Adjuster	309	268	278	350	340
Leader	927	886	896	608	598
Regulator	1236	1195	1205	917	907
General Governor	2472	2431	2441	2153	2143
High Overseer	190344	190303	190313	190025	190015

Fire - Sun

34	45	65	51	55	59
40	50	61	64	38	56
46	68	54	44	60	37
57	36	47	62	41	66
63	52	43	35	67	49
69	58	39	53	48	42

Earth - Sun

69	63	57	46	40	34
58	52	36	68	50	45
39	43	47	54	61	65
53	35	62	44	64	51
48	67	41	60	38	55
42	49	66	37	56	59

Occult Encyclopedia of Magic Squares

Air - Sun

42	48	53	39	58	69
49	67	35	43	52	63
66	41	62	47	36	57
37	60	44	54	68	46
56	38	64	61	50	40
59	55	51	65	45	34

Water - Sun

59	56	37	66	49	42
55	38	60	41	67	48
51	64	44	62	35	53
65	61	54	47	43	39
45	50	68	36	52	58
34	40	46	57	63	69

	Number	Angel Value (Arabic)	Angel Value (Hebrew)	Jinn Value (Arabic)	Jinn Value (Hebrew)
Usurper	34	353	3	75	65
Guide	69	28	38	110	100
Mystery	103	62	72	144	134
Adjuster	309	268	278	350	340
Leader	927	886	896	608	598
Regulator	1236	1195	1205	917	907
General Governor	2472	2431	2441	2153	2143
High Overseer	170568	170527	170537	170249	170239

Fire - Venus

20	61	46	31	51	65	35
66	36	21	55	47	32	52
33	53	67	37	22	56	41
57	42	27	54	68	38	23
39	24	58	43	28	48	69
49	63	40	25	59	44	29
45	30	50	64	34	26	60

Air - Venus

60	26	34	64	50	30	45
29	44	59	25	40	63	49
69	48	28	43	58	24	39
23	38	68	54	27	42	57
41	56	22	37	67	53	33
52	32	47	55	21	36	66
35	65	51	31	46	61	20

Earth - Venus

45	49	39	57	33	66	20
30	63	24	42	53	36	61
50	40	58	27	67	21	46
64	25	43	54	37	55	31
34	59	28	68	22	47	51
26	44	48	38	56	32	65
60	29	69	23	41	52	35

Water - Venus

35	52	41	23	69	29	60
65	32	56	38	48	44	26
51	47	22	68	28	59	34
31	55	37	54	43	25	64
46	21	67	27	58	40	50
61	36	53	42	24	63	30
20	66	33	57	39	49	45

	Number	Angel Value (Arabic)	Angel Value (Hebrew)	Jinn Value (Arabic)	Jinn Value (Hebrew)
Usurper	20	339	349	61	51
Guide	69	28	38	110	100
Mystery	89	48	58	130	120
Adjuster	309	268	278	350	340
Leader	927	886	896	608	598
Regulator	1236	1195	1205	917	907
General Governor	2472	2431	2441	2153	2143
High Overseer	170568	170527	170537	170249	170239

Fire - Mercury

7	23	69	52	41	57	38	22
15	31	60	44	49	66	30	14
58	42	21	37	24	8	51	68
67	50	13	29	32	16	43	59
36	20	39	55	71	54	9	25
28	12	47	64	62	46	17	33
53	70	26	10	19	35	56	40
45	61	34	18	11	27	65	48

Earth - Mercury

45	53	28	36	67	58	15	7
61	70	12	20	50	42	31	23
34	26	47	39	13	21	60	69
18	10	64	55	29	37	44	52
11	19	62	71	32	24	49	41
27	35	46	54	16	8	66	57
65	56	17	9	43	51	30	38
48	40	33	25	59	68	14	22

Air - Mercury

48	65	27	11	18	34	61	45
40	56	35	19	10	26	70	53
33	17	46	62	64	47	12	28
25	9	54	71	55	39	20	36
59	43	16	32	29	13	50	67
68	51	8	24	37	21	42	58
14	30	66	49	44	60	31	15
22	38	57	41	52	69	23	7

Water - Mercury

22	14	68	59	25	33	40	48
38	30	51	43	9	17	56	65
57	66	8	16	54	46	35	27
41	49	24	32	71	62	19	11
52	44	37	29	55	64	10	18
69	60	21	13	39	47	26	34
23	31	42	50	20	12	70	61
7	15	58	67	36	28	53	45

	Number	Angel Value (Arabic)	Angel Value (Hebrew)	Jinn Value (Arabic)	Jinn Value (Hebrew)
Usurper	7	326	336	48	38
Guide	71	30	40	112	102
Mystery	78	37	47	119	109
Adjuster	309	268	278	350	340
Leader	927	886	896	608	598
Regulator	1236	1195	1205	917	907
General Governor	2472	2431	2441	2153	2143
High Overseer	175512	175471	175481	175193	175183

ANGEL OF THIRD QUINANCE: NEMAMIAH (145)

יה	מ	מ	נ
49	41	43	12
42	13	48	42
39	51	14	41

ה	י	מ	מ	נ
מ	מ	נ	ה	י
נ	ה	י	מ	מ
י	מ	מ	נ	ה
מ	נ	ה	י	מ

Fire - Jupiter

28	39	33	45
44	34	36	31
38	29	46	32
35	43	30	37

Air - Jupiter

37	30	43	35
32	46	29	38
31	36	34	44
45	33	39	28

Earth - Jupiter

35	38	44	28
43	29	34	39
30	46	36	33
37	32	31	45

Water - Jupiter

45	31	32	37
33	36	46	30
39	34	29	43
28	44	38	35

	Number	Angel Value (Arabic)	Angel Value (Hebrew)	Jinn Value (Arabic)	Jinn Value (Hebrew)
Usurper	28	347	357	69	59
Guide	46	5	15	87	77
Mystery	74	33	43	115	105
Adjuster	1160	1119	1129	841	831
Leader	3480	3439	3449	3161	3151
Regulator	4640	4599	4609	4321	4311
General Governor	9280	9239	9249	8961	8951
High Overseer	426880	426839	426849	426561	426551

Occult Encyclopedia of Magic Squares

Fire - Mars

17	41	35	29	23
30	24	18	37	36
38	32	31	25	19
26	20	39	33	27
34	28	22	21	40

Air - Mars

34	26	38	30	17
28	20	32	24	41
22	39	31	18	35
21	33	25	37	29
40	27	19	36	23

Earth - Mars

40	21	22	28	34
27	33	39	20	26
19	25	31	32	38
36	37	18	24	30
23	29	35	41	17

Water - Mars

23	36	19	27	40
29	37	25	33	21
35	18	31	39	22
41	24	32	20	28
17	30	38	26	34

	Number	Angel Value (Arabic)	Angel Value (Hebrew)	Jinn Value (Arabic)	Jinn Value (Hebrew)
Usurper	17	336	346	58	48
Guide	41	360	10	82	72
Mystery	58	17	27	99	89
Adjuster	145	104	114	186	176
Leader	435	394	404	116	106
Regulator	580	539	549	261	251
General Governor	1160	1119	1129	841	831
High Overseer	47560	47519	47529	47241	47231

Fire - Sun

6	17	41	23	27	31
12	22	33	40	10	28
18	44	26	16	32	9
29	8	19	34	13	42
35	24	15	7	43	21
45	30	11	25	20	14

Earth - Sun

45	35	29	18	12	6
30	24	8	44	22	17
11	15	19	26	33	41
25	7	34	16	40	23
20	43	13	32	10	27
14	21	42	9	28	31

Air - Sun

14	20	25	11	30	45
21	43	7	15	24	35
42	13	34	19	8	29
9	32	16	26	44	18
28	10	40	33	22	12
31	27	23	41	17	6

Water - Sun

31	28	9	42	21	14
27	10	32	13	43	20
23	40	16	34	7	25
41	33	26	19	15	11
17	22	44	8	24	30
6	12	18	29	35	45

	Number	Angel Value (Arabic)	Angel Value (Hebrew)	Jinn Value (Arabic)	Jinn Value (Hebrew)
Usurper	6	325	335	47	37
Guide	45	4	14	86	76
Mystery	51	10	20	92	82
Adjuster	145	104	114	186	176
Leader	435	394	404	116	106
Regulator	580	539	549	261	251
General Governor	1160	1119	1129	841	831
High Overseer	52200	52159	52169	51881	51871

ANGEL OF FOURTH QUINANCE: YEYALEL (81)

ל אך	ל	'	'
9	11	33	28
32	29	8	12
9	11	30	31

ל	א	ל	'	'
ל	'	'	ל	א
'	ל	א	ל	'
א	ל	'	'	ל
'	'	ל	א	ל

Fire - Saturn

28	23	30
29	27	25
24	31	26

Air - Saturn

26	31	24
25	27	29
30	23	28

Earth - Saturn

24	29	28
31	27	23
26	25	30

Water - Saturn

30	25	26
23	27	31
28	29	24

	Number	Angel Value (Arabic)	Angel Value (Hebrew)	Jinn Value (Arabic)	Jinn Value (Hebrew)
Usurper	23	342	352	64	54
Guide	31	350	360	72	62
Mystery	54	13	23	95	85
Adjuster	81	40	50	122	112
Leader	243	202	212	284	274
Regulator	324	283	293	5	355
General Governor	648	607	617	329	319
High Overseer	20088	20047	20057	19769	19759

Fire - Jupiter

12	23	17	29
28	18	20	15
22	13	30	16
19	27	14	21

Air - Jupiter

21	14	27	19
16	30	13	22
15	20	18	28
29	17	23	12

Earth - Jupiter

19	22	28	12
27	13	18	23
14	30	20	17
21	16	15	29

Water - Jupiter

29	15	16	21
17	20	30	14
23	18	13	27
12	28	22	19

Occult Encyclopedia of Magic Squares

	Number	Angel Value (Arabic)	Angel Value (Hebrew)	Jinn Value (Arabic)	Jinn Value (Hebrew)
Usurper	12	331	341	53	43
Guide	30	349	359	71	61
Mystery	42	1	11	83	73
Adjuster	648	607	617	329	319
Leader	1944	1903	1913	1625	1615
Regulator	2592	2551	2561	2273	2263
General Governor	5184	5143	5153	4865	4855
High Overseer	155520	155479	155489	155201	155191

Fire - Mars

4	29	22	16	10
17	11	5	25	23
26	19	18	12	6
13	7	27	20	14
21	15	9	8	28

Air - Mars

21	13	26	17	4
15	7	19	11	29
9	27	18	5	22
8	20	12	25	16
28	14	6	23	10

Earth - Mars

28	8	9	15	21
14	20	27	7	13
6	12	18	19	26
23	25	5	11	17
10	16	22	29	4

Water - Mars

10	23	6	14	28
16	25	12	20	8
22	5	18	27	9
29	11	19	7	15
4	17	26	13	21

	Number	Angel Value (Arabic)	Angel Value (Hebrew)	Jinn Value (Arabic)	Jinn Value (Hebrew)
Usurper	4	323	333	45	35
Guide	29	348	358	70	60
Mystery	33	352	2	74	64
Adjuster	81	40	50	122	112
Leader	243	202	212	284	274
Regulator	324	283	293	5	355
General Governor	648	607	617	329	319
High Overseer	18792	18751	18761	18473	18463

ANGEL OF THIRD DECANATE: YAKASAGANOTZ (239)

צ	נר	סצ	יכ
29	64	59	87
58	88	28	65
62	31	89	57

א	ו	נ	ס	כ	י
כ	ס	א	י	נ	ו
נ	י	ו	כ	א	ס
י	כ	ס	נ	ו	א
ס	א	כ	ו	י	נ
ו	נ	י	א	ס	כ

Fire - Jupiter

52	63	57	67
66	58	60	55
62	53	68	56
59	65	54	61

Air - Jupiter

61	54	65	59
56	68	53	62
55	60	58	66
67	57	63	52

Earth - Jupiter

59	62	66	52
65	53	58	63
54	68	60	57
61	56	55	67

Water - Jupiter

67	55	56	61
57	60	68	54
63	58	53	65
52	66	62	59

	Number	Angel Value (Arabic)	Angel Value (Hebrew)	Jinn Value (Arabic)	Jinn Value (Hebrew)
Usurper	52	11	21	93	83
Guide	68	27	37	109	99
Mystery	120	79	89	161	151
Adjuster	1912	1871	1881	1593	1583
Leader	5736	5695	5705	5417	5407
Regulator	7648	7607	7617	7329	7319
General Governor	15296	15255	15265	14977	14967
High Overseer	1040128	1040087	1040097	1039809	1039799

Occult Encyclopedia of Magic Squares

Fire - Mars

35	63	53	47	41
48	42	36	59	54
60	50	49	43	37
44	38	61	51	45
52	46	40	39	62

Air - Mars

52	44	60	48	35
46	38	50	42	63
40	61	49	36	53
39	51	43	59	47
62	45	37	54	41

Earth - Mars

62	39	40	46	52
45	51	61	38	44
37	43	49	50	60
54	59	36	42	48
41	47	53	63	35

Water - Mars

41	54	37	45	62
47	59	43	51	39
53	36	49	61	40
63	42	50	38	46
35	48	60	44	52

	Number	Angel Value (Arabic)	Angel Value (Hebrew)	Jinn Value (Arabic)	Jinn Value (Hebrew)
Usurper	35	354	4	76	66
Guide	63	22	32	104	94
Mystery	98	57	67	139	129
Adjuster	239	198	208	280	270
Leader	717	676	686	398	388
Regulator	956	915	925	637	627
General Governor	1912	1871	1881	1593	1583
High Overseer	120456	120415	120425	120137	120127

Fire - Sun

22	33	55	39	43	47
28	38	49	54	26	44
34	58	42	32	48	25
45	24	35	50	29	56
51	40	31	23	57	37
59	46	27	41	36	30

Earth - Sun

59	51	45	34	28	22
46	40	24	58	38	33
27	31	35	42	49	55
41	23	50	32	54	39
36	57	29	48	26	43
30	37	56	25	44	47

Occult Encyclopedia of Magic Squares

Air - Sun

30	36	41	27	46	59
37	57	23	31	40	51
56	29	50	35	24	45
25	48	32	42	58	34
44	26	54	49	38	28
47	43	39	55	33	22

Water - Sun

47	44	25	56	37	30
43	26	48	29	57	36
39	54	32	50	23	41
55	49	42	35	31	27
33	38	58	24	40	46
22	28	34	45	51	59

	Number	Angel Value (Arabic)	Angel Value (Hebrew)	Jinn Value (Arabic)	Jinn Value (Hebrew)
Usurper	22	341	351	63	53
Guide	59	18	28	100	90
Mystery	81	40	50	122	112
Adjuster	239	198	208	280	270
Leader	717	676	686	398	388
Regulator	956	915	925	637	627
General Governor	1912	1871	1881	1593	1583
High Overseer	112808	112767	112777	112489	112479

Fire - Venus

10	51	36	21	41	55	25
56	26	11	45	37	22	42
23	43	57	27	12	46	31
47	32	17	44	58	28	13
29	14	48	33	18	38	59
39	53	30	15	49	34	19
35	20	40	54	24	16	50

Air - Venus

50	16	24	54	40	20	35
19	34	49	15	30	53	39
59	38	18	33	48	14	29
13	28	58	44	17	32	47
31	46	12	27	57	43	23
42	22	37	45	11	26	56
25	55	41	21	36	51	10

Earth - Venus

35	39	29	47	23	56	10
20	53	14	32	43	26	51
40	30	48	17	57	11	36
54	15	33	44	27	45	21
24	49	18	58	12	37	41
16	34	38	28	46	22	55
50	19	59	13	31	42	25

Water - Venus

25	42	31	13	59	19	50
55	22	46	28	38	34	16
41	37	12	58	18	49	24
21	45	27	44	33	15	54
36	11	57	17	48	30	40
51	26	43	32	14	53	20
10	56	23	47	29	39	35

	Number	Angel Value (Arabic)	Angel Value (Hebrew)	Jinn Value (Arabic)	Jinn Value (Hebrew)
Usurper	10	329	339	51	41
Guide	59	18	28	100	90
Mystery	69	28	38	110	100
Adjuster	239	198	208	280	270
Leader	717	676	686	398	388
Regulator	956	915	925	637	627
General Governor	1912	1871	1881	1593	1583
High Overseer	112808	112767	112777	112489	112479

ANGEL OF FIFTH QUINANCE: HERACHIEL (244)

א֗ל	ח	ר	ה
4	201	11	28
10	29	3	202
199	6	30	9

ל	א	ח	ר	ה
ח	ר	ה	ל	א
ה	ל	א	ח	ר
א	ח	ר	ה	ל
ר	ה	ל	א	ח

Fire - Jupiter

53	64	58	69
68	59	61	56
63	54	70	57
60	67	55	62

Air - Jupiter

62	55	67	60
57	70	54	63
56	61	59	68
69	58	64	53

Earth - Jupiter

60	63	68	53
67	54	59	64
55	70	61	58
62	57	56	69

Water - Jupiter

69	56	57	62
58	61	70	55
64	59	54	67
53	68	63	60

Occult Encyclopedia of Magic Squares

	Number	Angel Value (Arabic)	Angel Value (Hebrew)	Jinn Value (Arabic)	Jinn Value (Hebrew)
Usurper	53	12	22	94	84
Guide	70	29	39	111	101
Mystery	123	82	92	164	154
Adjuster	1952	1911	1921	1633	1623
Leader	5856	5815	5825	5537	5527
Regulator	7808	7767	7777	7489	7479
General Governor	15616	15575	15585	15297	15287
High Overseer	1093120	1093079	1093089	1092801	1092791

Fire - Mars

36	64	54	48	42
49	43	37	60	55
61	51	50	44	38
45	39	62	52	46
53	47	41	40	63

Air - Mars

53	45	61	49	36
47	39	51	43	64
41	62	50	37	54
40	52	44	60	48
63	46	38	55	42

Earth - Mars

63	40	41	47	53
46	52	62	39	45
38	44	50	51	61
55	60	37	43	49
42	48	54	64	36

Water - Mars

42	55	38	46	63
48	60	44	52	40
54	37	50	62	41
64	43	51	39	47
36	49	61	45	53

Occult Encyclopedia of Magic Squares

	Number	Angel Value (Arabic)	Angel Value (Hebrew)	Jinn Value (Arabic)	Jinn Value (Hebrew)
Usurper	36	355	5	77	67
Guide	64	23	33	105	95
Mystery	100	59	69	141	131
Adjuster	244	203	213	285	275
Leader	732	691	701	413	403
Regulator	976	935	945	657	647
General Governor	1952	1911	1921	1633	1623
High Overseer	124928	124887	124897	124609	124599

Fire - Sun

30	36	41	27	46	59
37	57	23	31	40	51
56	29	50	35	24	45
25	48	32	42	58	34
44	26	54	49	38	28
47	43	39	55	33	22

Air - Sun

31	37	42	28	47	59
38	57	24	32	41	52
56	30	51	36	25	46
26	49	33	43	58	35
45	27	54	50	39	29
48	44	40	55	34	23

Earth - Sun

59	52	46	35	29	23
47	41	25	58	39	34
28	32	36	43	50	55
42	24	51	33	54	40
37	57	30	49	27	44
31	38	56	26	45	48

Water - Sun

48	45	26	56	38	31
44	27	49	30	57	37
40	54	33	51	24	42
55	50	43	36	32	28
34	39	58	25	41	47
23	29	35	46	52	59

Occult Encyclopedia of Magic Squares

	Number	Angel Value (Arabic)	Angel Value (Hebrew)	Jinn Value (Arabic)	Jinn Value (Hebrew)
Usurper	23	342	352	64	54
Guide	59	18	28	100	90
Mystery	82	41	51	123	113
Adjuster	244	203	213	285	275
Leader	732	691	701	413	403
Regulator	976	935	945	657	647
General Governor	1952	1911	1921	1633	1623
High Overseer	115168	115127	115137	114849	114839

Fire - Venus

10	51	36	21	41	60	25
61	26	11	45	37	22	42
23	43	62	27	12	46	31
47	32	17	44	63	28	13
29	14	48	33	18	38	64
39	58	30	15	49	34	19
35	20	40	59	24	16	50

Air - Venus

50	16	24	59	40	20	35
19	34	49	15	30	58	39
64	38	18	33	48	14	29
13	28	63	44	17	32	47
31	46	12	27	62	43	23
42	22	37	45	11	26	61
25	60	41	21	36	51	10

Earth - Venus

35	39	29	47	23	61	10
20	58	14	32	43	26	51
40	30	48	17	62	11	36
59	15	33	44	27	45	21
24	49	18	63	12	37	41
16	34	38	28	46	22	60
50	19	64	13	31	42	25

Water - Venus

25	42	31	13	64	19	50
60	22	46	28	38	34	16
41	37	12	63	18	49	24
21	45	27	44	33	15	59
36	11	62	17	48	30	40
51	26	43	32	14	58	20
10	61	23	47	29	39	35

	Number	Angel Value (Arabic)	Angel Value (Hebrew)	Jinn Value (Arabic)	Jinn Value (Hebrew)
Usurper	10	329	339	51	41
Guide	64	23	33	105	95
Mystery	74	33	43	115	105
Adjuster	244	203	213	285	275
Leader	732	691	701	413	403
Regulator	976	935	945	657	647
General Governor	1952	1911	1921	1633	1623
High Overseer	124928	124887	124897	124609	124599

ANGEL OF SIX QUINANCE: MITZRAEL (361)

אל	ר	צ	מ
39	91	203	28
202	29	38	92
89	41	30	201

ל	א	ר	צ	מ
ר	צ	מ	ל	א
מ	ל	א	ר	צ
א	ר	צ	מ	ל
צ	מ	ל	א	ר

Fire - Jupiter

82	93	87	99
98	88	90	85
92	83	100	86
89	97	84	91

Air - Jupiter

91	84	97	89
86	100	83	92
85	90	88	98
99	87	93	82

Earth - Jupiter

89	92	98	82
97	83	88	93
84	100	90	87
91	86	85	99

Water - Jupiter

99	85	86	91
87	90	100	84
93	88	83	97
82	98	92	89

Occult Encyclopedia of Magic Squares

	Number	Angel Value (Arabic)	Angel Value (Hebrew)	Jinn Value (Arabic)	Jinn Value (Hebrew)
Usurper	82	41	51	123	113
Guide	100	59	69	141	131
Mystery	182	141	151	223	213
Adjuster	2888	2847	2857	2569	2559
Leader	8664	8623	8633	8345	8335
Regulator	11552	11511	11521	11233	11223
General Governor	23104	23063	23073	22785	22775
High Overseer	2310400	2310359	2310369	2310081	2310071

Fire - Mars

60	85	78	72	66
73	67	61	81	79
82	75	74	68	62
69	63	83	76	70
77	71	65	64	84

Air - Mars

77	69	82	73	60
71	63	75	67	85
65	83	74	61	78
64	76	68	81	72
84	70	62	79	66

Earth - Mars

84	64	65	71	77
70	76	83	63	69
62	68	74	75	82
79	81	61	67	73
66	72	78	85	60

Water - Mars

66	79	62	70	84
72	81	68	76	64
78	61	74	83	65
85	67	75	63	71
60	73	82	69	77

Occult Encyclopedia of Magic Squares

	Number	Angel Value (Arabic)	Angel Value (Hebrew)	Jinn Value (Arabic)	Jinn Value (Hebrew)
Usurper	60	19	29	101	91
Guide	85	44	54	126	116
Mystery	145	104	114	186	176
Adjuster	361	320	330	42	32
Leader	1083	1042	1052	764	754
Regulator	1444	1403	1413	1125	1115
General Governor	2888	2847	2857	2569	2559
High Overseer	245480	245439	245449	245161	245151

Fire - Sun

42	53	77	59	63	67
48	58	69	76	46	64
54	80	62	52	68	45
65	44	55	70	49	78
71	60	51	43	79	57
81	66	47	61	56	50

Air - Sun

50	56	61	47	66	81
57	79	43	51	60	71
78	49	70	55	44	65
45	68	52	62	80	54
64	46	76	69	58	48
67	63	59	77	53	42

Earth - Sun

81	71	65	54	48	42
66	60	44	80	58	53
47	51	55	62	69	77
61	43	70	52	76	59
56	79	49	68	46	63
50	57	78	45	64	67

Water - Sun

67	64	45	78	57	50
63	46	68	49	79	56
59	76	52	70	43	61
77	69	62	55	51	47
53	58	80	44	60	66
42	48	54	65	71	81

Occult Encyclopedia of Magic Squares

	Number	Angel Value (Arabic)	Angel Value (Hebrew)	Jinn Value (Arabic)	Jinn Value (Hebrew)
Usurper	42	1	11	83	73
Guide	81	40	50	122	112
Mystery	123	82	92	164	154
Adjuster	361	320	330	42	32
Leader	1083	1042	1052	764	754
Regulator	1444	1403	1413	1125	1115
General Governor	2888	2847	2857	2569	2559
High Overseer	233928	233887	233897	233609	233599

Fire - Venus

27	68	53	38	58	75	42
76	43	28	62	54	39	59
40	60	77	44	29	63	48
64	49	34	61	78	45	30
46	31	65	50	35	55	79
56	73	47	32	66	51	36
52	37	57	74	41	33	67

Air - Venus

67	33	41	74	57	37	52
36	51	66	32	47	73	56
79	55	35	50	65	31	46
30	45	78	61	34	49	64
48	63	29	44	77	60	40
59	39	54	62	28	43	76
42	75	58	38	53	68	27

Earth - Venus

52	56	46	64	40	76	27
37	73	31	49	60	43	68
57	47	65	34	77	28	53
74	32	50	61	44	62	38
41	66	35	78	29	54	58
33	51	55	45	63	39	75
67	36	79	30	48	59	42

Water - Venus

42	59	48	30	79	36	67
75	39	63	45	55	51	33
58	54	29	78	35	66	41
38	62	44	61	50	32	74
53	28	77	34	65	47	57
68	43	60	49	31	73	37
27	76	40	64	46	56	52

Occult Encyclopedia of Magic Squares

	Number	Angel Value (Arabic)	Angel Value (Hebrew)	Jinn Value (Arabic)	Jinn Value (Hebrew)
Usurper	27	346	356	68	58
Guide	79	38	48	120	110
Mystery	106	65	75	147	137
Adjuster	361	320	330	42	32
Leader	1083	1042	1052	764	754
Regulator	1444	1403	1413	1125	1115
General Governor	2888	2847	2857	2569	2559
High Overseer	228152	228111	228121	227833	227823

Fire - Mercury

13	29	79	58	47	63	44	28
21	37	66	50	55	76	36	20
64	48	27	43	30	14	57	78
77	56	19	35	38	22	49	65
42	26	45	61	81	60	15	31
34	18	53	74	68	52	23	39
59	80	32	16	25	41	62	46
51	67	40	24	17	33	75	54

Earth - Mercury

51	59	34	42	77	64	21	13
67	80	18	26	56	48	37	29
40	32	53	45	19	27	66	79
24	16	74	61	35	43	50	58
17	25	68	81	38	30	55	47
33	41	52	60	22	14	76	63
75	62	23	15	49	57	36	44
54	46	39	31	65	78	20	28

Occult Encyclopedia of Magic Squares

Air - Mercury

54	75	33	17	24	40	67	51
46	62	41	25	16	32	80	59
39	23	52	68	74	53	18	34
31	15	60	81	61	45	26	42
65	49	22	38	35	19	56	77
78	57	14	30	43	27	48	64
20	36	76	55	50	66	37	21
28	44	63	47	58	79	29	13

Water - Mercury

28	20	78	65	31	39	46	54
44	36	57	49	15	23	62	75
63	76	14	22	60	52	41	33
47	55	30	38	81	68	25	17
58	50	43	35	61	74	16	24
79	66	27	19	45	53	32	40
29	37	48	56	26	18	80	67
13	21	64	77	42	34	59	51

	Number	Angel Value (Arabic)	Angel Value (Hebrew)	Jinn Value (Arabic)	Jinn Value (Hebrew)
Usurper	13	332	342	54	44
Guide	81	40	50	122	112
Mystery	94	53	63	135	125
Adjuster	361	320	330	42	32
Leader	1083	1042	1052	764	754
Regulator	1444	1403	1413	1125	1115
General Governor	2888	2847	2857	2569	2559
High Overseer	233928	233887	233897	233609	233599

GEMINI

SIGN GEMINI: TEOMIM (497)

מ	י	מי	תא
400	47	13	37
12	38	399	48
45	402	39	11

מ	י	מ	ו	א	ת
א	ו	מ	ת	מ	י
מ	ת	י	א	מ	ו
ת	א	ו	מ	י	מ
ו	מ	א	י	ת	מ

Fire - Jupiter

116	127	121	133
132	122	124	119
126	117	134	120
123	131	118	125

Air - Jupiter

125	118	131	123
120	134	117	126
119	124	122	132
133	121	127	116

Earth - Jupiter

123	126	132	116
131	117	122	127
118	134	124	121
125	120	119	133

Water - Jupiter

133	119	120	125
121	124	134	118
127	122	117	131
116	132	126	123

	Number	Angel Value (Arabic)	Angel Value (Hebrew)	Jinn Value (Arabic)	Jinn Value (Hebrew)
Usurper	116	75	85	157	147
Guide	134	93	103	175	165
Mystery	250	209	219	291	281
Adjuster	3976	3935	3945	3657	3647
Leader	11928	11887	11897	11609	11599
Regulator	15904	15863	15873	15585	15575
General Governor	31808	31767	31777	31489	31479
High Overseer	4262272	4262231	4262241	4261953	4261943

Occult Encyclopedia of Magic Squares

Fire - Mars

87	113	105	99	93
100	94	88	109	106
110	102	101	95	89
96	90	111	103	97
104	98	92	91	112

Air - Mars

104	96	110	100	87
98	90	102	94	113
92	111	101	88	105
91	103	95	109	99
112	97	89	106	93

Earth - Mars

112	91	92	98	104
97	103	111	90	96
89	95	101	102	110
106	109	88	94	100
93	99	105	113	87

Water - Mars

93	106	89	97	112
99	109	95	103	91
105	88	101	111	92
113	94	102	90	98
87	100	110	96	104

	Number	Angel Value (Arabic)	Angel Value (Hebrew)	Jinn Value (Arabic)	Jinn Value (Hebrew)
Usurper	87	46	56	128	118
Guide	113	72	82	154	144
Mystery	200	159	169	241	231
Adjuster	497	456	466	178	168
Leader	1491	1450	1460	1172	1162
Regulator	1988	1947	1957	1669	1659
General Governor	3976	3935	3945	3657	3647
High Overseer	449288	449247	449257	448969	448959

Fire - Sun

65	76	98	82	86	90
71	81	92	97	69	87
77	101	85	75	91	68
88	67	78	93	72	99
94	83	74	66	100	80
102	89	70	84	79	73

Earth - Sun

102	94	88	77	71	65
89	83	67	101	81	76
70	74	78	85	92	98
84	66	93	75	97	82
79	100	72	91	69	86
73	80	99	68	87	90

Occult Encyclopedia of Magic Squares

Air - Sun

73	79	84	70	89	102
80	100	66	74	83	94
99	72	93	78	67	88
68	91	75	85	101	77
87	69	97	92	81	71
90	86	82	98	76	65

Water - Sun

90	87	68	99	80	73
86	69	91	72	100	79
82	97	75	93	66	84
98	92	85	78	74	70
76	81	101	67	83	89
65	71	77	88	94	102

	Number	Angel Value (Arabic)	Angel Value (Hebrew)	Jinn Value (Arabic)	Jinn Value (Hebrew)
Usurper	65	24	34	106	96
Guide	102	61	71	143	133
Mystery	167	126	136	208	198
Adjuster	497	456	466	178	168
Leader	1491	1450	1460	1172	1162
Regulator	1988	1947	1957	1669	1659
General Governor	3976	3935	3945	3657	3647
High Overseer	405552	405511	405521	405233	405223

Fire - Venus

47	88	73	58	78	91	62
92	63	48	82	74	59	79
60	80	93	64	49	83	68
84	69	54	81	94	65	50
66	51	85	70	55	75	95
76	89	67	52	86	71	56
72	57	77	90	61	53	87

Earth - Venus

72	76	66	84	60	92	47
57	89	51	69	80	63	88
77	67	85	54	93	48	73
90	52	70	81	64	82	58
61	86	55	94	49	74	78
53	71	75	65	83	59	91
87	56	95	50	68	79	62

Occult Encyclopedia of Magic Squares

Fire - Venus

47	88	73	58	78	91	62
92	63	48	82	74	59	79
60	80	93	64	49	83	68
84	69	54	81	94	65	50
66	51	85	70	55	75	95
76	89	67	52	86	71	56
72	57	77	90	61	53	87

Earth - Venus

72	76	66	84	60	92	47
57	89	51	69	80	63	88
77	67	85	54	93	48	73
90	52	70	81	64	82	58
61	86	55	94	49	74	78
53	71	75	65	83	59	91
87	56	95	50	68	79	62

	Number	Angel Value (Arabic)	Angel Value (Hebrew)	Jinn Value (Arabic)	Jinn Value (Hebrew)
Usurper	47	6	16	88	78
Guide	95	54	64	136	126
Mystery	142	101	111	183	173
Adjuster	497	456	466	178	168
Leader	1491	1450	1460	1172	1162
Regulator	1988	1947	1957	1669	1659
General Governor	3976	3935	3945	3657	3647
High Overseer	377720	377679	377689	377401	377391

Fire - Mercury

30	46	96	75	64	80	61	45
38	54	83	67	72	93	53	37
81	65	44	60	47	31	74	95
94	73	36	52	55	39	66	82
59	43	62	78	98	77	32	48
51	35	70	91	85	69	40	56
76	97	49	33	42	58	79	63
68	84	57	41	34	50	92	71

Occult Encyclopedia of Magic Squares

Earth - Mercury

68	76	51	59	94	81	38	30
84	97	35	43	73	65	54	46
57	49	70	62	36	44	83	96
41	33	91	78	52	60	67	75
34	42	85	98	55	47	72	64
50	58	69	77	39	31	93	80
92	79	40	32	66	74	53	61
71	63	56	48	82	95	37	45

Air - Mercury

71	92	50	34	41	57	84	68
63	79	58	42	33	49	97	76
56	40	69	85	91	70	35	51
48	32	77	98	78	62	43	59
82	66	39	55	52	36	73	94
95	74	31	47	60	44	65	81
37	53	93	72	67	83	54	38
45	61	80	64	75	96	46	30

Water - Mercury

45	37	95	82	48	56	63	71
61	53	74	66	32	40	79	92
80	93	31	39	77	69	58	50
64	72	47	55	98	85	42	34
75	67	60	52	78	91	33	41
96	83	44	36	62	70	49	57
46	54	65	73	43	35	97	84
30	38	81	94	59	51	76	68

Occult Encyclopedia of Magic Squares

	Number	Angel Value (Arabic)	Angel Value (Hebrew)	Jinn Value (Arabic)	Jinn Value (Hebrew)
Usurper	30	349	359	71	61
Guide	98	57	67	139	129
Mystery	128	87	97	169	159
Adjuster	497	456	466	178	168
Leader	1491	1450	1460	1172	1162
Regulator	1988	1947	1957	1669	1659
General Governor	3976	3935	3945	3657	3647
High Overseer	389648	389607	389617	389329	389319

Fire - Moon

59	72	34	43	97	27	63	79	23
19	62	84	39	55	71	26	48	93
89	31	47	83	15	67	76	38	51
86	18	61	70	41	54	92	25	50
46	91	30	66	82	17	53	75	37
33	58	74	29	42	96	22	65	78
32	45	90	16	68	81	36	52	77
73	35	57	95	28	44	80	21	64
60	85	20	56	69	40	49	94	24

Earth - Moon

23	93	51	50	37	78	77	64	24
79	48	38	25	75	65	52	21	94
63	26	76	92	53	22	36	80	49
27	71	67	54	17	96	81	44	40
97	55	15	41	82	42	68	28	69
43	39	83	70	66	29	16	95	56
34	84	47	61	30	74	90	57	20
72	62	31	18	91	58	45	35	85
59	19	89	86	46	33	32	73	60

Air - Moon

24	94	49	40	69	56	20	85	60
64	21	80	44	28	95	57	35	73
77	52	36	81	68	16	90	45	32
78	65	22	96	42	29	74	58	33
37	75	53	17	82	66	30	91	46
50	25	92	54	41	70	61	18	86
51	38	76	67	15	83	47	31	89
93	48	26	71	55	39	84	62	19
23	79	63	27	97	43	34	72	59

Water - Moon

60	73	32	33	46	86	89	19	59
85	35	45	58	91	18	31	62	72
20	57	90	74	30	61	47	84	34
56	95	16	29	66	70	83	39	43
69	28	68	42	82	41	15	55	97
40	44	81	96	17	54	67	71	27
49	80	36	22	53	92	76	26	63
94	21	52	65	75	25	38	48	79
24	64	77	78	37	50	51	93	23

	Number	Angel Value (Arabic)	Angel Value (Hebrew)	Jinn Value (Arabic)	Jinn Value (Hebrew)
Usurper	15	334	344	56	46
Guide	97	56	66	138	128
Mystery	112	71	81	153	143
Adjuster	497	456	466	178	168
Leader	1491	1450	1460	1172	1162
Regulator	1988	1947	1957	1669	1659
General Governor	3976	3935	3945	3657	3647
High Overseer	385672	385631	385641	385353	385343

ARCHANGEL OF GEMINI: AMBRIEL (284)

אל	י	בר	אם
40	203	13	28
12	29	39	204
201	42	30	11

ל	א	י	ר	ב	מ	א
י	ר	ב	מ	א	ל	א
ב	מ	א	ל	א	י	ר
א	ל	א	י	ר	ב	מ
א	י	ר	ב	מ	א	ל
ר	ב	מ	א	ל	א	י

Fire - Jupiter

63	74	68	79
78	69	71	66
73	64	80	67
70	77	65	72

Air - Jupiter

72	65	77	70
67	80	64	73
66	71	69	78
79	68	74	63

Earth - Jupiter

70	73	78	63
77	64	69	74
65	80	71	68
72	67	66	79

Water - Jupiter

79	66	67	72
68	71	80	65
74	69	64	77
63	78	73	70

	Number	Angel Value (Arabic)	Angel Value (Hebrew)	Jinn Value (Arabic)	Jinn Value (Hebrew)
Usurper	63	22	32	104	94
Guide	80	39	49	121	111
Mystery	143	102	112	184	174
Adjuster	2272	2231	2241	1953	1943
Leader	6816	6775	6785	6497	6487
Regulator	9088	9047	9057	8769	8759
General Governor	18176	18135	18145	17857	17847
High Overseer	1454080	1454039	1454049	1453761	1453751

Occult Encyclopedia of Magic Squares

Fire - Mars

44	72	62	56	50
57	51	45	68	63
69	59	58	52	46
53	47	70	60	54
61	55	49	48	71

Air - Mars

61	53	69	57	44
55	47	59	51	72
49	70	58	45	62
48	60	52	68	56
71	54	46	63	50

Earth - Mars

71	48	49	55	61
54	60	70	47	53
46	52	58	59	69
63	68	45	51	57
50	56	62	72	44

Water - Mars

50	63	46	54	71
56	68	52	60	48
62	45	58	70	49
72	51	59	47	55
44	57	69	53	61

	Number	Angel Value (Arabic)	Angel Value (Hebrew)	Jinn Value (Arabic)	Jinn Value (Hebrew)
Usurper	44	3	13	85	75
Guide	72	31	41	113	103
Mystery	116	75	85	157	147
Adjuster	284	243	253	325	315
Leader	852	811	821	533	523
Regulator	1136	1095	1105	817	807
General Governor	2272	2231	2241	1953	1943
High Overseer	163584	163543	163553	163265	163255

Occult Encyclopedia of Magic Squares

Fire - Sun

29	40	65	46	50	54
35	45	56	64	33	51
41	68	49	39	55	32
52	31	42	57	36	66
58	47	38	30	67	44
69	53	34	48	43	37

Air - Sun

37	43	48	34	53	69
44	67	30	38	47	58
66	36	57	42	31	52
32	55	39	49	68	41
51	33	64	56	45	35
54	50	46	65	40	29

Earth - Sun

69	58	52	41	35	29
53	47	31	68	45	40
34	38	42	49	56	65
48	30	57	39	64	46
43	67	36	55	33	50
37	44	66	32	51	54

Water - Sun

54	51	32	66	44	37
50	33	55	36	67	43
46	64	39	57	30	48
65	56	49	42	38	34
40	45	68	31	47	53
29	35	41	52	58	69

	Number	Angel Value (Arabic)	Angel Value (Hebrew)	Jinn Value (Arabic)	Jinn Value (Hebrew)
Usurper	29	348	358	70	60
Guide	69	28	38	110	100
Mystery	98	57	67	139	129
Adjuster	284	243	253	325	315
Leader	852	811	821	533	523
Regulator	1136	1095	1105	817	807
General Governor	2272	2231	2241	1953	1943
High Overseer	156768	156727	156737	156449	156439

Fire - Venus

16	57	42	27	47	64	31
65	32	17	51	43	28	48
29	49	66	33	18	52	37
53	38	23	50	67	34	19
35	20	54	39	24	44	68
45	62	36	21	55	40	25
41	26	46	63	30	22	56

Air - Venus

56	22	30	63	46	26	41
25	40	55	21	36	62	45
68	44	24	39	54	20	35
19	34	67	50	23	38	53
37	52	18	33	66	49	29
48	28	43	51	17	32	65
31	64	47	27	42	57	16

Earth - Venus

41	45	35	53	29	65	16
26	62	20	38	49	32	57
46	36	54	23	66	17	42
63	21	39	50	33	51	27
30	55	24	67	18	43	47
22	40	44	34	52	28	64
56	25	68	19	37	48	31

Water - Venus

31	48	37	19	68	25	56
64	28	52	34	44	40	22
47	43	18	67	24	55	30
27	51	33	50	39	21	63
42	17	66	23	54	36	46
57	32	49	38	20	62	26
16	65	29	53	35	45	41

	Number	Angel Value (Arabic)	Angel Value (Hebrew)	Jinn Value (Arabic)	Jinn Value (Hebrew)
Usurper	16	335	345	57	47
Guide	68	27	37	109	99
Mystery	84	43	53	125	115
Adjuster	284	243	253	325	315
Leader	852	811	821	533	523
Regulator	1136	1095	1105	817	807
General Governor	2272	2231	2241	1953	1943
High Overseer	154496	154455	154465	154177	154167

Occult Encyclopedia of Magic Squares

Fire - Mercury

4	20	65	49	38	54	35	19
12	28	57	41	46	62	27	11
55	39	18	34	21	5	48	64
63	47	10	26	29	13	40	56
33	17	36	52	67	51	6	22
25	9	44	60	59	43	14	30
50	66	23	7	16	32	53	37
42	58	31	15	8	24	61	45

Earth - Mercury

42	50	25	33	63	55	12	4
58	66	9	17	47	39	28	20
31	23	44	36	10	18	57	65
15	7	60	52	26	34	41	49
8	16	59	67	29	21	46	38
24	32	43	51	13	5	62	54
61	53	14	6	40	48	27	35
45	37	30	22	56	64	11	19

Air - Mercury

45	61	24	8	15	31	58	42
37	53	32	16	7	23	66	50
30	14	43	59	60	44	9	25
22	6	51	67	52	36	17	33
56	40	13	29	26	10	47	63
64	48	5	21	34	18	39	55
11	27	62	46	41	57	28	12
19	35	54	38	49	65	20	4

Water - Mercury

19	11	64	56	22	30	37	45
35	27	48	40	6	14	53	61
54	62	5	13	51	43	32	24
38	46	21	29	67	59	16	8
49	41	34	26	52	60	7	15
65	57	18	10	36	44	23	31
20	28	39	47	17	9	66	58
4	12	55	63	33	25	50	42

	Number	Angel Value (Arabic)	Angel Value (Hebrew)	Jinn Value (Arabic)	Jinn Value (Hebrew)
Usurper	4	323	333	45	35
Guide	67	26	36	108	98
Mystery	71	30	40	112	102
Adjuster	284	243	253	325	315
Leader	852	811	821	533	523
Regulator	1136	1095	1105	817	807
General Governor	2272	2231	2241	1953	1943
High Overseer	152224	152183	152193	151905	151895

ANGEL OF GEMINI : SARAYEL (302)

אל	אי	ר	ם
59	201	14	28
13	29	58	202
199	61	30	12

ל	א	י	א	ר	ם
ר	א	ל	ם	י	א
י	ם	א	ר	ל	א
ם	ר	א	י	א	ל
א	ל	ר	א	ם	י
א	י	ם	ל	א	ר

Fire - Jupiter

68	79	73	82
81	74	76	71
78	69	83	72
75	80	70	77

Air - Jupiter

77	70	80	75
72	83	69	78
71	76	74	81
82	73	79	68

Earth - Jupiter

75	78	81	68
80	69	74	79
70	83	76	73
77	72	71	82

Water - Jupiter

82	71	72	77
73	76	83	70
79	74	69	80
68	81	78	75

Occult Encyclopedia of Magic Squares

	Number	Angel Value (Arabic)	Angel Value (Hebrew)	Jinn Value (Arabic)	Jinn Value (Hebrew)
Usurper	68	27	37	109	99
Guide	83	42	52	124	114
Mystery	151	110	120	192	182
Adjuster	2416	2375	2385	2097	2087
Leader	7248	7207	7217	6929	6919
Regulator	9664	9623	9633	9345	9335
General Governor	19328	19287	19297	19009	18999
High Overseer	1604224	1604183	1604193	1603905	1603895

Fire - Mars

48	74	66	60	54
61	55	49	70	67
71	63	62	56	50
57	51	72	64	58
65	59	53	52	73

Air - Mars

65	57	71	61	48
59	51	63	55	74
53	72	62	49	66
52	64	56	70	60
73	58	50	67	54

Earth - Mars

73	52	53	59	65
58	64	72	51	57
50	56	62	63	71
67	70	49	55	61
54	60	66	74	48

Water - Mars

54	67	50	58	73
60	70	56	64	52
66	49	62	72	53
74	55	63	51	59
48	61	71	57	65

Occult Encyclopedia of Magic Squares

	Number	Angel Value (Arabic)	Angel Value (Hebrew)	Jinn Value (Arabic)	Jinn Value (Hebrew)
Usurper	48	7	17	89	79
Guide	74	33	43	115	105
Mystery	122	81	91	163	153
Adjuster	302	261	271	343	333
Leader	906	865	875	587	577
Regulator	1208	1167	1177	889	879
General Governor	2416	2375	2385	2097	2087
High Overseer	178784	178743	178753	178465	178455

Fire - Sun

32	43	68	49	53	57
38	48	59	67	36	54
44	71	52	42	58	35
55	34	45	60	39	69
61	50	41	33	70	47
72	56	37	51	46	40

Air - Sun

40	46	51	37	56	72
47	70	33	41	50	61
69	39	60	45	34	55
35	58	42	52	71	44
54	36	67	59	48	38
57	53	49	68	43	32

Earth - Sun

72	61	55	44	38	32
56	50	34	71	48	43
37	41	45	52	59	68
51	33	60	42	67	49
46	70	39	58	36	53
40	47	69	35	54	57

Water - Sun

57	54	35	69	47	40
53	36	58	39	70	46
49	67	42	60	33	51
68	59	52	45	41	37
43	48	71	34	50	56
32	38	44	55	61	72

Occult Encyclopedia of Magic Squares

	Number	Angel Value (Arabic)	Angel Value (Hebrew)	Jinn Value (Arabic)	Jinn Value (Hebrew)
Usurper	32	351	1	73	63
Guide	72	31	41	113	103
Mystery	104	63	73	145	135
Adjuster	302	261	271	343	333
Leader	906	865	875	587	577
Regulator	1208	1167	1177	889	879
General Governor	2416	2375	2385	2097	2087
High Overseer	173952	173911	173921	173633	173623

Fire - Venus

19	60	45	30	50	64	34
65	35	20	54	46	31	51
32	52	66	36	21	55	40
56	41	26	53	67	37	22
38	23	57	42	27	47	68
48	62	39	24	58	43	28
44	29	49	63	33	25	59

Air - Venus

59	25	33	63	49	29	44
28	43	58	24	39	62	48
68	47	27	42	57	23	38
22	37	67	53	26	41	56
40	55	21	36	66	52	32
51	31	46	54	20	35	65
34	64	50	30	45	60	19

Earth - Venus

44	48	38	56	32	65	19
29	62	23	41	52	35	60
49	39	57	26	66	20	45
63	24	42	53	36	54	30
33	58	27	67	21	46	50
25	43	47	37	55	31	64
59	28	68	22	40	51	34

Water - Venus

34	51	40	22	68	28	59
64	31	55	37	47	43	25
50	46	21	67	27	58	33
30	54	36	53	42	24	63
45	20	66	26	57	39	49
60	35	52	41	23	62	29
19	65	32	56	38	48	44

	Number	Angel Value (Arabic)	Angel Value (Hebrew)	Jinn Value (Arabic)	Jinn Value (Hebrew)
Usurper	19	338	348	60	50
Guide	68	27	37	109	99
Mystery	87	46	56	128	118
Adjuster	302	261	271	343	333
Leader	906	865	875	587	577
Regulator	1208	1167	1177	889	879
General Governor	2416	2375	2385	2097	2087
High Overseer	164288	164247	164257	163969	163959

Fire - Mercury

6	22	69	51	40	56	37	21
14	30	59	43	48	66	29	13
57	41	20	36	23	7	50	68
67	49	12	28	31	15	42	58
35	19	38	54	71	53	8	24
27	11	46	64	61	45	16	32
52	70	25	9	18	34	55	39
44	60	33	17	10	26	65	47

Earth - Mercury

44	52	27	35	67	57	14	6
60	70	11	19	49	41	30	22
33	25	46	38	12	20	59	69
17	9	64	54	28	36	43	51
10	18	61	71	31	23	48	40
26	34	45	53	15	7	66	56
65	55	16	8	42	50	29	37
47	39	32	24	58	68	13	21

Occult Encyclopedia of Magic Squares

Air - Mercury

47	65	26	10	17	33	60	44
39	55	34	18	9	25	70	52
32	16	45	61	64	46	11	27
24	8	53	71	54	38	19	35
58	42	15	31	28	12	49	67
68	50	7	23	36	20	41	57
13	29	66	48	43	59	30	14
21	37	56	40	51	69	22	6

Water - Mercury

21	13	68	58	24	32	39	47
37	29	50	42	8	16	55	65
56	66	7	15	53	45	34	26
40	48	23	31	71	61	18	10
51	43	36	28	54	64	9	17
69	59	20	12	38	46	25	33
22	30	41	49	19	11	70	60
6	14	57	67	35	27	52	44

	Number	Angel Value (Arabic)	Angel Value (Hebrew)	Jinn Value (Arabic)	Jinn Value (Hebrew)
Usurper	6	325	335	47	37
Guide	71	30	40	112	102
Mystery	77	36	46	118	108
Adjuster	302	261	271	343	333
Leader	906	865	875	587	577
Regulator	1208	1167	1177	889	879
General Governor	2416	2375	2385	2097	2087
High Overseer	171536	171495	171505	171217	171207

LORD OF TRIPLICITY BY DAY: SARASH (630)

ש	ר	ע	ם
59	71	203	297
202	298	58	72
69	61	299	201

ש	ר	ע	ם
ם	ע	ר	ש
ר	ש	ם	ע
ע	ם	ש	ר

Fire - Saturn

211	206	213
212	210	208
207	214	209

Air - Saturn

209	214	207
208	210	212
213	206	211

Earth - Saturn

207	212	211
214	210	206
209	208	213

Water - Saturn

213	208	209
206	210	214
211	212	207

	Number	Angel Value (Arabic)	Angel Value (Hebrew)	Jinn Value (Arabic)	Jinn Value (Hebrew)
Usurper	206	165	175	247	237
Guide	214	173	183	255	245
Mystery	420	379	389	101	91
Adjuster	630	589	599	311	301
Leader	1890	1849	1859	1571	1561
Regulator	2520	2479	2489	2201	2191
General Governor	5040	4999	5009	4721	4711
High Overseer	1078560	1078519	1078529	1078241	1078231

Occult Encyclopedia of Magic Squares

Fire - Jupiter

150	161	155	164
163	156	158	153
160	151	165	154
157	162	152	159

Air - Jupiter

159	152	162	157
154	165	151	160
153	158	156	163
164	155	161	150

Earth - Jupiter

157	160	163	150
162	151	156	161
152	165	158	155
159	154	153	164

Water - Jupiter

164	153	154	159
155	158	165	152
161	156	151	162
150	163	160	157

	Number	Angel Value (Arabic)	Angel Value (Hebrew)	Jinn Value (Arabic)	Jinn Value (Hebrew)
Usurper	150	109	119	191	181
Guide	165	124	134	206	196
Mystery	315	274	284	356	346
Adjuster	5040	4999	5009	4721	4711
Leader	15120	15079	15089	14801	14791
Regulator	20160	20119	20129	19841	19831
General Governor	40320	40279	40289	40001	39991
High Overseer	6652800	6652759	6652769	6652481	6652471

Fire - Mars

114	138	132	126	120
127	121	115	134	133
135	129	128	122	116
123	117	136	130	124
131	125	119	118	137

Earth - Mars

137	118	119	125	131
124	130	136	117	123
116	122	128	129	135
133	134	115	121	127
120	126	132	138	114

Air - Mars

131	123	135	127	114
125	117	129	121	138
119	136	128	115	132
118	130	122	134	126
137	124	116	133	120

Water - Mars

120	133	116	124	137
126	134	122	130	118
132	115	128	136	119
138	121	129	117	125
114	127	135	123	131

	Number	Angel Value (Arabic)	Angel Value (Hebrew)	Jinn Value (Arabic)	Jinn Value (Hebrew)
Usurper	114	73	83	155	145
Guide	138	97	107	179	169
Mystery	252	211	221	293	283
Adjuster	630	589	599	311	301
Leader	1890	1849	1859	1571	1561
Regulator	2520	2479	2489	2201	2191
General Governor	5040	4999	5009	4721	4711
High Overseer	695520	695479	695489	695201	695191

Fire - Sun

87	98	121	104	108	112
93	103	114	120	91	109
99	124	107	97	113	90
110	89	100	115	94	122
116	105	96	88	123	102
125	111	92	106	101	95

Earth - Sun

125	116	110	99	93	87
111	105	89	124	103	98
92	96	100	107	114	121
106	88	115	97	120	104
101	123	94	113	91	108
95	102	122	90	109	112

Air - Sun

95	101	106	92	111	125
102	123	88	96	105	116
122	94	115	100	89	110
90	113	97	107	124	99
109	91	120	114	103	93
112	108	104	121	98	87

Water - Sun

112	109	90	122	102	95
108	91	113	94	123	101
104	120	97	115	88	106
121	114	107	100	96	92
98	103	124	89	105	111
87	93	99	110	116	125

	Number	Angel Value (Arabic)	Angel Value (Hebrew)	Jinn Value (Arabic)	Jinn Value (Hebrew)
Usurper	87	46	56	128	118
Guide	125	84	94	166	156
Mystery	212	171	181	253	243
Adjuster	630	589	599	311	301
Leader	1890	1849	1859	1571	1561
Regulator	2520	2479	2489	2201	2191
General Governor	5040	4999	5009	4721	4711
High Overseer	630000	629959	629969	629681	629671

Fire - Venus

66	107	92	77	97	110	81
111	82	67	101	93	78	98
79	99	112	83	68	102	87
103	88	73	100	113	84	69
85	70	104	89	74	94	114
95	108	86	71	105	90	75
91	76	96	109	80	72	106

Earth - Venus

91	95	85	103	79	111	66
76	108	70	88	99	82	107
96	86	104	73	112	67	92
109	71	89	100	83	101	77
80	105	74	113	68	93	97
72	90	94	84	102	78	110
106	75	114	69	87	98	81

Air - Venus

106	72	80	109	96	76	91
75	90	105	71	86	108	95
114	94	74	89	104	70	85
69	84	113	100	73	88	103
87	102	68	83	112	99	79
98	78	93	101	67	82	111
81	110	97	77	92	107	66

Water - Venus

81	98	87	69	114	75	106
110	78	102	84	94	90	72
97	93	68	113	74	105	80
77	101	83	100	89	71	109
92	67	112	73	104	86	96
107	82	99	88	70	108	76
66	111	79	103	85	95	91

Occult Encyclopedia of Magic Squares

	Number	Angel Value (Arabic)	Angel Value (Hebrew)	Jinn Value (Arabic)	Jinn Value (Hebrew)
Usurper	66	25	35	107	97
Guide	114	73	83	155	145
Mystery	180	139	149	221	211
Adjuster	630	589	599	311	301
Leader	1890	1849	1859	1571	1561
Regulator	2520	2479	2489	2201	2191
General Governor	5040	4999	5009	4721	4711
High Overseer	574560	574519	574529	574241	574231

Fire - Mercury

47	63	110	92	81	97	78	62
55	71	100	84	89	107	70	54
98	82	61	77	64	48	91	109
108	90	53	69	72	56	83	99
76	60	79	95	112	94	49	65
68	52	87	105	102	86	57	73
93	111	66	50	59	75	96	80
85	101	74	58	51	67	106	88

Earth - Mercury

85	93	68	76	108	98	55	47
101	111	52	60	90	82	71	63
74	66	87	79	53	61	100	110
58	50	105	95	69	77	84	92
51	59	102	112	72	64	89	81
67	75	86	94	56	48	107	97
106	96	57	49	83	91	70	78
88	80	73	65	99	109	54	62

Occult Encyclopedia of Magic Squares

Air - Mercury

88	106	67	51	58	74	101	85
80	96	75	59	50	66	111	93
73	57	86	102	105	87	52	68
65	49	94	112	95	79	60	76
99	83	56	72	69	53	90	108
109	91	48	64	77	61	82	98
54	70	107	89	84	100	71	55
62	78	97	81	92	110	63	47

Water - Mercury

62	54	109	99	65	73	80	88
78	70	91	83	49	57	96	106
97	107	48	56	94	86	75	67
81	89	64	72	112	102	59	51
92	84	77	69	95	105	50	58
110	100	61	53	79	87	66	74
63	71	82	90	60	52	111	101
47	55	98	108	76	68	93	85

	Number	Angel Value (Arabic)	Angel Value (Hebrew)	Jinn Value (Arabic)	Jinn Value (Hebrew)
Usurper	47	6	16	88	78
Guide	112	71	81	153	143
Mystery	159	118	128	200	190
Adjuster	630	589	599	311	301
Leader	1890	1849	1859	1571	1561
Regulator	2520	2479	2489	2201	2191
General Governor	5040	4999	5009	4721	4711
High Overseer	564480	564439	564449	564161	564151

Occult Encyclopedia of Magic Squares

Fire - Moon

74	87	49	58	110	42	78	94	38
34	77	99	54	70	86	41	63	106
102	46	62	98	30	82	91	53	66
101	33	76	85	56	69	105	40	65
61	104	45	81	97	32	68	90	52
48	73	89	44	57	109	37	80	93
47	60	103	31	83	96	51	67	92
88	50	72	108	43	59	95	36	79
75	100	35	71	84	55	64	107	39

Earth - Moon

38	106	66	65	52	93	92	79	39
94	63	53	40	90	80	67	36	107
78	41	91	105	68	37	51	95	64
42	86	82	69	32	109	96	59	55
110	70	30	56	97	57	83	43	84
58	54	98	85	81	44	31	108	71
49	99	62	76	45	89	103	72	35
87	77	46	33	104	73	60	50	100
74	34	102	101	61	48	47	88	75

Air - Moon

39	107	64	55	84	71	35	100	75
79	36	95	59	43	108	72	50	88
92	67	51	96	83	31	103	60	47
93	80	37	109	57	44	89	73	48
52	90	68	32	97	81	45	104	61
65	40	105	69	56	85	76	33	101
66	53	91	82	30	98	62	46	102
106	63	41	86	70	54	99	77	34
38	94	78	42	110	58	49	87	74

Occult Encyclopedia of Magic Squares

Water - Moon

75	88	47	48	61	101	102	34	74
100	50	60	73	104	33	46	77	87
35	72	103	89	45	76	62	99	49
71	108	31	44	81	85	98	54	58
84	43	83	57	97	56	30	70	110
55	59	96	109	32	69	82	86	42
64	95	51	37	68	105	91	41	78
107	36	67	80	90	40	53	63	94
39	79	92	93	52	65	66	106	38

	Number	Angel Value (Arabic)	Angel Value (Hebrew)	Jinn Value (Arabic)	Jinn Value (Hebrew)
Usurper	30	349	359	71	61
Guide	110	69	79	151	141
Mystery	140	99	109	181	171
Adjuster	630	589	599	311	301
Leader	1890	1849	1859	1571	1561
Regulator	2520	2479	2489	2201	2191
General Governor	5040	4999	5009	4721	4711
High Overseer	554400	554359	554369	554081	554071

Fire - Saturn

13	31	38	76	67	110	60	52	84	99
24	88	81	72	112	97	15	57	43	41
39	44	68	111	98	83	32	20	61	74
45	70	109	100	33	79	87	28	17	62
58	108	102	37	48	71	75	85	30	16
65	22	23	90	78	54	50	40	95	113
77	59	19	26	92	47	35	96	116	63
91	80	55	14	25	42	93	115	66	49
101	34	46	53	21	29	114	64	82	86
117	94	89	51	56	18	69	73	36	27

Occult Encyclopedia of Magic Squares

Earth - Saturn

117	101	91	77	65	58	45	39	24	13
94	34	80	59	22	108	70	44	88	31
89	46	55	19	23	102	109	68	81	38
51	53	14	26	90	37	100	111	72	76
56	21	25	92	78	48	33	98	112	67
18	29	42	47	54	71	79	83	97	110
69	114	93	35	50	75	87	32	15	60
73	64	115	96	40	85	28	20	57	52
36	82	66	116	95	30	17	61	43	84
27	86	49	63	113	16	62	74	41	99

Air - Saturn

27	36	73	69	18	56	51	89	94	117
86	82	64	114	29	21	53	46	34	101
49	66	115	93	42	25	14	55	80	91
63	116	96	35	47	92	26	19	59	77
113	95	40	50	54	78	90	23	22	65
16	30	85	75	71	48	37	102	108	58
62	17	28	87	79	33	100	109	70	45
74	61	20	32	83	98	111	68	44	39
41	43	57	15	97	112	72	81	88	24
99	84	52	60	110	67	76	38	31	13

Water - Saturn

99	41	74	62	16	113	63	49	86	27
84	43	61	17	30	95	116	66	82	36
52	57	20	28	85	40	96	115	64	73
60	**15**	32	87	75	50	35	93	114	69
110	97	83	79	71	54	47	42	29	18
67	112	98	33	48	78	92	25	21	56
76	72	111	100	37	90	26	14	53	51
38	81	68	109	102	23	19	55	46	89
31	88	44	70	108	22	59	80	34	94
13	24	39	45	58	65	77	91	101	117

	Number	Angel Value (Arabic)	Angel Value (Hebrew)	Jinn Value (Arabic)	Jinn Value (Hebrew)
Usurper	13	332	342	54	44
Guide	117	76	86	158	148
Mystery	130	89	99	171	161
Adjuster	630	589	599	311	301
Leader	1890	1849	1859	1571	1561
Regulator	2520	2479	2489	2201	2191
General Governor	5040	4999	5009	4721	4711
High Overseer	589680	589639	589649	589361	589351

LORD OF TRIPLICITY BY NIGHT: OGARMAN (439)

נ	ע	רמ	עוג
78	241	73	47
72	48	77	242
239	80	49	71

Fire - Jupiter

102	113	107	117
116	108	110	105
112	103	118	106
109	115	104	111

Earth - Jupiter

109	112	116	102
115	103	108	113
104	118	110	107
111	106	105	117

Occult Encyclopedia of Magic Squares

Air - Jupiter

111	104	115	109
106	118	103	112
105	110	108	116
117	107	113	102

Water - Jupiter

117	105	106	111
107	110	118	104
113	108	103	115
102	116	112	109

	Number	Angel Value (Arabic)	Angel Value (Hebrew)	Jinn Value (Arabic)	Jinn Value (Hebrew)
Usurper	102	61	71	143	133
Guide	118	77	87	159	149
Mystery	220	179	189	261	251
Adjuster	3512	3471	3481	3193	3183
Leader	10536	10495	10505	10217	10207
Regulator	14048	14007	14017	13729	13719
General Governor	28096	28055	28065	27777	27767
High Overseer	3315328	3315287	3315297	3315009	3314999

Fire - Mars

75	103	93	87	81
88	82	76	99	94
100	90	89	83	77
84	78	101	91	85
92	86	80	79	102

Air - Mars

92	84	100	88	75
86	78	90	82	103
80	101	89	76	93
79	91	83	99	87
102	85	77	94	81

Earth - Mars

102	79	80	86	92
85	91	101	78	84
77	83	89	90	100
94	99	76	82	88
81	87	93	103	75

Water - Mars

81	94	77	85	102
87	99	83	91	79
93	76	89	101	80
103	82	90	78	86
75	88	100	84	92

Occult Encyclopedia of Magic Squares

	Number	Angel Value (Arabic)	Angel Value (Hebrew)	Jinn Value (Arabic)	Jinn Value (Hebrew)
Usurper	75	34	44	116	106
Guide	103	62	72	144	134
Mystery	178	137	147	219	209
Adjuster	439	398	408	120	110
Leader	1317	1276	1286	998	988
Regulator	1756	1715	1725	1437	1427
General Governor	3512	3471	3481	3193	3183
High Overseer	361736	361695	361705	361417	361407

Fire - Sun

55	66	90	72	76	80
61	71	82	89	59	77
67	93	75	65	81	58
78	57	68	83	62	91
84	73	64	56	92	70
94	79	60	74	69	63

Air - Sun

63	69	74	60	79	94
70	92	56	64	73	84
91	62	83	68	57	78
58	81	65	75	93	67
77	59	89	82	71	61
80	76	72	90	66	55

Earth - Sun

94	84	78	67	61	55
79	73	57	93	71	66
60	64	68	75	82	90
74	56	83	65	89	72
69	92	62	81	59	76
63	70	91	58	77	80

Water - Sun

80	77	58	91	70	63
76	59	81	62	92	69
72	89	65	83	56	74
90	82	75	68	64	60
66	71	93	57	73	79
55	61	67	78	84	94

	Number	Angel Value (Arabic)	Angel Value (Hebrew)	Jinn Value (Arabic)	Jinn Value (Hebrew)
Usurper	55	14	24	96	86
Guide	94	53	63	135	125
Mystery	149	108	118	190	180
Adjuster	439	398	408	120	110
Leader	1317	1276	1286	998	988
Regulator	1756	1715	1725	1437	1427
General Governor	3512	3471	3481	3193	3183
High Overseer	330128	330087	330097	329809	329799

Fire - Venus

38	79	64	49	69	87	53
88	54	39	73	65	50	70
51	71	89	55	40	74	59
75	60	45	72	90	56	41
57	42	76	61	46	66	91
67	85	58	43	77	62	47
63	48	68	86	52	44	78

Air - Venus

78	44	52	86	68	48	63
47	62	77	43	58	85	67
91	66	46	61	76	42	57
41	56	90	72	45	60	75
59	74	40	55	89	71	51
70	50	65	73	39	54	88
53	87	69	49	64	79	38

Earth - Venus

63	67	57	75	51	88	38
48	85	42	60	71	54	79
68	58	76	45	89	39	64
86	43	61	72	55	73	49
52	77	46	90	40	65	69
44	62	66	56	74	50	87
78	47	91	41	59	70	53

Water - Venus

53	70	59	41	91	47	78
87	50	74	56	66	62	44
69	65	40	90	46	77	52
49	73	55	72	61	43	86
64	39	89	45	76	58	68
79	54	71	60	42	85	48
38	88	51	75	57	67	63

Occult Encyclopedia of Magic Squares

	Number	Angel Value (Arabic)	Angel Value (Hebrew)	Jinn Value (Arabic)	Jinn Value (Hebrew)
Usurper	38	357	7	79	69
Guide	91	50	60	132	122
Mystery	129	88	98	170	160
Adjuster	439	398	408	120	110
Leader	1317	1276	1286	998	988
Regulator	1756	1715	1725	1437	1427
General Governor	3512	3471	3481	3193	3183
High Overseer	319592	319551	319561	319273	319263

Fire - Mercury

23	39	87	68	57	73	54	38
31	47	76	60	65	84	46	30
74	58	37	53	40	24	67	86
85	66	29	45	48	32	59	75
52	36	55	71	89	70	25	41
44	28	63	82	78	62	33	49
69	88	42	26	35	51	72	56
61	77	50	34	27	43	83	64

Earth - Mercury

61	69	44	52	85	74	31	23
77	88	28	36	66	58	47	39
50	42	63	55	29	37	76	87
34	26	82	71	45	53	60	68
27	35	78	89	48	40	65	57
43	51	62	70	32	24	84	73
83	72	33	25	59	67	46	54
64	56	49	41	75	86	30	38

Occult Encyclopedia of Magic Squares

Air - Mercury

64	83	43	27	34	50	77	61
56	72	51	35	26	42	88	69
49	33	62	78	82	63	28	44
41	25	70	89	71	55	36	52
75	59	32	48	45	29	66	85
86	67	24	40	53	37	58	74
30	46	84	65	60	76	47	31
38	54	73	57	68	87	39	23

Water - Mercury

38	30	86	75	41	49	56	64
54	46	67	59	25	33	72	83
73	84	24	32	70	62	51	43
57	65	40	48	89	78	35	27
68	60	53	45	71	82	26	34
87	76	37	29	55	63	42	50
39	47	58	66	36	28	88	77
23	31	74	85	52	44	69	61

	Number	Angel Value (Arabic)	Angel Value (Hebrew)	Jinn Value (Arabic)	Jinn Value (Hebrew)
Usurper	23	342	352	64	54
Guide	89	48	58	130	120
Mystery	112	71	81	153	143
Adjuster	439	398	408	120	110
Leader	1317	1276	1286	998	988
Regulator	1756	1715	1725	1437	1427
General Governor	3512	3471	3481	3193	3183
High Overseer	312568	312527	312537	312249	312239

Fire - Moon

52	65	27	36	95	20	56	72	16
12	55	77	32	48	64	19	41	91
87	24	40	76	8	60	69	31	44
79	11	54	63	34	47	90	18	43
39	89	23	59	75	10	46	68	30
26	51	67	22	35	94	15	58	71
25	38	88	9	61	74	29	45	70
66	28	50	93	21	37	73	14	57
53	78	13	49	62	33	42	92	17

Earth - Moon

16	91	44	43	30	71	70	57	17
72	41	31	18	68	58	45	14	92
56	19	69	90	46	15	29	73	42
20	64	60	47	10	94	74	37	33
95	48	8	34	75	35	61	21	62
36	32	76	63	59	22	9	93	49
27	77	40	54	23	67	88	50	13
65	55	24	11	89	51	38	28	78
52	12	87	79	39	26	25	66	53

Air - Moon

17	92	42	33	62	49	13	78	53
57	14	73	37	21	93	50	28	66
70	45	29	74	61	9	88	38	25
71	58	15	94	35	22	67	51	26
30	68	46	10	75	59	23	89	39
43	18	90	47	34	63	54	11	79
44	31	69	60	8	76	40	24	87
91	41	19	64	48	32	77	55	12
16	72	56	20	95	36	27	65	52

Water - Moon

53	66	25	26	39	79	87	12	52
78	28	38	51	89	11	24	55	65
13	50	88	67	23	54	40	77	27
49	93	9	22	59	63	76	32	36
62	21	61	35	75	34	8	48	95
33	37	74	94	10	47	60	64	20
42	73	29	15	46	90	69	19	56
92	14	45	58	68	18	31	41	72
17	57	70	71	30	43	44	91	16

	Number	Angel Value (Arabic)	Angel Value (Hebrew)	Jinn Value (Arabic)	Jinn Value (Hebrew)
Usurper	8	327	337	49	39
Guide	95	54	64	136	126
Mystery	103	62	72	144	134
Adjuster	439	398	408	120	110
Leader	1317	1276	1286	998	988
Regulator	1756	1715	1725	1437	1427
General Governor	3512	3471	3481	3193	3183
High Overseer	333640	333599	333609	333321	333311

ANGEL RULING 3ʳᴰ HOUSE: GIEL (44)

ל	א	י	ג
2	11	4	27
3	28	1	12
9	4	29	2

ל	א	י	ג
ג	י	א	ל
א	ל	ג	י
י	ג	ל	א

Numerical Squares See Page: 1

ANGEL OF FIRST DECANATE: SAGARASH (563)

ש	ר	ג	ס
59	4	203	297
202	298	58	5
2	61	299	201

ש	ר	ג	ס
ס	ג	ר	ש
ר	ש	ס	ג
ג	ס	ש	ר

Fire - Jupiter

133	144	138	148
147	139	141	136
143	134	149	137
140	146	135	142

Air - Jupiter

142	135	146	140
137	149	134	143
136	141	139	147
148	138	144	133

Earth - Jupiter

140	143	147	133
146	134	139	144
135	149	141	138
142	137	136	148

Water - Jupiter

148	136	137	142
138	141	149	135
144	139	134	146
133	147	143	140

	Number	Angel Value (Arabic)	Angel Value (Hebrew)	Jinn Value (Arabic)	Jinn Value (Hebrew)
Usurper	133	92	102	174	164
Guide	149	108	118	190	180
Mystery	282	241	251	323	313
Adjuster	4504	4463	4473	4185	4175
Leader	13512	13471	13481	13193	13183
Regulator	18016	17975	17985	17697	17687
General Governor	36032	35991	36001	35713	35703
High Overseer	5368768	5368727	5368737	5368449	5368439

Occult Encyclopedia of Magic Squares

Fire - Mars

100	127	118	112	106
113	107	101	123	119
124	115	114	108	102
109	103	125	116	110
117	111	105	104	126

Air - Mars

117	109	124	113	100
111	103	115	107	127
105	125	114	101	118
104	116	108	123	112
126	110	102	119	106

Earth - Mars

126	104	105	111	117
110	116	125	103	109
102	108	114	115	124
119	123	101	107	113
106	112	118	127	100

Water - Mars

106	119	102	110	126
112	123	108	116	104
118	101	114	125	105
127	107	115	103	111
100	113	124	109	117

	Number	Angel Value (Arabic)	Angel Value (Hebrew)	Jinn Value (Arabic)	Jinn Value (Hebrew)
Usurper	100	59	69	141	131
Guide	127	86	96	168	158
Mystery	227	186	196	268	258
Adjuster	563	522	532	244	234
Leader	1689	1648	1658	1370	1360
Regulator	2252	2211	2221	1933	1923
General Governor	4504	4463	4473	4185	4175
High Overseer	572008	571967	571977	571689	571679

Fire - Sun

76	87	109	93	97	101
82	92	103	108	80	98
88	112	96	86	102	79
99	78	89	104	83	110
105	94	85	77	111	91
113	100	81	95	90	84

Earth - Sun

113	105	99	88	82	76
100	94	78	112	92	87
81	85	89	96	103	109
95	77	104	86	108	93
90	111	83	102	80	97
84	91	110	79	98	101

Occult Encyclopedia of Magic Squares

Air - Sun

84	90	95	81	100	113
91	111	77	85	94	105
110	83	104	89	78	99
79	102	86	96	112	88
98	80	108	103	92	82
101	97	93	109	87	76

Water - Sun

101	98	79	110	91	84
97	80	102	83	111	90
93	108	86	104	77	95
109	103	96	89	85	81
87	92	112	78	94	100
76	82	88	99	105	113

	Number	Angel Value (Arabic)	Angel Value (Hebrew)	Jinn Value (Arabic)	Jinn Value (Hebrew)
Usurper	76	35	45	117	107
Guide	113	72	82	154	144
Mystery	189	148	158	230	220
Adjuster	563	522	532	244	234
Leader	1689	1648	1658	1370	1360
Regulator	2252	2211	2221	1933	1923
General Governor	4504	4463	4473	4185	4175
High Overseer	508952	508911	508921	508633	508623

Fire - Venus

56	97	82	67	87	103	71
104	72	57	91	83	68	88
69	89	105	73	58	92	77
93	78	63	90	106	74	59
75	60	94	79	64	84	107
85	101	76	61	95	80	65
81	66	86	102	70	62	96

Occult Encyclopedia of Magic Squares

Earth - Venus

81	85	75	93	69	104	56
66	101	60	78	89	72	97
86	76	94	63	105	57	82
102	61	79	90	73	91	67
70	95	64	106	58	83	87
62	80	84	74	92	68	103
96	65	107	59	77	88	71

Air - Venus

96	62	70	102	86	66	81
65	80	95	61	76	101	85
107	84	64	79	94	60	75
59	74	106	90	63	78	93
77	92	58	73	105	89	69
88	68	83	91	57	72	104
71	103	87	67	82	97	56

Water - Venus

71	88	77	59	107	65	96
103	68	92	74	84	80	62
87	83	58	106	64	95	70
67	91	73	90	79	61	102
82	57	105	63	94	76	86
97	72	89	78	60	101	66
56	104	69	93	75	85	81

	Number	Angel Value (Arabic)	Angel Value (Hebrew)	Jinn Value (Arabic)	Jinn Value (Hebrew)
Usurper	56	15	25	97	87
Guide	107	66	76	148	138
Mystery	163	122	132	204	194
Adjuster	563	522	532	244	234
Leader	1689	1648	1658	1370	1360
Regulator	2252	2211	2221	1933	1923
General Governor	4504	4463	4473	4185	4175
High Overseer	481928	481887	481897	481609	481599

Fire - Mercury

38	54	106	83	72	88	69	53
46	62	91	75	80	103	61	45
89	73	52	68	55	39	82	105
104	81	44	60	63	47	74	90
67	51	70	86	108	85	40	56
59	43	78	101	93	77	48	64
84	107	57	41	50	66	87	71
76	92	65	49	42	58	102	79

Earth - Mercury

76	84	59	67	104	89	46	38
92	107	43	51	81	73	62	54
65	57	78	70	44	52	91	106
49	41	101	86	60	68	75	83
42	50	93	108	63	55	80	72
58	66	77	85	47	39	103	88
102	87	48	40	74	82	61	69
79	71	64	56	90	105	45	53

Air - Mercury

79	102	58	42	49	65	92	76
71	87	66	50	41	57	107	84
64	48	77	93	101	78	43	59
56	40	85	108	86	70	51	67
90	74	47	63	60	44	81	104
105	82	39	55	68	52	73	89
45	61	103	80	75	91	62	46
53	69	88	72	83	106	54	38

Water - Mercury

53	45	105	90	56	64	71	79
69	61	82	74	40	48	87	102
88	103	39	47	85	77	66	58
72	80	55	63	108	93	50	42
83	75	68	60	86	101	41	49
106	91	52	44	70	78	57	65
54	62	73	81	51	43	107	92
38	46	89	104	67	59	84	76

Occult Encyclopedia of Magic Squares

	Number	Angel Value (Arabic)	Angel Value (Hebrew)	Jinn Value (Arabic)	Jinn Value (Hebrew)
Usurper	38	357	7	79	69
Guide	108	67	77	149	139
Mystery	146	105	115	187	177
Adjuster	563	522	532	244	234
Leader	1689	1648	1658	1370	1360
Regulator	2252	2211	2221	1933	1923
General Governor	4504	4463	4473	4185	4175
High Overseer	486432	486391	486401	486113	486103

Fire - Moon

66	79	41	50	107	34	70	86	30
26	69	91	46	62	78	33	55	103
99	38	54	90	22	74	83	45	58
93	25	68	77	48	61	102	32	57
53	101	37	73	89	24	60	82	44
40	65	81	36	49	106	29	72	85
39	52	100	23	75	88	43	59	84
80	42	64	105	35	51	87	28	71
67	92	27	63	76	47	56	104	31

Earth - Moon

30	103	58	57	44	85	84	71	31
86	55	45	32	82	72	59	28	104
70	33	83	102	60	29	43	87	56
34	78	74	61	24	106	88	51	47
107	62	22	48	89	49	75	35	76
50	46	90	77	73	36	23	105	63
41	91	54	68	37	81	100	64	27
79	69	38	25	101	65	52	42	92
66	26	99	93	53	40	39	80	67

Occult Encyclopedia of Magic Squares

Air - Moon

31	104	56	47	76	63	27	92	67
71	28	87	51	35	105	64	42	80
84	59	43	88	75	23	100	52	39
85	72	29	106	49	36	81	65	40
44	82	60	24	89	73	37	101	53
57	32	102	61	48	77	68	25	93
58	45	83	74	22	90	54	38	99
103	55	33	78	62	46	91	69	26
30	86	70	34	107	50	41	79	66

Water - Moon

67	80	39	40	53	93	99	26	66
92	42	52	65	101	25	38	69	79
27	64	100	81	37	68	54	91	41
63	105	23	36	73	77	90	46	50
76	35	75	49	89	48	22	62	107
47	51	88	106	24	61	74	78	34
56	87	43	29	60	102	83	33	70
104	28	59	72	82	32	45	55	86
31	71	84	85	44	57	58	103	30

	Number	Angel Value (Arabic)	Angel Value (Hebrew)	Jinn Value (Arabic)	Jinn Value (Hebrew)
Usurper	22	341	351	63	53
Guide	107	66	76	148	138
Mystery	129	88	98	170	160
Adjuster	563	522	532	244	234
Leader	1689	1648	1658	1370	1360
Regulator	2252	2211	2221	1933	1923
General Governor	4504	4463	4473	4185	4175
High Overseer	481928	481887	481897	481609	481599

Occult Encyclopedia of Magic Squares

Fire - Saturn

6	24	31	69	60	106	53	45	77	92
17	81	74	65	108	90	8	50	36	34
32	37	61	107	91	76	25	13	54	67
38	63	105	93	26	72	80	21	10	55
51	104	95	30	41	64	68	78	23	9
58	15	16	83	71	47	43	33	88	109
70	52	12	19	85	40	28	89	112	56
84	73	48	7	18	35	86	111	59	42
94	27	39	46	14	22	110	57	75	79
113	87	82	44	49	11	62	66	29	20

Earth - Saturn

113	94	84	70	58	51	38	32	17	6
87	27	73	52	15	104	63	37	81	24
82	39	48	12	16	95	105	61	74	31
44	46	7	19	83	30	93	107	65	69
49	14	18	85	71	41	26	91	108	60
11	22	35	40	47	64	72	76	90	106
62	110	86	28	43	68	80	25	8	53
66	57	111	89	33	78	21	13	50	45
29	75	59	112	88	23	10	54	36	77
20	79	42	56	109	9	55	67	34	92

Air - Saturn

20	29	66	62	11	49	44	82	87	113
79	75	57	110	22	14	46	39	27	94
42	59	111	86	35	18	7	48	73	84
56	112	89	28	40	85	19	12	52	70
109	88	33	43	47	71	83	16	15	58
9	23	78	68	64	41	30	95	104	51
55	10	21	80	72	26	93	105	63	38
67	54	13	25	76	91	107	61	37	32
34	36	50	8	90	108	65	74	81	17
92	77	45	53	106	60	69	31	24	6

Occult Encyclopedia of Magic Squares

Water - Saturn

92	34	67	55	9	109	56	42	79	20
77	36	54	10	23	88	112	59	75	29
45	50	13	21	78	33	89	111	57	66
53	**8**	25	80	68	43	28	86	110	62
106	90	76	72	64	47	40	35	22	11
60	108	91	26	41	71	85	18	14	49
69	65	107	93	30	83	19	7	46	44
31	74	61	105	95	16	12	48	39	82
24	81	37	63	104	15	52	73	27	87
6	17	32	38	51	58	70	84	94	113

	Number	Angel Value (Arabic)	Angel Value (Hebrew)	Jinn Value (Arabic)	Jinn Value (Hebrew)
Usurper	6	325	335	47	37
Guide	113	72	82	154	144
Mystery	119	78	88	160	150
Adjuster	563	522	532	244	234
Leader	1689	1648	1658	1370	1360
Regulator	2252	2211	2221	1933	1923
General Governor	4504	4463	4473	4185	4175
High Overseer	508952	508911	508921	508633	508623

ANGEL OF FIRST QUINANCE: VEMIBAEL (79)

אל	ב	מ	ו
5	41	5	28
4	29	4	42
39	7	30	3

ל	א	ב	מ	ו
ב	מ	ו	ל	א
ו	ל	א	ב	מ
א	ב	מ	ו	ל
מ	ו	ל	א	ב

Fire - Jupiter

12	23	17	27
26	18	20	15
22	13	28	16
19	25	14	21

Air - Jupiter

21	14	25	19
16	28	13	22
15	20	18	26
27	17	23	12

Earth - Jupiter

19	22	26	12
25	13	18	23
14	28	20	17
21	16	15	27

Water - Jupiter

27	15	16	21
17	20	28	14
23	18	13	25
12	26	22	19

	Number	Angel Value (Arabic)	Angel Value (Hebrew)	Jinn Value (Arabic)	Jinn Value (Hebrew)
Usurper	12	331	341	53	43
Guide	28	347	357	69	59
Mystery	40	359	9	81	71
Adjuster	632	591	601	313	303
Leader	1896	1855	1865	1577	1567
Regulator	2528	2487	2497	2209	2199
General Governor	5056	5015	5025	4737	4727
High Overseer	141568	141527	141537	141249	141239

Fire - Mars

3	31	21	15	9
16	10	4	27	22
28	18	17	11	5
12	6	29	19	13
20	14	8	7	30

Air - Mars

20	12	28	16	3
14	6	18	10	31
8	29	17	4	21
7	19	11	27	15
30	13	5	22	9

Earth - Mars

30	7	8	14	20
13	19	29	6	12
5	11	17	18	28
22	27	4	10	16
9	15	21	31	3

Water - Mars

9	22	5	13	30
15	27	11	19	7
21	4	17	29	8
31	10	18	6	14
3	16	28	12	20

	Number	Angel Value (Arabic)	Angel Value (Hebrew)	Jinn Value (Arabic)	Jinn Value (Hebrew)
Usurper	3	322	332	44	34
Guide	31	350	360	72	62
Mystery	34	353	3	75	65
Adjuster	79	38	48	120	110
Leader	237	196	206	278	268
Regulator	316	275	285	357	347
General Governor	632	591	601	313	303
High Overseer	19592	19551	19561	19273	19263

ANGEL OF SECOND QUINANCE: YEHOHEL (51)

אל	ה	ה	י
9	6	8	28
7	29	8	7
4	11	30	6

ל	א	ה	ה	י
ה	ה	י	ל	א
י	ל	א	ה	ה
א	ה	ה	י	ל
ה	י	ל	א	ה

Fire - Saturn

18	13	20
19	17	15
14	21	16

Air - Saturn

16	21	14
15	17	19
20	13	18

Earth - Saturn

14	19	18
21	17	13
16	15	20

Water - Saturn

20	15	16
13	17	21
18	19	14

	Number	Angel Value (Arabic)	Angel Value (Hebrew)	Jinn Value (Arabic)	Jinn Value (Hebrew)
Usurper	13	332	342	54	44
Guide	21	340	350	62	52
Mystery	34	353	3	75	65
Adjuster	51	10	20	92	82
Leader	153	112	122	194	184
Regulator	204	163	173	245	235
General Governor	408	367	377	89	79
High Overseer	8568	8527	8537	8249	8239

Fire - Jupiter

5	16	10	20
19	11	13	8
15	6	21	9
12	18	7	14

Air - Jupiter

14	7	18	12
9	21	6	15
8	13	11	19
20	10	16	5

Earth - Jupiter

12	15	19	5
18	6	11	16
7	21	13	10
14	9	8	20

Water - Jupiter

20	8	9	14
10	13	21	7
16	11	6	18
5	19	15	12

	Number	Angel Value (Arabic)	Angel Value (Hebrew)	Jinn Value (Arabic)	Jinn Value (Hebrew)
Usurper	5	324	334	46	36
Guide	21	340	350	62	52
Mystery	26	345	355	67	57
Adjuster	408	367	377	89	79
Leader	1224	1183	1193	905	895
Regulator	1632	1591	1601	1313	1303
General Governor	3264	3223	3233	2945	2935
High Overseer	68544	68503	68513	68225	68215

ANGEL OF SECOND DECANATE: SHEHADANI (369)

י	נ	ד	שׂה
304	5	53	7
52	8	303	6
3	306	9	51

י	נ	ד	ה	שׂ
ד	ה	שׂ	י	נ
שׂ	י	נ	ד	ה
נ	ד	ה	שׂ	י
ה	שׂ	י	נ	ד

Fire - Saturn

124	119	126
125	123	121
120	127	122

Air - Saturn

122	127	120
121	123	125
126	119	124

Earth - Saturn

120	125	124
127	123	119
122	121	126

Water - Saturn

126	121	122
119	123	127
124	125	120

	Number	Angel Value (Arabic)	Angel Value (Hebrew)	Jinn Value (Arabic)	Jinn Value (Hebrew)
Usurper	119	78	88	160	150
Guide	127	86	96	168	158
Mystery	246	205	215	287	277
Adjuster	369	328	338	50	40
Leader	1107	1066	1076	788	778
Regulator	1476	1435	1445	1157	1147
General Governor	2952	2911	2921	2633	2623
High Overseer	374904	374863	374873	374585	374575

Occult Encyclopedia of Magic Squares

Fire - Jupiter

84	95	89	101
100	90	92	87
94	85	102	88
91	99	86	93

Air - Jupiter

93	86	99	91
88	102	85	94
87	92	90	100
101	89	95	84

Earth - Jupiter

91	94	100	84
99	85	90	95
86	102	92	89
93	88	87	101

Water - Jupiter

101	87	88	93
89	92	102	86
95	90	85	99
84	100	94	91

	Number	Angel Value (Arabic)	Angel Value (Hebrew)	Jinn Value (Arabic)	Jinn Value (Hebrew)
Usurper	84	43	53	125	115
Guide	102	61	71	143	133
Mystery	186	145	155	227	217
Adjuster	2952	2911	2921	2633	2623
Leader	8856	8815	8825	8537	8527
Regulator	11808	11767	11777	11489	11479
General Governor	23616	23575	23585	23297	23287
High Overseer	2408832	2408791	2408801	2408513	2408503

Fire - Mars

61	89	79	73	67
74	68	62	85	80
86	76	75	69	63
70	64	87	77	71
78	72	66	65	88

Earth - Mars

88	65	66	72	78
71	77	87	64	70
63	69	75	76	86
80	85	62	68	74
67	73	79	89	61

Occult Encyclopedia of Magic Squares

Air - Mars

78	70	86	74	61
72	64	76	68	89
66	87	75	62	79
65	77	69	85	73
88	71	63	80	67

Water - Mars

67	80	63	71	88
73	85	69	77	65
79	62	75	87	66
89	68	76	64	72
61	74	86	70	78

	Number	Angel Value (Arabic)	Angel Value (Hebrew)	Jinn Value (Arabic)	Jinn Value (Hebrew)
Usurper	61	20	30	102	92
Guide	89	48	58	130	120
Mystery	150	109	119	191	181
Adjuster	369	328	338	50	40
Leader	1107	1066	1076	788	778
Regulator	1476	1435	1445	1157	1147
General Governor	2952	2911	2921	2633	2623
High Overseer	262728	262687	262697	262409	262399

Fire - Sun

44	55	75	61	65	69
50	60	71	74	48	66
56	78	64	54	70	47
67	46	57	72	51	76
73	62	53	45	77	59
79	68	49	63	58	52

Earth - Sun

79	73	67	56	50	44
68	62	46	78	60	55
49	53	57	64	71	75
63	45	72	54	74	61
58	77	51	70	48	65
52	59	76	47	66	69

Occult Encyclopedia of Magic Squares

Air - Sun

52	58	63	49	68	79
59	77	45	53	62	73
76	51	72	57	46	67
47	70	54	64	78	56
66	48	74	71	60	50
69	65	61	75	55	44

Water - Sun

69	66	47	76	59	52
65	48	70	51	77	58
61	74	54	72	45	63
75	71	64	57	53	49
55	60	78	46	62	68
44	50	56	67	73	79

	Number	Angel Value (Arabic)	Angel Value (Hebrew)	Jinn Value (Arabic)	Jinn Value (Hebrew)
Usurper	44	3	13	85	75
Guide	79	38	48	120	110
Mystery	123	82	92	164	154
Adjuster	369	328	338	50	40
Leader	1107	1066	1076	788	778
Regulator	1476	1435	1445	1157	1147
General Governor	2952	2911	2921	2633	2623
High Overseer	233208	233167	233177	232889	232879

Fire - Venus

28	69	54	39	59	77	43
78	44	29	63	55	40	60
41	61	79	45	30	64	49
65	50	35	62	80	46	31
47	32	66	51	36	56	81
57	75	48	33	67	52	37
53	38	58	76	42	34	68

Earth - Venus

53	57	47	65	41	78	28
38	75	32	50	61	44	69
58	48	66	35	79	29	54
76	33	51	62	45	63	39
42	67	36	80	30	55	59
34	52	56	46	64	40	77
68	37	81	31	49	60	43

Occult Encyclopedia of Magic Squares

Air - Venus

68	34	42	76	58	38	53
37	52	67	33	48	75	57
81	56	36	51	66	32	47
31	46	80	62	35	50	65
49	64	30	45	79	61	41
60	40	55	63	29	44	78
43	77	59	39	54	69	28

Water - Venus

43	60	49	31	81	37	68
77	40	64	46	56	52	34
59	55	30	80	36	67	42
39	63	45	62	51	33	76
54	29	79	35	66	48	58
69	44	61	50	32	75	38
28	78	41	65	47	57	53

	Number	Angel Value (Arabic)	Angel Value (Hebrew)	Jinn Value (Arabic)	Jinn Value (Hebrew)
Usurper	28	347	357	69	59
Guide	81	40	50	122	112
Mystery	109	68	78	150	140
Adjuster	369	328	338	50	40
Leader	1107	1066	1076	788	778
Regulator	1476	1435	1445	1157	1147
General Governor	2952	2911	2921	2633	2623
High Overseer	239112	239071	239081	238793	238783

Fire - Mercury

14	30	80	59	48	64	45	29
22	38	67	51	56	77	37	21
65	49	28	44	31	15	58	79
78	57	20	36	39	23	50	66
43	27	46	62	82	61	16	32
35	19	54	75	69	53	24	40
60	81	33	17	26	42	63	47
52	68	41	25	18	34	76	55

Occult Encyclopedia of Magic Squares

Earth - Mercury

52	60	35	43	78	65	22	14
68	81	19	27	57	49	38	30
41	33	54	46	20	28	67	80
25	17	75	62	36	44	51	59
18	26	69	82	39	31	56	48
34	42	53	61	23	15	77	64
76	63	24	16	50	58	37	45
55	47	40	32	66	79	21	29

Air - Mercury

55	76	34	18	25	41	68	52
47	63	42	26	17	33	81	60
40	24	53	69	75	54	19	35
32	16	61	82	62	46	27	43
66	50	23	39	36	20	57	78
79	58	15	31	44	28	49	65
21	37	77	56	51	67	38	22
29	45	64	48	59	80	30	14

Water - Mercury

29	21	79	66	32	40	47	55
45	37	58	50	16	24	63	76
64	77	15	23	61	53	42	34
48	56	31	39	82	69	26	18
59	51	44	36	62	75	17	25
80	67	28	20	46	54	33	41
30	38	49	57	27	19	81	68
14	22	65	78	43	35	60	52

Fire - Moon

45	58	20	29	81	13	49	65	9
5	48	70	25	41	57	12	34	77
73	17	33	69	1	53	62	24	37
72	4	47	56	27	40	76	11	36
32	75	16	52	68	3	39	61	23
19	44	60	15	28	80	8	51	64
18	31	74	2	54	67	22	38	63
59	21	43	79	14	30	66	7	50
46	71	6	42	55	26	35	78	10

Earth - Moon

9	77	37	36	23	64	63	50	10
65	34	24	11	61	51	38	7	78
49	12	62	76	39	8	22	66	35
13	57	53	40	3	80	67	30	26
81	41	1	27	68	28	54	14	55
29	25	69	56	52	15	2	79	42
20	70	33	47	16	60	74	43	6
58	48	17	4	75	44	31	21	71
45	5	73	72	32	19	18	59	46

Air - Moon

10	78	35	26	55	42	6	71	46
50	7	66	30	14	79	43	21	59
63	38	22	67	54	2	74	31	18
64	51	8	80	28	15	60	44	19
23	61	39	3	68	52	16	75	32
36	11	76	40	27	56	47	4	72
37	24	62	53	1	69	33	17	73
77	34	12	57	41	25	70	48	5
9	65	49	13	81	29	20	58	45

Water - Moon

46	59	18	19	32	72	73	5	45
71	21	31	44	75	4	17	48	58
6	43	74	60	16	47	33	70	20
42	79	2	15	52	56	69	25	29
55	14	54	28	68	27	1	41	81
26	30	67	80	3	40	53	57	13
35	66	22	8	39	76	62	12	49
78	7	38	51	61	11	24	34	65
10	50	63	64	23	36	37	77	9

	Number	Angel Value (Arabic)	Angel Value (Hebrew)	Jinn Value (Arabic)	Jinn Value (Hebrew)
Usurper	1	320	330	42	32
Guide	81	40	50	122	112
Mystery	82	41	51	123	113
Adjuster	369	328	338	50	40
Leader	1107	1066	1076	788	778
Regulator	1476	1435	1445	1157	1147
General Governor	2952	2911	2921	2633	2623
High Overseer	239112	239071	239081	238793	238783

ANGEL OF THIRD QUINANCE: ANEVEL (157)

אל	ו	נ	ע
69	51	9	28
8	29	68	52
49	71	30	7

ל	א	ו	נ	ע
ו	נ	ע	ל	א
ע	ל	א	ו	נ
א	ו	נ	ע	ל
נ	ע	ל	א	ו

Fire - Jupiter

31	42	36	48
47	37	39	34
41	32	49	35
38	46	33	40

Earth - Jupiter

38	41	47	31
46	32	37	42
33	49	39	36
40	35	34	48

Occult Encyclopedia of Magic Squares

Air - Jupiter

40	33	46	38
35	49	32	41
34	39	37	47
48	36	42	31

Water - Jupiter

48	34	35	40
36	39	49	33
42	37	32	46
31	47	41	38

	Number	Angel Value (Arabic)	Angel Value (Hebrew)	Jinn Value (Arabic)	Jinn Value (Hebrew)
Usurper	31	350	360	72	62
Guide	49	8	18	90	80
Mystery	80	39	49	121	111
Adjuster	1256	1215	1225	937	927
Leader	3768	3727	3737	3449	3439
Regulator	5024	4983	4993	4705	4695
General Governor	10048	10007	10017	9729	9719
High Overseer	492352	492311	492321	492033	492023

Fire - Mars

19	45	37	31	25
32	26	20	41	38
42	34	33	27	21
28	22	43	35	29
36	30	24	23	44

Air - Mars

36	28	42	32	19
30	22	34	26	45
24	43	33	20	37
23	35	27	41	31
44	29	21	38	25

Earth - Mars

44	23	24	30	36
29	35	43	22	28
21	27	33	34	42
38	41	20	26	32
25	31	37	45	19

Water - Mars

25	38	21	29	44
31	41	27	35	23
37	20	33	43	24
45	26	34	22	30
19	32	42	28	36

Occult Encyclopedia of Magic Squares

	Number	Angel Value (Arabic)	Angel Value (Hebrew)	Jinn Value (Arabic)	Jinn Value (Hebrew)
Usurper	19	338	348	60	50
Guide	45	4	14	86	76
Mystery	64	23	33	105	95
Adjuster	157	116	126	198	188
Leader	471	430	440	152	142
Regulator	628	587	597	309	299
General Governor	1256	1215	1225	937	927
High Overseer	56520	56479	56489	56201	56191

Fire - Sun

8	19	43	25	29	33
14	24	35	42	12	30
20	46	28	18	34	11
31	10	21	36	15	44
37	26	17	9	45	23
47	32	13	27	22	16

Air - Sun

16	22	27	13	32	47
23	45	9	17	26	37
44	15	36	21	10	31
11	34	18	28	46	20
30	12	42	35	24	14
33	29	25	43	19	8

Earth - Sun

47	37	31	20	14	8
32	26	10	46	24	19
13	17	21	28	35	43
27	9	36	18	42	25
22	45	15	34	12	29
16	23	44	11	30	33

Water - Sun

33	30	11	44	23	16
29	12	34	15	45	22
25	42	18	36	9	27
43	35	28	21	17	13
19	24	46	10	26	32
8	14	20	31	37	47

	Number	Angel Value (Arabic)	Angel Value (Hebrew)	Jinn Value (Arabic)	Jinn Value (Hebrew)
Usurper	8	327	337	49	39
Guide	47	6	16	88	78
Mystery	55	14	24	96	86
Adjuster	157	116	126	198	188
Leader	471	430	440	152	142
Regulator	628	587	597	309	299
General Governor	1256	1215	1225	937	927
High Overseer	59032	58991	59001	58713	58703

ANGEL OF FOURTH QUINANCE: MOCHAYEL (89)

אל	י	ה	מ
39	9	13	28
12	29	38	10
7	41	30	11

ל	א	י	ה	מ
י	ה	מ	ל	א
מ	ל	א	י	ה
א	י	ה	מ	ל
ה	מ	ל	א	י

Fire - Jupiter

14	25	19	31
30	20	22	17
24	15	32	18
21	29	16	23

Air - Jupiter

23	16	29	21
18	32	15	24
17	22	20	30
31	19	25	14

Earth - Jupiter

21	24	30	14
29	15	20	25
16	32	22	19
23	18	17	31

Water - Jupiter

31	17	18	23
19	22	32	16
25	20	15	29
14	30	24	21

	Number	Angel Value (Arabic)	Angel Value (Hebrew)	Jinn Value (Arabic)	Jinn Value (Hebrew)
Usurper	14	333	343	55	45
Guide	32	351	1	73	63
Mystery	46	5	15	87	77
Adjuster	712	671	681	393	383
Leader	2136	2095	2105	1817	1807
Regulator	2848	2807	2817	2529	2519
General Governor	5696	5655	5665	5377	5367
High Overseer	182272	182231	182241	181953	181943

Fire - Mars

5	33	23	17	11
18	12	6	29	24
30	20	19	13	7
14	8	31	21	15
22	16	10	9	32

Air - Mars

22	14	30	18	5
16	8	20	12	33
10	31	19	6	23
9	21	13	29	17
32	15	7	24	11

Earth - Mars

32	9	10	16	22
15	21	31	8	14
7	13	19	20	30
24	29	6	12	18
11	17	23	33	5

Water - Mars

11	24	7	15	32
17	29	13	21	9
23	6	19	31	10
33	12	20	8	16
5	18	30	14	22

	Number	Angel Value (Arabic)	Angel Value (Hebrew)	Jinn Value (Arabic)	Jinn Value (Hebrew)
Usurper	5	324	334	46	36
Guide	33	352	2	74	64
Mystery	38	357	7	79	69
Adjuster	89	48	58	130	120
Leader	267	226	236	308	298
Regulator	356	315	325	37	27
General Governor	712	671	681	393	383
High Overseer	23496	23455	23465	23177	23167

ANGEL OF THIRD DECANATE: BETHON (468)

נ	ו	ת	בי
11	401	9	47
8	48	10	402
399	13	49	7

נ	ו	ת	י	ב
ת	י	ב	נ	ו
ב	נ	ו	ת	י
ו	ת	י	ב	נ
י	ב	נ	ו	ת

Fire - Saturn

157	152	159
158	156	154
153	160	155

Air - Saturn

155	160	153
154	156	158
159	152	157

Earth - Saturn

153	158	157
160	156	152
155	154	159

Water - Saturn

159	154	155
152	156	160
157	158	153

	Number	Angel Value (Arabic)	Angel Value (Hebrew)	Jinn Value (Arabic)	Jinn Value (Hebrew)
Usurper	152	111	121	193	183
Guide	160	119	129	201	191
Mystery	312	271	281	353	343
Adjuster	468	427	437	149	139
Leader	1404	1363	1373	1085	1075
Regulator	1872	1831	1841	1553	1543
General Governor	3744	3703	3713	3425	3415
High Overseer	599040	598999	599009	598721	598711

Fire - Jupiter

109	120	114	125
124	115	117	112
119	110	126	113
116	123	111	118

Air - Jupiter

118	111	123	116
113	126	110	119
112	117	115	124
125	114	120	109

Earth - Jupiter

116	119	124	109
123	110	115	120
111	126	117	114
118	113	112	125

Water - Jupiter

125	112	113	118
114	117	126	111
120	115	110	123
109	124	119	116

Occult Encyclopedia of Magic Squares

	Number	Angel Value (Arabic)	Angel Value (Hebrew)	Jinn Value (Arabic)	Jinn Value (Hebrew)
Usurper	109	68	78	150	140
Guide	126	85	95	167	157
Mystery	235	194	204	276	266
Adjuster	3744	3703	3713	3425	3415
Leader	11232	11191	11201	10913	10903
Regulator	14976	14935	14945	14657	14647
General Governor	29952	29911	29921	29633	29623
High Overseer	3773952	3773911	3773921	3773633	3773623

Fire - Mars

81	108	99	93	87
94	88	82	104	100
105	96	95	89	83
90	84	106	97	91
98	92	86	85	107

Air - Mars

98	90	105	94	81
92	84	96	88	108
86	106	95	82	99
85	97	89	104	93
107	91	83	100	87

Earth - Mars

107	85	86	92	98
91	97	106	84	90
83	89	95	96	105
100	104	82	88	94
87	93	99	108	81

Water - Mars

87	100	83	91	107
93	104	89	97	85
99	82	95	106	86
108	88	96	84	92
81	94	105	90	98

	Number	Angel Value (Arabic)	Angel Value (Hebrew)	Jinn Value (Arabic)	Jinn Value (Hebrew)
Usurper	81	40	50	122	112
Guide	108	67	77	149	139
Mystery	189	148	158	230	220
Adjuster	468	427	437	149	139
Leader	1404	1363	1373	1085	1075
Regulator	1872	1831	1841	1553	1543
General Governor	3744	3703	3713	3425	3415
High Overseer	404352	404311	404321	404033	404023

Fire - Sun

60	71	94	77	81	85
66	76	87	93	64	82
72	97	80	70	86	63
83	62	73	88	67	95
89	78	69	61	96	75
98	84	65	79	74	68

Air - Sun

68	74	79	65	84	98
75	96	61	69	78	89
95	67	88	73	62	83
63	86	70	80	97	72
82	64	93	87	76	66
85	81	77	94	71	60

Earth - Sun

98	89	83	72	66	60
84	78	62	97	76	71
65	69	73	80	87	94
79	61	88	70	93	77
74	96	67	86	64	81
68	75	95	63	82	85

Water - Sun

85	82	63	95	75	68
81	64	86	67	96	74
77	93	70	88	61	79
94	87	80	73	69	65
71	76	97	62	78	84
60	66	72	83	89	98

Occult Encyclopedia of Magic Squares

	Number	Angel Value (Arabic)	Angel Value (Hebrew)	Jinn Value (Arabic)	Jinn Value (Hebrew)
Usurper	60	19	29	101	91
Guide	98	57	67	139	129
Mystery	158	117	127	199	189
Adjuster	468	427	437	149	139
Leader	1404	1363	1373	1085	1075
Regulator	1872	1831	1841	1553	1543
General Governor	3744	3703	3713	3425	3415
High Overseer	366912	366871	366881	366593	366583

Fire - Venus

42	83	68	53	73	92	57
93	58	43	77	69	54	74
55	75	94	59	44	78	63
79	64	49	76	95	60	45
61	46	80	65	50	70	96
71	90	62	47	81	66	51
67	52	72	91	56	48	82

Air - Venus

82	48	56	91	72	52	67
51	66	81	47	62	90	71
96	70	50	65	80	46	61
45	60	95	76	49	64	79
63	78	44	59	94	75	55
74	54	69	77	43	58	93
57	92	73	53	68	83	42

Earth - Venus

67	71	61	79	55	93	42
52	90	46	64	75	58	83
72	62	80	49	94	43	68
91	47	65	76	59	77	53
56	81	50	95	44	69	73
48	66	70	60	78	54	92
82	51	96	45	63	74	57

Water - Venus

57	74	63	45	96	51	82
92	54	78	60	70	66	48
73	69	44	95	50	81	56
53	77	59	76	65	47	91
68	43	94	49	80	62	72
83	58	75	64	46	90	52
42	93	55	79	61	71	67

	Number	Angel Value (Arabic)	Angel Value (Hebrew)	Jinn Value (Arabic)	Jinn Value (Hebrew)
Usurper	42	1	11	83	73
Guide	96	55	65	137	127
Mystery	138	97	107	179	169
Adjuster	468	427	437	149	139
Leader	1404	1363	1373	1085	1075
Regulator	1872	1831	1841	1553	1543
General Governor	3744	3703	3713	3425	3415
High Overseer	359424	359383	359393	359105	359095

Fire - Mercury

27	43	88	72	61	77	58	42
35	51	80	64	69	85	50	34
78	62	41	57	44	28	71	87
86	70	33	49	52	36	63	79
56	40	59	75	90	74	29	45
48	32	67	83	82	66	37	53
73	89	46	30	39	55	76	60
65	81	54	38	31	47	84	68

Earth - Mercury

65	73	48	56	86	78	35	27
81	89	32	40	70	62	51	43
54	46	67	59	33	41	80	88
38	30	83	75	49	57	64	72
31	39	82	90	52	44	69	61
47	55	66	74	36	28	85	77
84	76	37	29	63	71	50	58
68	60	53	45	79	87	34	42

Occult Encyclopedia of Magic Squares

Air - Mercury

68	84	47	31	38	54	81	65
60	76	55	39	30	46	89	73
53	37	66	82	83	67	32	48
45	29	74	90	75	59	40	56
79	63	36	52	49	33	70	86
87	71	28	44	57	41	62	78
34	50	85	69	64	80	51	35
42	58	77	61	72	88	43	27

Water - Mercury

42	34	87	79	45	53	60	68
58	50	71	63	29	37	76	84
77	85	28	36	74	66	55	47
61	69	44	52	90	82	39	31
72	64	57	49	75	83	30	38
88	80	41	33	59	67	46	54
43	51	62	70	40	32	89	81
27	35	78	86	56	48	73	65

	Number	Angel Value (Arabic)	Angel Value (Hebrew)	Jinn Value (Arabic)	Jinn Value (Hebrew)
Usurper	27	346	356	68	58
Guide	90	49	59	131	121
Mystery	117	76	86	158	148
Adjuster	468	427	437	149	139
Leader	1404	1363	1373	1085	1075
Regulator	1872	1831	1841	1553	1543
General Governor	3744	3703	3713	3425	3415
High Overseer	336960	336919	336929	336641	336631

Fire - Moon

56	69	31	40	92	24	60	76	20
16	59	81	36	52	68	23	45	88
84	28	44	80	12	64	73	35	48
83	15	58	67	38	51	87	22	47
43	86	27	63	79	14	50	72	34
30	55	71	26	39	91	19	62	75
29	42	85	13	65	78	33	49	74
70	32	54	90	25	41	77	18	61
57	82	17	53	66	37	46	89	21

Earth - Moon

20	88	48	47	34	75	74	61	21
76	45	35	22	72	62	49	18	89
60	23	73	87	50	19	33	77	46
24	68	64	51	14	91	78	41	37
92	52	12	38	79	39	65	25	66
40	36	80	67	63	26	13	90	53
31	81	44	58	27	71	85	54	17
69	59	28	15	86	55	42	32	82
56	16	84	83	43	30	29	70	57

Air - Moon

21	89	46	37	66	53	17	82	57
61	18	77	41	25	90	54	32	70
74	49	33	78	65	13	85	42	29
75	62	19	91	39	26	71	55	30
34	72	50	14	79	63	27	86	43
47	22	87	51	38	67	58	15	83
48	35	73	64	12	80	44	28	84
88	45	23	68	52	36	81	59	16
20	76	60	24	92	40	31	69	56

Water - Moon

57	70	29	30	43	83	84	16	56
82	32	42	55	86	15	28	59	69
17	54	85	71	27	58	44	81	31
53	90	13	26	63	67	80	36	40
66	25	65	39	79	38	12	52	92
37	41	78	91	14	51	64	68	24
46	77	33	19	50	87	73	23	60
89	18	49	62	72	22	35	45	76
21	61	74	75	34	47	48	88	20

	Number	Angel Value (Arabic)	Angel Value (Hebrew)	Jinn Value (Arabic)	Jinn Value (Hebrew)
Usurper	12	331	341	53	43
Guide	92	51	61	133	123
Mystery	104	63	73	145	135
Adjuster	468	427	437	149	139
Leader	1404	1363	1373	1085	1075
Regulator	1872	1831	1841	1553	1543
General Governor	3744	3703	3713	3425	3415
High Overseer	344448	344407	344417	344129	344119

ANGEL OF FIFTH QUINANCE: DAMABIAH (61)

יח	ב	מ	ד
3	41	5	12
4	13	2	42
39	5	14	3

ה	י	ב	מ	ד
ב	מ	ד	ה	י
ד	ה	י	ב	מ
י	ב	מ	ד	ה
מ	ד	ה	י	ב

Fire - Jupiter

7	18	12	24
23	13	15	10
17	8	25	11
14	22	9	16

Air - Jupiter

16	9	22	14
11	25	8	17
10	15	13	23
24	12	18	7

Earth - Jupiter

14	17	23	7
22	8	13	18
9	25	15	12
16	11	10	24

Water - Jupiter

24	10	11	16
12	15	25	9
18	13	8	22
7	23	17	14

	Number	Angel Value (Arabic)	Angel Value (Hebrew)	Jinn Value (Arabic)	Jinn Value (Hebrew)
Usurper	7	326	336	48	38
Guide	25	344	354	66	56
Mystery	32	351	1	73	63
Adjuster	488	447	457	169	159
Leader	1464	1423	1433	1145	1135
Regulator	1952	1911	1921	1633	1623
General Governor	3904	3863	3873	3585	3575
High Overseer	97600	97559	97569	97281	97271

ANGEL OF SIX QUINANCE: MENQEL (221)

אל	ק	נ	ם
39	51	103	28
102	29	38	52
49	41	30	101

ל	א	ק	נ	ם
ק	נ	ם	ל	א
ם	ל	א	ק	נ
א	ק	נ	ם	ל

Occult Encyclopedia of Magic Squares

Fire - Jupiter

47	58	52	64
63	53	55	50
57	48	65	51
54	62	49	56

Air - Jupiter

56	49	62	54
51	65	48	57
50	55	53	63
64	52	58	47

Earth - Jupiter

54	57	63	47
62	48	53	58
49	65	55	52
56	51	50	64

Water - Jupiter

64	50	51	56
52	55	65	49
58	53	48	62
47	63	57	54

	Number	Angel Value (Arabic)	Angel Value (Hebrew)	Jinn Value (Arabic)	Jinn Value (Hebrew)
Usurper	47	6	16	88	78
Guide	65	24	34	106	96
Mystery	112	71	81	153	143
Adjuster	1768	1727	1737	1449	1439
Leader	5304	5263	5273	4985	4975
Regulator	7072	7031	7041	6753	6743
General Governor	14144	14103	14113	13825	13815
High Overseer	919360	919319	919329	919041	919031

Fire - Mars

32	57	50	44	38
45	39	33	53	51
54	47	46	40	34
41	35	55	48	42
49	43	37	36	56

Air - Mars

49	41	54	45	32
43	35	47	39	57
37	55	46	33	50
36	48	40	53	44
56	42	34	51	38

Earth - Mars

56	36	37	43	49
42	48	55	35	41
34	40	46	47	54
51	53	33	39	45
38	44	50	57	32

Water - Mars

38	51	34	42	56
44	53	40	48	36
50	33	46	55	37
57	39	47	35	43
32	45	54	41	49

	Number	Angel Value (Arabic)	Angel Value (Hebrew)	Jinn Value (Arabic)	Jinn Value (Hebrew)
Usurper	32	351	1	73	63
Guide	57	16	26	98	88
Mystery	89	48	58	130	120
Adjuster	221	180	190	262	252
Leader	663	622	632	344	334
Regulator	884	843	853	565	555
General Governor	1768	1727	1737	1449	1439
High Overseer	100776	100735	100745	100457	100447

Fire - Sun

19	30	52	36	40	44
25	35	46	51	23	41
31	55	39	29	45	22
42	21	32	47	26	53
48	37	28	20	54	34
56	43	24	38	33	27

Air - Sun

27	33	38	24	43	56
34	54	20	28	37	48
53	26	47	32	21	42
22	45	29	39	55	31
41	23	51	46	35	25
44	40	36	52	30	19

Earth - Sun

56	48	42	31	25	19
43	37	21	55	35	30
24	28	32	39	46	52
38	20	47	29	51	36
33	54	26	45	23	40
27	34	53	22	41	44

Water - Sun

44	41	22	53	34	27
40	23	45	26	54	33
36	51	29	47	20	38
52	46	39	32	28	24
30	35	55	21	37	43
19	25	31	42	48	56

Occult Encyclopedia of Magic Squares

	Number	Angel Value (Arabic)	Angel Value (Hebrew)	Jinn Value (Arabic)	Jinn Value (Hebrew)
Usurper	19	338	348	60	50
Guide	56	15	25	97	87
Mystery	75	34	44	116	106
Adjuster	221	180	190	262	252
Leader	663	622	632	344	334
Regulator	884	843	853	565	555
General Governor	1768	1727	1737	1449	1439
High Overseer	99008	98967	98977	98689	98679

Fire - Venus

7	48	33	18	38	55	22
56	23	8	42	34	19	39
20	40	57	24	9	43	28
44	29	14	41	58	25	10
26	11	45	30	15	35	59
36	53	27	12	46	31	16
32	17	37	54	21	13	47

Air - Venus

47	13	21	54	37	17	32
16	31	46	12	27	53	36
59	35	15	30	45	11	26
10	25	58	41	14	29	44
28	43	9	24	57	40	20
39	19	34	42	8	23	56
22	55	38	18	33	48	7

Earth - Venus

32	36	26	44	20	56	7
17	53	11	29	40	23	48
37	27	45	14	57	8	33
54	12	30	41	24	42	18
21	46	15	58	9	34	38
13	31	35	25	43	19	55
47	16	59	10	28	39	22

Water - Venus

22	39	28	10	59	16	47
55	19	43	25	35	31	13
38	34	9	58	15	46	21
18	42	24	41	30	12	54
33	8	57	14	45	27	37
48	23	40	29	11	53	17
7	56	20	44	26	36	32

	Number	Angel Value (Arabic)	Angel Value (Hebrew)	Jinn Value (Arabic)	Jinn Value (Hebrew)
Usurper	7	326	336	48	38
Guide	59	18	28	100	90
Mystery	66	25	35	107	97
Adjuster	221	180	190	262	252
Leader	663	622	632	344	334
Regulator	884	843	853	565	555
General Governor	1768	1727	1737	1449	1439
High Overseer	104312	104271	104281	103993	103983

CANCER

SIGN CANCER: SARTON (319)

נ	ת	ר	ם
59	201	403	47
402	48	58	202
199	61	49	401

נ	ת	ר	ם
ם	ר	ת	נ
ת	נ	ם	ר
ר	ם	נ	ת

Fire - Jupiter

72	83	77	87
86	78	80	75
82	73	88	76
79	85	74	81

Air - Jupiter

81	74	85	79
76	88	73	82
75	80	78	86
87	77	83	72

Earth - Jupiter

79	82	86	72
85	73	78	83
74	88	80	77
81	76	75	87

Water - Jupiter

87	75	76	81
77	80	88	74
83	78	73	85
72	86	82	79

	Number	Angel Value (Arabic)	Angel Value (Hebrew)	Jinn Value (Arabic)	Jinn Value (Hebrew)
Usurper	72	31	41	113	103
Guide	88	47	57	129	119
Mystery	160	119	129	201	191
Adjuster	2552	2511	2521	2233	2223
Leader	7656	7615	7625	7337	7327
Regulator	10208	10167	10177	9889	9879
General Governor	20416	20375	20385	20097	20087
High Overseer	1796608	1796567	1796577	1796289	1796279

Occult Encyclopedia of Magic Squares

Fire - Mars

51	79	69	63	57
64	58	52	75	70
76	66	65	59	53
60	54	77	67	61
68	62	56	55	78

Air - Mars

68	60	76	64	51
62	54	66	58	79
56	77	65	52	69
55	67	59	75	63
78	61	53	70	57

Earth - Mars

78	55	56	62	68
61	67	77	54	60
53	59	65	66	76
70	75	52	58	64
57	63	69	79	51

Water - Mars

57	70	53	61	78
63	75	59	67	55
69	52	65	77	56
79	58	66	54	62
51	64	76	60	68

	Number	Angel Value (Arabic)	Angel Value (Hebrew)	Jinn Value (Arabic)	Jinn Value (Hebrew)
Usurper	51	10	20	92	82
Guide	79	38	48	120	110
Mystery	130	89	99	171	161
Adjuster	319	278	288	360	350
Leader	957	916	926	638	628
Regulator	1276	1235	1245	957	947
General Governor	2552	2511	2521	2233	2223
High Overseer	201608	201567	201577	201289	201279

Occult Encyclopedia of Magic Squares

Fire - Sun

35	46	70	52	56	60
41	51	62	69	39	57
47	73	55	45	61	38
58	37	48	63	42	71
64	53	44	36	72	50
74	59	40	54	49	43

Air - Sun

43	49	54	40	59	74
50	72	36	44	53	64
71	42	63	48	37	58
38	61	45	55	73	47
57	39	69	62	51	41
60	56	52	70	46	35

Earth - Sun

74	64	58	47	41	35
59	53	37	73	51	46
40	44	48	55	62	70
54	36	63	45	69	52
49	72	42	61	39	56
43	50	71	38	57	60

Water - Sun

60	57	38	71	50	43
56	39	61	42	72	49
52	69	45	63	36	54
70	62	55	48	44	40
46	51	73	37	53	59
35	41	47	58	64	74

	Number	Angel Value (Arabic)	Angel Value (Hebrew)	Jinn Value (Arabic)	Jinn Value (Hebrew)
Usurper	35	354	4	76	66
Guide	74	33	43	115	105
Mystery	109	68	78	150	140
Adjuster	319	278	288	360	350
Leader	957	916	926	638	628
Regulator	1276	1235	1245	957	947
General Governor	2552	2511	2521	2233	2223
High Overseer	188848	188807	188817	188529	188519

Fire - Venus

21	62	47	32	52	69	36
70	37	22	56	48	33	53
34	54	71	38	23	57	42
58	43	28	55	72	39	24
40	25	59	44	29	49	73
50	67	41	26	60	45	30
46	31	51	68	35	27	61

Air - Venus

61	27	35	68	51	31	46
30	45	60	26	41	67	50
73	49	29	44	59	25	40
24	39	72	55	28	43	58
42	57	23	38	71	54	34
53	33	48	56	22	37	70
36	69	52	32	47	62	21

Earth - Venus

46	50	40	58	34	70	21
31	67	25	43	54	37	62
51	41	59	28	71	22	47
68	26	44	55	38	56	32
35	60	29	72	23	48	52
27	45	49	39	57	33	69
61	30	73	24	42	53	36

Water - Venus

36	53	42	24	73	30	61
69	33	57	39	49	45	27
52	48	23	72	29	60	35
32	56	38	55	44	26	68
47	22	71	28	59	41	51
62	37	54	43	25	67	31
21	70	34	58	40	50	46

Fire - Mercury

8	24	72	53	42	58	39	23
16	32	61	45	50	69	31	15
59	43	22	38	25	9	52	71
70	51	14	30	33	17	44	60
37	21	40	56	74	55	10	26
29	13	48	67	63	47	18	34
54	73	27	11	20	36	57	41
46	62	35	19	12	28	68	49

Earth - Mercury

46	54	29	37	70	59	16	8
62	73	13	21	51	43	32	24
35	27	48	40	14	22	61	72
19	11	67	56	30	38	45	53
12	20	63	74	33	25	50	42
28	36	47	55	17	9	69	58
68	57	18	10	44	52	31	39
49	41	34	26	60	71	15	23

Occult Encyclopedia of Magic Squares

Air - Mercury

49	68	28	12	19	35	62	46
41	57	36	20	11	27	73	54
34	18	47	63	67	48	13	29
26	10	55	74	56	40	21	37
60	44	17	33	30	14	51	70
71	52	9	25	38	22	43	59
15	31	69	50	45	61	32	16
23	39	58	42	53	72	24	8

Water - Mercury

23	15	71	60	26	34	41	49
39	31	52	44	10	18	57	68
58	69	9	17	55	47	36	28
42	50	25	33	74	63	20	12
53	45	38	30	56	67	11	19
72	61	22	14	40	48	27	35
24	32	43	51	21	13	73	62
8	16	59	70	37	29	54	46

	Number	Angel Value (Arabic)	Angel Value (Hebrew)	Jinn Value (Arabic)	Jinn Value (Hebrew)
Usurper	8	327	337	49	39
Guide	74	33	43	115	105
Mystery	82	41	51	123	113
Adjuster	319	278	288	360	350
Leader	957	916	926	638	628
Regulator	1276	1235	1245	957	947
General Governor	2552	2511	2521	2233	2223
High Overseer	188848	188807	188817	188529	188519

ARCHANGEL OF CANCER: MURIEL (287)

אל	י	ר	מו
45	201	13	28
12	29	44	202
199	47	30	11

ל	א	י	ר	ו	מ
ו	ר	ל	מ	י	א
י	מ	א	ו	ל	ר
מ	ו	ר	י	א	ל
ר	ל	ו	א	מ	י
א	י	מ	ל	ר	ו

Fire - Jupiter

64	75	69	79
78	70	72	67
74	65	80	68
71	77	66	73

Air - Jupiter

73	66	77	71
68	80	65	74
67	72	70	78
79	69	75	64

Earth - Jupiter

71	74	78	64
77	65	70	75
66	80	72	69
73	68	67	79

Water - Jupiter

79	67	68	73
69	72	80	66
75	70	65	77
64	78	74	71

	Number	Angel Value (Arabic)	Angel Value (Hebrew)	Jinn Value (Arabic)	Jinn Value (Hebrew)
Usurper	64	23	33	105	95
Guide	80	39	49	121	111
Mystery	144	103	113	185	175
Adjuster	2296	2255	2265	1977	1967
Leader	6888	6847	6857	6569	6559
Regulator	9184	9143	9153	8865	8855
General Governor	18368	18327	18337	18049	18039
High Overseer	1469440	1469399	1469409	1469121	1469111

Occult Encyclopedia of Magic Squares

Fire - Mars

45	71	63	57	51
58	52	46	67	64
68	60	59	53	47
54	48	69	61	55
62	56	50	49	70

Air - Mars

62	54	68	58	45
56	48	60	52	71
50	69	59	46	63
49	61	53	67	57
70	55	47	64	51

Earth - Mars

70	49	50	56	62
55	61	69	48	54
47	53	59	60	68
64	67	46	52	58
51	57	63	71	45

Water - Mars

51	64	47	55	70
57	67	53	61	49
63	46	59	69	50
71	52	60	48	56
45	58	68	54	62

	Number	Angel Value (Arabic)	Angel Value (Hebrew)	Jinn Value (Arabic)	Jinn Value (Hebrew)
Usurper	45	4	14	86	76
Guide	71	30	40	112	102
Mystery	116	75	85	157	147
Adjuster	287	246	256	328	318
Leader	861	820	830	542	532
Regulator	1148	1107	1117	829	819
General Governor	2296	2255	2265	1977	1967
High Overseer	163016	162975	162985	162697	162687

Occult Encyclopedia of Magic Squares

Fire - Sun

30	41	63	47	51	55
36	46	57	62	34	52
42	66	50	40	56	33
53	32	43	58	37	64
59	48	39	31	65	45
67	54	35	49	44	38

Air - Sun

38	44	49	35	54	67
45	65	31	39	48	59
64	37	58	43	32	53
33	56	40	50	66	42
52	34	62	57	46	36
55	51	47	63	41	30

Earth - Sun

67	59	53	42	36	30
54	48	32	66	46	41
35	39	43	50	57	63
49	31	58	40	62	47
44	65	37	56	34	51
38	45	64	33	52	55

Water - Sun

55	52	33	64	45	38
51	34	56	37	65	44
47	62	40	58	31	49
63	57	50	43	39	35
41	46	66	32	48	54
30	36	42	53	59	67

	Number	Angel Value (Arabic)	Angel Value (Hebrew)	Jinn Value (Arabic)	Jinn Value (Hebrew)
Usurper	30	349	359	71	61
Guide	67	26	36	108	98
Mystery	97	56	66	138	128
Adjuster	287	246	256	328	318
Leader	861	820	830	542	532
Regulator	1148	1107	1117	829	819
General Governor	2296	2255	2265	1977	1967
High Overseer	153832	153791	153801	153513	153503

Occult Encyclopedia of Magic Squares

Fire - Venus

17	58	43	28	48	61	32
62	33	18	52	44	29	49
30	50	63	34	19	53	38
54	39	24	51	64	35	20
36	21	55	40	25	45	65
46	59	37	22	56	41	26
42	27	47	60	31	23	57

Air - Venus

57	23	31	60	47	27	42
26	41	56	22	37	59	46
65	45	25	40	55	21	36
20	35	64	51	24	39	54
38	53	19	34	63	50	30
49	29	44	52	18	33	62
32	61	48	28	43	58	17

Earth - Venus

42	46	36	54	30	62	17
27	59	21	39	50	33	58
47	37	55	24	63	18	43
60	22	40	51	34	52	28
31	56	25	64	19	44	48
23	41	45	35	53	29	61
57	26	65	20	38	49	32

Water - Venus

32	49	38	20	65	26	57
61	29	53	35	45	41	23
48	44	19	64	25	56	31
28	52	34	51	40	22	60
43	18	63	24	55	37	47
58	33	50	39	21	59	27
17	62	30	54	36	46	42

	Number	Angel Value (Arabic)	Angel Value (Hebrew)	Jinn Value (Arabic)	Jinn Value (Hebrew)
Usurper	17	336	346	58	48
Guide	65	24	34	106	96
Mystery	82	41	51	123	113
Adjuster	287	246	256	328	318
Leader	861	820	830	542	532
Regulator	1148	1107	1117	829	819
General Governor	2296	2255	2265	1977	1967
High Overseer	149240	149199	149209	148921	148911

Occult Encyclopedia of Magic Squares

Fire - Mercury

4	20	68	49	38	54	35	19
12	28	57	41	46	65	27	11
55	39	18	34	21	5	48	67
66	47	10	26	29	13	40	56
33	17	36	52	70	51	6	22
25	9	44	63	59	43	14	30
50	69	23	7	16	32	53	37
42	58	31	15	8	24	64	45

Earth - Mercury

42	50	25	33	66	55	12	4
58	69	9	17	47	39	28	20
31	23	44	36	10	18	57	68
15	7	63	52	26	34	41	49
8	16	59	70	29	21	46	38
24	32	43	51	13	5	65	54
64	53	14	6	40	48	27	35
45	37	30	22	56	67	11	19

Air - Mercury

45	64	24	8	15	31	58	42
37	53	32	16	7	23	69	50
30	14	43	59	63	44	9	25
22	6	51	70	52	36	17	33
56	40	13	29	26	10	47	66
67	48	5	21	34	18	39	55
11	27	65	46	41	57	28	12
19	35	54	38	49	68	20	4

Water - Mercury

19	11	67	56	22	30	37	45
35	27	48	40	6	14	53	64
54	65	5	13	51	43	32	24
38	46	21	29	70	59	16	8
49	41	34	26	52	63	7	15
68	57	18	10	36	44	23	31
20	28	39	47	17	9	69	58

	Number	Angel Value (Arabic)	Angel Value (Hebrew)	Jinn Value (Arabic)	Jinn Value (Hebrew)
Usurper	4	323	333	45	35
Guide	70	29	39	111	101
Mystery	74	33	43	115	105
Adjuster	287	246	256	328	318
Leader	861	820	830	542	532
Regulator	1148	1107	1117	829	819
General Governor	2296	2255	2265	1977	1967
High Overseer	160720	160679	160689	160401	160391

ANGEL OF CANCER: PAKIEL (141)

אל	י	כ	פ
79	21	13	28
12	29	78	22
19	81	30	11

ל	א	י	כ	פ
י	כ	פ	ל	א
פ	ל	א	י	כ
א	י	כ	פ	ל
כ	פ	ל	א	י

Fire - Saturn

48	43	50
49	47	45
44	51	46

Air - Saturn

46	51	44
45	47	49
50	43	48

Earth - Saturn

44	49	48
51	47	43
46	45	50

Water - Saturn

50	45	46
43	47	51
48	49	44

Occult Encyclopedia of Magic Squares

	Number	Angel Value (Arabic)	Angel Value (Hebrew)	Jinn Value (Arabic)	Jinn Value (Hebrew)
Usurper	43	2	12	84	74
Guide	51	10	20	92	82
Mystery	94	53	63	135	125
Adjuster	141	100	110	182	172
Leader	423	382	392	104	94
Regulator	564	523	533	245	235
General Governor	1128	1087	1097	809	799
High Overseer	57528	57487	57497	57209	57199

Fire - Jupiter

27	38	32	44
43	33	35	30
37	28	45	31
34	42	29	36

Air - Jupiter

36	29	42	34
31	45	28	37
30	35	33	43
44	32	38	27

Earth - Jupiter

34	37	43	27
42	28	33	38
29	45	35	32
36	31	30	44

Water - Jupiter

44	30	31	36
32	35	45	29
38	33	28	42
27	43	37	34

Occult Encyclopedia of Magic Squares

	Number	Angel Value (Arabic)	Angel Value (Hebrew)	Jinn Value (Arabic)	Jinn Value (Hebrew)
Usurper	27	346	356	68	58
Guide	45	4	14	86	76
Mystery	72	31	41	113	103
Adjuster	1128	1087	1097	809	799
Leader	3384	3343	3353	3065	3055
Regulator	4512	4471	4481	4193	4183
General Governor	9024	8983	8993	8705	8695
High Overseer	406080	406039	406049	405761	405751

Fire - Mars

16	41	34	28	22
29	23	17	37	35
38	31	30	24	18
25	19	39	32	26
33	27	21	20	40

Air - Mars

33	25	38	29	16
27	19	31	23	41
21	39	30	17	34
20	32	24	37	28
40	26	18	35	22

Earth - Mars

40	20	21	27	33
26	32	39	19	25
18	24	30	31	38
35	37	17	23	29
22	28	34	41	16

Water - Mars

22	35	18	26	40
28	37	24	32	20
34	17	30	39	21
41	23	31	19	27
16	29	38	25	33

Occult Encyclopedia of Magic Squares

	Number	Angel Value (Arabic)	Angel Value (Hebrew)	Jinn Value (Arabic)	Jinn Value (Hebrew)
Usurper	16	335	345	57	47
Guide	41	360	10	82	72
Mystery	57	16	26	98	88
Adjuster	141	100	110	182	172
Leader	423	382	392	104	94
Regulator	564	523	533	245	235
General Governor	1128	1087	1097	809	799
High Overseer	46248	46207	46217	45929	45919

Fire - Sun

6	17	37	23	27	31
12	22	33	36	10	28
18	40	26	16	32	9
29	8	19	34	13	38
35	24	15	7	39	21
41	30	11	25	20	14

Air - Sun

14	20	25	11	30	41
21	39	7	15	24	35
38	13	34	19	8	29
9	32	16	26	40	18
28	10	36	33	22	12
31	27	23	37	17	6

Earth - Sun

41	35	29	18	12	6
30	24	8	40	22	17
11	15	19	26	33	37
25	7	34	16	36	23
20	39	13	32	10	27
14	21	38	9	28	31

Water - Sun

31	28	9	38	21	14
27	10	32	13	39	20
23	36	16	34	7	25
37	33	26	19	15	11
17	22	40	8	24	30
6	12	18	29	35	41

Occult Encyclopedia of Magic Squares

	Number	Angel Value (Arabic)	Angel Value (Hebrew)	Jinn Value (Arabic)	Jinn Value (Hebrew)
Usurper	6	325	335	47	37
Guide	41	360	10	82	72
Mystery	47	6	16	88	78
Adjuster	141	100	110	182	172
Leader	423	382	392	104	94
Regulator	564	523	533	245	235
General Governor	1128	1087	1097	809	799
High Overseer	46248	46207	46217	45929	45919

LORD OF TRIPLICITY BY DAY: RAADAR (474)

ר	ע	ד	ר
199	71	7	197
6	198	198	72
69	201	199	5

ר	ע	ד	ר
ר	ד	ע	ר
ע	ר	ר	ר
ד	ר	ר	ע

Fire - Saturn

159	154	161
160	158	156
155	162	157

Air - Saturn

157	162	155
156	158	160
161	154	159

Earth - Saturn

155	160	159
162	158	154
157	156	161

Water - Saturn

161	156	157
154	158	162
159	160	155

	Number	Angel Value (Arabic)	Angel Value (Hebrew)	Jinn Value (Arabic)	Jinn Value (Hebrew)
Usurper	154	113	123	195	185
Guide	162	121	131	203	193
Mystery	316	275	285	357	347
Adjuster	474	433	443	155	145
Leader	1422	1381	1391	1103	1093
Regulator	1896	1855	1865	1577	1567
General Governor	3792	3751	3761	3473	3463
High Overseer	614304	614263	614273	613985	613975

Fire - Jupiter

111	122	116	125
124	117	119	114
121	112	126	115
118	123	113	120

Air - Jupiter

120	113	123	118
115	126	112	121
114	119	117	124
125	116	122	111

Earth - Jupiter

118	121	124	111
123	112	117	122
113	126	119	116
120	115	114	125

Water - Jupiter

125	114	115	120
116	119	126	113
122	117	112	123
111	124	121	118

	Number	Angel Value (Arabic)	Angel Value (Hebrew)	Jinn Value (Arabic)	Jinn Value (Hebrew)
Usurper	111	70	80	152	142
Guide	126	85	95	167	157
Mystery	237	196	206	278	268
Adjuster	3792	3751	3761	3473	3463
Leader	11376	11335	11345	11057	11047
Regulator	15168	15127	15137	14849	14839
General Governor	30336	30295	30305	30017	30007
High Overseer	3822336	3822295	3822305	3822017	3822007

Occult Encyclopedia of Magic Squares

Fire - Mars

82	110	100	94	88
95	89	83	106	101
107	97	96	90	84
91	85	108	98	92
99	93	87	86	109

Air - Mars

99	91	107	95	82
93	85	97	89	110
87	108	96	83	100
86	98	90	106	94
109	92	84	101	88

Earth - Mars

109	86	87	93	99
92	98	108	85	91
84	90	96	97	107
101	106	83	89	95
88	94	100	110	82

Water - Mars

88	101	84	92	109
94	106	90	98	86
100	83	96	108	87
110	89	97	85	93
82	95	107	91	99

	Number	Angel Value (Arabic)	Angel Value (Hebrew)	Jinn Value (Arabic)	Jinn Value (Hebrew)
Usurper	82	41	51	123	113
Guide	110	69	79	151	141
Mystery	192	151	161	233	223
Adjuster	474	433	443	155	145
Leader	1422	1381	1391	1103	1093
Regulator	1896	1855	1865	1577	1567
General Governor	3792	3751	3761	3473	3463
High Overseer	417120	417079	417089	416801	416791

Fire - Sun

61	72	95	78	82	86
67	77	88	94	65	83
73	98	81	71	87	64
84	63	74	89	68	96
90	79	70	62	97	76
99	85	66	80	75	69

Earth - Sun

99	90	84	73	67	61
85	79	63	98	77	72
66	70	74	81	88	95
80	62	89	71	94	78
75	97	68	87	65	82
69	76	96	64	83	86

Air - Sun

69	75	80	66	85	99
76	97	62	70	79	90
96	68	89	74	63	84
64	87	71	81	98	73
83	65	94	88	77	67
86	82	78	95	72	61

Water - Sun

86	83	64	96	76	69
82	65	87	68	97	75
78	94	71	89	62	80
95	88	81	74	70	66
72	77	98	63	79	85
61	67	73	84	90	99

	Number	Angel Value (Arabic)	Angel Value (Hebrew)	Jinn Value (Arabic)	Jinn Value (Hebrew)
Usurper	61	20	30	102	92
Guide	99	58	68	140	130
Mystery	160	119	129	201	191
Adjuster	474	433	443	155	145
Leader	1422	1381	1391	1103	1093
Regulator	1896	1855	1865	1577	1567
General Governor	3792	3751	3761	3473	3463
High Overseer	375408	375367	375377	375089	375079

Fire - Venus

43	84	69	54	74	92	58
93	59	44	78	70	55	75
56	76	94	60	45	79	64
80	65	50	77	95	61	46
62	47	81	66	51	71	96
72	90	63	48	82	67	52
68	53	73	91	57	49	83

Air - Venus

83	49	57	91	73	53	68
52	67	82	48	63	90	72
96	71	51	66	81	47	62
46	61	95	77	50	65	80
64	79	45	60	94	76	56
75	55	70	78	44	59	93
58	92	74	54	69	84	43

Earth - Venus

68	72	62	80	56	93	43
53	90	47	65	76	59	84
73	63	81	50	94	44	69
91	48	66	77	60	78	54
57	82	51	95	45	70	74
49	67	71	61	79	55	92
83	52	96	46	64	75	58

Water - Venus

58	75	64	46	96	52	83
92	55	79	61	71	67	49
74	70	45	95	51	82	57
54	78	60	77	66	48	91
69	44	94	50	81	63	73
84	59	76	65	47	90	53
43	93	56	80	62	72	68

Occult Encyclopedia of Magic Squares

	Number	Angel Value (Arabic)	Angel Value (Hebrew)	Jinn Value (Arabic)	Jinn Value (Hebrew)
Usurper	43	2	12	84	74
Guide	96	55	65	137	127
Mystery	139	98	108	180	170
Adjuster	474	433	443	155	145
Leader	1422	1381	1391	1103	1093
Regulator	1896	1855	1865	1577	1567
General Governor	3792	3751	3761	3473	3463
High Overseer	364032	363991	364001	363713	363703

Fire - Mercury

27	43	94	72	61	77	58	42
35	51	80	64	69	91	50	34
78	62	41	57	44	28	71	93
92	70	33	49	52	36	63	79
56	40	59	75	96	74	29	45
48	32	67	89	82	66	37	53
73	95	46	30	39	55	76	60
65	81	54	38	31	47	90	68

Earth - Mercury

65	73	48	56	92	78	35	27
81	95	32	40	70	62	51	43
54	46	67	59	33	41	80	94
38	30	89	75	49	57	64	72
31	39	82	96	52	44	69	61
47	55	66	74	36	28	91	77
90	76	37	29	63	71	50	58
68	60	53	45	79	93	34	42

Air - Mercury

68	90	47	31	38	54	81	65
60	76	55	39	30	46	95	73
53	37	66	82	89	67	32	48
45	29	74	96	75	59	40	56
79	63	36	52	49	33	70	92
93	71	28	44	57	41	62	78
34	50	91	69	64	80	51	35
42	58	77	61	72	94	43	27

Water - Mercury

42	34	93	79	45	53	60	68
58	50	71	63	29	37	76	90
77	91	28	36	74	66	55	47
61	69	44	52	96	82	39	31
72	64	57	49	75	89	30	38
94	80	41	33	59	67	46	54
43	51	62	70	40	32	95	81
27	35	78	92	56	48	73	65

	Number	Angel Value (Arabic)	Angel Value (Hebrew)	Jinn Value (Arabic)	Jinn Value (Hebrew)
Usurper	27	346	356	68	58
Guide	96	55	65	137	127
Mystery	123	82	92	164	154
Adjuster	474	433	443	155	145
Leader	1422	1381	1391	1103	1093
Regulator	1896	1855	1865	1577	1567
General Governor	3792	3751	3761	3473	3463
High Overseer	364032	363991	364001	363713	363703

Occult Encyclopedia of Magic Squares

Fire - Moon

56	69	31	40	98	24	60	76	20
16	59	81	36	52	68	23	45	94
90	28	44	80	12	64	73	35	48
83	15	58	67	38	51	93	22	47
43	92	27	63	79	14	50	72	34
30	55	71	26	39	97	19	62	75
29	42	91	13	65	78	33	49	74
70	32	54	96	25	41	77	18	61
57	82	17	53	66	37	46	95	21

Earth - Moon

20	94	48	47	34	75	74	61	21
76	45	35	22	72	62	49	18	95
60	23	73	93	50	19	33	77	46
24	68	64	51	14	97	78	41	37
98	52	12	38	79	39	65	25	66
40	36	80	67	63	26	13	96	53
31	81	44	58	27	71	91	54	17
69	59	28	15	92	55	42	32	82
56	16	90	83	43	30	29	70	57

Air - Moon

21	95	46	37	66	53	17	82	57
61	18	77	41	25	96	54	32	70
74	49	33	78	65	13	91	42	29
75	62	19	97	39	26	71	55	30
34	72	50	14	79	63	27	92	43
47	22	93	51	38	67	58	15	83
48	35	73	64	12	80	44	28	90
94	45	23	68	52	36	81	59	16
20	76	60	24	98	40	31	69	56

Water - Moon

57	70	29	30	43	83	90	16	56
82	32	42	55	92	15	28	59	69
17	54	91	71	27	58	44	81	31
53	96	13	26	63	67	80	36	40
66	25	65	39	79	38	12	52	98
37	41	78	97	14	51	64	68	24
46	77	33	19	50	93	73	23	60
95	18	49	62	72	22	35	45	76
21	61	74	75	34	47	48	94	20

	Number	Angel Value (Arabic)	Angel Value (Hebrew)	Jinn Value (Arabic)	Jinn Value (Hebrew)
Usurper	12	331	341	53	43
Guide	98	57	67	139	129
Mystery	110	69	79	151	141
Adjuster	474	433	443	155	145
Leader	1422	1381	1391	1103	1093
Regulator	1896	1855	1865	1577	1567
General Governor	3792	3751	3761	3473	3463
High Overseer	371616	371575	371585	371297	371287

LORD OF TRIPLICITY BY NIGHT: AKEL (121)

ל	א	ב	ע
69	21	4	27
3	28	68	22
19	71	29	2

ל	א	ב	ע
ע	ב	א	ל
א	ל	ע	ב
ב	ע	ל	א

Occult Encyclopedia of Magic Squares

Fire - Jupiter

22	33	27	39
38	28	30	25
32	23	40	26
29	37	24	31

Air - Jupiter

31	24	37	29
26	40	23	32
25	30	28	38
39	27	33	22

Earth - Jupiter

29	32	38	22
37	23	28	33
24	40	30	27
31	26	25	39

Water - Jupiter

39	25	26	31
27	30	40	24
33	28	23	37
22	38	32	29

	Number	Angel Value (Arabic)	Angel Value (Hebrew)	Jinn Value (Arabic)	Jinn Value (Hebrew)
Usurper	22	341	351	63	53
Guide	40	359	9	81	71
Mystery	62	21	31	103	93
Adjuster	968	927	937	649	639
Leader	2904	2863	2873	2585	2575
Regulator	3872	3831	3841	3553	3543
General Governor	7744	7703	7713	7425	7415
High Overseer	309760	309719	309729	309441	309431

Fire - Mars

12	37	30	24	18
25	19	13	33	31
34	27	26	20	14
21	15	35	28	22
29	23	17	16	36

Earth - Mars

36	16	17	23	29
22	28	35	15	21
14	20	26	27	34
31	33	13	19	25
18	24	30	37	12

Occult Encyclopedia of Magic Squares

Air - Mars

29	21	34	25	12
23	15	27	19	37
17	35	26	13	30
16	28	20	33	24
36	22	14	31	18

Water - Mars

18	31	14	22	36
24	33	20	28	16
30	13	26	35	17
37	19	27	15	23
12	25	34	21	29

	Number	Angel Value (Arabic)	Angel Value (Hebrew)	Jinn Value (Arabic)	Jinn Value (Hebrew)
Usurper	12	331	341	53	43
Guide	37	356	6	78	68
Mystery	49	8	18	90	80
Adjuster	121	80	90	162	152
Leader	363	322	332	44	34
Regulator	484	443	453	165	155
General Governor	968	927	937	649	639
High Overseer	35816	35775	35785	35497	35487

Fire - Sun

2	13	37	19	23	27
8	18	29	36	6	24
14	40	22	12	28	5
25	4	15	30	9	38
31	20	11	3	39	17
41	26	7	21	16	10

Air - Sun

10	16	21	7	26	41
17	39	3	11	20	31
38	9	30	15	4	25
5	28	12	22	40	14
24	6	36	29	18	8
27	23	19	37	13	2

Earth - Sun

41	31	25	14	8	2
26	20	4	40	18	13
7	11	15	22	29	37
21	3	30	12	36	19
16	39	9	28	6	23
10	17	38	5	24	27

Water - Sun

27	24	5	38	17	10
23	6	28	9	39	16
19	36	12	30	3	21
37	29	22	15	11	7
13	18	40	4	20	26
2	8	14	25	31	41

	Number	Angel Value (Arabic)	Angel Value (Hebrew)	Jinn Value (Arabic)	Jinn Value (Hebrew)
Usurper	2	321	331	43	33
Guide	41	360	10	82	72
Mystery	43	2	12	84	74
Adjuster	121	80	90	162	152
Leader	363	322	332	44	34
Regulator	484	443	453	165	155
General Governor	968	927	937	649	639
High Overseer	39688	39647	39657	39369	39359

ANGEL RULING 4TH HOUSE: KAEL (121)

ל	א	ע	כ
19	71	4	27
3	28	18	72
69	21	29	2

ל	א	ע	כ
כ	ע	א	ל
א	ל	כ	ע
ע	כ	ל	א

Numerical Squares See Page: 216

ANGEL OF FIRST DECANATE: MATHRAVASH (947)

ש	ו	רא	מת
439	202	9	297
8	298	438	203
200	441	299	7

ש	ו	א	ר	ת	מ
ת	ר	ש	מ	א	ו
א	מ	ו	ת	ש	ר
מ	ת	ר	א	ו	ש
ר	ש	ת	ו	מ	א
ו	א	מ	ש	ר	ת

219

Occult Encyclopedia of Magic Squares

Fire - Jupiter

229	240	234	244
243	235	237	232
239	230	245	233
236	242	231	238

Air - Jupiter

238	231	242	236
233	245	230	239
232	237	235	243
244	234	240	229

Earth - Jupiter

236	239	243	229
242	230	235	240
231	245	237	234
238	233	232	244

Water - Jupiter

244	232	233	238
234	237	245	231
240	235	230	242
229	243	239	236

	Number	Angel Value (Arabic)	Angel Value (Hebrew)	Jinn Value (Arabic)	Jinn Value (Hebrew)
Usurper	229	188	198	270	260
Guide	245	204	214	286	276
Mystery	474	433	443	155	145
Adjuster	7576	7535	7545	7257	7247
Leader	22728	22687	22697	22409	22399
Regulator	30304	30263	30273	29985	29975
General Governor	60608	60567	60577	60289	60279
High Overseer	14848960	14848919	14848929	14848641	14848631

Fire - Mars

177	203	195	189	183
190	184	178	199	196
200	192	191	185	179
186	180	201	193	187
194	188	182	181	202

Air - Mars

194	186	200	190	177
188	180	192	184	203
182	201	191	178	195
181	193	185	199	189
202	187	179	196	183

Earth - Mars

202	181	182	188	194
187	193	201	180	186
179	185	191	192	200
196	199	178	184	190
183	189	195	203	177

Water - Mars

183	196	179	187	202
189	199	185	193	181
195	178	191	201	182
203	184	192	180	188
177	190	200	186	194

	Number	Angel Value (Arabic)	Angel Value (Hebrew)	Jinn Value (Arabic)	Jinn Value (Hebrew)
Usurper	177	136	146	218	208
Guide	203	162	172	244	234
Mystery	380	339	349	61	51
Adjuster	947	906	916	628	618
Leader	2841	2800	2810	2522	2512
Regulator	3788	3747	3757	3469	3459
General Governor	7576	7535	7545	7257	7247
High Overseer	1537928	1537887	1537897	1537609	1537599

Fire - Sun

140	151	173	157	161	165
146	156	167	172	144	162
152	176	160	150	166	143
163	142	153	168	147	174
169	158	149	141	175	155
177	164	145	159	154	148

Air - Sun

148	154	159	145	164	177
155	175	141	149	158	169
174	147	168	153	142	163
143	166	150	160	176	152
162	144	172	167	156	146
165	161	157	173	151	140

Earth - Sun

177	169	163	152	146	140
164	158	142	176	156	151
145	149	153	160	167	173
159	141	168	150	172	157
154	175	147	166	144	161
148	155	174	143	162	165

Water - Sun

165	162	143	174	155	148
161	144	166	147	175	154
157	172	150	168	141	159
173	167	160	153	149	145
151	156	176	142	158	164
140	146	152	163	169	177

	Number	Angel Value (Arabic)	Angel Value (Hebrew)	Jinn Value (Arabic)	Jinn Value (Hebrew)
Usurper	140	99	109	181	171
Guide	177	136	146	218	208
Mystery	317	276	286	358	348
Adjuster	947	906	916	628	618
Leader	2841	2800	2810	2522	2512
Regulator	3788	3747	3757	3469	3459
General Governor	7576	7535	7545	7257	7247
High Overseer	1340952	1340911	1340921	1340633	1340623

Fire - Venus

111	152	137	122	142	157	126
158	127	112	146	138	123	143
124	144	159	128	113	147	132
148	133	118	145	160	129	114
130	115	149	134	119	139	161
140	155	131	116	150	135	120
136	121	141	156	125	117	151

Earth - Venus

136	140	130	148	124	158	111
121	155	115	133	144	127	152
141	131	149	118	159	112	137
156	116	134	145	128	146	122
125	150	119	160	113	138	142
117	135	139	129	147	123	157
151	120	161	114	132	143	126

Air - Venus

151	117	125	156	141	121	136
120	135	150	116	131	155	140
161	139	119	134	149	115	130
114	129	160	145	118	133	148
132	147	113	128	159	144	124
143	123	138	146	112	127	158
126	157	142	122	137	152	111

Water - Venus

126	143	132	114	161	120	151
157	123	147	129	139	135	117
142	138	113	160	119	150	125
122	146	128	145	134	116	156
137	112	159	118	149	131	141
152	127	144	133	115	155	121
111	158	124	148	130	140	136

	Number	Angel Value (Arabic)	Angel Value (Hebrew)	Jinn Value (Arabic)	Jinn Value (Hebrew)
Usurper	111	70	80	152	142
Guide	161	120	130	202	192
Mystery	272	231	241	313	303
Adjuster	947	906	916	628	618
Leader	2841	2800	2810	2522	2512
Regulator	3788	3747	3757	3469	3459
General Governor	7576	7535	7545	7257	7247
High Overseer	1219736	1219695	1219705	1219417	1219407

Fire - Mercury

86	102	154	131	120	136	117	101
94	110	139	123	128	151	109	93
137	121	100	116	103	87	130	153
152	129	92	108	111	95	122	138
115	99	118	134	156	133	88	104
107	91	126	149	141	125	96	112
132	155	105	89	98	114	135	119
124	140	113	97	90	106	150	127

Earth - Mercury

124	132	107	115	152	137	94	86
140	155	91	99	129	121	110	102
113	105	126	118	92	100	139	154
97	89	149	134	108	116	123	131
90	98	141	156	111	103	128	120
106	114	125	133	95	87	151	136
150	135	96	88	122	130	109	117
127	119	112	104	138	153	93	101

Occult Encyclopedia of Magic Squares

Air - Mercury

127	150	106	90	97	113	140	124
119	135	114	98	89	105	155	132
112	96	125	141	149	126	91	107
104	88	133	156	134	118	99	115
138	122	95	111	108	92	129	152
153	130	87	103	116	100	121	137
93	109	151	128	123	139	110	94
101	117	136	120	131	154	102	86

Water - Mercury

101	93	153	138	104	112	119	127
117	109	130	122	88	96	135	150
136	151	87	95	133	125	114	106
120	128	103	111	156	141	98	90
131	123	116	108	134	149	89	97
154	139	100	92	118	126	105	113
102	110	121	129	99	91	155	140
86	94	137	152	115	107	132	124

	Number	Angel Value (Arabic)	Angel Value (Hebrew)	Jinn Value (Arabic)	Jinn Value (Hebrew)
Usurper	86	45	55	127	117
Guide	156	115	125	197	187
Mystery	242	201	211	283	273
Adjuster	947	906	916	628	618
Leader	2841	2800	2810	2522	2512
Regulator	3788	3747	3757	3469	3459
General Governor	7576	7535	7545	7257	7247
High Overseer	1181856	1181815	1181825	1181537	1181527

Fire - Moon

109	122	84	93	147	77	113	129	73
69	112	134	89	105	121	76	98	143
139	81	97	133	65	117	126	88	101
136	68	111	120	91	104	142	75	100
96	141	80	116	132	67	103	125	87
83	108	124	79	92	146	72	115	128
82	95	140	66	118	131	86	102	127
123	85	107	145	78	94	130	71	114
110	135	70	106	119	90	99	144	74

Earth - Moon

73	143	101	100	87	128	127	114	74
129	98	88	75	125	115	102	71	144
113	76	126	142	103	72	86	130	99
77	121	117	104	67	146	131	94	90
147	105	65	91	132	92	118	78	119
93	89	133	120	116	79	66	145	106
84	134	97	111	80	124	140	107	70
122	112	81	68	141	108	95	85	135
109	69	139	136	96	83	82	123	110

Air - Moon

74	144	99	90	119	106	70	135	110
114	71	130	94	78	145	107	85	123
127	102	86	131	118	66	140	95	82
128	115	72	146	92	79	124	108	83
87	125	103	67	132	116	80	141	96
100	75	142	104	91	120	111	68	136
101	88	126	117	65	133	97	81	139
143	98	76	121	105	89	134	112	69
73	129	113	77	147	93	84	122	109

Water - Moon

110	123	82	83	96	136	139	69	109
135	85	95	108	141	68	81	112	122
70	107	140	124	80	111	97	134	84
106	145	66	79	116	120	133	89	93
119	78	118	92	132	91	65	105	147
90	94	131	146	67	104	117	121	77
99	130	86	72	103	142	126	76	113
144	71	102	115	125	75	88	98	129
74	114	127	128	87	100	101	143	73

	Number	Angel Value (Arabic)	Angel Value (Hebrew)	Jinn Value (Arabic)	Jinn Value (Hebrew)
Usurper	65	24	34	106	96
Guide	147	106	116	188	178
Mystery	212	171	181	253	243
Adjuster	947	906	916	628	618
Leader	2841	2800	2810	2522	2512
Regulator	3788	3747	3757	3469	3459
General Governor	7576	7535	7545	7257	7247
High Overseer	1113672	1113631	1113641	1113353	1113343

Fire - Saturn

45	63	70	108	99	139	92	84	116	131
56	120	113	104	141	129	47	89	75	73
71	76	100	140	130	115	64	52	93	106
77	102	138	132	65	111	119	60	49	94
90	137	134	69	80	103	107	117	62	48
97	54	55	122	110	86	82	72	127	142
109	91	51	58	124	79	67	128	145	95
123	112	87	46	57	74	125	144	98	81
133	66	78	85	53	61	143	96	114	118
146	126	121	83	88	50	101	105	68	59

Earth - Saturn

146	133	123	109	97	90	77	71	56	45
126	66	112	91	54	137	102	76	120	63
121	78	87	51	55	134	138	100	113	70
83	85	46	58	122	69	132	140	104	108
88	53	57	124	110	80	65	130	141	99
50	61	74	79	86	103	111	115	129	139
101	143	125	67	82	107	119	64	47	92
105	96	144	128	72	117	60	52	89	84
68	114	98	145	127	62	49	93	75	116
59	118	81	95	142	48	94	106	73	131

Occult Encyclopedia of Magic Squares

Air - Saturn

59	68	105	101	50	88	83	121	126	146
118	114	96	143	61	53	85	78	66	133
81	98	144	125	74	57	46	87	112	123
95	145	128	67	79	124	58	51	91	109
142	127	72	82	86	110	122	55	54	97
48	62	117	107	103	80	69	134	137	90
94	49	60	119	111	65	132	138	102	77
106	93	52	64	115	130	140	100	76	71
73	75	89	47	129	141	104	113	120	56
131	116	84	92	139	99	108	70	63	45

Water - Saturn

131	73	106	94	48	142	95	81	118	59
116	75	93	49	62	127	145	98	114	68
84	89	52	60	117	72	128	144	96	105
92	**47**	64	119	107	82	67	125	143	101
139	129	115	111	103	86	79	74	61	50
99	141	130	65	80	110	124	57	53	88
108	104	140	132	69	122	58	46	85	83
70	113	100	138	134	55	51	87	78	121
63	120	76	102	137	54	91	112	66	126
45	56	71	77	90	97	109	123	133	146

	Number	Angel Value (Arabic)	Angel Value (Hebrew)	Jinn Value (Arabic)	Jinn Value (Hebrew)
Usurper	45	4	14	86	76
Guide	146	105	115	187	177
Mystery	191	150	160	232	222
Adjuster	947	906	916	628	618
Leader	2841	2800	2810	2522	2512
Regulator	3788	3747	3757	3469	3459
General Governor	7576	7535	7545	7257	7247
High Overseer	1106096	1106055	1106065	1105777	1105767

ANGEL OF FIRST QUINANCE: AYOEL (112)

ל	ב	׳	ע
69	11	5	27
4	28	68	12
9	71	29	3

ל	ב	׳	ע
ע	׳	ב	ל
ב	ל	ע	׳
׳	ע	ל	ב

Fire - Jupiter

20	31	25	36
35	26	28	23
30	21	37	24
27	34	22	29

Air - Jupiter

29	22	34	27
24	37	21	30
23	28	26	35
36	25	31	20

Earth - Jupiter

27	30	35	20
34	21	26	31
22	37	28	25
29	24	23	36

Water - Jupiter

36	23	24	29
25	28	37	22
31	26	21	34
20	35	30	27

	Number	Angel Value (Arabic)	Angel Value (Hebrew)	Jinn Value (Arabic)	Jinn Value (Hebrew)
Usurper	20	339	349	61	51
Guide	37	356	6	78	68
Mystery	57	16	26	98	88
Adjuster	896	855	865	577	567
Leader	2688	2647	2657	2369	2359
Regulator	3584	3543	3553	3265	3255
General Governor	7168	7127	7137	6849	6839
High Overseer	265216	265175	265185	264897	264887

Occult Encyclopedia of Magic Squares

Fire - Mars

10	36	28	22	16
23	17	11	32	29
33	25	24	18	12
19	13	34	26	20
27	21	15	14	35

Air - Mars

27	19	33	23	10
21	13	25	17	36
15	34	24	11	28
14	26	18	32	22
35	20	12	29	16

Earth - Mars

35	14	15	21	27
20	26	34	13	19
12	18	24	25	33
29	32	11	17	23
16	22	28	36	10

Water - Mars

16	29	12	20	35
22	32	18	26	14
28	11	24	34	15
36	17	25	13	21
10	23	33	19	27

	Number	Angel Value (Arabic)	Angel Value (Hebrew)	Jinn Value (Arabic)	Jinn Value (Hebrew)
Usurper	10	329	339	51	41
Guide	36	355	5	77	67
Mystery	46	5	15	87	77
Adjuster	112	71	81	153	143
Leader	336	295	305	17	7
Regulator	448	407	417	129	119
General Governor	896	855	865	577	567
High Overseer	32256	32215	32225	31937	31927

Fire - Sun

1	12	33	18	22	26
7	17	28	32	5	23
13	36	21	11	27	4
24	3	14	29	8	34
30	19	10	2	35	16
37	25	6	20	15	9

Earth - Sun

37	30	24	13	7	1
25	19	3	36	17	12
6	10	14	21	28	33
20	2	29	11	32	18
15	35	8	27	5	22
9	16	34	4	23	26

Air - Sun

9	15	20	6	25	37
16	35	2	10	19	30
34	8	29	14	3	24
4	27	11	21	36	13
23	5	32	28	17	7
26	22	18	33	12	1

Water - Sun

26	23	4	34	16	9
22	5	27	8	35	15
18	32	11	29	2	20
33	28	21	14	10	6
12	17	36	3	19	25
1	7	13	24	30	37

	Number	Angel Value (Arabic)	Angel Value (Hebrew)	Jinn Value (Arabic)	Jinn Value (Hebrew)
Usurper	1	320	330	42	32
Guide	37	356	6	78	68
Mystery	38	357	7	79	69
Adjuster	112	71	81	153	143
Leader	336	295	305	17	7
Regulator	448	407	417	129	119
General Governor	896	855	865	577	567
High Overseer	33152	33111	33121	32833	32823

ANGEL OF SECOND QUINANCE: CHABUYAH (31)

יה	ו	ב	ח
7	3	9	12
8	13	6	4
1	9	14	7

ה	י	ו	ב	ח
ו	ב	ח	ה	י
ח	ה	י	ו	ב
י	ו	ב	ח	ה
ב	ח	ה	י	ו

No Numerical Squares Available

ANGEL OF SECOND DECANATE: RAHADETZ (299)

צ	ד	ה	ר
199	6	7	87
6	88	198	7
4	201	89	5

צ	ד	ה	ר
ר	ה	ד	צ
ד	צ	ר	ה
ה	ר	צ	ד

Fire - Jupiter

67	78	72	82
81	73	75	70
77	68	83	71
74	80	69	76

Air - Jupiter

76	69	80	74
71	83	68	77
70	75	73	81
82	72	78	67

Earth - Jupiter

74	77	81	67
80	68	73	78
69	83	75	72
76	71	70	82

Water - Jupiter

82	70	71	76
72	75	83	69
78	73	68	80
67	81	77	74

	Number	Angel Value (Arabic)	Angel Value (Hebrew)	Jinn Value (Arabic)	Jinn Value (Hebrew)
Usurper	67	26	36	108	98
Guide	83	42	52	124	114
Mystery	150	109	119	191	181
Adjuster	2392	2351	2361	2073	2063
Leader	7176	7135	7145	6857	6847
Regulator	9568	9527	9537	9249	9239
General Governor	19136	19095	19105	18817	18807
High Overseer	1588288	1588247	1588257	1587969	1587959

Occult Encyclopedia of Magic Squares

Fire - Mars

47	75	65	59	53
60	54	48	71	66
72	62	61	55	49
56	50	73	63	57
64	58	52	51	74

Air - Mars

64	56	72	60	47
58	50	62	54	75
52	73	61	48	65
51	63	55	71	59
74	57	49	66	53

Earth - Mars

74	51	52	58	64
57	63	73	50	56
49	55	61	62	72
66	71	48	54	60
53	59	65	75	47

Water - Mars

53	66	49	57	74
59	71	55	63	51
65	48	61	73	52
75	54	62	50	58
47	60	72	56	64

	Number	Angel Value (Arabic)	Angel Value (Hebrew)	Jinn Value (Arabic)	Jinn Value (Hebrew)
Usurper	47	6	16	88	78
Guide	75	34	44	116	106
Mystery	122	81	91	163	153
Adjuster	299	258	268	340	330
Leader	897	856	866	578	568
Regulator	1196	1155	1165	877	867
General Governor	2392	2351	2361	2073	2063
High Overseer	179400	179359	179369	179081	179071

Fire - Sun

32	43	65	49	53	57
38	48	59	64	36	54
44	68	52	42	58	35
55	34	45	60	39	66
61	50	41	33	67	47
69	56	37	51	46	40

Earth - Sun

69	61	55	44	38	32
56	50	34	68	48	43
37	41	45	52	59	65
51	33	60	42	64	49
46	67	39	58	36	53
40	47	66	35	54	57

Occult Encyclopedia of Magic Squares

Air - Sun

40	46	51	37	56	69
47	67	33	41	50	61
66	39	60	45	34	55
35	58	42	52	68	44
54	36	64	59	48	38
57	53	49	65	43	32

Water - Sun

57	54	35	66	47	40
53	36	58	39	67	46
49	64	42	60	33	51
65	59	52	45	41	37
43	48	68	34	50	56
32	38	44	55	61	69

	Number	Angel Value (Arabic)	Angel Value (Hebrew)	Jinn Value (Arabic)	Jinn Value (Hebrew)
Usurper	32	351	1	73	63
Guide	69	28	38	110	100
Mystery	101	60	70	142	132
Adjuster	299	258	268	340	330
Leader	897	856	866	578	568
Regulator	1196	1155	1165	877	867
General Governor	2392	2351	2361	2073	2063
High Overseer	165048	165007	165017	164729	164719

Fire - Venus

18	59	44	29	49	67	33
68	34	19	53	45	30	50
31	51	69	35	20	54	39
55	40	25	52	70	36	21
37	22	56	41	26	46	71
47	65	38	23	57	42	27
43	28	48	66	32	24	58

Air - Venus

58	24	32	66	48	28	43
27	42	57	23	38	65	47
71	46	26	41	56	22	37
21	36	70	52	25	40	55
39	54	20	35	69	51	31
50	30	45	53	19	34	68
33	67	49	29	44	59	18

Earth - Venus

43	47	37	55	31	68	18
28	65	22	40	51	34	59
48	38	56	25	69	19	44
66	23	41	52	35	53	29
32	57	26	70	20	45	49
24	42	46	36	54	30	67
58	27	71	21	39	50	33

Water - Venus

33	50	39	21	71	27	58
67	30	54	36	46	42	24
49	45	20	70	26	57	32
29	53	35	52	41	23	66
44	19	69	25	56	38	48
59	34	51	40	22	65	28
18	68	31	55	37	47	43

	Number	Angel Value (Arabic)	Angel Value (Hebrew)	Jinn Value (Arabic)	Jinn Value (Hebrew)
Usurper	18	337	347	59	49
Guide	71	30	40	112	102
Mystery	89	48	58	130	120
Adjuster	299	258	268	340	330
Leader	897	856	866	578	568
Regulator	1196	1155	1165	877	867
General Governor	2392	2351	2361	2073	2063
High Overseer	169832	169791	169801	169513	169503

Fire - Mercury

5	21	73	50	39	55	36	20
13	29	58	42	47	70	28	12
56	40	19	35	22	6	49	72
71	48	11	27	30	14	41	57
34	18	37	53	75	52	7	23
26	10	45	68	60	44	15	31
51	74	24	8	17	33	54	38
43	59	32	16	9	25	69	46

Earth - Mercury

43	51	26	34	71	56	13	5
59	74	10	18	48	40	29	21
32	24	45	37	11	19	58	73
16	8	68	53	27	35	42	50
9	17	60	75	30	22	47	39
25	33	44	52	14	6	70	55
69	54	15	7	41	49	28	36
46	38	31	23	57	72	12	20

Occult Encyclopedia of Magic Squares

Air - Mercury

46	69	25	9	16	32	59	43
38	54	33	17	8	24	74	51
31	15	44	60	68	45	10	26
23	7	52	75	53	37	18	34
57	41	14	30	27	11	48	71
72	49	6	22	35	19	40	56
12	28	70	47	42	58	29	13
20	36	55	39	50	73	21	5

Water - Mercury

20	12	72	57	23	31	38	46
36	28	49	41	7	15	54	69
55	70	6	14	52	44	33	25
39	47	22	30	75	60	17	9
50	42	35	27	53	68	8	16
73	58	19	11	37	45	24	32
21	29	40	48	18	10	74	59
5	13	56	71	34	26	51	43

	Number	Angel Value (Arabic)	Angel Value (Hebrew)	Jinn Value (Arabic)	Jinn Value (Hebrew)
Usurper	5	324	334	46	36
Guide	75	34	44	116	106
Mystery	80	39	49	121	111
Adjuster	299	258	268	340	330
Leader	897	856	866	578	568
Regulator	1196	1155	1165	877	867
General Governor	2392	2351	2361	2073	2063
High Overseer	179400	179359	179369	179081	179071

ANGEL OF THIRD QUINANCE: RAHAEL (237)

אל	ה	א	ר
199	2	4	32
3	29	202	3
4	201	30	2

ל	א	ה	א	ר
ה	א	ר	ל	א
ר	ל	א	ה	א
א	ה	א	ר	ל
א	ר	ל	א	ה

Fire - Saturn

80	75	82
81	79	77
76	83	78

Earth - Saturn

76	81	80
83	79	75
78	77	82

Air - Saturn

78	83	76
77	79	81
82	75	80

Water - Saturn

82	77	78
75	79	83
80	81	76

	Number	Angel Value (Arabic)	Angel Value (Hebrew)	Jinn Value (Arabic)	Jinn Value (Hebrew)
Usurper	75	44	44	116	106
Guide	83	52	52	124	114
Mystery	158	117	127	199	189
Adjuster	237	196	206	278	268
Leader	711	670	680	392	382
Regulator	948	907	917	629	619
General Governor	1896	1855	1865	1577	1567
High Overseer	157368	157327	157337	157049	157039

Fire - Jupiter

51	62	56	68
67	57	59	54
61	52	69	55
58	66	53	60

Earth - Jupiter

58	61	67	51
66	52	57	62
53	69	59	56
60	55	54	68

Occult Encyclopedia of Magic Squares

Air - Jupiter

60	53	66	58
55	69	52	61
54	59	57	67
68	56	62	51

Water - Jupiter

68	54	55	60
56	59	69	53
62	57	52	66
51	67	61	58

	Number	Angel Value (Arabic)	Angel Value (Hebrew)	Jinn Value (Arabic)	Jinn Value (Hebrew)
Usurper	51	10	20	92	82
Guide	69	28	38	110	100
Mystery	120	79	89	161	151
Adjuster	1896	1855	1865	1577	1567
Leader	5688	5647	5657	5369	5359
Regulator	7584	7543	7553	7265	7255
General Governor	15168	15127	15137	14849	14839
High Overseer	1046592	1046551	1046561	1046273	1046263

Fire - Mars

35	61	53	47	41
48	42	36	57	54
58	50	49	43	37
44	38	59	51	45
52	46	40	39	60

Air - Mars

52	44	58	48	35
46	38	50	42	61
40	59	49	36	53
39	51	43	57	47
60	45	37	54	41

Earth - Mars

60	39	40	46	52
45	51	59	38	44
37	43	49	50	58
54	57	36	42	48
41	47	53	61	35

Water - Mars

41	54	37	45	60
47	57	43	51	39
53	36	49	59	40
61	42	50	38	46
35	48	58	44	52

Occult Encyclopedia of Magic Squares

	Number	Angel Value (Arabic)	Angel Value (Hebrew)	Jinn Value (Arabic)	Jinn Value (Hebrew)
Usurper	35	354	4	76	66
Guide	61	20	30	102	92
Mystery	96	55	65	137	127
Adjuster	237	196	206	278	268
Leader	711	670	680	392	382
Regulator	948	907	917	629	619
General Governor	1896	1855	1865	1577	1567
High Overseer	115656	115615	115625	115337	115327

Fire - Sun

22	33	53	39	43	47
28	38	49	52	26	44
34	56	42	32	48	25
45	24	35	50	29	54
51	40	31	23	55	37
57	46	27	41	36	30

Air - Sun

30	36	41	27	46	57
37	55	23	31	40	51
54	29	50	35	24	45
25	48	32	42	56	34
44	26	52	49	38	28
47	43	39	53	33	22

Earth - Sun

57	51	45	34	28	22
46	40	24	56	38	33
27	31	35	42	49	53
41	23	50	32	52	39
36	55	29	48	26	43
30	37	54	25	44	47

Water - Sun

47	44	25	54	37	30
43	26	48	29	55	36
39	52	32	50	23	41
53	49	42	35	31	27
33	38	56	24	40	46
22	28	34	45	51	57

	Number	Angel Value (Arabic)	Angel Value (Hebrew)	Jinn Value (Arabic)	Jinn Value (Hebrew)
Usurper	22	341	351	63	53
Guide	57	16	26	98	88
Mystery	79	38	48	120	110
Adjuster	237	196	206	278	268
Leader	711	670	680	392	382
Regulator	948	907	917	629	619
General Governor	1896	1855	1865	1577	1567
High Overseer	108072	108031	108041	107753	107743

ANGEL OF FOURTH QUINANCE: YEBAMIAH (67)

הי	מ	ב	י
9	3	43	12
42	13	8	4
1	11	14	41

ה	י	מ	ב	י
מ	ב	י	ה	י
י	ה	י	מ	ב
י	מ	ב	י	ה
ב	י	ה	י	מ

Fire - Jupiter

9	20	14	24
23	15	17	12
19	10	25	13
16	22	11	18

Air - Jupiter

18	11	22	16
13	25	10	19
12	17	15	23
24	14	20	9

Earth - Jupiter

16	19	23	9
22	10	15	20
11	25	17	14
18	13	12	24

Water - Jupiter

24	12	13	18
14	17	25	11
20	15	10	22
9	23	19	16

Occult Encyclopedia of Magic Squares

	Number	Angel Value (Arabic)	Angel Value (Hebrew)	Jinn Value (Arabic)	Jinn Value (Hebrew)
Usurper	9	328	338	50	40
Guide	25	344	354	66	56
Mystery	34	353	3	75	65
Adjuster	536	495	505	217	207
Leader	1608	1567	1577	1289	1279
Regulator	2144	2103	2113	1825	1815
General Governor	4288	4247	4257	3969	3959
High Overseer	107200	107159	107169	106881	106871

Fire - Mars

1	27	19	13	7
14	8	2	23	20
24	16	15	9	3
10	4	25	17	11
18	12	6	5	26

Air - Mars

18	10	24	14	1
12	4	16	8	27
6	25	15	2	19
5	17	9	23	13
26	11	3	20	7

Earth - Mars

26	5	6	12	18
11	17	25	4	10
3	9	15	16	24
20	23	2	8	14
7	13	19	27	1

Water - Mars

7	20	3	11	26
13	23	9	17	5
19	2	15	25	6
27	8	16	4	12
1	14	24	10	18

	Number	Angel Value (Arabic)	Angel Value (Hebrew)	Jinn Value (Arabic)	Jinn Value (Hebrew)
Usurper	1	320	330	42	32
Guide	27	346	356	68	58
Mystery	28	347	357	69	59
Adjuster	67	26	36	108	98
Leader	201	160	170	242	232
Regulator	268	227	237	309	299
General Governor	536	495	505	217	207
High Overseer	14472	14431	14441	14153	14143

ANGEL OF THIRD DECANATE: ALINKIR (321)

ר	כי	יג	אל
30	61	33	197
32	198	29	62
59	32	199	31

ר	י	כ	נ	י	ל	א
כ	נ	י	ל	א	ר	י
י	ל	א	ר	י	כ	נ
א	ר	י	כ	נ	י	ל
י	כ	נ	י	ל	א	ר
נ	י	ל	א	ר	י	כ
ל	א	ר	י	כ	נ	י

Fire - Saturn

108	103	110
109	107	105
104	111	106

Earth - Saturn

104	109	108
111	107	103
106	105	110

Air - Saturn

106	111	104
105	107	109
110	103	108

Water - Saturn

110	105	106
103	107	111
108	109	104

	Number	Angel Value (Arabic)	Angel Value (Hebrew)	Jinn Value (Arabic)	Jinn Value (Hebrew)
Usurper	103	62	72	144	134
Guide	111	70	80	152	142
Mystery	214	173	183	255	245
Adjuster	321	280	290	2	352
Leader	963	922	932	644	634
Regulator	1284	1243	1253	965	955
General Governor	2568	2527	2537	2249	2239
High Overseer	285048	285007	285017	284729	284719

Fire - Jupiter

72	83	77	89
88	78	80	75
82	73	90	76
79	87	74	81

Earth - Jupiter

79	82	88	72
87	73	78	83
74	90	80	77
81	76	75	89

Occult Encyclopedia of Magic Squares

Air - Jupiter

81	74	87	79
76	90	73	82
75	80	78	88
89	77	83	72

Water - Jupiter

89	75	76	81
77	80	90	74
83	78	73	87
72	88	82	79

	Number	Angel Value (Arabic)	Angel Value (Hebrew)	Jinn Value (Arabic)	Jinn Value (Hebrew)
Usurper	72	31	41	113	103
Guide	90	49	59	131	121
Mystery	162	121	131	203	193
Adjuster	2568	2527	2537	2249	2239
Leader	7704	7663	7673	7385	7375
Regulator	10272	10231	10241	9953	9943
General Governor	20544	20503	20513	20225	20215
High Overseer	1848960	1848919	1848929	1848641	1848631

Fire - Mars

52	77	70	64	58
65	59	53	73	71
74	67	66	60	54
61	55	75	68	62
69	63	57	56	76

Air - Mars

69	61	74	65	52
63	55	67	59	77
57	75	66	53	70
56	68	60	73	64
76	62	54	71	58

Earth - Mars

76	56	57	63	69
62	68	75	55	61
54	60	66	67	74
71	73	53	59	65
58	64	70	77	52

Water - Mars

58	71	54	62	76
64	73	60	68	56
70	53	66	75	57
77	59	67	55	63
52	65	74	61	69

Occult Encyclopedia of Magic Squares

	Number	Angel Value (Arabic)	Angel Value (Hebrew)	Jinn Value (Arabic)	Jinn Value (Hebrew)
Usurper	52	11	21	93	83
Guide	77	36	46	118	108
Mystery	129	88	98	170	160
Adjuster	321	280	290	2	352
Leader	963	922	932	644	634
Regulator	1284	1243	1253	965	955
General Governor	2568	2527	2537	2249	2239
High Overseer	197736	197695	197705	197417	197407

Fire - Sun

36	47	67	53	57	61
42	52	63	66	40	58
48	70	56	46	62	39
59	38	49	64	43	68
65	54	45	37	69	51
71	60	41	55	50	44

Air - Sun

44	50	55	41	60	71
51	69	37	45	54	65
68	43	64	49	38	59
39	62	46	56	70	48
58	40	66	63	52	42
61	57	53	67	47	36

Earth - Sun

71	65	59	48	42	36
60	54	38	70	52	47
41	45	49	56	63	67
55	37	64	46	66	53
50	69	43	62	40	57
44	51	68	39	58	61

Water - Sun

61	58	39	68	51	44
57	40	62	43	69	50
53	66	46	64	37	55
67	63	56	49	45	41
47	52	70	38	54	60
36	42	48	59	65	71

	Number	Angel Value (Arabic)	Angel Value (Hebrew)	Jinn Value (Arabic)	Jinn Value (Hebrew)
Usurper	36	355	5	77	67
Guide	71	30	40	112	102
Mystery	107	66	76	148	138
Adjuster	321	280	290	2	352
Leader	963	922	932	644	634
Regulator	1284	1243	1253	965	955
General Governor	2568	2527	2537	2249	2239
High Overseer	182328	182287	182297	182009	181999

Occult Encyclopedia of Magic Squares

Fire - Venus

21	62	47	32	52	71	36
72	37	22	56	48	33	53
34	54	73	38	23	57	42
58	43	28	55	74	39	24
40	25	59	44	29	49	75
50	69	41	26	60	45	30
46	31	51	70	35	27	61

Air - Venus

61	27	35	70	51	31	46
30	45	60	26	41	69	50
75	49	29	44	59	25	40
24	39	74	55	28	43	58
42	57	23	38	73	54	34
53	33	48	56	22	37	72
36	71	52	32	47	62	21

Earth - Venus

46	50	40	58	34	72	21
31	69	25	43	54	37	62
51	41	59	28	73	22	47
70	26	44	55	38	56	32
35	60	29	74	23	48	52
27	45	49	39	57	33	71
61	30	75	24	42	53	36

Water - Venus

36	53	42	24	75	30	61
71	33	57	39	49	45	27
52	48	23	74	29	60	35
32	56	38	55	44	26	70
47	22	73	28	59	41	51
62	37	54	43	25	69	31
21	72	34	58	40	50	46

	Number	Angel Value (Arabic)	Angel Value (Hebrew)	Jinn Value (Arabic)	Jinn Value (Hebrew)
Usurper	21	340	350	62	52
Guide	75	34	44	116	106
Mystery	96	55	65	137	127
Adjuster	321	280	290	2	352
Leader	963	922	932	644	634
Regulator	1284	1243	1253	965	955
General Governor	2568	2527	2537	2249	2239
High Overseer	192600	192559	192569	192281	192271

Fire - Mercury

8	24	74	53	42	58	39	23
16	32	61	45	50	71	31	15
59	43	22	38	25	9	52	73
72	51	14	30	33	17	44	60
37	21	40	56	76	55	10	26
29	13	48	69	63	47	18	34
54	75	27	11	20	36	57	41
46	62	35	19	12	28	70	49

Occult Encyclopedia of Magic Squares

Earth - Mercury

46	54	29	37	72	59	16	8
62	75	13	21	51	43	32	24
35	27	48	40	14	22	61	74
19	11	69	56	30	38	45	53
12	20	63	76	33	25	50	42
28	36	47	55	17	9	71	58
70	57	18	10	44	52	31	39
49	41	34	26	60	73	15	23

Air - Mercury

49	70	28	12	19	35	62	46
41	57	36	20	11	27	75	54
34	18	47	63	69	48	13	29
26	10	55	76	56	40	21	37
60	44	17	33	30	14	51	72
73	52	9	25	38	22	43	59
15	31	71	50	45	61	32	16
23	39	58	42	53	74	24	8

Water - Mercury

23	15	73	60	26	34	41	49
39	31	52	44	10	18	57	70
58	71	9	17	55	47	36	28
42	50	25	33	76	63	20	12
53	45	38	30	56	69	11	19
74	61	22	14	40	48	27	35
24	32	43	51	21	13	75	62
8	16	59	72	37	29	54	46

	Number	Angel Value (Arabic)	Angel Value (Hebrew)	Jinn Value (Arabic)	Jinn Value (Hebrew)
Usurper	8	327	337	49	39
Guide	76	35	45	117	107
Mystery	84	43	53	125	115
Adjuster	321	280	290	2	352
Leader	963	922	932	644	634
Regulator	1284	1243	1253	965	955
General Governor	2568	2527	2537	2249	2239
High Overseer	195168	195127	195137	194849	194839

ANGEL OF FIFTH QUINANCE: HAYAYEL (56)

אל	י	י	ה
4	11	13	28
12	29	3	12
9	6	30	11

ל	א	י	י	ה
י	י	ה	ל	א
ה	ל	א	י	י
א	י	י	ה	ל
י	ה	ל	א	י

Fire - Jupiter

6	17	11	22
21	12	14	9
16	7	23	10
13	20	8	15

Air - Jupiter

15	8	20	13
10	23	7	16
9	14	12	21
22	11	17	6

Earth - Jupiter

13	16	21	6
20	7	12	17
8	23	14	11
15	10	9	22

Water - Jupiter

22	9	10	15
11	14	23	8
17	12	7	20
6	21	16	13

	Number	Angel Value (Arabic)	Angel Value (Hebrew)	Jinn Value (Arabic)	Jinn Value (Hebrew)
Usurper	6	325	335	47	37
Guide	23	342	352	64	54
Mystery	29	348	358	70	60
Adjuster	448	407	417	129	119
Leader	1344	1303	1313	1025	1015
Regulator	1792	1751	1761	1473	1463
General Governor	3584	3543	3553	3265	3255
High Overseer	82432	82391	82401	82113	82103

ANGEL OF SIX QUINANCE: MEVAMIAH (101)

הי	מ	ו	מ
39	7	43	12
42	13	38	8
5	41	14	41

ה	י	מ	ו	מ
מ	ו	מ	ה	י
מ	ה	י	מ	ו
י	מ	ו	מ	ה
ו	מ	ה	י	מ

Fire - Jupiter

17	28	22	34
33	23	25	20
27	18	35	21
24	32	19	26

Air - Jupiter

26	19	32	24
21	35	18	27
20	25	23	33
34	22	28	17

Earth - Jupiter

24	27	33	17
32	18	23	28
19	35	25	22
26	21	20	34

Water - Jupiter

34	20	21	26
22	25	35	19
28	23	18	32
17	33	27	24

Occult Encyclopedia of Magic Squares

	Number	Angel Value (Arabic)	Angel Value (Hebrew)	Jinn Value (Arabic)	Jinn Value (Hebrew)
Usurper	17	336	346	58	48
Guide	35	354	4	76	66
Mystery	52	11	21	93	83
Adjuster	808	767	777	489	479
Leader	2424	2383	2393	2105	2095
Regulator	3232	3191	3201	2913	2903
General Governor	6464	6423	6433	6145	6135
High Overseer	226240	226199	226209	225921	225911

Fire - Mars

8	33	26	20	14
21	15	9	29	27
30	23	22	16	10
17	11	31	24	18
25	19	13	12	32

Air - Mars

25	17	30	21	8
19	11	23	15	33
13	31	22	9	26
12	24	16	29	20
32	18	10	27	14

Earth - Mars

32	12	13	19	25
18	24	31	11	17
10	16	22	23	30
27	29	9	15	21
14	20	26	33	8

Water - Mars

14	27	10	18	32
20	29	16	24	12
26	9	22	31	13
33	15	23	11	19
8	21	30	17	25

	Number	Angel Value (Arabic)	Angel Value (Hebrew)	Jinn Value (Arabic)	Jinn Value (Hebrew)
Usurper	8	327	337	49	39
Guide	33	352	2	74	64
Mystery	41	360	10	82	72
Adjuster	101	60	70	142	132
Leader	303	262	272	344	334
Regulator	404	363	373	85	75
General Governor	808	767	777	489	479
High Overseer	26664	26623	26633	26345	26335

LEO

SIGN LEO: ARI (216)

ה	י	ר	א
199	2	4	11
3	202	8	3
9	2	4	201

ה	י	ר	א
א	ר	י	ה
י	ה	א	ר
ר	א	ה	י

Fire - Saturn		
73	68	75
74	72	70
69	76	71

Earth - Saturn		
69	74	73
76	72	68
71	70	75

Air - Saturn		
71	76	69
70	72	74
75	68	73

Water - Saturn		
75	70	71
68	72	76
73	74	69

	Number	Angel Value (Arabic)	Angel Value (Hebrew)	Jinn Value (Arabic)	Jinn Value (Hebrew)
Usurper	68	27	37	109	99
Guide	76	35	45	117	107
Mystery	144	103	113	185	175
Adjuster	216	175	185	257	247
Leader	648	607	617	329	319
Regulator	864	823	833	545	535
General Governor	1728	1687	1697	1409	1399
High Overseer	131328	131287	131297	131009	130999

Fire - Jupiter

46	57	51	62
61	52	54	49
56	47	63	50
53	60	48	55

Air - Jupiter

55	48	60	53
50	63	47	56
49	54	52	61
62	51	57	46

Earth - Jupiter

53	56	61	46
60	47	52	57
48	63	54	51
55	50	49	62

Water - Jupiter

62	49	50	55
51	54	63	48
57	52	47	60
46	61	56	53

	Number	Angel Value (Arabic)	Angel Value (Hebrew)	Jinn Value (Arabic)	Jinn Value (Hebrew)
Usurper	46	5	15	87	77
Guide	63	22	32	104	94
Mystery	109	68	78	150	140
Adjuster	1728	1687	1697	1409	1399
Leader	5184	5143	5153	4865	4855
Regulator	6912	6871	6881	6593	6583
General Governor	13824	13783	13793	13505	13495
High Overseer	870912	870871	870881	870593	870583

Fire - Mars

31	56	49	43	37
44	38	32	52	50
53	46	45	39	33
40	34	54	47	41
48	42	36	35	55

Air - Mars

48	40	53	44	31
42	34	46	38	56
36	54	45	32	49
35	47	39	52	43
55	41	33	50	37

Earth - Mars

55	35	36	42	48
41	47	54	34	40
33	39	45	46	53
50	52	32	38	44
37	43	49	56	31

Water - Mars

37	50	33	41	55
43	52	39	47	35
49	32	45	54	36
56	38	46	34	42
31	44	53	40	48

	Number	Angel Value (Arabic)	Angel Value (Hebrew)	Jinn Value (Arabic)	Jinn Value (Hebrew)
Usurper	31	350	360	72	62
Guide	56	15	25	97	87
Mystery	87	46	56	128	118
Adjuster	216	175	185	257	247
Leader	648	607	617	329	319
Regulator	864	823	833	545	535
General Governor	1728	1687	1697	1409	1399
High Overseer	96768	96727	96737	96449	96439

Fire - Sun

18	29	52	35	39	43
24	34	45	51	22	40
30	55	38	28	44	21
41	20	31	46	25	53
47	36	27	19	54	33
56	42	23	37	32	26

Air - Sun

26	32	37	23	42	56
33	54	19	27	36	47
53	25	46	31	20	41
21	44	28	38	55	30
40	22	51	45	34	24
43	39	35	52	29	18

Earth - Sun

56	47	41	30	24	18
42	36	20	55	34	29
23	27	31	38	45	52
37	19	46	28	51	35
32	54	25	44	22	39
26	33	53	21	40	43

Water - Sun

43	40	21	53	33	26
39	22	44	25	54	32
35	51	28	46	19	37
52	45	38	31	27	23
29	34	55	20	36	42
18	24	30	41	47	56

	Number	Angel Value (Arabic)	Angel Value (Hebrew)	Jinn Value (Arabic)	Jinn Value (Hebrew)
Usurper	18	337	347	59	49
Guide	56	15	25	97	87
Mystery	74	33	43	115	105
Adjuster	216	175	185	257	247
Leader	648	607	617	329	319
Regulator	864	823	833	545	535
General Governor	1728	1687	1697	1409	1399
High Overseer	96768	96727	96737	96449	96439

Fire - Venus

6	47	32	17	37	56	21
57	22	7	41	33	18	38
19	39	58	23	8	42	27
43	28	13	40	59	24	9
25	10	44	29	14	34	60
35	54	26	11	45	30	15
31	16	36	55	20	12	46

Air - Venus

46	12	20	55	36	16	31
15	30	45	11	26	54	35
60	34	14	29	44	10	25
9	24	59	40	13	28	43
27	42	8	23	58	39	19
38	18	33	41	7	22	57
21	56	37	17	32	47	6

Earth - Venus

31	35	25	43	19	57	6
16	54	10	28	39	22	47
36	26	44	13	58	7	32
55	11	29	40	23	41	17
20	45	14	59	8	33	37
12	30	34	24	42	18	56
46	15	60	9	27	38	21

Water - Venus

21	38	27	9	60	15	46
56	18	42	24	34	30	12
37	33	8	59	14	45	20
17	41	23	40	29	11	55
32	7	58	13	44	26	36
47	22	39	28	10	54	16
6	57	19	43	25	35	31

	Number	Angel Value (Arabic)	Angel Value (Hebrew)	Jinn Value (Arabic)	Jinn Value (Hebrew)
Usurper	6	325	335	47	37
Guide	60	19	29	101	91
Mystery	66	25	35	107	97
Adjuster	216	175	185	257	247
Leader	648	607	617	329	319
Regulator	864	823	833	545	535
General Governor	1728	1687	1697	1409	1399
High Overseer	103680	103639	103649	103361	103351

ARCHANGEL OF LEO: VERKIEL (267)

אל	י	כ	ור
205	21	13	28
12	29	204	22
19	207	30	11

ל	א	י	כ	ר	ו
ר	כ	ל	ו	י	א
י	ו	א	ר	ל	כ
ו	ר	כ	י	א	ל
כ	ל	ר	א	ו	י
א	י	ו	ל	כ	ר

Fire - Saturn

90	85	92
91	89	87
86	93	88

Air - Saturn

88	93	86
87	89	91
92	85	90

Earth - Saturn

86	91	90
93	89	85
88	87	92

Water - Saturn

92	87	88
85	89	93
90	91	86

	Number	Angel Value (Arabic)	Angel Value (Hebrew)	Jinn Value (Arabic)	Jinn Value (Hebrew)
Usurper	85	54	54	126	116
Guide	93	62	62	134	124
Mystery	178	137	147	219	209
Adjuster	267	226	236	308	298
Leader	801	760	770	482	472
Regulator	1068	1027	1037	749	739
General Governor	2136	2095	2105	1817	1807
High Overseer	198648	198607	198617	198329	198319

Fire - Jupiter

59	70	64	74
73	65	67	62
69	60	75	63
66	72	61	68

Air - Jupiter

68	61	72	66
63	75	60	69
62	67	65	73
74	64	70	59

Earth - Jupiter

66	69	73	59
72	60	65	70
61	75	67	64
68	63	62	74

Water - Jupiter

74	62	63	68
64	67	75	61
70	65	60	72
59	73	69	66

	Number	Angel Value (Arabic)	Angel Value (Hebrew)	Jinn Value (Arabic)	Jinn Value (Hebrew)
Usurper	59	18	28	100	90
Guide	75	34	44	116	106
Mystery	134	93	103	175	165
Adjuster	2136	2095	2105	1817	1807
Leader	6408	6367	6377	6089	6079
Regulator	8544	8503	8513	8225	8215
General Governor	17088	17047	17057	16769	16759
High Overseer	1281600	1281559	1281569	1281281	1281271

Occult Encyclopedia of Magic Squares

Fire - Mars

41	67	59	53	47
54	48	42	63	60
64	56	55	49	43
50	44	65	57	51
58	52	46	45	66

Air - Mars

58	50	64	54	41
52	44	56	48	67
46	65	55	42	59
45	57	49	63	53
66	51	43	60	47

Earth - Mars

66	45	46	52	58
51	57	65	44	50
43	49	55	56	64
60	63	42	48	54
47	53	59	67	41

Water - Mars

47	60	43	51	66
53	63	49	57	45
59	42	55	65	46
67	48	56	44	52
41	54	64	50	58

	Number	Angel Value (Arabic)	Angel Value (Hebrew)	Jinn Value (Arabic)	Jinn Value (Hebrew)
Usurper	41	360	10	82	72
Guide	67	26	36	108	98
Mystery	108	67	77	149	139
Adjuster	267	226	236	308	298
Leader	801	760	770	482	472
Regulator	1068	1027	1037	749	739
General Governor	2136	2095	2105	1817	1807
High Overseer	143112	143071	143081	142793	142783

Fire - Sun

27	38	58	44	48	52
33	43	54	57	31	49
39	61	47	37	53	30
50	29	40	55	34	59
56	45	36	28	60	42
62	51	32	46	41	35

Earth - Sun

62	56	50	39	33	27
51	45	29	61	43	38
32	36	40	47	54	58
46	28	55	37	57	44
41	60	34	53	31	48
35	42	59	30	49	52

Air - Sun

35	41	46	32	51	62
42	60	28	36	45	56
59	34	55	40	29	50
30	53	37	47	61	39
49	31	57	54	43	33
52	48	44	58	38	27

Water - Sun

52	49	30	59	42	35
48	31	53	34	60	41
44	57	37	55	28	46
58	54	47	40	36	32
38	43	61	29	45	51
27	33	39	50	56	62

	Number	Angel Value (Arabic)	Angel Value (Hebrew)	Jinn Value (Arabic)	Jinn Value (Hebrew)
Usurper	27	346	356	68	58
Guide	62	21	31	103	93
Mystery	89	48	58	130	120
Adjuster	267	226	236	308	298
Leader	801	760	770	482	472
Regulator	1068	1027	1037	749	739
General Governor	2136	2095	2105	1817	1807
High Overseer	132432	132391	132401	132113	132103

Fire - Venus

14	55	40	25	45	59	29
60	30	15	49	41	26	46
27	47	61	31	16	50	35
51	36	21	48	62	32	17
33	18	52	37	22	42	63
43	57	34	19	53	38	23
39	24	44	58	28	20	54

Air - Venus

54	20	28	58	44	24	39
23	38	53	19	34	57	43
63	42	22	37	52	18	33
17	32	62	48	21	36	51
35	50	16	31	61	47	27
46	26	41	49	15	30	60
29	59	45	25	40	55	14

Earth - Venus

39	43	33	51	27	60	14
24	57	18	36	47	30	55
44	34	52	21	61	15	40
58	19	37	48	31	49	25
28	53	22	62	16	41	45
20	38	42	32	50	26	59
54	23	63	17	35	46	29

Water - Venus

29	46	35	17	63	23	54
59	26	50	32	42	38	20
45	41	16	62	22	53	28
25	49	31	48	37	19	58
40	15	61	21	52	34	44
55	30	47	36	18	57	24
14	60	27	51	33	43	39

Occult Encyclopedia of Magic Squares

	Number	Angel Value (Arabic)	Angel Value (Hebrew)	Jinn Value (Arabic)	Jinn Value (Hebrew)
Usurper	14	333	343	55	45
Guide	63	22	32	104	94
Mystery	77	36	46	118	108
Adjuster	267	226	236	308	298
Leader	801	760	770	482	472
Regulator	1068	1027	1037	749	739
General Governor	2136	2095	2105	1817	1807
High Overseer	134568	134527	134537	134249	134239

Fire - Mercury

1	17	69	46	35	51	32	16
9	25	54	38	43	66	24	8
52	36	15	31	18	2	45	68
67	44	7	23	26	10	37	53
30	14	33	49	71	48	3	19
22	6	41	64	56	40	11	27
47	70	20	4	13	29	50	34
39	55	28	12	5	21	65	42

Earth - Mercury

39	47	22	30	67	52	9	1
55	70	6	14	44	36	25	17
28	20	41	33	7	15	54	69
12	4	64	49	23	31	38	46
5	13	56	71	26	18	43	35
21	29	40	48	10	2	66	51
65	50	11	3	37	45	24	32
42	34	27	19	53	68	8	16

Occult Encyclopedia of Magic Squares

Air - Mercury

42	65	21	5	12	28	55	39
34	50	29	13	4	20	70	47
27	11	40	56	64	41	6	22
19	3	48	71	49	33	14	30
53	37	10	26	23	7	44	67
68	45	2	18	31	15	36	52
8	24	66	43	38	54	25	9
16	32	51	35	46	69	17	1

Water - Mercury

16	8	68	53	19	27	34	42
32	24	45	37	3	11	50	65
51	66	2	10	48	40	29	21
35	43	18	26	71	56	13	5
46	38	31	23	49	64	4	12
69	54	15	7	33	41	20	28
17	25	36	44	14	6	70	55
1	9	52	67	30	22	47	39

	Number	Angel Value (Arabic)	Angel Value (Hebrew)	Jinn Value (Arabic)	Jinn Value (Hebrew)
Usurper	1	320	330	42	32
Guide	71	30	40	112	102
Mystery	72	31	41	113	103
Adjuster	267	226	236	308	298
Leader	801	760	770	482	472
Regulator	1068	1027	1037	749	739
General Governor	2136	2095	2105	1817	1807
High Overseer	151656	151615	151625	151337	151327

ANGEL OF LEO: SHARATIEL (550)

יאל	ט	ר	ש
299	201	12	38
11	39	298	202
199	301	40	10

ל	א	י	ט	ר	ש	מ
ר	ט	ל	ש	י	א	א
י	ש	א	ר	ל	ט	י
ש	ר	ט	י	א	ל	ל
ט	ל	ר	א	ש	י	ל
א	י	ש	ל	ט	ר	ד
ל	מ	ל	א	ד	י	כ

Fire - Jupiter

130	141	135	144
143	136	138	133
140	131	145	134
137	142	132	139

Air - Jupiter

139	132	142	137
134	145	131	140
133	138	136	143
144	135	141	130

Earth - Jupiter

137	140	143	130
142	131	136	141
132	145	138	135
139	134	133	144

Water - Jupiter

144	133	134	139
135	138	145	132
141	136	131	142
130	143	140	137

	Number	Angel Value (Arabic)	Angel Value (Hebrew)	Jinn Value (Arabic)	Jinn Value (Hebrew)
Usurper	130	89	99	171	161
Guide	145	104	114	186	176
Mystery	275	234	244	316	306
Adjuster	4400	4359	4369	4081	4071
Leader	13200	13159	13169	12881	12871
Regulator	17600	17559	17569	17281	17271
General Governor	35200	35159	35169	34881	34871
High Overseer	5104000	5103959	5103969	5103681	5103671

Occult Encyclopedia of Magic Squares

Fire - Mars

98	122	116	110	104
111	105	99	118	117
119	113	112	106	100
107	101	120	114	108
115	109	103	102	121

Air - Mars

115	107	119	111	98
109	101	113	105	122
103	120	112	99	116
102	114	106	118	110
121	108	100	117	104

Earth - Mars

121	102	103	109	115
108	114	120	101	107
100	106	112	113	119
117	118	99	105	111
104	110	116	122	98

Water - Mars

104	117	100	108	121
110	118	106	114	102
116	99	112	120	103
122	105	113	101	109
98	111	119	107	115

	Number	Angel Value (Arabic)	Angel Value (Hebrew)	Jinn Value (Arabic)	Jinn Value (Hebrew)
Usurper	98	57	67	139	129
Guide	122	81	91	163	153
Mystery	220	179	189	261	251
Adjuster	550	509	519	231	221
Leader	1650	1609	1619	1331	1321
Regulator	2200	2159	2169	1881	1871
General Governor	4400	4359	4369	4081	4071
High Overseer	536800	536759	536769	536481	536471

Fire - Sun

74	85	106	91	95	99
80	90	101	105	78	96
86	109	94	84	100	77
97	76	87	102	81	107
103	92	83	75	108	89
110	98	79	93	88	82

Earth - Sun

110	103	97	86	80	74
98	92	76	109	90	85
79	83	87	94	101	106
93	75	102	84	105	91
88	108	81	100	78	95
82	89	107	77	96	99

Occult Encyclopedia of Magic Squares

Air - Sun

82	88	93	79	98	110
89	108	75	83	92	103
107	81	102	87	76	97
77	100	84	94	109	86
96	78	105	101	90	80
99	95	91	106	85	74

Water - Sun

99	96	77	107	89	82
95	78	100	81	108	88
91	105	84	102	75	93
106	101	94	87	83	79
85	90	109	76	92	98
74	80	86	97	103	110

	Number	Angel Value (Arabic)	Angel Value (Hebrew)	Jinn Value (Arabic)	Jinn Value (Hebrew)
Usurper	74	33	43	115	105
Guide	110	69	79	151	141
Mystery	184	143	153	225	215
Adjuster	550	509	519	231	221
Leader	1650	1609	1619	1331	1321
Regulator	2200	2159	2169	1881	1871
General Governor	4400	4359	4369	4081	4071
High Overseer	484000	483959	483969	483681	483671

Fire - Venus

54	95	80	65	85	102	69
103	70	55	89	81	66	86
67	87	104	71	56	90	75
91	76	61	88	105	72	57
73	58	92	77	62	82	106
83	100	74	59	93	78	63
79	64	84	101	68	60	94

Earth - Venus

79	83	73	91	67	103	54
64	100	58	76	87	70	95
84	74	92	61	104	55	80
101	59	77	88	71	89	65
68	93	62	105	56	81	85
60	78	82	72	90	66	102
94	63	106	57	75	86	69

Air - Venus

94	60	68	101	84	64	79
63	78	93	59	74	100	83
106	82	62	77	92	58	73
57	72	105	88	61	76	91
75	90	56	71	104	87	67
86	66	81	89	55	70	103
69	102	85	65	80	95	54

Water - Venus

69	86	75	57	106	63	94
102	66	90	72	82	78	60
85	81	56	105	62	93	68
65	89	71	88	77	59	101
80	55	104	61	92	74	84
95	70	87	76	58	100	64
54	103	67	91	73	83	79

	Number	Angel Value (Arabic)	Angel Value (Hebrew)	Jinn Value (Arabic)	Jinn Value (Hebrew)
Usurper	54	13	23	95	85
Guide	106	65	75	147	137
Mystery	160	119	129	201	191
Adjuster	550	509	519	231	221
Leader	1650	1609	1619	1331	1321
Regulator	2200	2159	2169	1881	1871
General Governor	4400	4359	4369	4081	4071
High Overseer	466400	466359	466369	466081	466071

Occult Encyclopedia of Magic Squares

Fire - Mercury

37	53	100	82	71	87	68	52
45	61	90	74	79	97	60	44
88	72	51	67	54	38	81	99
98	80	43	59	62	46	73	89
66	50	69	85	102	84	39	55
58	42	77	95	92	76	47	63
83	101	56	40	49	65	86	70
75	91	64	48	41	57	96	78

Earth - Mercury

75	83	58	66	98	88	45	37
91	101	42	50	80	72	61	53
64	56	77	69	43	51	90	100
48	40	95	85	59	67	74	82
41	49	92	102	62	54	79	71
57	65	76	84	46	38	97	87
96	86	47	39	73	81	60	68
78	70	63	55	89	99	44	52

Air - Mercury

78	96	57	41	48	64	91	75
70	86	65	49	40	56	101	83
63	47	76	92	95	77	42	58
55	39	84	102	85	69	50	66
89	73	46	62	59	43	80	98
99	81	38	54	67	51	72	88
44	60	97	79	74	90	61	45
52	68	87	71	82	100	53	37

Water - Mercury

52	44	99	89	55	63	70	78
68	60	81	73	39	47	86	96
87	97	38	46	84	76	65	57
71	79	54	62	102	92	49	41
82	74	67	59	85	95	40	48
100	90	51	43	69	77	56	64
53	61	72	80	50	42	101	91
37	45	88	98	66	58	83	75

	Number	Angel Value (Arabic)	Angel Value (Hebrew)	Jinn Value (Arabic)	Jinn Value (Hebrew)
Usurper	37	356	6	78	68
Guide	102	61	71	143	133
Mystery	139	98	108	180	170
Adjuster	550	509	519	231	221
Leader	1650	1609	1619	1331	1321
Regulator	2200	2159	2169	1881	1871
General Governor	4400	4359	4369	4081	4071
High Overseer	448800	448759	448769	448481	448471

Fire - Moon

65	78	40	49	102	33	69	85	29
25	68	90	45	61	77	32	54	98
94	37	53	89	21	73	82	44	57
92	24	67	76	47	60	97	31	56
52	96	36	72	88	23	59	81	43
39	64	80	35	48	101	28	71	84
38	51	95	22	74	87	42	58	83
79	41	63	100	34	50	86	27	70
66	91	26	62	75	46	55	99	30

Earth - Moon

29	98	57	56	43	84	83	70	30
85	54	44	31	81	71	58	27	99
69	32	82	97	59	28	42	86	55
33	77	73	60	23	101	87	50	46
102	61	21	47	88	48	74	34	75
49	45	89	76	72	35	22	100	62
40	90	53	67	36	80	95	63	26
78	68	37	24	96	64	51	41	91
65	25	94	92	52	39	38	79	66

Occult Encyclopedia of Magic Squares

Air - Moon

30	99	55	46	75	62	26	91	66
70	27	86	50	34	100	63	41	79
83	58	42	87	74	22	95	51	38
84	71	28	101	48	35	80	64	39
43	81	59	23	88	72	36	96	52
56	31	97	60	47	76	67	24	92
57	44	82	73	21	89	53	37	94
98	54	32	77	61	45	90	68	25
29	85	69	33	102	49	40	78	65

Water - Moon

66	79	38	39	52	92	94	25	65
91	41	51	64	96	24	37	68	78
26	63	95	80	36	67	53	90	40
62	100	22	35	72	76	89	45	49
75	34	74	48	88	47	21	61	102
46	50	87	101	23	60	73	77	33
55	86	42	28	59	97	82	32	69
99	27	58	71	81	31	44	54	85
30	70	83	84	43	56	57	98	29

	Number	Angel Value (Arabic)	Angel Value (Hebrew)	Jinn Value (Arabic)	Jinn Value (Hebrew)
Usurper	21	340	350	62	52
Guide	102	61	71	143	133
Mystery	123	82	92	164	154
Adjuster	550	509	519	231	221
Leader	1650	1609	1619	1331	1321
Regulator	2200	2159	2169	1881	1871
General Governor	4400	4359	4369	4081	4071
High Overseer	448800	448759	448769	448481	448471

Occult Encyclopedia of Magic Squares

Fire - Saturn

5	23	30	68	59	102	52	44	76	91
16	80	73	64	104	89	7	49	35	33
31	36	60	103	90	75	24	12	53	66
37	62	101	92	25	71	79	20	9	54
50	100	94	29	40	63	67	77	22	8
57	14	15	82	70	46	42	32	87	105
69	51	11	18	84	39	27	88	108	55
83	72	47	6	17	34	85	107	58	41
93	26	38	45	13	21	106	56	74	78
109	86	81	43	48	10	61	65	28	19

Earth - Saturn

109	93	83	69	57	50	37	31	16	5
86	26	72	51	14	100	62	36	80	23
81	38	47	11	15	94	101	60	73	30
43	45	6	18	82	29	92	103	64	68
48	13	17	84	70	40	25	90	104	59
10	21	34	39	46	63	71	75	89	102
61	106	85	27	42	67	79	24	7	52
65	56	107	88	32	77	20	12	49	44
28	74	58	108	87	22	9	53	35	76
19	78	41	55	105	8	54	66	33	91

Air - Saturn

19	28	65	61	10	48	43	81	86	109
78	74	56	106	21	13	45	38	26	93
41	58	107	85	34	17	6	47	72	83
55	108	88	27	39	84	18	11	51	69
105	87	32	42	46	70	82	15	14	57
8	22	77	67	63	40	29	94	100	50
54	9	20	79	71	25	92	101	62	37
66	53	12	24	75	90	103	60	36	31
33	35	49	7	89	104	64	73	80	16
91	76	44	52	102	59	68	30	23	5

Water - Saturn

91	33	66	54	8	105	55	41	78	19
76	35	53	9	22	87	108	58	74	28
44	49	12	20	77	32	88	107	56	65
52	7	24	79	67	42	27	85	106	61
102	89	75	71	63	46	39	34	21	10
59	104	90	25	40	70	84	17	13	48
68	64	103	92	29	82	18	6	45	43
30	73	60	101	94	15	11	47	38	81
23	80	36	62	100	14	51	72	26	86
5	16	31	37	50	57	69	83	93	109

	Number	Angel Value (Arabic)	Angel Value (Hebrew)	Jinn Value (Arabic)	Jinn Value (Hebrew)
Usurper	5	324	324	46	36
Guide	109	68	68	150	140
Mystery	114	73	73	155	145
Adjuster	550	509	509	231	221
Leader	1650	1609	1609	1331	1321
Regulator	2200	2159	2159	1881	1871
General Governor	4400	4359	4359	4081	4071
High Overseer	479600	479559	479559	479281	479271

LORD OF TRIPLICITY BY DAY: SANAHEM (155)

מ	ה	נ	ס
59	51	8	37
7	38	58	52
49	61	39	6

מ	ה	נ	ס
ס	נ	ה	מ
ה	מ	ס	נ
נ	ס	מ	ה

Fire - Jupiter

31	42	36	46
45	37	39	34
41	32	47	35
38	44	33	40

Air - Jupiter

40	33	44	38
35	47	32	41
34	39	37	45
46	36	42	31

Earth - Jupiter

38	41	45	31
44	32	37	42
33	47	39	36
40	35	34	46

Water - Jupiter

46	34	35	40
36	39	47	33
42	37	32	44
31	45	41	38

	Number	Angel Value (Arabic)	Angel Value (Hebrew)	Jinn Value (Arabic)	Jinn Value (Hebrew)
Usurper	31	350	360	72	62
Guide	47	6	16	88	78
Mystery	78	37	47	119	109
Adjuster	1240	1199	1209	921	911
Leader	3720	3679	3689	3401	3391
Regulator	4960	4919	4929	4641	4631
General Governor	9920	9879	9889	9601	9591
High Overseer	466240	466199	466209	465921	465911

Fire - Mars

19	43	37	31	25
32	26	20	39	38
40	34	33	27	21
28	22	41	35	29
36	30	24	23	42

Air - Mars

36	28	40	32	19
30	22	34	26	43
24	41	33	20	37
23	35	27	39	31
42	29	21	38	25

Earth - Mars

42	23	24	30	36
29	35	41	22	28
21	27	33	34	40
38	39	20	26	32
25	31	37	43	19

Water - Mars

25	38	21	29	42
31	39	27	35	23
37	20	33	41	24
43	26	34	22	30
19	32	40	28	36

Occult Encyclopedia of Magic Squares

	Number	Angel Value (Arabic)	Angel Value (Hebrew)	Jinn Value (Arabic)	Jinn Value (Hebrew)
Usurper	19	338	348	60	50
Guide	43	2	12	84	74
Mystery	62	21	31	103	93
Adjuster	155	114	124	196	186
Leader	465	424	434	146	136
Regulator	620	579	589	301	291
General Governor	1240	1199	1209	921	911
High Overseer	53320	53279	53289	53001	52991

Fire - Sun

8	19	41	25	29	33
14	24	35	40	12	30
20	44	28	18	34	11
31	10	21	36	15	42
37	26	17	9	43	23
45	32	13	27	22	16

Air - Sun

16	22	27	13	32	45
23	43	9	17	26	37
42	15	36	21	10	31
11	34	18	28	44	20
30	12	40	35	24	14
33	29	25	41	19	8

Earth - Sun

45	37	31	20	14	8
32	26	10	44	24	19
13	17	21	28	35	41
27	9	36	18	40	25
22	43	15	34	12	29
16	23	42	11	30	33

Water - Sun

33	30	11	42	23	16
29	12	34	15	43	22
25	40	18	36	9	27
41	35	28	21	17	13
19	24	44	10	26	32
8	14	20	31	37	45

	Number	Angel Value (Arabic)	Angel Value (Hebrew)	Jinn Value (Arabic)	Jinn Value (Hebrew)
Usurper	8	327	337	49	39
Guide	45	4	14	86	76
Mystery	53	12	22	94	84
Adjuster	155	114	124	196	186
Leader	465	424	434	146	136
Regulator	620	579	589	301	291
General Governor	1240	1199	1209	921	911
High Overseer	55800	55759	55769	55481	55471

LORD OF TRIPLICITY BY NIGHT: ZALBARHITH (654)

זל	בר	חי	ת
397	18	203	36
204	35	398	17
16	399	38	201

ו	ל	ב	ר	ה	י	ת
י	ת	ז	ל	ב	ר	ה
ר	ה	י	ת	ז	ל	ב
ל	ב	ר	ה	י	ת	ז
ת	ז	ל	ב	ר	ה	י
ה	י	ת	ז	ל	ב	ר
ב	ר	ה	י	ת	ז	ל

Fire - Saturn

219	214	221
220	218	216
215	222	217

Earth - Saturn

215	220	219
222	218	214
217	216	221

Air - Saturn

217	222	215
216	218	220
221	214	219

Water - Saturn

221	216	217
214	218	222
219	220	215

	Number	Angel Value (Arabic)	Angel Value (Hebrew)	Jinn Value (Arabic)	Jinn Value (Hebrew)
Usurper	214	183	183	255	245
Guide	222	191	191	263	253
Mystery	436	395	405	117	107
Adjuster	654	613	623	335	325
Leader	1962	1921	1931	1643	1633
Regulator	2616	2575	2585	2297	2287
General Governor	5232	5191	5201	4913	4903
High Overseer	1161504	1161463	1161473	1161185	1161175

Occult Encyclopedia of Magic Squares

Fire - Jupiter

156	167	161	170
169	162	164	159
166	157	171	160
163	168	158	165

Air - Jupiter

165	158	168	163
160	171	157	166
159	164	162	169
170	161	167	156

Earth - Jupiter

163	166	169	156
168	157	162	167
158	171	164	161
165	160	159	170

Water - Jupiter

170	159	160	165
161	164	171	158
167	162	157	168
156	169	166	163

	Number	Angel Value (Arabic)	Angel Value (Hebrew)	Jinn Value (Arabic)	Jinn Value (Hebrew)
Usurper	156	115	125	197	187
Guide	171	130	140	212	202
Mystery	327	286	296	8	358
Adjuster	5232	5191	5201	4913	4903
Leader	15696	15655	15665	15377	15367
Regulator	20928	20887	20897	20609	20599
General Governor	41856	41815	41825	41537	41527
High Overseer	7157376	7157335	7157345	7157057	7157047

Fire - Mars

118	146	136	130	124
131	125	119	142	137
143	133	132	126	120
127	121	144	134	128
135	129	123	122	145

Air - Mars

135	127	143	131	118
129	121	133	125	146
123	144	132	119	136
122	134	126	142	130
145	128	120	137	124

Earth - Mars

145	122	123	129	135
128	134	144	121	127
120	126	132	133	143
137	142	119	125	131
124	130	136	146	118

Water - Mars

124	137	120	128	145
130	142	126	134	122
136	119	132	144	123
146	125	133	121	129
118	131	143	127	135

	Number	Angel Value (Arabic)	Angel Value (Hebrew)	Jinn Value (Arabic)	Jinn Value (Hebrew)
Usurper	118	77	87	159	149
Guide	146	105	115	187	177
Mystery	264	223	233	305	295
Adjuster	654	613	623	335	325
Leader	1962	1921	1931	1643	1633
Regulator	2616	2575	2585	2297	2287
General Governor	5232	5191	5201	4913	4903
High Overseer	763872	763831	763841	763553	763543

Fire - Sun

91	102	125	108	112	116
97	107	118	124	95	113
103	128	111	101	117	94
114	93	104	119	98	126
120	109	100	92	127	106
129	115	96	110	105	99

Earth - Sun

129	120	114	103	97	91
115	109	93	128	107	102
96	100	104	111	118	125
110	92	119	101	124	108
105	127	98	117	95	112
99	106	126	94	113	116

Air - Sun

99	105	110	96	115	129
106	127	92	100	109	120
126	98	119	104	93	114
94	117	101	111	128	103
113	95	124	118	107	97
116	112	108	125	102	91

Water - Sun

116	113	94	126	106	99
112	95	117	98	127	105
108	124	101	119	92	110
125	118	111	104	100	96
102	107	128	93	109	115
91	97	103	114	120	129

	Number	Angel Value (Arabic)	Angel Value (Hebrew)	Jinn Value (Arabic)	Jinn Value (Hebrew)
Usurper	91	50	60	132	122
Guide	129	88	98	170	160
Mystery	220	179	189	261	251
Adjuster	654	613	623	335	325
Leader	1962	1921	1931	1643	1633
Regulator	2616	2575	2585	2297	2287
General Governor	5232	5191	5201	4913	4903
High Overseer	674928	674887	674897	674609	674599

Fire - Venus

69	110	95	80	100	116	84
117	85	70	104	96	81	101
82	102	118	86	71	105	90
106	91	76	103	119	87	72
88	73	107	92	77	97	120
98	114	89	74	108	93	78
94	79	99	115	83	75	109

Earth - Venus

94	98	88	106	82	117	69
79	114	73	91	102	85	110
99	89	107	76	118	70	95
115	74	92	103	86	104	80
83	108	77	119	71	96	100
75	93	97	87	105	81	116
109	78	120	72	90	101	84

Air - Venus

109	75	83	115	99	79	94
78	93	108	74	89	114	98
120	97	77	92	107	73	88
72	87	119	103	76	91	106
90	105	71	86	118	102	82
101	81	96	104	70	85	117
84	116	100	80	95	110	69

Water - Venus

84	101	90	72	120	78	109
116	81	105	87	97	93	75
100	96	71	119	77	108	83
80	104	86	103	92	74	115
95	70	118	76	107	89	99
110	85	102	91	73	114	79
69	117	82	106	88	98	94

	Number	Angel Value (Arabic)	Angel Value (Hebrew)	Jinn Value (Arabic)	Jinn Value (Hebrew)
Usurper	69	28	38	110	100
Guide	120	79	89	161	151
Mystery	189	148	158	230	220
Adjuster	654	613	623	335	325
Leader	1962	1921	1931	1643	1633
Regulator	2616	2575	2585	2297	2287
General Governor	5232	5191	5201	4913	4903
High Overseer	627840	627799	627809	627521	627511

Fire - Mercury

50	66	113	95	84	100	81	65
58	74	103	87	92	110	73	57
101	85	64	80	67	51	94	112
111	93	56	72	75	59	86	102
79	63	82	98	115	97	52	68
71	55	90	108	105	89	60	76
96	114	69	53	62	78	99	83
88	104	77	61	54	70	109	91

Occult Encyclopedia of Magic Squares

Fire - Mercury

50	66	113	95	84	100	81	65
58	74	103	87	92	110	73	57
101	85	64	80	67	51	94	112
111	93	56	72	75	59	86	102
79	63	82	98	115	97	52	68
71	55	90	108	105	89	60	76
96	114	69	53	62	78	99	83
88	104	77	61	54	70	109	91

Earth - Mercury

88	96	71	79	111	101	58	50
104	114	55	63	93	85	74	66
77	69	90	82	56	64	103	113
61	53	108	98	72	80	87	95
54	62	105	115	75	67	92	84
70	78	89	97	59	51	110	100
109	99	60	52	86	94	73	81
91	83	76	68	102	112	57	65

Air - Mercury

91	109	70	54	61	77	104	88
83	99	78	62	53	69	114	96
76	60	89	105	108	90	55	71
68	52	97	115	98	82	63	79
102	86	59	75	72	56	93	111
112	94	51	67	80	64	85	101
57	73	110	92	87	103	74	58
65	81	100	84	95	113	66	50

	Number	Angel Value (Arabic)	Angel Value (Hebrew)	Jinn Value (Arabic)	Jinn Value (Hebrew)
Usurper	50	9	19	91	81
Guide	115	74	84	156	146
Mystery	165	124	134	206	196
Adjuster	654	613	623	335	325
Leader	1962	1921	1931	1643	1633
Regulator	2616	2575	2585	2297	2287
General Governor	5232	5191	5201	4913	4903
High Overseer	601680	601639	601649	601361	601351

Occult Encyclopedia of Magic Squares

Fire - Moon

76	89	51	60	118	44	80	96	40
36	79	101	56	72	88	43	65	114
110	48	64	100	32	84	93	55	68
103	35	78	87	58	71	113	42	67
63	112	47	83	99	34	70	92	54
50	75	91	46	59	117	39	82	95
49	62	111	33	85	98	53	69	94
90	52	74	116	45	61	97	38	81
77	102	37	73	86	57	66	115	41

Earth - Moon

40	114	68	67	54	95	94	81	41
96	65	55	42	92	82	69	38	115
80	43	93	113	70	39	53	97	66
44	88	84	71	34	117	98	61	57
118	72	32	58	99	59	85	45	86
60	56	100	87	83	46	33	116	73
51	101	64	78	47	91	111	74	37
89	79	48	35	112	75	62	52	102
76	36	110	103	63	50	49	90	77

Air - Moon

41	115	66	57	86	73	37	102	77
81	38	97	61	45	116	74	52	90
94	69	53	98	85	33	111	62	49
95	82	39	117	59	46	91	75	50
54	92	70	34	99	83	47	112	63
67	42	113	71	58	87	78	35	103
68	55	93	84	32	100	64	48	110
114	65	43	88	72	56	101	79	36
40	96	80	44	118	60	51	89	76

Water - Moon

77	90	49	50	63	103	110	36	76
102	52	62	75	112	35	48	79	89
37	74	111	91	47	78	64	101	51
73	116	33	46	83	87	100	56	60
86	45	85	59	99	58	32	72	118
57	61	98	117	34	71	84	88	44
66	97	53	39	70	113	93	43	80
115	38	69	82	92	42	55	65	96
41	81	94	95	54	67	68	114	40

Occult Encyclopedia of Magic Squares

	Number	Angel Value (Arabic)	Angel Value (Hebrew)	Jinn Value (Arabic)	Jinn Value (Hebrew)
Usurper	32	351	1	73	63
Guide	118	77	87	159	149
Mystery	150	109	119	191	181
Adjuster	654	613	623	335	325
Leader	1962	1921	1931	1643	1633
Regulator	2616	2575	2585	2297	2287
General Governor	5232	5191	5201	4913	4903
High Overseer	617376	617335	617345	617057	617047

Fire - Saturn

15	33	40	78	69	116	62	54	86	101
26	90	83	74	118	99	17	59	45	43
41	46	70	117	100	85	34	22	63	76
47	72	115	102	35	81	89	30	19	64
60	114	104	39	50	73	77	87	32	18
67	24	25	92	80	56	52	42	97	119
79	61	21	28	94	49	37	98	122	65
93	82	57	16	27	44	95	121	68	51
103	36	48	55	23	31	120	66	84	88
123	96	91	53	58	20	71	75	38	29

Earth - Saturn

123	103	93	79	67	60	47	41	26	15
96	36	82	61	24	114	72	46	90	33
91	48	57	21	25	104	115	70	83	40
53	55	16	28	92	39	102	117	74	78
58	23	27	94	80	50	35	100	118	69
20	31	44	49	56	73	81	85	99	116
71	120	95	37	52	77	89	34	17	62
75	66	121	98	42	87	30	22	59	54
38	84	68	122	97	32	19	63	45	86
29	88	51	65	119	18	64	76	43	101

Air - Saturn

29	38	75	71	20	58	53	91	96	123
88	84	66	120	31	23	55	48	36	103
51	68	121	95	44	27	16	57	82	93
65	122	98	37	49	94	28	21	61	79
119	97	42	52	56	80	92	25	24	67
18	32	87	77	73	50	39	104	114	60
64	19	30	89	81	35	102	115	72	47
76	63	22	34	85	100	117	70	46	41
43	45	59	17	99	118	74	83	90	26
101	86	54	62	116	69	78	40	33	15

Water - Saturn

101	43	76	64	18	119	65	51	88	29
86	45	63	19	32	97	122	68	84	38
54	59	22	30	87	42	98	121	66	75
62	**17**	34	89	77	52	37	95	120	71
116	99	85	81	73	56	49	44	31	20
69	118	100	35	50	80	94	27	23	58
78	74	117	102	39	92	28	16	55	53
40	83	70	115	104	25	21	57	48	91
33	90	46	72	114	24	61	82	36	96
15	26	41	47	60	67	79	93	103	123

	Number	Angel Value (Arabic)	Angel Value (Hebrew)	Jinn Value (Arabic)	Jinn Value (Hebrew)
Usurper	15	334	344	56	46
Guide	123	82	92	164	154
Mystery	138	97	107	179	169
Adjuster	654	613	623	335	325
Leader	1962	1921	1931	1643	1633
Regulator	2616	2575	2585	2297	2287
General Governor	5232	5191	5201	4913	4903
High Overseer	643536	643495	643505	643217	643207

ANGEL RULING 5TH HOUSE: OEL (107)

ל	א	ו	ע
69	7	4	27
3	28	68	8
5	71	29	2

ל	א	ו	ע
ע	ו	א	ל
א	ל	ע	ו
ו	ע	ל	א

Fire - Jupiter

19	30	24	34
33	25	27	22
29	20	35	23
26	32	21	28

Air - Jupiter

28	21	32	26
23	35	20	29
22	27	25	33
34	24	30	19

Earth - Jupiter

26	29	33	19
32	20	25	30
21	35	27	24
28	23	22	34

Water - Jupiter

34	22	23	28
24	27	35	21
30	25	20	32
19	33	29	26

	Number	Angel Value (Arabic)	Angel Value (Hebrew)	Jinn Value (Arabic)	Jinn Value (Hebrew)
Usurper	19	338	348	60	50
Guide	35	354	4	76	66
Mystery	54	13	23	95	85
Adjuster	856	815	825	537	527
Leader	2568	2527	2537	2249	2239
Regulator	3424	3383	3393	3105	3095
General Governor	6848	6807	6817	6529	6519
High Overseer	239680	239639	239649	239361	239351

Fire - Mars

9	35	27	21	15
22	16	10	31	28
32	24	23	17	11
18	12	33	25	19
26	20	14	13	34

Air - Mars

26	18	32	22	9
20	12	24	16	35
14	33	23	10	27
13	25	17	31	21
34	19	11	28	15

Earth - Mars

34	13	14	20	26
19	25	33	12	18
11	17	23	24	32
28	31	10	16	22
15	21	27	35	9

Water - Mars

15	28	11	19	34
21	31	17	25	13
27	10	23	33	14
35	16	24	12	20
9	22	32	18	26

	Number	Angel Value (Arabic)	Angel Value (Hebrew)	Jinn Value (Arabic)	Jinn Value (Hebrew)
Usurper	9	328	338	50	40
Guide	35	354	4	76	66
Mystery	44	3	13	85	75
Adjuster	107	66	76	148	138
Leader	321	280	290	2	352
Regulator	428	387	397	109	99
General Governor	856	815	825	537	527
High Overseer	29960	29919	29929	29641	29631

ANGEL OF FIRST DECANATE: LOSANAHAR (351)

ר	ה	מנ	לו
35	111	8	197
7	198	34	112
109	37	199	6

ר	ה	נ	ס	ו	ל
ו	ס	ר	ל	נ	ה
נ	ל	ה	ו	ר	ס
ל	ו	ס	נ	ה	ר
ס	ר	ו	ה	ל	נ
ה	נ	ל	ר	ס	ו

Occult Encyclopedia of Magic Squares

Fire - Saturn

118	113	120
119	117	115
114	121	116

Earth - Saturn

114	119	118
121	117	113
116	115	120

Air - Saturn

116	121	114
115	117	119
120	113	118

Water - Saturn

120	115	116
113	117	121
118	119	114

	Number	Angel Value (Arabic)	Angel Value (Hebrew)	Jinn Value (Arabic)	Jinn Value (Hebrew)
Usurper	113	72	82	154	144
Guide	121	80	90	162	152
Mystery	234	193	203	275	265
Adjuster	351	310	320	32	22
Leader	1053	1012	1022	734	724
Regulator	1404	1363	1373	1085	1075
General Governor	2808	2767	2777	2489	2479
High Overseer	339768	339727	339737	339449	339439

Fire - Jupiter

80	91	85	95
94	86	88	83
90	81	96	84
87	93	82	89

Air - Jupiter

89	82	93	87
84	96	81	90
83	88	86	94
95	85	91	80

Earth - Jupiter

87	90	94	80
93	81	86	91
82	96	88	85
89	84	83	95

Water - Jupiter

95	83	84	89
85	88	96	82
91	86	81	93
80	94	90	87

	Number	Angel Value (Arabic)	Angel Value (Hebrew)	Jinn Value (Arabic)	Jinn Value (Hebrew)
Usurper	80	39	49	121	111
Guide	96	55	65	137	127
Mystery	176	135	145	217	207
Adjuster	2808	2767	2777	2489	2479
Leader	8424	8383	8393	8105	8095
Regulator	11232	11191	11201	10913	10903
General Governor	22464	22423	22433	22145	22135
High Overseer	2156544	2156503	2156513	2156225	2156215

Occult Encyclopedia of Magic Squares

Fire - Mars

58	83	76	70	64
71	65	59	79	77
80	73	72	66	60
67	61	81	74	68
75	69	63	62	82

Air - Mars

75	67	80	71	58
69	61	73	65	83
63	81	72	59	76
62	74	66	79	70
82	68	60	77	64

Earth - Mars

82	62	63	69	75
68	74	81	61	67
60	66	72	73	80
77	79	59	65	71
64	70	76	83	58

Water - Mars

64	77	60	68	82
70	79	66	74	62
76	59	72	81	63
83	65	73	61	69
58	71	80	67	75

	Number	Angel Value (Arabic)	Angel Value (Hebrew)	Jinn Value (Arabic)	Jinn Value (Hebrew)
Usurper	58	17	27	99	89
Guide	83	42	52	124	114
Mystery	141	100	110	182	172
Adjuster	351	310	320	32	22
Leader	1053	1012	1022	734	724
Regulator	1404	1363	1373	1085	1075
General Governor	2808	2767	2777	2489	2479
High Overseer	233064	233023	233033	232745	232735

Fire - Sun

41	52	72	58	62	66
47	57	68	71	45	63
53	75	61	51	67	44
64	43	54	69	48	73
70	59	50	42	74	56
76	65	46	60	55	49

Earth - Sun

76	70	64	53	47	41
65	59	43	75	57	52
46	50	54	61	68	72
60	42	69	51	71	58
55	74	48	67	45	62
49	56	73	44	63	66

Occult Encyclopedia of Magic Squares

Air - Sun

49	55	60	46	65	76
56	74	42	50	59	70
73	48	69	54	43	64
44	67	51	61	75	53
63	45	71	68	57	47
66	62	58	72	52	41

Water - Sun

66	63	44	73	56	49
62	45	67	48	74	55
58	71	51	69	42	60
72	68	61	54	50	46
52	57	75	43	59	65
41	47	53	64	70	76

	Number	Angel Value (Arabic)	Angel Value (Hebrew)	Jinn Value (Arabic)	Jinn Value (Hebrew)
Usurper	41	360	10	82	72
Guide	76	35	45	117	107
Mystery	117	76	86	158	148
Adjuster	351	310	320	32	22
Leader	1053	1012	1022	734	724
Regulator	1404	1363	1373	1085	1075
General Governor	2808	2767	2777	2489	2479
High Overseer	213408	213367	213377	213089	213079

Fire - Venus

26	67	52	37	57	71	41
72	42	27	61	53	38	58
39	59	73	43	28	62	47
63	48	33	60	74	44	29
45	30	64	49	34	54	75
55	69	46	31	65	50	35
51	36	56	70	40	32	66

Air - Venus

66	32	40	70	56	36	51
35	50	65	31	46	69	55
75	54	34	49	64	30	45
29	44	74	60	33	48	63
47	62	28	43	73	59	39
58	38	53	61	27	42	72
41	71	57	37	52	67	26

Earth - Venus

51	55	45	63	39	72	26
36	69	30	48	59	42	67
56	46	64	33	73	27	52
70	31	49	60	43	61	37
40	65	34	74	28	53	57
32	50	54	44	62	38	71
66	35	75	29	47	58	41

Water - Venus

41	58	47	29	75	35	66
71	38	62	44	54	50	32
57	53	28	74	34	65	40
37	61	43	60	49	31	70
52	27	73	33	64	46	56
67	42	59	48	30	69	36
26	72	39	63	45	55	51

Occult Encyclopedia of Magic Squares

	Number	Angel Value (Arabic)	Angel Value (Hebrew)	Jinn Value (Arabic)	Jinn Value (Hebrew)
Usurper	26	345	355	67	57
Guide	75	34	44	116	106
Mystery	101	60	70	142	132
Adjuster	351	310	320	32	22
Leader	1053	1012	1022	734	724
Regulator	1404	1363	1373	1085	1075
General Governor	2808	2767	2777	2489	2479
High Overseer	210600	210559	210569	210281	210271

Fire - Mercury

12	28	76	57	46	62	43	27
20	36	65	49	54	73	35	19
63	47	26	42	29	13	56	75
74	55	18	34	37	21	48	64
41	25	44	60	78	59	14	30
33	17	52	71	67	51	22	38
58	77	31	15	24	40	61	45
50	66	39	23	16	32	72	53

Earth - Mercury

50	58	33	41	74	63	20	12
66	77	17	25	55	47	36	28
39	31	52	44	18	26	65	76
23	15	71	60	34	42	49	57
16	24	67	78	37	29	54	46
32	40	51	59	21	13	73	62
72	61	22	14	48	56	35	43
53	45	38	30	64	75	19	27

Air - Mercury

53	72	32	16	23	39	66	50
45	61	40	24	15	31	77	58
38	22	51	67	71	52	17	33
30	14	59	78	60	44	25	41
64	48	21	37	34	18	55	74
75	56	13	29	42	26	47	63
19	35	73	54	49	65	36	20
27	43	62	46	57	76	28	12

Water - Mercury

27	19	75	64	30	38	45	53
43	35	56	48	14	22	61	72
62	73	13	21	59	51	40	32
46	54	29	37	78	67	24	16
57	49	42	34	60	71	15	23
76	65	26	18	44	52	31	39
28	36	47	55	25	17	77	66
12	20	63	74	41	33	58	50

	Number	Angel Value (Arabic)	Angel Value (Hebrew)	Jinn Value (Arabic)	Jinn Value (Hebrew)
Usurper	12	331	341	53	43
Guide	78	37	47	119	109
Mystery	90	49	59	131	121
Adjuster	351	310	320	32	22
Leader	1053	1012	1022	734	724
Regulator	1404	1363	1373	1085	1075
General Governor	2808	2767	2777	2489	2479
High Overseer	219024	218983	218993	218705	218695

ANGEL OF FIRST QUINANCE: VAHAVIAH (32)

יה	ו	ה	י
5	6	9	12
8	13	4	7
4	7	14	7

ה	י	ו	ה	ו
ו	ה	ו	ה	י
ו	ה	י	ו	ה
י	ו	ה	ו	ה
ה	ו	ה	י	ו

No Numerical Squares Available

ANGEL OF SECOND QUINANCE: YELAYEL (81)

אל	י	ל	י
9	31	13	28
12	29	8	32
29	11	30	11

ל	א	י	ל	י
י	ל	י	ל	א
י	ל	א	י	ל
א	י	ל	י	ל
ל	י	ל	א	י

Numerical Squares See Page: 104

ANGEL OF SECOND DECANATE: ZACHI (95)

י	ע	ח	ז
6	9	73	7
72	8	5	10
7	8	9	71

י	ע	ח	ז
ז	ח	ע	י
ע	י	ז	ח
ח	ז	י	ע

Occult Encyclopedia of Magic Squares

Fire - Jupiter

16	27	21	31
30	22	24	19
26	17	32	20
23	29	18	25

Air - Jupiter

25	18	29	23
20	32	17	26
19	24	22	30
31	21	27	16

Earth - Jupiter

23	26	30	16
29	17	22	27
18	32	24	21
25	20	19	31

Water - Jupiter

31	19	20	25
21	24	32	18
27	22	17	29
16	30	26	23

	Number	Angel Value (Arabic)	Angel Value (Hebrew)	Jinn Value (Arabic)	Jinn Value (Hebrew)
Usurper	16	335	345	57	47
Guide	32	351	1	73	63
Mystery	48	7	17	89	79
Adjuster	760	719	729	441	431
Leader	2280	2239	2249	1961	1951
Regulator	3040	2999	3009	2721	2711
General Governor	6080	6039	6049	5761	5751
High Overseer	194560	194519	194529	194241	194231

Fire - Mars

7	31	25	19	13
20	14	8	27	26
28	22	21	15	9
16	10	29	23	17
24	18	12	11	30

Air - Mars

24	16	28	20	7
18	10	22	14	31
12	29	21	8	25
11	23	15	27	19
30	17	9	26	13

Earth - Mars

30	11	12	18	24
17	23	29	10	16
9	15	21	22	28
26	27	8	14	20
13	19	25	31	7

Water - Mars

13	26	9	17	30
19	27	15	23	11
25	8	21	29	12
31	14	22	10	18
7	20	28	16	24

	Number	Angel Value (Arabic)	Angel Value (Hebrew)	Jinn Value (Arabic)	Jinn Value (Hebrew)
Usurper	7	326	336	48	38
Guide	31	350	360	72	62
Mystery	38	357	7	79	69
Adjuster	95	54	64	136	126
Leader	285	244	254	326	316
Regulator	380	339	349	61	51
General Governor	760	719	729	441	431
High Overseer	23560	23519	23529	23241	23231

ANGEL OF THIRD QUINANCE: SITAEL (110)

אל	ט	י	ס
59	11	12	28
11	29	58	12
9	61	30	10

ל	א	ט	י	ס
ט	י	ס	ל	א
ס	ל	א	ט	י
א	ט	י	ס	ל
י	ס	ל	א	ט

Fire - Jupiter

20	31	25	34
33	26	28	23
30	21	35	24
27	32	22	29

Air - Jupiter

29	22	32	27
24	35	21	30
23	28	26	33
34	25	31	20

Earth - Jupiter

27	30	33	20
32	21	26	31
22	35	28	25
29	24	23	34

Water - Jupiter

34	23	24	29
25	28	35	22
31	26	21	32
20	33	30	27

Occult Encyclopedia of Magic Squares

	Number	Angel Value (Arabic)	Angel Value (Hebrew)	Jinn Value (Arabic)	Jinn Value (Hebrew)
Usurper	20	339	349	61	51
Guide	35	354	4	76	66
Mystery	55	14	24	96	86
Adjuster	880	839	849	561	551
Leader	2640	2599	2609	2321	2311
Regulator	3520	3479	3489	3201	3191
General Governor	7040	6999	7009	6721	6711
High Overseer	246400	246359	246369	246081	246071

Fire - Mars

10	34	28	22	16
23	17	11	30	29
31	25	24	18	12
19	13	32	26	20
27	21	15	14	33

Air - Mars

27	19	31	23	10
21	13	25	17	34
15	32	24	11	28
14	26	18	30	22
33	20	12	29	16

Earth - Mars

33	14	15	21	27
20	26	32	13	19
12	18	24	25	31
29	30	11	17	23
16	22	28	34	10

Water - Mars

16	29	12	20	33
22	30	18	26	14
28	11	24	32	15
34	17	25	13	21
10	23	31	19	27

	Number	Angel Value (Arabic)	Angel Value (Hebrew)	Jinn Value (Arabic)	Jinn Value (Hebrew)
Usurper	10	329	339	51	41
Guide	34	353	3	75	65
Mystery	44	3	13	85	75
Adjuster	110	69	79	151	141
Leader	330	289	299	11	1
Regulator	440	399	409	121	111
General Governor	880	839	849	561	551
High Overseer	29920	29879	29889	29601	29591

ANGEL OF FOURTH QUINANCE: ELEMIAH (155)

יה	מ	ל	ע
69	31	43	12
42	13	68	32
29	71	14	41

ה	י	מ	ל	ע
מ	ל	ע	ה	י
ע	ה	י	מ	ל
י	מ	ל	ע	ה
ל	ע	ה	י	מ

Numerical Squares See Page: 267

ANGEL OF THIRD DECANATE: SAHIBER (277)

ר	יב	ה	ס
59	6	15	197
14	198	58	7
4	61	199	13

ר	ב	י	ה	ס
י	ה	ס	ר	ב
ס	ר	ב	י	ה
ב	י	ה	ס	ר
ה	ס	ר	ב	י

Fire - Jupiter

61	72	66	78
77	67	69	64
71	62	79	65
68	76	63	70

Air - Jupiter

70	63	76	68
65	79	62	71
64	69	67	77
78	66	72	61

Earth - Jupiter

68	71	77	61
76	62	67	72
63	79	69	66
70	65	64	78

Water - Jupiter

78	64	65	70
66	69	79	63
72	67	62	76
61	77	71	68

Occult Encyclopedia of Magic Squares

	Number	Angel Value (Arabic)	Angel Value (Hebrew)	Jinn Value (Arabic)	Jinn Value (Hebrew)
Usurper	61	20	30	102	92
Guide	79	38	48	120	110
Mystery	140	99	109	181	171
Adjuster	2216	2175	2185	1897	1887
Leader	6648	6607	6617	6329	6319
Regulator	8864	8823	8833	8545	8535
General Governor	17728	17687	17697	17409	17399
High Overseer	1400512	1400471	1400481	1400193	1400183

Fire - Mars

43	69	61	55	49
56	50	44	65	62
66	58	57	51	45
52	46	67	59	53
60	54	48	47	68

Air - Mars

60	52	66	56	43
54	46	58	50	69
48	67	57	44	61
47	59	51	65	55
68	53	45	62	49

Earth - Mars

68	47	48	54	60
53	59	67	46	52
45	51	57	58	66
62	65	44	50	56
49	55	61	69	43

Water - Mars

49	62	45	53	68
55	65	51	59	47
61	44	57	67	48
69	50	58	46	54
43	56	66	52	60

	Number	Angel Value (Arabic)	Angel Value (Hebrew)	Jinn Value (Arabic)	Jinn Value (Hebrew)
Usurper	43	2	12	84	74
Guide	69	28	38	110	100
Mystery	112	71	81	153	143
Adjuster	277	236	246	318	308
Leader	831	790	800	512	502
Regulator	1108	1067	1077	789	779
General Governor	2216	2175	2185	1897	1887
High Overseer	152904	152863	152873	152585	152575

291

Fire - Sun

28	39	63	45	49	53
34	44	55	62	32	50
40	66	48	38	54	31
51	30	41	56	35	64
57	46	37	29	65	43
67	52	33	47	42	36

Air - Sun

36	42	47	33	52	67
43	65	29	37	46	57
64	35	56	41	30	51
31	54	38	48	66	40
50	32	62	55	44	34
53	49	45	63	39	28

Earth - Sun

67	57	51	40	34	28
52	46	30	66	44	39
33	37	41	48	55	63
47	29	56	38	62	45
42	65	35	54	32	49
36	43	64	31	50	53

Water - Sun

53	50	31	64	43	36
49	32	54	35	65	42
45	62	38	56	29	47
63	55	48	41	37	33
39	44	66	30	46	52
28	34	40	51	57	67

	Number	Angel Value (Arabic)	Angel Value (Hebrew)	Jinn Value (Arabic)	Jinn Value (Hebrew)
Usurper	28	347	357	69	59
Guide	67	26	36	108	98
Mystery	95	54	64	136	126
Adjuster	277	236	246	318	308
Leader	831	790	800	512	502
Regulator	1108	1067	1077	789	779
General Governor	2216	2175	2185	1897	1887
High Overseer	148472	148431	148441	148153	148143

Occult Encyclopedia of Magic Squares

Fire - Venus

15	56	41	26	46	63	30
64	31	16	50	42	27	47
28	48	65	32	17	51	36
52	37	22	49	66	33	18
34	19	53	38	23	43	67
44	61	35	20	54	39	24
40	25	45	62	29	21	55

Air - Venus

55	21	29	62	45	25	40
24	39	54	20	35	61	44
67	43	23	38	53	19	34
18	33	66	49	22	37	52
36	51	17	32	65	48	28
47	27	42	50	16	31	64
30	63	46	26	41	56	15

Earth - Venus

40	44	34	52	28	64	15
25	61	19	37	48	31	56
45	35	53	22	65	16	41
62	20	38	49	32	50	26
29	54	23	66	17	42	46
21	39	43	33	51	27	63
55	24	67	18	36	47	30

Water - Venus

30	47	36	18	67	24	55
63	27	51	33	43	39	21
46	42	17	66	23	54	29
26	50	32	49	38	20	62
41	16	65	22	53	35	45
56	31	48	37	19	61	25
15	64	28	52	34	44	40

	Number	Angel Value (Arabic)	Angel Value (Hebrew)	Jinn Value (Arabic)	Jinn Value (Hebrew)
Usurper	15	334	344	56	46
Guide	67	26	36	108	98
Mystery	82	41	51	123	113
Adjuster	277	236	246	318	308
Leader	831	790	800	512	502
Regulator	1108	1067	1077	789	779
General Governor	2216	2175	2185	1897	1887
High Overseer	148472	148431	148441	148153	148143

Fire - Mercury

3	19	65	48	37	53	34	18
11	27	56	40	45	62	26	10
54	38	17	33	20	4	47	64
63	46	9	25	28	12	39	55
32	16	35	51	67	50	5	21
24	8	43	60	58	42	13	29
49	66	22	6	15	31	52	36
41	57	30	14	7	23	61	44

Earth - Mercury

41	49	24	32	63	54	11	3
57	66	8	16	46	38	27	19
30	22	43	35	9	17	56	65
14	6	60	51	25	33	40	48
7	15	58	67	28	20	45	37
23	31	42	50	12	4	62	53
61	52	13	5	39	47	26	34
44	36	29	21	55	64	10	18

Air - Mercury

44	61	23	7	14	30	57	41
36	52	31	15	6	22	66	49
29	13	42	58	60	43	8	24
21	5	50	67	51	35	16	32
55	39	12	28	25	9	46	63
64	47	4	20	33	17	38	54
10	26	62	45	40	56	27	11
18	34	53	37	48	65	19	3

Water - Mercury

18	10	64	55	21	29	36	44
34	26	47	39	5	13	52	61
53	62	4	12	50	42	31	23
37	45	20	28	67	58	15	7
48	40	33	25	51	60	6	14
65	56	17	9	35	43	22	30
19	27	38	46	16	8	66	57
3	11	54	63	32	24	49	41

	Number	Angel Value (Arabic)	Angel Value (Hebrew)	Jinn Value (Arabic)	Jinn Value (Hebrew)
Usurper	3	322	332	44	34
Guide	67	26	36	108	98
Mystery	70	29	39	111	101
Adjuster	277	236	246	318	308
Leader	831	790	800	512	502
Regulator	1108	1067	1077	789	779
General Governor	2216	2175	2185	1897	1887
High Overseer	148472	148431	148441	148153	148143

ANGEL OF FIFTH QUINANCE: MAHASHIAH (360)

יה	שׁ	ה	מ
39	6	303	12
302	13	38	7
4	41	14	301

ה	י	שׁ	ה	מ
שׁ	ה	מ	ה	י
מ	ה	י	שׁ	ה
י	שׁ	ה	מ	ה
ה	מ	ה	י	שׁ

Fire - Saturn

121	116	123
122	120	118
117	124	119

Air - Saturn

119	124	117
118	120	122
123	116	121

Earth - Saturn

117	122	121
124	120	116
119	118	123

Water - Saturn

123	118	119
116	120	124
121	122	117

	Number	Angel Value (Arabic)	Angel Value (Hebrew)	Jinn Value (Arabic)	Jinn Value (Hebrew)
Usurper	116	75	85	157	147
Guide	124	83	93	165	155
Mystery	240	199	209	281	271
Adjuster	360	319	329	41	31
Leader	1080	1039	1049	761	751
Regulator	1440	1399	1409	1121	1111
General Governor	2880	2839	2849	2561	2551
High Overseer	357120	357079	357089	356801	356791

Fire - Jupiter

82	93	87	98
97	88	90	85
92	83	99	86
89	96	84	91

Air - Jupiter

91	84	96	89
86	99	83	92
85	90	88	97
98	87	93	82

Earth - Jupiter

89	92	97	82
96	83	88	93
84	99	90	87
91	86	85	98

Water - Jupiter

98	85	86	91
87	90	99	84
93	88	83	96
82	97	92	89

	Number	Angel Value (Arabic)	Angel Value (Hebrew)	Jinn Value (Arabic)	Jinn Value (Hebrew)
Usurper	82	41	51	123	113
Guide	99	58	68	140	130
Mystery	181	140	150	222	212
Adjuster	2880	2839	2849	2561	2551
Leader	8640	8599	8609	8321	8311
Regulator	11520	11479	11489	11201	11191
General Governor	23040	22999	23009	22721	22711
High Overseer	2280960	2280919	2280929	2280641	2280631

Occult Encyclopedia of Magic Squares

Fire - Mars

60	84	78	72	66
73	67	61	80	79
81	75	74	68	62
69	63	82	76	70
77	71	65	64	83

Air - Mars

77	69	81	73	60
71	63	75	67	84
65	82	74	61	78
64	76	68	80	72
83	70	62	79	66

Earth - Mars

83	64	65	71	77
70	76	82	63	69
62	68	74	75	81
79	80	61	67	73
66	72	78	84	60

Water - Mars

66	79	62	70	83
72	80	68	76	64
78	61	74	82	65
84	67	75	63	71
60	73	81	69	77

	Number	Angel Value (Arabic)	Angel Value (Hebrew)	Jinn Value (Arabic)	Jinn Value (Hebrew)
Usurper	60	19	29	101	91
Guide	84	43	53	125	115
Mystery	144	103	113	185	175
Adjuster	360	319	329	41	31
Leader	1080	1039	1049	761	751
Regulator	1440	1399	1409	1121	1111
General Governor	2880	2839	2849	2561	2551
High Overseer	241920	241879	241889	241601	241591

Fire - Sun

42	53	76	59	63	67
48	58	69	75	46	64
54	79	62	52	68	45
65	44	55	70	49	77
71	60	51	43	78	57
80	66	47	61	56	50

Earth - Sun

80	71	65	54	48	42
66	60	44	79	58	53
47	51	55	62	69	76
61	43	70	52	75	59
56	78	49	68	46	63
50	57	77	45	64	67

Air - Sun

50	56	61	47	66	80
57	78	43	51	60	71
77	49	70	55	44	65
45	68	52	62	79	54
64	46	75	69	58	48
67	63	59	76	53	42

Water - Sun

67	64	45	77	57	50
63	46	68	49	78	56
59	75	52	70	43	61
76	69	62	55	51	47
53	58	79	44	60	66
42	48	54	65	71	80

	Number	Angel Value (Arabic)	Angel Value (Hebrew)	Jinn Value (Arabic)	Jinn Value (Hebrew)
Usurper	42	1	11	83	73
Guide	80	39	49	121	111
Mystery	122	81	91	163	153
Adjuster	360	319	329	41	31
Leader	1080	1039	1049	761	751
Regulator	1440	1399	1409	1121	1111
General Governor	2880	2839	2849	2561	2551
High Overseer	230400	230359	230369	230081	230071

Fire - Venus

27	68	53	38	58	74	42
75	43	28	62	54	39	59
40	60	76	44	29	63	48
64	49	34	61	77	45	30
46	31	65	50	35	55	78
56	72	47	32	66	51	36
52	37	57	73	41	33	67

Air - Venus

67	33	41	73	57	37	52
36	51	66	32	47	72	56
78	55	35	50	65	31	46
30	45	77	61	34	49	64
48	63	29	44	76	60	40
59	39	54	62	28	43	75
42	74	58	38	53	68	27

Earth - Venus

52	56	46	64	40	75	27
37	72	31	49	60	43	68
57	47	65	34	76	28	53
73	32	50	61	44	62	38
41	66	35	77	29	54	58
33	51	55	45	63	39	74
67	36	78	30	48	59	42

Water - Venus

42	59	48	30	78	36	67
74	39	63	45	55	51	33
58	54	29	77	35	66	41
38	62	44	61	50	32	73
53	28	76	34	65	47	57
68	43	60	49	31	72	37
27	75	40	64	46	56	52

Occult Encyclopedia of Magic Squares

	Number	Angel Value (Arabic)	Angel Value (Hebrew)	Jinn Value (Arabic)	Jinn Value (Hebrew)
Usurper	27	346	356	68	58
Guide	78	37	47	119	109
Mystery	105	64	74	146	136
Adjuster	360	319	329	41	31
Leader	1080	1039	1049	761	751
Regulator	1440	1399	1409	1121	1111
General Governor	2880	2839	2849	2561	2551
High Overseer	224640	224599	224609	224321	224311

Fire - Mercury

13	29	78	58	47	63	44	28
21	37	66	50	55	75	36	20
64	48	27	43	30	14	57	77
76	56	19	35	38	22	49	65
42	26	45	61	80	60	15	31
34	18	53	73	68	52	23	39
59	79	32	16	25	41	62	46
51	67	40	24	17	33	74	54

Earth - Mercury

51	59	34	42	76	64	21	13
67	79	18	26	56	48	37	29
40	32	53	45	19	27	66	78
24	16	73	61	35	43	50	58
17	25	68	80	38	30	55	47
33	41	52	60	22	14	75	63
74	62	23	15	49	57	36	44
54	46	39	31	65	77	20	28

Air - Mercury

54	74	33	17	24	40	67	51
46	62	41	25	16	32	79	59
39	23	52	68	73	53	18	34
31	15	60	80	61	45	26	42
65	49	22	38	35	19	56	76
77	57	14	30	43	27	48	64
20	36	75	55	50	66	37	21
28	44	63	47	58	78	29	13

Water - Mercury

28	20	77	65	31	39	46	54
44	36	57	49	15	23	62	74
63	75	14	22	60	52	41	33
47	55	30	38	80	68	25	17
58	50	43	35	61	73	16	24
78	66	27	19	45	53	32	40
29	37	48	56	26	18	79	67
13	21	64	76	42	34	59	51

	Number	Angel Value (Arabic)	Angel Value (Hebrew)	Jinn Value (Arabic)	Jinn Value (Hebrew)
Usurper	13	332	342	54	44
Guide	80	39	49	121	111
Mystery	93	52	62	134	124
Adjuster	360	319	329	41	31
Leader	1080	1039	1049	761	751
Regulator	1440	1399	1409	1121	1111
General Governor	2880	2839	2849	2561	2551
High Overseer	230400	230359	230369	230081	230071

ANGEL OF SIX QUINANCE: LELAHEL (96)

אל	ה	ל	ל
29	31	8	28
7	29	28	32
29	31	30	6

ל	א	ה	ל	ל
ה	ל	ל	ל	א
ל	ל	א	ה	ל
א	ה	ל	ל	ל
ל	ל	ל	א	ה

Occult Encyclopedia of Magic Squares

Fire - Saturn

33	28	35
34	32	30
29	36	31

Air - Saturn

31	36	29
30	32	34
35	28	33

Earth - Saturn

29	34	33
36	32	28
31	30	35

Water - Saturn

35	30	31
28	32	36
33	34	29

	Number	Angel Value (Arabic)	Angel Value (Hebrew)	Jinn Value (Arabic)	Jinn Value (Hebrew)
Usurper	28	347	357	69	59
Guide	36	355	5	77	67
Mystery	64	23	33	105	95
Adjuster	96	55	65	137	127
Leader	288	247	257	329	319
Regulator	384	343	353	65	55
General Governor	768	727	737	449	439
High Overseer	27648	27607	27617	27329	27319

Fire - Jupiter

16	27	21	32
31	22	24	19
26	17	33	20
23	30	18	25

Air - Jupiter

25	18	30	23
20	33	17	26
19	24	22	31
32	21	27	16

Earth - Jupiter

23	26	31	16
30	17	22	27
18	33	24	21
25	20	19	32

Water - Jupiter

32	19	20	25
21	24	33	18
27	22	17	30
16	31	26	23

	Number	Angel Value (Arabic)	Angel Value (Hebrew)	Jinn Value (Arabic)	Jinn Value (Hebrew)
Usurper	16	335	345	57	47
Guide	33	352	2	74	64
Mystery	49	8	18	90	80
Adjuster	768	727	737	449	439
Leader	2304	2263	2273	1985	1975
Regulator	3072	3031	3041	2753	2743
General Governor	6144	6103	6113	5825	5815
High Overseer	202752	202711	202721	202433	202423

Fire - Mars

7	32	25	19	13
20	14	8	28	26
29	22	21	15	9
16	10	30	23	17
24	18	12	11	31

Air - Mars

24	16	29	20	7
18	10	22	14	32
12	30	21	8	25
11	23	15	28	19
31	17	9	26	13

Earth - Mars

31	11	12	18	24
17	23	30	10	16
9	15	21	22	29
26	28	8	14	20
13	19	25	32	7

Water - Mars

13	26	9	17	31
19	28	15	23	11
25	8	21	30	12
32	14	22	10	18
7	20	29	16	24

	Number	Angel Value (Arabic)	Angel Value (Hebrew)	Jinn Value (Arabic)	Jinn Value (Hebrew)
Usurper	7	326	336	48	38
Guide	32	351	1	73	63
Mystery	39	358	8	80	70
Adjuster	96	55	65	137	127
Leader	288	247	257	329	319
Regulator	384	343	353	65	55
General Governor	768	727	737	449	439
High Overseer	24576	24535	24545	24257	24247

VIRGO

SIGN VIRGO: BETULAH (443)

ה	ל	ו	בת
401	7	33	2
32	3	400	8
5	403	4	31

ה	ל	ו	ת	ב	ל
ו	ת	ב	ה	ל	ה
ב	ה	ל	ו	ת	ס
ל	ו	ת	ב	ה	ר
ת	ב	ה	ל	ו	נ
ה	נ	ל	ר	ס	ו

Fire - Jupiter

103	114	108	118
117	109	111	106
113	104	119	107
110	116	105	112

Air - Jupiter

112	105	116	110
107	119	104	113
106	111	109	117
118	108	114	103

Earth - Jupiter

110	113	117	103
116	104	109	114
105	119	111	108
112	107	106	118

Water - Jupiter

118	106	107	112
108	111	119	105
114	109	104	116
103	117	113	110

	Number	Angel Value (Arabic)	Angel Value (Hebrew)	Jinn Value (Arabic)	Jinn Value (Hebrew)
Usurper	103	62	72	144	134
Guide	119	78	88	160	150
Mystery	222	181	191	263	253
Adjuster	3544	3503	3513	3225	3215
Leader	10632	10591	10601	10313	10303
Regulator	14176	14135	14145	13857	13847
General Governor	28352	28311	28321	28033	28023
High Overseer	3373888	3373847	3373857	3373569	3373559

Fire - Mars

76	103	94	88	82
89	83	77	99	95
100	91	90	84	78
85	79	101	92	86
93	87	81	80	102

Air - Mars

93	85	100	89	76
87	79	91	83	103
81	101	90	77	94
80	92	84	99	88
102	86	78	95	82

Earth - Mars

102	80	81	87	93
86	92	101	79	85
78	84	90	91	100
95	99	77	83	89
82	88	94	103	76

Water - Mars

82	95	78	86	102
88	99	84	92	80
94	77	90	101	81
103	83	91	79	87
76	89	100	85	93

	Number	Angel Value (Arabic)	Angel Value (Hebrew)	Jinn Value (Arabic)	Jinn Value (Hebrew)
Usurper	76	35	45	117	107
Guide	103	62	72	144	134
Mystery	179	138	148	220	210
Adjuster	443	402	412	124	114
Leader	1329	1288	1298	1010	1000
Regulator	1772	1731	1741	1453	1443
General Governor	3544	3503	3513	3225	3215
High Overseer	365032	364991	365001	364713	364703

Occult Encyclopedia of Magic Squares

Fire - Sun

56	67	89	73	77	81
62	72	83	88	60	78
68	92	76	66	82	59
79	58	69	84	63	90
85	74	65	57	91	71
93	80	61	75	70	64

Air - Sun

64	70	75	61	80	93
71	91	57	65	74	85
90	63	84	69	58	79
59	82	66	76	92	68
78	60	88	83	72	62
81	77	73	89	67	56

Earth - Sun

93	85	79	68	62	56
80	74	58	92	72	67
61	65	69	76	83	89
75	57	84	66	88	73
70	91	63	82	60	77
64	71	90	59	78	81

Water - Sun

81	78	59	90	71	64
77	60	82	63	91	70
73	88	66	84	57	75
89	83	76	69	65	61
67	72	92	58	74	80
56	62	68	79	85	93

	Number	Angel Value (Arabic)	Angel Value (Hebrew)	Jinn Value (Arabic)	Jinn Value (Hebrew)
Usurper	56	15	25	97	87
Guide	93	52	62	134	124
Mystery	149	108	118	190	180
Adjuster	443	402	412	124	114
Leader	1329	1288	1298	1010	1000
Regulator	1772	1731	1741	1453	1443
General Governor	3544	3503	3513	3225	3215
High Overseer	329592	329551	329561	329273	329263

Fire - Venus

39	80	65	50	70	85	54
86	55	40	74	66	51	71
52	72	87	56	41	75	60
76	61	46	73	88	57	42
58	43	77	62	47	67	89
68	83	59	44	78	63	48
64	49	69	84	53	45	79

Earth - Venus

64	68	58	76	52	86	39
49	83	43	61	72	55	80
69	59	77	46	87	40	65
84	44	62	73	56	74	50
53	78	47	88	41	66	70
45	63	67	57	75	51	85
79	48	89	42	60	71	54

Occult Encyclopedia of Magic Squares

Air - Venus

79	45	53	84	69	49	64
48	63	78	44	59	83	68
89	67	47	62	77	43	58
42	57	88	73	46	61	76
60	75	41	56	87	72	52
71	51	66	74	40	55	86
54	85	70	50	65	80	39

Water - Venus

54	71	60	42	89	48	79
85	51	75	57	67	63	45
70	66	41	88	47	78	53
50	74	56	73	62	44	84
65	40	87	46	77	59	69
80	55	72	61	43	83	49
39	86	52	76	58	68	64

	Number	Angel Value (Arabic)	Angel Value (Hebrew)	Jinn Value (Arabic)	Jinn Value (Hebrew)
Usurper	39	358	8	80	70
Guide	89	48	58	130	120
Mystery	128	87	97	169	159
Adjuster	443	402	412	124	114
Leader	1329	1288	1298	1010	1000
Regulator	1772	1731	1741	1453	1443
General Governor	3544	3503	3513	3225	3215
High Overseer	315416	315375	315385	315097	315087

Fire - Mercury

23	39	91	68	57	73	54	38
31	47	76	60	65	88	46	30
74	58	37	53	40	24	67	90
89	66	29	45	48	32	59	75
52	36	55	71	93	70	25	41
44	28	63	86	78	62	33	49
69	92	42	26	35	51	72	56
61	77	50	34	27	43	87	64

Earth - Mercury

61	69	44	52	89	74	31	23
77	92	28	36	66	58	47	39
50	42	63	55	29	37	76	91
34	26	86	71	45	53	60	68
27	35	78	93	48	40	65	57
43	51	62	70	32	24	88	73
87	72	33	25	59	67	46	54
64	56	49	41	75	90	30	38

Air - Mercury

64	87	43	27	34	50	77	61
56	72	51	35	26	42	92	69
49	33	62	78	86	63	28	44
41	25	70	93	71	55	36	52
75	59	32	48	45	29	66	89
90	67	24	40	53	37	58	74
30	46	88	65	60	76	47	31
38	54	73	57	68	91	39	23

Water - Mercury

38	30	90	75	41	49	56	64
54	46	67	59	25	33	72	87
73	88	24	32	70	62	51	43
57	65	40	48	93	78	35	27
68	60	53	45	71	86	26	34
91	76	37	29	55	63	42	50
39	47	58	66	36	28	92	77
23	31	74	89	52	44	69	61

Occult Encyclopedia of Magic Squares

	Number	Angel Value (Arabic)	Angel Value (Hebrew)	Jinn Value (Arabic)	Jinn Value (Hebrew)
Usurper	23	342	352	64	54
Guide	93	52	62	134	124
Mystery	116	75	85	157	147
Adjuster	443	402	412	124	114
Leader	1329	1288	1298	1010	1000
Regulator	1772	1731	1741	1453	1443
General Governor	3544	3503	3513	3225	3215
High Overseer	329592	329551	329561	329273	329263

Fire - Moon

53	66	28	37	91	21	57	73	17
13	56	78	33	49	65	20	42	87
83	25	41	77	9	61	70	32	45
80	12	55	64	35	48	86	19	44
40	85	24	60	76	11	47	69	31
27	52	68	23	36	90	16	59	72
26	39	84	10	62	75	30	46	71
67	29	51	89	22	38	74	15	58
54	79	14	50	63	34	43	88	18

Earth - Moon

17	87	45	44	31	72	71	58	18
73	42	32	19	69	59	46	15	88
57	20	70	86	47	16	30	74	43
21	65	61	48	11	90	75	38	34
91	49	9	35	76	36	62	22	63
37	33	77	64	60	23	10	89	50
28	78	41	55	24	68	84	51	14
66	56	25	12	85	52	39	29	79
53	13	83	80	40	27	26	67	54

Air - Moon

18	88	43	34	63	50	14	79	54
58	15	74	38	22	89	51	29	67
71	46	30	75	62	10	84	39	26
72	59	16	90	36	23	68	52	27
31	69	47	11	76	60	24	85	40
44	19	86	48	35	64	55	12	80
45	32	70	61	9	77	41	25	83
87	42	20	65	49	33	78	56	13
17	73	57	21	91	37	28	66	53

Water - Moon

54	67	26	27	40	80	83	13	53
79	29	39	52	85	12	25	56	66
14	51	84	68	24	55	41	78	28
50	89	10	23	60	64	77	33	37
63	22	62	36	76	35	9	49	91
34	38	75	90	11	48	61	65	21
43	74	30	16	47	86	70	20	57
88	15	46	59	69	19	32	42	73
18	58	71	72	31	44	45	87	17

	Number	Angel Value (Arabic)	Angel Value (Hebrew)	Jinn Value (Arabic)	Jinn Value (Hebrew)
Usurper	9	328	338	50	40
Guide	91	50	60	132	122
Mystery	100	59	69	141	131
Adjuster	443	402	412	124	114
Leader	1329	1288	1298	1010	1000
Regulator	1772	1731	1741	1453	1443
General Governor	3544	3503	3513	3225	3215
High Overseer	322504	322463	322473	322185	322175

ARCHANGEL OF VIRGO: HAMALIEL (116)

אל	י	ל	הם
44	31	13	28
12	29	43	32
29	46	30	11

ל	א	י	ל	מ	ה
מ	ל	ל	ה	י	א
י	ה	א	מ	ל	ל
ה	מ	ל	י	א	ל
ל	ל	מ	א	ה	י
א	י	ה	ל	ל	מ

Fire - Jupiter

21	32	26	37
36	27	29	24
31	22	38	25
28	35	23	30

Air - Jupiter

30	23	35	28
25	38	22	31
24	29	27	36
37	26	32	21

Earth - Jupiter

28	31	36	21
35	22	27	32
23	38	29	26
30	25	24	37

Water - Jupiter

37	24	25	30
26	29	38	23
32	27	22	35
21	36	31	28

	Number	Angel Value (Arabic)	Angel Value (Hebrew)	Jinn Value (Arabic)	Jinn Value (Hebrew)
Usurper	21	340	350	62	52
Guide	38	357	7	79	69
Mystery	59	18	28	100	90
Adjuster	928	887	897	609	599
Leader	2784	2743	2753	2465	2455
Regulator	3712	3671	3681	3393	3383
General Governor	7424	7383	7393	7105	7095
High Overseer	282112	282071	282081	281793	281783

Fire - Mars

11	36	29	23	17
24	18	12	32	30
33	26	25	19	13
20	14	34	27	21
28	22	16	15	35

Air - Mars

28	20	33	24	11
22	14	26	18	36
16	34	25	12	29
15	27	19	32	23
35	21	13	30	17

Earth - Mars

35	15	16	22	28
21	27	34	14	20
13	19	25	26	33
30	32	12	18	24
17	23	29	36	11

Water - Mars

17	30	13	21	35
23	32	19	27	15
29	12	25	34	16
36	18	26	14	22
11	24	33	20	28

	Number	Angel Value (Arabic)	Angel Value (Hebrew)	Jinn Value (Arabic)	Jinn Value (Hebrew)
Usurper	11	330	340	52	42
Guide	36	355	5	77	67
Mystery	47	6	16	88	78
Adjuster	116	75	85	157	147
Leader	348	307	317	29	19
Regulator	464	423	433	145	135
General Governor	928	887	897	609	599
High Overseer	33408	33367	33377	33089	33079

Fire - Sun

1	12	37	18	22	26
7	17	28	36	5	23
13	40	21	11	27	4
24	3	14	29	8	38
30	19	10	2	39	16
41	25	6	20	15	9

Earth - Sun

41	30	24	13	7	1
25	19	3	40	17	12
6	10	14	21	28	37
20	2	29	11	36	18
15	39	8	27	5	22
9	16	38	4	23	26

Air - Sun

9	15	20	6	25	41
16	39	2	10	19	30
38	8	29	14	3	24
4	27	11	21	40	13
23	5	36	28	17	7
26	22	18	37	12	1

Water - Sun

26	23	4	38	16	9
22	5	27	8	39	15
18	36	11	29	2	20
37	28	21	14	10	6
12	17	40	3	19	25
1	7	13	24	30	41

ANGEL OF VIRGO: SHELATHIEL (771)

יאל	ת	ל	ש
299	31	403	38
402	39	298	32
29	301	40	401

ל	א	י	ת	ל	ש
ל	ת	ל	ש	י	א
י	ש	א	ל	ל	ת
ש	ל	ת	י	א	ל
ת	ל	ל	א	ש	י
א	י	ש	ל	ת	ל

Fire - Saturn

258	253	260
259	257	255
254	261	256

Earth - Saturn

254	259	258
261	257	253
256	255	260

Air - Saturn

256	261	254
255	257	259
260	253	258

Water - Saturn

260	255	256
253	257	261
258	259	254

	Number	Angel Value (Arabic)	Angel Value (Hebrew)	Jinn Value (Arabic)	Jinn Value (Hebrew)
Usurper	253	212	222	294	284
Guide	261	220	230	302	292
Mystery	514	473	483	195	185
Adjuster	771	730	740	452	442
Leader	2313	2272	2282	1994	1984
Regulator	3084	3043	3053	2765	2755
General Governor	6168	6127	6137	5849	5839
High Overseer	1609848	1609807	1609817	1609529	1609519

Occult Encyclopedia of Magic Squares

Fire - Jupiter

185	196	190	200
199	191	193	188
195	186	201	189
192	198	187	194

Air - Jupiter

194	187	198	192
189	201	186	195
188	193	191	199
200	190	196	185

Earth - Jupiter

192	195	199	185
198	186	191	196
187	201	193	190
194	189	188	200

Water - Jupiter

200	188	189	194
190	193	201	187
196	191	186	198
185	199	195	192

	Number	Angel Value (Arabic)	Angel Value (Hebrew)	Jinn Value (Arabic)	Jinn Value (Hebrew)
Usurper	185	144	154	226	216
Guide	201	160	170	242	232
Mystery	386	345	355	67	57
Adjuster	6168	6127	6137	5849	5839
Leader	18504	18463	18473	18185	18175
Regulator	24672	24631	24641	24353	24343
General Governor	49344	49303	49313	49025	49015
High Overseer	9918144	9918103	9918113	9917825	9917815

Fire - Mars

142	167	160	154	148
155	149	143	163	161
164	157	156	150	144
151	145	165	158	152
159	153	147	146	166

Air - Mars

159	151	164	155	142
153	145	157	149	167
147	165	156	143	160
146	158	150	163	154
166	152	144	161	148

Earth - Mars

166	146	147	153	159
152	158	165	145	151
144	150	156	157	164
161	163	143	149	155
148	154	160	167	142

Water - Mars

148	161	144	152	166
154	163	150	158	146
160	143	156	165	147
167	149	157	145	153
142	155	164	151	159

	Number	Angel Value (Arabic)	Angel Value (Hebrew)	Jinn Value (Arabic)	Jinn Value (Hebrew)
Usurper	142	101	111	183	173
Guide	167	126	136	208	198
Mystery	309	268	278	350	340
Adjuster	771	730	740	452	442
Leader	2313	2272	2282	1994	1984
Regulator	3084	3043	3053	2765	2755
General Governor	6168	6127	6137	5849	5839
High Overseer	1030056	1030015	1030025	1029737	1029727

Fire - Sun

111	122	142	128	132	136
117	127	138	141	115	133
123	145	131	121	137	114
134	113	124	139	118	143
140	129	120	112	144	126
146	135	116	130	125	119

Air - Sun

119	125	130	116	135	146
126	144	112	120	129	140
143	118	139	124	113	134
114	137	121	131	145	123
133	115	141	138	127	117
136	132	128	142	122	111

Earth - Sun

146	140	134	123	117	111
135	129	113	145	127	122
116	120	124	131	138	142
130	112	139	121	141	128
125	144	118	137	115	132
119	126	143	114	133	136

Water - Sun

136	133	114	143	126	119
132	115	137	118	144	125
128	141	121	139	112	130
142	138	131	124	120	116
122	127	145	113	129	135
111	117	123	134	140	146

	Number	Angel Value (Arabic)	Angel Value (Hebrew)	Jinn Value (Arabic)	Jinn Value (Hebrew)
Usurper	111	70	80	152	142
Guide	146	105	115	187	177
Mystery	257	216	226	298	288
Adjuster	771	730	740	452	442
Leader	2313	2272	2282	1994	1984
Regulator	3084	3043	3053	2765	2755
General Governor	6168	6127	6137	5849	5839
High Overseer	900528	900487	900497	900209	900199

Fire - Venus

86	127	112	97	117	131	101
132	102	87	121	113	98	118
99	119	133	103	88	122	107
123	108	93	120	134	104	89
105	90	124	109	94	114	135
115	129	106	91	125	110	95
111	96	116	130	100	92	126

Earth - Venus

111	115	105	123	99	132	86
96	129	90	108	119	102	127
116	106	124	93	133	87	112
130	91	109	120	103	121	97
100	125	94	134	88	113	117
92	110	114	104	122	98	131
126	95	135	89	107	118	101

Air - Venus

126	92	100	130	116	96	111
95	110	125	91	106	129	115
135	114	94	109	124	90	105
89	104	134	120	93	108	123
107	122	88	103	133	119	99
118	98	113	121	87	102	132
101	131	117	97	112	127	86

Water - Venus

101	118	107	89	135	95	126
131	98	122	104	114	110	92
117	113	88	134	94	125	100
97	121	103	120	109	91	130
112	87	133	93	124	106	116
127	102	119	108	90	129	96
86	132	99	123	105	115	111

	Number	Angel Value (Arabic)	Angel Value (Hebrew)	Jinn Value (Arabic)	Jinn Value (Hebrew)
Usurper	86	45	55	127	117
Guide	135	94	104	176	166
Mystery	221	180	190	262	252
Adjuster	771	730	740	452	442
Leader	2313	2272	2282	1994	1984
Regulator	3084	3043	3053	2765	2755
General Governor	6168	6127	6137	5849	5839
High Overseer	832680	832639	832649	832361	832351

Fire - Mercury

64	80	132	109	98	114	95	79
72	88	117	101	106	129	87	71
115	99	78	94	81	65	108	131
130	107	70	86	89	73	100	116
93	77	96	112	134	111	66	82
85	69	104	127	119	103	74	90
110	133	83	67	76	92	113	97
102	118	91	75	68	84	128	105

Earth - Mercury

102	110	85	93	130	115	72	64
118	133	69	77	107	99	88	80
91	83	104	96	70	78	117	132
75	67	127	112	86	94	101	109
68	76	119	134	89	81	106	98
84	92	103	111	73	65	129	114
128	113	74	66	100	108	87	95
105	97	90	82	116	131	71	79

Occult Encyclopedia of Magic Squares

Air - Mercury

105	128	84	68	75	91	118	102
97	113	92	76	67	83	133	110
90	74	103	119	127	104	69	85
82	66	111	134	112	96	77	93
116	100	73	89	86	70	107	130
131	108	65	81	94	78	99	115
71	87	129	106	101	117	88	72
79	95	114	98	109	132	80	64

Water - Mercury

79	71	131	116	82	90	97	105
95	87	108	100	66	74	113	128
114	129	65	73	111	103	92	84
98	106	81	89	134	119	76	68
109	101	94	86	112	127	67	75
132	117	78	70	96	104	83	91
80	88	99	107	77	69	133	118
64	72	115	130	93	85	110	102

	Number	Angel Value (Arabic)	Angel Value (Hebrew)	Jinn Value (Arabic)	Jinn Value (Hebrew)
Usurper	64	23	33	105	95
Guide	134	93	103	175	165
Mystery	198	157	167	239	229
Adjuster	771	730	740	452	442
Leader	2313	2272	2282	1994	1984
Regulator	3084	3043	3053	2765	2755
General Governor	6168	6127	6137	5849	5839
High Overseer	826512	826471	826481	826193	826183

Fire - Moon

89	102	64	73	131	57	93	109	53
49	92	114	69	85	101	56	78	127
123	61	77	113	45	97	106	68	81
116	48	91	100	71	84	126	55	80
76	125	60	96	112	47	83	105	67
63	88	104	59	72	130	52	95	108
62	75	124	46	98	111	66	82	107
103	65	87	129	58	74	110	51	94
90	115	50	86	99	70	79	128	54

Earth - Moon

53	127	81	80	67	108	107	94	54
109	78	68	55	105	95	82	51	128
93	56	106	126	83	52	66	110	79
57	101	97	84	47	130	111	74	70
131	85	45	71	112	72	98	58	99
73	69	113	100	96	59	46	129	86
64	114	77	91	60	104	124	87	50
102	92	61	48	125	88	75	65	115
89	49	123	116	76	63	62	103	90

Air - Moon

54	128	79	70	99	86	50	115	90
94	51	110	74	58	129	87	65	103
107	82	66	111	98	46	124	75	62
108	95	52	130	72	59	104	88	63
67	105	83	47	112	96	60	125	76
80	55	126	84	71	100	91	48	116
81	68	106	97	45	113	77	61	123
127	78	56	101	85	69	114	92	49
53	109	93	57	131	73	64	102	89

Occult Encyclopedia of Magic Squares

Water - Moon

90	103	62	63	76	116	123	49	89
115	65	75	88	125	48	61	92	102
50	87	124	104	60	91	77	114	64
86	129	46	59	96	100	113	69	73
99	58	98	72	112	71	45	85	131
70	74	111	130	47	84	97	101	57
79	110	66	52	83	126	106	56	93
128	51	82	95	105	55	68	78	109
54	94	107	108	67	80	81	127	53

	Number	Angel Value (Arabic)	Angel Value (Hebrew)	Jinn Value (Arabic)	Jinn Value (Hebrew)
Usurper	45	4	14	86	76
Guide	131	90	100	172	162
Mystery	176	135	145	217	207
Adjuster	771	730	740	452	442
Leader	2313	2272	2282	1994	1984
Regulator	3084	3043	3053	2765	2755
General Governor	6168	6127	6137	5849	5839
High Overseer	808008	807967	807977	807689	807679

Fire - Saturn

27	45	52	90	81	125	74	66	98	113
38	102	95	86	127	111	29	71	57	55
53	58	82	126	112	97	46	34	75	88
59	84	124	114	47	93	101	42	31	76
72	123	116	51	62	85	89	99	44	30
79	36	37	104	92	68	64	54	109	128
91	73	33	40	106	61	49	110	131	77
105	94	69	28	39	56	107	130	80	63
115	48	60	67	35	43	129	78	96	100
132	108	103	65	70	32	83	87	50	41

Earth - Saturn

132	115	105	91	79	72	59	53	38	27
108	48	94	73	36	123	84	58	102	45
103	60	69	33	37	116	124	82	95	52
65	67	28	40	104	51	114	126	86	90
70	35	39	106	92	62	47	112	127	81
32	43	56	61	68	85	93	97	111	125
83	129	107	49	64	89	101	46	29	74
87	78	130	110	54	99	42	34	71	66
50	96	80	131	109	44	31	75	57	98
41	100	63	77	128	30	76	88	55	113

Air - Saturn

41	50	87	83	32	70	65	103	108	132
100	96	78	129	43	35	67	60	48	115
63	80	130	107	56	39	28	69	94	105
77	131	110	49	61	106	40	33	73	91
128	109	54	64	68	92	104	37	36	79
30	44	99	89	85	62	51	116	123	72
76	31	42	101	93	47	114	124	84	59
88	75	34	46	97	112	126	82	58	53
55	57	71	29	111	127	86	95	102	38
113	98	66	74	125	81	90	52	45	27

Water - Saturn

113	55	88	76	30	128	77	63	100	41
98	57	75	31	44	109	131	80	96	50
66	71	34	42	99	54	110	130	78	87
74	**29**	46	101	89	64	49	107	129	83
125	111	97	93	85	68	61	56	43	32
81	127	112	47	62	92	106	39	35	70
90	86	126	114	51	104	40	28	67	65
52	95	82	124	116	37	33	69	60	103
45	102	58	84	123	36	73	94	48	108
27	38	53	59	72	79	91	105	115	132

	Number	Angel Value (Arabic)	Angel Value (Hebrew)	Jinn Value (Arabic)	Jinn Value (Hebrew)
Usurper	27	346	356	68	58
Guide	132	91	101	173	163
Mystery	159	118	128	200	190
Adjuster	771	730	740	452	442
Leader	2313	2272	2282	1994	1984
Regulator	3084	3043	3053	2765	2755
General Governor	6168	6127	6137	5849	5839
High Overseer	814176	814135	814145	813857	813847

LORD OF TRIPLICITY BY DAY: LASLARA (321)

א‏ר	ל	מ	ל
29	61	33	198
32	199	28	62
59	31	200	31

א	ר	ל	מ	ל
ל	מ	ל	א	ר
ל	א	ר	ל	מ
ר	ל	מ	ל	א
מ	ל	א	ר	ל

Numerical Squares See Page: 241

LORD OF TRIPLICITY BY NIGHT: SASIA (131)

א	י	מ	מ
61	59	2	9
58	58	12	3
11	4	57	59

א	י	מ	מ
מ	מ	י	א
י	א	מ	מ
מ	מ	א	י

Occult Encyclopedia of Magic Squares

Fire - Jupiter

25	36	30	40
39	31	33	28
35	26	41	29
32	38	27	34

Air - Jupiter

34	27	38	32
29	41	26	35
28	33	31	39
40	30	36	25

Earth - Jupiter

32	35	39	25
38	26	31	36
27	41	33	30
34	29	28	40

Water - Jupiter

40	28	29	34
30	33	41	27
36	31	26	38
25	39	35	32

	Number	Angel Value (Arabic)	Angel Value (Hebrew)	Jinn Value (Arabic)	Jinn Value (Hebrew)
Usurper	25	344	354	66	56
Guide	41	360	10	82	72
Mystery	66	25	35	107	97
Adjuster	1048	1007	1017	729	719
Leader	3144	3103	3113	2825	2815
Regulator	4192	4151	4161	3873	3863
General Governor	8384	8343	8353	8065	8055
High Overseer	343744	343703	343713	343425	343415

Fire - Mars

14	39	32	26	20
27	21	15	35	33
36	29	28	22	16
23	17	37	30	24
31	25	19	18	38

Air - Mars

31	23	36	27	14
25	17	29	21	39
19	37	28	15	32
18	30	22	35	26
38	24	16	33	20

Earth - Mars

38	18	19	25	31
24	30	37	17	23
16	22	28	29	36
33	35	15	21	27
20	26	32	39	14

Water - Mars

20	33	16	24	38
26	35	22	30	18
32	15	28	37	19
39	21	29	17	25
14	27	36	23	31

Occult Encyclopedia of Magic Squares

	Number	Angel Value (Arabic)	Angel Value (Hebrew)	Jinn Value (Arabic)	Jinn Value (Hebrew)
Usurper	14	333	343	55	45
Guide	39	358	8	80	70
Mystery	53	12	22	94	84
Adjuster	131	90	100	172	162
Leader	393	352	362	74	64
Regulator	524	483	493	205	195
General Governor	1048	1007	1017	729	719
High Overseer	40872	40831	40841	40553	40543

Fire - Sun

4	15	37	21	25	29
10	20	31	36	8	26
16	40	24	14	30	7
27	6	17	32	11	38
33	22	13	5	39	19
41	28	9	23	18	12

Air - Sun

12	18	23	9	28	41
19	39	5	13	22	33
38	11	32	17	6	27
7	30	14	24	40	16
26	8	36	31	20	10
29	25	21	37	15	4

Earth - Sun

41	33	27	16	10	4
28	22	6	40	20	15
9	13	17	24	31	37
23	5	32	14	36	21
18	39	11	30	8	25
12	19	38	7	26	29

Water - Sun

29	26	7	38	19	12
25	8	30	11	39	18
21	36	14	32	5	23
37	31	24	17	13	9
15	20	40	6	22	28
4	10	16	27	33	41

	Number	Angel Value (Arabic)	Angel Value (Hebrew)	Jinn Value (Arabic)	Jinn Value (Hebrew)
Usurper	4	323	333	45	35
Guide	41	360	10	82	72
Mystery	45	4	14	86	76
Adjuster	131	90	100	172	162
Leader	393	352	362	74	64
Regulator	524	483	493	205	195
General Governor	1048	1007	1017	729	719
High Overseer	42968	42927	42937	42649	42639

ANGEL RULING 6ᵀᴴ HOUSE: VEYEL (47)

ל	א	י	ו
5	11	4	27
3	28	4	12
9	7	29	2

ל	א	י	ו
ו	י	א	ל
א	ל	ו	י
י	ו	ל	א

Fire - Jupiter

4	15	9	19
18	10	12	7
14	5	20	8
11	17	6	13

Air - Jupiter

13	6	17	11
8	20	5	14
7	12	10	18
19	9	15	4

Earth - Jupiter

11	14	18	4
17	5	10	15
6	20	12	9
13	8	7	19

Water - Jupiter

19	7	8	13
9	12	20	6
15	10	5	17
4	18	14	11

	Number	Angel Value (Arabic)	Angel Value (Hebrew)	Jinn Value (Arabic)	Jinn Value (Hebrew)
Usurper	4	323	333	45	35
Guide	20	339	349	61	51
Mystery	24	343	353	65	55
Adjuster	376	335	345	57	47
Leader	1128	1087	1097	809	799
Regulator	1504	1463	1473	1185	1175
General Governor	3008	2967	2977	2689	2679
High Overseer	60160	60119	60129	59841	59831

ANGEL OF FIRST DECANATE: ANANAURAH (313)

ה	ור	נא	אנ
50	52	209	2
208	3	49	53
50	52	4	207

ה	ר	ו	א	נ	נ	א
ו	א	נ	נ	א	ה	ר
נ	נ	א	ה	ר	ו	א
א	ה	ר	ו	א	נ	נ
ר	ו	א	נ	נ	א	ה
א	נ	נ	א	ה	ר	ו
נ	א	ה	ר	ו	א	נ

Fire - Jupiter

70	81	75	87
86	76	78	73
80	71	88	74
77	85	72	79

Air - Jupiter

79	72	85	77
74	88	71	80
73	78	76	86
87	75	81	70

Earth - Jupiter

77	80	86	70
85	71	76	81
72	88	78	75
79	74	73	87

Water - Jupiter

87	73	74	79
75	78	88	72
81	76	71	85
70	86	80	77

Occult Encyclopedia of Magic Squares

	Number	Angel Value (Arabic)	Angel Value (Hebrew)	Jinn Value (Arabic)	Jinn Value (Hebrew)
Usurper	70	29	39	111	101
Guide	88	47	57	129	119
Mystery	158	117	127	199	189
Adjuster	2504	2463	2473	2185	2175
Leader	7512	7471	7481	7193	7183
Regulator	10016	9975	9985	9697	9687
General Governor	20032	19991	20001	19713	19703
High Overseer	1762816	1762775	1762785	1762497	1762487

Fire - Mars

50	77	68	62	56
63	57	51	73	69
74	65	64	58	52
59	53	75	66	60
67	61	55	54	76

Air - Mars

67	59	74	63	50
61	53	65	57	77
55	75	64	51	68
54	66	58	73	62
76	60	52	69	56

Earth - Mars

76	54	55	61	67
60	66	75	53	59
52	58	64	65	74
69	73	51	57	63
56	62	68	77	50

Water - Mars

56	69	52	60	76
62	73	58	66	54
68	51	64	75	55
77	57	65	53	61
50	63	74	59	67

	Number	Angel Value (Arabic)	Angel Value (Hebrew)	Jinn Value (Arabic)	Jinn Value (Hebrew)
Usurper	50	9	19	91	81
Guide	77	36	46	118	108
Mystery	127	86	96	168	158
Adjuster	313	272	282	354	344
Leader	939	898	908	620	610
Regulator	1252	1211	1221	933	923
General Governor	2504	2463	2473	2185	2175
High Overseer	192808	192767	192777	192489	192479

Occult Encyclopedia of Magic Squares

Fire - Sun

34	45	69	51	55	59
40	50	61	68	38	56
46	72	54	44	60	37
57	36	47	62	41	70
63	52	43	35	71	49
73	58	39	53	48	42

Air - Sun

42	48	53	39	58	73
49	71	35	43	52	63
70	41	62	47	36	57
37	60	44	54	72	46
56	38	68	61	50	40
59	55	51	69	45	34

Earth - Sun

73	63	57	46	40	34
58	52	36	72	50	45
39	43	47	54	61	69
53	35	62	44	68	51
48	71	41	60	38	55
42	49	70	37	56	59

Water - Sun

59	56	37	70	49	42
55	38	60	41	71	48
51	68	44	62	35	53
69	61	54	47	43	39
45	50	72	36	52	58
34	40	46	57	63	73

	Number	Angel Value (Arabic)	Angel Value (Hebrew)	Jinn Value (Arabic)	Jinn Value (Hebrew)
Usurper	34	353	3	75	65
Guide	73	32	42	114	104
Mystery	107	66	76	148	138
Adjuster	313	272	282	354	344
Leader	939	898	908	620	610
Regulator	1252	1211	1221	933	923
General Governor	2504	2463	2473	2185	2175
High Overseer	182792	182751	182761	182473	182463

Fire - Venus

20	61	46	31	51	69	35
70	36	21	55	47	32	52
33	53	71	37	22	56	41
57	42	27	54	72	38	23
39	24	58	43	28	48	73
49	67	40	25	59	44	29
45	30	50	68	34	26	60

Earth - Venus

45	49	39	57	33	70	20
30	67	24	42	53	36	61
50	40	58	27	71	21	46
68	25	43	54	37	55	31
34	59	28	72	22	47	51
26	44	48	38	56	32	69
60	29	73	23	41	52	35

Air - Venus

60	26	34	68	50	30	45
29	44	59	25	40	67	49
73	48	28	43	58	24	39
23	38	72	54	27	42	57
41	56	22	37	71	53	33
52	32	47	55	21	36	70
35	69	51	31	46	61	20

Water - Venus

35	52	41	23	73	29	60
69	32	56	38	48	44	26
51	47	22	72	28	59	34
31	55	37	54	43	25	68
46	21	71	27	58	40	50
61	36	53	42	24	67	30
20	70	33	57	39	49	45

	Number	Angel Value (Arabic)	Angel Value (Hebrew)	Jinn Value (Arabic)	Jinn Value (Hebrew)
Usurper	20	339	349	61	51
Guide	73	32	42	114	104
Mystery	93	52	62	134	124
Adjuster	313	272	282	354	344
Leader	939	898	908	620	610
Regulator	1252	1211	1221	933	923
General Governor	2504	2463	2473	2185	2175
High Overseer	182792	182751	182761	182473	182463

Fire - Mercury

7	23	73	52	41	57	38	22
15	31	60	44	49	70	30	14
58	42	21	37	24	8	51	72
71	50	13	29	32	16	43	59
36	20	39	55	75	54	9	25
28	12	47	68	62	46	17	33
53	74	26	10	19	35	56	40
45	61	34	18	11	27	69	48

Earth - Mercury

45	53	28	36	71	58	15	7
61	74	12	20	50	42	31	23
34	26	47	39	13	21	60	73
18	10	68	55	29	37	44	52
11	19	62	75	32	24	49	41
27	35	46	54	16	8	70	57
69	56	17	9	43	51	30	38
48	40	33	25	59	72	14	22

Air - Mercury

48	69	27	11	18	34	61	45
40	56	35	19	10	26	74	53
33	17	46	62	68	47	12	28
25	9	54	75	55	39	20	36
59	43	16	32	29	13	50	71
72	51	8	24	37	21	42	58
14	30	70	49	44	60	31	15
22	38	57	41	52	73	23	7

Water - Mercury

22	14	72	59	25	33	40	48
38	30	51	43	9	17	56	69
57	70	8	16	54	46	35	27
41	49	24	32	75	62	19	11
52	44	37	29	55	68	10	18
73	60	21	13	39	47	26	34
23	31	42	50	20	12	74	61
7	15	58	71	36	28	53	45

	Number	Angel Value (Arabic)	Angel Value (Hebrew)	Jinn Value (Arabic)	Jinn Value (Hebrew)
Usurper	7	326	336	48	38
Guide	75	34	44	116	106
Mystery	82	41	51	123	113
Adjuster	313	272	282	354	344
Leader	939	898	908	620	610
Regulator	1252	1211	1221	933	923
General Governor	2504	2463	2473	2185	2175
High Overseer	187800	187759	187769	187481	187471

329

ANGEL OF FIRST QUINANCE: AKAIAH (37)

ה	׳	א	אֵ
2	2	9	6
8	3	5	3
4	4	4	7

ה	׳	א	כ	א
א	כ	א	ה	׳
א	ה	׳	א	כ
׳	א	כ	א	ה
כ	א	ה	׳	א

Fire - Jupiter

1	12	6	18
17	7	9	4
11	2	19	5
8	16	3	10

Air - Jupiter

10	3	16	8
5	19	2	11
4	9	7	17
18	6	12	1

Earth - Jupiter

8	11	17	1
16	2	7	12
3	19	9	6
10	5	4	18

Water - Jupiter

18	4	5	10
6	9	19	3
12	7	2	16
1	17	11	8

	Number	Angel Value (Arabic)	Angel Value (Hebrew)	Jinn Value (Arabic)	Jinn Value (Hebrew)
Usurper	1	320	330	42	32
Guide	19	338	348	60	50
Mystery	20	339	349	61	51
Adjuster	296	255	265	337	327
Leader	888	847	857	569	559
Regulator	1184	1143	1153	865	855
General Governor	2368	2327	2337	2049	2039
High Overseer	44992	44951	44961	44673	44663

ANGEL OF SECOND QUINANCE: KEHETHEL (456)

אל	ת	ח	כ
19	6	403	28
402	29	18	7
4	21	30	401

ל	א	ת	ה	כ
ת	ה	כ	ל	א
כ	ל	א	ת	ה
א	ת	ה	כ	ל
ה	כ	ל	א	ת

Fire - Saturn

153	148	155
154	152	150
149	156	151

Air - Saturn

151	156	149
150	152	154
155	148	153

Earth - Saturn

149	154	153
156	152	148
151	150	155

Water - Saturn

155	150	151
148	152	156
153	154	149

	Number	Angel Value (Arabic)	Angel Value (Hebrew)	Jinn Value (Arabic)	Jinn Value (Hebrew)
Usurper	148	107	117	189	179
Guide	156	115	125	197	187
Mystery	304	263	273	345	335
Adjuster	456	415	425	137	127
Leader	1368	1327	1337	1049	1039
Regulator	1824	1783	1793	1505	1495
General Governor	3648	3607	3617	3329	3319
High Overseer	569088	569047	569057	568769	568759

Occult Encyclopedia of Magic Squares

Fire - Jupiter

106	117	111	122
121	112	114	109
116	107	123	110
113	120	108	115

Air - Jupiter

115	108	120	113
110	123	107	116
109	114	112	121
122	111	117	106

Earth - Jupiter

113	116	121	106
120	107	112	117
108	123	114	111
115	110	109	122

Water - Jupiter

122	109	110	115
111	114	123	108
117	112	107	120
106	121	116	113

	Number	Angel Value (Arabic)	Angel Value (Hebrew)	Jinn Value (Arabic)	Jinn Value (Hebrew)
Usurper	106	65	75	147	137
Guide	123	82	92	164	154
Mystery	229	188	198	270	260
Adjuster	3648	3607	3617	3329	3319
Leader	10944	10903	10913	10625	10615
Regulator	14592	14551	14561	14273	14263
General Governor	29184	29143	29153	28865	28855
High Overseer	3589632	3589591	3589601	3589313	3589303

Fire - Mars

79	104	97	91	85
92	86	80	100	98
101	94	93	87	81
88	82	102	95	89
96	90	84	83	103

Air - Mars

96	88	101	92	79
90	82	94	86	104
84	102	93	80	97
83	95	87	100	91
103	89	81	98	85

Earth - Mars

103	83	84	90	96
89	95	102	82	88
81	87	93	94	101
98	100	80	86	92
85	91	97	104	79

Water - Mars

85	98	81	89	103
91	100	87	95	83
97	80	93	102	84
104	86	94	82	90
79	92	101	88	96

	Number	Angel Value (Arabic)	Angel Value (Hebrew)	Jinn Value (Arabic)	Jinn Value (Hebrew)
Usurper	79	38	48	120	110
Guide	104	63	73	145	135
Mystery	183	142	152	224	214
Adjuster	456	415	425	137	127
Leader	1368	1327	1337	1049	1039
Regulator	1824	1783	1793	1505	1495
General Governor	3648	3607	3617	3329	3319
High Overseer	379392	379351	379361	379073	379063

Fire - Sun

58	69	92	75	79	83
64	74	85	91	62	80
70	95	78	68	84	61
81	60	71	86	65	93
87	76	67	59	94	73
96	82	63	77	72	66

Air - Sun

66	72	77	63	82	96
73	94	59	67	76	87
93	65	86	71	60	81
61	84	68	78	95	70
80	62	91	85	74	64
83	79	75	92	69	58

Earth - Sun

96	87	81	70	64	58
82	76	60	95	74	69
63	67	71	78	85	92
77	59	86	68	91	75
72	94	65	84	62	79
66	73	93	61	80	83

Water - Sun

83	80	61	93	73	66
79	62	84	65	94	72
75	91	68	86	59	77
92	85	78	71	67	63
69	74	95	60	76	82
58	64	70	81	87	96

	Number	Angel Value (Arabic)	Angel Value (Hebrew)	Jinn Value (Arabic)	Jinn Value (Hebrew)
Usurper	58	17	27	99	89
Guide	96	55	65	137	127
Mystery	154	113	123	195	185
Adjuster	456	415	425	137	127
Leader	1368	1327	1337	1049	1039
Regulator	1824	1783	1793	1505	1495
General Governor	3648	3607	3617	3329	3319
High Overseer	350208	350167	350177	349889	349879

Occult Encyclopedia of Magic Squares

Fire - Venus

41	82	67	52	72	86	56
87	57	42	76	68	53	73
54	74	88	58	43	77	62
78	63	48	75	89	59	44
60	45	79	64	49	69	90
70	84	61	46	80	65	50
66	51	71	85	55	47	81

Air - Venus

81	47	55	85	71	51	66
50	65	80	46	61	84	70
90	69	49	64	79	45	60
44	59	89	75	48	63	78
62	77	43	58	88	74	54
73	53	68	76	42	57	87
56	86	72	52	67	82	41

Earth - Venus

66	70	60	78	54	87	41
51	84	45	63	74	57	82
71	61	79	48	88	42	67
85	46	64	75	58	76	52
55	80	49	89	43	68	72
47	65	69	59	77	53	86
81	50	90	44	62	73	56

Water - Venus

56	73	62	44	90	50	81
86	53	77	59	69	65	47
72	68	43	89	49	80	55
52	76	58	75	64	46	85
67	42	88	48	79	61	71
82	57	74	63	45	84	51
41	87	54	78	60	70	66

	Number	Angel Value (Arabic)	Angel Value (Hebrew)	Jinn Value (Arabic)	Jinn Value (Hebrew)
Usurper	41	360	10	82	72
Guide	90	49	59	131	121
Mystery	131	90	100	172	162
Adjuster	456	415	425	137	127
Leader	1368	1327	1337	1049	1039
Regulator	1824	1783	1793	1505	1495
General Governor	3648	3607	3617	3329	3319
High Overseer	328320	328279	328289	328001	327991

Occult Encyclopedia of Magic Squares

Fire - Mercury

25	41	90	70	59	75	56	40
33	49	78	62	67	87	48	32
76	60	39	55	42	26	69	89
88	68	31	47	50	34	61	77
54	38	57	73	92	72	27	43
46	30	65	85	80	64	35	51
71	91	44	28	37	53	74	58
63	79	52	36	29	45	86	66

Air - Mercury

66	86	45	29	36	52	79	63
58	74	53	37	28	44	91	71
51	35	64	80	85	65	30	46
43	27	72	92	73	57	38	54
77	61	34	50	47	31	68	88
89	69	26	42	55	39	60	76
32	48	87	67	62	78	49	33
40	56	75	59	70	90	41	25

Earth - Mercury

63	71	46	54	88	76	33	25
79	91	30	38	68	60	49	41
52	44	65	57	31	39	78	90
36	28	85	73	47	55	62	70
29	37	80	92	50	42	67	59
45	53	64	72	34	26	87	75
86	74	35	27	61	69	48	56
66	58	51	43	77	89	32	40

Water - Mercury

40	32	89	77	43	51	58	66
56	48	69	61	27	35	74	86
75	87	26	34	72	64	53	45
59	67	42	50	92	80	37	29
70	62	55	47	73	85	28	36
90	78	39	31	57	65	44	52
41	49	60	68	38	30	91	79
25	33	76	88	54	46	71	63

	Number	Angel Value (Arabic)	Angel Value (Hebrew)	Jinn Value (Arabic)	Jinn Value (Hebrew)
Usurper	25	344	354	66	56
Guide	92	51	61	133	123
Mystery	117	76	86	158	148
Adjuster	456	415	425	137	127
Leader	1368	1327	1337	1049	1039
Regulator	1824	1783	1793	1505	1495
General Governor	3648	3607	3617	3329	3319
High Overseer	335616	335575	335585	335297	335287

Occult Encyclopedia of Magic Squares

Fire - Moon

54	67	29	38	96	22	58	74	18
14	57	79	34	50	66	21	43	92
88	26	42	78	10	62	71	33	46
81	13	56	65	36	49	91	20	45
41	90	25	61	77	12	48	70	32
28	53	69	24	37	95	17	60	73
27	40	89	11	63	76	31	47	72
68	30	52	94	23	39	75	16	59
55	80	15	51	64	35	44	93	19

Earth - Moon

18	92	46	45	32	73	72	59	19
74	43	33	20	70	60	47	16	93
58	21	71	91	48	17	31	75	44
22	66	62	49	12	95	76	39	35
96	50	10	36	77	37	63	23	64
38	34	78	65	61	24	11	94	51
29	79	42	56	25	69	89	52	15
67	57	26	13	90	53	40	30	80
54	14	88	81	41	28	27	68	55

Air - Moon

19	93	44	35	64	51	15	80	55
59	16	75	39	23	94	52	30	68
72	47	31	76	63	11	89	40	27
73	60	17	95	37	24	69	53	28
32	70	48	12	77	61	25	90	41
45	20	91	49	36	65	56	13	81
46	33	71	62	10	78	42	26	88
92	43	21	66	50	34	79	57	14
18	74	58	22	96	38	29	67	54

Water - Moon

55	68	27	28	41	81	88	14	54
80	30	40	53	90	13	26	57	67
15	52	89	69	25	56	42	79	29
51	94	11	24	61	65	78	34	38
64	23	63	37	77	36	10	50	96
35	39	76	95	12	49	62	66	22
44	75	31	17	48	91	71	21	58
93	16	47	60	70	20	33	43	74
19	59	72	73	32	45	46	92	18

	Number	Angel Value (Arabic)	Angel Value (Hebrew)	Jinn Value (Arabic)	Jinn Value (Hebrew)
Usurper	10	329	339	51	41
Guide	96	55	65	137	127
Mystery	106	65	75	147	137
Adjuster	456	415	425	137	127
Leader	1368	1327	1337	1049	1039
Regulator	1824	1783	1793	1505	1495
General Governor	3648	3607	3617	3329	3319
High Overseer	350208	350167	350177	349889	349879

ANGEL OF SECOND DECANATE: RAYADYAH (230)

יה	ד	י	רא
200	11	7	12
6	13	199	12
9	202	14	5

ה	י	ד	י	א	ר
א	י	ה	ר	ד	י
ד	ר	י	א	ה	י
ר	א	י	ד	י	ה
י	ה	א	י	ר	ד
י	ד	ר	ה	י	א

Fire - Jupiter

50	61	55	64
63	56	58	53
60	51	65	54
57	62	52	59

Air - Jupiter

59	52	62	57
54	65	51	60
53	58	56	63
64	55	61	50

Earth - Jupiter

57	60	63	50
62	51	56	61
52	65	58	55
59	54	53	64

Water - Jupiter

64	53	54	59
55	58	65	52
61	56	51	62
50	63	60	57

Occult Encyclopedia of Magic Squares

	Number	Angel Value (Arabic)	Angel Value (Hebrew)	Jinn Value (Arabic)	Jinn Value (Hebrew)
Usurper	50	9	19	91	81
Guide	65	24	34	106	96
Mystery	115	74	84	156	146
Adjuster	1840	1799	1809	1521	1511
Leader	5520	5479	5489	5201	5191
Regulator	7360	7319	7329	7041	7031
General Governor	14720	14679	14689	14401	14391
High Overseer	956800	956759	956769	956481	956471

Fire - Mars

34	58	52	46	40
47	41	35	54	53
55	49	48	42	36
43	37	56	50	44
51	45	39	38	57

Air - Mars

51	43	55	47	34
45	37	49	41	58
39	56	48	35	52
38	50	42	54	46
57	44	36	53	40

Earth - Mars

57	38	39	45	51
44	50	56	37	43
36	42	48	49	55
53	54	35	41	47
40	46	52	58	34

Water - Mars

40	53	36	44	57
46	54	42	50	38
52	35	48	56	39
58	41	49	37	45
34	47	55	43	51

	Number	Angel Value (Arabic)	Angel Value (Hebrew)	Jinn Value (Arabic)	Jinn Value (Hebrew)
Usurper	34	353	3	75	65
Guide	58	17	27	99	89
Mystery	92	51	61	133	123
Adjuster	230	189	199	271	261
Leader	690	649	659	371	361
Regulator	920	879	889	601	591
General Governor	1840	1799	1809	1521	1511
High Overseer	106720	106679	106689	106401	106391

Occult Encyclopedia of Magic Squares

Fire - Sun

20	31	56	37	41	45
26	36	47	55	24	42
32	59	40	30	46	23
43	22	33	48	27	57
49	38	29	21	58	35
60	44	25	39	34	28

Air - Sun

28	34	39	25	44	60
35	58	21	29	38	49
57	27	48	33	22	43
23	46	30	40	59	32
42	24	55	47	36	26
45	41	37	56	31	20

Earth - Sun

60	49	43	32	26	20
44	38	22	59	36	31
25	29	33	40	47	56
39	21	48	30	55	37
34	58	27	46	24	41
28	35	57	23	42	45

Water - Sun

45	42	23	57	35	28
41	24	46	27	58	34
37	55	30	48	21	39
56	47	40	33	29	25
31	36	59	22	38	44
20	26	32	43	49	60

	Number	Angel Value (Arabic)	Angel Value (Hebrew)	Jinn Value (Arabic)	Jinn Value (Hebrew)
Usurper	20	339	349	61	51
Guide	60	19	29	101	91
Mystery	80	39	49	121	111
Adjuster	230	189	199	271	261
Leader	690	649	659	371	361
Regulator	920	879	889	601	591
General Governor	1840	1799	1809	1521	1511
High Overseer	110400	110359	110369	110081	110071

Fire - Venus

8	49	34	19	39	58	23
59	24	9	43	35	20	40
21	41	60	25	10	44	29
45	30	15	42	61	26	11
27	12	46	31	16	36	62
37	56	28	13	47	32	17
33	18	38	57	22	14	48

Earth - Venus

33	37	27	45	21	59	8
18	56	12	30	41	24	49
38	28	46	15	60	9	34
57	13	31	42	25	43	19
22	47	16	61	10	35	39
14	32	36	26	44	20	58
48	17	62	11	29	40	23

Air - Venus

48	14	22	57	38	18	33
17	32	47	13	28	56	37
62	36	16	31	46	12	27
11	26	61	42	15	30	45
29	44	10	25	60	41	21
40	20	35	43	9	24	59
23	58	39	19	34	49	8

Water - Venus

23	40	29	11	62	17	48
58	20	44	26	36	32	14
39	35	10	61	16	47	22
19	43	25	42	31	13	57
34	9	60	15	46	28	38
49	24	41	30	12	56	18
8	59	21	45	27	37	33

	Number	Angel Value (Arabic)	Angel Value (Hebrew)	Jinn Value (Arabic)	Jinn Value (Hebrew)
Usurper	8	327	337	49	39
Guide	62	21	31	103	93
Mystery	70	29	39	111	101
Adjuster	230	189	199	271	261
Leader	690	649	659	371	361
Regulator	920	879	889	601	591
General Governor	1840	1799	1809	1521	1511
High Overseer	114080	114039	114049	113761	113751

ANGEL OF THIRD QUINANCE: HAZIEL (53)

אל	י	ו	ה
4	8	13	28
12	29	3	9
6	6	30	11

ל	א	י	ו	ה
י	ו	ה	ל	א
ה	ל	א	י	ו
א	י	ו	ה	ל
ו	ה	ל	א	י

Occult Encyclopedia of Magic Squares

Fire - Jupiter

5	16	10	22
21	11	13	8
15	6	23	9
12	20	7	14

Air - Jupiter

14	7	20	12
9	23	6	15
8	13	11	21
22	10	16	5

Earth - Jupiter

12	15	21	5
20	6	11	16
7	23	13	10
14	9	8	22

Water - Jupiter

22	8	9	14
10	13	23	7
16	11	6	20
5	21	15	12

	Number	Angel Value (Arabic)	Angel Value (Hebrew)	Jinn Value (Arabic)	Jinn Value (Hebrew)
Usurper	5	324	334	46	36
Guide	23	342	352	64	54
Mystery	28	347	357	69	59
Adjuster	424	383	393	105	95
Leader	1272	1231	1241	953	943
Regulator	1696	1655	1665	1377	1367
General Governor	3392	3351	3361	3073	3063
High Overseer	78016	77975	77985	77697	77687

ANGEL OF FOURTH QUINANCE: ALDIAH (50)

ה	י	ד	אל
30	5	13	2
12	3	29	6
3	32	4	11

ה	י	ד	ל	א
ד	ל	א	ה	י
א	ה	י	ד	ל
י	ד	ל	א	ה
ל	א	ה	י	ד

Fire - Jupiter

5	16	10	19
18	11	13	8
15	6	20	9
12	17	7	14

Air - Jupiter

14	7	17	12
9	20	6	15
8	13	11	18
19	10	16	5

Earth - Jupiter

12	15	18	5
17	6	11	16
7	20	13	10
14	9	8	19

Water - Jupiter

19	8	9	14
10	13	20	7
16	11	6	17
5	18	15	12

	Number	Angel Value (Arabic)	Angel Value (Hebrew)	Jinn Value (Arabic)	Jinn Value (Hebrew)
Usurper	5	324	334	46	36
Guide	20	339	349	61	51
Mystery	25	344	354	66	56
Adjuster	400	359	369	81	71
Leader	1200	1159	1169	881	871
Regulator	1600	1559	1569	1281	1271
General Governor	3200	3159	3169	2881	2871
High Overseer	64000	63959	63969	63681	63671

ANGEL OF THIRD DECANATE: MISHPAR (620)

ר	פ	שׁ	מ
39	301	83	197
82	198	38	302
299	41	199	81

ר	פ	שׁ	מ
מ	שׁ	פ	ר
פ	ר	מ	שׁ
שׁ	מ	ר	פ

Fire - Jupiter

147	158	152	163
162	153	155	150
157	148	164	151
154	161	149	156

Air - Jupiter

156	149	161	154
151	164	148	157
150	155	153	162
163	152	158	147

Earth - Jupiter

154	157	162	147
161	148	153	158
149	164	155	152
156	151	150	163

Water - Jupiter

163	150	151	156
152	155	164	149
158	153	148	161
147	162	157	154

	Number	Angel Value (Arabic)	Angel Value (Hebrew)	Jinn Value (Arabic)	Jinn Value (Hebrew)
Usurper	147	106	116	188	178
Guide	164	123	133	205	195
Mystery	311	270	280	352	342
Adjuster	4960	4919	4929	4641	4631
Leader	14880	14839	14849	14561	14551
Regulator	19840	19799	19809	19521	19511
General Governor	39680	39639	39649	39361	39351
High Overseer	6507520	6507479	6507489	6507201	6507191

Fire - Mars

112	136	130	124	118
125	119	113	132	131
133	127	126	120	114
121	115	134	128	122
129	123	117	116	135

Air - Mars

129	121	133	125	112
123	115	127	119	136
117	134	126	113	130
116	128	120	132	124
135	122	114	131	118

Earth - Mars

135	116	117	123	129
122	128	134	115	121
114	120	126	127	133
131	132	113	119	125
118	124	130	136	112

Water - Mars

118	131	114	122	135
124	132	120	128	116
130	113	126	134	117
136	119	127	115	123
112	125	133	121	129

Occult Encyclopedia of Magic Squares

	Number	Angel Value (Arabic)	Angel Value (Hebrew)	Jinn Value (Arabic)	Jinn Value (Hebrew)
Usurper	112	71	81	153	143
Guide	136	95	105	177	167
Mystery	248	207	217	289	279
Adjuster	620	579	589	301	291
Leader	1860	1819	1829	1541	1531
Regulator	2480	2439	2449	2161	2151
General Governor	4960	4919	4929	4641	4631
High Overseer	674560	674519	674529	674241	674231

Fire - Sun

85	96	121	102	106	110
91	101	112	120	89	107
97	124	105	95	111	88
108	87	98	113	92	122
114	103	94	86	123	100
125	109	90	104	99	93

Air - Sun

93	99	104	90	109	125
100	123	86	94	103	114
122	92	113	98	87	108
88	111	95	105	124	97
107	89	120	112	101	91
110	106	102	121	96	85

Earth - Sun

125	114	108	97	91	85
109	103	87	124	101	96
90	94	98	105	112	121
104	86	113	95	120	102
99	123	92	111	89	106
93	100	122	88	107	110

Water - Sun

110	107	88	122	100	93
106	89	111	92	123	99
102	120	95	113	86	104
121	112	105	98	94	90
96	101	124	87	103	109
85	91	97	108	114	125

Occult Encyclopedia of Magic Squares

	Number	Angel Value (Arabic)	Angel Value (Hebrew)	Jinn Value (Arabic)	Jinn Value (Hebrew)
Usurper	85	44	54	126	116
Guide	125	84	94	166	156
Mystery	210	169	179	251	241
Adjuster	620	579	589	301	291
Leader	1860	1819	1829	1541	1531
Regulator	2480	2439	2449	2161	2151
General Governor	4960	4919	4929	4641	4631
High Overseer	620000	619959	619969	619681	619671

Fire - Venus

64	105	90	75	95	112	79
113	80	65	99	91	76	96
77	97	114	81	66	100	85
101	86	71	98	115	82	67
83	68	102	87	72	92	116
93	110	84	69	103	88	73
89	74	94	111	78	70	104

Earth - Venus

89	93	83	101	77	113	64
74	110	68	86	97	80	105
94	84	102	71	114	65	90
111	69	87	98	81	99	75
78	103	72	115	66	91	95
70	88	92	82	100	76	112
104	73	116	67	85	96	79

Air - Venus

104	70	78	111	94	74	89
73	88	103	69	84	110	93
116	92	72	87	102	68	83
67	82	115	98	71	86	101
85	100	66	81	114	97	77
96	76	91	99	65	80	113
79	112	95	75	90	105	64

Occult Encyclopedia of Magic Squares

Water - Venus

79	96	85	67	116	73	104
112	76	100	82	92	88	70
95	91	66	115	72	103	78
75	99	81	98	87	69	111
90	65	114	71	102	84	94
105	80	97	86	68	110	74
64	113	77	101	83	93	89

	Number	Angel Value (Arabic)	Angel Value (Hebrew)	Jinn Value (Arabic)	Jinn Value (Hebrew)
Usurper	64	23	33	105	95
Guide	116	75	85	157	147
Mystery	180	139	149	221	211
Adjuster	620	579	589	301	291
Leader	1860	1819	1829	1541	1531
Regulator	2480	2439	2449	2161	2151
General Governor	4960	4919	4929	4641	4631
High Overseer	575360	575319	575329	575041	575031

Fire - Mercury

46	62	107	91	80	96	77	61
54	70	99	83	88	104	69	53
97	81	60	76	63	47	90	106
105	89	52	68	71	55	82	98
75	59	78	94	109	93	48	64
67	51	86	102	101	85	56	72
92	108	65	49	58	74	95	79
84	100	73	57	50	66	103	87

Earth - Mercury

84	92	67	75	105	97	54	46
100	108	51	59	89	81	70	62
73	65	86	78	52	60	99	107
57	49	102	94	68	76	83	91
50	58	101	109	71	63	88	80
66	74	85	93	55	47	104	96
103	95	56	48	82	90	69	77
87	79	72	64	98	106	53	61

Occult Encyclopedia of Magic Squares

Air - Mercury

87	103	66	50	57	73	100	84
79	95	74	58	49	65	108	92
72	56	85	101	102	86	51	67
64	48	93	109	94	78	59	75
98	82	55	71	68	52	89	105
106	90	47	63	76	60	81	97
53	69	104	88	83	99	70	54
61	77	96	80	91	107	62	46

Water - Mercury

61	53	106	98	64	72	79	87
77	69	90	82	48	56	95	103
96	104	47	55	93	85	74	66
80	88	63	71	109	101	58	50
91	83	76	68	94	102	49	57
107	99	60	52	78	86	65	73
62	70	81	89	59	51	108	100
46	54	97	105	75	67	92	84

	Number	Angel Value (Arabic)	Angel Value (Hebrew)	Jinn Value (Arabic)	Jinn Value (Hebrew)
Usurper	46	5	15	87	77
Guide	109	68	78	150	140
Mystery	155	114	124	196	186
Adjuster	620	579	589	301	291
Leader	1860	1819	1829	1541	1531
Regulator	2480	2439	2449	2161	2151
General Governor	4960	4919	4929	4641	4631
High Overseer	540640	540599	540609	540321	540311

Occult Encyclopedia of Magic Squares

Fire - Moon

72	85	47	56	116	40	76	92	36
32	75	97	52	68	84	39	61	112
108	44	60	96	28	80	89	51	64
99	31	74	83	54	67	111	38	63
59	110	43	79	95	30	66	88	50
46	71	87	42	55	115	35	78	91
45	58	109	29	81	94	49	65	90
86	48	70	114	41	57	93	34	77
73	98	33	69	82	53	62	113	37

Earth - Moon

36	112	64	63	50	91	90	77	37
92	61	51	38	88	78	65	34	113
76	39	89	111	66	35	49	93	62
40	84	80	67	30	115	94	57	53
116	68	28	54	95	55	81	41	82
56	52	96	83	79	42	29	114	69
47	97	60	74	43	87	109	70	33
85	75	44	31	110	71	58	48	98
72	32	108	99	59	46	45	86	73

Air - Moon

37	113	62	53	82	69	33	98	73
77	34	93	57	41	114	70	48	86
90	65	49	94	81	29	109	58	45
91	78	35	115	55	42	87	71	46
50	88	66	30	95	79	43	110	59
63	38	111	67	54	83	74	31	99
64	51	89	80	28	96	60	44	108
112	61	39	84	68	52	97	75	32
36	92	76	40	116	56	47	85	72

Occult Encyclopedia of Magic Squares

Water - Moon

73	86	45	46	59	99	108	32	72
98	48	58	71	110	31	44	75	85
33	70	109	87	43	74	60	97	47
69	114	29	42	79	83	96	52	56
82	41	81	55	95	54	28	68	116
53	57	94	115	30	67	80	84	40
62	93	49	35	66	111	89	39	76
113	34	65	78	88	38	51	61	92
37	77	90	91	50	63	64	112	36

	Number	Angel Value (Arabic)	Angel Value (Hebrew)	Jinn Value (Arabic)	Jinn Value (Hebrew)
Usurper	28	347	357	69	59
Guide	116	75	85	157	147
Mystery	144	103	113	185	175
Adjuster	620	579	589	301	291
Leader	1860	1819	1829	1541	1531
Regulator	2480	2439	2449	2161	2151
General Governor	4960	4919	4929	4641	4631
High Overseer	575360	575319	575329	575041	575031

Fire - Saturn

12	30	37	75	66	109	59	51	83	98
23	87	80	71	111	96	14	56	42	40
38	43	67	110	97	82	31	19	60	73
44	69	108	99	32	78	86	27	16	61
57	107	101	36	47	70	74	84	29	15
64	21	22	89	77	53	49	39	94	112
76	58	18	25	91	46	34	95	115	62
90	79	54	13	24	41	92	114	65	48
100	33	45	52	20	28	113	63	81	85
116	93	88	50	55	17	68	72	35	26

Occult Encyclopedia of Magic Squares

Earth - Saturn

116	100	90	76	64	57	44	38	23	12
93	33	79	58	21	107	69	43	87	30
88	45	54	18	22	101	108	67	80	37
50	52	13	25	89	36	99	110	71	75
55	20	24	91	77	47	32	97	111	66
17	28	41	46	53	70	78	82	96	109
68	113	92	34	49	74	86	31	14	59
72	63	114	95	39	84	27	19	56	51
35	81	65	115	94	29	16	60	42	83
26	85	48	62	112	15	61	73	40	98

Air - Saturn

26	35	72	68	17	55	50	88	93	116
85	81	63	113	28	20	52	45	33	100
48	65	114	92	41	24	13	54	79	90
62	115	95	34	46	91	25	18	58	76
112	94	39	49	53	77	89	22	21	64
15	29	84	74	70	47	36	101	107	57
61	16	27	86	78	32	99	108	69	44
73	60	19	31	82	97	110	67	43	38
40	42	56	14	96	111	71	80	87	23
98	83	51	59	109	66	75	37	30	12

Water - Saturn

98	40	73	61	15	112	62	48	85	26
83	42	60	16	29	94	115	65	81	35
51	56	19	27	84	39	95	114	63	72
59	**14**	31	86	74	49	34	92	113	68
109	96	82	78	70	53	46	41	28	17
66	111	97	32	47	77	91	24	20	55
75	71	110	99	36	89	25	13	52	50
37	80	67	108	101	22	18	54	45	88
30	87	43	69	107	21	58	79	33	93
12	23	38	44	57	64	76	90	100	116

	Number	Angel Value (Arabic)	Angel Value (Hebrew)	Jinn Value (Arabic)	Jinn Value (Hebrew)
Usurper	12	331	341	53	43
Guide	116	75	85	157	147
Mystery	128	87	97	169	159
Adjuster	620	579	589	301	291
Leader	1860	1819	1829	1541	1531
Regulator	2480	2439	2449	2161	2151
General Governor	4960	4919	4929	4641	4631
High Overseer	575360	575319	575329	575041	575031

ANGEL OF FIFTH QUINANCE: LAVIAH (52)

ה	י	ו	אל
30	7	13	2
12	3	29	8
5	32	4	11

ה	י	ו	א	ל
ו	א	ל	ה	י
ל	ה	י	ו	א
י	ו	א	ל	ה
א	ל	ה	י	ו

Fire - Jupiter

5	16	10	21
20	11	13	8
15	6	22	9
12	19	7	14

Air - Jupiter

14	7	19	12
9	22	6	15
8	13	11	20
21	10	16	5

Earth - Jupiter

12	15	20	5
19	6	11	16
7	22	13	10
14	9	8	21

Water - Jupiter

21	8	9	14
10	13	22	7
16	11	6	19
5	20	15	12

	Number	Angel Value (Arabic)	Angel Value (Hebrew)	Jinn Value (Arabic)	Jinn Value (Hebrew)
Usurper	5	324	334	46	36
Guide	22	341	351	63	53
Mystery	27	346	356	68	58
Adjuster	416	375	385	97	87
Leader	1248	1207	1217	929	919
Regulator	1664	1623	1633	1345	1335
General Governor	3328	3287	3297	3009	2999
High Overseer	73216	73175	73185	72897	72887

ANGEL OF SIX QUINANCE: HIHAYAH (95)

ה	י	ע	הה
9	71	13	2
12	3	8	72
69	11	4	11

ה	י	ע	ה	ה
ע	ה	ה	ה	י
ה	ה	י	ע	ה
י	ע	ה	ה	ה
ה	ה	ה	י	ע

Fire - Jupiter

29	40	34	45
44	35	37	32
39	30	46	33
36	43	31	38

Air - Jupiter

38	31	43	36
33	46	30	39
32	37	35	44
45	34	40	29

Earth - Jupiter

36	39	44	29
43	30	35	40
31	46	37	34
38	33	32	45

Water - Jupiter

45	32	33	38
34	37	46	31
40	35	30	43
29	44	39	36

LIBRA

SIGN LIBRA: MOZNAIM (148)

מ	י	גּו	מא
40	58	13	37
12	38	39	59
56	42	39	11

מת	י	נ	ו	א	מ
א	ו	מ	מ	נ	י
נ	מ	י	א	מ	ו
מ	א	ו	נ	י	מ
ו	מ	א	י	מ	נ
י	נ	מ	מ	ו	א

	Number	Angel Value (Arabic)	Angel Value (Hebrew)	Jinn Value (Arabic)	Jinn Value (Hebrew)
Usurper	29	348	358	70	60
Guide	46	5	15	87	77
Mystery	75	34	44	116	106
Adjuster	1184	1143	1153	865	855
Leader	3552	3511	3521	3233	3223
Regulator	4736	4695	4705	4417	4407
General Governor	9472	9431	9441	9153	9143
High Overseer	435712	435671	435681	435393	435383

Fire - Mars

17	44	35	29	23
30	24	18	40	36
41	32	31	25	19
26	20	42	33	27
34	28	22	21	43

Earth - Mars

43	21	22	28	34
27	33	42	20	26
19	25	31	32	41
36	40	18	24	30
23	29	35	44	17

Occult Encyclopedia of Magic Squares

Air - Mars

34	26	41	30	17
28	20	32	24	44
22	42	31	18	35
21	33	25	40	29
43	27	19	36	23

Water - Mars

23	36	19	27	43
29	40	25	33	21
35	18	31	42	22
44	24	32	20	28
17	30	41	26	34

	Number	Angel Value (Arabic)	Angel Value (Hebrew)	Jinn Value (Arabic)	Jinn Value (Hebrew)
Usurper	17	336	346	58	48
Guide	44	3	13	85	75
Mystery	61	20	30	102	92
Adjuster	148	107	117	189	179
Leader	444	403	413	125	115
Regulator	592	551	561	273	263
General Governor	1184	1143	1153	865	855
High Overseer	52096	52055	52065	51777	51767

Fire - Sun

7	18	39	24	28	32
13	23	34	38	11	29
19	42	27	17	33	10
30	9	20	35	14	40
36	25	16	8	41	22
43	31	12	26	21	15

Air - Sun

15	21	26	12	31	43
22	41	8	16	25	36
40	14	35	20	9	30
10	33	17	27	42	19
29	11	38	34	23	13
32	28	24	39	18	7

Earth - Sun

43	36	30	19	13	7
31	25	9	42	23	18
12	16	20	27	34	39
26	8	35	17	38	24
21	41	14	33	11	28
15	22	40	10	29	32

Water - Sun

32	29	10	40	22	15
28	11	33	14	41	21
24	38	17	35	8	26
39	34	27	20	16	12
18	23	42	9	25	31
7	13	19	30	36	43

	Number	Angel Value (Arabic)	Angel Value (Hebrew)	Jinn Value (Arabic)	Jinn Value (Hebrew)
Usurper	7	326	336	48	38
Guide	43	2	12	84	74
Mystery	50	9	19	91	81
Adjuster	148	107	117	189	179
Leader	444	403	413	125	115
Regulator	592	551	561	273	263
General Governor	1184	1143	1153	865	855
High Overseer	50912	50871	50881	50593	50583

ARCHANGEL OF LIBRA: ZURIEL (254)

לא	י	ור	ז
6	207	13	28
12	29	5	208
205	8	30	11

ל	א	'	ר	ו	ז
ו	ר	ל	ז	'	א
'	ז	א	ו	ל	ר
ז	ו	ר	'	א	ל
ר	ל	ו	א	ז	'
א	'	ז	ל	ר	ו

Fire - Jupiter

56	67	61	70
69	62	64	59
66	57	71	60
63	68	58	65

Air - Jupiter

65	58	68	63
60	71	57	66
59	64	62	69
70	61	67	56

Earth - Jupiter

63	66	69	56
68	57	62	67
58	71	64	61
65	60	59	70

Water - Jupiter

70	59	60	65
61	64	71	58
67	62	57	68
56	69	66	63

Occult Encyclopedia of Magic Squares

	Number	Angel Value (Arabic)	Angel Value (Hebrew)	Jinn Value (Arabic)	Jinn Value (Hebrew)
Usurper	56	15	25	97	87
Guide	71	30	40	112	102
Mystery	127	86	96	168	158
Adjuster	2032	1991	2001	1713	1703
Leader	6096	6055	6065	5777	5767
Regulator	8128	8087	8097	7809	7799
General Governor	16256	16215	16225	15937	15927
High Overseer	1154176	1154135	1154145	1153857	1153847

Fire - Mars

38	66	56	50	44
51	45	39	62	57
63	53	52	46	40
47	41	64	54	48
55	49	43	42	65

Air - Mars

55	47	63	51	38
49	41	53	45	66
43	64	52	39	56
42	54	46	62	50
65	48	40	57	44

Earth - Mars

65	42	43	49	55
48	54	64	41	47
40	46	52	53	63
57	62	39	45	51
44	50	56	66	38

Water - Mars

44	57	40	48	65
50	62	46	54	42
56	39	52	64	43
66	45	53	41	49
38	51	63	47	55

	Number	Angel Value (Arabic)	Angel Value (Hebrew)	Jinn Value (Arabic)	Jinn Value (Hebrew)
Usurper	38	357	7	79	69
Guide	66	25	35	107	97
Mystery	104	63	73	145	135
Adjuster	254	213	223	295	285
Leader	762	721	731	443	433
Regulator	1016	975	985	697	687
General Governor	2032	1991	2001	1713	1703
High Overseer	134112	134071	134081	133793	133783

Occult Encyclopedia of Magic Squares

Fire - Sun

24	35	60	41	45	49
30	40	51	59	28	46
36	63	44	34	50	27
47	26	37	52	31	61
53	42	33	25	62	39
64	48	29	43	38	32

Air - Sun

32	38	43	29	48	64
39	62	25	33	42	53
61	31	52	37	26	47
27	50	34	44	63	36
46	28	59	51	40	30
49	45	41	60	35	24

Earth - Sun

64	53	47	36	30	24
48	42	26	63	40	35
29	33	37	44	51	60
43	25	52	34	59	41
38	62	31	50	28	45
32	39	61	27	46	49

Water - Sun

49	46	27	61	39	32
45	28	50	31	62	38
41	59	34	52	25	43
60	51	44	37	33	29
35	40	63	26	42	48
24	30	36	47	53	64

	Number	Angel Value (Arabic)	Angel Value (Hebrew)	Jinn Value (Arabic)	Jinn Value (Hebrew)
Usurper	24	343	353	65	55
Guide	64	23	33	105	95
Mystery	88	47	57	129	119
Adjuster	254	213	223	295	285
Leader	762	721	731	443	433
Regulator	1016	975	985	697	687
General Governor	2032	1991	2001	1713	1703
High Overseer	130048	130007	130017	129729	129719

Fire - Venus

12	53	38	23	43	58	27
59	28	13	47	39	24	44
25	45	60	29	14	48	33
49	34	19	46	61	30	15
31	16	50	35	20	40	62
41	56	32	17	51	36	21
37	22	42	57	26	18	52

Earth - Venus

37	41	31	49	25	59	12
22	56	16	34	45	28	53
42	32	50	19	60	13	38
57	17	35	46	29	47	23
26	51	20	61	14	39	43
18	36	40	30	48	24	58
52	21	62	15	33	44	27

Air - Venus

52	18	26	57	42	22	37
21	36	51	17	32	56	41
62	40	20	35	50	16	31
15	30	61	46	19	34	49
33	48	14	29	60	45	25
44	24	39	47	13	28	59
27	58	43	23	38	53	12

Water - Venus

27	44	33	15	62	21	52
58	24	48	30	40	36	18
43	39	14	61	20	51	26
23	47	29	46	35	17	57
38	13	60	19	50	32	42
53	28	45	34	16	56	22
12	59	25	49	31	41	37

	Number	Angel Value (Arabic)	Angel Value (Hebrew)	Jinn Value (Arabic)	Jinn Value (Hebrew)
Usurper	12	331	341	53	43
Guide	62	21	31	103	93
Mystery	74	33	43	115	105
Adjuster	254	213	223	295	285
Leader	762	721	731	443	433
Regulator	1016	975	985	697	687
General Governor	2032	1991	2001	1713	1703
High Overseer	125984	125943	125953	125665	125655

ANGEL OF LIBRA: CHEDEQIEL (153)

אל	י	דק	ח
7	105	13	28
12	29	6	106
103	9	30	11

ל	א	י	ק	ד	ח
ד	ק	ל	ח	י	א
י	ח	א	ד	ל	ק
ח	ד	ק	י	א	ל
ק	ל	ד	א	ח	י
א	י	ח	ל	ק	ד

Occult Encyclopedia of Magic Squares

Fire - Saturn

52	47	54
53	51	49
48	55	50

Air - Saturn

50	55	48
49	51	53
54	47	52

Earth - Saturn

48	53	52
55	51	47
50	49	54

Water - Saturn

54	49	50
47	51	55
52	53	48

	Number	Angel Value (Arabic)	Angel Value (Hebrew)	Jinn Value (Arabic)	Jinn Value (Hebrew)
Usurper	47	6	16	88	78
Guide	55	14	24	96	86
Mystery	102	61	71	143	133
Adjuster	153	112	122	194	184
Leader	459	418	428	140	130
Regulator	612	571	581	293	283
General Governor	1224	1183	1193	905	895
High Overseer	67320	67279	67289	67001	66991

Fire - Jupiter

30	41	35	47
46	36	38	33
40	31	48	34
37	45	32	39

Air - Jupiter

39	32	45	37
34	48	31	40
33	38	36	46
47	35	41	30

Earth - Jupiter

37	40	46	30
45	31	36	41
32	48	38	35
39	34	33	47

Water - Jupiter

47	33	34	39
35	38	48	32
41	36	31	45
30	46	40	37

Occult Encyclopedia of Magic Squares

	Number	Angel Value (Arabic)	Angel Value (Hebrew)	Jinn Value (Arabic)	Jinn Value (Hebrew)
Usurper	30	349	359	71	61
Guide	48	7	17	89	79
Mystery	78	37	47	119	109
Adjuster	1224	1183	1193	905	895
Leader	3672	3631	3641	3353	3343
Regulator	4896	4855	4865	4577	4567
General Governor	9792	9751	9761	9473	9463
High Overseer	470016	469975	469985	469697	469687

Fire - Mars

18	45	36	30	24
31	25	19	41	37
42	33	32	26	20
27	21	43	34	28
35	29	23	22	44

Air - Mars

35	27	42	31	18
29	21	33	25	45
23	43	32	19	36
22	34	26	41	30
44	28	20	37	24

Earth - Mars

44	22	23	29	35
28	34	43	21	27
20	26	32	33	42
37	41	19	25	31
24	30	36	45	18

Water - Mars

24	37	20	28	44
30	41	26	34	22
36	19	32	43	23
45	25	33	21	29
18	31	42	27	35

	Number	Angel Value (Arabic)	Angel Value (Hebrew)	Jinn Value (Arabic)	Jinn Value (Hebrew)
Usurper	18	337	347	59	49
Guide	45	4	14	86	76
Mystery	63	22	32	104	94
Adjuster	153	112	122	194	184
Leader	459	418	428	140	130
Regulator	612	571	581	293	283
General Governor	1224	1183	1193	905	895
High Overseer	55080	55039	55049	54761	54751

Occult Encyclopedia of Magic Squares

Fire - Sun

8	19	39	25	29	33
14	24	35	38	12	30
20	42	28	18	34	11
31	10	21	36	15	40
37	26	17	9	41	23
43	32	13	27	22	16

Air - Sun

16	22	27	13	32	43
23	41	9	17	26	37
40	15	36	21	10	31
11	34	18	28	42	20
30	12	38	35	24	14
33	29	25	39	19	8

Earth - Sun

43	37	31	20	14	8
32	26	10	42	24	19
13	17	21	28	35	39
27	9	36	18	38	25
22	41	15	34	12	29
16	23	40	11	30	33

Water - Sun

33	30	11	40	23	16
29	12	34	15	41	22
25	38	18	36	9	27
39	35	28	21	17	13
19	24	42	10	26	32
8	14	20	31	37	43

	Number	Angel Value (Arabic)	Angel Value (Hebrew)	Jinn Value (Arabic)	Jinn Value (Hebrew)
Usurper	8	327	337	49	39
Guide	43	2	12	84	74
Mystery	51	10	20	92	82
Adjuster	153	112	122	194	184
Leader	459	418	428	140	130
Regulator	612	571	581	293	283
General Governor	1224	1183	1193	905	895
High Overseer	52632	52591	52601	52313	52303

LORD OF TRIPLICITY BY DAY: THERGEBON (661)

נו	גב	ר	ת
399	201	8	53
7	54	398	202
199	401	55	6

נ	ו	ב	ג	ר	ת
ר	ג	נ	ת	ב	ו
ב	ת	ו	ר	נ	ג
ת	ר	ג	ב	ו	נ
ג	נ	ר	ו	ת	ב
ו	ב	ת	נ	ג	ר

Fire - Jupiter

157	168	162	174
173	163	165	160
167	158	175	161
164	172	159	166

Air - Jupiter

166	159	172	164
161	175	158	167
160	165	163	173
174	162	168	157

Earth - Jupiter

164	167	173	157
172	158	163	168
159	175	165	162
166	161	160	174

Water - Jupiter

174	160	161	166
162	165	175	159
168	163	158	172
157	173	167	164

	Number	Angel Value (Arabic)	Angel Value (Hebrew)	Jinn Value (Arabic)	Jinn Value (Hebrew)
Usurper	157	116	126	198	188
Guide	175	134	144	216	206
Mystery	332	291	301	13	3
Adjuster	5288	5247	5257	4969	4959
Leader	15864	15823	15833	15545	15535
Regulator	21152	21111	21121	20833	20823
General Governor	42304	42263	42273	41985	41975
High Overseer	7403200	7403159	7403169	7402881	7402871

Occult Encyclopedia of Magic Squares

Fire - Mars

120	145	138	132	126
133	127	121	141	139
142	135	134	128	122
129	123	143	136	130
137	131	125	124	144

Air - Mars

137	129	142	133	120
131	123	135	127	145
125	143	134	121	138
124	136	128	141	132
144	130	122	139	126

Earth - Mars

144	124	125	131	137
130	136	143	123	129
122	128	134	135	142
139	141	121	127	133
126	132	138	145	120

Water - Mars

126	139	122	130	144
132	141	128	136	124
138	121	134	143	125
145	127	135	123	131
120	133	142	129	137

	Number	Angel Value (Arabic)	Angel Value (Hebrew)	Jinn Value (Arabic)	Jinn Value (Hebrew)
Usurper	120	79	89	161	151
Guide	145	104	114	186	176
Mystery	265	224	234	306	296
Adjuster	661	620	630	342	332
Leader	1983	1942	1952	1664	1654
Regulator	2644	2603	2613	2325	2315
General Governor	5288	5247	5257	4969	4959
High Overseer	766760	766719	766729	766441	766431

Fire - Sun

92	103	127	109	113	117
98	108	119	126	96	114
104	130	112	102	118	95
115	94	105	120	99	128
121	110	101	93	129	107
131	116	97	111	106	100

Earth - Sun

131	121	115	104	98	92
116	110	94	130	108	103
97	101	105	112	119	127
111	93	120	102	126	109
106	129	99	118	96	113
100	107	128	95	114	117

Occult Encyclopedia of Magic Squares

Air - Sun

100	106	111	97	116	131
107	129	93	101	110	121
128	99	120	105	94	115
95	118	102	112	130	104
114	96	126	119	108	98
117	113	109	127	103	92

Water - Sun

117	114	95	128	107	100
113	96	118	99	129	106
109	126	102	120	93	111
127	119	112	105	101	97
103	108	130	94	110	116
92	98	104	115	121	131

	Number	Angel Value (Arabic)	Angel Value (Hebrew)	Jinn Value (Arabic)	Jinn Value (Hebrew)
Usurper	92	51	61	133	123
Guide	131	90	100	172	162
Mystery	223	182	192	264	254
Adjuster	661	620	630	342	332
Leader	1983	1942	1952	1664	1654
Regulator	2644	2603	2613	2325	2315
General Governor	5288	5247	5257	4969	4959
High Overseer	692728	692687	692697	692409	692399

Fire - Venus

70	111	96	81	101	117	85
118	86	71	105	97	82	102
83	103	119	87	72	106	91
107	92	77	104	120	88	73
89	74	108	93	78	98	121
99	115	90	75	109	94	79
95	80	100	116	84	76	110

Earth - Venus

95	99	89	107	83	118	70
80	115	74	92	103	86	111
100	90	108	77	119	71	96
116	75	93	104	87	105	81
84	109	78	120	72	97	101
76	94	98	88	106	82	117
110	79	121	73	91	102	85

Occult Encyclopedia of Magic Squares

Air - Venus

110	76	84	116	100	80	95
79	94	109	75	90	115	99
121	98	78	93	108	74	89
73	88	120	104	77	92	107
91	106	72	87	119	103	83
102	82	97	105	71	86	118
85	117	101	81	96	111	70

Water - Venus

85	102	91	73	121	79	110
117	82	106	88	98	94	76
101	97	72	120	78	109	84
81	105	87	104	93	75	116
96	71	119	77	108	90	100
111	86	103	92	74	115	80
70	118	83	107	89	99	95

	Number	Angel Value (Arabic)	Angel Value (Hebrew)	Jinn Value (Arabic)	Jinn Value (Hebrew)
Usurper	70	29	39	111	101
Guide	121	80	90	162	152
Mystery	191	150	160	232	222
Adjuster	661	620	630	342	332
Leader	1983	1942	1952	1664	1654
Regulator	2644	2603	2613	2325	2315
General Governor	5288	5247	5257	4969	4959
High Overseer	639848	639807	639817	639529	639519

Fire - Mercury

51	67	113	96	85	101	82	66
59	75	104	88	93	110	74	58
102	86	65	81	68	52	95	112
111	94	57	73	76	60	87	103
80	64	83	99	115	98	53	69
72	56	91	108	106	90	61	77
97	114	70	54	63	79	100	84
89	105	78	62	55	71	109	92

Earth - Mercury

89	97	72	80	111	102	59	51
105	114	56	64	94	86	75	67
78	70	91	83	57	65	104	113
62	54	108	99	73	81	88	96
55	63	106	115	76	68	93	85
71	79	90	98	60	52	110	101
109	100	61	53	87	95	74	82
92	84	77	69	103	112	58	66

Air - Mercury

92	109	71	55	62	78	105	89
84	100	79	63	54	70	114	97
77	61	90	106	108	91	56	72
69	53	98	115	99	83	64	80
103	87	60	76	73	57	94	111
112	95	52	68	81	65	86	102
58	74	110	93	88	104	75	59
66	82	101	85	96	113	67	51

Water - Mercury

66	58	112	103	69	77	84	92
82	74	95	87	53	61	100	109
101	110	52	60	98	90	79	71
85	93	68	76	115	106	63	55
96	88	81	73	99	108	54	62
113	104	65	57	83	91	70	78
67	75	86	94	64	56	114	105
51	59	102	111	80	72	97	89

Occult Encyclopedia of Magic Squares

	Number	Angel Value (Arabic)	Angel Value (Hebrew)	Jinn Value (Arabic)	Jinn Value (Hebrew)
Usurper	51	10	20	92	82
Guide	115	74	84	156	146
Mystery	166	125	135	207	197
Adjuster	661	620	630	342	332
Leader	1983	1942	1952	1664	1654
Regulator	2644	2603	2613	2325	2315
General Governor	5288	5247	5257	4969	4959
High Overseer	608120	608079	608089	607801	607791

Fire - Moon

77	90	52	61	117	45	81	97	41
37	80	102	57	73	89	44	66	113
109	49	65	101	33	85	94	56	69
104	36	79	88	59	72	112	43	68
64	111	48	84	100	35	71	93	55
51	76	92	47	60	116	40	83	96
50	63	110	34	86	99	54	70	95
91	53	75	115	46	62	98	39	82
78	103	38	74	87	58	67	114	42

Earth - Moon

41	113	69	68	55	96	95	82	42
97	66	56	43	93	83	70	39	114
81	44	94	112	71	40	54	98	67
45	89	85	72	35	116	99	62	58
117	73	33	59	100	60	86	46	87
61	57	101	88	84	47	34	115	74
52	102	65	79	48	92	110	75	38
90	80	49	36	111	76	63	53	103
77	37	109	104	64	51	50	91	78

Occult Encyclopedia of Magic Squares

Air - Moon

42	114	67	58	87	74	38	103	78
82	39	98	62	46	115	75	53	91
95	70	54	99	86	34	110	63	50
96	83	40	116	60	47	92	76	51
55	93	71	35	100	84	48	111	64
68	43	112	72	59	88	79	36	104
69	56	94	85	33	101	65	49	109
113	66	44	89	73	57	102	80	37
41	97	81	45	117	61	52	90	77

Water - Moon

78	91	50	51	64	104	109	37	77
103	53	63	76	111	36	49	80	90
38	75	110	92	48	79	65	102	52
74	115	34	47	84	88	101	57	61
87	46	86	60	100	59	33	73	117
58	62	99	116	35	72	85	89	45
67	98	54	40	71	112	94	44	81
114	39	70	83	93	43	56	66	97
42	82	95	96	55	68	69	113	41

	Number	Angel Value (Arabic)	Angel Value (Hebrew)	Jinn Value (Arabic)	Jinn Value (Hebrew)
Usurper	33	352	2	74	64
Guide	117	76	86	158	148
Mystery	150	109	119	191	181
Adjuster	661	620	630	342	332
Leader	1983	1942	1952	1664	1654
Regulator	2644	2603	2613	2325	2315
General Governor	5288	5247	5257	4969	4959
High Overseer	618696	618655	618665	618377	618367

Occult Encyclopedia of Magic Squares

Fire - Saturn

16	34	41	79	70	114	63	55	87	102
27	91	84	75	116	100	18	60	46	44
42	47	71	115	101	86	35	23	64	77
48	73	113	103	36	82	90	31	20	65
61	112	105	40	51	74	78	88	33	19
68	25	26	93	81	57	53	43	98	117
80	62	22	29	95	50	38	99	120	66
94	83	58	17	28	45	96	119	69	52
104	37	49	56	24	32	118	67	85	89
121	97	92	54	59	21	72	76	39	30

Earth - Saturn

121	104	94	80	68	61	48	42	27	16
97	37	83	62	25	112	73	47	91	34
92	49	58	22	26	105	113	71	84	41
54	56	17	29	93	40	103	115	75	79
59	24	28	95	81	51	36	101	116	70
21	32	45	50	57	74	82	86	100	114
72	118	96	38	53	78	90	35	18	63
76	67	119	99	43	88	31	23	60	55
39	85	69	120	98	33	20	64	46	87
30	89	52	66	117	19	65	77	44	102

Air - Saturn

30	39	76	72	21	59	54	92	97	121
89	85	67	118	32	24	56	49	37	104
52	69	119	96	45	28	17	58	83	94
66	120	99	38	50	95	29	22	62	80
117	98	43	53	57	81	93	26	25	68
19	33	88	78	74	51	40	105	112	61
65	20	31	90	82	36	103	113	73	48
77	64	23	35	86	101	115	71	47	42
44	46	60	18	100	116	75	84	91	27
102	87	55	63	114	70	79	41	34	16

Occult Encyclopedia of Magic Squares

Water - Saturn

102	44	77	65	19	117	66	52	89	30
87	46	64	20	33	98	120	69	85	39
55	60	23	31	88	43	99	119	67	76
63	**18**	35	90	78	53	38	96	118	72
114	100	86	82	74	57	50	45	32	21
70	116	101	36	51	81	95	28	24	59
79	75	115	103	40	93	29	17	56	54
41	84	71	113	105	26	22	58	49	92
34	91	47	73	112	25	62	83	37	97
16	27	42	48	61	68	80	94	104	121

	Number	Angel Value (Arabic)	Angel Value (Hebrew)	Jinn Value (Arabic)	Jinn Value (Hebrew)
Usurper	16	335	345	57	47
Guide	121	80	90	162	152
Mystery	137	96	106	178	168
Adjuster	661	620	630	342	332
Leader	1983	1942	1952	1664	1654
Regulator	2644	2603	2613	2325	2315
General Governor	5288	5247	5257	4969	4959
High Overseer	639848	639807	639817	639529	639519

LORD OF TRIPLICITY BY NIGHT: ACHODRAON (276)

ג	ו	א	ר	ד	ו	ח	א
ו	א	ר	ד	א	ג	ו	ח
א	ר	ד	א	ח	ו	ג	ו
ו	ד	א	ח	ר	א	ו	ג
ר	ג	ו	א	ו	ח	א	ד
ח	ו	ג	ו	א	א	ד	ר
א	ח	ו	ג	ו	ד	ר	א
ד	א	ח	ו	ג	ר	א	ו

נג	רא	וד	אח
8	11	204	53
203	54	7	12
9	10	55	202

Fire - Saturn

93	88	95
94	92	90
89	96	91

Air - Saturn

91	96	89
90	92	94
95	88	93

Earth - Saturn

89	94	93
96	92	88
91	90	95

Water - Saturn

95	90	91
88	92	96
93	94	89

	Number	Angel Value (Arabic)	Angel Value (Hebrew)	Jinn Value (Arabic)	Jinn Value (Hebrew)
Usurper	88	47	57	129	119
Guide	96	55	65	137	127
Mystery	184	143	153	225	215
Adjuster	276	235	245	317	307
Leader	828	787	797	509	499
Regulator	1104	1063	1073	785	775
General Governor	2208	2167	2177	1889	1879
High Overseer	211968	211927	211937	211649	211639

Fire - Jupiter

61	72	66	77
76	67	69	64
71	62	78	65
68	75	63	70

Air - Jupiter

70	63	75	68
65	78	62	71
64	69	67	76
77	66	72	61

Earth - Jupiter

68	71	76	61
75	62	67	72
63	78	69	66
70	65	64	77

Water - Jupiter

77	64	65	70
66	69	78	63
72	67	62	75
61	76	71	68

	Number	Angel Value (Arabic)	Angel Value (Hebrew)	Jinn Value (Arabic)	Jinn Value (Hebrew)
Usurper	61	20	30	102	92
Guide	78	37	47	119	109
Mystery	139	98	108	180	170
Adjuster	2208	2167	2177	1889	1879
Leader	6624	6583	6593	6305	6295
Regulator	8832	8791	8801	8513	8503
General Governor	17664	17623	17633	17345	17335
High Overseer	1377792	1377751	1377761	1377473	1377463

Fire - Mars

43	68	61	55	49
56	50	44	64	62
65	58	57	51	45
52	46	66	59	53
60	54	48	47	67

Air - Mars

60	52	65	56	43
54	46	58	50	68
48	66	57	44	61
47	59	51	64	55
67	53	45	62	49

Earth - Mars

67	47	48	54	60
53	59	66	46	52
45	51	57	58	65
62	64	44	50	56
49	55	61	68	43

Water - Mars

49	62	45	53	67
55	64	51	59	47
61	44	57	66	48
68	50	58	46	54
43	56	65	52	60

Occult Encyclopedia of Magic Squares

	Number	Angel Value (Arabic)	Angel Value (Hebrew)	Jinn Value (Arabic)	Jinn Value (Hebrew)
Usurper	43	2	12	84	74
Guide	68	27	37	109	99
Mystery	111	70	80	152	142
Adjuster	276	235	245	317	307
Leader	828	787	797	509	499
Regulator	1104	1063	1073	785	775
General Governor	2208	2167	2177	1889	1879
High Overseer	150144	150103	150113	149825	149815

Fire - Sun

28	39	62	45	49	53
34	44	55	61	32	50
40	65	48	38	54	31
51	30	41	56	35	63
57	46	37	29	64	43
66	52	33	47	42	36

Air - Sun

36	42	47	33	52	66
43	64	29	37	46	57
63	35	56	41	30	51
31	54	38	48	65	40
50	32	61	55	44	34
53	49	45	62	39	28

Earth - Sun

66	57	51	40	34	28
52	46	30	65	44	39
33	37	41	48	55	62
47	29	56	38	61	45
42	64	35	54	32	49
36	43	63	31	50	53

Water - Sun

53	50	31	63	43	36
49	32	54	35	64	42
45	61	38	56	29	47
62	55	48	41	37	33
39	44	65	30	46	52
28	34	40	51	57	66

Occult Encyclopedia of Magic Squares

	Number	Angel Value (Arabic)	Angel Value (Hebrew)	Jinn Value (Arabic)	Jinn Value (Hebrew)
Usurper	28	347	357	69	59
Guide	66	25	35	107	97
Mystery	94	53	63	135	125
Adjuster	276	235	245	317	307
Leader	828	787	797	509	499
Regulator	1104	1063	1073	785	775
General Governor	2208	2167	2177	1889	1879
High Overseer	145728	145687	145697	145409	145399

Fire - Venus

15	56	41	26	46	62	30
63	31	16	50	42	27	47
28	48	64	32	17	51	36
52	37	22	49	65	33	18
34	19	53	38	23	43	66
44	60	35	20	54	39	24
40	25	45	61	29	21	55

Air - Venus

55	21	29	61	45	25	40
24	39	54	20	35	60	44
66	43	23	38	53	19	34
18	33	65	49	22	37	52
36	51	17	32	64	48	28
47	27	42	50	16	31	63
30	62	46	26	41	56	15

Earth - Venus

40	44	34	52	28	63	15
25	60	19	37	48	31	56
45	35	53	22	64	16	41
61	20	38	49	32	50	26
29	54	23	65	17	42	46
21	39	43	33	51	27	62
55	24	66	18	36	47	30

Water - Venus

30	47	36	18	66	24	55
62	27	51	33	43	39	21
46	42	17	65	23	54	29
26	50	32	49	38	20	61
41	16	64	22	53	35	45
56	31	48	37	19	60	25
15	63	28	52	34	44	40

	Number	Angel Value (Arabic)	Angel Value (Hebrew)	Jinn Value (Arabic)	Jinn Value (Hebrew)
Usurper	15	334	344	56	46
Guide	66	25	35	107	97
Mystery	81	40	50	122	112
Adjuster	276	235	245	317	307
Leader	828	787	797	509	499
Regulator	1104	1063	1073	785	775
General Governor	2208	2167	2177	1889	1879
High Overseer	145728	145687	145697	145409	145399

Fire - Mercury

3	19	64	48	37	53	34	18
11	27	56	40	45	61	26	10
54	38	17	33	20	4	47	63
62	46	9	25	28	12	39	55
32	16	35	51	66	50	5	21
24	8	43	59	58	42	13	29
49	65	22	6	15	31	52	36
41	57	30	14	7	23	60	44

Earth - Mercury

41	49	24	32	62	54	11	3
57	65	8	16	46	38	27	19
30	22	43	35	9	17	56	64
14	6	59	51	25	33	40	48
7	15	58	66	28	20	45	37
23	31	42	50	12	4	61	53
60	52	13	5	39	47	26	34
44	36	29	21	55	63	10	18

Air - Mercury

44	60	23	7	14	30	57	41
36	52	31	15	6	22	65	49
29	13	42	58	59	43	8	24
21	5	50	66	51	35	16	32
55	39	12	28	25	9	46	62
63	47	4	20	33	17	38	54
10	26	61	45	40	56	27	11
18	34	53	37	48	64	19	3

Water - Mercury

18	10	63	55	21	29	36	44
34	26	47	39	5	13	52	60
53	61	4	12	50	42	31	23
37	45	20	28	66	58	15	7
48	40	33	25	51	59	6	14
64	56	17	9	35	43	22	30
19	27	38	46	16	8	65	57
3	11	54	62	32	24	49	41

	Number	Angel Value (Arabic)	Angel Value (Hebrew)	Jinn Value (Arabic)	Jinn Value (Hebrew)
Usurper	3	322	332	44	34
Guide	66	25	35	107	97
Mystery	69	28	38	110	100
Adjuster	276	235	245	317	307
Leader	828	787	797	509	499
Regulator	1104	1063	1073	785	775
General Governor	2208	2167	2177	1889	1879
High Overseer	145728	145687	145697	145409	145399

ANGEL RULING 7TH HOUSE: YAHEL (46)

ל	א	ה	י
9	6	4	27
3	28	8	7
4	11	29	2

ל	א	ה	י
י	ה	א	ל
א	ל	י	ה
ה	י	ל	א

Numerical Squares See Page: 90

ANGEL OF FIRST DECANATE: TARASNI (329)

נ	ס	ר	ש
8	201	63	57
62	58	7	202
199	10	59	61

י	נ	ס	ר	ש
ס	ר	ש	י	נ
ש	י	נ	ס	ר
נ	ס	ר	ש	י
ר	ש	י	נ	ס

Fire - Jupiter

74	85	79	91
90	80	82	77
84	75	92	78
81	89	76	83

Air - Jupiter

83	76	89	81
78	92	75	84
77	82	80	90
91	79	85	74

Earth - Jupiter

81	84	90	74
89	75	80	85
76	92	82	79
83	78	77	91

Water - Jupiter

91	77	78	83
79	82	92	76
85	80	75	89
74	90	84	81

	Number	Angel Value (Arabic)	Angel Value (Hebrew)	Jinn Value (Arabic)	Jinn Value (Hebrew)
Usurper	74	33	43	115	105
Guide	92	51	61	133	123
Mystery	166	125	135	207	197
Adjuster	2632	2591	2601	2313	2303
Leader	7896	7855	7865	7577	7567
Regulator	10528	10487	10497	10209	10199
General Governor	21056	21015	21025	20737	20727
High Overseer	1937152	1937111	1937121	1936833	1936823

Occult Encyclopedia of Magic Squares

Fire - Mars

53	81	71	65	59
66	60	54	77	72
78	68	67	61	55
62	56	79	69	63
70	64	58	57	80

Air - Mars

70	62	78	66	53
64	56	68	60	81
58	79	67	54	71
57	69	61	77	65
80	63	55	72	59

Earth - Mars

80	57	58	64	70
63	69	79	56	62
55	61	67	68	78
72	77	54	60	66
59	65	71	81	53

Water - Mars

59	72	55	63	80
65	77	61	69	57
71	54	67	79	58
81	60	68	56	64
53	66	78	62	70

	Number	Angel Value (Arabic)	Angel Value (Hebrew)	Jinn Value (Arabic)	Jinn Value (Hebrew)
Usurper	53	12	22	94	84
Guide	81	40	50	122	112
Mystery	134	93	103	175	165
Adjuster	329	288	298	10	360
Leader	987	946	956	668	658
Regulator	1316	1275	1285	997	987
General Governor	2632	2591	2601	2313	2303
High Overseer	213192	213151	213161	212873	212863

Fire - Sun

37	48	70	54	58	62
43	53	64	69	41	59
49	73	57	47	63	40
60	39	50	65	44	71
66	55	46	38	72	52
74	61	42	56	51	45

Earth - Sun

74	66	60	49	43	37
61	55	39	73	53	48
42	46	50	57	64	70
56	38	65	47	69	54
51	72	44	63	41	58
45	52	71	40	59	62

Occult Encyclopedia of Magic Squares

Air - Sun

45	51	56	42	61	74
52	72	38	46	55	66
71	44	65	50	39	60
40	63	47	57	73	49
59	41	69	64	53	43
62	58	54	70	48	37

Water - Sun

62	59	40	71	52	45
58	41	63	44	72	51
54	69	47	65	38	56
70	64	57	50	46	42
48	53	73	39	55	61
37	43	49	60	66	74

	Number	Angel Value (Arabic)	Angel Value (Hebrew)	Jinn Value (Arabic)	Jinn Value (Hebrew)
Usurper	37	356	6	78	68
Guide	74	33	43	115	105
Mystery	111	70	80	152	142
Adjuster	329	288	298	10	360
Leader	987	946	956	668	658
Regulator	1316	1275	1285	997	987
General Governor	2632	2591	2601	2313	2303
High Overseer	194768	194727	194737	194449	194439

Fire - Venus

23	64	49	34	54	67	38
68	39	24	58	50	35	55
36	56	69	40	25	59	44
60	45	30	57	70	41	26
42	27	61	46	31	51	71
52	65	43	28	62	47	32
48	33	53	66	37	29	63

Air - Venus

63	29	37	66	53	33	48
32	47	62	28	43	65	52
71	51	31	46	61	27	42
26	41	70	57	30	45	60
44	59	25	40	69	56	36
55	35	50	58	24	39	68
38	67	54	34	49	64	23

Earth - Venus

48	52	42	60	36	68	23
33	65	27	45	56	39	64
53	43	61	30	69	24	49
66	28	46	57	40	58	34
37	62	31	70	25	50	54
29	47	51	41	59	35	67
63	32	71	26	44	55	38

Water - Venus

38	55	44	26	71	32	63
67	35	59	41	51	47	29
54	50	25	70	31	62	37
34	58	40	57	46	28	66
49	24	69	30	61	43	53
64	39	56	45	27	65	33
23	68	36	60	42	52	48

Occult Encyclopedia of Magic Squares

	Number	Angel Value (Arabic)	Angel Value (Hebrew)	Jinn Value (Arabic)	Jinn Value (Hebrew)
Usurper	23	342	352	64	54
Guide	71	30	40	112	102
Mystery	94	53	63	135	125
Adjuster	329	288	298	10	360
Leader	987	946	956	668	658
Regulator	1316	1275	1285	997	987
General Governor	2632	2591	2601	2313	2303
High Overseer	186872	186831	186841	186553	186543

Fire - Mercury

9	25	75	54	43	59	40	24
17	33	62	46	51	72	32	16
60	44	23	39	26	10	53	74
73	52	15	31	34	18	45	61
38	22	41	57	77	56	11	27
30	14	49	70	64	48	19	35
55	76	28	12	21	37	58	42
47	63	36	20	13	29	71	50

Earth - Mercury

47	55	30	38	73	60	17	9
63	76	14	22	52	44	33	25
36	28	49	41	15	23	62	75
20	12	70	57	31	39	46	54
13	21	64	77	34	26	51	43
29	37	48	56	18	10	72	59
71	58	19	11	45	53	32	40
50	42	35	27	61	74	16	24

Air - Mercury

50	71	29	13	20	36	63	47
42	58	37	21	12	28	76	55
35	19	48	64	70	49	14	30
27	11	56	77	57	41	22	38
61	45	18	34	31	15	52	73
74	53	10	26	39	23	44	60
16	32	72	51	46	62	33	17
24	40	59	43	54	75	25	9

Water - Mercury

24	16	74	61	27	35	42	50
40	32	53	45	11	19	58	71
59	72	10	18	56	48	37	29
43	51	26	34	77	64	21	13
54	46	39	31	57	70	12	20
75	62	23	15	41	49	28	36
25	33	44	52	22	14	76	63
9	17	60	73	38	30	55	47

ANGEL OF FIRST QUINANCE: YEZALEL (78)

ל	א	ל	ד
16	31	4	27
3	28	15	32
29	18	29	2

ל	א	ל	ו	י
ל	ו	י	ל	א
י	ל	א	ל	ו
א	ל	ו	י	ל
ו	י	ל	א	ל

Numerical Squares See Page: 91

ANGEL OF SECOND QUINANCE: MEBAHEL (78)

אל	ה	ב	מ
39	3	8	28
7	29	38	4
1	41	30	6

ל	א	ה	ב	מ
ה	ב	מ	ל	א
מ	ל	א	ה	ב
א	ה	ב	מ	ל
ב	מ	ל	א	ה

Numerical Squares See Page: 91

ANGEL OF SECOND DECANATE: SAHARNATZ (405)

צ	נ	ר	סה
64	201	53	87
52	88	63	202
199	66	89	51

צ	נ	ר	ה	ס
ר	ה	ס	צ	נ
ס	צ	נ	ר	ה
נ	ר	ה	ס	צ
ה	ס	צ	נ	ר

Fire - Saturn

136	131	138
137	135	133
132	139	134

Air - Saturn

134	139	132
133	135	137
138	131	136

Earth - Saturn

132	137	136
139	135	131
134	133	138

Water - Saturn

138	133	134
131	135	139
136	137	132

Occult Encyclopedia of Magic Squares

	Number	Angel Value (Arabic)	Angel Value (Hebrew)	Jinn Value (Arabic)	Jinn Value (Hebrew)
Usurper	131	90	100	172	162
Guide	139	98	108	180	170
Mystery	270	229	239	311	301
Adjuster	405	364	374	86	76
Leader	1215	1174	1184	896	886
Regulator	1620	1579	1589	1301	1291
General Governor	3240	3199	3209	2921	2911
High Overseer	450360	450319	450329	450041	450031

Fire - Jupiter

93	104	98	110
109	99	101	96
103	94	111	97
100	108	95	102

Air - Jupiter

102	95	108	100
97	111	94	103
96	101	99	109
110	98	104	93

Earth - Jupiter

100	103	109	93
108	94	99	104
95	111	101	98
102	97	96	110

Water - Jupiter

110	96	97	102
98	101	111	95
104	99	94	108
93	109	103	100

	Number	Angel Value (Arabic)	Angel Value (Hebrew)	Jinn Value (Arabic)	Jinn Value (Hebrew)
Usurper	93	52	62	134	124
Guide	111	70	80	152	142
Mystery	204	163	173	245	235
Adjuster	3240	3199	3209	2921	2911
Leader	9720	9679	9689	9401	9391
Regulator	12960	12919	12929	12641	12631
General Governor	25920	25879	25889	25601	25591
High Overseer	2877120	2877079	2877089	2876801	2876791

Fire - Mars

69	93	87	81	75
82	76	70	89	88
90	84	83	77	71
78	72	91	85	79
86	80	74	73	92

Air - Mars

86	78	90	82	69
80	72	84	76	93
74	91	83	70	87
73	85	77	89	81
92	79	71	88	75

Earth - Mars

92	73	74	80	86
79	85	91	72	78
71	77	83	84	90
88	89	70	76	82
75	81	87	93	69

Water - Mars

75	88	71	79	92
81	89	77	85	73
87	70	83	91	74
93	76	84	72	80
69	82	90	78	86

	Number	Angel Value (Arabic)	Angel Value (Hebrew)	Jinn Value (Arabic)	Jinn Value (Hebrew)
Usurper	69	28	38	110	100
Guide	93	52	62	134	124
Mystery	162	121	131	203	193
Adjuster	405	364	374	86	76
Leader	1215	1174	1184	896	886
Regulator	1620	1579	1589	1301	1291
General Governor	3240	3199	3209	2921	2911
High Overseer	301320	301279	301289	301001	300991

Fire - Sun

50	61	81	67	71	75
56	66	77	80	54	72
62	84	70	60	76	53
73	52	63	78	57	82
79	68	59	51	83	65
85	74	55	69	64	58

Earth - Sun

85	79	73	62	56	50
74	68	52	84	66	61
55	59	63	70	77	81
69	51	78	60	80	67
64	83	57	76	54	71
58	65	82	53	72	75

Air - Sun

58	64	69	55	74	85
65	83	51	59	68	79
82	57	78	63	52	73
53	76	60	70	84	62
72	54	80	77	66	56
75	71	67	81	61	50

Water - Sun

75	72	53	82	65	58
71	54	76	57	83	64
67	80	60	78	51	69
81	77	70	63	59	55
61	66	84	52	68	74
50	56	62	73	79	85

	Number	Angel Value (Arabic)	Angel Value (Hebrew)	Jinn Value (Arabic)	Jinn Value (Hebrew)
Usurper	50	9	19	91	81
Guide	85	44	54	126	116
Mystery	135	94	104	176	166
Adjuster	405	364	374	86	76
Leader	1215	1174	1184	896	886
Regulator	1620	1579	1589	1301	1291
General Governor	3240	3199	3209	2921	2911
High Overseer	275400	275359	275369	275081	275071

Fire - Venus

33	74	59	44	64	83	48
84	49	34	68	60	45	65
46	66	85	50	35	69	54
70	55	40	67	86	51	36
52	37	71	56	41	61	87
62	81	53	38	72	57	42
58	43	63	82	47	39	73

Earth - Venus

58	62	52	70	46	84	33
43	81	37	55	66	49	74
63	53	71	40	85	34	59
82	38	56	67	50	68	44
47	72	41	86	35	60	64
39	57	61	51	69	45	83
73	42	87	36	54	65	48

Occult Encyclopedia of Magic Squares

Air - Venus

73	39	47	82	63	43	58
42	57	72	38	53	81	62
87	61	41	56	71	37	52
36	51	86	67	40	55	70
54	69	35	50	85	66	46
65	45	60	68	34	49	84
48	83	64	44	59	74	33

Water - Venus

48	65	54	36	87	42	73
83	45	69	51	61	57	39
64	60	35	86	41	72	47
44	68	50	67	56	38	82
59	34	85	40	71	53	63
74	49	66	55	37	81	43
33	84	46	70	52	62	58

	Number	Angel Value (Arabic)	Angel Value (Hebrew)	Jinn Value (Arabic)	Jinn Value (Hebrew)
Usurper	33	352	2	74	64
Guide	87	46	56	128	118
Mystery	120	79	89	161	151
Adjuster	405	364	374	86	76
Leader	1215	1174	1184	896	886
Regulator	1620	1579	1589	1301	1291
General Governor	3240	3199	3209	2921	2911
High Overseer	281880	281839	281849	281561	281551

Fire - Mercury

19	35	81	64	53	69	50	34
27	43	72	56	61	78	42	26
70	54	33	49	36	20	63	80
79	62	25	41	44	28	55	71
48	32	51	67	83	66	21	37
40	24	59	76	74	58	29	45
65	82	38	22	31	47	68	52
57	73	46	30	23	39	77	60

Occult Encyclopedia of Magic Squares

Earth - Mercury

57	65	40	48	79	70	27	19
73	82	24	32	62	54	43	35
46	38	59	51	25	33	72	81
30	22	76	67	41	49	56	64
23	31	74	83	44	36	61	53
39	47	58	66	28	20	78	69
77	68	29	21	55	63	42	50
60	52	45	37	71	80	26	34

Air - Mercury

60	77	39	23	30	46	73	57
52	68	47	31	22	38	82	65
45	29	58	74	76	59	24	40
37	21	66	83	67	51	32	48
71	55	28	44	41	25	62	79
80	63	20	36	49	33	54	70
26	42	78	61	56	72	43	27
34	50	69	53	64	81	35	19

Water - Mercury

34	26	80	71	37	45	52	60
50	42	63	55	21	29	68	77
69	78	20	28	66	58	47	39
53	61	36	44	83	74	31	23
64	56	49	41	67	76	22	30
81	72	33	25	51	59	38	46
35	43	54	62	32	24	82	73
19	27	70	79	48	40	65	57

	Number	Angel Value (Arabic)	Angel Value (Hebrew)	Jinn Value (Arabic)	Jinn Value (Hebrew)
Usurper	19	338	348	60	50
Guide	83	42	52	124	114
Mystery	102	61	71	143	133
Adjuster	405	364	374	86	76
Leader	1215	1174	1184	896	886
Regulator	1620	1579	1589	1301	1291
General Governor	3240	3199	3209	2921	2911
High Overseer	268920	268879	268889	268601	268591

Fire - Moon

49	62	24	33	85	17	53	69	13
9	52	74	29	45	61	16	38	81
77	21	37	73	5	57	66	28	41
76	8	51	60	31	44	80	15	40
36	79	20	56	72	7	43	65	27
23	48	64	19	32	84	12	55	68
22	35	78	6	58	71	26	42	67
63	25	47	83	18	34	70	11	54
50	75	10	46	59	30	39	82	14

Earth - Moon

13	81	41	40	27	68	67	54	14
69	38	28	15	65	55	42	11	82
53	16	66	80	43	12	26	70	39
17	61	57	44	7	84	71	34	30
85	45	5	31	72	32	58	18	59
33	29	73	60	56	19	6	83	46
24	74	37	51	20	64	78	47	10
62	52	21	8	79	48	35	25	75
49	9	77	76	36	23	22	63	50

Air - Moon

14	82	39	30	59	46	10	75	50
54	11	70	34	18	83	47	25	63
67	42	26	71	58	6	78	35	22
68	55	12	84	32	19	64	48	23
27	65	43	7	72	56	20	79	36
40	15	80	44	31	60	51	8	76
41	28	66	57	5	73	37	21	77
81	38	16	61	45	29	74	52	9
13	69	53	17	85	33	24	62	49

Water - Moon

50	63	22	23	36	76	77	9	49
75	25	35	48	79	8	21	52	62
10	47	78	64	20	51	37	74	24
46	83	6	19	56	60	73	29	33
59	18	58	32	72	31	5	45	85
30	34	71	84	7	44	57	61	17
39	70	26	12	43	80	66	16	53
82	11	42	55	65	15	28	38	69
14	54	67	68	27	40	41	81	13

	Number	Angel Value (Arabic)	Angel Value (Hebrew)	Jinn Value (Arabic)	Jinn Value (Hebrew)
Usurper	5	324	334	46	36
Guide	85	44	54	126	116
Mystery	90	49	59	131	121
Adjuster	405	364	374	86	76
Leader	1215	1174	1184	896	886
Regulator	1620	1579	1589	1301	1291
General Governor	3240	3199	3209	2921	2911
High Overseer	275400	275359	275369	275081	275071

ANGEL OF THIRD QUINANCE: HARIEL (246)

אל	י	ר	ה
4	201	13	28
12	29	3	202
199	6	30	11

ל	א	י	ר	ה
י	ר	ה	ל	א
ה	ל	א	י	ר
א	י	ר	ה	ל
ר	ה	ל	א	י

Numerical Squares See Page: 79

ANGEL OF FOURTH QUINANCE: HAQMIAH (160)

יה	מ	ק	ה
4	101	43	12
42	13	3	102
99	6	14	41

ה	י	מ	ק	ה
מ	ק	ה	ה	י
ה	ה	י	מ	ק
י	מ	ק	ה	ה
ק	ה	ה	י	מ

Fire - Jupiter

32	43	37	48
47	38	40	35
42	33	49	36
39	46	34	41

Air - Jupiter

41	34	46	39
36	49	33	42
35	40	38	47
48	37	43	32

Earth - Jupiter

39	42	47	32
46	33	38	43
34	49	40	37
41	36	35	48

Water - Jupiter

48	35	36	41
37	40	49	34
43	38	33	46
32	47	42	39

	Number	Angel Value (Arabic)	Angel Value (Hebrew)	Jinn Value (Arabic)	Jinn Value (Hebrew)
Usurper	32	351	1	73	63
Guide	49	8	18	90	80
Mystery	81	40	50	122	112
Adjuster	1280	1239	1249	961	951
Leader	3840	3799	3809	3521	3511
Regulator	5120	5079	5089	4801	4791
General Governor	10240	10199	10209	9921	9911
High Overseer	501760	501719	501729	501441	501431

Occult Encyclopedia of Magic Squares

Fire - Mars

20	44	38	32	26
33	27	21	40	39
41	35	34	28	22
29	23	42	36	30
37	31	25	24	43

Air - Mars

37	29	41	33	20
31	23	35	27	44
25	42	34	21	38
24	36	28	40	32
43	30	22	39	26

Earth - Mars

43	24	25	31	37
30	36	42	23	29
22	28	34	35	41
39	40	21	27	33
26	32	38	44	20

Water - Mars

26	39	22	30	43
32	40	28	36	24
38	21	34	42	25
44	27	35	23	31
20	33	41	29	37

	Number	Angel Value (Arabic)	Angel Value (Hebrew)	Jinn Value (Arabic)	Jinn Value (Hebrew)
Usurper	20	339	349	61	51
Guide	44	3	13	85	75
Mystery	64	23	33	105	95
Adjuster	160	119	129	201	191
Leader	480	439	449	161	151
Regulator	640	599	609	321	311
General Governor	1280	1239	1249	961	951
High Overseer	56320	56279	56289	56001	55991

Fire - Sun

9	20	41	26	30	34
15	25	36	40	13	31
21	44	29	19	35	12
32	11	22	37	16	42
38	27	18	10	43	24
45	33	14	28	23	17

Earth - Sun

45	38	32	21	15	9
33	27	11	44	25	20
14	18	22	29	36	41
28	10	37	19	40	26
23	43	16	35	13	30
17	24	42	12	31	34

Air - Sun

17	23	28	14	33	45
24	43	10	18	27	38
42	16	37	22	11	32
12	35	19	29	44	21
31	13	40	36	25	15
34	30	26	41	20	9

Water - Sun

34	31	12	42	24	17
30	13	35	16	43	23
26	40	19	37	10	28
41	36	29	22	18	14
20	25	44	11	27	33
9	15	21	32	38	45

	Number	Angel Value (Arabic)	Angel Value (Hebrew)	Jinn Value (Arabic)	Jinn Value (Hebrew)
Usurper	9	328	338	50	40
Guide	45	4	14	86	76
Mystery	54	13	23	95	85
Adjuster	160	119	129	201	191
Leader	480	439	449	161	151
Regulator	640	599	609	321	311
General Governor	1280	1239	1249	961	951
High Overseer	57600	57559	57569	57281	57271

ANGEL OF THIRD DECANATE: SHACHDAR (512)

ר	ד	ח	שׁ
299	9	7	197
6	198	298	10
7	301	199	5

ר	ד	ח	שׁ
שׁ	ח	ד	ר
ד	ר	שׁ	ח
ח	שׁ	ר	ד

Occult Encyclopedia of Magic Squares

Fire - Jupiter

120	131	125	136
135	126	128	123
130	121	137	124
127	134	122	129

Air - Jupiter

129	122	134	127
124	137	121	130
123	128	126	135
136	125	131	120

Earth - Jupiter

127	130	135	120
134	121	126	131
122	137	128	125
129	124	123	136

Water - Jupiter

136	123	124	129
125	128	137	122
131	126	121	134
120	135	130	127

	Number	Angel Value (Arabic)	Angel Value (Hebrew)	Jinn Value (Arabic)	Jinn Value (Hebrew)
Usurper	120	79	89	161	151
Guide	137	96	106	178	168
Mystery	257	216	226	298	288
Adjuster	4096	4055	4065	3777	3767
Leader	12288	12247	12257	11969	11959
Regulator	16384	16343	16353	16065	16055
General Governor	32768	32727	32737	32449	32439
High Overseer	4489216	4489175	4489185	4488897	4488887

Fire - Mars

90	116	108	102	96
103	97	91	112	109
113	105	104	98	92
99	93	114	106	100
107	101	95	94	115

Air - Mars

107	99	113	103	90
101	93	105	97	116
95	114	104	91	108
94	106	98	112	102
115	100	92	109	96

Earth - Mars

115	94	95	101	107
100	106	114	93	99
92	98	104	105	113
109	112	91	97	103
96	102	108	116	90

Water - Mars

96	109	92	100	115
102	112	98	106	94
108	91	104	114	95
116	97	105	93	101
90	103	113	99	107

Occult Encyclopedia of Magic Squares

	Number	Angel Value (Arabic)	Angel Value (Hebrew)	Jinn Value (Arabic)	Jinn Value (Hebrew)
Usurper	90	49	59	131	121
Guide	116	75	85	157	147
Mystery	206	165	175	247	237
Adjuster	512	471	481	193	183
Leader	1536	1495	1505	1217	1207
Regulator	2048	2007	2017	1729	1719
General Governor	4096	4055	4065	3777	3767
High Overseer	475136	475095	475105	474817	474807

Fire - Sun

67	78	103	84	88	92
73	83	94	102	71	89
79	106	87	77	93	70
90	69	80	95	74	104
96	85	76	68	105	82
107	91	72	86	81	75

Air - Sun

75	81	86	72	91	107
82	105	68	76	85	96
104	74	95	80	69	90
70	93	77	87	106	79
89	71	102	94	83	73
92	88	84	103	78	67

Earth - Sun

107	96	90	79	73	67
91	85	69	106	83	78
72	76	80	87	94	103
86	68	95	77	102	84
81	105	74	93	71	88
75	82	104	70	89	92

Water - Sun

92	89	70	104	82	75
88	71	93	74	105	81
84	102	77	95	68	86
103	94	87	80	76	72
78	83	106	69	85	91
67	73	79	90	96	107

	Number	Angel Value (Arabic)	Angel Value (Hebrew)	Jinn Value (Arabic)	Jinn Value (Hebrew)
Usurper	67	26	36	108	98
Guide	107	66	76	148	138
Mystery	174	133	143	215	205
Adjuster	512	471	481	193	183
Leader	1536	1495	1505	1217	1207
Regulator	2048	2007	2017	1729	1719
General Governor	4096	4055	4065	3777	3767
High Overseer	438272	438231	438241	437953	437943

Fire - Venus

49	90	75	60	80	94	64
95	65	50	84	76	61	81
62	82	96	66	51	85	70
86	71	56	83	97	67	52
68	53	87	72	57	77	98
78	92	69	54	88	73	58
74	59	79	93	63	55	89

Air - Venus

89	55	63	93	79	59	74
58	73	88	54	69	92	78
98	77	57	72	87	53	68
52	67	97	83	56	71	86
70	85	51	66	96	82	62
81	61	76	84	50	65	95
64	94	80	60	75	90	49

Earth - Venus

74	78	68	86	62	95	49
59	92	53	71	82	65	90
79	69	87	56	96	50	75
93	54	72	83	66	84	60
63	88	57	97	51	76	80
55	73	77	67	85	61	94
89	58	98	52	70	81	64

Water - Venus

64	81	70	52	98	58	89
94	61	85	67	77	73	55
80	76	51	97	57	88	63
60	84	66	83	72	54	93
75	50	96	56	87	69	79
90	65	82	71	53	92	59
49	95	62	86	68	78	74

	Number	Angel Value (Arabic)	Angel Value (Hebrew)	Jinn Value (Arabic)	Jinn Value (Hebrew)
Usurper	49	8	18	90	80
Guide	98	57	67	139	129
Mystery	147	106	116	188	178
Adjuster	512	471	481	193	183
Leader	1536	1495	1505	1217	1207
Regulator	2048	2007	2017	1729	1719
General Governor	4096	4055	4065	3777	3767
High Overseer	401408	401367	401377	401089	401079

Fire - Mercury

32	48	97	77	66	82	63	47
40	56	85	69	74	94	55	39
83	67	46	62	49	33	76	96
95	75	38	54	57	41	68	84
61	45	64	80	99	79	34	50
53	37	72	92	87	71	42	58
78	98	51	35	44	60	81	65
70	86	59	43	36	52	93	73

Earth - Mercury

70	78	53	61	95	83	40	32
86	98	37	45	75	67	56	48
59	51	72	64	38	46	85	97
43	35	92	80	54	62	69	77
36	44	87	99	57	49	74	66
52	60	71	79	41	33	94	82
93	81	42	34	68	76	55	63
73	65	58	50	84	96	39	47

Occult Encyclopedia of Magic Squares

Air - Mercury

73	93	52	36	43	59	86	70
65	81	60	44	35	51	98	78
58	42	71	87	92	72	37	53
50	34	79	99	80	64	45	61
84	68	41	57	54	38	75	95
96	76	33	49	62	46	67	83
39	55	94	74	69	85	56	40
47	63	82	66	77	97	48	32

Water - Mercury

47	39	96	84	50	58	65	73
63	55	76	68	34	42	81	93
82	94	33	41	79	71	60	52
66	74	49	57	99	87	44	36
77	69	62	54	80	92	35	43
97	85	46	38	64	72	51	59
48	56	67	75	45	37	98	86
32	40	83	95	61	53	78	70

	Number	Angel Value (Arabic)	Angel Value (Hebrew)	Jinn Value (Arabic)	Jinn Value (Hebrew)
Usurper	32	351	1	73	63
Guide	99	58	68	140	130
Mystery	131	90	100	172	162
Adjuster	512	471	481	193	183
Leader	1536	1495	1505	1217	1207
Regulator	2048	2007	2017	1729	1719
General Governor	4096	4055	4065	3777	3767
High Overseer	405504	405463	405473	405185	405175

Fire - Moon

60	73	35	44	104	28	64	80	24
20	63	85	40	56	72	27	49	100
96	32	48	84	16	68	77	39	52
87	19	62	71	42	55	99	26	51
47	98	31	67	83	18	54	76	38
34	59	75	30	43	103	23	66	79
33	46	97	17	69	82	37	53	78
74	36	58	102	29	45	81	22	65
61	86	21	57	70	41	50	101	25

Earth - Moon

24	100	52	51	38	79	78	65	25
80	49	39	26	76	66	53	22	101
64	27	77	99	54	23	37	81	50
28	72	68	55	18	103	82	45	41
104	56	16	42	83	43	69	29	70
44	40	84	71	67	30	17	102	57
35	85	48	62	31	75	97	58	21
73	63	32	19	98	59·	46	36	86
60	20	96	87	47	34	33	74	61

Air - Moon

25	101	50	41	70	57	21	86	61
65	22	81	45	29	102	58	36	74
78	53	37	82	69	17	97	46	33
79	66	23	103	43	30	75	59	34
38	76	54	18	83	67	31	98	47
51	26	99	55	42	71	62	19	87
52	39	77	68	16	84	48	32	96
100	49	27	72	56	40	85	63	20
24	80	64	28	104	44	35	73	60

Occult Encyclopedia of Magic Squares

Water - Moon

61	74	33	34	47	87	96	20	60
86	36	46	59	98	19	32	63	73
21	58	97	75	31	62	48	85	35
57	102	17	30	67	71	84	40	44
70	29	69	43	83	42	16	56	104
41	45	82	103	18	55	68	72	28
50	81	37	23	54	99	77	27	64
101	22	53	66	76	26	39	49	80
25	65	78	79	38	51	52	100	24

	Number	Angel Value (Arabic)	Angel Value (Hebrew)	Jinn Value (Arabic)	Jinn Value (Hebrew)
Usurper	16	335	345	57	47
Guide	104	63	73	145	135
Mystery	120	79	89	161	151
Adjuster	512	471	481	193	183
Leader	1536	1495	1505	1217	1207
Regulator	2048	2007	2017	1729	1719
General Governor	4096	4055	4065	3777	3767
High Overseer	425984	425943	425953	425665	425655

Fire - Saturn

1	19	26	64	55	100	48	40	72	87
12	76	69	60	102	85	3	45	31	29
27	32	56	101	86	71	20	8	49	62
33	58	99	88	21	67	75	16	5	50
46	98	90	25	36	59	63	73	18	4
53	10	11	78	66	42	38	28	83	103
65	47	7	14	80	35	23	84	106	51
79	68	43	2	13	30	81	105	54	37
89	22	34	41	9	17	104	52	70	74
107	82	77	39	44	6	57	61	24	15

Occult Encyclopedia of Magic Squares

Earth - Saturn

107	89	79	65	53	46	33	27	12	1
82	22	68	47	10	98	58	32	76	19
77	34	43	7	11	90	99	56	69	26
39	41	2	14	78	25	88	101	60	64
44	9	13	80	66	36	21	86	102	55
6	17	30	35	42	59	67	71	85	100
57	104	81	23	38	63	75	20	3	48
61	52	105	84	28	73	16	8	45	40
24	70	54	106	83	18	5	49	31	72
15	74	37	51	103	4	50	62	29	87

Air - Saturn

15	24	61	57	6	44	39	77	82	107
74	70	52	104	17	9	41	34	22	89
37	54	105	81	30	13	2	43	68	79
51	106	84	23	35	80	14	7	47	65
103	83	28	38	42	66	78	11	10	53
4	18	73	63	59	36	25	90	98	46
50	5	16	75	67	21	88	99	58	33
62	49	8	20	71	86	101	56	32	27
29	31	45	3	85	102	60	69	76	12
87	72	40	48	100	55	64	26	19	1

Water - Saturn

87	29	62	50	4	103	51	37	74	15
72	31	49	5	18	83	106	54	70	24
40	45	8	16	73	28	84	105	52	61
48	**3**	20	75	63	38	23	81	104	57
100	85	71	67	59	42	35	30	17	6
55	102	86	21	36	66	80	13	9	44
64	60	101	88	25	78	14	2	41	39
26	69	56	99	90	11	7	43	34	77
19	76	32	58	98	10	47	68	22	82
1	12	27	33	46	53	65	79	89	107

Occult Encyclopedia of Magic Squares

	Number	Angel Value (Arabic)	Angel Value (Hebrew)	Jinn Value (Arabic)	Jinn Value (Hebrew)
Usurper	1	320	330	42	32
Guide	107	66	76	148	138
Mystery	108	67	77	149	139
Adjuster	512	471	481	193	183
Leader	1536	1495	1505	1217	1207
Regulator	2048	2007	2017	1729	1719
General Governor	4096	4055	4065	3777	3767
High Overseer	438272	438231	438241	437953	437943

ANGEL OF FIFTH QUINANCE: LAVIAH (52)

Hebrew Squares See Page: 351

Numerical Squares See Page: 351

ANGEL OF SIX QUINANCE: KALIEL (91)

אל	י	ל	ב
19	31	13	28
12	29	18	32
29	21	30	11

ל	א	י	ל	ב
י	ל	ב	ל	א
ב	ל	א	י	ל
א	י	ל	ב	ל
ל	ב	ל	א	י

401

Fire - Jupiter

15	26	20	30
29	21	23	18
25	16	31	19
22	28	17	24

Air - Jupiter

24	17	28	22
19	31	16	25
18	23	21	29
30	20	26	15

Earth - Jupiter

22	25	29	15
28	16	21	26
17	31	23	20
24	19	18	30

Water - Jupiter

30	18	19	24
20	23	31	17
26	21	16	28
15	29	25	22

	Number	Angel Value (Arabic)	Angel Value (Hebrew)	Jinn Value (Arabic)	Jinn Value (Hebrew)
Usurper	15	334	344	56	46
Guide	31	350	360	72	62
Mystery	46	5	15	87	77
Adjuster	728	687	697	409	399
Leader	2184	2143	2153	1865	1855
Regulator	2912	2871	2881	2593	2583
General Governor	5824	5783	5793	5505	5495
High Overseer	180544	180503	180513	180225	180215

Fire - Mars

6	31	24	18	12
19	13	7	27	25
28	21	20	14	8
15	9	29	22	16
23	17	11	10	30

Air - Mars

23	15	28	19	6
17	9	21	13	31
11	29	20	7	24
10	22	14	27	18
30	16	8	25	12

Earth - Mars

30	10	11	17	23
16	22	29	9	15
8	14	20	21	28
25	27	7	13	19
12	18	24	31	6

Water - Mars

12	25	8	16	30
18	27	14	22	10
24	7	20	29	11
31	13	21	9	17
6	19	28	15	23

Occult Encyclopedia of Magic Squares

	Number	Angel Value (Arabic)	Angel Value (Hebrew)	Jinn Value (Arabic)	Jinn Value (Hebrew)
Usurper	6	325	335	47	37
Guide	31	350	360	72	62
Mystery	37	356	6	78	68
Adjuster	91	50	60	132	122
Leader	273	232	242	314	304
Regulator	364	323	333	45	35
General Governor	728	687	697	409	399
High Overseer	22568	22527	22537	22249	22239

SCORPIO

SIGN SCORPIO: AKRAB (372)

ב	ר	ק	ע
71	102	198	1
198	3	69	102
101	67	5	199

ב	ר	ק	ע
ע	ק	ר	ב
ר	ב	ע	ק
ק	ע	ב	ר

Fire - Saturn

125	120	127
126	124	122
121	128	123

Air - Saturn

123	128	121
122	124	126
127	120	125

Earth - Saturn

121	126	125
128	124	120
123	122	127

Water - Saturn

127	122	123
120	124	128
125	126	121

	Number	Angel Value (Arabic)	Angel Value (Hebrew)	Jinn Value (Arabic)	Jinn Value (Hebrew)
Usurper	120	79	89	161	151
Guide	128	87	97	169	159
Mystery	248	207	217	289	279
Adjuster	372	331	341	53	43
Leader	1116	1075	1085	797	787
Regulator	1488	1447	1457	1169	1159
General Governor	2976	2935	2945	2657	2647
High Overseer	380928	380887	380897	380609	380599

Occult Encyclopedia of Magic Squares

Fire - Jupiter

85	96	90	101
100	91	93	88
95	86	102	89
92	99	87	94

Air - Jupiter

94	87	99	92
89	102	86	95
88	93	91	100
101	90	96	85

Earth - Jupiter

92	95	100	85
99	86	91	96
87	102	93	90
94	89	88	101

Water - Jupiter

101	88	89	94
90	93	102	87
96	91	86	99
85	100	95	92

	Number	Angel Value (Arabic)	Angel Value (Hebrew)	Jinn Value (Arabic)	Jinn Value (Hebrew)
Usurper	85	44	54	126	116
Guide	102	61	71	143	133
Mystery	187	146	156	228	218
Adjuster	2976	2935	2945	2657	2647
Leader	8928	8887	8897	8609	8599
Regulator	11904	11863	11873	11585	11575
General Governor	23808	23767	23777	23489	23479
High Overseer	2428416	2428375	2428385	2428097	2428087

Fire - Mars

62	88	80	74	68
75	69	63	84	81
85	77	76	70	64
71	65	86	78	72
79	73	67	66	87

Air - Mars

79	71	85	75	62
73	65	77	69	88
67	86	76	63	80
66	78	70	84	74
87	72	64	81	68

Earth - Mars

87	66	67	73	79
72	78	86	65	71
64	70	76	77	85
81	84	63	69	75
68	74	80	88	62

Water - Mars

68	81	64	72	87
74	84	70	78	66
80	63	76	86	67
88	69	77	65	73
62	75	85	71	79

Occult Encyclopedia of Magic Squares

	Number	Angel Value (Arabic)	Angel Value (Hebrew)	Jinn Value (Arabic)	Jinn Value (Hebrew)
Usurper	62	21	31	103	93
Guide	88	47	57	129	119
Mystery	150	109	119	191	181
Adjuster	372	331	341	53	43
Leader	1116	1075	1085	797	787
Regulator	1488	1447	1457	1169	1159
General Governor	2976	2935	2945	2657	2647
High Overseer	261888	261847	261857	261569	261559

Fire - Sun

44	55	78	61	65	69
50	60	71	77	48	66
56	81	64	54	70	47
67	46	57	72	51	79
73	62	53	45	80	59
82	68	49	63	58	52

Air - Sun

52	58	63	49	68	82
59	80	45	53	62	73
79	51	72	57	46	67
47	70	54	64	81	56
66	48	77	71	60	50
69	65	61	78	55	44

Earth - Sun

82	73	67	56	50	44
68	62	46	81	60	55
49	53	57	64	71	78
63	45	72	54	77	61
58	80	51	70	48	65
52	59	79	47	66	69

Water - Sun

69	66	47	79	59	52
65	48	70	51	80	58
61	77	54	72	45	63
78	71	64	57	53	49
55	60	81	46	62	68
44	50	56	67	73	82

Occult Encyclopedia of Magic Squares

	Number	Angel Value (Arabic)	Angel Value (Hebrew)	Jinn Value (Arabic)	Jinn Value (Hebrew)
Usurper	44	3	13	85	75
Guide	82	41	51	123	113
Mystery	126	85	95	167	157
Adjuster	372	331	341	53	43
Leader	1116	1075	1085	797	787
Regulator	1488	1447	1457	1169	1159
General Governor	2976	2935	2945	2657	2647
High Overseer	244032	243991	244001	243713	243703

Fire - Venus

29	70	55	40	60	74	44
75	45	30	64	56	41	61
42	62	76	46	31	65	50
66	51	36	63	77	47	32
48	33	67	52	37	57	78
58	72	49	34	68	53	38
54	39	59	73	43	35	69

Air - Venus

69	35	43	73	59	39	54
38	53	68	34	49	72	58
78	57	37	52	67	33	48
32	47	77	63	36	51	66
50	65	31	46	76	62	42
61	41	56	64	30	45	75
44	74	60	40	55	70	29

Earth - Venus

54	58	48	66	42	75	29
39	72	33	51	62	45	70
59	49	67	36	76	30	55
73	34	52	63	46	64	40
43	68	37	77	31	56	60
35	53	57	47	65	41	74
69	38	78	32	50	61	44

Water - Venus

44	61	50	32	78	38	69
74	41	65	47	57	53	35
60	56	31	77	37	68	43
40	64	46	63	52	34	73
55	30	76	36	67	49	59
70	45	62	51	33	72	39
29	75	42	66	48	58	54

Occult Encyclopedia of Magic Squares

	Number	Angel Value (Arabic)	Angel Value (Hebrew)	Jinn Value (Arabic)	Jinn Value (Hebrew)
Usurper	29	348	358	70	60
Guide	78	37	47	119	109
Mystery	107	66	76	148	138
Adjuster	372	331	341	53	43
Leader	1116	1075	1085	797	787
Regulator	1488	1447	1457	1169	1159
General Governor	2976	2935	2945	2657	2647
High Overseer	232128	232087	232097	231809	231799

Fire - Mercury

15	31	76	60	49	65	46	30
23	39	68	52	57	73	38	22
66	50	29	45	32	16	59	75
74	58	21	37	40	24	51	67
44	28	47	63	78	62	17	33
36	20	55	71	70	54	25	41
61	77	34	18	27	43	64	48
53	69	42	26	19	35	72	56

Earth - Mercury

53	61	36	44	74	66	23	15
69	77	20	28	58	50	39	31
42	34	55	47	21	29	68	76
26	18	71	63	37	45	52	60
19	27	70	78	40	32	57	49
35	43	54	62	24	16	73	65
72	64	25	17	51	59	38	46
56	48	41	33	67	75	22	30

Air - Mercury

56	72	35	19	26	42	69	53
48	64	43	27	18	34	77	61
41	25	54	70	71	55	20	36
33	17	62	78	63	47	28	44
67	51	24	40	37	21	58	74
75	59	16	32	45	29	50	66
22	38	73	57	52	68	39	23
30	46	65	49	60	76	31	15

Water - Mercury

30	22	75	67	33	41	48	56
46	38	59	51	17	25	64	72
65	73	16	24	62	54	43	35
49	57	32	40	78	70	27	19
60	52	45	37	63	71	18	26
76	68	29	21	47	55	34	42
31	39	50	58	28	20	77	69
15	23	66	74	44	36	61	53

	Number	Angel Value (Arabic)	Angel Value (Hebrew)	Jinn Value (Arabic)	Jinn Value (Hebrew)
Usurper	15	334	344	56	46
Guide	78	37	47	119	109
Mystery	93	52	62	134	124
Adjuster	372	331	341	53	43
Leader	1116	1075	1085	797	787
Regulator	1488	1447	1457	1169	1159
General Governor	2976	2935	2945	2657	2647
High Overseer	232128	232087	232097	231809	231799

Occult Encyclopedia of Magic Squares

Fire - Moon

45	58	20	29	84	13	49	65	9
5	48	70	25	41	57	12	34	80
76	17	33	69	1	53	62	24	37
72	4	47	56	27	40	79	11	36
32	78	16	52	68	3	39	61	23
19	44	60	15	28	83	8	51	64
18	31	77	2	54	67	22	38	63
59	21	43	82	14	30	66	7	50
46	71	6	42	55	26	35	81	10

Earth - Moon

9	80	37	36	23	64	63	50	10
65	34	24	11	61	51	38	7	81
49	12	62	79	39	8	22	66	35
13	57	53	40	3	83	67	30	26
84	41	1	27	68	28	54	14	55
29	25	69	56	52	15	2	82	42
20	70	33	47	16	60	77	43	6
58	48	17	4	78	44	31	21	71
45	5	76	72	32	19	18	59	46

Air - Moon

10	81	35	26	55	42	6	71	46
50	7	66	30	14	82	43	21	59
63	38	22	67	54	2	77	31	18
64	51	8	83	28	15	60	44	19
23	61	39	3	68	52	16	78	32
36	11	79	40	27	56	47	4	72
37	24	62	53	1	69	33	17	76
80	34	12	57	41	25	70	48	5
9	65	49	13	84	29	20	58	45

Water - Moon

46	59	18	19	32	72	76	5	45
71	21	31	44	78	4	17	48	58
6	43	77	60	16	47	33	70	20
42	82	2	15	52	56	69	25	29
55	14	54	28	68	27	1	41	84
26	30	67	83	3	40	53	57	13
35	66	22	8	39	79	62	12	49
81	7	38	51	61	11	24	34	65
10	50	63	64	23	36	37	80	9

	Number	Angel Value (Arabic)	Angel Value (Hebrew)	Jinn Value (Arabic)	Jinn Value (Hebrew)
Usurper	1	320	330	42	32
Guide	84	43	53	125	115
Mystery	85	44	54	126	116
Adjuster	372	331	341	53	43
Leader	1116	1075	1085	797	787
Regulator	1488	1447	1457	1169	1159
General Governor	2976	2935	2945	2657	2647
High Overseer	249984	249943	249953	249665	249655

ARCHANGEL OF SCORPIO: BARKIEL (263)

אל	י	כב	בר
201	21	13	28
12	29	200	22
19	203	30	11

ל	א	י	ב	ר	כ
ר	ב	ל	כ	י	א
י	ב	א	ר	ל	כ
כ	ר	ב	י	א	ל
ב	ל	ר	א	כ	י
א	י	כ	ל	ב	ר

Occult Encyclopedia of Magic Squares

Fire - Jupiter

58	69	63	73
72	64	66	61
68	59	74	62
65	71	60	67

Air - Jupiter

67	60	71	65
62	74	59	68
61	66	64	72
73	63	69	58

Earth - Jupiter

65	68	72	58
71	59	64	69
60	74	66	63
67	62	61	73

Water - Jupiter

73	61	62	67
63	66	74	60
69	64	59	71
58	72	68	65

	Number	Angel Value (Arabic)	Angel Value (Hebrew)	Jinn Value (Arabic)	Jinn Value (Hebrew)
Usurper	58	17	27	99	89
Guide	74	33	43	115	105
Mystery	132	91	101	173	163
Adjuster	2104	2063	2073	1785	1775
Leader	6312	6271	6281	5993	5983
Regulator	8416	8375	8385	8097	8087
General Governor	16832	16791	16801	16513	16503
High Overseer	1245568	1245527	1245537	1245249	1245239

Fire - Mars

40	67	58	52	46
53	47	41	63	59
64	55	54	48	42
49	43	65	56	50
57	51	45	44	66

Air - Mars

57	49	64	53	40
51	43	55	47	67
45	65	54	41	58
44	56	48	63	52
66	50	42	59	46

Earth - Mars

66	44	45	51	57
50	56	65	43	49
42	48	54	55	64
59	63	41	47	53
46	52	58	67	40

Water - Mars

46	59	42	50	66
52	63	48	56	44
58	41	54	65	45
67	47	55	43	51
40	53	64	49	57

Occult Encyclopedia of Magic Squares

	Number	Angel Value (Arabic)	Angel Value (Hebrew)	Jinn Value (Arabic)	Jinn Value (Hebrew)
Usurper	40	359	9	81	71
Guide	67	26	36	108	98
Mystery	107	66	76	148	138
Adjuster	263	222	232	304	294
Leader	789	748	758	470	460
Regulator	1052	1011	1021	733	723
General Governor	2104	2063	2073	1785	1775
High Overseer	140968	140927	140937	140649	140639

Fire - Sun

26	37	59	43	47	51
32	42	53	58	30	48
38	62	46	36	52	29
49	28	39	54	33	60
55	44	35	27	61	41
63	50	31	45	40	34

Air - Sun

34	40	45	31	50	63
41	61	27	35	44	55
60	33	54	39	28	49
29	52	36	46	62	38
48	30	58	53	42	32
51	47	43	59	37	26

Earth - Sun

63	55	49	38	32	26
50	44	28	62	42	37
31	35	39	46	53	59
45	27	54	36	58	43
40	61	33	52	30	47
34	41	60	29	48	51

Water - Sun

51	48	29	60	41	34
47	30	52	33	61	40
43	58	36	54	27	45
59	53	46	39	35	31
37	42	62	28	44	50
26	32	38	49	55	63

	Number	Angel Value (Arabic)	Angel Value (Hebrew)	Jinn Value (Arabic)	Jinn Value (Hebrew)
Usurper	26	345	355	67	57
Guide	63	22	32	104	94
Mystery	89	48	58	130	120
Adjuster	263	222	232	304	294
Leader	789	748	758	470	460
Regulator	1052	1011	1021	733	723
General Governor	2104	2063	2073	1785	1775
High Overseer	132552	132511	132521	132233	132223

Fire - Venus

13	54	39	24	44	61	28
62	29	14	48	40	25	45
26	46	63	30	15	49	34
50	35	20	47	64	31	16
32	17	51	36	21	41	65
42	59	33	18	52	37	22
38	23	43	60	27	19	53

Earth - Venus

38	42	32	50	26	62	13
23	59	17	35	46	29	54
43	33	51	20	63	14	39
60	18	36	47	30	48	24
27	52	21	64	15	40	44
19	37	41	31	49	25	61
53	22	65	16	34	45	28

Air - Venus

53	19	27	60	43	23	38
22	37	52	18	33	59	42
65	41	21	36	51	17	32
16	31	64	47	20	35	50
34	49	15	30	63	46	26
45	25	40	48	14	29	62
28	61	44	24	39	54	13

Water - Venus

28	45	34	16	65	22	53
61	25	49	31	41	37	19
44	40	15	64	21	52	27
24	48	30	47	36	18	60
39	14	63	20	51	33	43
54	29	46	35	17	59	23
13	62	26	50	32	42	38

	Number	Angel Value (Arabic)	Angel Value (Hebrew)	Jinn Value (Arabic)	Jinn Value (Hebrew)
Usurper	13	332	342	54	44
Guide	65	24	34	106	96
Mystery	78	37	47	119	109
Adjuster	263	222	232	304	294
Leader	789	748	758	470	460
Regulator	1052	1011	1021	733	723
General Governor	2104	2063	2073	1785	1775
High Overseer	136760	136719	136729	136441	136431

Fire - Mercury

1	17	65	46	35	51	32	16
9	25	54	38	43	62	24	8
52	36	15	31	18	2	45	64
63	44	7	23	26	10	37	53
30	14	33	49	67	48	3	19
22	6	41	60	56	40	11	27
47	66	20	4	13	29	50	34
39	55	28	12	5	21	61	42

Earth - Mercury

39	47	22	30	63	52	9	1
55	66	6	14	44	36	25	17
28	20	41	33	7	15	54	65
12	4	60	49	23	31	38	46
5	13	56	67	26	18	43	35
21	29	40	48	10	2	62	51
61	50	11	3	37	45	24	32
42	34	27	19	53	64	8	16

Occult Encyclopedia of Magic Squares

Air - Mercury

42	61	21	5	12	28	55	39
34	50	29	13	4	20	66	47
27	11	40	56	60	41	6	22
19	3	48	67	49	33	14	30
53	37	10	26	23	7	44	63
64	45	2	18	31	15	36	52
8	24	62	43	38	54	25	9
16	32	51	35	46	65	17	1

Water - Mercury

16	8	64	53	19	27	34	42
32	24	45	37	3	11	50	61
51	62	2	10	48	40	29	21
35	43	18	26	67	56	13	5
46	38	31	23	49	60	4	12
65	54	15	7	33	41	20	28
17	25	36	44	14	6	66	55
1	9	52	63	30	22	47	39

	Number	Angel Value (Arabic)	Angel Value (Hebrew)	Jinn Value (Arabic)	Jinn Value (Hebrew)
Usurper	1	320	330	42	32
Guide	67	26	36	108	98
Mystery	68	27	37	109	99
Adjuster	263	222	232	304	294
Leader	789	748	758	470	460
Regulator	1052	1011	1021	733	723
General Governor	2104	2063	2073	1785	1775
High Overseer	140968	140927	140937	140649	140639

ANGEL OF SCORPIO: SAITZEL (202)

ל	י״	צ״	מא
60	101	14	27
13	28	59	102
99	62	29	12

Fire - Jupiter

43	54	48	57
56	49	51	46
53	44	58	47
50	55	45	52

Air - Jupiter

52	45	55	50
47	58	44	53
46	51	49	56
57	48	54	43

Earth - Jupiter

50	53	56	43
55	44	49	54
45	58	51	48
52	47	46	57

Water - Jupiter

57	46	47	52
48	51	58	45
54	49	44	55
43	56	53	50

	Number	Angel Value (Arabic)	Angel Value (Hebrew)	Jinn Value (Arabic)	Jinn Value (Hebrew)
Usurper	43	2	12	84	74
Guide	58	17	27	99	89
Mystery	101	60	70	142	132
Adjuster	1616	1575	1585	1297	1287
Leader	4848	4807	4817	4529	4519
Regulator	6464	6423	6433	6145	6135
General Governor	12928	12887	12897	12609	12599
High Overseer	749824	749783	749793	749505	749495

Occult Encyclopedia of Magic Squares

Fire - Mars

28	54	46	40	34
41	35	29	50	47
51	43	42	36	30
37	31	52	44	38
45	39	33	32	53

Air - Mars

45	37	51	41	28
39	31	43	35	54
33	52	42	29	46
32	44	36	50	40
53	38	30	47	34

Earth - Mars

53	32	33	39	45
38	44	52	31	37
30	36	42	43	51
47	50	29	35	41
34	40	46	54	28

Water - Mars

34	47	30	38	53
40	50	36	44	32
46	29	42	52	33
54	35	43	31	39
28	41	51	37	45

	Number	Angel Value (Arabic)	Angel Value (Hebrew)	Jinn Value (Arabic)	Jinn Value (Hebrew)
Usurper	28	347	357	69	59
Guide	54	13	23	95	85
Mystery	82	41	51	123	113
Adjuster	202	161	171	243	233
Leader	606	565	575	287	277
Regulator	808	767	777	489	479
General Governor	1616	1575	1585	1297	1287
High Overseer	87264	87223	87233	86945	86935

Fire - Sun

16	27	48	33	37	41
22	32	43	47	20	38
28	51	36	26	42	19
39	18	29	44	23	49
45	34	25	17	50	31
52	40	21	35	30	24

Earth - Sun

52	45	39	28	22	16
40	34	18	51	32	27
21	25	29	36	43	48
35	17	44	26	47	33
30	50	23	42	20	37
24	31	49	19	38	41

Occult Encyclopedia of Magic Squares

Air - Sun

24	30	35	21	40	52
31	50	17	25	34	45
49	23	44	29	18	39
19	42	26	36	51	28
38	20	47	43	32	22
41	37	33	48	27	16

Water - Sun

41	38	19	49	31	24
37	20	42	23	50	30
33	47	26	44	17	35
48	43	36	29	25	21
27	32	51	18	34	40
16	22	28	39	45	52

	Number	Angel Value (Arabic)	Angel Value (Hebrew)	Jinn Value (Arabic)	Jinn Value (Hebrew)
Usurper	16	335	345	57	47
Guide	52	11	21	93	83
Mystery	68	27	37	109	99
Adjuster	202	161	171	243	233
Leader	606	565	575	287	277
Regulator	808	767	777	489	479
General Governor	1616	1575	1585	1297	1287
High Overseer	84032	83991	84001	83713	83703

Fire - Venus

4	45	30	15	35	54	19
55	20	5	39	31	16	36
17	37	56	21	6	40	25
41	26	11	38	57	22	7
23	8	42	27	12	32	58
33	52	24	9	43	28	13
29	14	34	53	18	10	44

Air - Venus

44	10	18	53	34	14	29
13	28	43	9	24	52	33
58	32	12	27	42	8	23
7	22	57	38	11	26	41
25	40	6	21	56	37	17
36	16	31	39	5	20	55
19	54	35	15	30	45	4

Earth - Venus

29	33	23	41	17	55	4
14	52	8	26	37	20	45
34	24	42	11	56	5	30
53	9	27	38	21	39	15
18	43	12	57	6	31	35
10	28	32	22	40	16	54
44	13	58	7	25	36	19

Water - Venus

19	36	25	7	58	13	44
54	16	40	22	32	28	10
35	31	6	57	12	43	18
15	39	21	38	27	9	53
30	5	56	11	42	24	34
45	20	37	26	8	52	14
4	55	17	41	23	33	29

	Number	Angel Value (Arabic)	Angel Value (Hebrew)	Jinn Value (Arabic)	Jinn Value (Hebrew)
Usurper	4	323	333	45	35
Guide	58	17	27	99	89
Mystery	62	21	31	103	93
Adjuster	202	161	171	243	233
Leader	606	565	575	287	277
Regulator	808	767	777	489	479
General Governor	1616	1575	1585	1297	1287
High Overseer	93728	93687	93697	93409	93399

LORD OF TRIPLICITY BY DAY: BETHCHON (476)

נ	חו	ת	בי
11	401	17	47
16	48	10	402
399	13	49	15

נ	ו	ח	ת	י	ב
י	ת	נ	ב	ח	ו
ח	ב	ו	י	נ	ת
ב	י	ת	ח	ו	נ
ת	נ	י	ו	ב	ח
ו	ח	ב	נ	ת	י

Fire - Jupiter

111	122	116	127
126	117	119	114
121	112	128	115
118	125	113	120

Air - Jupiter

120	113	125	118
115	128	112	121
114	119	117	126
127	116	122	111

Earth - Jupiter

118	121	126	111
125	112	117	122
113	128	119	116
120	115	114	127

Water - Jupiter

127	114	115	120
116	119	128	113
122	117	112	125
111	126	121	118

Occult Encyclopedia of Magic Squares

	Number	Angel Value (Arabic)	Angel Value (Hebrew)	Jinn Value (Arabic)	Jinn Value (Hebrew)
Usurper	111	70	80	152	142
Guide	128	87	97	169	159
Mystery	239	198	208	280	270
Adjuster	3808	3767	3777	3489	3479
Leader	11424	11383	11393	11105	11095
Regulator	15232	15191	15201	14913	14903
General Governor	30464	30423	30433	30145	30135
High Overseer	3899392	3899351	3899361	3899073	3899063

Fire - Mars

83	108	101	95	89
96	90	84	104	102
105	98	97	91	85
92	86	106	99	93
100	94	88	87	107

Air - Mars

100	92	105	96	83
94	86	98	90	108
88	106	97	84	101
87	99	91	104	95
107	93	85	102	89

Earth - Mars

107	87	88	94	100
93	99	106	86	92
85	91	97	98	105
102	104	84	90	96
89	95	101	108	83

Water - Mars

89	102	85	93	107
95	104	91	99	87
101	84	97	106	88
108	90	98	86	94
83	96	105	92	100

	Number	Angel Value (Arabic)	Angel Value (Hebrew)	Jinn Value (Arabic)	Jinn Value (Hebrew)
Usurper	83	42	52	124	114
Guide	108	67	77	149	139
Mystery	191	150	160	232	222
Adjuster	476	435	445	157	147
Leader	1428	1387	1397	1109	1099
Regulator	1904	1863	1873	1585	1575
General Governor	3808	3767	3777	3489	3479
High Overseer	411264	411223	411233	410945	410935

Occult Encyclopedia of Magic Squares

Fire - Sun

61	72	97	78	82	86
67	77	88	96	65	83
73	100	81	71	87	64
84	63	74	89	68	98
90	79	70	62	99	76
101	85	66	80	75	69

Air - Sun

69	75	80	66	85	101
76	99	62	70	79	90
98	68	89	74	63	84
64	87	71	81	100	73
83	65	96	88	77	67
86	82	78	97	72	61

Earth - Sun

101	90	84	73	67	61
85	79	63	100	77	72
66	70	74	81	88	97
80	62	89	71	96	78
75	99	68	87	65	82
69	76	98	64	83	86

Water - Sun

86	83	64	98	76	69
82	65	87	68	99	75
78	96	71	89	62	80
97	88	81	74	70	66
72	77	100	63	79	85
61	67	73	84	90	101

	Number	Angel Value (Arabic)	Angel Value (Hebrew)	Jinn Value (Arabic)	Jinn Value (Hebrew)
Usurper	61	20	30	102	92
Guide	101	60	70	142	132
Mystery	162	121	131	203	193
Adjuster	476	435	445	157	147
Leader	1428	1387	1397	1109	1099
Regulator	1904	1863	1873	1585	1575
General Governor	3808	3767	3777	3489	3479
High Overseer	384608	384567	384577	384289	384279

Fire - Venus

44	85	70	55	75	88	59
89	60	45	79	71	56	76
57	77	90	61	46	80	65
81	66	51	78	91	62	47
63	48	82	67	52	72	92
73	86	64	49	83	68	53
69	54	74	87	58	50	84

Earth - Venus

69	73	63	81	57	89	44
54	86	48	66	77	60	85
74	64	82	51	90	45	70
87	49	67	78	61	79	55
58	83	52	91	46	71	75
50	68	72	62	80	56	88
84	53	92	47	65	76	59

Occult Encyclopedia of Magic Squares

Air - Venus

84	50	58	87	74	54	69
53	68	83	49	64	86	73
92	72	52	67	82	48	63
47	62	91	78	51	66	81
65	80	46	61	90	77	57
76	56	71	79	45	60	89
59	88	75	55	70	85	44

Water - Venus

59	76	65	47	92	53	84
88	56	80	62	72	68	50
75	71	46	91	52	83	58
55	79	61	78	67	49	87
70	45	90	51	82	64	74
85	60	77	66	48	86	54
44	89	57	81	63	73	69

	Number	Angel Value (Arabic)	Angel Value (Hebrew)	Jinn Value (Arabic)	Jinn Value (Hebrew)
Usurper	44	3	13	85	75
Guide	92	51	61	133	123
Mystery	136	95	105	177	167
Adjuster	476	435	445	157	147
Leader	1428	1387	1397	1109	1099
Regulator	1904	1863	1873	1585	1575
General Governor	3808	3767	3777	3489	3479
High Overseer	350336	350295	350305	350017	350007

Fire - Mercury

28	44	89	73	62	78	59	43
36	52	81	65	70	86	51	35
79	63	42	58	45	29	72	88
87	71	34	50	53	37	64	80
57	41	60	76	91	75	30	46
49	33	68	84	83	67	38	54
74	90	47	31	40	56	77	61
66	82	55	39	32	48	85	69

Earth - Mercury

66	74	49	57	87	79	36	28
82	90	33	41	71	63	52	44
55	47	68	60	34	42	81	89
39	31	84	76	50	58	65	73
32	40	83	91	53	45	70	62
48	56	67	75	37	29	86	78
85	77	38	30	64	72	51	59
69	61	54	46	80	88	35	43

Occult Encyclopedia of Magic Squares

Air - Mercury

69	85	48	32	39	55	82	66
61	77	56	40	31	47	90	74
54	38	67	83	84	68	33	49
46	30	75	91	76	60	41	57
80	64	37	53	50	34	71	87
88	72	29	45	58	42	63	79
35	51	86	70	65	81	52	36
43	59	78	62	73	89	44	28

Water - Mercury

43	35	88	80	46	54	61	69
59	51	72	64	30	38	77	85
78	86	29	37	75	67	56	48
62	70	45	53	91	83	40	32
73	65	58	50	76	84	31	39
89	81	42	34	60	68	47	55
44	52	63	71	41	33	90	82
28	36	79	87	57	49	74	66

	Number	Angel Value (Arabic)	Angel Value (Hebrew)	Jinn Value (Arabic)	Jinn Value (Hebrew)
Usurper	28	347	357	69	59
Guide	91	50	60	132	122
Mystery	119	78	88	160	150
Adjuster	476	435	445	157	147
Leader	1428	1387	1397	1109	1099
Regulator	1904	1863	1873	1585	1575
General Governor	3808	3767	3777	3489	3479
High Overseer	346528	346487	346497	346209	346199

Fire - Moon

56	69	31	40	100	24	60	76	20
16	59	81	36	52	68	23	45	96
92	28	44	80	12	64	73	35	48
83	15	58	67	38	51	95	22	47
43	94	27	63	79	14	50	72	34
30	55	71	26	39	99	19	62	75
29	42	93	13	65	78	33	49	74
70	32	54	98	25	41	77	18	61
57	82	17	53	66	37	46	97	21

Occult Encyclopedia of Magic Squares

Earth - Moon

20	96	48	47	34	75	74	61	21
76	45	35	22	72	62	49	18	97
60	23	73	95	50	19	33	77	46
24	68	64	51	14	99	78	41	37
100	52	12	38	79	39	65	25	66
40	36	80	67	63	26	13	98	53
31	81	44	58	27	71	93	54	17
69	59	28	15	94	55	42	32	82
56	16	92	83	43	30	29	70	57

Air - Moon

21	97	46	37	66	53	17	82	57
61	18	77	41	25	98	54	32	70
74	49	33	78	65	13	93	42	29
75	62	19	99	39	26	71	55	30
34	72	50	14	79	63	27	94	43
47	22	95	51	38	67	58	15	83
48	35	73	64	12	80	44	28	92
96	45	23	68	52	36	81	59	16
20	76	60	24	100	40	31	69	56

Water - Moon

57	70	29	30	43	83	92	16	56
82	32	42	55	94	15	28	59	69
17	54	93	71	27	58	44	81	31
53	98	13	26	63	67	80	36	40
66	25	65	39	79	38	12	52	100
37	41	78	99	14	51	64	68	24
46	77	33	19	50	95	73	23	60
97	18	49	62	72	22	35	45	76
21	61	74	75	34	47	48	96	20

	Number	Angel Value (Arabic)	Angel Value (Hebrew)	Jinn Value (Arabic)	Jinn Value (Hebrew)
Usurper	12	331	341	53	43
Guide	100	59	69	141	131
Mystery	112	71	81	153	143
Adjuster	476	435	445	157	147
Leader	1428	1387	1397	1109	1099
Regulator	1904	1863	1873	1585	1575
General Governor	3808	3767	3777	3489	3479
High Overseer	380800	380759	380769	380481	380471

LORD OF TRIPLICITY BY NIGHT: SAHAQNAB (217)

נב	ק	ה	ס
59	6	103	49
102	50	58	7
4	61	51	101

ב	נ	ק	ה	ס
ק	ה	ס	ב	נ
ס	ב	נ	ק	ה
נ	ק	ה	ס	ב
ה	ס	ב	נ	ק

Fire - Jupiter

46	57	51	63
62	52	54	49
56	47	64	50
53	61	48	55

Air - Jupiter

55	48	61	53
50	64	47	56
49	54	52	62
63	51	57	46

Earth - Jupiter

53	56	62	46
61	47	52	57
48	64	54	51
55	50	49	63

Water - Jupiter

63	49	50	55
51	54	64	48
57	52	47	61
46	62	56	53

Occult Encyclopedia of Magic Squares

	Number	Angel Value (Arabic)	Angel Value (Hebrew)	Jinn Value (Arabic)	Jinn Value (Hebrew)
Usurper	46	5	15	87	77
Guide	64	23	33	105	95
Mystery	110	69	79	151	141
Adjuster	1736	1695	1705	1417	1407
Leader	5208	5167	5177	4889	4879
Regulator	6944	6903	6913	6625	6615
General Governor	13888	13847	13857	13569	13559
High Overseer	888832	888791	888801	888513	888503

Fire - Mars

31	57	49	43	37
44	38	32	53	50
54	46	45	39	33
40	34	55	47	41
48	42	36	35	56

Air - Mars

48	40	54	44	31
42	34	46	38	57
36	55	45	32	49
35	47	39	53	43
56	41	33	50	37

Earth - Mars

56	35	36	42	48
41	47	55	34	40
33	39	45	46	54
50	53	32	38	44
37	43	49	57	31

Water - Mars

37	50	33	41	56
43	53	39	47	35
49	32	45	55	36
57	38	46	34	42
31	44	54	40	48

	Number	Angel Value (Arabic)	Angel Value (Hebrew)	Jinn Value (Arabic)	Jinn Value (Hebrew)
Usurper	31	350	360	72	62
Guide	57	16	26	98	88
Mystery	88	47	57	129	119
Adjuster	217	176	186	258	248
Leader	651	610	620	332	322
Regulator	868	827	837	549	539
General Governor	1736	1695	1705	1417	1407
High Overseer	98952	98911	98921	98633	98623

Fire - Sun

18	29	53	35	39	43
24	34	45	52	22	40
30	56	38	28	44	21
41	20	31	46	25	54
47	36	27	19	55	33
57	42	23	37	32	26

Air - Sun

26	32	37	23	42	57
33	55	19	27	36	47
54	25	46	31	20	41
21	44	28	38	56	30
40	22	52	45	34	24
43	39	35	53	29	18

Earth - Sun

57	47	41	30	24	18
42	36	20	56	34	29
23	27	31	38	45	53
37	19	46	28	52	35
32	55	25	44	22	39
26	33	54	21	40	43

Water - Sun

43	40	21	54	33	26
39	22	44	25	55	32
35	52	28	46	19	37
53	45	38	31	27	23
29	34	56	20	36	42
18	24	30	41	47	57

	Number	Angel Value (Arabic)	Angel Value (Hebrew)	Jinn Value (Arabic)	Jinn Value (Hebrew)
Usurper	18	337	347	59	49
Guide	57	16	26	98	88
Mystery	75	34	44	116	106
Adjuster	217	176	186	258	248
Leader	651	610	620	332	322
Regulator	868	827	837	549	539
General Governor	1736	1695	1705	1417	1407
High Overseer	98952	98911	98921	98633	98623

Fire - Venus

7	48	33	18	38	51	22
52	23	8	42	34	19	39
20	40	53	24	9	43	28
44	29	14	41	54	25	10
26	11	45	30	15	35	55
36	49	27	12	46	31	16
32	17	37	50	21	13	47

Air - Venus

47	13	21	50	37	17	32
16	31	46	12	27	49	36
55	35	15	30	45	11	26
10	25	54	41	14	29	44
28	43	9	24	53	40	20
39	19	34	42	8	23	52
22	51	38	18	33	48	7

Earth - Venus

32	36	26	44	20	52	7
17	49	11	29	40	23	48
37	27	45	14	53	8	33
50	12	30	41	24	42	18
21	46	15	54	9	34	38
13	31	35	25	43	19	51
47	16	55	10	28	39	22

Water - Venus

22	39	28	10	55	16	47
51	19	43	25	35	31	13
38	34	9	54	15	46	21
18	42	24	41	30	12	50
33	8	53	14	45	27	37
48	23	40	29	11	49	17
7	52	20	44	26	36	32

	Number	Angel Value (Arabic)	Angel Value (Hebrew)	Jinn Value (Arabic)	Jinn Value (Hebrew)
Usurper	7	326	336	48	38
Guide	55	14	24	96	86
Mystery	62	21	31	103	93
Adjuster	217	176	186	258	248
Leader	651	610	620	332	322
Regulator	868	827	837	549	539
General Governor	1736	1695	1705	1417	1407
High Overseer	95480	95439	95449	95161	95151

ANGEL RULING 8ᵀᴴ HOUSE: SOSUL (162)

ל	ו	ם	טם
65	61	9	27
8	28	64	62
59	67	29	7

ל	ו	ם	ו	ם
ם	ו	ם	ל	ו
ם	ל	ו	ם	ו
ו	ם	ו	ם	ל
ו	ם	ל	ו	ם

Fire - Saturn

55	50	57
56	54	52
51	58	53

Air - Saturn

53	58	51
52	54	56
57	50	55

Earth - Saturn

51	56	55
58	54	50
53	52	57

Water - Saturn

57	52	53
50	54	58
55	56	51

	Number	Angel Value (Arabic)	Angel Value (Hebrew)	Jinn Value (Arabic)	Jinn Value (Hebrew)
Usurper	50	9	19	91	81
Guide	58	17	27	99	89
Mystery	108	67	77	149	139
Adjuster	162	121	131	203	193
Leader	486	445	455	167	157
Regulator	648	607	617	329	319
General Governor	1296	1255	1265	977	967
High Overseer	75168	75127	75137	74849	74839

Occult Encyclopedia of Magic Squares

Fire - Jupiter

33	44	38	47
46	39	41	36
43	34	48	37
40	45	35	42

Air - Jupiter

42	35	45	40
37	48	34	43
36	41	39	46
47	38	44	33

Earth - Jupiter

40	43	46	33
45	34	39	44
35	48	41	38
42	37	36	47

Water - Jupiter

47	36	37	42
38	41	48	35
44	39	34	45
33	46	43	40

	Number	Angel Value (Arabic)	Angel Value (Hebrew)	Jinn Value (Arabic)	Jinn Value (Hebrew)
Usurper	33	352	2	74	64
Guide	48	7	17	89	79
Mystery	81	40	50	122	112
Adjuster	1296	1255	1265	977	967
Leader	3888	3847	3857	3569	3559
Regulator	5184	5143	5153	4865	4855
General Governor	10368	10327	10337	10049	10039
High Overseer	497664	497623	497633	497345	497335

Fire - Mars

20	46	38	32	26
33	27	21	42	39
43	35	34	28	22
29	23	44	36	30
37	31	25	24	45

Air - Mars

37	29	43	33	20
31	23	35	27	46
25	44	34	21	38
24	36	28	42	32
45	30	22	39	26

Earth - Mars

45	24	25	31	37
30	36	44	23	29
22	28	34	35	43
39	42	21	27	33
26	32	38	46	20

Water - Mars

26	39	22	30	45
32	42	28	36	24
38	21	34	44	25
46	27	35	23	31
20	33	43	29	37

	Number	Angel Value (Arabic)	Angel Value (Hebrew)	Jinn Value (Arabic)	Jinn Value (Hebrew)
Usurper	20	339	349	61	51
Guide	46	5	15	87	77
Mystery	66	25	35	107	97
Adjuster	162	121	131	203	193
Leader	486	445	455	167	157
Regulator	648	607	617	329	319
General Governor	1296	1255	1265	977	967
High Overseer	59616	59575	59585	59297	59287

Fire - Sun

9	20	43	26	30	34
15	25	36	42	13	31
21	46	29	19	35	12
32	11	22	37	16	44
38	27	18	10	45	24
47	33	14	28	23	17

Air - Sun

17	23	28	14	33	47
24	45	10	18	27	38
44	16	37	22	11	32
12	35	19	29	46	21
31	13	42	36	25	15
34	30	26	43	20	9

Earth - Sun

47	38	32	21	15	9
33	27	11	46	25	20
14	18	22	29	36	43
28	10	37	19	42	26
23	45	16	35	13	30
17	24	44	12	31	34

Water - Sun

34	31	12	44	24	17
30	13	35	16	45	23
26	42	19	37	10	28
43	36	29	22	18	14
20	25	46	11	27	33
9	15	21	32	38	47

	Number	Angel Value (Arabic)	Angel Value (Hebrew)	Jinn Value (Arabic)	Jinn Value (Hebrew)
Usurper	9	328	338	50	40
Guide	47	6	16	88	78
Mystery	56	15	25	97	87
Adjuster	162	121	131	203	193
Leader	486	445	455	167	157
Regulator	648	607	617	329	319
General Governor	1296	1255	1265	977	967
High Overseer	60912	60871	60881	60593	60583

ANGEL OF FIRST DECANATE: KAMOTZ (156)

צ	ו	מ	כ
19	41	9	87
8	88	18	42
39	21	89	7

צ	ו	מ	כ
כ	מ	ו	צ
ו	צ	כ	מ
מ	כ	צ	ו

Fire - Saturn

53	48	55
54	52	50
49	56	51

Air - Saturn

51	56	49
50	52	54
55	48	53

Earth - Saturn

49	54	53
56	52	48
51	50	55

Water - Saturn

55	50	51
48	52	56
53	54	49

Occult Encyclopedia of Magic Squares

	Number	Angel Value (Arabic)	Angel Value (Hebrew)	Jinn Value (Arabic)	Jinn Value (Hebrew)
Usurper	48	7	17	89	79
Guide	56	15	25	97	87
Mystery	104	63	73	145	135
Adjuster	156	115	125	197	187
Leader	468	427	437	149	139
Regulator	624	583	593	305	295
General Governor	1248	1207	1217	929	919
High Overseer	69888	69847	69857	69569	69559

Fire - Jupiter

31	42	36	47
46	37	39	34
41	32	48	35
38	45	33	40

Air - Jupiter

40	33	45	38
35	48	32	41
34	39	37	46
47	36	42	31

Earth - Jupiter

38	41	46	31
45	32	37	42
33	48	39	36
40	35	34	47

Water - Jupiter

47	34	35	40
36	39	48	33
42	37	32	45
31	46	41	38

	Number	Angel Value (Arabic)	Angel Value (Hebrew)	Jinn Value (Arabic)	Jinn Value (Hebrew)
Usurper	31	350	360	72	62
Guide	48	7	17	89	79
Mystery	79	38	48	120	110
Adjuster	1248	1207	1217	929	919
Leader	3744	3703	3713	3425	3415
Regulator	4992	4951	4961	4673	4663
General Governor	9984	9943	9953	9665	9655
High Overseer	479232	479191	479201	478913	478903

Occult Encyclopedia of Magic Squares

Fire - Mars

19	44	37	31	25
32	26	20	40	38
41	34	33	27	21
28	22	42	35	29
36	30	24	23	43

Air - Mars

36	28	41	32	19
30	22	34	26	44
24	42	33	20	37
23	35	27	40	31
43	29	21	38	25

Earth - Mars

43	23	24	30	36
29	35	42	22	28
21	27	33	34	41
38	40	20	26	32
25	31	37	44	19

Water - Mars

25	38	21	29	43
31	40	27	35	23
37	20	33	42	24
44	26	34	22	30
19	32	41	28	36

	Number	Angel Value (Arabic)	Angel Value (Hebrew)	Jinn Value (Arabic)	Jinn Value (Hebrew)
Usurper	19	338	348	60	50
Guide	44	3	13	85	75
Mystery	63	22	32	104	94
Adjuster	156	115	125	197	187
Leader	468	427	437	149	139
Regulator	624	583	593	305	295
General Governor	1248	1207	1217	929	919
High Overseer	54912	54871	54881	54593	54583

Fire - Sun

8	19	42	25	29	33
14	24	35	41	12	30
20	45	28	18	34	11
31	10	21	36	15	43
37	26	17	9	44	23
46	32	13	27	22	16

Earth - Sun

46	37	31	20	14	8
32	26	10	45	24	19
13	17	21	28	35	42
27	9	36	18	41	25
22	44	15	34	12	29
16	23	43	11	30	33

Air - Sun

16	22	27	13	32	46
23	44	9	17	26	37
43	15	36	21	10	31
11	34	18	28	45	20
30	12	41	35	24	14
33	29	25	42	19	8

Water - Sun

33	30	11	43	23	16
29	12	34	15	44	22
25	41	18	36	9	27
42	35	28	21	17	13
19	24	45	10	26	32
8	14	20	31	37	46

	Number	Angel Value (Arabic)	Angel Value (Hebrew)	Jinn Value (Arabic)	Jinn Value (Hebrew)
Usurper	8	327	337	49	39
Guide	46	5	15	87	77
Mystery	54	13	23	95	85
Adjuster	156	115	125	197	187
Leader	468	427	437	149	139
Regulator	624	583	593	305	295
General Governor	1248	1207	1217	929	919
High Overseer	57408	57367	57377	57089	57079

ANGEL OF FIRST QUINANCE: LUVIAH (57)

ה	י	ו	לו
35	7	13	2
12	3	34	8
5	37	4	11

ה	י	ו	ו	ל
ו	ו	ל	ה	י
ל	ה	י	ו	ו
י	ו	ו	ל	ה
ו	ל	ה	י	ו

Occult Encyclopedia of Magic Squares

Fire - Saturn

20	15	22
21	19	17
16	23	18

Air - Saturn

18	23	16
17	19	21
22	15	20

Earth - Saturn

16	21	20
23	19	15
18	17	22

Water - Saturn

22	17	18
15	19	23
20	21	16

	Number	Angel Value (Arabic)	Angel Value (Hebrew)	Jinn Value (Arabic)	Jinn Value (Hebrew)
Usurper	15	334	344	56	46
Guide	23	342	352	64	54
Mystery	38	357	7	79	69
Adjuster	57	16	26	98	88
Leader	171	130	140	212	202
Regulator	228	187	197	269	259
General Governor	456	415	425	137	127
High Overseer	10488	10447	10457	10169	10159

Fire - Jupiter

6	17	11	23
22	12	14	9
16	7	24	10
13	21	8	15

Air - Jupiter

15	8	21	13
10	24	7	16
9	14	12	22
23	11	17	6

Earth - Jupiter

13	16	22	6
21	7	12	17
8	24	14	11
15	10	9	23

Water - Jupiter

23	9	10	15
11	14	24	8
17	12	7	21
6	22	16	13

	Number	Angel Value (Arabic)	Angel Value (Hebrew)	Jinn Value (Arabic)	Jinn Value (Hebrew)
Usurper	6	325	335	47	37
Guide	24	343	353	65	55
Mystery	30	349	359	71	61
Adjuster	456	415	425	137	127
Leader	1368	1327	1337	1049	1039
Regulator	1824	1783	1793	1505	1495
General Governor	3648	3607	3617	3329	3319
High Overseer	87552	87511	87521	87233	87223

ANGEL OF SECOND QUINANCE: PAHALIAH (130)

יה	ל	ה	פ
79	6	33	12
32	13	78	7
4	81	14	31

ה	י	ל	ה	פ
ל	ה	פ	ה	י
פ	ה	י	ל	ה
י	ל	ה	פ	ה
ה	פ	ה	י	ל

Fire - Jupiter

25	36	30	39
38	31	33	28
35	26	40	29
32	37	27	34

Air - Jupiter

34	27	37	32
29	40	26	35
28	33	31	38
39	30	36	25

Earth - Jupiter

32	35	38	25
37	26	31	36
27	40	33	30
34	29	28	39

Water - Jupiter

39	28	29	34
30	33	40	27
36	31	26	37
25	38	35	32

	Number	Angel Value (Arabic)	Angel Value (Hebrew)	Jinn Value (Arabic)	Jinn Value (Hebrew)
Usurper	25	344	354	66	56
Guide	40	359	9	81	71
Mystery	65	24	34	106	96
Adjuster	1040	999	1009	721	711
Leader	3120	3079	3089	2801	2791
Regulator	4160	4119	4129	3841	3831
General Governor	8320	8279	8289	8001	7991
High Overseer	332800	332759	332769	332481	332471

Fire - Mars

14	38	32	26	20
27	21	15	34	33
35	29	28	22	16
23	17	36	30	24
31	25	19	18	37

Air - Mars

31	23	35	27	14
25	17	29	21	38
19	36	28	15	32
18	30	22	34	26
37	24	16	33	20

Earth - Mars

37	18	19	25	31
24	30	36	17	23
16	22	28	29	35
33	34	15	21	27
20	26	32	38	14

Water - Mars

20	33	16	24	37
26	34	22	30	18
32	15	28	36	19
38	21	29	17	25
14	27	35	23	31

	Number	Angel Value (Arabic)	Angel Value (Hebrew)	Jinn Value (Arabic)	Jinn Value (Hebrew)
Usurper	14	333	343	55	45
Guide	38	357	7	79	69
Mystery	52	11	21	93	83
Adjuster	130	89	99	171	161
Leader	390	349	359	71	61
Regulator	520	479	489	201	191
General Governor	1040	999	1009	721	711
High Overseer	39520	39479	39489	39201	39191

Fire - Sun

4	15	36	21	25	29
10	20	31	35	8	26
16	39	24	14	30	7
27	6	17	32	11	37
33	22	13	5	38	19
40	28	9	23	18	12

Air - Sun

12	18	23	9	28	40
19	38	5	13	22	33
37	11	32	17	6	27
7	30	14	24	39	16
26	8	35	31	20	10
29	25	21	36	15	4

Earth - Sun

40	33	27	16	10	4
28	22	6	39	20	15
9	13	17	24	31	36
23	5	32	14	35	21
18	38	11	30	8	25
12	19	37	7	26	29

Water - Sun

29	26	7	37	19	12
25	8	30	11	38	18
21	35	14	32	5	23
36	31	24	17	13	9
15	20	39	6	22	28
4	10	16	27	33	40

	Number	Angel Value (Arabic)	Angel Value (Hebrew)	Jinn Value (Arabic)	Jinn Value (Hebrew)
Usurper	4	323	333	45	35
Guide	40	359	9	81	71
Mystery	44	3	13	85	75
Adjuster	130	89	99	171	161
Leader	390	349	359	71	61
Regulator	520	479	489	201	191
General Governor	1040	999	1009	721	711
High Overseer	41600	41559	41569	41281	41271

ANGEL OF SECOND DECANATE: NUNDOHAR (325)

ר	וה	נד	ני
59	55	14	197
13	198	58	56
53	61	199	12

ר	ה	ו	ד	נ	י	נ
ו	ד	נ	י	נ	ר	ה
נ	י	נ	ר	ה	ו	ד
נ	ר	ה	ו	ד	נ	י
ה	ו	ד	נ	י	נ	ר
ד	נ	י	נ	ר	ה	ו
י	נ	ר	ה	ו	ד	נ

Fire - Jupiter

73	84	78	90
89	79	81	76
83	74	91	77
80	88	75	82

Air - Jupiter

82	75	88	80
77	91	74	83
76	81	79	89
90	78	84	73

Earth - Jupiter

80	83	89	73
88	74	79	84
75	91	81	78
82	77	76	90

Water - Jupiter

90	76	77	82
78	81	91	75
84	79	74	88
73	89	83	80

	Number	Angel Value (Arabic)	Angel Value (Hebrew)	Jinn Value (Arabic)	Jinn Value (Hebrew)
Usurper	73	32	42	114	104
Guide	91	50	60	132	122
Mystery	164	123	133	205	195
Adjuster	2600	2559	2569	2281	2271
Leader	7800	7759	7769	7481	7471
Regulator	10400	10359	10369	10081	10071
General Governor	20800	20759	20769	20481	20471
High Overseer	1892800	1892759	1892769	1892481	1892471

Occult Encyclopedia of Magic Squares

Fire - Mars

53	77	71	65	59
66	60	54	73	72
74	68	67	61	55
62	56	75	69	63
70	64	58	57	76

Air - Mars

70	62	74	66	53
64	56	68	60	77
58	75	67	54	71
57	69	61	73	65
76	63	55	72	59

Earth - Mars

76	57	58	64	70
63	69	75	56	62
55	61	67	68	74
72	73	54	60	66
59	65	71	77	53

Water - Mars

59	72	55	63	76
65	73	61	69	57
71	54	67	75	58
77	60	68	56	64
53	66	74	62	70

	Number	Angel Value (Arabic)	Angel Value (Hebrew)	Jinn Value (Arabic)	Jinn Value (Hebrew)
Usurper	53	12	22	94	84
Guide	77	36	46	118	108
Mystery	130	89	99	171	161
Adjuster	325	284	294	6	356
Leader	975	934	944	656	646
Regulator	1300	1259	1269	981	971
General Governor	2600	2559	2569	2281	2271
High Overseer	200200	200159	200169	199881	199871

Fire - Sun

36	47	71	53	57	61
42	52	63	70	40	58
48	74	56	46	62	39
59	38	49	64	43	72
65	54	45	37	73	51
75	60	41	55	50	44

Earth - Sun

75	65	59	48	42	36
60	54	38	74	52	47
41	45	49	56	63	71
55	37	64	46	70	53
50	73	43	62	40	57
44	51	72	39	58	61

Occult Encyclopedia of Magic Squares

Air - Sun

44	50	55	41	60	75
51	73	37	45	54	65
72	43	64	49	38	59
39	62	46	56	74	48
58	40	70	63	52	42
61	57	53	71	47	36

Water - Sun

61	58	39	72	51	44
57	40	62	43	73	50
53	70	46	64	37	55
71	63	56	49	45	41
47	52	74	38	54	60
36	42	48	59	65	75

	Number	Angel Value (Arabic)	Angel Value (Hebrew)	Jinn Value (Arabic)	Jinn Value (Hebrew)
Usurper	36	355	5	77	67
Guide	75	34	44	116	106
Mystery	111	70	80	152	142
Adjuster	325	284	294	6	356
Leader	975	934	944	656	646
Regulator	1300	1259	1269	981	971
General Governor	2600	2559	2569	2281	2271
High Overseer	195000	194959	194969	194681	194671

Fire - Venus

22	63	48	33	53	69	37
70	38	23	57	49	34	54
35	55	71	39	24	58	43
59	44	29	56	72	40	25
41	26	60	45	30	50	73
51	67	42	27	61	46	31
47	32	52	68	36	28	62

Air - Venus

62	28	36	68	52	32	47
31	46	61	27	42	67	51
73	50	30	45	60	26	41
25	40	72	56	29	44	59
43	58	24	39	71	55	35
54	34	49	57	23	38	70
37	69	53	33	48	63	22

Earth - Venus

47	51	41	59	35	70	22
32	67	26	44	55	38	63
52	42	60	29	71	23	48
68	27	45	56	39	57	33
36	61	30	72	24	49	53
28	46	50	40	58	34	69
62	31	73	25	43	54	37

Water - Venus

37	54	43	25	73	31	62
69	34	58	40	50	46	28
53	49	24	72	30	61	36
33	57	39	56	45	27	68
48	23	71	29	60	42	52
63	38	55	44	26	67	32
22	70	35	59	41	51	47

	Number	Angel Value (Arabic)	Angel Value (Hebrew)	Jinn Value (Arabic)	Jinn Value (Hebrew)
Usurper	22	341	351	63	53
Guide	73	32	42	114	104
Mystery	95	54	64	136	126
Adjuster	325	284	294	6	356
Leader	975	934	944	656	646
Regulator	1300	1259	1269	981	971
General Governor	2600	2559	2569	2281	2271
High Overseer	189800	189759	189769	189481	189471

Fire - Mercury

47	55	30	38	69	60	17	9
63	72	14	22	52	44	33	25
36	28	49	41	15	23	62	71
20	12	66	57	31	39	46	54
13	21	64	73	34	26	51	43
29	37	48	56	18	10	68	59
67	58	19	11	45	53	32	40
50	42	35	27	61	70	16	24

Earth - Mercury

47	55	30	38	69	60	17	9
63	72	14	22	52	44	33	25
36	28	49	41	15	23	62	71
20	12	66	57	31	39	46	54
13	21	64	73	34	26	51	43
29	37	48	56	18	10	68	59
67	58	19	11	45	53	32	40
50	42	35	27	61	70	16	24

Occult Encyclopedia of Magic Squares

Air - Mercury

50	67	29	13	20	36	63	47
42	58	37	21	12	28	72	55
35	19	48	64	66	49	14	30
27	11	56	73	57	41	22	38
61	45	18	34	31	15	52	69
70	53	10	26	39	23	44	60
16	32	68	51	46	62	33	17
24	40	59	43	54	71	25	9

Water - Mercury

24	16	70	61	27	35	42	50
40	32	53	45	11	19	58	67
59	68	10	18	56	48	37	29
43	51	26	34	73	64	21	13
54	46	39	31	57	66	12	20
71	62	23	15	41	49	28	36
25	33	44	52	22	14	72	63
9	17	60	69	38	30	55	47

	Number	Angel Value (Arabic)	Angel Value (Hebrew)	Jinn Value (Arabic)	Jinn Value (Hebrew)
Usurper	9	328	338	50	40
Guide	73	32	42	114	104
Mystery	82	41	51	123	113
Adjuster	325	284	294	6	356
Leader	975	934	944	656	646
Regulator	1300	1259	1269	981	971
General Governor	2600	2559	2569	2281	2271
High Overseer	189800	189759	189769	189481	189471

ANGEL OF THIRD QUINANCE: NELAKIEL (131)

אל	ב	ל	נ
49	31	23	28
22	29	48	32
29	51	30	21

ל	א	ב	ל	נ
ב	ל	נ	ל	א
נ	ל	א	ב	ל
א	ב	ל	נ	ל
ל	נ	ל	א	ב

Numerical Squares See Page: 321

ANGEL OF FOURTH QUINANCE: YEYAYEL (61)

ל	א	י	יי
19	11	4	28
3	29	18	12
9	21	30	2

ל	א	י	י	י
י	י	י	ל	א
י	ל	א	י	י
א	י	י	י	ל
י	י	ל	א	י

Numerical Squares See Page: 189

ANGEL OF THIRD DECANATE: UTHRODIEL (657)

יאל	וד	ר	ות
405	201	13	38
12	39	404	202
199	407	40	11

ל	א	י	ד	ו	ר	ת	ו
א	י	ד	ו	ו	ל	ר	ת
י	ד	ו	ו	ת	א	ל	ר
ר	ו	ו	ת	ד	י	א	ל
ד	ל	א	י	ר	ת	ו	ו
ת	ר	ל	א	י	ו	ו	ד
ו	ת	ר	ל	א	ו	ד	י
ו	ו	ת	ר	ל	ד	י	א

Fire - Saturn

220	215	222
221	219	217
216	223	218

Air - Saturn

218	223	216
217	219	221
222	215	220

Earth - Saturn

216	221	220
223	219	215
218	217	222

Water - Saturn

222	217	218
215	219	223
220	221	216

	Number	Angel Value (Arabic)	Angel Value (Hebrew)	Jinn Value (Arabic)	Jinn Value (Hebrew)
Usurper	215	174	184	256	246
Guide	223	182	192	264	254
Mystery	438	397	407	119	109
Adjuster	657	616	626	338	328
Leader	1971	1930	1940	1652	1642
Regulator	2628	2587	2597	2309	2299
General Governor	5256	5215	5225	4937	4927
High Overseer	1172088	1172047	1172057	1171769	1171759

Fire - Jupiter

156	167	161	173
172	162	164	159
166	157	174	160
163	171	158	165

Air - Jupiter

165	158	171	163
160	174	157	166
159	164	162	172
173	161	167	156

Earth - Jupiter

163	166	172	156
171	157	162	167
158	174	164	161
165	160	159	173

Water - Jupiter

173	159	160	165
161	164	174	158
167	162	157	171
156	172	166	163

Occult Encyclopedia of Magic Squares

	Number	Angel Value (Arabic)	Angel Value (Hebrew)	Jinn Value (Arabic)	Jinn Value (Hebrew)
Usurper	156	115	125	197	187
Guide	174	133	143	215	205
Mystery	330	289	299	11	1
Adjuster	5256	5215	5225	4937	4927
Leader	15768	15727	15737	15449	15439
Regulator	21024	20983	20993	20705	20695
General Governor	42048	42007	42017	41729	41719
High Overseer	7316352	7316311	7316321	7316033	7316023

Fire - Mars

119	145	137	131	125
132	126	120	141	138
142	134	133	127	121
128	122	143	135	129
136	130	124	123	144

Air - Mars

136	128	142	132	119
130	122	134	126	145
124	143	133	120	137
123	135	127	141	131
144	129	121	138	125

Earth - Mars

144	123	124	130	136
129	135	143	122	128
121	127	133	134	142
138	141	120	126	132
125	131	137	145	119

Water - Mars

125	138	121	129	144
131	141	127	135	123
137	120	133	143	124
145	126	134	122	130
119	132	142	128	136

	Number	Angel Value (Arabic)	Angel Value (Hebrew)	Jinn Value (Arabic)	Jinn Value (Hebrew)
Usurper	119	78	88	160	150
Guide	145	104	114	186	176
Mystery	264	223	233	305	295
Adjuster	657	616	626	338	328
Leader	1971	1930	1940	1652	1642
Regulator	2628	2587	2597	2309	2299
General Governor	5256	5215	5225	4937	4927
High Overseer	762120	762079	762089	761801	761791

Occult Encyclopedia of Magic Squares

Fire - Sun

92	103	123	109	113	117
98	108	119	122	96	114
104	126	112	102	118	95
115	94	105	120	99	124
121	110	101	93	125	107
127	116	97	111	106	100

Air - Sun

100	106	111	97	116	127
107	125	93	101	110	121
124	99	120	105	94	115
95	118	102	112	126	104
114	96	122	119	108	98
117	113	109	123	103	92

Earth - Sun

127	121	115	104	98	92
116	110	94	126	108	103
97	101	105	112	119	123
111	93	120	102	122	109
106	125	99	118	96	113
100	107	124	95	114	117

Water - Sun

117	114	95	124	107	100
113	96	118	99	125	106
109	122	102	120	93	111
123	119	112	105	101	97
103	108	126	94	110	116
92	98	104	115	121	127

	Number	Angel Value (Arabic)	Angel Value (Hebrew)	Jinn Value (Arabic)	Jinn Value (Hebrew)
Usurper	92	51	61	133	123
Guide	127	86	96	168	158
Mystery	219	178	188	260	250
Adjuster	657	616	626	338	328
Leader	1971	1930	1940	1652	1642
Regulator	2628	2587	2597	2309	2299
General Governor	5256	5215	5225	4937	4927
High Overseer	667512	667471	667481	667193	667183

Fire - Venus

69	110	95	80	100	119	84
120	85	70	104	96	81	101
82	102	121	86	71	105	90
106	91	76	103	122	87	72
88	73	107	92	77	97	123
98	117	89	74	108	93	78
94	79	99	118	83	75	109

Occult Encyclopedia of Magic Squares

Earth - Venus

94	98	88	106	82	120	69
79	117	73	91	102	85	110
99	89	107	76	121	70	95
118	74	92	103	86	104	80
83	108	77	122	71	96	100
75	93	97	87	105	81	119
109	78	123	72	90	101	84

Air - Venus

109	75	83	118	99	79	94
78	93	108	74	89	117	98
123	97	77	92	107	73	88
72	87	122	103	76	91	106
90	105	71	86	121	102	82
101	81	96	104	70	85	120
84	119	100	80	95	110	69

Water - Venus

84	101	90	72	123	78	109
119	81	105	87	97	93	75
100	96	71	122	77	108	83
80	104	86	103	92	74	118
95	70	121	76	107	89	99
110	85	102	91	73	117	79
69	120	82	106	88	98	94

	Number	Angel Value (Arabic)	Angel Value (Hebrew)	Jinn Value (Arabic)	Jinn Value (Hebrew)
Usurper	69	28	38	110	100
Guide	123	82	92	164	154
Mystery	192	151	161	233	223
Adjuster	657	616	626	338	328
Leader	1971	1930	1940	1652	1642
Regulator	2628	2587	2597	2309	2299
General Governor	5256	5215	5225	4937	4927
High Overseer	646488	646447	646457	646169	646159

Occult Encyclopedia of Magic Squares

Fire - Mercury

50	66	116	95	84	100	81	65
58	74	103	87	92	113	73	57
101	85	64	80	67	51	94	115
114	93	56	72	75	59	86	102
79	63	82	98	118	97	52	68
71	55	90	111	105	89	60	76
96	117	69	53	62	78	99	83
88	104	77	61	54	70	112	91

Earth - Mercury

88	96	71	79	114	101	58	50
104	117	55	63	93	85	74	66
77	69	90	82	56	64	103	116
61	53	111	98	72	80	87	95
54	62	105	118	75	67	92	84
70	78	89	97	59	51	113	100
112	99	60	52	86	94	73	81
91	83	76	68	102	115	57	65

Air - Mercury

91	112	70	54	61	77	104	88
83	99	78	62	53	69	117	96
76	60	89	105	111	90	55	71
68	52	97	118	98	82	63	79
102	86	59	75	72	56	93	114
115	94	51	67	80	64	85	101
57	73	113	92	87	103	74	58
65	81	100	84	95	116	66	50

Water - Mercury

65	57	115	102	68	76	83	91
81	73	94	86	52	60	99	112
100	113	51	59	97	89	78	70
84	92	67	75	118	105	62	54
95	87	80	72	98	111	53	61
116	103	64	56	82	90	69	77
66	74	85	93	63	55	117	104
50	58	101	114	79	71	96	88

	Number	Angel Value (Arabic)	Angel Value (Hebrew)	Jinn Value (Arabic)	Jinn Value (Hebrew)
Usurper	50	9	19	91	81
Guide	118	77	87	159	149
Mystery	168	127	137	209	199
Adjuster	657	616	626	338	328
Leader	1971	1930	1940	1652	1642
Regulator	2628	2587	2597	2309	2299
General Governor	5256	5215	5225	4937	4927
High Overseer	620208	620167	620177	619889	619879

Fire - Moon

77	90	52	61	113	45	81	97	41
37	80	102	57	73	89	44	66	109
105	49	65	101	33	85	94	56	69
104	36	79	88	59	72	108	43	68
64	107	48	84	100	35	71	93	55
51	76	92	47	60	112	40	83	96
50	63	106	34	86	99	54	70	95
91	53	75	111	46	62	98	39	82
78	103	38	74	87	58	67	110	42

Earth - Moon

41	109	69	68	55	96	95	82	42
97	66	56	43	93	83	70	39	110
81	44	94	108	71	40	54	98	67
45	89	85	72	35	112	99	62	58
113	73	33	59	100	60	86	46	87
61	57	101	88	84	47	34	111	74
52	102	65	79	48	92	106	75	38
90	80	49	36	107	76	63	53	103
77	37	105	104	64	51	50	91	78

Occult Encyclopedia of Magic Squares

Air - Moon

42	110	67	58	87	74	38	103	78
82	39	98	62	46	111	75	53	91
95	70	54	99	86	34	106	63	50
96	83	40	112	60	47	92	76	51
55	93	71	35	100	84	48	107	64
68	43	108	72	59	88	79	36	104
69	56	94	85	33	101	65	49	105
109	66	44	89	73	57	102	80	37
41	97	81	45	113	61	52	90	77

Water - Moon

78	91	50	51	64	104	105	37	77
103	53	63	76	107	36	49	80	90
38	75	106	92	48	79	65	102	52
74	111	34	47	84	88	101	57	61
87	46	86	60	100	59	33	73	113
58	62	99	112	35	72	85	89	45
67	98	54	40	71	108	94	44	81
110	39	70	83	93	43	56	66	97
42	82	95	96	55	68	69	109	41

	Number	Angel Value (Arabic)	Angel Value (Hebrew)	Jinn Value (Arabic)	Jinn Value (Hebrew)
Usurper	33	352	2	74	64
Guide	113	72	82	154	144
Mystery	146	105	115	187	177
Adjuster	657	616	626	338	328
Leader	1971	1930	1940	1652	1642
Regulator	2628	2587	2597	2309	2299
General Governor	5256	5215	5225	4937	4927
High Overseer	593928	593887	593897	593609	593599

Fire - Saturn

16	34	41	79	70	110	63	55	87	102
27	91	84	75	112	100	18	60	46	44
42	47	71	111	101	86	35	23	64	77
48	73	109	103	36	82	90	31	20	65
61	108	105	40	51	74	78	88	33	19
68	25	26	93	81	57	53	43	98	113
80	62	22	29	95	50	38	99	116	66
94	83	58	17	28	45	96	115	69	52
104	37	49	56	24	32	114	67	85	89
117	97	92	54	59	21	72	76	39	30

Earth - Saturn

117	104	94	80	68	61	48	42	27	16
97	37	83	62	25	108	73	47	91	34
92	49	58	22	26	105	109	71	84	41
54	56	17	29	93	40	103	111	75	79
59	24	28	95	81	51	36	101	112	70
21	32	45	50	57	74	82	86	100	110
72	114	96	38	53	78	90	35	18	63
76	67	115	99	43	88	31	23	60	55
39	85	69	116	98	33	20	64	46	87
30	89	52	66	113	19	65	77	44	102

Air - Saturn

30	39	76	72	21	59	54	92	97	117
89	85	67	114	32	24	56	49	37	104
52	69	115	96	45	28	17	58	83	94
66	116	99	38	50	95	29	22	62	80
113	98	43	53	57	81	93	26	25	68
19	33	88	78	74	51	40	105	108	61
65	20	31	90	82	36	103	109	73	48
77	64	23	35	86	101	111	71	47	42
44	46	60	18	100	112	75	84	91	27
102	87	55	63	110	70	79	41	34	16

Water - Saturn

102	44	77	65	19	113	66	52	89	30
87	46	64	20	33	98	116	69	85	39
55	60	23	31	88	43	99	115	67	76
63	**18**	35	90	78	53	38	96	114	72
110	100	86	82	74	57	50	45	32	21
70	112	101	36	51	81	95	28	24	59
79	75	111	103	40	93	29	17	56	54
41	84	71	109	105	26	22	58	49	92
34	91	47	73	108	25	62	83	37	97
16	27	42	48	61	68	80	94	104	117

	Number	Angel Value (Arabic)	Angel Value (Hebrew)	Jinn Value (Arabic)	Jinn Value (Hebrew)
Usurper	16	325	335	57	47
Guide	117	66	76	158	148
Mystery	133	92	92	174	164
Adjuster	657	616	616	338	328
Leader	1971	1930	1930	1652	1642
Regulator	2628	2587	2587	2309	2299
General Governor	5256	5215	5215	4937	4927
High Overseer	614952	614911	614911	614633	614623

ANGEL OF FIFTH QUINANCE: MELAHEL (106)

אל	ה	ל	מ
39	31	8	28
7	29	38	32
29	41	30	6

ל	א	ה	ל	מ
ה	ל	מ	ל	א
מ	ל	א	ה	ל
א	ה	ל	מ	ל
ל	מ	ל	א	ה

Fire - Jupiter

19	30	24	33
32	25	27	22
29	20	34	23
26	31	21	28

Air - Jupiter

28	21	31	26
23	34	20	29
22	27	25	32
33	24	30	19

Earth - Jupiter

26	29	32	19
31	20	25	30
21	34	27	24
28	23	22	33

Water - Jupiter

33	22	23	28
24	27	34	21
30	25	20	31
19	32	29	26

	Number	Angel Value (Arabic)	Angel Value (Hebrew)	Jinn Value (Arabic)	Jinn Value (Hebrew)
Usurper	19	338	348	60	50
Guide	34	353	3	75	65
Mystery	53	12	22	94	84
Adjuster	848	807	817	529	519
Leader	2544	2503	2513	2225	2215
Regulator	3392	3351	3361	3073	3063
General Governor	6784	6743	6753	6465	6455
High Overseer	230656	230615	230625	230337	230327

Fire - Mars

9	34	27	21	15
22	16	10	30	28
31	24	23	17	11
18	12	32	25	19
26	20	14	13	33

Air - Mars

26	18	31	22	9
20	12	24	16	34
14	32	23	10	27
13	25	17	30	21
33	19	11	28	15

Earth - Mars

33	13	14	20	26
19	25	32	12	18
11	17	23	24	31
28	30	10	16	22
15	21	27	34	9

Water - Mars

15	28	11	19	33
21	30	17	25	13
27	10	23	32	14
34	16	24	12	20
9	22	31	18	26

	Number	Angel Value (Arabic)	Angel Value (Hebrew)	Jinn Value (Arabic)	Jinn Value (Hebrew)
Usurper	9	328	338	50	40
Guide	34	353	3	75	65
Mystery	43	2	12	84	74
Adjuster	106	65	75	147	137
Leader	318	277	287	359	349
Regulator	424	383	393	105	95
General Governor	848	807	817	529	519
High Overseer	28832	28791	28801	28513	28503

ANGEL OF SIX QUINANCE: CHAHAVIAH (34)

י	ו	ה	ה
7	6	9	12
8	13	6	7
4	9	14	7

ה	י	ו	ה	ה
ו	ה	ה	ה	י
ה	ה	י	ו	ה
י	ו	ה	ה	ה
ה	ה	ה	י	ו

Fire - Jupiter

1	12	6	15
14	7	9	4
11	2	16	5
8	13	3	10

Air - Jupiter

10	3	13	8
5	16	2	11
4	9	7	14
15	6	12	1

Earth - Jupiter

8	11	14	1
13	2	7	12
3	16	9	6
10	5	4	15

Water - Jupiter

15	4	5	10
6	9	16	3
12	7	2	13
1	14	11	8

	Number	Angel Value (Arabic)	Angel Value (Hebrew)	Jinn Value (Arabic)	Jinn Value (Hebrew)
Usurper	1	320	330	42	32
Guide	16	335	345	57	47
Mystery	17	336	346	58	48
Adjuster	272	231	241	313	303
Leader	816	775	785	497	487
Regulator	1088	1047	1057	769	759
General Governor	2176	2135	2145	1857	1847
High Overseer	34816	34775	34785	34497	34487

SAGITTARIUS

SIGN SAGITTARIUS: QASHAT (800)

No Hebrew Squares Possible

Fire - Jupiter

192	203	197	208
207	198	200	195
202	193	209	196
199	206	194	201

Air - Jupiter

201	194	206	199
196	209	193	202
195	200	198	207
208	197	203	192

Earth - Jupiter

199	202	207	192
206	193	198	203
194	209	200	197
201	196	195	208

Water - Jupiter

208	195	196	201
197	200	209	194
203	198	193	206
192	207	202	199

Occult Encyclopedia of Magic Squares

	Number	Angel Value (Arabic)	Angel Value (Hebrew)	Jinn Value (Arabic)	Jinn Value (Hebrew)
Usurper	192	151	161	233	223
Guide	209	168	178	250	240
Mystery	401	360	370	82	72
Adjuster	6400	6359	6369	6081	6071
Leader	19200	19159	19169	18881	18871
Regulator	25600	25559	25569	25281	25271
General Governor	51200	51159	51169	50881	50871
High Overseer	10700800	10700759	10700769	10700481	10700471

Fire - Mars

148	172	166	160	154
161	155	149	168	167
169	163	162	156	150
157	151	170	164	158
165	159	153	152	171

Air - Mars

165	157	169	161	148
159	151	163	155	172
153	170	162	149	166
152	164	156	168	160
171	158	150	167	154

Earth - Mars

171	152	153	159	165
158	164	170	151	157
150	156	162	163	169
167	168	149	155	161
154	160	166	172	148

Water - Mars

154	167	150	158	171
160	168	156	164	152
166	149	162	170	153
172	155	163	151	159
148	161	169	157	165

	Number	Angel Value (Arabic)	Angel Value (Hebrew)	Jinn Value (Arabic)	Jinn Value (Hebrew)
Usurper	148	107	117	189	179
Guide	172	131	141	213	203
Mystery	320	279	289	1	351
Adjuster	800	759	769	481	471
Leader	2400	2359	2369	2081	2071
Regulator	3200	3159	3169	2881	2871
General Governor	6400	6359	6369	6081	6071
High Overseer	1100800	1100759	1100769	1100481	1100471

Occult Encyclopedia of Magic Squares

Fire - Sun

115	126	151	132	136	140
121	131	142	150	119	137
127	154	135	125	141	118
138	117	128	143	122	152
144	133	124	116	153	130
155	139	120	134	129	123

Air - Sun

123	129	134	120	139	155
130	153	116	124	133	144
152	122	143	128	117	138
118	141	125	135	154	127
137	119	150	142	131	121
140	136	132	151	126	115

Earth - Sun

155	144	138	127	121	115
139	133	117	154	131	126
120	124	128	135	142	151
134	116	143	125	150	132
129	153	122	141	119	136
123	130	152	118	137	140

Water - Sun

140	137	118	152	130	123
136	119	141	122	153	129
132	150	125	143	116	134
151	142	135	128	124	120
126	131	154	117	133	139
115	121	127	138	144	155

	Number	Angel Value (Arabic)	Angel Value (Hebrew)	Jinn Value (Arabic)	Jinn Value (Hebrew)
Usurper	115	74	84	156	146
Guide	155	114	124	196	186
Mystery	270	229	239	311	301
Adjuster	800	759	769	481	471
Leader	2400	2359	2369	2081	2071
Regulator	3200	3159	3169	2881	2871
General Governor	6400	6359	6369	6081	6071
High Overseer	992000	991959	991969	991681	991671

Fire - Venus

90	131	116	101	121	136	105
137	106	91	125	117	102	122
103	123	138	107	92	126	111
127	112	97	124	139	108	93
109	94	128	113	98	118	140
119	134	110	95	129	114	99
115	100	120	135	104	96	130

Earth - Venus

115	119	109	127	103	137	90
100	134	94	112	123	106	131
120	110	128	97	138	91	116
135	95	113	124	107	125	101
104	129	98	139	92	117	121
96	114	118	108	126	102	136
130	99	140	93	111	122	105

Air - Venus

130	96	104	135	120	100	115
99	114	129	95	110	134	119
140	118	98	113	128	94	109
93	108	139	124	97	112	127
111	126	92	107	138	123	103
122	102	117	125	91	106	137
105	136	121	101	116	131	90

Water - Venus

105	122	111	93	140	99	130
136	102	126	108	118	114	96
121	117	92	139	98	129	104
101	125	107	124	113	95	135
116	91	138	97	128	110	120
131	106	123	112	94	134	100
90	137	103	127	109	119	115

Occult Encyclopedia of Magic Squares

	Number	Angel Value (Arabic)	Angel Value (Hebrew)	Jinn Value (Arabic)	Jinn Value (Hebrew)
Usurper	90	49	59	131	121
Guide	140	99	109	181	171
Mystery	230	189	199	271	261
Adjuster	800	759	769	481	471
Leader	2400	2359	2369	2081	2071
Regulator	3200	3159	3169	2881	2871
General Governor	6400	6359	6369	6081	6071
High Overseer	896000	895959	895969	895681	895671

Fire - Mercury

68	84	133	113	102	118	99	83
76	92	121	105	110	130	91	75
119	103	82	98	85	69	112	132
131	111	74	90	93	77	104	120
97	81	100	116	135	115	70	86
89	73	108	128	123	107	78	94
114	134	87	71	80	96	117	101
106	122	95	79	72	88	129	109

Earth - Mercury

106	114	89	97	131	119	76	68
122	134	73	81	111	103	92	84
95	87	108	100	74	82	121	133
79	71	128	116	90	98	105	113
72	80	123	135	93	85	110	102
88	96	107	115	77	69	130	118
129	117	78	70	104	112	91	99
109	101	94	86	120	132	75	83

Air - Mercury

109	129	88	72	79	95	122	106
101	117	96	80	71	87	134	114
94	78	107	123	128	108	73	89
86	70	115	135	116	100	81	97
120	104	77	93	90	74	111	131
132	112	69	85	98	82	103	119
75	91	130	110	105	121	92	76
83	99	118	102	113	133	84	68

Water - Mercury

83	75	132	120	86	94	101	109
99	91	112	104	70	78	117	129
118	130	69	77	115	107	96	88
102	110	85	93	135	123	80	72
113	105	98	90	116	128	71	79
133	121	82	74	100	108	87	95
84	92	103	111	81	73	134	122
68	76	119	131	97	89	114	106

	Number	Angel Value (Arabic)	Angel Value (Hebrew)	Jinn Value (Arabic)	Jinn Value (Hebrew)
Usurper	68	27	37	109	99
Guide	135	94	104	176	166
Mystery	203	162	172	244	234
Adjuster	800	759	769	481	471
Leader	2400	2359	2369	2081	2071
Regulator	3200	3159	3169	2881	2871
General Governor	6400	6359	6369	6081	6071
High Overseer	864000	863959	863969	863681	863671

Occult Encyclopedia of Magic Squares

Fire - Moon

92	105	67	76	136	60	96	112	56
52	95	117	72	88	104	59	81	132
128	64	80	116	48	100	109	71	84
119	51	94	103	74	87	131	58	83
79	130	63	99	115	50	86	108	70
66	91	107	62	75	135	55	98	111
65	78	129	49	101	114	69	85	110
106	68	90	134	61	77	113	54	97
93	118	53	89	102	73	82	133	57

Earth - Moon

56	132	84	83	70	111	110	97	57
112	81	71	58	108	98	85	54	133
96	59	109	131	86	55	69	113	82
60	104	100	87	50	135	114	77	73
136	88	48	74	115	75	101	61	102
76	72	116	103	99	62	49	134	89
67	117	80	94	63	107	129	90	53
105	95	64	51	130	91	78	68	118
92	52	128	119	79	66	65	106	93

Air - Moon

57	133	82	73	102	89	53	118	93
97	54	113	77	61	134	90	68	106
110	85	69	114	101	49	129	78	65
111	98	55	135	75	62	107	91	66
70	108	86	50	115	99	63	130	79
83	58	131	87	74	103	94	51	119
84	71	109	100	48	116	80	64	128
132	81	59	104	88	72	117	95	52
56	112	96	60	136	76	67	105	92

Occult Encyclopedia of Magic Squares

Water - Moon

93	106	65	66	79	119	128	52	92
118	68	78	91	130	51	64	95	105
53	90	129	107	63	94	80	117	67
89	134	49	62	99	103	116	72	76
102	61	101	75	115	74	48	88	136
73	77	114	135	50	87	100	104	60
82	113	69	55	86	131	109	59	96
133	54	85	98	108	58	71	81	112
57	97	110	111	70	83	84	132	56

	Number	Angel Value (Arabic)	Angel Value (Hebrew)	Jinn Value (Arabic)	Jinn Value (Hebrew)
Usurper	48	7	17	89	79
Guide	136	95	105	177	167
Mystery	184	143	153	225	215
Adjuster	800	759	769	481	471
Leader	2400	2359	2369	2081	2071
Regulator	3200	3159	3169	2881	2871
General Governor	6400	6359	6369	6081	6071
High Overseer	870400	870359	870369	870081	870071

Fire - Saturn

30	48	55	93	84	127	77	69	101	116
41	105	98	89	129	114	32	74	60	58
56	61	85	128	115	100	49	37	78	91
62	87	126	117	50	96	104	45	34	79
75	125	119	54	65	88	92	102	47	33
82	39	40	107	95	71	67	57	112	130
94	76	36	43	109	64	52	113	133	80
108	97	72	31	42	59	110	132	83	66
118	51	63	70	38	46	131	81	99	103
134	111	106	68	73	35	86	90	53	44

Occult Encyclopedia of Magic Squares

Earth - Saturn

134	118	108	94	82	75	62	56	41	30
111	51	97	76	39	125	87	61	105	48
106	63	72	36	40	119	126	85	98	55
68	70	31	43	107	54	117	128	89	93
73	38	42	109	95	65	50	115	129	84
35	46	59	64	71	88	96	100	114	127
86	131	110	52	67	92	104	49	32	77
90	81	132	113	57	102	45	37	74	69
53	99	83	133	112	47	34	78	60	101
44	103	66	80	130	33	79	91	58	116

Air - Saturn

44	53	90	86	35	73	68	106	111	134
103	99	81	131	46	38	70	63	51	118
66	83	132	110	59	42	31	72	97	108
80	133	113	52	64	109	43	36	76	94
130	112	57	67	71	95	107	40	39	82
33	47	102	92	88	65	54	119	125	75
79	34	45	104	96	50	117	126	87	62
91	78	37	49	100	115	128	85	61	56
58	60	74	32	114	129	89	98	105	41
116	101	69	77	127	84	93	55	48	30

Water - Saturn

116	58	91	79	33	130	80	66	103	44
101	60	78	34	47	112	133	83	99	53
69	74	37	45	102	57	113	132	81	90
77	**32**	49	104	92	67	52	110	131	86
127	114	100	96	88	71	64	59	46	35
84	129	115	50	65	95	109	42	38	73
93	89	128	117	54	107	43	31	70	68
55	98	85	126	119	40	36	72	63	106
48	105	61	87	125	39	76	97	51	111
30	41	56	62	75	82	94	108	118	134

	Number	Angel Value (Arabic)	Angel Value (Hebrew)	Jinn Value (Arabic)	Jinn Value (Hebrew)
Usurper	30	349	359	71	61
Guide	134	93	103	175	165
Mystery	164	123	133	205	195
Adjuster	800	759	769	481	471
Leader	2400	2359	2369	2081	2071
Regulator	3200	3159	3169	2881	2871
General Governor	6400	6359	6369	6081	6071
High Overseer	857600	857559	857569	857281	857271

ARCHANGEL OF SAGITTARIUS: ADVAKIEL (72)

אל	ב	ו	אד
4	7	23	38
22	39	3	8
5	6	40	21

ל	א	י	כ	ו	ד	א
י	כ	ו	ד	א	ל	א
ו	ד	א	ל	א	י	כ
א	ל	א	י	כ	ו	ד
א	י	כ	ו	ד	א	ל
כ	ו	ד	א	ל	א	י
ד	א	ל	א	י	כ	ו

Fire - Saturn

25	20	27
26	24	22
21	28	23

Air - Saturn

23	28	21
22	24	26
27	20	25

Earth - Saturn

21	26	25
28	24	20
23	22	27

Water - Saturn

27	22	23
20	24	28
25	26	21

Occult Encyclopedia of Magic Squares

	Number	Angel Value (Arabic)	Angel Value (Hebrew)	Jinn Value (Arabic)	Jinn Value (Hebrew)
Usurper	20	339	349	61	51
Guide	28	347	357	69	59
Mystery	48	7	17	89	79
Adjuster	72	31	41	113	103
Leader	216	175	185	257	247
Regulator	288	247	257	329	319
General Governor	576	535	545	257	247
High Overseer	16128	16087	16097	15809	15799

Fire - Jupiter

10	21	15	26
25	16	18	13
20	11	27	14
17	24	12	19

Air - Jupiter

19	12	24	17
14	27	11	20
13	18	16	25
26	15	21	10

Earth - Jupiter

17	20	25	10
24	11	16	21
12	27	18	15
19	14	13	26

Water - Jupiter

26	13	14	19
15	18	27	12
21	16	11	24
10	25	20	17

	Number	Angel Value (Arabic)	Angel Value (Hebrew)	Jinn Value (Arabic)	Jinn Value (Hebrew)
Usurper	10	329	339	51	41
Guide	27	346	356	68	58
Mystery	37	356	6	78	68
Adjuster	576	535	545	257	247
Leader	1728	1687	1697	1409	1399
Regulator	2304	2263	2273	1985	1975
General Governor	4608	4567	4577	4289	4279
High Overseer	124416	124375	124385	124097	124087

Fire - Mars

2	28	20	14	8
15	9	3	24	21
25	17	16	10	4
11	5	26	18	12
19	13	7	6	27

Air - Mars

19	11	25	15	2
13	5	17	9	28
7	26	16	3	20
6	18	10	24	14
27	12	4	21	8

Earth - Mars

27	6	7	13	19
12	18	26	5	11
4	10	16	17	25
21	24	3	9	15
8	14	20	28	2

Water - Mars

8	21	4	12	27
14	24	10	18	6
20	3	16	26	7
28	9	17	5	13
2	15	25	11	19

	Number	Angel Value (Arabic)	Angel Value (Hebrew)	Jinn Value (Arabic)	Jinn Value (Hebrew)
Usurper	2	321	331	43	33
Guide	28	347	357	69	59
Mystery	30	349	359	71	61
Adjuster	72	31	41	113	103
Leader	216	175	185	257	247
Regulator	288	247	257	329	319
General Governor	576	535	545	257	247
High Overseer	16128	16087	16097	15809	15799

ANGEL OF SAGITTARIUS: SARITIEL (320)

יאל	יט	ר	ס
59	201	22	38
21	39	58	202
199	61	40	20

ל	א	י	ט	י	ר	ס
י	ט	י	ר	ס	ל	א
י	ר	ס	ל	א	י	ט
ס	ל	א	י	ט	י	ר
א	י	ט	י	ר	ס	ל
ט	י	ר	ס	ל	א	י
ר	ס	ל	א	י	ט	י

Occult Encyclopedia of Magic Squares

Fire - Jupiter

72	83	77	88
87	78	80	75
82	73	89	76
79	86	74	81

Air - Jupiter

81	74	86	79
76	89	73	82
75	80	78	87
88	77	83	72

Earth - Jupiter

79	82	87	72
86	73	78	83
74	89	80	77
81	76	75	88

Water - Jupiter

88	75	76	81
77	80	89	74
83	78	73	86
72	87	82	79

	Number	Angel Value (Arabic)	Angel Value (Hebrew)	Jinn Value (Arabic)	Jinn Value (Hebrew)
Usurper	72	31	41	113	103
Guide	89	48	58	130	120
Mystery	161	120	130	202	192
Adjuster	2560	2519	2529	2241	2231
Leader	7680	7639	7649	7361	7351
Regulator	10240	10199	10209	9921	9911
General Governor	20480	20439	20449	20161	20151
High Overseer	1822720	1822679	1822689	1822401	1822391

Fire - Mars

52	76	70	64	58
65	59	53	72	71
73	67	66	60	54
61	55	74	68	62
69	63	57	56	75

Air - Mars

69	61	73	65	52
63	55	67	59	76
57	74	66	53	70
56	68	60	72	64
75	62	54	71	58

Earth - Mars

75	56	57	63	69
62	68	74	55	61
54	60	66	67	73
71	72	53	59	65
58	64	70	76	52

Water - Mars

58	71	54	62	75
64	72	60	68	56
70	53	66	74	57
76	59	67	55	63
52	65	73	61	69

Occult Encyclopedia of Magic Squares

	Number	Angel Value (Arabic)	Angel Value (Hebrew)	Jinn Value (Arabic)	Jinn Value (Hebrew)
Usurper	52	11	21	93	83
Guide	76	35	45	117	107
Mystery	128	87	97	169	159
Adjuster	320	279	289	1	351
Leader	960	919	929	641	631
Regulator	1280	1239	1249	961	951
General Governor	2560	2519	2529	2241	2231
High Overseer	194560	194519	194529	194241	194231

Fire - Sun

35	46	71	52	56	60
41	51	62	70	39	57
47	74	55	45	61	38
58	37	48	63	42	72
64	53	44	36	73	50
75	59	40	54	49	43

Air - Sun

43	49	54	40	59	75
50	73	36	44	53	64
72	42	63	48	37	58
38	61	45	55	74	47
57	39	70	62	51	41
60	56	52	71	46	35

Earth - Sun

75	64	58	47	41	35
59	53	37	74	51	46
40	44	48	55	62	71
54	36	63	45	70	52
49	73	42	61	39	56
43	50	72	38	57	60

Water - Sun

60	57	38	72	50	43
56	39	61	42	73	49
52	70	45	63	36	54
71	62	55	48	44	40
46	51	74	37	53	59
35	41	47	58	64	75

	Number	Angel Value (Arabic)	Angel Value (Hebrew)	Jinn Value (Arabic)	Jinn Value (Hebrew)
Usurper	35	354	4	76	66
Guide	75	34	44	116	106
Mystery	110	69	79	151	141
Adjuster	320	279	289	1	351
Leader	960	919	929	641	631
Regulator	1280	1239	1249	961	951
General Governor	2560	2519	2529	2241	2231
High Overseer	192000	191959	191969	191681	191671

Fire - Venus

21	62	47	32	52	70	36
71	37	22	56	48	33	53
34	54	72	38	23	57	42
58	43	28	55	73	39	24
40	25	59	44	29	49	74
50	68	41	26	60	45	30
46	31	51	69	35	27	61

Air - Venus

61	27	35	69	51	31	46
30	45	60	26	41	68	50
74	49	29	44	59	25	40
24	39	73	55	28	43	58
42	57	23	38	72	54	34
53	33	48	56	22	37	71
36	70	52	32	47	62	21

Earth - Venus

46	50	40	58	34	71	21
31	68	25	43	54	37	62
51	41	59	28	72	22	47
69	26	44	55	38	56	32
35	60	29	73	23	48	52
27	45	49	39	57	33	70
61	30	74	24	42	53	36

Water - Venus

36	53	42	24	74	30	61
70	33	57	39	49	45	27
52	48	23	73	29	60	35
32	56	38	55	44	26	69
47	22	72	28	59	41	51
62	37	54	43	25	68	31
21	71	34	58	40	50	46

	Number	Angel Value (Arabic)	Angel Value (Hebrew)	Jinn Value (Arabic)	Jinn Value (Hebrew)
Usurper	21	340	350	62	52
Guide	74	33	43	115	105
Mystery	95	54	64	136	126
Adjuster	320	279	289	1	351
Leader	960	919	929	641	631
Regulator	1280	1239	1249	961	951
General Governor	2560	2519	2529	2241	2231
High Overseer	189440	189399	189409	189121	189111

Fire - Mercury

8	24	73	53	42	58	39	23
16	32	61	45	50	70	31	15
59	43	22	38	25	9	52	72
71	51	14	30	33	17	44	60
37	21	40	56	75	55	10	26
29	13	48	68	63	47	18	34
54	74	27	11	20	36	57	41
46	62	35	19	12	28	69	49

Occult Encyclopedia of Magic Squares

Earth - Mercury

46	54	29	37	71	59	16	8
62	74	13	21	51	43	32	24
35	27	48	40	14	22	61	73
19	11	68	56	30	38	45	53
12	20	63	75	33	25	50	42
28	36	47	55	17	9	70	58
69	57	18	10	44	52	31	39
49	41	34	26	60	72	15	23

Air - Mercury

49	69	28	12	19	35	62	46
41	57	36	20	11	27	74	54
34	18	47	63	68	48	13	29
26	10	55	75	56	40	21	37
60	44	17	33	30	14	51	71
72	52	9	25	38	22	43	59
15	31	70	50	45	61	32	16
23	39	58	42	53	73	24	8

Water - Mercury

23	15	72	60	26	34	41	49
39	31	52	44	10	18	57	69
58	70	9	17	55	47	36	28
42	50	25	33	75	63	20	12
53	45	38	30	56	68	11	19
73	61	22	14	40	48	27	35
24	32	43	51	21	13	74	62
8	16	59	71	37	29	54	46

	Number	Angel Value (Arabic)	Angel Value (Hebrew)	Jinn Value (Arabic)	Jinn Value (Hebrew)
Usurper	8	327	337	49	39
Guide	75	34	44	116	106
Mystery	83	42	52	124	114
Adjuster	320	279	289	1	351
Leader	960	919	929	641	631
Regulator	1280	1239	1249	961	951
General Governor	2560	2519	2529	2241	2231
High Overseer	192000	191959	191969	191681	191671

LORD OF TRIPLICITY BY DAY: AHOZ (19)

ו	ו	ה	א
4	2	5	8
4	9	3	3
4	2	6	7

ו	ו	ה	א
א	ה	ו	ו
ו	ו	א	ה
ה	א	ו	ו

No Hebrew Squares Available

LORD OF TRIPLICITY BY LEBARMIM (322)

מ	מי	ר	לב
31	201	53	37
52	38	30	202
199	33	39	51

מ	י	מ	ר	ב	ל
ב	ר	מ	ל	מ	י
מ	ל	י	ב	מ	ר
ל	ב	ר	מ	י	מ
ר	מ	ב	י	ל	מ
י	מ	ל	מ	ר	ב

Fire - Jupiter

73	84	78	87
86	79	81	76
83	74	88	77
80	85	75	82

Air - Jupiter

82	75	85	80
77	88	74	83
76	81	79	86
87	78	84	73

Earth - Jupiter

80	83	86	73
85	74	79	84
75	88	81	78
82	77	76	87

Water - Jupiter

87	76	77	82
78	81	88	75
84	79	74	85
73	86	83	80

	Number	Angel Value (Arabic)	Angel Value (Hebrew)	Jinn Value (Arabic)	Jinn Value (Hebrew)
Usurper	73	32	42	114	104
Guide	88	47	57	129	119
Mystery	161	120	130	202	192
Adjuster	2576	2535	2545	2257	2247
Leader	7728	7687	7697	7409	7399
Regulator	10304	10263	10273	9985	9975
General Governor	20608	20567	20577	20289	20279
High Overseer	1813504	1813463	1813473	1813185	1813175

Fire - Mars

52	78	70	64	58
65	59	53	74	71
75	67	66	60	54
61	55	76	68	62
69	63	57	56	77

Air - Mars

69	61	75	65	52
63	55	67	59	78
57	76	66	53	70
56	68	60	74	64
77	62	54	71	58

Earth - Mars

77	56	57	63	69
62	68	76	55	61
54	60	66	67	75
71	74	53	59	65
58	64	70	78	52

Water - Mars

58	71	54	62	77
64	74	60	68	56
70	53	66	76	57
78	59	67	55	63
52	65	75	61	69

Occult Encyclopedia of Magic Squares

	Number	Angel Value (Arabic)	Angel Value (Hebrew)	Jinn Value (Arabic)	Jinn Value (Hebrew)
Usurper	52	11	21	93	83
Guide	78	37	47	119	109
Mystery	130	89	99	171	161
Adjuster	322	281	291	3	353
Leader	966	925	935	647	637
Regulator	1288	1247	1257	969	959
General Governor	2576	2535	2545	2257	2247
High Overseer	200928	200887	200897	200609	200599

Fire - Sun

36	47	68	53	57	61
42	52	63	67	40	58
48	71	56	46	62	39
59	38	49	64	43	69
65	54	45	37	70	51
72	60	41	55	50	44

Air - Sun

44	50	55	41	60	72
51	70	37	45	54	65
69	43	64	49	38	59
39	62	46	56	71	48
58	40	67	63	52	42
61	57	53	68	47	36

Earth - Sun

72	65	59	48	42	36
60	54	38	71	52	47
41	45	49	56	63	68
55	37	64	46	67	53
50	70	43	62	40	57
44	51	69	39	58	61

Water - Sun

61	58	39	69	51	44
57	40	62	43	70	50
53	67	46	64	37	55
68	63	56	49	45	41
47	52	71	38	54	60
36	42	48	59	65	72

	Number	Angel Value (Arabic)	Angel Value (Hebrew)	Jinn Value (Arabic)	Jinn Value (Hebrew)
Usurper	36	355	5	77	67
Guide	72	31	41	113	103
Mystery	108	67	77	149	139
Adjuster	322	281	291	3	353
Leader	966	925	935	647	637
Regulator	1288	1247	1257	969	959
General Governor	2576	2535	2545	2257	2247
High Overseer	185472	185431	185441	185153	185143

Occult Encyclopedia of Magic Squares

Fire - Venus

22	63	48	33	53	66	37
67	38	23	57	49	34	54
35	55	68	39	24	58	43
59	44	29	56	69	40	25
41	26	60	45	30	50	70
51	64	42	27	61	46	31
47	32	52	65	36	28	62

Air - Venus

62	28	36	65	52	32	47
31	46	61	27	42	64	51
70	50	30	45	60	26	41
25	40	69	56	29	44	59
43	58	24	39	68	55	35
54	34	49	57	23	38	67
37	66	53	33	48	63	22

Earth - Venus

47	51	41	59	35	67	22
32	64	26	44	55	38	63
52	42	60	29	68	23	48
65	27	45	56	39	57	33
36	61	30	69	24	49	53
28	46	50	40	58	34	66
62	31	70	25	43	54	37

Water - Venus

37	54	43	25	70	31	62
66	34	58	40	50	46	28
53	49	24	69	30	61	36
33	57	39	56	45	27	65
48	23	68	29	60	42	52
63	38	55	44	26	64	32
22	67	35	59	41	51	47

	Number	Angel Value (Arabic)	Angel Value (Hebrew)	Jinn Value (Arabic)	Jinn Value (Hebrew)
Usurper	22	341	351	63	53
Guide	70	29	39	111	101
Mystery	92	51	61	133	123
Adjuster	322	281	291	3	353
Leader	966	925	935	647	637
Regulator	1288	1247	1257	969	959
General Governor	2576	2535	2545	2257	2247
High Overseer	180320	180279	180289	180001	179991

Fire - Mercury

8	24	75	53	42	58	39	23
16	32	61	45	50	72	31	15
59	43	22	38	25	9	52	74
73	51	14	30	33	17	44	60
37	21	40	56	77	55	10	26
29	13	48	70	63	47	18	34
54	76	27	11	20	36	57	41
46	62	35	19	12	28	71	49

Earth - Mercury

46	54	29	37	73	59	16	8
62	76	13	21	51	43	32	24
35	27	48	40	14	22	61	75
19	11	70	56	30	38	45	53
12	20	63	77	33	25	50	42
28	36	47	55	17	9	72	58
71	57	18	10	44	52	31	39
49	41	34	26	60	74	15	23

Air - Mercury

49	71	28	12	19	35	62	46
41	57	36	20	11	27	76	54
34	18	47	63	70	48	13	29
26	10	55	77	56	40	21	37
60	44	17	33	30	14	51	73
74	52	9	25	38	22	43	59
15	31	72	50	45	61	32	16
23	39	58	42	53	75	24	8

Water - Mercury

23	15	74	60	26	34	41	49
39	31	52	44	10	18	57	71
58	72	9	17	55	47	36	28
42	50	25	33	77	63	20	12
53	45	38	30	56	70	11	19
75	61	22	14	40	48	27	35
24	32	43	51	21	13	76	62
8	16	59	73	37	29	54	46

	Number	Angel Value (Arabic)	Angel Value (Hebrew)	Jinn Value (Arabic)	Jinn Value (Hebrew)
Usurper	8	327	337	49	39
Guide	77	36	46	118	108
Mystery	85	44	54	126	116
Adjuster	322	281	291	3	353
Leader	966	925	935	647	637
Regulator	1288	1247	1257	969	959
General Governor	2576	2535	2545	2257	2247
High Overseer	198352	198311	198321	198033	198023

ANGEL RULING 9ᵀᴴ HOUSE: SOYASEL (237)

לא	ם	יע	םם
65	81	63	28
62	29	64	82
79	67	30	61

ל	א	ם	ע	י	ו	ם
ם	ע	י	ו	ם	ל	א
י	ו	ם	ל	א	ם	ע
ם	ל	א	ם	ע	י	ו
א	ם	ע	י	ו	ם	ל
ע	י	ו	ם	ל	א	ם
ו	ם	ל	א	ם	ע	י

Numerical Squares See Page: 236

ANGEL OF FIRST DECANATE: MISHRATH (941)

את	ר	ש	ם
39	301	203	398
202	399	38	302
299	41	400	201

ת	א	ר	ש	ם
ר	ש	ם	ת	א
ם	ת	א	ר	ש
א	ר	ש	ם	ת
ש	ם	ת	א	ר

Occult Encyclopedia of Magic Squares

Fire - Jupiter

227	238	232	244
243	233	235	230
237	228	245	231
234	242	229	236

Air - Jupiter

236	229	242	234
231	245	228	237
230	235	233	243
244	232	238	227

Earth - Jupiter

234	237	243	227
242	228	233	238
229	245	235	232
236	231	230	244

Water - Jupiter

244	230	231	236
232	235	245	229
238	233	228	242
227	243	237	234

	Number	Angel Value (Arabic)	Angel Value (Hebrew)	Jinn Value (Arabic)	Jinn Value (Hebrew)
Usurper	227	186	196	268	258
Guide	245	204	214	286	276
Mystery	472	431	441	153	143
Adjuster	7528	7487	7497	7209	7199
Leader	22584	22543	22553	22265	22255
Regulator	30112	30071	30081	29793	29783
General Governor	60224	60183	60193	59905	59895
High Overseer	14754880	14754839	14754849	14754561	14754551

Fire - Mars

176	201	194	188	182
189	183	177	197	195
198	191	190	184	178
185	179	199	192	186
193	187	181	180	200

Air - Mars

193	185	198	189	176
187	179	191	183	201
181	199	190	177	194
180	192	184	197	188
200	186	178	195	182

Earth - Mars

200	180	181	187	193
186	192	199	179	185
178	184	190	191	198
195	197	177	183	189
182	188	194	201	176

Water - Mars

182	195	178	186	200
188	197	184	192	180
194	177	190	199	181
201	183	191	179	187
176	189	198	185	193

Occult Encyclopedia of Magic Squares

	Number	Angel Value (Arabic)	Angel Value (Hebrew)	Jinn Value (Arabic)	Jinn Value (Hebrew)
Usurper	176	135	145	217	207
Guide	201	160	170	242	232
Mystery	377	336	346	58	48
Adjuster	941	900	910	622	612
Leader	2823	2782	2792	2504	2494
Regulator	3764	3723	3733	3445	3435
General Governor	7528	7487	7497	7209	7199
High Overseer	1513128	1513087	1513097	1512809	1512799

Fire - Sun

139	150	172	156	160	164
145	155	166	171	143	161
151	175	159	149	165	142
162	141	152	167	146	173
168	157	148	140	174	154
176	163	144	158	153	147

Air - Sun

147	153	158	144	163	176
154	174	140	148	157	168
173	146	167	152	141	162
142	165	149	159	175	151
161	143	171	166	155	145
164	160	156	172	150	139

Earth - Sun

176	168	162	151	145	139
163	157	141	175	155	150
144	148	152	159	166	172
158	140	167	149	171	156
153	174	146	165	143	160
147	154	173	142	161	164

Water - Sun

164	161	142	173	154	147
160	143	165	146	174	153
156	171	149	167	140	158
172	166	159	152	148	144
150	155	175	141	157	163
139	145	151	162	168	176

Occult Encyclopedia of Magic Squares

	Number	Angel Value (Arabic)	Angel Value (Hebrew)	Jinn Value (Arabic)	Jinn Value (Hebrew)
Usurper	139	98	108	180	170
Guide	176	135	145	217	207
Mystery	315	274	284	356	346
Adjuster	941	900	910	622	612
Leader	2823	2782	2792	2504	2494
Regulator	3764	3723	3733	3445	3435
General Governor	7528	7487	7497	7209	7199
High Overseer	1324928	1324887	1324897	1324609	1324599

Fire - Venus

110	151	136	121	141	157	125
158	126	111	145	137	122	142
123	143	159	127	112	146	131
147	132	117	144	160	128	113
129	114	148	133	118	138	161
139	155	130	115	149	134	119
135	120	140	156	124	116	150

Earth - Venus

135	139	129	147	123	158	110
120	155	114	132	143	126	151
140	130	148	117	159	111	136
156	115	133	144	127	145	121
124	149	118	160	112	137	141
116	134	138	128	146	122	157
150	119	161	113	131	142	125

Occult Encyclopedia of Magic Squares

Air - Venus

150	116	124	156	140	120	135
119	134	149	115	130	155	139
161	138	118	133	148	114	129
113	128	160	144	117	132	147
131	146	112	127	159	143	123
142	122	137	145	111	126	158
125	157	141	121	136	151	110

Water - Venus

125	142	131	113	161	119	150
157	122	146	128	138	134	116
141	137	112	160	118	149	124
121	145	127	144	133	115	156
136	111	159	117	148	130	140
151	126	143	132	114	155	120
110	158	123	147	129	139	135

	Number	Angel Value (Arabic)	Angel Value (Hebrew)	Jinn Value (Arabic)	Jinn Value (Hebrew)
Usurper	110	69	79	151	141
Guide	161	120	130	202	192
Mystery	271	230	240	312	302
Adjuster	941	900	910	622	612
Leader	2823	2782	2792	2504	2494
Regulator	3764	3723	3733	3445	3435
General Governor	7528	7487	7497	7209	7199
High Overseer	1212008	1211967	1211977	1211689	1211679

Fire - Mercury

86	102	148	131	120	136	117	101
94	110	139	123	128	145	109	93
137	121	100	116	103	87	130	147
146	129	92	108	111	95	122	138
115	99	118	134	150	133	88	104
107	91	126	143	141	125	96	112
132	149	105	89	98	114	135	119
124	140	113	97	90	106	144	127

Earth - Mercury

124	132	107	115	146	137	94	86
140	149	91	99	129	121	110	102
113	105	126	118	92	100	139	148
97	89	143	134	108	116	123	131
90	98	141	150	111	103	128	120
106	114	125	133	95	87	145	136
144	135	96	88	122	130	109	117
127	119	112	104	138	147	93	101

Air - Mercury

127	144	106	90	97	113	140	124
119	135	114	98	89	105	149	132
112	96	125	141	143	126	91	107
104	88	133	150	134	118	99	115
138	122	95	111	108	92	129	146
147	130	87	103	116	100	121	137
93	109	145	128	123	139	110	94
101	117	136	120	131	148	102	86

Water - Mercury

101	93	147	138	104	112	119	127
117	109	130	122	88	96	135	144
136	145	87	95	133	125	114	106
120	128	103	111	150	141	98	90
131	123	116	108	134	143	89	97
148	139	100	92	118	126	105	113
102	110	121	129	99	91	149	140
86	94	137	146	115	107	132	124

	Number	Angel Value (Arabic)	Angel Value (Hebrew)	Jinn Value (Arabic)	Jinn Value (Hebrew)
Usurper	86	45	55	127	117
Guide	150	109	119	191	181
Mystery	236	195	205	277	267
Adjuster	941	900	910	622	612
Leader	2823	2782	2792	2504	2494
Regulator	3764	3723	3733	3445	3435
General Governor	7528	7487	7497	7209	7199
High Overseer	1129200	1129159	1129169	1128881	1128871

Fire - Moon

108	121	83	92	149	76	112	128	72
68	111	133	88	104	120	75	97	145
141	80	96	132	64	116	125	87	100
135	67	110	119	90	103	144	74	99
95	143	79	115	131	66	102	124	86
82	107	123	78	91	148	71	114	127
81	94	142	65	117	130	85	101	126
122	84	106	147	77	93	129	70	113
109	134	69	105	118	89	98	146	73

Earth - Moon

72	145	100	99	86	127	126	113	73
128	97	87	74	124	114	101	70	146
112	75	125	144	102	71	85	129	98
76	120	116	103	66	148	130	93	89
149	104	64	90	131	91	117	77	118
92	88	132	119	115	78	65	147	105
83	133	96	110	79	123	142	106	69
121	111	80	67	143	107	94	84	134
108	68	141	135	95	82	81	122	109

Occult Encyclopedia of Magic Squares

Air - Moon

73	146	98	89	118	105	69	134	109
113	70	129	93	77	147	106	84	122
126	101	85	130	117	65	142	94	81
127	114	71	148	91	78	123	107	82
86	124	102	66	131	115	79	143	95
99	74	144	103	90	119	110	67	135
100	87	125	116	64	132	96	80	141
145	97	75	120	104	88	133	111	68
72	128	112	76	149	92	83	121	108

Water - Moon

109	122	81	82	95	135	141	68	108
134	84	94	107	143	67	80	111	121
69	106	142	123	79	110	96	133	83
105	147	65	78	115	119	132	88	92
118	77	117	91	131	90	64	104	149
89	93	130	148	66	103	116	120	76
98	129	85	71	102	144	125	75	112
146	70	101	114	124	74	87	97	128
73	113	126	127	86	99	100	145	72

	Number	Angel Value (Arabic)	Angel Value (Hebrew)	Jinn Value (Arabic)	Jinn Value (Hebrew)
Usurper	64	23	33	105	95
Guide	149	108	118	190	180
Mystery	213	172	182	254	244
Adjuster	941	900	910	622	612
Leader	2823	2782	2792	2504	2494
Regulator	3764	3723	3733	3445	3435
General Governor	7528	7487	7497	7209	7199
High Overseer	1121672	1121631	1121641	1121353	1121343

Fire - Saturn

44	62	69	107	98	142	91	83	115	130
55	119	112	103	144	128	46	88	74	72
70	75	99	143	129	114	63	51	92	105
76	101	141	131	64	110	118	59	48	93
89	140	133	68	79	102	106	116	61	47
96	53	54	121	109	85	81	71	126	145
108	90	50	57	123	78	66	127	148	94
122	111	86	45	56	73	124	147	97	80
132	65	77	84	52	60	146	95	113	117
149	125	120	82	87	49	100	104	67	58

Earth - Saturn

149	132	122	108	96	89	76	70	55	44
125	65	111	90	53	140	101	75	119	62
120	77	86	50	54	133	141	99	112	69
82	84	45	57	121	68	131	143	103	107
87	52	56	123	109	79	64	129	144	98
49	60	73	78	85	102	110	114	128	142
100	146	124	66	81	106	118	63	46	91
104	95	147	127	71	116	59	51	88	83
67	113	97	148	126	61	48	92	74	115
58	117	80	94	145	47	93	105	72	130

Air - Saturn

58	67	104	100	49	87	82	120	125	149
117	113	95	146	60	52	84	77	65	132
80	97	147	124	73	56	45	86	111	122
94	148	127	66	78	123	57	50	90	108
145	126	71	81	85	109	121	54	53	96
47	61	116	106	102	79	68	133	140	89
93	48	59	118	110	64	131	141	101	76
105	92	51	63	114	129	143	99	75	70
72	74	88	46	128	144	103	112	119	55
130	115	83	91	142	98	107	69	62	44

Water - Saturn

130	72	105	93	47	145	94	80	117	58
115	74	92	48	61	126	148	97	113	67
83	88	51	59	116	71	127	147	95	104
91	**46**	63	118	106	81	66	124	146	100
142	128	114	110	102	85	78	73	60	49
98	144	129	64	79	109	123	56	52	87
107	103	143	131	68	121	57	45	84	82
69	112	99	141	133	54	50	86	77	120
62	119	75	101	140	53	90	111	65	125
44	55	70	76	89	96	108	122	132	149

	Number	Angel Value (Arabic)	Angel Value (Hebrew)	Jinn Value (Arabic)	Jinn Value (Hebrew)
Usurper	44	3	13	85	75
Guide	149	108	118	190	180
Mystery	193	152	162	234	224
Adjuster	941	900	910	622	612
Leader	2823	2782	2792	2504	2494
Regulator	3764	3723	3733	3445	3435
General Governor	7528	7487	7497	7209	7199
High Overseer	1121672	1121631	1121641	1121353	1121343

ANGEL OF FIRST QUINANCE: NITHAHIAH (470)

יה	ה	ת	נ
49	401	8	12
7	13	48	402
399	51	14	6

ה	י	ה	ת	נ
ה	ת	נ	ה	י
נ	ה	י	ה	ת
י	ה	ת	נ	ה
ת	נ	ה	י	ה

Occult Encyclopedia of Magic Squares

Fire - Jupiter

110	121	115	124
123	116	118	113
120	111	125	114
117	122	112	119

Air - Jupiter

119	112	122	117
114	125	111	120
113	118	116	123
124	115	121	110

Earth - Jupiter

117	120	123	110
122	111	116	121
112	125	118	115
119	114	113	124

Water - Jupiter

124	113	114	119
115	118	125	112
121	116	111	122
110	123	120	117

	Number	Angel Value (Arabic)	Angel Value (Hebrew)	Jinn Value (Arabic)	Jinn Value (Hebrew)
Usurper	110	69	79	151	141
Guide	125	84	94	166	156
Mystery	235	194	204	276	266
Adjuster	3760	3719	3729	3441	3431
Leader	11280	11239	11249	10961	10951
Regulator	15040	14999	15009	14721	14711
General Governor	30080	30039	30049	29761	29751
High Overseer	3760000	3759959	3759969	3759681	3759671

Fire - Mars

82	106	100	94	88
95	89	83	102	101
103	97	96	90	84
91	85	104	98	92
99	93	87	86	105

Air - Mars

99	91	103	95	82
93	85	97	89	106
87	104	96	83	100
86	98	90	102	94
105	92	84	101	88

Earth - Mars

105	86	87	93	99
92	98	104	85	91
84	90	96	97	103
101	102	83	89	95
88	94	100	106	82

Water - Mars

88	101	84	92	105
94	102	90	98	86
100	83	96	104	87
106	89	97	85	93
82	95	103	91	99

Occult Encyclopedia of Magic Squares

	Number	Angel Value (Arabic)	Angel Value (Hebrew)	Jinn Value (Arabic)	Jinn Value (Hebrew)
Usurper	82	41	51	123	113
Guide	106	65	75	147	137
Mystery	188	147	157	229	219
Adjuster	470	429	439	151	141
Leader	1410	1369	1379	1091	1081
Regulator	1880	1839	1849	1561	1551
General Governor	3760	3719	3729	3441	3431
High Overseer	398560	398519	398529	398241	398231

Fire - Sun

60	71	96	77	81	85
66	76	87	95	64	82
72	99	80	70	86	63
83	62	73	88	67	97
89	78	69	61	98	75
100	84	65	79	74	68

Air - Sun

68	74	79	65	84	100
75	98	61	69	78	89
97	67	88	73	62	83
63	86	70	80	99	72
82	64	95	87	76	66
85	81	77	96	71	60

Earth - Sun

100	89	83	72	66	60
84	78	62	99	76	71
65	69	73	80	87	96
79	61	88	70	95	77
74	98	67	86	64	81
68	75	97	63	82	85

Water - Sun

85	82	63	97	75	68
81	64	86	67	98	74
77	95	70	88	61	79
96	87	80	73	69	65
71	76	99	62	78	84
60	66	72	83	89	100

	Number	Angel Value (Arabic)	Angel Value (Hebrew)	Jinn Value (Arabic)	Jinn Value (Hebrew)
Usurper	60	19	29	101	91
Guide	100	59	69	141	131
Mystery	160	119	129	201	191
Adjuster	470	429	439	151	141
Leader	1410	1369	1379	1091	1081
Regulator	1880	1839	1849	1561	1551
General Governor	3760	3719	3729	3441	3431
High Overseer	376000	375959	375969	375681	375671

Occult Encyclopedia of Magic Squares

Fire - Venus

43	84	69	54	74	88	58
89	59	44	78	70	55	75
56	76	90	60	45	79	64
80	65	50	77	91	61	46
62	47	81	66	51	71	92
72	86	63	48	82	67	52
68	53	73	87	57	49	83

Air - Venus

83	49	57	87	73	53	68
52	67	82	48	63	86	72
92	71	51	66	81	47	62
46	61	91	77	50	65	80
64	79	45	60	90	76	56
75	55	70	78	44	59	89
58	88	74	54	69	84	43

Earth - Venus

68	72	62	80	56	89	43
53	86	47	65	76	59	84
73	63	81	50	90	44	69
87	48	66	77	60	78	54
57	82	51	91	45	70	74
49	67	71	61	79	55	88
83	52	92	46	64	75	58

Water - Venus

58	75	64	46	92	52	83
88	55	79	61	71	67	49
74	70	45	91	51	82	57
54	78	60	77	66	48	87
69	44	90	50	81	63	73
84	59	76	65	47	86	53
43	89	56	80	62	72	68

	Number	Angel Value (Arabic)	Angel Value (Hebrew)	Jinn Value (Arabic)	Jinn Value (Hebrew)
Usurper	43	2	12	84	74
Guide	92	51	61	133	123
Mystery	135	94	104	176	166
Adjuster	470	429	439	151	141
Leader	1410	1369	1379	1091	1081
Regulator	1880	1839	1849	1561	1551
General Governor	3760	3719	3729	3441	3431
High Overseer	345920	345879	345889	345601	345591

Fire - Mercury

27	43	90	72	61	77	58	42
35	51	80	64	69	87	50	34
78	62	41	57	44	28	71	89
88	70	33	49	52	36	63	79
56	40	59	75	92	74	29	45
48	32	67	85	82	66	37	53
73	91	46	30	39	55	76	60
65	81	54	38	31	47	86	68

Earth - Mercury

65	73	48	56	88	78	35	27
81	91	32	40	70	62	51	43
54	46	67	59	33	41	80	90
38	30	85	75	49	57	64	72
31	39	82	92	52	44	69	61
47	55	66	74	36	28	87	77
86	76	37	29	63	71	50	58
68	60	53	45	79	89	34	42

Air - Mercury

68	86	47	31	38	54	81	65
60	76	55	39	30	46	91	73
53	37	66	82	85	67	32	48
45	29	74	92	75	59	40	56
79	63	36	52	49	33	70	88
89	71	28	44	57	41	62	78
34	50	87	69	64	80	51	35
42	58	77	61	72	90	43	27

Water - Mercury

42	34	89	79	45	53	60	68
58	50	71	63	29	37	76	86
77	87	28	36	74	66	55	47
61	69	44	52	92	82	39	31
72	64	57	49	75	85	30	38
90	80	41	33	59	67	46	54
43	51	62	70	40	32	91	81
27	35	78	88	56	48	73	65

Occult Encyclopedia of Magic Squares

	Number	Angel Value (Arabic)	Angel Value (Hebrew)	Jinn Value (Arabic)	Jinn Value (Hebrew)
Usurper	27	346	356	68	58
Guide	92	51	61	133	123
Mystery	119	78	88	160	150
Adjuster	470	429	439	151	141
Leader	1410	1369	1379	1091	1081
Regulator	1880	1839	1849	1561	1551
General Governor	3760	3719	3729	3441	3431
High Overseer	345920	345879	345889	345601	345591

Fire - Moon

56	69	31	40	94	24	60	76	20
16	59	81	36	52	68	23	45	90
86	28	44	80	12	64	73	35	48
83	15	58	67	38	51	89	22	47
43	88	27	63	79	14	50	72	34
30	55	71	26	39	93	19	62	75
29	42	87	13	65	78	33	49	74
70	32	54	92	25	41	77	18	61
57	82	17	53	66	37	46	91	21

Earth - Moon

20	90	48	47	34	75	74	61	21
76	45	35	22	72	62	49	18	91
60	23	73	89	50	19	33	77	46
24	68	64	51	14	93	78	41	37
94	52	12	38	79	39	65	25	66
40	36	80	67	63	26	13	92	53
31	81	44	58	27	71	87	54	17
69	59	28	15	88	55	42	32	82
56	16	86	83	43	30	29	70	57

Air - Moon

21	91	46	37	66	53	17	82	57
61	18	77	41	25	92	54	32	70
74	49	33	78	65	13	87	42	29
75	62	19	93	39	26	71	55	30
34	72	50	14	79	63	27	88	43
47	22	89	51	38	67	58	15	83
48	35	73	64	12	80	44	28	86
90	45	23	68	52	36	81	59	16
20	76	60	24	94	40	31	69	56

Water - Moon

57	70	29	30	43	83	86	16	56
82	32	42	55	88	15	28	59	69
17	54	87	71	27	58	44	81	31
53	92	13	26	63	67	80	36	40
66	25	65	39	79	38	12	52	94
37	41	78	93	14	51	64	68	24
46	77	33	19	50	89	73	23	60
91	18	49	62	72	22	35	45	76
21	61	74	75	34	47	48	90	20

	Number	Angel Value (Arabic)	Angel Value (Hebrew)	Jinn Value (Arabic)	Jinn Value (Hebrew)
Usurper	12	331	341	53	43
Guide	94	53	63	135	125
Mystery	106	65	75	147	137
Adjuster	470	429	439	151	141
Leader	1410	1369	1379	1091	1081
Regulator	1880	1839	1849	1561	1551
General Governor	3760	3719	3729	3441	3431
High Overseer	353440	353399	353409	353121	353111

ANGEL OF SECOND QUINANCE: HAAYAH (22)

ה	'	אא	ה
4	3	13	2
12	3	3	4
1	6	4	11

ה	'	א	א	ה
א	א	ה	ה	'
ה	ה	'	א	א
'	א	א	ה	ה
א	ה	ה	'	א

No Numerical Squares Available

ANGEL OF SECOND DECANATE: VEHRIN (271)

נ	'	ר	וה
10	201	13	47
12	48	9	202
199	12	49	11

נ	'	ר	ה	ו
ר	ה	ו	נ	'
ו	נ	'	ר	ה
'	ר	ה	ו	נ
ה	ו	נ	'	ר

Fire - Jupiter

60	71	65	75
74	66	68	63
70	61	76	64
67	73	62	69

Air - Jupiter

69	62	73	67
64	76	61	70
63	68	66	74
75	65	71	60

Earth - Jupiter

67	70	74	60
73	61	66	71
62	76	68	65
69	64	63	75

Water - Jupiter

75	63	64	69
65	68	76	62
71	66	61	73
60	74	70	67

Occult Encyclopedia of Magic Squares

	Number	Angel Value (Arabic)	Angel Value (Hebrew)	Jinn Value (Arabic)	Jinn Value (Hebrew)
Usurper	60	19	29	101	91
Guide	76	35	45	117	107
Mystery	136	95	105	177	167
Adjuster	2168	2127	2137	1849	1839
Leader	6504	6463	6473	6185	6175
Regulator	8672	8631	8641	8353	8343
General Governor	17344	17303	17313	17025	17015
High Overseer	1318144	1318103	1318113	1317825	1317815

Fire - Mars

42	67	60	54	48
55	49	43	63	61
64	57	56	50	44
51	45	65	58	52
59	53	47	46	66

Air - Mars

59	51	64	55	42
53	45	57	49	67
47	65	56	43	60
46	58	50	63	54
66	52	44	61	48

Earth - Mars

66	46	47	53	59
52	58	65	45	51
44	50	56	57	64
61	63	43	49	55
48	54	60	67	42

Water - Mars

48	61	44	52	66
54	63	50	58	46
60	43	56	65	47
67	49	57	45	53
42	55	64	51	59

	Number	Angel Value (Arabic)	Angel Value (Hebrew)	Jinn Value (Arabic)	Jinn Value (Hebrew)
Usurper	42	1	11	83	73
Guide	67	26	36	108	98
Mystery	109	68	78	150	140
Adjuster	271	230	240	312	302
Leader	813	772	782	494	484
Regulator	1084	1043	1053	765	755
General Governor	2168	2127	2137	1849	1839
High Overseer	145256	145215	145225	144937	144927

Occult Encyclopedia of Magic Squares

Fire - Sun

27	38	62	44	48	52
33	43	54	61	31	49
39	65	47	37	53	30
50	29	40	55	34	63
56	45	36	28	64	42
66	51	32	46	41	35

Air - Sun

35	41	46	32	51	66
42	64	28	36	45	56
63	34	55	40	29	50
30	53	37	47	65	39
49	31	61	54	43	33
52	48	44	62	38	27

Earth - Sun

66	56	50	39	33	27
51	45	29	65	43	38
32	36	40	47	54	62
46	28	55	37	61	44
41	64	34	53	31	48
35	42	63	30	49	52

Water - Sun

52	49	30	63	42	35
48	31	53	34	64	41
44	61	37	55	28	46
62	54	47	40	36	32
38	43	65	29	45	51
27	33	39	50	56	66

	Number	Angel Value (Arabic)	Angel Value (Hebrew)	Jinn Value (Arabic)	Jinn Value (Hebrew)
Usurper	27	346	356	68	58
Guide	66	25	35	107	97
Mystery	93	52	62	134	124
Adjuster	271	230	240	312	302
Leader	813	772	782	494	484
Regulator	1084	1043	1053	765	755
General Governor	2168	2127	2137	1849	1839
High Overseer	143088	143047	143057	142769	142759

Fire - Venus

14	55	40	25	45	63	29
64	30	15	49	41	26	46
27	47	65	31	16	50	35
51	36	21	48	66	32	17
33	18	52	37	22	42	67
43	61	34	19	53	38	23
39	24	44	62	28	20	54

Earth - Venus

39	43	33	51	27	64	14
24	61	18	36	47	30	55
44	34	52	21	65	15	40
62	19	37	48	31	49	25
28	53	22	66	16	41	45
20	38	42	32	50	26	63
54	23	67	17	35	46	29

Occult Encyclopedia of Magic Squares

Air - Venus

54	20	28	62	44	24	39
23	38	53	19	34	61	43
67	42	22	37	52	18	33
17	32	66	48	21	36	51
35	50	16	31	65	47	27
46	26	41	49	15	30	64
29	63	45	25	40	55	14

Water - Venus

29	46	35	17	67	23	54
63	26	50	32	42	38	20
45	41	16	66	22	53	28
25	49	31	48	37	19	62
40	15	65	21	52	34	44
55	30	47	36	18	61	24
14	64	27	51	33	43	39

	Number	Angel Value (Arabic)	Angel Value (Hebrew)	Jinn Value (Arabic)	Jinn Value (Hebrew)
Usurper	14	333	343	55	45
Guide	67	26	36	108	98
Mystery	81	40	50	122	112
Adjuster	271	230	240	312	302
Leader	813	772	782	494	484
Regulator	1084	1043	1053	765	755
General Governor	2168	2127	2137	1849	1839
High Overseer	145256	145215	145225	144937	144927

Fire - Mercury

2	18	66	47	36	52	33	17
10	26	55	39	44	63	25	9
53	37	16	32	19	3	46	65
64	45	8	24	27	11	38	54
31	15	34	50	68	49	4	20
23	7	42	61	57	41	12	28
48	67	21	5	14	30	51	35
40	56	29	13	6	22	62	43

Earth - Mercury

40	48	23	31	64	53	10	2
56	67	7	15	45	37	26	18
29	21	42	34	8	16	55	66
13	5	61	50	24	32	39	47
6	14	57	68	27	19	44	36
22	30	41	49	11	3	63	52
62	51	12	4	38	46	25	33
43	35	28	20	54	65	9	17

Air - Mercury

43	62	22	6	13	29	56	40
35	51	30	14	5	21	67	48
28	12	41	57	61	42	7	23
20	4	49	68	50	34	15	31
54	38	11	27	24	8	45	64
65	46	3	19	32	16	37	53
9	25	63	44	39	55	26	10
17	33	52	36	47	66	18	2

Water - Mercury

17	9	65	54	20	28	35	43
33	25	46	38	4	12	51	62
52	63	3	11	49	41	30	22
36	44	19	27	68	57	14	6
47	39	32	24	50	61	5	13
66	55	16	8	34	42	21	29
18	26	37	45	15	7	67	56
2	10	53	64	31	23	48	40

	Number	Angel Value (Arabic)	Angel Value (Hebrew)	Jinn Value (Arabic)	Jinn Value (Hebrew)
Usurper	2	321	331	43	33
Guide	68	27	37	109	99
Mystery	70	29	39	111	101
Adjuster	271	230	240	312	302
Leader	813	772	782	494	484
Regulator	1084	1043	1053	765	755
General Governor	2168	2127	2137	1849	1839
High Overseer	147424	147383	147393	147105	147095

ANGEL OF THIRD QUINANCE: YERATHEL (641)

אל	ה	ר	י
9	201	403	28
402	29	8	202
199	11	30	401

ל	א	ה	ר	י
ה	ר	י	ל	א
י	ל	א	ה	ר
א	ה	ר	י	ל
ר	י	ל	א	ה

Occult Encyclopedia of Magic Squares

Fire - Jupiter

152	163	157	169
168	158	160	155
162	153	170	156
159	167	154	161

Air - Jupiter

161	154	167	159
156	170	153	162
155	160	158	168
169	157	163	152

Earth - Jupiter

159	162	168	152
167	153	158	163
154	170	160	157
161	156	155	169

Water - Jupiter

169	155	156	161
157	160	170	154
163	158	153	167
152	168	162	159

	Number	Angel Value (Arabic)	Angel Value (Hebrew)	Jinn Value (Arabic)	Jinn Value (Hebrew)
Usurper	152	111	121	193	183
Guide	170	129	139	211	201
Mystery	322	281	291	3	353
Adjuster	5128	5087	5097	4809	4799
Leader	15384	15343	15353	15065	15055
Regulator	20512	20471	20481	20193	20183
General Governor	41024	40983	40993	40705	40695
High Overseer	6974080	6974039	6974049	6973761	6973751

Fire - Mars

116	141	134	128	122
129	123	117	137	135
138	131	130	124	118
125	119	139	132	126
133	127	121	120	140

Air - Mars

133	125	138	129	116
127	119	131	123	141
121	139	130	117	134
120	132	124	137	128
140	126	118	135	122

Earth - Mars

140	120	121	127	133
126	132	139	119	125
118	124	130	131	138
135	137	117	123	129
122	128	134	141	116

Water - Mars

122	135	118	126	140
128	137	124	132	120
134	117	130	139	121
141	123	131	119	127
116	129	138	125	133

Occult Encyclopedia of Magic Squares

	Number	Angel Value (Arabic)	Angel Value (Hebrew)	Jinn Value (Arabic)	Jinn Value (Hebrew)
Usurper	116	75	85	157	147
Guide	141	100	110	182	172
Mystery	257	216	226	298	288
Adjuster	641	600	610	322	312
Leader	1923	1882	1892	1604	1594
Regulator	2564	2523	2533	2245	2235
General Governor	5128	5087	5097	4809	4799
High Overseer	723048	723007	723017	722729	722719

Fire - Sun

97	103	108	94	113	126
104	124	90	98	107	118
123	96	117	102	91	112
92	115	99	109	125	101
111	93	121	116	105	95
114	110	106	122	100	89

Air - Sun

97	103	108	94	113	126
104	124	90	98	107	118
123	96	117	102	91	112
92	115	99	109	125	101
111	93	121	116	105	95
114	110	106	122	100	89

Earth - Sun

126	118	112	101	95	89
113	107	91	125	105	100
94	98	102	109	116	122
108	90	117	99	121	106
103	124	96	115	93	110
97	104	123	92	111	114

Water - Sun

114	111	92	123	104	97
110	93	115	96	124	103
106	121	99	117	90	108
122	116	109	102	98	94
100	105	125	91	107	113
89	95	101	112	118	126

	Number	Angel Value (Arabic)	Angel Value (Hebrew)	Jinn Value (Arabic)	Jinn Value (Hebrew)
Usurper	89	48	58	130	120
Guide	126	85	95	167	157
Mystery	215	174	184	256	246
Adjuster	641	600	610	322	312
Leader	1923	1882	1892	1604	1594
Regulator	2564	2523	2533	2245	2235
General Governor	5128	5087	5097	4809	4799
High Overseer	646128	646087	646097	645809	645799

Fire - Venus

67	108	93	78	98	115	82
116	83	68	102	94	79	99
80	100	117	84	69	103	88
104	89	74	101	118	85	70
86	71	105	90	75	95	119
96	113	87	72	106	91	76
92	77	97	114	81	73	107

Earth - Venus

92	96	86	104	80	116	67
77	113	71	89	100	83	108
97	87	105	74	117	68	93
114	72	90	101	84	102	78
81	106	75	118	69	94	98
73	91	95	85	103	79	115
107	76	119	70	88	99	82

Air - Venus

107	73	81	114	97	77	92
76	91	106	72	87	113	96
119	95	75	90	105	71	86
70	85	118	101	74	89	104
88	103	69	84	117	100	80
99	79	94	102	68	83	116
82	115	98	78	93	108	67

Water - Venus

82	99	88	70	119	76	107
115	79	103	85	95	91	73
98	94	69	118	75	106	81
78	102	84	101	90	72	114
93	68	117	74	105	87	97
108	83	100	89	71	113	77
67	116	80	104	86	96	92

	Number	Angel Value (Arabic)	Angel Value (Hebrew)	Jinn Value (Arabic)	Jinn Value (Hebrew)
Usurper	67	26	36	108	98
Guide	119	78	88	160	150
Mystery	186	145	155	227	217
Adjuster	641	600	610	322	312
Leader	1923	1882	1892	1604	1594
Regulator	2564	2523	2533	2245	2235
General Governor	5128	5087	5097	4809	4799
High Overseer	610232	610191	610201	609913	609903

Fire - Mercury

48	64	114	93	82	98	79	63
56	72	101	85	90	111	71	55
99	83	62	78	65	49	92	113
112	91	54	70	73	57	84	100
77	61	80	96	116	95	50	66
69	53	88	109	103	87	58	74
94	115	67	51	60	76	97	81
86	102	75	59	52	68	110	89

Earth - Mercury

86	94	69	77	112	99	56	48
102	115	53	61	91	83	72	64
75	67	88	80	54	62	101	114
59	51	109	96	70	78	85	93
52	60	103	116	73	65	90	82
68	76	87	95	57	49	111	98
110	97	58	50	84	92	71	79
89	81	74	66	100	113	55	63

Air - Mercury

89	110	68	52	59	75	102	86
81	97	76	60	51	67	115	94
74	58	87	103	109	88	53	69
66	50	95	116	96	80	61	77
100	84	57	73	70	54	91	112
113	92	49	65	78	62	83	99
55	71	111	90	85	101	72	56
63	79	98	82	93	114	64	48

Water - Mercury

63	55	113	100	66	74	81	89
79	71	92	84	50	58	97	110
98	111	49	57	95	87	76	68
82	90	65	73	116	103	60	52
93	85	78	70	96	109	51	59
114	101	62	54	80	88	67	75
64	72	83	91	61	53	115	102
48	56	99	112	77	69	94	86

	Number	Angel Value (Arabic)	Angel Value (Hebrew)	Jinn Value (Arabic)	Jinn Value (Hebrew)
Usurper	48	7	17	89	79
Guide	116	75	85	157	147
Mystery	164	123	133	205	195
Adjuster	641	600	610	322	312
Leader	1923	1882	1892	1604	1594
Regulator	2564	2523	2533	2245	2235
General Governor	5128	5087	5097	4809	4799
High Overseer	594848	594807	594817	594529	594519

Fire - Moon

75	88	50	59	113	43	79	95	39
35	78	100	55	71	87	42	64	109
105	47	63	99	31	83	92	54	67
102	34	77	86	57	70	108	41	66
62	107	46	82	98	33	69	91	53
49	74	90	45	58	112	38	81	94
48	61	106	32	84	97	52	68	93
89	51	73	111	44	60	96	37	80
76	101	36	72	85	56	65	110	40

Earth - Moon

39	109	67	66	53	94	93	80	40
95	64	54	41	91	81	68	37	110
79	42	92	108	69	38	52	96	65
43	87	83	70	33	112	97	60	56
113	71	31	57	98	58	84	44	85
59	55	99	86	82	45	32	111	72
50	100	63	77	46	90	106	73	36
88	78	47	34	107	74	61	51	101
75	35	105	102	62	49	48	89	76

Air - Moon

40	110	65	56	85	72	36	101	76
80	37	96	60	44	111	73	51	89
93	68	52	97	84	32	106	61	48
94	81	38	112	58	45	90	74	49
53	91	69	33	98	82	46	107	62
66	41	108	70	57	86	77	34	102
67	54	92	83	31	99	63	47	105
109	64	42	87	71	55	100	78	35
39	95	79	43	113	59	50	88	75

Water - Moon

76	89	48	49	62	102	105	35	75
101	51	61	74	107	34	47	78	88
36	73	106	90	46	77	63	100	50
72	111	32	45	82	86	99	55	59
85	44	84	58	98	57	31	71	113
56	60	97	112	33	70	83	87	43
65	96	52	38	69	108	92	42	79
110	37	68	81	91	41	54	64	95
40	80	93	94	53	66	67	109	39

Occult Encyclopedia of Magic Squares

	Number	Angel Value (Arabic)	Angel Value (Hebrew)	Jinn Value (Arabic)	Jinn Value (Hebrew)
Usurper	31	350	360	72	62
Guide	113	72	82	154	144
Mystery	144	103	113	185	175
Adjuster	641	600	610	322	312
Leader	1923	1882	1892	1604	1594
Regulator	2564	2523	2533	2245	2235
General Governor	5128	5087	5097	4809	4799
High Overseer	579464	579423	579433	579145	579135

Fire - Saturn

14	32	39	77	68	112	61	53	85	100
25	89	82	73	114	98	16	58	44	42
40	45	69	113	99	84	33	21	62	75
46	71	111	101	34	80	88	29	18	63
59	110	103	38	49	72	76	86	31	17
66	23	24	91	79	55	51	41	96	115
78	60	20	27	93	48	36	97	118	64
92	81	56	15	26	43	94	117	67	50
102	35	47	54	22	30	116	65	83	87
119	95	90	52	57	19	70	74	37	28

Earth - Saturn

119	102	92	78	66	59	46	40	25	14
95	35	81	60	23	110	71	45	89	32
90	47	56	20	24	103	111	69	82	39
52	54	15	27	91	38	101	113	73	77
57	22	26	93	79	49	34	99	114	68
19	30	43	48	55	72	80	84	98	112
70	116	94	36	51	76	88	33	16	61
74	65	117	97	41	86	29	21	58	53
37	83	67	118	96	31	18	62	44	85
28	87	50	64	115	17	63	75	42	100

Occult Encyclopedia of Magic Squares

Air - Saturn

28	37	74	70	19	57	52	90	95	119
87	83	65	116	30	22	54	47	35	102
50	67	117	94	43	26	15	56	81	92
64	118	97	36	48	93	27	20	60	78
115	96	41	51	55	79	91	24	23	66
17	31	86	76	72	49	38	103	110	59
63	18	29	88	80	34	101	111	71	46
75	62	21	33	84	99	113	69	45	40
42	44	58	16	98	114	73	82	89	25
100	85	53	61	112	68	77	39	32	14

Water - Saturn

100	42	75	63	17	115	64	50	87	28
85	44	62	18	31	96	118	67	83	37
53	58	21	29	86	41	97	117	65	74
61	**16**	33	88	76	51	36	94	116	70
112	98	84	80	72	55	48	43	30	19
68	114	99	34	49	79	93	26	22	57
77	73	113	101	38	91	27	15	54	52
39	82	69	111	103	24	20	56	47	90
32	89	45	71	110	23	60	81	35	95
14	25	40	46	59	66	78	92	102	119

	Number	Angel Value (Arabic)	Angel Value (Hebrew)	Jinn Value (Arabic)	Jinn Value (Hebrew)
Usurper	14	333	343	55	45
Guide	119	78	88	160	150
Mystery	133	92	102	174	164
Adjuster	641	600	610	322	312
Leader	1923	1882	1892	1604	1594
Regulator	2564	2523	2533	2245	2235
General Governor	5128	5087	5097	4809	4799
High Overseer	610232	610191	610201	609913	609903

ANGEL OF FOURTH QUINANCE: SAHIAH (321)

ה	׳	ה	שא
300	6	13	2
12	3	299	7
4	302	4	11

ה	׳	ה	א	ש
ה	א	ש	ה	׳
ש	ה	׳	ה	א
׳	ה	א	ש	ה
א	ש	ה	׳	ה

Numerical Squares See Page: 321

ANGEL OF THIRD DECANATE: ABOHA (15)

This Square Not Available

א	ה	ו	ב	א
׳	ב	א	א	ה
א	א	ה	ו	ב
ה	ו	ב	א	א
ב	א	א	ה	ו

Fire - Saturn

6	1	8
7	5	3
2	9	4

Earth - Saturn

2	7	6
9	5	1
4	3	8

Air - Saturn

4	9	2
3	5	7
8	1	6

Water - Saturn

8	3	4
1	5	9
6	7	2

	Number	Angel Value (Arabic)	Angel Value (Hebrew)	Jinn Value (Arabic)	Jinn Value (Hebrew)
Usurper	1	320	330	42	32
Guide	9	328	338	50	40
Mystery	10	329	339	51	41
Adjuster	15	334	344	56	46
Leader	45	4	14	86	76
Regulator	60	19	29	101	91
General Governor	120	79	89	161	151
High Overseer	1080	1039	1049	761	751

ANGEL OF FIFTH QUINANCE: REYAYEL (251)

אל	י	י	ר
199	11	13	28
12	29	198	12
9	201	30	11

ל	א	י	י	ר
י	י	ר	ל	א
ר	ל	א	י	י
א	י	י	ר	ל
י	ר	ל	א	י

Fire - Jupiter

55	66	60	70
69	61	63	58
65	56	71	59
62	68	57	64

Air - Jupiter

64	57	68	62
59	71	56	65
58	63	61	69
70	60	66	55

Earth - Jupiter

62	65	69	55
68	56	61	66
57	71	63	60
64	59	58	70

Water - Jupiter

70	58	59	64
60	63	71	57
66	61	56	68
55	69	65	62

Occult Encyclopedia of Magic Squares

	Number	Angel Value (Arabic)	Angel Value (Hebrew)	Jinn Value (Arabic)	Jinn Value (Hebrew)
Usurper	55	14	24	96	86
Guide	71	30	40	112	102
Mystery	126	85	95	167	157
Adjuster	2008	1967	1977	1689	1679
Leader	6024	5983	5993	5705	5695
Regulator	8032	7991	8001	7713	7703
General Governor	16064	16023	16033	15745	15735
High Overseer	1140544	1140503	1140513	1140225	1140215

Fire - Mars

38	63	56	50	44
51	45	39	59	57
60	53	52	46	40
47	41	61	54	48
55	49	43	42	62

Air - Mars

55	47	60	51	38
49	41	53	45	63
43	61	52	39	56
42	54	46	59	50
62	48	40	57	44

Earth - Mars

62	42	43	49	55
48	54	61	41	47
40	46	52	53	60
57	59	39	45	51
44	50	56	63	38

Water - Mars

44	57	40	48	62
50	59	46	54	42
56	39	52	61	43
63	45	53	41	49
38	51	60	47	55

	Number	Angel Value (Arabic)	Angel Value (Hebrew)	Jinn Value (Arabic)	Jinn Value (Hebrew)
Usurper	38	357	7	79	69
Guide	63	22	32	104	94
Mystery	101	60	70	142	132
Adjuster	251	210	220	292	282
Leader	753	712	722	434	424
Regulator	1004	963	973	685	675
General Governor	2008	1967	1977	1689	1679
High Overseer	126504	126463	126473	126185	126175

Occult Encyclopedia of Magic Squares

Fire - Sun

24	35	57	41	45	49
30	40	51	56	28	46
36	60	44	34	50	27
47	26	37	52	31	58
53	42	33	25	59	39
61	48	29	43	38	32

Air - Sun

32	38	43	29	48	61
39	59	25	33	42	53
58	31	52	37	26	47
27	50	34	44	60	36
46	28	56	51	40	30
49	45	41	57	35	24

Earth - Sun

61	53	47	36	30	24
48	42	26	60	40	35
29	33	37	44	51	57
43	25	52	34	56	41
38	59	31	50	28	45
32	39	58	27	46	49

Water - Sun

49	46	27	58	39	32
45	28	50	31	59	38
41	56	34	52	25	43
57	51	44	37	33	29
35	40	60	26	42	48
24	30	36	47	53	61

	Number	Angel Value (Arabic)	Angel Value (Hebrew)	Jinn Value (Arabic)	Jinn Value (Hebrew)
Usurper	24	343	353	65	55
Guide	61	20	30	102	92
Mystery	85	44	54	126	116
Adjuster	251	210	220	292	282
Leader	753	712	722	434	424
Regulator	1004	963	973	685	675
General Governor	2008	1967	1977	1689	1679
High Overseer	122488	122447	122457	122169	122159

Fire - Venus

11	52	37	22	42	61	26
62	27	12	46	38	23	43
24	44	63	28	13	47	32
48	33	18	45	64	29	14
30	15	49	34	19	39	65
40	59	31	16	50	35	20
36	21	41	60	25	17	51

Earth - Venus

36	40	30	48	24	62	11
21	59	15	33	44	27	52
41	31	49	18	63	12	37
60	16	34	45	28	46	22
25	50	19	64	13	38	42
17	35	39	29	47	23	61
51	20	65	14	32	43	26

Air - Venus

51	17	25	60	41	21	36
20	35	50	16	31	59	40
65	39	19	34	49	15	30
14	29	64	45	18	33	48
32	47	13	28	63	44	24
43	23	38	46	12	27	62
26	61	42	22	37	52	11

Water - Venus

26	43	32	14	65	20	51
61	23	47	29	39	35	17
42	38	13	64	19	50	25
22	46	28	45	34	16	60
37	12	63	18	49	31	41
52	27	44	33	15	59	21
11	62	24	48	30	40	36

	Number	Angel Value (Arabic)	Angel Value (Hebrew)	Jinn Value (Arabic)	Jinn Value (Hebrew)
Usurper	11	330	340	52	42
Guide	65	24	34	106	96
Mystery	76	35	45	117	107
Adjuster	251	210	220	292	282
Leader	753	712	722	434	424
Regulator	1004	963	973	685	675
General Governor	2008	1967	1977	1689	1679
High Overseer	130520	130479	130489	130201	130191

ANGEL OF SIX QUINANCE: AVAMEL (78)

ל	א	מ	אׁ
6	41	4	27
3	28	5	42
39	8	29	2

ל	א	מ	ו	א
מ	ו	א	ל	א
א	ל	א	מ	ו
א	מ	ו	א	ל
ו	א	ל	א	מ

Numerical Squares See Page: 91

CAPRICORN

SIGN CAPRICORN: GEDI (17)

No Hebrew Squares Available

ARCHANGEL OF CAPRICORN: HANAEL (86)

ל	א	נ	ה
4	51	4	27
3	28	3	52
49	6	29	2

ל	א	נ	ה
ה	נ	א	ל
א	ל	ה	נ
נ	ה	ל	א

Fire - Jupiter

14	25	19	28
27	20	22	17
24	15	29	18
21	26	16	23

Air - Jupiter

23	16	26	21
18	29	15	24
17	22	20	27
28	19	25	14

Earth - Jupiter

21	24	27	14
26	15	20	25
16	29	22	19
23	18	17	28

Water - Jupiter

28	17	18	23
19	22	29	16
25	20	15	26
14	27	24	21

Occult Encyclopedia of Magic Squares

	Number	Angel Value (Arabic)	Angel Value (Hebrew)	Jinn Value (Arabic)	Jinn Value (Hebrew)
Usurper	14	333	343	55	45
Guide	29	348	358	70	60
Mystery	43	2	12	84	74
Adjuster	688	647	657	369	359
Leader	2064	2023	2033	1745	1735
Regulator	2752	2711	2721	2433	2423
General Governor	5504	5463	5473	5185	5175
High Overseer	159616	159575	159585	159297	159287

Fire - Mars

5	30	23	17	11
18	12	6	26	24
27	20	19	13	7
14	8	28	21	15
22	16	10	9	29

Air - Mars

22	14	27	18	5
16	8	20	12	30
10	28	19	6	23
9	21	13	26	17
29	15	7	24	11

Earth - Mars

29	9	10	16	22
15	21	28	8	14
7	13	19	20	27
24	26	6	12	18
11	17	23	30	5

Water - Mars

11	24	7	15	29
17	26	13	21	9
23	6	19	28	10
30	12	20	8	16
5	18	27	14	22

	Number	Angel Value (Arabic)	Angel Value (Hebrew)	Jinn Value (Arabic)	Jinn Value (Hebrew)
Usurper	5	324	334	46	36
Guide	30	349	359	71	61
Mystery	35	354	4	76	66
Adjuster	86	45	55	127	117
Leader	258	217	227	299	289
Regulator	344	303	313	25	15
General Governor	688	647	657	369	359
High Overseer	20640	20599	20609	20321	20311

ANGEL OF CAPRICORN: SAMEQIEL (241)

יאל	ק	מ	ס
59	41	103	38
102	39	58	42
39	61	40	101

ל	א	י	ק	מ	ס
מ	ק	ל	ס	י	א
י	ס	א	מ	ל	ק
ס	מ	ק	י	א	ל
ק	ל	מ	א	ס	י
א	י	ס	ל	ק	מ

Fire - Jupiter

52	63	57	69
68	58	60	55
62	53	70	56
59	67	54	61

Air - Jupiter

61	54	67	59
56	70	53	62
55	60	58	68
69	57	63	52

Earth - Jupiter

59	62	68	52
67	53	58	63
54	70	60	57
61	56	55	69

Water - Jupiter

69	55	56	61
57	60	70	54
63	58	53	67
52	68	62	59

	Number	Angel Value (Arabic)	Angel Value (Hebrew)	Jinn Value (Arabic)	Jinn Value (Hebrew)
Usurper	52	11	21	93	83
Guide	70	29	39	111	101
Mystery	122	81	91	163	153
Adjuster	1928	1887	1897	1609	1599
Leader	5784	5743	5753	5465	5455
Regulator	7712	7671	7681	7393	7383
General Governor	15424	15383	15393	15105	15095
High Overseer	1079680	1079639	1079649	1079361	1079351

Occult Encyclopedia of Magic Squares

Fire - Mars

36	61	54	48	42
49	43	37	57	55
58	51	50	44	38
45	39	59	52	46
53	47	41	40	60

Air - Mars

53	45	58	49	36
47	39	51	43	61
41	59	50	37	54
40	52	44	57	48
60	46	38	55	42

Earth - Mars

60	40	41	47	53
46	52	59	39	45
38	44	50	51	58
55	57	37	43	49
42	48	54	61	36

Water - Mars

42	55	38	46	60
48	57	44	52	40
54	37	50	59	41
61	43	51	39	47
36	49	58	45	53

	Number	Angel Value (Arabic)	Angel Value (Hebrew)	Jinn Value (Arabic)	Jinn Value (Hebrew)
Usurper	36	355	5	77	67
Guide	61	20	30	102	92
Mystery	97	56	66	138	128
Adjuster	241	200	210	282	272
Leader	723	682	692	404	394
Regulator	964	923	933	645	635
General Governor	1928	1887	1897	1609	1599
High Overseer	117608	117567	117577	117289	117279

Fire - Sun

47	44	25	58	37	30
43	26	48	29	59	36
39	56	32	50	23	41
57	49	42	35	31	27
33	38	60	24	40	46
22	28	34	45	51	61

Earth - Sun

61	51	45	34	28	22
46	40	24	60	38	33
27	31	35	42	49	57
41	23	50	32	56	39
36	59	29	48	26	43
30	37	58	25	44	47

Air - Sun

30	36	41	27	46	61
37	59	23	31	40	51
58	29	50	35	24	45
25	48	32	42	60	34
44	26	56	49	38	28
47	43	39	57	33	22

Water - Sun

47	44	25	58	37	30
43	26	48	29	59	36
39	56	32	50	23	41
57	49	42	35	31	27
33	38	60	24	40	46
22	28	34	45	51	61

	Number	Angel Value (Arabic)	Angel Value (Hebrew)	Jinn Value (Arabic)	Jinn Value (Hebrew)
Usurper	22	341	351	63	53
Guide	61	20	30	102	92
Mystery	83	42	52	124	114
Adjuster	241	200	210	282	272
Leader	723	682	692	404	394
Regulator	964	923	933	645	635
General Governor	1928	1887	1897	1609	1599
High Overseer	117608	117567	117577	117289	117279

Fire - Venus

10	51	36	21	41	57	25
58	26	11	45	37	22	42
23	43	59	27	12	46	31
47	32	17	44	60	28	13
29	14	48	33	18	38	61
39	55	30	15	49	34	19
35	20	40	56	24	16	50

Earth - Venus

35	39	29	47	23	58	10
20	55	14	32	43	26	51
40	30	48	17	59	11	36
56	15	33	44	27	45	21
24	49	18	60	12	37	41
16	34	38	28	46	22	57
50	19	61	13	31	42	25

Air - Venus

50	16	24	56	40	20	35
19	34	49	15	30	55	39
61	38	18	33	48	14	29
13	28	60	44	17	32	47
31	46	12	27	59	43	23
42	22	37	45	11	26	58
25	57	41	21	36	51	10

Water - Venus

25	42	31	13	61	19	50
57	22	46	28	38	34	16
41	37	12	60	18	49	24
21	45	27	44	33	15	56
36	11	59	17	48	30	40
51	26	43	32	14	55	20
10	58	23	47	29	39	35

	Number	Angel Value (Arabic)	Angel Value (Hebrew)	Jinn Value (Arabic)	Jinn Value (Hebrew)
Usurper	10	329	339	51	41
Guide	61	20	30	102	92
Mystery	71	30	40	112	102
Adjuster	241	200	210	282	272
Leader	723	682	692	404	394
Regulator	964	923	933	645	635
General Governor	1928	1887	1897	1609	1599
High Overseer	117608	117567	117577	117289	117279

LORD OF TRIPLICITY BY DAY: SANDALI (224)

ע	ל	נד	ס
59	55	33	77
32	78	58	56
53	61	79	31

י	ע	ל	ד	נ	ס
נ	ד	י	ס	ל	ע
ל	ס	ע	נ	י	ד
ס	נ	ד	ל	ע	י
ד	י	נ	ע	ס	ל
ע	ל	ס	י	ד	נ

Occult Encyclopedia of Magic Squares

Fire - Jupiter

48	59	53	64
63	54	56	51
58	49	65	52
55	62	50	57

Air - Jupiter

57	50	62	55
52	65	49	58
51	56	54	63
64	53	59	48

Earth - Jupiter

55	58	63	48
62	49	54	59
50	65	56	53
57	52	51	64

Water - Jupiter

64	51	52	57
53	56	65	50
59	54	49	62
48	63	58	55

	Number	Angel Value (Arabic)	Angel Value (Hebrew)	Jinn Value (Arabic)	Jinn Value (Hebrew)
Usurper	48	7	17	89	79
Guide	65	24	34	106	96
Mystery	113	72	82	154	144
Adjuster	1792	1751	1761	1473	1463
Leader	5376	5335	5345	5057	5047
Regulator	7168	7127	7137	6849	6839
General Governor	14336	14295	14305	14017	14007
High Overseer	931840	931799	931809	931521	931511

Fire - Mars

32	60	50	44	38
45	39	33	56	51
57	47	46	40	34
41	35	58	48	42
49	43	37	36	59

Air - Mars

49	41	57	45	32
43	35	47	39	60
37	58	46	33	50
36	48	40	56	44
59	42	34	51	38

Earth - Mars

59	36	37	43	49
42	48	58	35	41
34	40	46	47	57
51	56	33	39	45
38	44	50	60	32

Water - Mars

38	51	34	42	59
44	56	40	48	36
50	33	46	58	37
60	39	47	35	43
32	45	57	41	49

	Number	Angel Value (Arabic)	Angel Value (Hebrew)	Jinn Value (Arabic)	Jinn Value (Hebrew)
Usurper	32	351	1	73	63
Guide	60	19	29	101	91
Mystery	92	51	61	133	123
Adjuster	224	183	193	265	255
Leader	672	631	641	353	343
Regulator	896	855	865	577	567
General Governor	1792	1751	1761	1473	1463
High Overseer	107520	107479	107489	107201	107191

Fire - Sun

19	30	55	36	40	44
25	35	46	54	23	41
31	58	39	29	45	22
42	21	32	47	26	56
48	37	28	20	57	34
59	43	24	38	33	27

Air - Sun

27	33	38	24	43	59
34	57	20	28	37	48
56	26	47	32	21	42
22	45	29	39	58	31
41	23	54	46	35	25
44	40	36	55	30	19

Earth - Sun

59	48	42	31	25	19
43	37	21	58	35	30
24	28	32	39	46	55
38	20	47	29	54	36
33	57	26	45	23	40
27	34	56	22	41	44

Water - Sun

44	41	22	56	34	27
40	23	45	26	57	33
36	54	29	47	20	38
55	46	39	32	28	24
30	35	58	21	37	43
19	25	31	42	48	59

	Number	Angel Value (Arabic)	Angel Value (Hebrew)	Jinn Value (Arabic)	Jinn Value (Hebrew)
Usurper	19	338	348	60	50
Guide	59	18	28	100	90
Mystery	78	37	47	119	109
Adjuster	224	183	193	265	255
Leader	672	631	641	353	343
Regulator	896	855	865	577	567
General Governor	1792	1751	1761	1473	1463
High Overseer	105728	105687	105697	105409	105399

Fire - Venus

8	49	34	19	39	52	23
53	24	9	43	35	20	40
21	41	54	25	10	44	29
45	30	15	42	55	26	11
27	12	46	31	16	36	56
37	50	28	13	47	32	17
33	18	38	51	22	14	48

Air - Venus

48	14	22	51	38	18	33
17	32	47	13	28	50	37
56	36	16	31	46	12	27
11	26	55	42	15	30	45
29	44	10	25	54	41	21
40	20	35	43	9	24	53
23	52	39	19	34	49	8

Earth - Venus

33	37	27	45	21	53	8
18	50	12	30	41	24	49
38	28	46	15	54	9	34
51	13	31	42	25	43	19
22	47	16	55	10	35	39
14	32	36	26	44	20	52
48	17	56	11	29	40	23

Water - Venus

23	40	29	11	56	17	48
52	20	44	26	36	32	14
39	35	10	55	16	47	22
19	43	25	42	31	13	51
34	9	54	15	46	28	38
49	24	41	30	12	50	18
8	53	21	45	27	37	33

	Number	Angel Value (Arabic)	Angel Value (Hebrew)	Jinn Value (Arabic)	Jinn Value (Hebrew)
Usurper	8	327	337	49	39
Guide	56	15	25	97	87
Mystery	64	23	33	105	95
Adjuster	224	183	193	265	255
Leader	672	631	641	353	343
Regulator	896	855	865	577	567
General Governor	1792	1751	1761	1473	1463
High Overseer	100352	100311	100321	100033	100023

LORD OF TRIPLICITY BY NIGHT: ALOYAR (247)

ר	י	נ	אל
30	7	13	197
12	198	29	8
5	32	199	11

ר	י	ן	ל	א
ן	ל	א	ר	י
א	ר	י	ן	ל
י	ן	ל	א	ר
ל	א	ר	י	ן

Fire - Jupiter

54	65	59	69
68	60	62	57
64	55	70	58
61	67	56	63

Air - Jupiter

63	56	67	61
58	70	55	64
57	62	60	68
69	59	65	54

Earth - Jupiter

61	64	68	54
67	55	60	65
56	70	62	59
63	58	57	69

Water - Jupiter

69	57	58	63
59	62	70	56
65	60	55	67
54	68	64	61

	Number	Angel Value (Arabic)	Angel Value (Hebrew)	Jinn Value (Arabic)	Jinn Value (Hebrew)
Usurper	54	13	23	95	85
Guide	70	29	39	111	101
Mystery	124	83	93	165	155
Adjuster	1976	1935	1945	1657	1647
Leader	5928	5887	5897	5609	5599
Regulator	7904	7863	7873	7585	7575
General Governor	15808	15767	15777	15489	15479
High Overseer	1106560	1106519	1106529	1106241	1106231

Fire - Mars

37	63	55	49	43
50	44	38	59	56
60	52	51	45	39
46	40	61	53	47
54	48	42	41	62

Air - Mars

54	46	60	50	37
48	40	52	44	63
42	61	51	38	55
41	53	45	59	49
62	47	39	56	43

Earth - Mars

62	41	42	48	54
47	53	61	40	46
39	45	51	52	60
56	59	38	44	50
43	49	55	63	37

Water - Mars

43	56	39	47	62
49	59	45	53	41
55	38	51	61	42
63	44	52	40	48
37	50	60	46	54

	Number	Angel Value (Arabic)	Angel Value (Hebrew)	Jinn Value (Arabic)	Jinn Value (Hebrew)
Usurper	37	356	6	78	68
Guide	63	22	32	104	94
Mystery	100	59	69	141	131
Adjuster	247	206	216	288	278
Leader	741	700	710	422	412
Regulator	988	947	957	669	659
General Governor	1976	1935	1945	1657	1647
High Overseer	124488	124447	124457	124169	124159

Fire - Sun

23	34	58	40	44	48
29	39	50	57	27	45
35	61	43	33	49	26
46	25	36	51	30	59
52	41	32	24	60	38
62	47	28	42	37	31

Earth - Sun

62	52	46	35	29	23
47	41	25	61	39	34
28	32	36	43	50	58
42	24	51	33	57	40
37	60	30	49	27	44
31	38	59	26	45	48

Air - Sun

31	37	42	28	47	62
38	60	24	32	41	52
59	30	51	36	25	46
26	49	33	43	61	35
45	27	57	50	39	29
48	44	40	58	34	23

Water - Sun

48	45	26	59	38	31
44	27	49	30	60	37
40	57	33	51	24	42
58	50	43	36	32	28
34	39	61	25	41	47
23	29	35	46	52	62

	Number	Angel Value (Arabic)	Angel Value (Hebrew)	Jinn Value (Arabic)	Jinn Value (Hebrew)
Usurper	23	342	352	64	54
Guide	62	21	31	103	93
Mystery	85	44	54	126	116
Adjuster	247	206	216	288	278
Leader	741	700	710	422	412
Regulator	988	947	957	669	659
General Governor	1976	1935	1945	1657	1647
High Overseer	122512	122471	122481	122193	122183

Fire - Venus

11	52	37	22	42	57	26
58	27	12	46	38	23	43
24	44	59	28	13	47	32
48	33	18	45	60	29	14
30	15	49	34	19	39	61
40	55	31	16	50	35	20
36	21	41	56	25	17	51

Air - Venus

51	17	25	56	41	21	36
20	35	50	16	31	55	40
61	39	19	34	49	15	30
14	29	60	45	18	33	48
32	47	13	28	59	44	24
43	23	38	46	12	27	58
26	57	42	22	37	52	11

Earth - Venus

36	40	30	48	24	58	11
21	55	15	33	44	27	52
41	31	49	18	59	12	37
56	16	34	45	28	46	22
25	50	19	60	13	38	42
17	35	39	29	47	23	57
51	20	61	14	32	43	26

Water - Venus

26	43	32	14	61	20	51
57	23	47	29	39	35	17
42	38	13	60	19	50	25
22	46	28	45	34	16	56
37	12	59	18	49	31	41
52	27	44	33	15	55	21
11	58	24	48	30	40	36

	Number	Angel Value (Arabic)	Angel Value (Hebrew)	Jinn Value (Arabic)	Jinn Value (Hebrew)
Usurper	11	330	340	52	42
Guide	61	20	30	102	92
Mystery	72	31	41	113	103
Adjuster	247	206	216	288	278
Leader	741	700	710	422	412
Regulator	988	947	957	669	659
General Governor	1976	1935	1945	1657	1647
High Overseer	120536	120495	120505	120217	120207

ANGEL RULING 10TH HOUSE: KASHENYAYAH (465)

יה	יע	נ	בש
319	51	83	12
82	13	318	52
49	321	14	81

ה	י	ע	י	נ	ש	ב
ע	י	נ	ש	ב	ה	י
נ	ש	ב	ה	י	ע	י
ב	ה	י	ע	י	נ	ש
י	ע	י	נ	ש	ב	ה
י	נ	ש	ב	ה	י	ע
ש	ב	ה	י	ע	י	נ

Fire - Saturn

156	151	158
157	155	153
152	159	154

Air - Saturn

154	159	152
153	155	157
158	151	156

Earth - Saturn

152	157	156
159	155	151
154	153	158

Water - Saturn

158	153	154
151	155	159
156	157	152

Occult Encyclopedia of Magic Squares

	Number	Angel Value (Arabic)	Angel Value (Hebrew)	Jinn Value (Arabic)	Jinn Value (Hebrew)
Usurper	151	120	120	192	182
Guide	159	128	128	200	190
Mystery	310	269	279	351	341
Adjuster	465	424	434	146	136
Leader	1395	1354	1364	1076	1066
Regulator	1860	1819	1829	1541	1531
General Governor	3720	3679	3689	3401	3391
High Overseer	591480	591439	591449	591161	591151

Fire - Jupiter

108	119	113	125
124	114	116	111
118	109	126	112
115	123	110	117

Air - Jupiter

117	110	123	115
112	126	109	118
111	116	114	124
125	113	119	108

Earth - Jupiter

115	118	124	108
123	109	114	119
110	126	116	113
117	112	111	125

Water - Jupiter

125	111	112	117
113	116	126	110
119	114	109	123
108	124	118	115

	Number	Angel Value (Arabic)	Angel Value (Hebrew)	Jinn Value (Arabic)	Jinn Value (Hebrew)
Usurper	108	67	77	149	139
Guide	126	85	95	167	157
Mystery	234	193	203	275	265
Adjuster	3720	3679	3689	3401	3391
Leader	11160	11119	11129	10841	10831
Regulator	14880	14839	14849	14561	14551
General Governor	29760	29719	29729	29441	29431
High Overseer	3749760	3749719	3749729	3749441	3749431

Fire - Mars

81	105	99	93	87
94	88	82	101	100
102	96	95	89	83
90	84	103	97	91
98	92	86	85	104

Air - Mars

98	90	102	94	81
92	84	96	88	105
86	103	95	82	99
85	97	89	101	93
104	91	83	100	87

Earth - Mars

104	85	86	92	98
91	97	103	84	90
83	89	95	96	102
100	101	82	88	94
87	93	99	105	81

Water - Mars

87	100	83	91	104
93	101	89	97	85
99	82	95	103	86
105	88	96	84	92
81	94	102	90	98

	Number	Angel Value (Arabic)	Angel Value (Hebrew)	Jinn Value (Arabic)	Jinn Value (Hebrew)
Usurper	81	40	50	122	112
Guide	105	64	74	146	136
Mystery	186	145	155	227	217
Adjuster	465	424	434	146	136
Leader	1395	1354	1364	1076	1066
Regulator	1860	1819	1829	1541	1531
General Governor	3720	3679	3689	3401	3391
High Overseer	390600	390559	390569	390281	390271

Fire - Sun

60	71	91	77	81	85
66	76	87	90	64	82
72	94	80	70	86	63
83	62	73	88	67	92
89	78	69	61	93	75
95	84	65	79	74	68

Earth - Sun

95	89	83	72	66	60
84	78	62	94	76	71
65	69	73	80	87	91
79	61	88	70	90	77
74	93	67	86	64	81
68	75	92	63	82	85

Air - Sun

68	74	79	65	84	95
75	93	61	69	78	89
92	67	88	73	62	83
63	86	70	80	94	72
82	64	90	87	76	66
85	81	77	91	71	60

Water - Sun

85	82	63	92	75	68
81	64	86	67	93	74
77	90	70	88	61	79
91	87	80	73	69	65
71	76	94	62	78	84
60	66	72	83	89	95

	Number	Angel Value (Arabic)	Angel Value (Hebrew)	Jinn Value (Arabic)	Jinn Value (Hebrew)
Usurper	60	19	29	101	91
Guide	95	54	64	136	126
Mystery	155	114	124	196	186
Adjuster	465	424	434	146	136
Leader	1395	1354	1364	1076	1066
Regulator	1860	1819	1829	1541	1531
General Governor	3720	3679	3689	3401	3391
High Overseer	353400	353359	353369	353081	353071

Fire - Venus

42	83	68	53	73	89	57
90	58	43	77	69	54	74
55	75	91	59	44	78	63
79	64	49	76	92	60	45
61	46	80	65	50	70	93
71	87	62	47	81	66	51
67	52	72	88	56	48	82

Air - Venus

82	48	56	88	72	52	67
51	66	81	47	62	87	71
93	70	50	65	80	46	61
45	60	92	76	49	64	79
63	78	44	59	91	75	55
74	54	69	77	43	58	90
57	89	73	53	68	83	42

Earth - Venus

67	71	61	79	55	90	42
52	87	46	64	75	58	83
72	62	80	49	91	43	68
88	47	65	76	59	77	53
56	81	50	92	44	69	73
48	66	70	60	78	54	89
82	51	93	45	63	74	57

Water - Venus

57	74	63	45	93	51	82
89	54	78	60	70	66	48
73	69	44	92	50	81	56
53	77	59	76	65	47	88
68	43	91	49	80	62	72
83	58	75	64	46	87	52
42	90	55	79	61	71	67

Occult Encyclopedia of Magic Squares

	Number	Angel Value (Arabic)	Angel Value (Hebrew)	Jinn Value (Arabic)	Jinn Value (Hebrew)
Usurper	42	1	11	83	73
Guide	93	52	62	134	124
Mystery	135	94	104	176	166
Adjuster	465	424	434	146	136
Leader	1395	1354	1364	1076	1066
Regulator	1860	1819	1829	1541	1531
General Governor	3720	3679	3689	3401	3391
High Overseer	345960	345919	345929	345641	345631

Fire - Mercury

26	42	92	71	60	76	57	41
34	50	79	63	68	89	49	33
77	61	40	56	43	27	70	91
90	69	32	48	51	35	62	78
55	39	58	74	94	73	28	44
47	31	66	87	81	65	36	52
72	93	45	29	38	54	75	59
64	80	53	37	30	46	88	67

Earth - Mercury

64	72	47	55	90	77	34	26
80	93	31	39	69	61	50	42
53	45	66	58	32	40	79	92
37	29	87	74	48	56	63	71
30	38	81	94	51	43	68	60
46	54	65	73	35	27	89	76
88	75	36	28	62	70	49	57
67	59	52	44	78	91	33	41

Air - Mercury

67	88	46	30	37	53	80	64
59	75	54	38	29	45	93	72
52	36	65	81	87	66	31	47
44	28	73	94	74	58	39	55
78	62	35	51	48	32	69	90
91	70	27	43	56	40	61	77
33	49	89	68	63	79	50	34
41	57	76	60	71	92	42	26

Water - Mercury

41	33	91	78	44	52	59	67
57	49	70	62	28	36	75	88
76	89	27	35	73	65	54	46
60	68	43	51	94	81	38	30
71	63	56	48	74	87	29	37
92	79	40	32	58	66	45	53
42	50	61	69	39	31	93	80
26	34	77	90	55	47	72	64

	Number	Angel Value (Arabic)	Angel Value (Hebrew)	Jinn Value (Arabic)	Jinn Value (Hebrew)
Usurper	26	345	355	67	57
Guide	94	53	63	135	125
Mystery	120	79	89	161	151
Adjuster	465	424	434	146	136
Leader	1395	1354	1364	1076	1066
Regulator	1860	1819	1829	1541	1531
General Governor	3720	3679	3689	3401	3391
High Overseer	349680	349639	349649	349361	349351

Fire - Moon

55	68	30	39	97	23	59	75	19
15	58	80	35	51	67	22	44	93
89	27	43	79	11	63	72	34	47
82	14	57	66	37	50	92	21	46
42	91	26	62	78	13	49	71	33
29	54	70	25	38	96	18	61	74
28	41	90	12	64	77	32	48	73
69	31	53	95	24	40	76	17	60
56	81	16	52	65	36	45	94	20

Earth - Moon

19	93	47	46	33	74	73	60	20
75	44	34	21	71	61	48	17	94
59	22	72	92	49	18	32	76	45
23	67	63	50	13	96	77	40	36
97	51	11	37	78	38	64	24	65
39	35	79	66	62	25	12	95	52
30	80	43	57	26	70	90	53	16
68	58	27	14	91	54	41	31	81
55	15	89	82	42	29	28	69	56

Air - Moon

20	94	45	36	65	52	16	81	56
60	17	76	40	24	95	53	31	69
73	48	32	77	64	12	90	41	28
74	61	18	96	38	25	70	54	29
33	71	49	13	78	62	26	91	42
46	21	92	50	37	66	57	14	82
47	34	72	63	11	79	43	27	89
93	44	22	67	51	35	80	58	15
19	75	59	23	97	39	30	68	55

Water - Moon

56	69	28	29	42	82	89	15	55
81	31	41	54	91	14	27	58	68
16	53	90	70	26	57	43	80	30
52	95	12	25	62	66	79	35	39
65	24	64	38	78	37	11	51	97
36	40	77	96	13	50	63	67	23
45	76	32	18	49	92	72	22	59
94	17	48	61	71	21	34	44	75
20	60	73	74	33	46	47	93	19

	Number	Angel Value (Arabic)	Angel Value (Hebrew)	Jinn Value (Arabic)	Jinn Value (Hebrew)
Usurper	11	330	340	52	42
Guide	97	56	66	138	128
Mystery	108	67	77	149	139
Adjuster	465	424	434	146	136
Leader	1395	1354	1364	1076	1066
Regulator	1860	1819	1829	1541	1531
General Governor	3720	3679	3689	3401	3391
High Overseer	360840	360799	360809	360521	360511

ANGEL OF FIRST DECANATE: MISNIN (210)

נ	ג	ס	מ
39	61	63	47
62	48	38	62
59	41	49	61

ג	י	ג	ס	מ
ג	ס	מ	ג	י
מ	ג	י	ג	ס
י	ג	ס	מ	ג
ס	מ	ג	י	ג

Occult Encyclopedia of Magic Squares

Fire - Saturn

71	66	73
72	70	68
67	74	69

Earth - Saturn

67	72	71
74	70	66
69	68	73

Air - Saturn

69	74	67
68	70	72
73	66	71

Water - Saturn

73	68	69
66	70	74
71	72	67

	Number	Angel Value (Arabic)	Angel Value (Hebrew)	Jinn Value (Arabic)	Jinn Value (Hebrew)
Usurper	66	35	45	107	97
Guide	74	43	53	115	105
Mystery	140	99	119	181	171
Adjuster	210	169	189	251	241
Leader	630	589	609	311	301
Regulator	840	799	819	521	511
General Governor	1680	1639	1659	1361	1351
High Overseer	124320	124279	124299	124001	123991

Fire - Jupiter

45	56	50	59
58	51	53	48
55	46	60	49
52	57	47	54

Air - Jupiter

54	47	57	52
49	60	46	55
48	53	51	58
59	50	56	45

Earth - Jupiter

52	55	58	45
57	46	51	56
47	60	53	50
54	49	48	59

Water - Jupiter

59	48	49	54
50	53	60	47
56	51	46	57
45	58	55	52

Occult Encyclopedia of Magic Squares

	Number	Angel Value (Arabic)	Angel Value (Hebrew)	Jinn Value (Arabic)	Jinn Value (Hebrew)
Usurper	45	4	14	86	76
Guide	60	19	29	101	91
Mystery	105	64	74	146	136
Adjuster	1680	1639	1649	1361	1351
Leader	5040	4999	5009	4721	4711
Regulator	6720	6679	6689	6401	6391
General Governor	13440	13399	13409	13121	13111
High Overseer	806400	806359	806369	806081	806071

Fire - Mars

30	54	48	42	36
43	37	31	50	49
51	45	44	38	32
39	33	52	46	40
47	41	35	34	53

Air - Mars

47	39	51	43	30
41	33	45	37	54
35	52	44	31	48
34	46	38	50	42
53	40	32	49	36

Earth - Mars

53	34	35	41	47
40	46	52	33	39
32	38	44	45	51
49	50	31	37	43
36	42	48	54	30

Water - Mars

36	49	32	40	53
42	50	38	46	34
48	31	44	52	35
54	37	45	33	41
30	43	51	39	47

	Number	Angel Value (Arabic)	Angel Value (Hebrew)	Jinn Value (Arabic)	Jinn Value (Hebrew)
Usurper	30	349	359	71	61
Guide	54	13	23	95	85
Mystery	84	43	53	125	115
Adjuster	210	169	179	251	241
Leader	630	589	599	311	301
Regulator	840	799	809	521	511
General Governor	1680	1639	1649	1361	1351
High Overseer	90720	90679	90689	90401	90391

Occult Encyclopedia of Magic Squares

Fire - Sun

17	28	51	34	38	42
23	33	44	50	21	39
29	54	37	27	43	20
40	19	30	45	24	52
46	35	26	18	53	32
55	41	22	36	31	25

Air - Sun

25	31	36	22	41	55
32	53	18	26	35	46
52	24	45	30	19	40
20	43	27	37	54	29
39	21	50	44	33	23
42	38	34	51	28	17

Earth - Sun

55	46	40	29	23	17
41	35	19	54	33	28
22	26	30	37	44	51
36	18	45	27	50	34
31	53	24	43	21	38
25	32	52	20	39	42

Water - Sun

42	39	20	52	32	25
38	21	43	24	53	31
34	50	27	45	18	36
51	44	37	30	26	22
28	33	54	19	35	41
17	23	29	40	46	55

	Number	Angel Value (Arabic)	Angel Value (Hebrew)	Jinn Value (Arabic)	Jinn Value (Hebrew)
Usurper	17	336	346	58	48
Guide	55	14	24	96	86
Mystery	72	31	41	113	103
Adjuster	210	169	179	251	241
Leader	630	589	599	311	301
Regulator	840	799	809	521	511
General Governor	1680	1639	1649	1361	1351
High Overseer	92400	92359	92369	92081	92071

Fire - Venus

6	47	32	17	37	50	21
51	22	7	41	33	18	38
19	39	52	23	8	42	27
43	28	13	40	53	24	9
25	10	44	29	14	34	54
35	48	26	11	45	30	15
31	16	36	49	20	12	46

Earth - Venus

31	35	25	43	19	51	6
16	48	10	28	39	22	47
36	26	44	13	52	7	32
49	11	29	40	23	41	17
20	45	14	53	8	33	37
12	30	34	24	42	18	50
46	15	54	9	27	38	21

Air - Venus

46	12	20	49	36	16	31
15	30	45	11	26	48	35
54	34	14	29	44	10	25
9	24	53	40	13	28	43
27	42	8	23	52	39	19
38	18	33	41	7	22	51
21	50	37	17	32	47	6

Water - Venus

21	38	27	9	54	15	46
50	18	42	24	34	30	12
37	33	8	53	14	45	20
17	41	23	40	29	11	49
32	7	52	13	44	26	36
47	22	39	28	10	48	16
6	51	19	43	25	35	31

	Number	Angel Value (Arabic)	Angel Value (Hebrew)	Jinn Value (Arabic)	Jinn Value (Hebrew)
Usurper	6	325	335	47	37
Guide	54	13	23	95	85
Mystery	60	19	29	101	91
Adjuster	210	169	179	251	241
Leader	630	589	599	311	301
Regulator	840	799	809	521	511
General Governor	1680	1639	1649	1361	1351
High Overseer	90720	90679	90689	90401	90391

ANGEL OF FIRST QUINANCE: LEKABEL (83)

אל	ב	ב	ל
29	21	5	28
4	29	28	22
19	31	30	3

ל	א	ב	ב	ל
ב	ב	ל	ל	א
ל	ל	א	ב	ב
א	ב	ב	ל	ל
ב	ל	ל	א	ב

Occult Encyclopedia of Magic Squares

Fire - Jupiter

13	24	18	28
27	19	21	16
23	14	29	17
20	26	15	22

Air - Jupiter

22	15	26	20
17	29	14	23
16	21	19	27
28	18	24	13

Earth - Jupiter

20	23	27	13
26	14	19	24
15	29	21	18
22	17	16	28

Water - Jupiter

28	16	17	22
18	21	29	15
24	19	14	26
13	27	23	20

	Number	Angel Value (Arabic)	Angel Value (Hebrew)	Jinn Value (Arabic)	Jinn Value (Hebrew)
Usurper	13	332	342	54	44
Guide	29	348	358	70	60
Mystery	42	1	11	83	73
Adjuster	664	623	633	345	335
Leader	1992	1951	1961	1673	1663
Regulator	2656	2615	2625	2337	2327
General Governor	5312	5271	5281	4993	4983
High Overseer	154048	154007	154017	153729	153719

Fire - Mars

4	31	22	16	10
17	11	5	27	23
28	19	18	12	6
13	7	29	20	14
21	15	9	8	30

Air - Mars

21	13	28	17	4
15	7	19	11	31
9	29	18	5	22
8	20	12	27	16
30	14	6	23	10

Earth - Mars

30	8	9	15	21
14	20	29	7	13
6	12	18	19	28
23	27	5	11	17
10	16	22	31	4

Water - Mars

10	23	6	14	30
16	27	12	20	8
22	5	18	29	9
31	11	19	7	15
4	17	28	13	21

	Number	Angel Value (Arabic)	Angel Value (Hebrew)	Jinn Value (Arabic)	Jinn Value (Hebrew)
Usurper	4	323	333	45	35
Guide	31	350	360	72	62
Mystery	35	354	4	76	66
Adjuster	83	42	52	124	114
Leader	249	208	218	290	280
Regulator	332	291	301	13	3
General Governor	664	623	633	345	335
High Overseer	20584	20543	20553	20265	20255

ANGEL OF SECOND QUINANCE: VESHRIAH (521)

יה	ר	שׁ	ו
5	301	203	12
202	13	4	302
299	7	14	201

ה	י	ר	שׁ	ו
ר	שׁ	ו	ה	י
ו	ה	י	ר	שׁ
י	ר	שׁ	ו	ה
שׁ	ו	ה	י	ר

Fire - Jupiter

122	133	127	139
138	128	130	125
132	123	140	126
129	137	124	131

Air - Jupiter

131	124	137	129
126	140	123	132
125	130	128	138
139	127	133	122

Earth - Jupiter

129	132	138	122
137	123	128	133
124	140	130	127
131	126	125	139

Water - Jupiter

139	125	126	131
127	130	140	124
133	128	123	137
122	138	132	129

	Number	Angel Value (Arabic)	Angel Value (Hebrew)	Jinn Value (Arabic)	Jinn Value (Hebrew)
Usurper	122	81	91	163	153
Guide	140	99	109	181	171
Mystery	262	221	231	303	293
Adjuster	4168	4127	4137	3849	3839
Leader	12504	12463	12473	12185	12175
Regulator	16672	16631	16641	16353	16343
General Governor	33344	33303	33313	33025	33015
High Overseer	4668160	4668119	4668129	4667841	4667831

Fire - Mars

92	117	110	104	98
105	99	93	113	111
114	107	106	100	94
101	95	115	108	102
109	103	97	96	116

Air - Mars

109	101	114	105	92
103	95	107	99	117
97	115	106	93	110
96	108	100	113	104
116	102	94	111	98

Earth - Mars

116	96	97	103	109
102	108	115	95	101
94	100	106	107	114
111	113	93	99	105
98	104	110	117	92

Water - Mars

98	111	94	102	116
104	113	100	108	96
110	93	106	115	97
117	99	107	95	103
92	105	114	101	109

	Number	Angel Value (Arabic)	Angel Value (Hebrew)	Jinn Value (Arabic)	Jinn Value (Hebrew)
Usurper	92	51	61	133	123
Guide	117	76	86	158	148
Mystery	209	168	178	250	240
Adjuster	521	480	490	202	192
Leader	1563	1522	1532	1244	1234
Regulator	2084	2043	2053	1765	1755
General Governor	4168	4127	4137	3849	3839
High Overseer	487656	487615	487625	487337	487327

Occult Encyclopedia of Magic Squares

Fire - Sun

69	80	102	86	90	94
75	85	96	101	73	91
81	105	89	79	95	72
92	71	82	97	76	103
98	87	78	70	104	84
106	93	74	88	83	77

Air - Sun

77	83	88	74	93	106
84	104	70	78	87	98
103	76	97	82	71	92
72	95	79	89	105	81
91	73	101	96	85	75
94	90	86	102	80	69

Earth - Sun

106	98	92	81	75	69
93	87	71	105	85	80
74	78	82	89	96	102
88	70	97	79	101	86
83	104	76	95	73	90
77	84	103	72	91	94

Water - Sun

94	91	72	103	84	77
90	73	95	76	104	83
86	101	79	97	70	88
102	96	89	82	78	74
80	85	105	71	87	93
69	75	81	92	98	106

	Number	Angel Value (Arabic)	Angel Value (Hebrew)	Jinn Value (Arabic)	Jinn Value (Hebrew)
Usurper	69	28	38	110	100
Guide	106	65	75	147	137
Mystery	175	134	144	216	206
Adjuster	521	480	490	202	192
Leader	1563	1522	1532	1244	1234
Regulator	2084	2043	2053	1765	1755
General Governor	4168	4127	4137	3849	3839
High Overseer	441808	441767	441777	441489	441479

Fire - Venus

50	91	76	61	81	97	65
98	66	51	85	77	62	82
63	83	99	67	52	86	71
87	72	57	84	100	68	53
69	54	88	73	58	78	101
79	95	70	55	89	74	59
75	60	80	96	64	56	90

Occult Encyclopedia of Magic Squares

Earth - Venus

75	79	69	87	63	98	50
60	95	54	72	83	66	91
80	70	88	57	99	51	76
96	55	73	84	67	85	61
64	89	58	100	52	77	81
56	74	78	68	86	62	97
90	59	101	53	71	82	65

Air - Venus

90	56	64	96	80	60	75
59	74	89	55	70	95	79
101	78	58	73	88	54	69
53	68	100	84	57	72	87
71	86	52	67	99	83	63
82	62	77	85	51	66	98
65	97	81	61	76	91	50

Water - Venus

65	82	71	53	101	59	90
97	62	86	68	78	74	56
81	77	52	100	58	89	64
61	85	67	84	73	55	96
76	51	99	57	88	70	80
91	66	83	72	54	95	60
50	98	63	87	69	79	75

	Number	Angel Value (Arabic)	Angel Value (Hebrew)	Jinn Value (Arabic)	Jinn Value (Hebrew)
Usurper	50	9	19	91	81
Guide	101	60	70	142	132
Mystery	151	110	120	192	182
Adjuster	521	480	490	202	192
Leader	1563	1522	1532	1244	1234
Regulator	2084	2043	2053	1765	1755
General Governor	4168	4127	4137	3849	3839
High Overseer	420968	420927	420937	420649	420639

Occult Encyclopedia of Magic Squares

Fire - Mercury

33	49	99	78	67	83	64	48
41	57	86	70	75	96	56	40
84	68	47	63	50	34	77	98
97	76	39	55	58	42	69	85
62	46	65	81	101	80	35	51
54	38	73	94	88	72	43	59
79	100	52	36	45	61	82	66
71	87	60	44	37	53	95	74

Earth - Mercury

71	79	54	62	97	84	41	33
87	100	38	46	76	68	57	49
60	52	73	65	39	47	86	99
44	36	94	81	55	63	70	78
37	45	88	101	58	50	75	67
53	61	72	80	42	34	96	83
95	82	43	35	69	77	56	64
74	66	59	51	85	98	40	48

Air - Mercury

74	95	53	37	44	60	87	71
66	82	61	45	36	52	100	79
59	43	72	88	94	73	38	54
51	35	80	101	81	65	46	62
85	69	42	58	55	39	76	97
98	77	34	50	63	47	68	84
40	56	96	75	70	86	57	41
48	64	83	67	78	99	49	33

Water - Mercury

48	40	98	85	51	59	66	74
64	56	77	69	35	43	82	95
83	96	34	42	80	72	61	53
67	75	50	58	101	88	45	37
78	70	63	55	81	94	36	44
99	86	47	39	65	73	52	60
49	57	68	76	46	38	100	87
33	41	84	97	62	54	79	71

Occult Encyclopedia of Magic Squares

	Number	Angel Value (Arabic)	Angel Value (Hebrew)	Jinn Value (Arabic)	Jinn Value (Hebrew)
Usurper	33	352	2	74	64
Guide	101	60	70	142	132
Mystery	134	93	103	175	165
Adjuster	521	480	490	202	192
Leader	1563	1522	1532	1244	1234
Regulator	2084	2043	2053	1765	1755
General Governor	4168	4127	4137	3849	3839
High Overseer	420968	420927	420937	420649	420639

Fire - Moon

61	74	36	45	105	29	65	81	25
21	64	86	41	57	73	28	50	101
97	33	49	85	17	69	78	40	53
88	20	63	72	43	56	100	27	52
48	99	32	68	84	19	55	77	39
35	60	76	31	44	104	24	67	80
34	47	98	18	70	83	38	54	79
75	37	59	103	30	46	82	23	66
62	87	22	58	71	42	51	102	26

Earth - Moon

25	101	53	52	39	80	79	66	26
81	50	40	27	77	67	54	23	102
65	28	78	100	55	24	38	82	51
29	73	69	56	19	104	83	46	42
105	57	17	43	84	44	70	30	71
45	41	85	72	68	31	18	103	58
36	86	49	63	32	76	98	59	22
74	64	33	20	99	60	47	37	87
61	21	97	88	48	35	34	75	62

Occult Encyclopedia of Magic Squares

Air - Moon

26	102	51	42	71	58	22	87	62
66	23	82	46	30	103	59	37	75
79	54	38	83	70	18	98	47	34
80	67	24	104	44	31	76	60	35
39	77	55	19	84	68	32	99	48
52	27	100	56	43	72	63	20	88
53	40	78	69	17	85	49	33	97
101	50	28	73	57	41	86	64	21
25	81	65	29	105	45	36	74	61

Water - Moon

62	75	34	35	48	88	97	21	61
87	37	47	60	99	20	33	64	74
22	59	98	76	32	63	49	86	36
58	103	18	31	68	72	85	41	45
71	30	70	44	84	43	17	57	105
42	46	83	104	19	56	69	73	29
51	82	38	24	55	100	78	28	65
102	23	54	67	77	27	40	50	81
26	66	79	80	39	52	53	101	25

	Number	Angel Value (Arabic)	Angel Value (Hebrew)	Jinn Value (Arabic)	Jinn Value (Hebrew)
Usurper	17	336	346	58	48
Guide	105	64	74	146	136
Mystery	122	81	91	163	153
Adjuster	521	480	490	202	192
Leader	1563	1522	1532	1244	1234
Regulator	2084	2043	2053	1765	1755
General Governor	4168	4127	4137	3849	3839
High Overseer	437640	437599	437609	437321	437311

Occult Encyclopedia of Magic Squares

Fire - Saturn

2	20	27	65	56	100	49	41	73	88
13	77	70	61	102	86	4	46	32	30
28	33	57	101	87	72	21	9	50	63
34	59	99	89	22	68	76	17	6	51
47	98	91	26	37	60	64	74	19	5
54	11	12	79	67	43	39	29	84	103
66	48	8	15	81	36	24	85	106	52
80	69	44	3	14	31	82	105	55	38
90	23	35	42	10	18	104	53	71	75
107	83	78	40	45	7	58	62	25	16

Earth - Saturn

107	90	80	66	54	47	34	28	13	2
83	23	69	48	11	98	59	33	77	20
78	35	44	8	12	91	99	57	70	27
40	42	3	15	79	26	89	101	61	65
45	10	14	81	67	37	22	87	102	56
7	18	31	36	43	60	68	72	86	100
58	104	82	24	39	64	76	21	4	49
62	53	105	85	29	74	17	9	46	41
25	71	55	106	84	19	6	50	32	73
16	75	38	52	103	5	51	63	30	88

Air - Saturn

16	25	62	58	7	45	40	78	83	107
75	71	53	104	18	10	42	35	23	90
38	55	105	82	31	14	3	44	69	80
52	106	85	24	36	81	15	8	48	66
103	84	29	39	43	67	79	12	11	54
5	19	74	64	60	37	26	91	98	47
51	6	17	76	68	22	89	99	59	34
63	50	9	21	72	87	101	57	33	28
30	32	46	4	86	102	61	70	77	13
88	73	41	49	100	56	65	27	20	2

Water - Saturn

88	30	63	51	5	103	52	38	75	16
73	32	50	6	19	84	106	55	71	25
41	46	9	17	74	29	85	105	53	62
49	4	21	76	64	39	24	82	104	58
100	86	72	68	60	43	36	31	18	7
56	102	87	22	37	67	81	14	10	45
65	61	101	89	26	79	15	3	42	40
27	70	57	99	91	12	8	44	35	78
20	77	33	59	98	11	48	69	23	83
2	13	28	34	47	54	66	80	90	107

	Number	Angel Value (Arabic)	Angel Value (Hebrew)	Jinn Value (Arabic)	Jinn Value (Hebrew)
Usurper	2	321	331	43	33
Guide	107	66	76	148	138
Mystery	109	68	78	150	140
Adjuster	521	480	490	202	192
Leader	1563	1522	1532	1244	1234
Regulator	2084	2043	2053	1765	1755
General Governor	4168	4127	4137	3849	3839
High Overseer	445976	445935	445945	445657	445647

ANGEL OF SECOND DECANATE: YASYASYAH (155)

יה	ס׳	ס	׳
9	61	73	12
72	13	8	62
59	11	14	71

ה	׳	ס	׳	ס	׳
ס	׳	ה	׳	ס	׳
ס	׳	׳	ס	ה	׳
׳	ס	׳	ס	׳	ה
׳	ה	ס	׳	׳	ס
׳	ס	׳	ה	׳	ס

Numerical Squares See Page: 267

ANGEL OF THIRD QUINANCE: YECHAVIAH (39)

<table>
<tr><td>יה</td><td>ו</td><td>ח</td><td>י</td></tr>
<tr><td>9</td><td>9</td><td>9</td><td>12</td></tr>
<tr><td>8</td><td>13</td><td>8</td><td>10</td></tr>
<tr><td>7</td><td>11</td><td>14</td><td>7</td></tr>
</table>

<table>
<tr><td>ה</td><td>י</td><td>ו</td><td>ח</td><td>י</td></tr>
<tr><td>ו</td><td>ח</td><td>י</td><td>ה</td><td>י</td></tr>
<tr><td>י</td><td>ה</td><td>י</td><td>ו</td><td>ח</td></tr>
<tr><td>י</td><td>ו</td><td>ח</td><td>י</td><td>ה</td></tr>
<tr><td>ח</td><td>י</td><td>ה</td><td>י</td><td>ו</td></tr>
</table>

Fire - Saturn

14	9	16
15	13	11
10	17	12

Earth - Saturn

10	15	14
17	13	9
12	11	16

Air - Saturn

12	17	10
11	13	15
16	9	14

Water - Saturn

16	11	12
9	13	17
14	15	10

	Number	Angel Value (Arabic)	Angel Value (Hebrew)	Jinn Value (Arabic)	Jinn Value (Hebrew)
Usurper	9	328	338	50	40
Guide	17	336	346	58	48
Mystery	26	345	355	67	57
Adjuster	39	358	8	80	70
Leader	117	76	86	158	148
Regulator	156	115	125	197	187
General Governor	312	271	281	353	343
High Overseer	5304	5263	5273	4985	4975

Fire - Jupiter

2	13	7	17
16	8	10	5
12	3	18	6
9	15	4	11

Air - Jupiter

11	4	15	9
6	18	3	12
5	10	8	16
17	7	13	2

Earth - Jupiter

9	12	16	2
15	3	8	13
4	18	10	7
11	6	5	17

Water - Jupiter

17	5	6	11
7	10	18	4
13	8	3	15
2	16	12	9

	Number	Angel Value (Arabic)	Angel Value (Hebrew)	Jinn Value (Arabic)	Jinn Value (Hebrew)
Usurper	2	321	331	43	33
Guide	18	337	347	59	49
Mystery	20	339	349	61	51
Adjuster	312	271	281	353	343
Leader	936	895	905	617	607
Regulator	1248	1207	1217	929	919
General Governor	2496	2455	2465	2177	2167
High Overseer	44928	44887	44897	44609	44599

ANGEL OF FOURTH QUINANCE: LEHACHIAH (58)

יה	ח	ה	ל
29	6	11	12
10	13	28	7
4	31	14	9

ה	י	ח	ה	ל
ח	ה	ל	ה	י
ל	ה	י	ח	ה
י	ה	ה	ל	ה
ה	ל	ה	י	ח

Fire - Jupiter

7	18	12	21
20	13	15	10
17	8	22	11
14	19	9	16

Air - Jupiter

16	9	19	14
11	22	8	17
10	15	13	20
21	12	18	7

Earth - Jupiter

14	17	20	7
19	8	13	18
9	22	15	12
16	11	10	21

Water - Jupiter

21	10	11	16
12	15	22	9
18	13	8	19
7	20	17	14

	Number	Angel Value (Arabic)	Angel Value (Hebrew)	Jinn Value (Arabic)	Jinn Value (Hebrew)
Usurper	7	326	336	48	38
Guide	22	341	351	63	53
Mystery	29	348	358	70	60
Adjuster	464	423	433	145	135
Leader	1392	1351	1361	1073	1063
Regulator	1856	1815	1825	1537	1527
General Governor	3712	3671	3681	3393	3383
High Overseer	81664	81623	81633	81345	81335

ANGEL OF THIRD DECANATE: YASGEDIBARODIEL (340)

ל	א	י	ד	ו	ר	ב	י	ד	ג	ס	י
א	י	ד	ו	ר	ב	י	ל	י	ד	ג	ס
י	ד	ו	ר	ב	י	ס	א	ל	י	ד	ג
ד	ו	ר	ב	י	ס	ג	י	א	ל	י	ד
ו	ר	ב	י	ס	ג	ד	ר	י	א	ל	י
י	ב	י	ס	ג	ד	ר	ו	ד	י	א	ל
ר	ל	א	י	ד	ו	י	ד	ג	ס	י	ב
ד	י	ל	א	י	ד	ו	ג	ס	י	ב	ר
ג	ד	י	ל	א	י	ד	ס	י	ב	ר	ו
ס	ג	ד	י	ל	א	י	י	ב	ר	ו	ד
י	ס	ג	ד	ר	ל	א	ב	ר	ו	ד	י
ב	י	ס	ג	ד	י	ל	ר	ו	ד	י	א

יסג	דיב	רוד	יאל
72	17	213	38
212	39	71	18
15	74	40	211

Occult Encyclopedia of Magic Squares

Fire - Jupiter

77	88	82	93
92	83	85	80
87	78	94	81
84	91	79	86

Air - Jupiter

86	79	91	84
81	94	78	87
80	85	83	92
93	82	88	77

Earth - Jupiter

84	87	92	77
91	78	83	88
79	94	85	82
86	81	80	93

Water - Jupiter

93	80	81	86
82	85	94	79
88	83	78	91
77	92	87	84

	Number	Angel Value (Arabic)	Angel Value (Hebrew)	Jinn Value (Arabic)	Jinn Value (Hebrew)
Usurper	77	36	46	118	108
Guide	94	53	63	135	125
Mystery	171	130	140	212	202
Adjuster	2720	2679	2689	2401	2391
Leader	8160	8119	8129	7841	7831
Regulator	10880	10839	10849	10561	10551
General Governor	21760	21719	21729	21441	21431
High Overseer	2045440	2045399	2045409	2045121	2045111

Fire - Mars

56	80	74	68	62
69	63	57	76	75
77	71	70	64	58
65	59	78	72	66
73	67	61	60	79

Air - Mars

73	65	77	69	56
67	59	71	63	80
61	78	70	57	74
60	72	64	76	68
79	66	58	75	62

Earth - Mars

79	60	61	67	73
66	72	78	59	65
58	64	70	71	77
75	76	57	63	69
62	68	74	80	56

Water - Mars

62	75	58	66	79
68	76	64	72	60
74	57	70	78	61
80	63	71	59	67
56	69	77	65	73

	Number	Angel Value (Arabic)	Angel Value (Hebrew)	Jinn Value (Arabic)	Jinn Value (Hebrew)
Usurper	56	15	25	97	87
Guide	80	39	49	121	111
Mystery	136	95	105	177	167
Adjuster	340	299	309	21	11
Leader	1020	979	989	701	691
Regulator	1360	1319	1329	1041	1031
General Governor	2720	2679	2689	2401	2391
High Overseer	217600	217559	217569	217281	217271

Fire - Sun

39	50	71	56	60	64
45	55	66	70	43	61
51	74	59	49	65	42
62	41	52	67	46	72
68	57	48	40	73	54
75	63	44	58	53	47

Air - Sun

47	53	58	44	63	75
54	73	40	48	57	68
72	46	67	52	41	62
42	65	49	59	74	51
61	43	70	66	55	45
64	60	56	71	50	39

Earth - Sun

75	68	62	51	45	39
63	57	41	74	55	50
44	48	52	59	66	71
58	40	67	49	70	56
53	73	46	65	43	60
47	54	72	42	61	64

Water - Sun

64	61	42	72	54	47
60	43	65	46	73	53
56	70	49	67	40	58
71	66	59	52	48	44
50	55	74	41	57	63
39	45	51	62	68	75

Occult Encyclopedia of Magic Squares

	Number	Angel Value (Arabic)	Angel Value (Hebrew)	Jinn Value (Arabic)	Jinn Value (Hebrew)
Usurper	39	358	8	80	70
Guide	75	34	44	116	106
Mystery	114	73	83	155	145
Adjuster	340	299	309	21	11
Leader	1020	979	989	701	691
Regulator	1360	1319	1329	1041	1031
General Governor	2720	2679	2689	2401	2391
High Overseer	204000	203959	203969	203681	203671

Fire - Venus

24	65	50	35	55	72	39
73	40	25	59	51	36	56
37	57	74	41	26	60	45
61	46	31	58	75	42	27
43	28	62	47	32	52	76
53	70	44	29	63	48	33
49	34	54	71	38	30	64

Air - Venus

64	30	38	71	54	34	49
33	48	63	29	44	70	53
76	52	32	47	62	28	43
27	42	75	58	31	46	61
45	60	26	41	74	57	37
56	36	51	59	25	40	73
39	72	55	35	50	65	24

Earth - Venus

49	53	43	61	37	73	24
34	70	28	46	57	40	65
54	44	62	31	74	25	50
71	29	47	58	41	59	35
38	63	32	75	26	51	55
30	48	52	42	60	36	72
64	33	76	27	45	56	39

Water - Venus

39	56	45	27	76	33	64
72	36	60	42	52	48	30
55	51	26	75	32	63	38
35	59	41	58	47	29	71
50	25	74	31	62	44	54
65	40	57	46	28	70	34
24	73	37	61	43	53	49

Occult Encyclopedia of Magic Squares

	Number	Angel Value (Arabic)	Angel Value (Hebrew)	Jinn Value (Arabic)	Jinn Value (Hebrew)
Usurper	24	343	353	65	55
Guide	76	35	45	117	107
Mystery	100	59	69	141	131
Adjuster	340	299	309	21	11
Leader	1020	979	989	701	691
Regulator	1360	1319	1329	1041	1031
General Governor	2720	2679	2689	2401	2391
High Overseer	206720	206679	206689	206401	206391

Fire - Mercury

11	27	72	56	45	61	42	26
19	35	64	48	53	69	34	18
62	46	25	41	28	12	55	71
70	54	17	33	36	20	47	63
40	24	43	59	74	58	13	29
32	16	51	67	66	50	21	37
57	73	30	14	23	39	60	44
49	65	38	22	15	31	68	52

Earth - Mercury

49	57	32	40	70	62	19	11
65	73	16	24	54	46	35	27
38	30	51	43	17	25	64	72
22	14	67	59	33	41	48	56
15	23	66	74	36	28	53	45
31	39	50	58	20	12	69	61
68	60	21	13	47	55	34	42
52	44	37	29	63	71	18	26

Occult Encyclopedia of Magic Squares

Air - Mercury

52	68	31	15	22	38	65	49
44	60	39	23	14	30	73	57
37	21	50	66	67	51	16	32
29	13	58	74	59	43	24	40
63	47	20	36	33	17	54	70
71	55	12	28	41	25	46	62
18	34	69	53	48	64	35	19
26	42	61	45	56	72	27	11

Water - Mercury

26	18	71	63	29	37	44	52
42	34	55	47	13	21	60	68
61	69	12	20	58	50	39	31
45	53	28	36	74	66	23	15
56	48	41	33	59	67	14	22
72	64	25	17	43	51	30	38
27	35	46	54	24	16	73	65
11	19	62	70	40	32	57	49

	Number	Angel Value (Arabic)	Angel Value (Hebrew)	Jinn Value (Arabic)	Jinn Value (Hebrew)
Usurper	11	330	340	52	42
Guide	74	33	43	115	105
Mystery	85	44	54	126	116
Adjuster	340	299	309	21	11
Leader	1020	979	989	701	691
Regulator	1360	1319	1329	1041	1031
General Governor	2720	2679	2689	2401	2391
High Overseer	201280	201239	201249	200961	200951

ANGEL OF FIFTH QUINANCE: KEVEQIAH (141)

יה	ק	ו	ב
19	7	103	12
102	13	18	8
5	21	14	101

ה	י	ק	ו	ב
ק	ו	ב	ה	י
ב	ה	י	ק	ו
י	ק	ו	ב	ה
ו	ב	ה	י	ק

Numerical Squares See Page: 205

ANGEL OF SIX QUINANCE: MENDEL (125)

אל	ד	נ	מ
39	51	7	28
6	29	38	52
49	41	30	5

ל	א	ד	נ	מ
ד	נ	מ	ל	א
מ	ל	א	ד	נ
א	ד	נ	מ	ל
נ	מ	ל	א	ד

Fire - Jupiter

23	34	28	40
39	29	31	26
33	24	41	27
30	38	25	32

Air - Jupiter

32	25	38	30
27	41	24	33
26	31	29	39
40	28	34	23

Earth - Jupiter

30	33	39	23
38	24	29	34
25	41	31	28
32	27	26	40

water - Jupiter

40	26	27	32
28	31	41	25
34	29	24	38
23	39	33	30

Occult Encyclopedia of Magic Squares

	Number	Angel Value (Arabic)	Angel Value (Hebrew)	Jinn Value (Arabic)	Jinn Value (Hebrew)
Usurper	23	342	352	64	54
Guide	41	360	10	82	72
Mystery	64	23	33	105	95
Adjuster	1000	959	969	681	671
Leader	3000	2959	2969	2681	2671
Regulator	4000	3959	3969	3681	3671
General Governor	8000	7959	7969	7681	7671
High Overseer	328000	327959	327969	327681	327671

Fire - Mars

13	37	31	25	19
26	20	14	33	32
34	28	27	21	15
22	16	35	29	23
30	24	18	17	36

Air - Mars

30	22	34	26	13
24	16	28	20	37
18	35	27	14	31
17	29	21	33	25
36	23	15	32	19

Earth - Mars

36	17	18	24	30
23	29	35	16	22
15	21	27	28	34
32	33	14	20	26
19	25	31	37	13

Water - Mars

19	32	15	23	36
25	33	21	29	17
31	14	27	35	18
37	20	28	16	24
13	26	34	22	30

	Number	Angel Value (Arabic)	Angel Value (Hebrew)	Jinn Value (Arabic)	Jinn Value (Hebrew)
Usurper	13	332	342	54	44
Guide	37	356	6	78	68
Mystery	50	9	19	91	81
Adjuster	125	84	94	166	156
Leader	375	334	344	56	46
Regulator	500	459	469	181	171
General Governor	1000	959	969	681	671
High Overseer	37000	36959	36969	36681	36671

Fire - Sun

3	14	36	20	24	28
9	19	30	35	7	25
15	39	23	13	29	6
26	5	16	31	10	37
32	21	12	4	38	18
40	27	8	22	17	11

Air - Sun

11	17	22	8	27	40
18	38	4	12	21	32
37	10	31	16	5	26
6	29	13	23	39	15
25	7	35	30	19	9
28	24	20	36	14	3

Earth - Sun

40	32	26	15	9	3
27	21	5	39	19	14
8	12	16	23	30	36
22	4	31	13	35	20
17	38	10	29	7	24
11	18	37	6	25	28

Water - Sun

28	25	6	37	18	11
24	7	29	10	38	17
20	35	13	31	4	22
36	30	23	16	12	8
14	19	39	5	21	27
3	9	15	26	32	40

	Number	Angel Value (Arabic)	Angel Value (Hebrew)	Jinn Value (Arabic)	Jinn Value (Hebrew)
Usurper	3	322	332	44	34
Guide	40	359	9	81	71
Mystery	43	2	12	84	74
Adjuster	125	84	94	166	156
Leader	375	334	344	56	46
Regulator	500	459	469	181	171
General Governor	1000	959	969	681	671
High Overseer	40000	39959	39969	39681	39671

AQUARIUS

SIGN AQUARIUS: DELI (44)

No Hebrew Squares Available

Numerical Squares See Page: 1

ARCHANGEL OF AQUARIUS: KAMBRIEL (304)

אל	רי	מב	כא
20	43	213	28
212	29	19	44
41	22	30	211

ל	א	י	ר	ב	מ	א	כ
ר	ב	מ	א	כ	ל	א	י
א	כ	ל	א	י	ר	ב	מ
א	י	ר	ב	מ	א	כ	ל
ב	מ	א	כ	ל	א	י	ר
כ	ל	א	י	ר	ב	מ	א
י	ר	ב	מ	א	כ	ל	א
מ	א	כ	ל	א	י	ר	ב

Fire - Jupiter

68	79	73	84
83	74	76	71
78	69	85	72
75	82	70	77

Air - Jupiter

77	70	82	75
72	85	69	78
71	76	74	83
84	73	79	68

Earth - Jupiter

75	78	83	68
82	69	74	79
70	85	76	73
77	72	71	84

Water - Jupiter

84	71	72	77
73	76	85	70
79	74	69	82
68	83	78	75

	Number	Angel Value (Arabic)	Angel Value (Hebrew)	Jinn Value (Arabic)	Jinn Value (Hebrew)
Usurper	68	27	37	109	99
Guide	85	44	54	126	116
Mystery	153	112	122	194	184
Adjuster	2432	2391	2401	2113	2103
Leader	7296	7255	7265	6977	6967
Regulator	9728	9687	9697	9409	9399
General Governor	19456	19415	19425	19137	19127
High Overseer	1653760	1653719	1653729	1653441	1653431

Fire - Mars

48	76	66	60	54
61	55	49	72	67
73	63	62	56	50
57	51	74	64	58
65	59	53	52	75

Air - Mars

65	57	73	61	48
59	51	63	55	76
53	74	62	49	66
52	64	56	72	60
75	58	50	67	54

Earth - Mars

75	52	53	59	65
58	64	74	51	57
50	56	62	63	73
67	72	49	55	61
54	60	66	76	48

Water - Mars

54	67	50	58	75
60	72	56	64	52
66	49	62	74	53
76	55	63	51	59
48	61	73	57	65

	Number	Angel Value (Arabic)	Angel Value (Hebrew)	Jinn Value (Arabic)	Jinn Value (Hebrew)
Usurper	48	7	17	89	79
Guide	76	35	45	117	107
Mystery	124	83	93	165	155
Adjuster	304	263	273	345	335
Leader	912	871	881	593	583
Regulator	1216	1175	1185	897	887
General Governor	2432	2391	2401	2113	2103
High Overseer	184832	184791	184801	184513	184503

Occult Encyclopedia of Magic Squares

Fire - Sun

33	44	65	50	54	58
39	49	60	64	37	55
45	68	53	43	59	36
56	35	46	61	40	66
62	51	42	34	67	48
69	57	38	52	47	41

Air - Sun

41	47	52	38	57	69
48	67	34	42	51	62
66	40	61	46	35	56
36	59	43	53	68	45
55	37	64	60	49	39
58	54	50	65	44	33

Earth - Sun

69	62	56	45	39	33
57	51	35	68	49	44
38	42	46	53	60	65
52	34	61	43	64	50
47	67	40	59	37	54
41	48	66	36	55	58

Water - Sun

58	55	36	66	48	41
54	37	59	40	67	47
50	64	43	61	34	52
65	60	53	46	42	38
44	49	68	35	51	57
33	39	45	56	62	69

	Number	Angel Value (Arabic)	Angel Value (Hebrew)	Jinn Value (Arabic)	Jinn Value (Hebrew)
Usurper	33	352	2	74	64
Guide	69	28	38	110	100
Mystery	102	61	71	143	133
Adjuster	304	263	273	345	335
Leader	912	871	881	593	583
Regulator	1216	1175	1185	897	887
General Governor	2432	2391	2401	2113	2103
High Overseer	167808	167767	167777	167489	167479

Fire - Venus

19	60	45	30	50	66	34
67	35	20	54	46	31	51
32	52	68	36	21	55	40
56	41	26	53	69	37	22
38	23	57	42	27	47	70
48	64	39	24	58	43	28
44	29	49	65	33	25	59

Air - Venus

59	25	33	65	49	29	44
28	43	58	24	39	64	48
70	47	27	42	57	23	38
22	37	69	53	26	41	56
40	55	21	36	68	52	32
51	31	46	54	20	35	67
34	66	50	30	45	60	19

Earth - Venus

44	48	38	56	32	67	19
29	64	23	41	52	35	60
49	39	57	26	68	20	45
65	24	42	53	36	54	30
33	58	27	69	21	46	50
25	43	47	37	55	31	66
59	28	70	22	40	51	34

Water - Venus

34	51	40	22	70	28	59
66	31	55	37	47	43	25
50	46	21	69	27	58	33
30	54	36	53	42	24	65
45	20	68	26	57	39	49
60	35	52	41	23	64	29
19	67	32	56	38	48	44

	Number	Angel Value (Arabic)	Angel Value (Hebrew)	Jinn Value (Arabic)	Jinn Value (Hebrew)
Usurper	19	338	348	60	50
Guide	70	29	39	111	101
Mystery	89	48	58	130	120
Adjuster	304	263	273	345	335
Leader	912	871	881	593	583
Regulator	1216	1175	1185	897	887
General Governor	2432	2391	2401	2113	2103
High Overseer	170240	170199	170209	169921	169911

Fire - Mercury

6	22	71	51	40	56	37	21
14	30	59	43	48	68	29	13
57	41	20	36	23	7	50	70
69	49	12	28	31	15	42	58
35	19	38	54	73	53	8	24
27	11	46	66	61	45	16	32
52	72	25	9	18	34	55	39
44	60	33	17	10	26	67	47

Earth - Mercury

44	52	27	35	69	57	14	6
60	72	11	19	49	41	30	22
33	25	46	38	12	20	59	71
17	9	66	54	28	36	43	51
10	18	61	73	31	23	48	40
26	34	45	53	15	7	68	56
67	55	16	8	42	50	29	37
47	39	32	24	58	70	13	21

Air - Mercury

47	67	26	10	17	33	60	44
39	55	34	18	9	25	72	52
32	16	45	61	66	46	11	27
24	8	53	73	54	38	19	35
58	42	15	31	28	12	49	69
70	50	7	23	36	20	41	57
13	29	68	48	43	59	30	14
21	37	56	40	51	71	22	6

Water - Mercury

21	13	70	58	24	32	39	47
37	29	50	42	8	16	55	67
56	68	7	15	53	45	34	26
40	48	23	31	73	61	18	10
51	43	36	28	54	66	9	17
71	59	20	12	38	46	25	33
22	30	41	49	19	11	72	60
6	14	57	69	35	27	52	44

	Number	Angel Value (Arabic)	Angel Value (Hebrew)	Jinn Value (Arabic)	Jinn Value (Hebrew)
Usurper	6	325	335	47	37
Guide	73	32	42	114	104
Mystery	79	38	48	120	110
Adjuster	304	263	273	345	335
Leader	912	871	881	593	583
Regulator	1216	1175	1185	897	887
General Governor	2432	2391	2401	2113	2103
High Overseer	177536	177495	177505	177217	177207

ANGEL OF AQUARIUS: TZAKMIQIEL (291)

יאל	ק	מ	צב
109	41	103	38
102	39	108	42
39	111	40	101

ל	א	י	ק	מ	נ	א
י	ק	מ	נ	א	ל	א
מ	נ	א	ל	א	י	ק
א	ל	א	י	ק	מ	נ
א	י	ק	מ	נ	א	ל
ק	מ	נ	א	ל	א	י
נ	א	ל	א	י	ק	מ

Occult Encyclopedia of Magic Squares

Fire - Saturn

98	93	100
99	97	95
94	101	96

Earth - Saturn

94	99	98
101	97	93
96	95	100

Air - Saturn

96	101	94
95	97	99
100	93	98

Water - Saturn

100	95	96
93	97	101
98	99	94

	Number	Angel Value (Arabic)	Angel Value (Hebrew)	Jinn Value (Arabic)	Jinn Value (Hebrew)
Usurper	93	52	62	134	124
Guide	101	60	70	142	132
Mystery	194	153	163	235	225
Adjuster	291	250	260	332	322
Leader	873	832	842	554	544
Regulator	1164	1123	1133	845	835
General Governor	2328	2287	2297	2009	1999
High Overseer	235128	235087	235097	234809	234799

Fire - Jupiter

65	76	70	80
79	71	73	68
75	66	81	69
72	78	67	74

Air - Jupiter

74	67	78	72
69	81	66	75
68	73	71	79
80	70	76	65

Earth - Jupiter

72	75	79	65
78	66	71	76
67	81	73	70
74	69	68	80

Water - Jupiter

80	68	69	74
70	73	81	67
76	71	66	78
65	79	75	72

Occult Encyclopedia of Magic Squares

	Number	Angel Value (Arabic)	Angel Value (Hebrew)	Jinn Value (Arabic)	Jinn Value (Hebrew)
Usurper	65	24	34	106	96
Guide	81	40	50	122	112
Mystery	146	105	115	187	177
Adjuster	2328	2287	2297	2009	1999
Leader	6984	6943	6953	6665	6655
Regulator	9312	9271	9281	8993	8983
General Governor	18624	18583	18593	18305	18295
High Overseer	1508544	1508503	1508513	1508225	1508215

Fire - Mars

46	71	64	58	52
59	53	47	67	65
68	61	60	54	48
55	49	69	62	56
63	57	51	50	70

Air - Mars

63	55	68	59	46
57	49	61	53	71
51	69	60	47	64
50	62	54	67	58
70	56	48	65	52

Earth - Mars

70	50	51	57	63
56	62	69	49	55
48	54	60	61	68
65	67	47	53	59
52	58	64	71	46

Water - Mars

52	65	48	56	70
58	67	54	62	50
64	47	60	69	51
71	53	61	49	57
46	59	68	55	63

	Number	Angel Value (Arabic)	Angel Value (Hebrew)	Jinn Value (Arabic)	Jinn Value (Hebrew)
Usurper	46	5	15	87	77
Guide	71	30	40	112	102
Mystery	117	76	86	158	148
Adjuster	291	250	260	332	322
Leader	873	832	842	554	544
Regulator	1164	1123	1133	845	835
General Governor	2328	2287	2297	2009	1999
High Overseer	165288	165247	165257	164969	164959

Occult Encyclopedia of Magic Squares

Fire - Sun

31	42	62	48	52	56
37	47	58	61	35	53
43	65	51	41	57	34
54	33	44	59	38	63
60	49	40	32	64	46
66	55	36	50	45	39

Air - Sun

39	45	50	36	55	66
46	64	32	40	49	60
63	38	59	44	33	54
34	57	41	51	65	43
53	35	61	58	47	37
56	52	48	62	42	31

Earth - Sun

66	60	54	43	37	31
55	49	33	65	47	42
36	40	44	51	58	62
50	32	59	41	61	48
45	64	38	57	35	52
39	46	63	34	53	56

Water - Sun

56	53	34	63	46	39
52	35	57	38	64	45
48	61	41	59	32	50
62	58	51	44	40	36
42	47	65	33	49	55
31	37	43	54	60	66

	Number	Angel Value (Arabic)	Angel Value (Hebrew)	Jinn Value (Arabic)	Jinn Value (Hebrew)
Usurper	31	350	360	72	62
Guide	66	25	35	107	97
Mystery	97	56	66	138	128
Adjuster	291	250	260	332	322
Leader	873	832	842	554	544
Regulator	1164	1123	1133	845	835
General Governor	2328	2287	2297	2009	1999
High Overseer	153648	153607	153617	153329	153319

Occult Encyclopedia of Magic Squares

Fire - Venus

17	58	43	28	48	65	32
66	33	18	52	44	29	49
30	50	67	34	19	53	38
54	39	24	51	68	35	20
36	21	55	40	25	45	69
46	63	37	22	56	41	26
42	27	47	64	31	23	57

Air - Venus

57	23	31	64	47	27	42
26	41	56	22	37	63	46
69	45	25	40	55	21	36
20	35	68	51	24	39	54
38	53	19	34	67	50	30
49	29	44	52	18	33	66
32	65	48	28	43	58	17

Earth - Venus

42	46	36	54	30	66	17
27	63	21	39	50	33	58
47	37	55	24	67	18	43
64	22	40	51	34	52	28
31	56	25	68	19	44	48
23	41	45	35	53	29	65
57	26	69	20	38	49	32

Water - Venus

32	49	38	20	69	26	57
65	29	53	35	45	41	23
48	44	19	68	25	56	31
28	52	34	51	40	22	64
43	18	67	24	55	37	47
58	33	50	39	21	63	27
17	66	30	54	36	46	42

	Number	Angel Value (Arabic)	Angel Value (Hebrew)	Jinn Value (Arabic)	Jinn Value (Hebrew)
Usurper	17	336	346	58	48
Guide	69	28	38	110	100
Mystery	86	45	55	127	117
Adjuster	291	250	260	332	322
Leader	873	832	842	554	544
Regulator	1164	1123	1133	845	835
General Governor	2328	2287	2297	2009	1999
High Overseer	160632	160591	160601	160313	160303

Fire - Mercury

4	20	72	49	38	54	35	19
12	28	57	41	46	69	27	11
55	39	18	34	21	5	48	71
70	47	10	26	29	13	40	56
33	17	36	52	74	51	6	22
25	9	44	67	59	43	14	30
50	73	23	7	16	32	53	37
42	58	31	15	8	24	68	45

Earth - Mercury

42	50	25	33	70	55	12	4
58	73	9	17	47	39	28	20
31	23	44	36	10	18	57	72
15	7	67	52	26	34	41	49
8	16	59	74	29	21	46	38
24	32	43	51	13	5	69	54
68	53	14	6	40	48	27	35
45	37	30	22	56	71	11	19

Air - Mercury

45	68	24	8	15	31	58	42
37	53	32	16	7	23	73	50
30	14	43	59	67	44	9	25
22	6	51	74	52	36	17	33
56	40	13	29	26	10	47	70
71	48	5	21	34	18	39	55
11	27	69	46	41	57	28	12
19	35	54	38	49	72	20	4

Water - Mercury

19	11	71	56	22	30	37	45
35	27	48	40	6	14	53	68
54	69	5	13	51	43	32	24
38	46	21	29	74	59	16	8
49	41	34	26	52	67	7	15
72	57	18	10	36	44	23	31
20	28	39	47	17	9	73	58
4	12	55	70	33	25	50	42

	Number	Angel Value (Arabic)	Angel Value (Hebrew)	Jinn Value (Arabic)	Jinn Value (Hebrew)
Usurper	4	323	333	45	35
Guide	74	33	43	115	105
Mystery	78	37	47	119	109
Adjuster	291	250	260	332	322
Leader	873	832	842	554	544
Regulator	1164	1123	1133	845	835
General Governor	2328	2287	2297	2009	1999
High Overseer	172272	172231	172241	171953	171943

LORD OF TRIPLICITY BY DAY: ATHOR (676)

ר	ו	ה	ע
69	401	9	197
8	198	68	402
399	71	199	7

ר	ו	ה	ע
ע	ה	ו	ר
ו	ר	ע	ה
ה	ע	ר	ו

Fire - Jupiter

161	172	166	177
176	167	169	164
171	162	178	165
168	175	163	170

Air - Jupiter

177	164	165	170
166	169	178	163
172	167	162	175
161	176	171	168

Earth - Jupiter

168	171	176	161
175	162	167	172
163	178	169	166
170	165	164	177

Water - Jupiter

177	164	165	170
166	169	178	163
172	167	162	175
161	176	171	168

Occult Encyclopedia of Magic Squares

	Number	Angel Value (Arabic)	Angel Value (Hebrew)	Jinn Value (Arabic)	Jinn Value (Hebrew)
Usurper	161	120	130	202	192
Guide	178	137	147	219	209
Mystery	339	298	308	20	10
Adjuster	5408	5367	5377	5089	5079
Leader	16224	16183	16193	15905	15895
Regulator	21632	21591	21601	21313	21303
General Governor	43264	43223	43233	42945	42935
High Overseer	7700992	7700951	7700961	7700673	7700663

Fire - Mars

123	148	141	135	129
136	130	124	144	142
145	138	137	131	125
132	126	146	139	133
140	134	128	127	147

Air - Mars

140	132	145	136	123
134	126	138	130	148
128	146	137	124	141
127	139	131	144	135
147	133	125	142	129

Earth - Mars

147	127	128	134	140
133	139	146	126	132
125	131	137	138	145
142	144	124	130	136
129	135	141	148	123

Water - Mars

129	142	125	133	147
135	144	131	139	127
141	124	137	146	128
148	130	138	126	134
123	136	145	132	140

Occult Encyclopedia of Magic Squares

	Number	Angel Value (Arabic)	Angel Value (Hebrew)	Jinn Value (Arabic)	Jinn Value (Hebrew)
Usurper	123	82	92	164	154
Guide	148	107	117	189	179
Mystery	271	230	240	312	302
Adjuster	676	635	645	357	347
Leader	2028	1987	1997	1709	1699
Regulator	2704	2663	2673	2385	2375
General Governor	5408	5367	5377	5089	5079
High Overseer	800384	800343	800353	800065	800055

Fire - Sun

95	106	127	112	116	120
101	111	122	126	99	117
107	130	115	105	121	98
118	97	108	123	102	128
124	113	104	96	129	110
131	119	100	114	109	103

Earth - Sun

131	124	118	107	101	95
119	113	97	130	111	106
100	104	108	115	122	127
114	96	123	105	126	112
109	129	102	121	99	116
103	110	128	98	117	120

Air - Sun

103	109	114	100	119	131
110	129	96	104	113	124
128	102	123	108	97	118
98	121	105	115	130	107
117	99	126	122	111	101
120	116	112	127	106	95

Occult Encyclopedia of Magic Squares

Water - Sun

120	117	98	128	110	103
116	99	121	102	129	109
112	126	105	123	96	114
127	122	115	108	104	100
106	111	130	97	113	119
95	101	107	118	124	131

	Number	Angel Value (Arabic)	Angel Value (Hebrew)	Jinn Value (Arabic)	Jinn Value (Hebrew)
Usurper	95	54	64	136	126
Guide	131	90	100	172	162
Mystery	226	185	195	267	257
Adjuster	676	635	645	357	347
Leader	2028	1987	1997	1709	1699
Regulator	2704	2663	2673	2385	2375
General Governor	5408	5367	5377	5089	5079
High Overseer	708448	708407	708417	708129	708119

Fire - Venus

72	113	98	83	103	120	87
121	88	73	107	99	84	104
85	105	122	89	74	108	93
109	94	79	106	123	90	75
91	76	110	95	80	100	124
101	118	92	77	111	96	81
97	82	102	119	86	78	112

Earth - Venus

97	101	91	109	85	121	72
82	118	76	94	105	88	113
102	92	110	79	122	73	98
119	77	95	106	89	107	83
86	111	80	123	74	99	103
78	96	100	90	108	84	120
112	81	124	75	93	104	87

Occult Encyclopedia of Magic Squares

Air - Venus

112	78	86	119	102	82	97
81	96	111	77	92	118	101
124	100	80	95	110	76	91
75	90	123	106	79	94	109
93	108	74	89	122	105	85
104	84	99	107	73	88	121
87	120	103	83	98	113	72

Water - Venus

87	104	93	75	124	81	112
120	84	108	90	100	96	78
103	99	74	123	80	111	86
83	107	89	106	95	77	119
98	73	122	79	110	92	102
113	88	105	94	76	118	82
72	121	85	109	91	101	97

	Number	Angel Value (Arabic)	Angel Value (Hebrew)	Jinn Value (Arabic)	Jinn Value (Hebrew)
Usurper	72	31	41	113	103
Guide	124	83	93	165	155
Mystery	196	155	165	237	227
Adjuster	676	635	645	357	347
Leader	2028	1987	1997	1709	1699
Regulator	2704	2663	2673	2385	2375
General Governor	5408	5367	5377	5089	5079
High Overseer	670592	670551	670561	670273	670263

Occult Encyclopedia of Magic Squares

Fire - Mercury

53	69	114	98	87	103	84	68
61	77	106	90	95	111	76	60
104	88	67	83	70	54	97	113
112	96	59	75	78	62	89	105
82	66	85	101	116	100	55	71
74	58	93	109	108	92	63	79
99	115	72	56	65	81	102	86
91	107	80	64	57	73	110	94

Earth - Mercury

91	99	74	82	112	104	61	53
107	115	58	66	96	88	77	69
80	72	93	85	59	67	106	114
64	56	109	101	75	83	90	98
57	65	108	116	78	70	95	87
73	81	92	100	62	54	111	103
110	102	63	55	89	97	76	84
94	86	79	71	105	113	60	68

Air - Mercury

94	110	73	57	64	80	107	91
86	102	81	65	56	72	115	99
79	63	92	108	109	93	58	74
71	55	100	116	101	85	66	82
105	89	62	78	75	59	96	112
113	97	54	70	83	67	88	104
60	76	111	95	90	106	77	61
68	84	103	87	98	114	69	53

Water - Mercury

68	60	113	105	71	79	86	94
84	76	97	89	55	63	102	110
103	111	54	62	100	92	81	73
87	95	70	78	116	108	65	57
98	90	83	75	101	109	56	64
114	106	67	59	85	93	72	80
69	77	88	96	66	58	115	107
53	61	104	112	82	74	99	91

	Number	Angel Value (Arabic)	Angel Value (Hebrew)	Jinn Value (Arabic)	Jinn Value (Hebrew)
Usurper	53	12	22	94	84
Guide	116	75	85	157	147
Mystery	169	128	138	210	200
Adjuster	676	635	645	357	347
Leader	2028	1987	1997	1709	1699
Regulator	2704	2663	2673	2385	2375
General Governor	5408	5367	5377	5089	5079
High Overseer	627328	627287	627297	627009	626999

Fire - Moon

79	92	54	63	116	47	83	99	43
39	82	104	59	75	91	46	68	112
108	51	67	103	35	87	96	58	71
106	38	81	90	61	74	111	45	70
66	110	50	86	102	37	73	95	57
53	78	94	49	62	115	42	85	98
52	65	109	36	88	101	56	72	97
93	55	77	114	48	64	100	41	84
80	105	40	76	89	60	69	113	44

Earth - Moon

43	112	71	70	57	98	97	84	44
99	68	58	45	95	85	72	41	113
83	46	96	111	73	42	56	100	69
47	91	87	74	37	115	101	64	60
116	75	35	61	102	62	88	48	89
63	59	103	90	86	49	36	114	76
54	104	67	81	50	94	109	77	40
92	82	51	38	110	78	65	55	105
79	39	108	106	66	53	52	93	80

Occult Encyclopedia of Magic Squares

Air - Moon

44	113	69	60	89	76	40	105	80
84	41	100	64	48	114	77	55	93
97	72	56	101	88	36	109	65	52
98	85	42	115	62	49	94	78	53
57	95	73	37	102	86	50	110	66
70	45	111	74	61	90	81	38	106
71	58	96	87	35	103	67	51	108
112	68	46	91	75	59	104	82	39
43	99	83	47	116	63	54	92	79

Water - Moon

80	93	52	53	66	106	108	39	79
105	55	65	78	110	38	51	82	92
40	77	109	94	50	81	67	104	54
76	114	36	49	86	90	103	59	63
89	48	88	62	102	61	35	75	116
60	64	101	115	37	74	87	91	47
69	100	56	42	73	111	96	46	83
113	41	72	85	95	45	58	68	99
44	84	97	98	57	70	71	112	43

	Number	Angel Value (Arabic)	Angel Value (Hebrew)	Jinn Value (Arabic)	Jinn Value (Hebrew)
Usurper	35	354	4	76	66
Guide	116	75	85	157	147
Mystery	151	110	120	192	182
Adjuster	676	635	645	357	347
Leader	2028	1987	1997	1709	1699
Regulator	2704	2663	2673	2385	2375
General Governor	5408	5367	5377	5089	5079
High Overseer	627328	627287	627297	627009	626999

Fire - Saturn

18	36	43	81	72	111	65	57	89	104
29	93	86	77	113	102	20	62	48	46
44	49	73	112	103	88	37	25	66	79
50	75	110	105	38	84	92	33	22	67
63	109	107	42	53	76	80	90	35	21
70	27	28	95	83	59	55	45	100	114
82	64	24	31	97	52	40	101	117	68
96	85	60	19	30	47	98	116	71	54
106	39	51	58	26	34	115	69	87	91
118	99	94	56	61	23	74	78	41	32

Earth - Saturn

118	106	96	82	70	63	50	44	29	18
99	39	85	64	27	109	75	49	93	36
94	51	60	24	28	107	110	73	86	43
56	58	19	31	95	42	105	112	77	81
61	26	30	97	83	53	38	103	113	72
23	34	47	52	59	76	84	88	102	111
74	115	98	40	55	80	92	37	20	65
78	69	116	101	45	90	33	25	62	57
41	87	71	117	100	35	22	66	48	89
32	91	54	68	114	21	67	79	46	104

Air - Saturn

32	41	78	74	23	61	56	94	99	118
91	87	69	115	34	26	58	51	39	106
54	71	116	98	47	30	19	60	85	96
68	117	101	40	52	97	31	24	64	82
114	100	45	55	59	83	95	28	27	70
21	35	90	80	76	53	42	107	109	63
67	22	33	92	84	38	105	110	75	50
79	66	25	37	88	103	112	73	49	44
46	48	62	20	102	113	77	86	93	29
104	89	57	65	111	72	81	43	36	18

Water - Saturn

104	46	79	67	21	114	68	54	91	32
89	48	66	22	35	100	117	71	87	41
57	62	25	33	90	45	101	116	69	78
65	**20**	37	92	80	55	40	98	115	74
111	102	88	84	76	59	52	47	34	23
72	113	103	38	53	83	97	30	26	61
81	77	112	105	42	95	31	19	58	56
43	86	73	110	107	28	24	60	51	94
36	93	49	75	109	27	64	85	39	99
18	29	44	50	63	70	82	96	106	118

	Number	Angel Value (Arabic)	Angel Value (Hebrew)	Jinn Value (Arabic)	Jinn Value (Hebrew)
Usurper	18	337	347	59	49
Guide	118	77	87	159	149
Mystery	136	95	105	177	167
Adjuster	676	635	645	357	347
Leader	2028	1987	1997	1709	1699
Regulator	2704	2663	2673	2385	2375
General Governor	5408	5367	5377	5089	5079
High Overseer	638144	638103	638113	637825	637815

LORD OF TRIPLICITY BY NIGHT: POLAYAN (171)

נ	אי	ל	פ
79	31	14	47
13	48	78	32
29	81	49	12

נ	י	א	ל	פ
א	ל	פ	נ	י
פ	נ	י	א	ל
י	א	ל	פ	נ
ל	פ	נ	י	א

Fire - Saturn

58	53	60
59	57	55
54	61	56

Earth - Saturn

54	59	58
61	57	53
56	55	60

Air - Saturn

56	61	54
55	57	59
60	53	58

Water - Saturn

60	55	56
53	57	61
58	59	54

	Number	Angel Value (Arabic)	Angel Value (Hebrew)	Jinn Value (Arabic)	Jinn Value (Hebrew)
Usurper	53	12	22	94	84
Guide	61	20	30	102	92
Mystery	114	73	83	155	145
Adjuster	171	130	140	212	202
Leader	513	472	482	194	184
Regulator	684	643	653	365	355
General Governor	1368	1327	1337	1049	1039
High Overseer	83448	83407	83417	83129	83119

Fire - Jupiter

35	46	40	50
49	41	43	38
45	36	51	39
42	48	37	44

Air - Jupiter

44	37	48	42
39	51	36	45
38	43	41	49
50	40	46	35

Earth - Jupiter

42	45	49	35
48	36	41	46
37	51	43	40
44	39	38	50

Water - Jupiter

50	38	39	44
40	43	51	37
46	41	36	48
35	49	45	42

Occult Encyclopedia of Magic Squares

	Number	Angel Value (Arabic)	Angel Value (Hebrew)	Jinn Value (Arabic)	Jinn Value (Hebrew)
Usurper	35	354	4	76	66
Guide	51	10	20	92	82
Mystery	86	45	55	127	117
Adjuster	1368	1327	1337	1049	1039
Leader	4104	4063	4073	3785	3775
Regulator	5472	5431	5441	5153	5143
General Governor	10944	10903	10913	10625	10615
High Overseer	558144	558103	558113	557825	557815

Fire - Mars

22	47	40	34	28
35	29	23	43	41
44	37	36	30	24
31	25	45	38	32
39	33	27	26	46

Air - Mars

39	31	44	35	22
33	25	37	29	47
27	45	36	23	40
26	38	30	43	34
46	32	24	41	28

Earth - Mars

46	26	27	33	39
32	38	45	25	31
24	30	36	37	44
41	43	23	29	35
28	34	40	47	22

Water - Mars

28	41	24	32	46
34	43	30	38	26
40	23	36	45	27
47	29	37	25	33
22	35	44	31	39

	Number	Angel Value (Arabic)	Angel Value (Hebrew)	Jinn Value (Arabic)	Jinn Value (Hebrew)
Usurper	22	341	351	63	53
Guide	47	6	16	88	78
Mystery	69	28	38	110	100
Adjuster	171	130	140	212	202
Leader	513	472	482	194	184
Regulator	684	643	653	365	355
General Governor	1368	1327	1337	1049	1039
High Overseer	64296	64255	64265	63977	63967

Fire - Sun

11	22	42	28	32	36
17	27	38	41	15	33
23	45	31	21	37	14
34	13	24	39	18	43
40	29	20	12	44	26
46	35	16	30	25	19

Earth - Sun

46	40	34	23	17	11
35	29	13	45	27	22
16	20	24	31	38	42
30	12	39	21	41	28
25	44	18	37	15	32
19	26	43	14	33	36

Air - Sun

19	25	30	16	35	46
26	44	12	20	29	40
43	18	39	24	13	34
14	37	21	31	45	23
33	15	41	38	27	17
36	32	28	42	22	11

Water - Sun

36	33	14	43	26	19
32	15	37	18	44	25
28	41	21	39	12	30
42	38	31	24	20	16
22	27	45	13	29	35
11	17	23	34	40	46

	Number	Angel Value (Arabic)	Angel Value (Hebrew)	Jinn Value (Arabic)	Jinn Value (Hebrew)
Usurper	11	330	340	52	42
Guide	46	5	15	87	77
Mystery	57	16	26	98	88
Adjuster	171	130	140	212	202
Leader	513	472	482	194	184
Regulator	684	643	653	365	355
General Governor	1368	1327	1337	1049	1039
High Overseer	62928	62887	62897	62609	62599

ANGEL RULING 11ᵀᴴ HOUSE: ANSUEL (148)

אל	ו	ם	אן
50	61	9	28
8	29	49	62
59	52	30	7

ל	א	ו	ם	נ	א
נ	ם	ל	א	ו	א
ו	א	א	נ	ל	ם
א	נ	ם	ו	א	ל
ם	ל	נ	א	א	ו
א	ו	א	ל	ם	נ

Numerical Squares See Page: 353

583

ANGEL OF FIRST DECANATE: SASPAM (240)

צ	פ	ס	ס
59	61	83	37
82	38	58	62
59	61	39	81

צ	פ	ס	ס
ס	ס	פ	צ
פ	צ	ס	ס
ס	ס	צ	פ

Fire - Saturn

81	76	83
82	80	78
77	84	79

Earth - Saturn

77	82	81
84	80	76
79	78	83

Air - Saturn

79	84	77
78	80	82
83	76	81

Water - Saturn

83	78	79
76	80	84
81	82	77

	Number	Angel Value (Arabic)	Angel Value (Hebrew)	Jinn Value (Arabic)	Jinn Value (Hebrew)
Usurper	76	35	45	117	107
Guide	84	43	53	125	115
Mystery	160	119	129	201	191
Adjuster	240	199	209	281	271
Leader	720	679	689	401	391
Regulator	960	919	929	641	631
General Governor	1920	1879	1889	1601	1591
High Overseer	161280	161239	161249	160961	160951

Fire - Jupiter

52	63	57	68
67	58	60	55
62	53	69	56
59	66	54	61

Air - Jupiter

61	54	66	59
56	69	53	62
55	60	58	67
68	57	63	52

Earth - Jupiter

59	62	67	52
66	53	58	63
54	69	60	57
61	56	55	68

Water - Jupiter

68	55	56	61
57	60	69	54
63	58	53	66
52	67	62	59

	Number	Angel Value (Arabic)	Angel Value (Hebrew)	Jinn Value (Arabic)	Jinn Value (Hebrew)
Usurper	52	11	21	93	83
Guide	69	28	38	110	100
Mystery	121	80	90	162	152
Adjuster	1920	1879	1889	1601	1591
Leader	5760	5719	5729	5441	5431
Regulator	7680	7639	7649	7361	7351
General Governor	15360	15319	15329	15041	15031
High Overseer	1059840	1059799	1059809	1059521	1059511

Fire - Mars

36	60	54	48	42
49	43	37	56	55
57	51	50	44	38
45	39	58	52	46
53	47	41	40	59

Air - Mars

53	45	57	49	36
47	39	51	43	60
41	58	50	37	54
40	52	44	56	48
59	46	38	55	42

Earth - Mars

59	40	41	47	53
46	52	58	39	45
38	44	50	51	57
55	56	37	43	49
42	48	54	60	36

Water - Mars

42	55	38	46	59
48	56	44	52	40
54	37	50	58	41
60	43	51	39	47
36	49	57	45	53

Occult Encyclopedia of Magic Squares

	Number	Angel Value (Arabic)	Angel Value (Hebrew)	Jinn Value (Arabic)	Jinn Value (Hebrew)
Usurper	36	355	5	77	67
Guide	60	19	29	101	91
Mystery	96	55	65	137	127
Adjuster	240	199	209	281	271
Leader	720	679	689	401	391
Regulator	960	919	929	641	631
General Governor	1920	1879	1889	1601	1591
High Overseer	115200	115159	115169	114881	114871

Fire - Sun

22	33	56	39	43	47
28	38	49	55	26	44
34	59	42	32	48	25
45	24	35	50	29	57
51	40	31	23	58	37
60	46	27	41	36	30

Air - Sun

30	36	41	27	46	60
37	58	23	31	40	51
57	29	50	35	24	45
25	48	32	42	59	34
44	26	55	49	38	28
47	43	39	56	33	22

Earth - Sun

60	51	45	34	28	22
46	40	24	59	38	33
27	31	35	42	49	56
41	23	50	32	55	39
36	58	29	48	26	43
30	37	57	25	44	47

Water - Sun

47	44	25	57	37	30
43	26	48	29	58	36
39	55	32	50	23	41
56	49	42	35	31	27
33	38	59	24	40	46
22	28	34	45	51	60

Occult Encyclopedia of Magic Squares

	Number	Angel Value (Arabic)	Angel Value (Hebrew)	Jinn Value (Arabic)	Jinn Value (Hebrew)
Usurper	22	341	351	63	53
Guide	60	19	29	101	91
Mystery	82	41	51	123	113
Adjuster	240	199	209	281	271
Leader	720	679	689	401	391
Regulator	960	919	929	641	631
General Governor	1920	1879	1889	1601	1591
High Overseer	115200	115159	115169	114881	114871

Fire - Venus

10	51	36	21	41	56	25
57	26	11	45	37	22	42
23	43	58	27	12	46	31
47	32	17	44	59	28	13
29	14	48	33	18	38	60
39	54	30	15	49	34	19
35	20	40	55	24	16	50

Earth - Venus

35	39	29	47	23	57	10
20	54	14	32	43	26	51
40	30	48	17	58	11	36
55	15	33	44	27	45	21
24	49	18	59	12	37	41
16	34	38	28	46	22	56
50	19	60	13	31	42	25

Air - Venus

50	16	24	55	40	20	35
19	34	49	15	30	54	39
60	38	18	33	48	14	29
13	28	59	44	17	32	47
31	46	12	27	58	43	23
42	22	37	45	11	26	57
25	56	41	21	36	51	10

Water - Venus

25	42	31	13	60	19	50
56	22	46	28	38	34	16
41	37	12	59	18	49	24
21	45	27	44	33	15	55
36	11	58	17	48	30	40
51	26	43	32	14	54	20
10	57	23	47	29	39	35

	Number	Angel Value (Arabic)	Angel Value (Hebrew)	Jinn Value (Arabic)	Jinn Value (Hebrew)
Usurper	10	329	339	51	41
Guide	60	19	29	101	91
Mystery	70	29	39	111	101
Adjuster	240	199	209	281	271
Leader	720	679	689	401	391
Regulator	960	919	929	641	631
General Governor	1920	1879	1889	1601	1591
High Overseer	115200	115159	115169	114881	114871

ANGEL OF FIRST QUINANCE: ANIEL (92)

ל	א	י	אנ
50	11	4	27
3	28	49	12
9	52	29	2

ל	א	י	נ	א
י	נ	א	ל	א
א	ל	א	י	נ
א	י	נ	א	ל

Fire - Jupiter

15	26	20	31
30	21	23	18
25	16	32	19
22	29	17	24

Air - Jupiter

24	17	29	22
19	32	16	25
18	23	21	30
31	20	26	15

Earth - Jupiter

22	25	30	15
29	16	21	26
17	32	23	20
24	19	18	31

Water - Jupiter

31	18	19	24
20	23	32	17
26	21	16	29
15	30	25	22

	Number	Angel Value (Arabic)	Angel Value (Hebrew)	Jinn Value (Arabic)	Jinn Value (Hebrew)
Usurper	15	334	344	56	46
Guide	32	351	1	73	63
Mystery	47	6	16	88	78
Adjuster	736	695	705	417	407
Leader	2208	2167	2177	1889	1879
Regulator	2944	2903	2913	2625	2615
General Governor	5888	5847	5857	5569	5559
High Overseer	188416	188375	188385	188097	188087

Fire - Mars

6	32	24	18	12
19	13	7	28	25
29	21	20	14	8
15	9	30	22	16
23	17	11	10	31

Air - Mars

23	15	29	19	6
17	9	21	13	32
11	30	20	7	24
10	22	14	28	18
31	16	8	25	12

Earth - Mars

31	10	11	17	23
16	22	30	9	15
8	14	20	21	29
25	28	7	13	19
12	18	24	32	6

Water - Mars

12	25	8	16	31
18	28	14	22	10
24	7	20	30	11
32	13	21	9	17
6	19	29	15	23

	Number	Angel Value (Arabic)	Angel Value (Hebrew)	Jinn Value (Arabic)	Jinn Value (Hebrew)
Usurper	6	325	335	47	37
Guide	32	351	1	73	63
Mystery	38	357	7	79	69
Adjuster	92	51	61	133	123
Leader	276	235	245	317	307
Regulator	368	327	337	49	39
General Governor	736	695	705	417	407
High Overseer	23552	23511	23521	23233	23223

ANGEL OF SECOND QUINANCE: CHAMIAH (133)

יה	מ	ע	ח
7	71	43	12
42	13	6	72
69	9	14	41

ח	י	מ	ע	ח
מ	ע	ח	ה	י
ח	ה	י	מ	ע
י	מ	ע	ה	ה
ע	ח	ה	י	מ

Fire - Jupiter

25	36	30	42
41	31	33	28
35	26	43	29
32	40	27	34

Air - Jupiter

34	27	40	32
29	43	26	35
28	33	31	41
42	30	36	25

Earth - Jupiter

32	35	41	25
40	26	31	36
27	43	33	30
34	29	28	42

Water - Jupiter

42	28	29	34
30	33	43	27
36	31	26	40
25	41	35	32

Occult Encyclopedia of Magic Squares

	Number	Angel Value (Arabic)	Angel Value (Hebrew)	Jinn Value (Arabic)	Jinn Value (Hebrew)
Usurper	25	344	354	66	56
Guide	43	2	12	84	74
Mystery	68	27	37	109	99
Adjuster	1064	1023	1033	745	735
Leader	3192	3151	3161	2873	2863
Regulator	4256	4215	4225	3937	3927
General Governor	8512	8471	8481	8193	8183
High Overseer	366016	365975	365985	365697	365687

Fire - Mars

14	41	32	26	20
27	21	15	37	33
38	29	28	22	16
23	17	39	30	24
31	25	19	18	40

Air - Mars

31	23	38	27	14
25	17	29	21	41
19	39	28	15	32
18	30	22	37	26
40	24	16	33	20

Earth - Mars

40	18	19	25	31
24	30	39	17	23
16	22	28	29	38
33	37	15	21	27
20	26	32	41	14

Water - Mars

20	33	16	24	40
26	37	22	30	18
32	15	28	39	19
41	21	29	17	25
14	27	38	23	31

	Number	Angel Value (Arabic)	Angel Value (Hebrew)	Jinn Value (Arabic)	Jinn Value (Hebrew)
Usurper	14	333	343	55	45
Guide	41	360	10	82	72
Mystery	55	14	24	96	86
Adjuster	133	92	102	174	164
Leader	399	358	368	80	70
Regulator	532	491	501	213	203
General Governor	1064	1023	1033	745	735
High Overseer	43624	43583	43593	43305	43295

Occult Encyclopedia of Magic Squares

Fire - Sun

4	15	39	21	25	29
10	20	31	38	8	26
16	42	24	14	30	7
27	6	17	32	11	40
33	22	13	5	41	19
43	28	9	23	18	12

Air - Sun

12	18	23	9	28	43
19	41	5	13	22	33
40	11	32	17	6	27
7	30	14	24	42	16
26	8	38	31	20	10
29	25	21	39	15	4

Earth - Sun

43	33	27	16	10	4
28	22	6	42	20	15
9	13	17	24	31	39
23	5	32	14	38	21
18	41	11	30	8	25
12	19	40	7	26	29

Water - Sun

29	26	7	40	19	12
25	8	30	11	41	18
21	38	14	32	5	23
39	31	24	17	13	9
15	20	42	6	22	28
4	10	16	27	33	43

	Number	Angel Value (Arabic)	Angel Value (Hebrew)	Jinn Value (Arabic)	Jinn Value (Hebrew)
Usurper	4	323	333	45	35
Guide	43	2	12	84	74
Mystery	47	6	16	88	78
Adjuster	133	92	102	174	164
Leader	399	358	368	80	70
Regulator	532	491	501	213	203
General Governor	1064	1023	1033	745	735
High Overseer	45752	45711	45721	45433	45423

ANGEL OF SECOND DECANATE: ABDARON (263)

נ	ו	רד	אב
30	205	9	47
8	48	29	206
203	32	49	7

נ	ו	ר	ד	ב	א
ב	ד	נ	א	ר	ו
ר	א	ו	ב	נ	ד
א	ב	ד	ר	ו	נ
ד	נ	ב	ו	א	ר
ו	ר	א	נ	ד	ב

Numerical Squares See Page: 411

ANGEL OF THIRD QUINANCE: REHAEL (306)

אל	ו	ע	ר
199	71	9	28
8	29	198	72
69	201	30	7

ל	א	ו	ע	ר
ו	ע	ר	ל	א
ר	ל	א	ו	ע
א	ו	ע	ר	ל
ע	ר	ל	א	ו

Fire - Saturn			Earth - Saturn			Air - Saturn			Water - Saturn		
103	98	105	99	104	103	101	106	99	105	100	101
104	102	100	106	102	98	100	102	104	98	102	106
99	106	101	101	100	105	105	98	103	103	104	99

	Number	Angel Value (Arabic)	Angel Value (Hebrew)	Jinn Value (Arabic)	Jinn Value (Hebrew)
Usurper	98	57	67	139	129
Guide	106	65	75	147	137
Mystery	204	163	173	245	235
Adjuster	306	265	275	347	337
Leader	918	877	887	599	589
Regulator	1224	1183	1193	905	895
General Governor	2448	2407	2417	2129	2119
High Overseer	259488	259447	259457	259169	259159

Fire - Jupiter

69	80	74	83
82	75	77	72
79	70	84	73
76	81	71	78

Air - Jupiter

78	71	81	76
73	84	70	79
72	77	75	82
83	74	80	69

Earth - Jupiter

76	79	82	69
81	70	75	80
71	84	77	74
78	73	72	83

Water - Jupiter

83	72	73	78
74	77	84	71
80	75	70	81
69	82	79	76

	Number	Angel Value (Arabic)	Angel Value (Hebrew)	Jinn Value (Arabic)	Jinn Value (Hebrew)
Usurper	69	28	38	110	100
Guide	84	43	53	125	115
Mystery	153	112	122	194	184
Adjuster	2448	2407	2417	2129	2119
Leader	7344	7303	7313	7025	7015
Regulator	9792	9751	9761	9473	9463
General Governor	19584	19543	19553	19265	19255
High Overseer	1645056	1645015	1645025	1644737	1644727

Fire - Mars

49	74	67	61	55
62	56	50	70	68
71	64	63	57	51
58	52	72	65	59
66	60	54	53	73

Air - Mars

66	58	71	62	49
60	52	64	56	74
54	72	63	50	67
53	65	57	70	61
73	59	51	68	55

Earth - Mars

73	53	54	60	66
59	65	72	52	58
51	57	63	64	71
68	70	50	56	62
55	61	67	74	49

Water - Mars

55	68	51	59	73
61	70	57	65	53
67	50	63	72	54
74	56	64	52	60
49	62	71	58	66

	Number	Angel Value (Arabic)	Angel Value (Hebrew)	Jinn Value (Arabic)	Jinn Value (Hebrew)
Usurper	49	8	18	90	80
Guide	74	33	43	115	105
Mystery	123	82	92	164	154
Adjuster	306	265	275	347	337
Leader	918	877	887	599	589
Regulator	1224	1183	1193	905	895
General Governor	2448	2407	2417	2129	2119
High Overseer	181152	181111	181121	180833	180823

Occult Encyclopedia of Magic Squares

Fire - Sun

33	44	67	50	54	58
39	49	60	66	37	55
45	70	53	43	59	36
56	35	46	61	40	68
62	51	42	34	69	48
71	57	38	52	47	41

Air - Sun

41	47	52	38	57	71
48	69	34	42	51	62
68	40	61	46	35	56
36	59	43	53	70	45
55	37	66	60	49	39
58	54	50	67	44	33

Earth - Sun

71	62	56	45	39	33
57	51	35	70	49	44
38	42	46	53	60	67
52	34	61	43	66	50
47	69	40	59	37	54
41	48	68	36	55	58

Water - Sun

58	55	36	68	48	41
54	37	59	40	69	47
50	66	43	61	34	52
67	60	53	46	42	38
44	49	70	35	51	57
33	39	45	56	62	71

	Number	Angel Value (Arabic)	Angel Value (Hebrew)	Jinn Value (Arabic)	Jinn Value (Hebrew)
Usurper	33	352	2	74	64
Guide	71	30	40	112	102
Mystery	104	63	73	145	135
Adjuster	306	265	275	347	337
Leader	918	877	887	599	589
Regulator	1224	1183	1193	905	895
General Governor	2448	2407	2417	2129	2119
High Overseer	173808	173767	173777	173489	173479

Occult Encyclopedia of Magic Squares

Fire - Venus

19	60	45	30	50	68	34
69	35	20	54	46	31	51
32	52	70	36	21	55	40
56	41	26	53	71	37	22
38	23	57	42	27	47	72
48	66	39	24	58	43	28
44	29	49	67	33	25	59

Air - Venus

59	25	33	67	49	29	44
28	43	58	24	39	66	48
72	47	27	42	57	23	38
22	37	71	53	26	41	56
40	55	21	36	70	52	32
51	31	46	54	20	35	69
34	68	50	30	45	60	19

Earth - Venus

44	48	38	56	32	69	19
29	66	23	41	52	35	60
49	39	57	26	70	20	45
67	24	42	53	36	54	30
33	58	27	71	21	46	50
25	43	47	37	55	31	68
59	28	72	22	40	51	34

Water - Venus

34	51	40	22	72	28	59
68	31	55	37	47	43	25
50	46	21	71	27	58	33
30	54	36	53	42	24	67
45	20	70	26	57	39	49
60	35	52	41	23	66	29
19	69	32	56	38	48	44

	Number	Angel Value (Arabic)	Angel Value (Hebrew)	Jinn Value (Arabic)	Jinn Value (Hebrew)
Usurper	19	338	348	60	50
Guide	72	31	41	113	103
Mystery	91	50	60	132	122
Adjuster	306	265	275	347	337
Leader	918	877	887	599	589
Regulator	1224	1183	1193	905	895
General Governor	2448	2407	2417	2129	2119
High Overseer	176256	176215	176225	175937	175927

Fire - Mercury

6	22	73	51	40	56	37	21
14	30	59	43	48	70	29	13
57	41	20	36	23	7	50	72
71	49	12	28	31	15	42	58
35	19	38	54	75	53	8	24
27	11	46	68	61	45	16	32
52	74	25	9	18	34	55	39
44	60	33	17	10	26	69	47

Earth - Mercury

44	52	27	35	71	57	14	6
60	74	11	19	49	41	30	22
33	25	46	38	12	20	59	73
17	9	68	54	28	36	43	51
10	18	61	75	31	23	48	40
26	34	45	53	15	7	70	56
69	55	16	8	42	50	29	37
47	39	32	24	58	72	13	21

Air - Mercury

47	69	26	10	17	33	60	44
39	55	34	18	9	25	74	52
32	16	45	61	68	46	11	27
24	8	53	75	54	38	19	35
58	42	15	31	28	12	49	71
72	50	7	23	36	20	41	57
13	29	70	48	43	59	30	14
21	37	56	40	51	73	22	6

Water - Mercury

21	13	72	58	24	32	39	47
37	29	50	42	8	16	55	69
56	70	7	15	53	45	34	26
40	48	23	31	75	61	18	10
51	43	36	28	54	68	9	17
73	59	20	12	38	46	25	33
22	30	41	49	19	11	74	60
6	14	57	71	35	27	52	44

	Number	Angel Value (Arabic)	Angel Value (Hebrew)	Jinn Value (Arabic)	Jinn Value (Hebrew)
Usurper	6	325	335	47	37
Guide	75	34	44	116	106
Mystery	81	40	50	122	112
Adjuster	306	265	275	347	337
Leader	918	877	887	599	589
Regulator	1224	1183	1193	905	895
General Governor	2448	2407	2417	2129	2119
High Overseer	183600	183559	183569	183281	183271

ANGEL OF FOURTH QUINANCE: YEYAZEL (58)

אל	ו	י	י
9	11	10	28
9	29	8	12
9	11	30	8

ל	א	ו	י	י
ו	י	י	ל	א
י	ל	א	ו	י
א	ו	י	י	ל
י	י	ל	א	ו

Numerical Squares See Page: 549

ANGEL OF THIRD DECANATE: GERODIEL (254)

יאל	וד	ר	ג
2	201	13	38
12	39	1	202
199	4	40	11

ל	א	י	ד	ו	ר	ג
י	ד	ו	ר	ג	ל	א
ו	ר	ג	ל	א	י	ד
ג	ל	א	י	ד	ו	ר
א	י	ד	ו	ר	ג	ל
ד	ו	ר	ג	ל	א	י
ר	ג	ל	א	י	ד	ו

Numerical Squares See Page: 355

ANGEL OF FIFTH QUINANCE: HAHAHEL (46)

אל	ה	ה	ה
4	6	8	28
7	29	3	7
4	6	30	6

ל	א	ה	ה	ה
ה	ה	ה	ל	א
ה	ל	א	ה	ה
א	ה	ה	ה	ל
ה	ה	ל	א	ה

Numerical Squares See Page: 90

ANGEL OF SIX QUINANCE: MICHAEL (101)

אל	ב	י	מ
39	11	23	28
22	29	38	12
9	41	30	21

ל	א	ב	י	מ
ב	י	מ	ל	א
מ	ל	א	ב	י
א	ב	י	מ	ל
י	מ	ל	א	ב

Numerical Squares See Page: 247

PISCES

SIGN PISCES: DAGIM (57)

מ	י	ג	ד
3	4	13	37
12	38	2	5
2	5	39	11

מ	י	ג	ד
ד	ג	י	מ
י	מ	ד	ג
ג	ד	מ	י

Numerical Squares See Page: 436

ARCHANGEL OF PISCES: AMNITZIEL (232)

יאל	צ	ני	אמ
40	61	93	38
92	39	39	62
59	42	40	91

א	י	צ	י	א	ל	ג	מ
י	צ	י	א	מ	א	ל	ג
ג	י	א	מ	צ	י	א	ל
צ	ל	א	י	ג	מ	א	י
מ	ג	ל	א	י	א	י	צ
א	מ	ג	ל	א	י	צ	י
י	א	מ	ג	ל	צ	י	א

ל	א	י	צ	י	ג	מ	א

Occult Encyclopedia of Magic Squares

Fire - Jupiter

50	61	55	66
65	56	58	53
60	51	67	54
57	64	52	59

Air - Jupiter

59	52	64	57
54	67	51	60
53	58	56	65
66	55	61	50

Earth - Jupiter

57	60	65	50
64	51	56	61
52	67	58	55
59	54	53	66

Water - Jupiter

66	53	54	59
55	58	67	52
61	56	51	64
50	65	60	57

	Number	Angel Value (Arabic)	Angel Value (Hebrew)	Jinn Value (Arabic)	Jinn Value (Hebrew)
Usurper	50	9	19	91	81
Guide	67	26	36	108	98
Mystery	117	76	86	158	148
Adjuster	1856	1815	1825	1537	1527
Leader	5568	5527	5537	5249	5239
Regulator	7424	7383	7393	7105	7095
General Governor	14848	14807	14817	14529	14519
High Overseer	994816	994775	994785	994497	994487

Fire - Mars

34	60	52	46	40
47	41	35	56	53
57	49	48	42	36
43	37	58	50	44
51	45	39	38	59

Air - Mars

51	43	57	47	34
45	37	49	41	60
39	58	48	35	52
38	50	42	56	46
59	44	36	53	40

Earth - Mars

59	38	39	45	51
44	50	58	37	43
36	42	48	49	57
53	56	35	41	47
40	46	52	60	34

Water - Mars

40	53	36	44	59
46	56	42	50	38
52	35	48	58	39
60	41	49	37	45
34	47	57	43	51

	Number	Angel Value (Arabic)	Angel Value (Hebrew)	Jinn Value (Arabic)	Jinn Value (Hebrew)
Usurper	34	353	3	75	65
Guide	60	19	29	101	91
Mystery	94	53	63	135	125
Adjuster	232	191	201	273	263
Leader	696	655	665	377	367
Regulator	928	887	897	609	599
General Governor	1856	1815	1825	1537	1527
High Overseer	111360	111319	111329	111041	111031

Fire - Sun

21	32	53	38	42	46
27	37	48	52	25	43
33	56	41	31	47	24
44	23	34	49	28	54
50	39	30	22	55	36
57	45	26	40	35	29

Air - Sun

29	35	40	26	45	57
36	55	22	30	39	50
54	28	49	34	23	44
24	47	31	41	56	33
43	25	52	48	37	27
46	42	38	53	32	21

Earth - Sun

57	50	44	33	27	21
45	39	23	56	37	32
26	30	34	41	48	53
40	22	49	31	52	38
35	55	28	47	25	42
29	36	54	24	43	46

Water - Sun

46	43	24	54	36	29
42	25	47	28	55	35
38	52	31	49	22	40
53	48	41	34	30	26
32	37	56	23	39	45
21	27	33	44	50	57

	Number	Angel Value (Arabic)	Angel Value (Hebrew)	Jinn Value (Arabic)	Jinn Value (Hebrew)
Usurper	21	340	350	62	52
Guide	57	16	26	98	88
Mystery	78	37	47	119	109
Adjuster	232	191	201	273	263
Leader	696	655	665	377	367
Regulator	928	887	897	609	599
General Governor	1856	1815	1825	1537	1527
High Overseer	105792	105751	105761	105473	105463

Fire - Venus

9	50	35	20	40	54	24
55	25	10	44	36	21	41
22	42	56	26	11	45	30
46	31	16	43	57	27	12
28	13	47	32	17	37	58
38	52	29	14	48	33	18
34	19	39	53	23	15	49

Earth - Venus

34	38	28	46	22	55	9
19	52	13	31	42	25	50
39	29	47	16	56	10	35
53	14	32	43	26	44	20
23	48	17	57	11	36	40
15	33	37	27	45	21	54
49	18	58	12	30	41	24

Air - Venus

49	15	23	53	39	19	34
18	33	48	14	29	52	38
58	37	17	32	47	13	28
12	27	57	43	16	31	46
30	45	11	26	56	42	22
41	21	36	44	10	25	55
24	54	40	20	35	50	9

Water - Venus

24	41	30	12	58	18	49
54	21	45	27	37	33	15
40	36	11	57	17	48	23
20	44	26	43	32	14	53
35	10	56	16	47	29	39
50	25	42	31	13	52	19
9	55	22	46	28	38	34

	Number	Angel Value (Arabic)	Angel Value (Hebrew)	Jinn Value (Arabic)	Jinn Value (Hebrew)
Usurper	9	328	338	50	40
Guide	58	17	27	99	89
Mystery	67	26	36	108	98
Adjuster	232	191	201	273	263
Leader	696	655	665	377	367
Regulator	928	887	897	609	599
General Governor	1856	1815	1825	1537	1527
High Overseer	107648	107607	107617	107329	107319

ANGEL OF PISCES: VAKABIEL (69)

יאל	ב	כ	ו
5	21	5	38
4	39	4	22
19	7	40	3

ל	א	י	ב	כ	ו
ב	ב	ל	ו	י	א
י	ו	א	ב	ל	כ
ו	כ	ב	י	א	ל
כ	ל	כ	א	ו	י
א	י	ו	ל	ב	כ

Fire - Saturn

24	19	26
25	23	21
20	27	22

Earth - Saturn

20	25	24
27	23	19
22	21	26

Air - Saturn

22	27	20
21	23	25
26	19	24

Water - Saturn

26	21	22
19	23	27
24	25	20

Occult Encyclopedia of Magic Squares

	Number	Angel Value (Arabic)	Angel Value (Hebrew)	Jinn Value (Arabic)	Jinn Value (Hebrew)
Usurper	19	338	348	60	50
Guide	27	346	356	68	58
Mystery	46	5	15	87	77
Adjuster	69	28	38	110	100
Leader	207	166	176	248	238
Regulator	276	235	245	317	307
General Governor	552	511	521	233	223
High Overseer	14904	14863	14873	14585	14575

Fire - Jupiter

9	20	14	26
25	15	17	12
19	10	27	13
16	24	11	18

Air - Jupiter

18	11	24	16
13	27	10	19
12	17	15	25
26	14	20	9

Earth - Jupiter

16	19	25	9
24	10	15	20
11	27	17	14
18	13	12	26

Water - Jupiter

26	12	13	18
14	17	27	11
20	15	10	24
9	25	19	16

	Number	Angel Value (Arabic)	Angel Value (Hebrew)	Jinn Value (Arabic)	Jinn Value (Hebrew)
Usurper	9	328	338	50	40
Guide	27	346	356	68	58
Mystery	36	355	5	77	67
Adjuster	552	511	521	233	223
Leader	1656	1615	1625	1337	1327
Regulator	2208	2167	2177	1889	1879
General Governor	4416	4375	4385	4097	4087
High Overseer	119232	119191	119201	118913	118903

Fire - Mars

1	29	19	13	7
14	8	2	25	20
26	16	15	9	3
10	4	27	17	11
18	12	6	5	28

Air - Mars

18	10	26	14	1
12	4	16	8	29
6	27	15	2	19
5	17	9	25	13
28	11	3	20	7

Earth - Mars

28	5	6	12	18
11	17	27	4	10
3	9	15	16	26
20	25	2	8	14
7	13	19	29	1

Water - Mars

7	20	3	11	28
13	25	9	17	5
19	2	15	27	6
29	8	16	4	12
1	14	26	10	18

	Number	Angel Value (Arabic)	Angel Value (Hebrew)	Jinn Value (Arabic)	Jinn Value (Hebrew)
Usurper	1	320	330	42	32
Guide	29	348	358	70	60
Mystery	30	349	359	71	61
Adjuster	69	28	38	110	100
Leader	207	166	176	248	238
Regulator	276	235	245	317	307
General Governor	552	511	521	233	223
High Overseer	16008	15967	15977	15689	15679

LORD OF TRIPLICITY BY DAY: RAMARA (441)

א	ר	מ	ר
199	41	199	2
202	3	198	38
39	197	4	201

א	ר	מ	ר
ר	מ	ר	א
ר	א	ר	מ
מ	ר	א	ר

Occult Encyclopedia of Magic Squares

Fire - Saturn

148	143	150
149	147	145
144	151	146

Air - Saturn

146	151	144
145	147	149
150	143	148

Earth - Saturn

144	149	148
151	147	143
146	145	150

Water - Saturn

150	145	146
143	147	151
148	149	144

	Number	Angel Value (Arabic)	Angel Value (Hebrew)	Jinn Value (Arabic)	Jinn Value (Hebrew)
Usurper	143	102	112	184	174
Guide	151	110	120	192	182
Mystery	294	253	263	335	325
Adjuster	441	400	410	122	112
Leader	1323	1282	1292	1004	994
Regulator	1764	1723	1733	1445	1435
General Governor	3528	3487	3497	3209	3199
High Overseer	532728	532687	532697	532409	532399

Fire - Jupiter

102	113	107	119
118	108	110	105
112	103	120	106
109	117	104	111

Air - Jupiter

111	104	117	109
106	120	103	112
105	110	108	118
119	107	113	102

Earth - Jupiter

109	112	118	102
117	103	108	113
104	120	110	107
111	106	105	119

Water - Jupiter

119	105	106	111
107	110	120	104
113	108	103	117
102	118	112	109

Occult Encyclopedia of Magic Squares

	Number	Angel Value (Arabic)	Angel Value (Hebrew)	Jinn Value (Arabic)	Jinn Value (Hebrew)
Usurper	102	61	71	143	133
Guide	120	79	89	161	151
Mystery	222	181	191	263	253
Adjuster	3528	3487	3497	3209	3199
Leader	10584	10543	10553	10265	10255
Regulator	14112	14071	14081	13793	13783
General Governor	28224	28183	28193	27905	27895
High Overseer	3386880	3386839	3386849	3386561	3386551

Fire - Mars

76	101	94	88	82
89	83	77	97	95
98	91	90	84	78
85	79	99	92	86
93	87	81	80	100

Air - Mars

93	85	98	89	76
87	79	91	83	101
81	99	90	77	94
80	92	84	97	88
100	86	78	95	82

Earth - Mars

100	80	81	87	93
86	92	99	79	85
78	84	90	91	98
95	97	77	83	89
82	88	94	101	76

Water - Mars

82	95	78	86	100
88	97	84	92	80
94	77	90	99	81
101	83	91	79	87
76	89	98	85	93

	Number	Angel Value (Arabic)	Angel Value (Hebrew)	Jinn Value (Arabic)	Jinn Value (Hebrew)
Usurper	76	35	45	117	107
Guide	101	60	70	142	132
Mystery	177	136	146	218	208
Adjuster	441	400	410	122	112
Leader	1323	1282	1292	1004	994
Regulator	1764	1723	1733	1445	1435
General Governor	3528	3487	3497	3209	3199
High Overseer	356328	356287	356297	356009	355999

Occult Encyclopedia of Magic Squares

Fire - Sun

56	67	87	73	77	81
62	72	83	86	60	78
68	90	76	66	82	59
79	58	69	84	63	88
85	74	65	57	89	71
91	80	61	75	70	64

Air - Sun

64	70	75	61	80	91
71	89	57	65	74	85
88	63	84	69	58	79
59	82	66	76	90	68
78	60	86	83	72	62
81	77	73	87	67	56

Earth - Sun

91	85	79	68	62	56
80	74	58	90	72	67
61	65	69	76	83	87
75	57	84	66	86	73
70	89	63	82	60	77
64	71	88	59	78	81

Water - Sun

81	78	59	88	71	64
77	60	82	63	89	70
73	86	66	84	57	75
87	83	76	69	65	61
67	72	90	58	74	80
56	62	68	79	85	91

	Number	Angel Value (Arabic)	Angel Value (Hebrew)	Jinn Value (Arabic)	Jinn Value (Hebrew)
Usurper	56	15	25	97	87
Guide	91	50	60	132	122
Mystery	147	106	116	188	178
Adjuster	441	400	410	122	112
Leader	1323	1282	1292	1004	994
Regulator	1764	1723	1733	1445	1435
General Governor	3528	3487	3497	3209	3199
High Overseer	321048	321007	321017	320729	320719

Occult Encyclopedia of Magic Squares

Fire - Venus

39	80	65	50	70	83	54
84	55	40	74	66	51	71
52	72	85	56	41	75	60
76	61	46	73	86	57	42
58	43	77	62	47	67	87
68	81	59	44	78	63	48
64	49	69	82	53	45	79

Air - Venus

79	45	53	82	69	49	64
48	63	78	44	59	81	68
87	67	47	62	77	43	58
42	57	86	73	46	61	76
60	75	41	56	85	72	52
71	51	66	74	40	55	84
54	83	70	50	65	80	39

Earth - Venus

64	68	58	76	52	84	39
49	81	43	61	72	55	80
69	59	77	46	85	40	65
82	44	62	73	56	74	50
53	78	47	86	41	66	70
45	63	67	57	75	51	83
79	48	87	42	60	71	54

Water - Venus

54	71	60	42	87	48	79
83	51	75	57	67	63	45
70	66	41	86	47	78	53
50	74	56	73	62	44	82
65	40	85	46	77	59	69
80	55	72	61	43	81	49
39	84	52	76	58	68	64

	Number	Angel Value (Arabic)	Angel Value (Hebrew)	Jinn Value (Arabic)	Jinn Value (Hebrew)
Usurper	39	358	8	80	70
Guide	87	46	56	128	118
Mystery	126	85	95	167	157
Adjuster	441	400	410	122	112
Leader	1323	1282	1292	1004	994
Regulator	1764	1723	1733	1445	1435
General Governor	3528	3487	3497	3209	3199
High Overseer	306936	306895	306905	306617	306607

Fire - Mercury

23	39	89	68	57	73	54	38
31	47	76	60	65	86	46	30
74	58	37	53	40	24	67	88
87	66	29	45	48	32	59	75
52	36	55	71	91	70	25	41
44	28	63	84	78	62	33	49
69	90	42	26	35	51	72	56
61	77	50	34	27	43	85	64

Earth - Mercury

61	69	44	52	87	74	31	23
77	90	28	36	66	58	47	39
50	42	63	55	29	37	76	89
34	26	84	71	45	53	60	68
27	35	78	91	48	40	65	57
43	51	62	70	32	24	86	73
85	72	33	25	59	67	46	54
64	56	49	41	75	88	30	38

Air - Mercury

64	85	43	27	34	50	77	61
56	72	51	35	26	42	90	69
49	33	62	78	84	63	28	44
41	25	70	91	71	55	36	52
75	59	32	48	45	29	66	87
88	67	24	40	53	37	58	74
30	46	86	65	60	76	47	31
38	54	73	57	68	89	39	23

Water - Mercury

38	30	88	75	41	49	56	64
54	46	67	59	25	33	72	85
73	86	24	32	70	62	51	43
57	65	40	48	91	78	35	27
68	60	53	45	71	84	26	34
89	76	37	29	55	63	42	50
39	47	58	66	36	28	90	77
23	31	74	87	52	44	69	61

Occult Encyclopedia of Magic Squares

	Number	Angel Value (Arabic)	Angel Value (Hebrew)	Jinn Value (Arabic)	Jinn Value (Hebrew)
Usurper	23	342	352	64	54
Guide	91	50	60	132	122
Mystery	114	73	83	155	145
Adjuster	441	400	410	122	112
Leader	1323	1282	1292	1004	994
Regulator	1764	1723	1733	1445	1435
General Governor	3528	3487	3497	3209	3199
High Overseer	321048	321007	321017	320729	320719

Fire - Moon

53	66	28	37	89	21	57	73	17
13	56	78	33	49	65	20	42	85
81	25	41	77	9	61	70	32	45
80	12	55	64	35	48	84	19	44
40	83	24	60	76	11	47	69	31
27	52	68	23	36	88	16	59	72
26	39	82	10	62	75	30	46	71
67	29	51	87	22	38	74	15	58
54	79	14	50	63	34	43	86	18

Earth - Moon

17	85	45	44	31	72	71	58	18
73	42	32	19	69	59	46	15	86
57	20	70	84	47	16	30	74	43
21	65	61	48	11	88	75	38	34
89	49	9	35	76	36	62	22	63
37	33	77	64	60	23	10	87	50
28	78	41	55	24	68	82	51	14
66	56	25	12	83	52	39	29	79
53	13	81	80	40	27	26	67	54

Occult Encyclopedia of Magic Squares

Air - Moon

18	86	43	34	63	50	14	79	54
58	15	74	38	22	87	51	29	67
71	46	30	75	62	10	82	39	26
72	59	16	88	36	23	68	52	27
31	69	47	11	76	60	24	83	40
44	19	84	48	35	64	55	12	80
45	32	70	61	9	77	41	25	81
85	42	20	65	49	33	78	56	13
17	73	57	21	89	37	28	66	53

Water - Moon

54	67	26	27	40	80	81	13	53
79	29	39	52	83	12	25	56	66
14	51	82	68	24	55	41	78	28
50	87	10	23	60	64	77	33	37
63	22	62	36	76	35	9	49	89
34	38	75	88	11	48	61	65	21
43	74	30	16	47	84	70	20	57
86	15	46	59	69	19	32	42	73
18	58	71	72	31	44	45	85	17

	Number	Angel Value (Arabic)	Angel Value (Hebrew)	Jinn Value (Arabic)	Jinn Value (Hebrew)
Usurper	9	328	338	50	40
Guide	89	48	58	130	120
Mystery	98	57	67	139	129
Adjuster	441	400	410	122	112
Leader	1323	1282	1292	1004	994
Regulator	1764	1723	1733	1445	1435
General Governor	3528	3487	3497	3209	3199
High Overseer	313992	313951	313961	313673	313663

LORD OF TRIPLICITY BY NIGHT: NATHDORINEL (751)

נ	א	מ	נ	י	צא	י	א	ל
א	מ	נ	ל	א	י	צא	י	א
ו	נ	ל	א	מ	א	י	צא	י
מ	ל	א	י	צא	מ	א	י	נ
ל	י	א	מ	נ	י	א	ל	צא
ר	צא	י	א	י	א	ל	נ	מ
י	י	צא	י	א	ל	נ	מ	א
נ	א	י	צא	ל	נ	מ	א	י
ר	ו	נ	א	ל	ר	י	נ	מ

נתד	ור	ינ	אל
28	63	207	453
208	452	29	62
61	30	455	205

Fire - Jupiter

180	191	185	195
194	186	188	183
190	181	196	184
187	193	182	189

Air - Jupiter

189	182	193	187
184	196	181	190
183	188	186	194
195	185	191	180

Earth - Jupiter

187	190	194	180
193	181	186	191
182	196	188	185
189	184	183	195

Water - Jupiter

195	183	184	189
185	188	196	182
191	186	181	193
180	194	190	187

Occult Encyclopedia of Magic Squares

	Number	Angel Value (Arabic)	Angel Value (Hebrew)	Jinn Value (Arabic)	Jinn Value (Hebrew)
Usurper	180	139	149	221	211
Guide	196	155	165	237	227
Mystery	376	335	345	57	47
Adjuster	6008	5967	5977	5689	5679
Leader	18024	17983	17993	17705	17695
Regulator	24032	23991	24001	23713	23703
General Governor	48064	48023	48033	47745	47735
High Overseer	9420544	9420503	9420513	9420225	9420215

Fire - Mars

138	163	156	150	144
151	145	139	159	157
160	153	152	146	140
147	141	161	154	148
155	149	143	142	162

Air - Mars

155	147	160	151	138
149	141	153	145	163
143	161	152	139	156
142	154	146	159	150
162	148	140	157	144

Earth - Mars

162	142	143	149	155
148	154	161	141	147
140	146	152	153	160
157	159	139	145	151
144	150	156	163	138

Water - Mars

144	157	140	148	162
150	159	146	154	142
156	139	152	161	143
163	145	153	141	149
138	151	160	147	155

	Number	Angel Value (Arabic)	Angel Value (Hebrew)	Jinn Value (Arabic)	Jinn Value (Hebrew)
Usurper	138	97	107	179	169
Guide	163	122	132	204	194
Mystery	301	260	270	342	332
Adjuster	751	710	720	432	422
Leader	2253	2212	2222	1934	1924
Regulator	3004	2963	2973	2685	2675
General Governor	6008	5967	5977	5689	5679
High Overseer	979304	979263	979273	978985	978975

Fire - Sun

107	118	142	124	128	132
113	123	134	141	111	129
119	145	127	117	133	110
130	109	120	135	114	143
136	125	116	108	144	122
146	131	112	126	121	115

Air - Sun

115	121	126	112	131	146
122	144	108	116	125	136
143	114	135	120	109	130
110	133	117	127	145	119
129	111	141	134	123	113
132	128	124	142	118	107

Earth - Sun

146	136	130	119	113	107
131	125	109	145	123	118
112	116	120	127	134	142
126	108	135	117	141	124
121	144	114	133	111	128
115	122	143	110	129	132

Water - Sun

132	129	110	143	122	115
128	111	133	114	144	121
124	141	117	135	108	126
142	134	127	120	116	112
118	123	145	109	125	131
107	113	119	130	136	146

	Number	Angel Value (Arabic)	Angel Value (Hebrew)	Jinn Value (Arabic)	Jinn Value (Hebrew)
Usurper	107	66	76	148	138
Guide	146	105	115	187	177
Mystery	253	212	222	294	284
Adjuster	751	710	720	432	422
Leader	2253	2212	2222	1934	1924
Regulator	3004	2963	2973	2685	2675
General Governor	6008	5967	5977	5689	5679
High Overseer	877168	877127	877137	876849	876839

Fire - Venus

83	124	109	94	114	129	98
130	99	84	118	110	95	115
96	116	131	100	85	119	104
120	105	90	117	132	101	86
102	87	121	106	91	111	133
112	127	103	88	122	107	92
108	93	113	128	97	89	123

Occult Encyclopedia of Magic Squares

Earth - Venus

108	112	102	120	96	130	83
93	127	87	105	116	99	124
113	103	121	90	131	84	109
128	88	106	117	100	118	94
97	122	91	132	85	110	114
89	107	111	101	119	95	129
123	92	133	86	104	115	98

Air - Venus

123	89	97	128	113	93	108
92	107	122	88	103	127	112
133	111	91	106	121	87	102
86	101	132	117	90	105	120
104	119	85	100	131	116	96
115	95	110	118	84	99	130
98	129	114	94	109	124	83

Water - Venus

98	115	104	86	133	92	123
129	95	119	101	111	107	89
114	110	85	132	91	122	97
94	118	100	117	106	88	128
109	84	131	90	121	103	113
124	99	116	105	87	127	93
83	130	96	120	102	112	108

	Number	Angel Value (Arabic)	Angel Value (Hebrew)	Jinn Value (Arabic)	Jinn Value (Hebrew)
Usurper	83	42	52	124	114
Guide	133	92	102	174	164
Mystery	216	175	185	257	247
Adjuster	751	710	720	432	422
Leader	2253	2212	2222	1934	1924
Regulator	3004	2963	2973	2685	2675
General Governor	6008	5967	5977	5689	5679
High Overseer	799064	799023	799033	798745	798735

Fire - Mercury

62	78	126	107	96	112	93	77
70	86	115	99	104	123	85	69
113	97	76	92	79	63	106	125
124	105	68	84	87	71	98	114
91	75	94	110	128	109	64	80
83	67	102	121	117	101	72	88
108	127	81	65	74	90	111	95
100	116	89	73	66	82	122	103

Earth - Mercury

100	108	83	91	124	113	70	62
116	127	67	75	105	97	86	78
89	81	102	94	68	76	115	126
73	65	121	110	84	92	99	107
66	74	117	128	87	79	104	96
82	90	101	109	71	63	123	112
122	111	72	64	98	106	85	93
103	95	88	80	114	125	69	77

Air - Mercury

103	122	82	66	73	89	116	100
95	111	90	74	65	81	127	108
88	72	101	117	121	102	67	83
80	64	109	128	110	94	75	91
114	98	71	87	84	68	105	124
125	106	63	79	92	76	97	113
69	85	123	104	99	115	86	70
77	93	112	96	107	126	78	62

Water - Mercury

77	69	125	114	80	88	95	103
93	85	106	98	64	72	111	122
112	123	63	71	109	101	90	82
96	104	79	87	128	117	74	66
107	99	92	84	110	121	65	73
126	115	76	68	94	102	81	89
78	86	97	105	75	67	127	116
62	70	113	124	91	83	108	100

	Number	Angel Value (Arabic)	Angel Value (Hebrew)	Jinn Value (Arabic)	Jinn Value (Hebrew)
Usurper	62	21	31	103	93
Guide	128	87	97	169	159
Mystery	190	149	159	231	221
Adjuster	751	710	720	432	422
Leader	2253	2212	2222	1934	1924
Regulator	3004	2963	2973	2685	2675
General Governor	6008	5967	5977	5689	5679
High Overseer	769024	768983	768993	768705	768695

Fire - Moon

87	100	62	71	127	55	91	107	51
47	90	112	67	83	99	54	76	123
119	59	75	111	43	95	104	66	79
114	46	89	98	69	82	122	53	78
74	121	58	94	110	45	81	103	65
61	86	102	57	70	126	50	93	106
60	73	120	44	96	109	64	80	105
101	63	85	125	56	72	108	49	92
88	113	48	84	97	68	77	124	52

Earth - Moon

51	123	79	78	65	106	105	92	52
107	76	66	53	103	93	80	49	124
91	54	104	122	81	50	64	108	77
55	99	95	82	45	126	109	72	68
127	83	43	69	110	70	96	56	97
71	67	111	98	94	57	44	125	84
62	112	75	89	58	102	120	85	48
100	90	59	46	121	86	73	63	113
87	47	119	114	74	61	60	101	88

Air - Moon

52	124	77	68	97	84	48	113	88
92	49	108	72	56	125	85	63	101
105	80	64	109	96	44	120	73	60
106	93	50	126	70	57	102	86	61
65	103	81	45	110	94	58	121	74
78	53	122	82	69	98	89	46	114
79	66	104	95	43	111	75	59	119
123	76	54	99	83	67	112	90	47
51	107	91	55	127	71	62	100	87

Water - Moon

88	101	60	61	74	114	119	47	87
113	63	73	86	121	46	59	90	100
48	85	120	102	58	89	75	112	62
84	125	44	57	94	98	111	67	71
97	56	96	70	110	69	43	83	127
68	72	109	126	45	82	95	99	55
77	108	64	50	81	122	104	54	91
124	49	80	93	103	53	66	76	107
52	92	105	106	65	78	79	123	51

	Number	Angel Value (Arabic)	Angel Value (Hebrew)	Jinn Value (Arabic)	Jinn Value (Hebrew)
Usurper	43	2	12	84	74
Guide	127	86	96	168	158
Mystery	170	129	139	211	201
Adjuster	751	710	720	432	422
Leader	2253	2212	2222	1934	1924
Regulator	3004	2963	2973	2685	2675
General Governor	6008	5967	5977	5689	5679
High Overseer	763016	762975	762985	762697	762687

Occult Encyclopedia of Magic Squares

Fire - Saturn

25	43	50	88	79	123	72	64	96	111
36	100	93	84	125	109	27	69	55	53
51	56	80	124	110	95	44	32	73	86
57	82	122	112	45	91	99	40	29	74
70	121	114	49	60	83	87	97	42	28
77	34	35	102	90	66	62	52	107	126
89	71	31	38	104	59	47	108	129	75
103	92	67	26	37	54	105	128	78	61
113	46	58	65	33	41	127	76	94	98
130	106	101	63	68	30	81	85	48	39

Earth - Saturn

130	113	103	89	77	70	57	51	36	25
106	46	92	71	34	121	82	56	100	43
101	58	67	31	35	114	122	80	93	50
63	65	26	38	102	49	112	124	84	88
68	33	37	104	90	60	45	110	125	79
30	41	54	59	66	83	91	95	109	123
81	127	105	47	62	87	99	44	27	72
85	76	128	108	52	97	40	32	69	64
48	94	78	129	107	42	29	73	55	96
39	98	61	75	126	28	74	86	53	111

Air - Saturn

39	48	85	81	30	68	63	101	106	130
98	94	76	127	41	33	65	58	46	113
61	78	128	105	54	37	26	67	92	103
75	129	108	47	59	104	38	31	71	89
126	107	52	62	66	90	102	35	34	77
28	42	97	87	83	60	49	114	121	70
74	29	40	99	91	45	112	122	82	57
86	73	32	44	95	110	124	80	56	51
53	55	69	27	109	125	84	93	100	36
111	96	64	72	123	79	88	50	43	25

Water - Saturn

111	53	86	74	28	126	75	61	98	39
96	55	73	29	42	107	129	78	94	48
64	69	32	40	97	52	108	128	76	85
72	**27**	44	99	87	62	47	105	127	81
123	109	95	91	83	66	59	54	41	30
79	125	110	45	60	90	104	37	33	68
88	84	124	112	49	102	38	26	65	63
50	93	80	122	114	35	31	67	58	101
43	100	56	82	121	34	71	92	46	106
25	36	51	57	70	77	89	103	113	130

	Number	Angel Value (Arabic)	Angel Value (Hebrew)	Jinn Value (Arabic)	Jinn Value (Hebrew)
Usurper	25	344	354	66	56
Guide	130	89	99	171	161
Mystery	155	114	124	196	186
Adjuster	751	710	720	432	422
Leader	2253	2212	2222	1934	1924
Regulator	3004	2963	2973	2685	2675
General Governor	6008	5967	5977	5689	5679
High Overseer	781040	780999	781009	780721	780711

ANGEL RULING 12ᵀᴴ HOUSE: PASIEL (421)

אל	י	שׁ	פ
79	301	13	28
12	29	78	302
299	81	30	11

ל	א	י	שׁ	פ
י	שׁ	פ	ל	א
פ	ל	א	י	שׁ
א	י	שׁ	פ	ל
שׁ	פ	ל	א	י

Fire - Jupiter

97	108	102	114
113	103	105	100
107	98	115	101
104	112	99	106

Air - Jupiter

106	99	112	104
101	115	98	107
100	105	103	113
114	102	108	97

Earth - Jupiter

104	107	113	97
112	98	103	108
99	115	105	102
106	101	100	114

Water - Jupiter

114	100	101	106
102	105	115	99
108	103	98	112
97	113	107	104

	Number	Angel Value (Arabic)	Angel Value (Hebrew)	Jinn Value (Arabic)	Jinn Value (Hebrew)
Usurper	97	56	66	138	128
Guide	115	74	84	156	146
Mystery	212	171	181	253	243
Adjuster	3368	3327	3337	3049	3039
Leader	10104	10063	10073	9785	9775
Regulator	13472	13431	13441	13153	13143
General Governor	26944	26903	26913	26625	26615
High Overseer	3098560	3098519	3098529	3098241	3098231

Fire - Mars

72	97	90	84	78
85	79	73	93	91
94	87	86	80	74
81	75	95	88	82
89	83	77	76	96

Air - Mars

89	81	94	85	72
83	75	87	79	97
77	95	86	73	90
76	88	80	93	84
96	82	74	91	78

Earth - Mars

96	76	77	83	89
82	88	95	75	81
74	80	86	87	94
91	93	73	79	85
78	84	90	97	72

Water - Mars

78	91	74	82	96
84	93	80	88	76
90	73	86	95	77
97	79	87	75	83
72	85	94	81	89

Occult Encyclopedia of Magic Squares

	Number	Angel Value (Arabic)	Angel Value (Hebrew)	Jinn Value (Arabic)	Jinn Value (Hebrew)
Usurper	72	31	41	113	103
Guide	97	56	66	138	128
Mystery	169	128	138	210	200
Adjuster	421	380	390	102	92
Leader	1263	1222	1232	944	934
Regulator	1684	1643	1653	1365	1355
General Governor	3368	3327	3337	3049	3039
High Overseer	326696	326655	326665	326377	326367

Fire - Sun

52	63	87	69	73	77
58	68	79	86	56	74
64	90	72	62	78	55
75	54	65	80	59	88
81	70	61	53	89	67
91	76	57	71	66	60

Air - Sun

60	66	71	57	76	91
67	89	53	61	70	81
88	59	80	65	54	75
55	78	62	72	90	64
74	56	86	79	68	58
77	73	69	87	63	52

Earth - Sun

91	81	75	64	58	52
76	70	54	90	68	63
57	61	65	72	79	87
71	53	80	62	86	69
66	89	59	78	56	73
60	67	88	55	74	77

Water - Sun

77	74	55	88	67	60
73	56	78	59	89	66
69	86	62	80	53	71
87	79	72	65	61	57
63	68	90	54	70	76
52	58	64	75	81	91

	Number	Angel Value (Arabic)	Angel Value (Hebrew)	Jinn Value (Arabic)	Jinn Value (Hebrew)
Usurper	52	11	21	93	83
Guide	91	50	60	132	122
Mystery	143	102	112	184	174
Adjuster	421	380	390	102	92
Leader	1263	1222	1232	944	934
Regulator	1684	1643	1653	1365	1355
General Governor	3368	3327	3337	3049	3039
High Overseer	306488	306447	306457	306169	306159

Fire - Venus

36	77	62	47	67	81	51
82	52	37	71	63	48	68
49	69	83	53	38	72	57
73	58	43	70	84	54	39
55	40	74	59	44	64	85
65	79	56	41	75	60	45
61	46	66	80	50	42	76

Air - Venus

76	42	50	80	66	46	61
45	60	75	41	56	79	65
85	64	44	59	74	40	55
39	54	84	70	43	58	73
57	72	38	53	83	69	49
68	48	63	71	37	52	82
51	81	67	47	62	77	36

Earth - Venus

61	65	55	73	49	82	36
46	79	40	58	69	52	77
66	56	74	43	83	37	62
80	41	59	70	53	71	47
50	75	44	84	38	63	67
42	60	64	54	72	48	81
76	45	85	39	57	68	51

Water - Venus

51	68	57	39	85	45	76
81	48	72	54	64	60	42
67	63	38	84	44	75	50
47	71	53	70	59	41	80
62	37	83	43	74	56	66
77	52	69	58	40	79	46
36	82	49	73	55	65	61

	Number	Angel Value (Arabic)	Angel Value (Hebrew)	Jinn Value (Arabic)	Jinn Value (Hebrew)
Usurper	36	355	5	77	67
Guide	85	44	54	126	116
Mystery	121	80	90	162	152
Adjuster	421	380	390	102	92
Leader	1263	1222	1232	944	934
Regulator	1684	1643	1653	1365	1355
General Governor	3368	3327	3337	3049	3039
High Overseer	286280	286239	286249	285961	285951

Fire - Mercury

21	37	83	66	55	71	52	36
29	45	74	58	63	80	44	28
72	56	35	51	38	22	65	82
81	64	27	43	46	30	57	73
50	34	53	69	85	68	23	39
42	26	61	78	76	60	31	47
67	84	40	24	33	49	70	54
59	75	48	32	25	41	79	62

Earth - Mercury

59	67	42	50	81	72	29	21
75	84	26	34	64	56	45	37
48	40	61	53	27	35	74	83
32	24	78	69	43	51	58	66
25	33	76	85	46	38	63	55
41	49	60	68	30	22	80	71
79	70	31	23	57	65	44	52
62	54	47	39	73	82	28	36

Occult Encyclopedia of Magic Squares

Air - Mercury

62	79	41	25	32	48	75	59
54	70	49	33	24	40	84	67
47	31	60	76	78	61	26	42
39	23	68	85	69	53	34	50
73	57	30	46	43	27	64	81
82	65	22	38	51	35	56	72
28	44	80	63	58	74	45	29
36	52	71	55	66	83	37	21

Water - Mercury

36	28	82	73	39	47	54	62
52	44	65	57	23	31	70	79
71	80	22	30	68	60	49	41
55	63	38	46	85	76	33	25
66	58	51	43	69	78	24	32
83	74	35	27	53	61	40	48
37	45	56	64	34	26	84	75
21	29	72	81	50	42	67	59

	Number	Angel Value (Arabic)	Angel Value (Hebrew)	Jinn Value (Arabic)	Jinn Value (Hebrew)
Usurper	21	340	350	62	52
Guide	85	44	54	126	116
Mystery	106	65	75	147	137
Adjuster	421	380	390	102	92
Leader	1263	1222	1232	944	934
Regulator	1684	1643	1653	1365	1355
General Governor	3368	3327	3337	3049	3039
High Overseer	286280	286239	286249	285961	285951

Fire - Moon

50	63	25	34	93	18	54	70	14
10	53	75	30	46	62	17	39	89
85	22	38	74	6	58	67	29	42
77	9	52	61	32	45	88	16	41
37	87	21	57	73	8	44	66	28
24	49	65	20	33	92	13	56	69
23	36	86	7	59	72	27	43	68
64	26	48	91	19	35	71	12	55
51	76	11	47	60	31	40	90	15

Earth - Moon

14	89	42	41	28	69	68	55	15
70	39	29	16	66	56	43	12	90
54	17	67	88	44	13	27	71	40
18	62	58	45	8	92	72	35	31
93	46	6	32	73	33	59	19	60
34	30	74	61	57	20	7	91	47
25	75	38	52	21	65	86	48	11
63	53	22	9	87	49	36	26	76
50	10	85	77	37	24	23	64	51

Air - Moon

15	90	40	31	60	47	11	76	51
55	12	71	35	19	91	48	26	64
68	43	27	72	59	7	86	36	23
69	56	13	92	33	20	65	49	24
28	66	44	8	73	57	21	87	37
41	16	88	45	32	61	52	9	77
42	29	67	58	6	74	38	22	85
89	39	17	62	46	30	75	53	10
14	70	54	18	93	34	25	63	50

Water - Moon

51	64	23	24	37	77	85	10	50
76	26	36	49	87	9	22	53	63
11	48	86	65	21	52	38	75	25
47	91	7	20	57	61	74	30	34
60	19	59	33	73	32	6	46	93
31	35	72	92	8	45	58	62	18
40	71	27	13	44	88	67	17	54
90	12	43	56	66	16	29	39	70
15	55	68	69	28	41	42	89	14

	Number	Angel Value (Arabic)	Angel Value (Hebrew)	Jinn Value (Arabic)	Jinn Value (Hebrew)
Usurper	6	325	335	47	37
Guide	93	52	62	134	124
Mystery	99	58	68	140	130
Adjuster	421	380	390	102	92
Leader	1263	1222	1232	944	934
Regulator	1684	1643	1653	1365	1355
General Governor	3368	3327	3337	3049	3039
High Overseer	313224	313183	313193	312905	312895

ANGEL OF FIRST DECANATE: BIHELAMI (87)

י	מ	ל	בה
6	31	43	7
42	8	5	32
29	8	9	41

י	מ	ל	ה	ב
ל	ה	ב	י	מ
ב	י	מ	ל	ה
מ	ל	ה	ב	י
ה	ב	י	מ	ל

Occult Encyclopedia of Magic Squares

Fire - Saturn

30	25	32
31	29	27
26	33	28

Earth - Saturn

26	31	30
33	29	25
28	27	32

Air - Saturn

28	33	26
27	29	31
32	25	30

Water - Saturn

32	27	28
25	29	33
30	31	26

	Number	Angel Value (Arabic)	Angel Value (Hebrew)	Jinn Value (Arabic)	Jinn Value (Hebrew)
Usurper	25	344	354	66	56
Guide	33	352	2	74	64
Mystery	58	17	27	99	89
Adjuster	87	46	56	128	118
Leader	261	220	230	302	292
Regulator	348	307	317	29	19
General Governor	696	655	665	377	367
High Overseer	22968	22927	22937	22649	22639

Fire - Jupiter

14	25	19	29
28	20	22	17
24	15	30	18
21	27	16	23

Air - Jupiter

23	16	27	21
18	30	15	24
17	22	20	28
29	19	25	14

Earth - Jupiter

21	24	28	14
27	15	20	25
16	30	22	19
23	18	17	29

Water - Jupiter

29	17	18	23
19	22	30	16
25	20	15	27
14	28	24	21

Occult Encyclopedia of Magic Squares

	Number	Angel Value (Arabic)	Angel Value (Hebrew)	Jinn Value (Arabic)	Jinn Value (Hebrew)
Usurper	14	333	343	55	45
Guide	30	349	359	71	61
Mystery	44	3	13	85	75
Adjuster	696	655	665	377	367
Leader	2088	2047	2057	1769	1759
Regulator	2784	2743	2753	2465	2455
General Governor	5568	5527	5537	5249	5239
High Overseer	167040	166999	167009	166721	166711

Fire - Mars

5	31	23	17	11
18	12	6	27	24
28	20	19	13	7
14	8	29	21	15
22	16	10	9	30

Air - Mars

22	14	28	18	5
16	8	20	12	31
10	29	19	6	23
9	21	13	27	17
30	15	7	24	11

Earth - Mars

30	9	10	16	22
15	21	29	8	14
7	13	19	20	28
24	27	6	12	18
11	17	23	31	5

Water - Mars

11	24	7	15	30
17	27	13	21	9
23	6	19	29	10
31	12	20	8	16
5	18	28	14	22

	Number	Angel Value (Arabic)	Angel Value (Hebrew)	Jinn Value (Arabic)	Jinn Value (Hebrew)
Usurper	5	324	334	46	36
Guide	31	350	360	72	62
Mystery	36	355	5	77	67
Adjuster	87	46	56	128	118
Leader	261	220	230	302	292
Regulator	348	307	317	29	19
General Governor	696	655	665	377	367
High Overseer	21576	21535	21545	21257	21247

ANGEL OF FIRST QUINANCE: VAVALIAH (57)

יה	ל	ו	ו
5	7	33	12
32	13	4	8
5	7	14	31

ה	י	ל	ו	ו
ל	ו	ו	ה	י
ו	ה	י	ל	ו
י	ל	ו	ו	ה
ו	ו	ה	י	ל

Numerical Squares See Page: 436

ANGEL OF SECOND QUINANCE: YELAHIAH (60)

יה	ה	ל	י
9	31	8	12
7	13	8	32
29	11	14	6

ה	י	ה	ל	י
ה	ל	י	ה	י
י	ה	י	ה	ל
י	ה	ל	י	ה
ל	י	ה	י	ה

Fire - Saturn

21	16	23
22	20	18
17	24	19

Earth - Saturn

17	22	21
24	20	16
19	18	23

Air - Saturn

19	24	17
18	20	22
23	16	21

Water - Saturn

23	18	19
16	20	24
21	22	17

Occult Encyclopedia of Magic Squares

	Number	Angel Value (Arabic)	Angel Value (Hebrew)	Jinn Value (Arabic)	Jinn Value (Hebrew)
Usurper	16	335	345	57	47
Guide	24	343	353	65	55
Mystery	40	359	9	81	71
Adjuster	60	19	29	101	91
Leader	180	139	149	221	211
Regulator	240	199	209	281	271
General Governor	480	439	449	161	151
High Overseer	11520	11479	11489	11201	11191

Fire - Jupiter

7	18	12	23
22	13	15	10
17	8	24	11
14	21	9	16

Air - Jupiter

16	9	21	14
11	24	8	17
10	15	13	22
23	12	18	7

Earth - Jupiter

14	17	22	7
21	8	13	18
9	24	15	12
16	11	10	23

Water - Jupiter

23	10	11	16
12	15	24	9
18	13	8	21
7	22	17	14

	Number	Angel Value (Arabic)	Angel Value (Hebrew)	Jinn Value (Arabic)	Jinn Value (Hebrew)
Usurper	7	326	336	48	38
Guide	24	343	353	65	55
Mystery	31	350	360	72	62
Adjuster	480	439	449	161	151
Leader	1440	1399	1409	1121	1111
Regulator	1920	1879	1889	1601	1591
General Governor	3840	3799	3809	3521	3511
High Overseer	92160	92119	92129	91841	91831

ANGEL OF SECOND DECANATE: AVRON (263)

נ	ר	ר	אי
6	201	9	47
8	48	5	202
199	8	49	7

ו	ר	ו	א
א	ו	ר	ו
ר	ו	א	ו
ו	א	ו	ר

Numerical Squares See Page: 411

ANGEL OF THIRD QUINANCE: SALIAH (106)

ה	י	אל	ס
59	32	13	2
12	3	58	33
30	61	4	11

ה	י	ל	א	ס
ל	א	ס	ה	י
ס	ה	י	ל	א
י	ל	א	ס	ה
א	ס	ה	י	ל

Numerical Squares See Page: 455

ANGEL OF FOURTH QUINANCE: ARIEL (311)

אל	י	ר	ע
69	201	13	28
12	29	68	202
199	71	30	11

ל	א	י	ר	ע
י	ר	ע	ל	א
ע	ל	א	י	ר
א	י	ר	ע	ל
ר	ע	ל	א	י

Fire - Jupiter

70	81	75	85
84	76	78	73
80	71	86	74
77	83	72	79

Air - Jupiter

79	72	83	77
74	86	71	80
73	78	76	84
85	75	81	70

Earth - Jupiter

77	80	84	70
83	71	76	81
72	86	78	75
79	74	73	85

Water - Jupiter

85	73	74	79
75	78	86	72
81	76	71	83
70	84	80	77

	Number	Angel Value (Arabic)	Angel Value (Hebrew)	Jinn Value (Arabic)	Jinn Value (Hebrew)
Usurper	70	29	39	111	101
Guide	86	45	55	127	117
Mystery	156	115	125	197	187
Adjuster	2488	2447	2457	2169	2159
Leader	7464	7423	7433	7145	7135
Regulator	9952	9911	9921	9633	9623
General Governor	19904	19863	19873	19585	19575
High Overseer	1711744	1711703	1711713	1711425	1711415

Occult Encyclopedia of Magic Squares

Fire - Mars

50	75	68	62	56
63	57	51	71	69
72	65	64	58	52
59	53	73	66	60
67	61	55	54	74

Air - Mars

67	59	72	63	50
61	53	65	57	75
55	73	64	51	68
54	66	58	71	62
74	60	52	69	56

Earth - Mars

74	54	55	61	67
60	66	73	53	59
52	58	64	65	72
69	71	51	57	63
56	62	68	75	50

Water - Mars

56	69	52	60	74
62	71	58	66	54
68	51	64	73	55
75	57	65	53	61
50	63	72	59	67

	Number	Angel Value (Arabic)	Angel Value (Hebrew)	Jinn Value (Arabic)	Jinn Value (Hebrew)
Usurper	50	9	19	91	81
Guide	75	34	44	116	106
Mystery	125	84	94	166	156
Adjuster	311	270	280	352	342
Leader	933	892	902	614	604
Regulator	1244	1203	1213	925	915
General Governor	2488	2447	2457	2169	2159
High Overseer	186600	186559	186569	186281	186271

Occult Encyclopedia of Magic Squares

Fire - Sun

34	45	67	51	55	59
40	50	61	66	38	56
46	70	54	44	60	37
57	36	47	62	41	68
63	52	43	35	69	49
71	58	39	53	48	42

Air - Sun

42	48	53	39	58	71
49	69	35	43	52	63
68	41	62	47	36	57
37	60	44	54	70	46
56	38	66	61	50	40
59	55	51	67	45	34

Earth - Sun

71	63	57	46	40	34
58	52	36	70	50	45
39	43	47	54	61	67
53	35	62	44	66	51
48	69	41	60	38	55
42	49	68	37	56	59

Water - Sun

59	56	37	68	49	42
55	38	60	41	69	48
51	66	44	62	35	53
67	61	54	47	43	39
45	50	70	36	52	58
34	40	46	57	63	71

	Number	Angel Value (Arabic)	Angel Value (Hebrew)	Jinn Value (Arabic)	Jinn Value (Hebrew)
Usurper	34	353	3	75	65
Guide	71	30	40	112	102
Mystery	105	64	74	146	136
Adjuster	311	270	280	352	342
Leader	933	892	902	614	604
Regulator	1244	1203	1213	925	915
General Governor	2488	2447	2457	2169	2159
High Overseer	176648	176607	176617	176329	176319

Fire - Venus

20	61	46	31	51	67	35
68	36	21	55	47	32	52
33	53	69	37	22	56	41
57	42	27	54	70	38	23
39	24	58	43	28	48	71
49	65	40	25	59	44	29
45	30	50	66	34	26	60

Earth - Venus

45	49	39	57	33	68	20
30	65	24	42	53	36	61
50	40	58	27	69	21	46
66	25	43	54	37	55	31
34	59	28	70	22	47	51
26	44	48	38	56	32	67
60	29	71	23	41	52	35

Air - Venus

60	26	34	66	50	30	45
29	44	59	25	40	65	49
71	48	28	43	58	24	39
23	38	70	54	27	42	57
41	56	22	37	69	53	33
52	32	47	55	21	36	68
35	67	51	31	46	61	20

Water - Venus

35	52	41	23	71	29	60
67	32	56	38	48	44	26
51	47	22	70	28	59	34
31	55	37	54	43	25	66
46	21	69	27	58	40	50
61	36	53	42	24	65	30
20	68	33	57	39	49	45

	Number	Angel Value (Arabic)	Angel Value (Hebrew)	Jinn Value (Arabic)	Jinn Value (Hebrew)
Usurper	20	339	349	61	51
Guide	71	30	40	112	102
Mystery	91	50	60	132	122
Adjuster	311	270	280	352	342
Leader	933	892	902	614	604
Regulator	1244	1203	1213	925	915
General Governor	2488	2447	2457	2169	2159
High Overseer	176648	176607	176617	176329	176319

Fire - Mercury

7	23	71	52	41	57	38	22
15	31	60	44	49	68	30	14
58	42	21	37	24	8	51	70
69	50	13	29	32	16	43	59
36	20	39	55	73	54	9	25
28	12	47	66	62	46	17	33
53	72	26	10	19	35	56	40
45	61	34	18	11	27	67	48

Earth - Mercury

45	53	28	36	69	58	15	7
61	72	12	20	50	42	31	23
34	26	47	39	13	21	60	71
18	10	66	55	29	37	44	52
11	19	62	73	32	24	49	41
27	35	46	54	16	8	68	57
67	56	17	9	43	51	30	38
48	40	33	25	59	70	14	22

Air - Mercury

48	67	27	11	18	34	61	45
40	56	35	19	10	26	72	53
33	17	46	62	66	47	12	28
25	9	54	73	55	39	20	36
59	43	16	32	29	13	50	69
70	51	8	24	37	21	42	58
14	30	68	49	44	60	31	15
22	38	57	41	52	71	23	7

Water - Mercury

22	14	70	59	25	33	40	48
38	30	51	43	9	17	56	67
57	68	8	16	54	46	35	27
41	49	24	32	73	62	19	11
52	44	37	29	55	66	10	18
71	60	21	13	39	47	26	34
23	31	42	50	20	12	72	61
7	15	58	69	36	28	53	45

	Number	Angel Value (Arabic)	Angel Value (Hebrew)	Jinn Value (Arabic)	Jinn Value (Hebrew)
Usurper	7	326	336	48	38
Guide	73	32	42	114	104
Mystery	80	39	49	121	111
Adjuster	311	270	280	352	342
Leader	933	892	902	614	604
Regulator	1244	1203	1213	925	915
General Governor	2488	2447	2457	2169	2159
High Overseer	181624	181583	181593	181305	181295

ANGEL OF THIRD DECANATE: SATRIP (359)

מ	ר	ט	פ
59	10	203	87
202	88	58	11
8	61	89	201

פ	י	ר	ט	פ
ר	ט	פ	פ	י
פ	פ	י	ר	ט
י	ר	ט	פ	פ
ט	פ	פ	י	ר

Fire - Jupiter

82	93	87	97
96	88	90	85
92	83	98	86
89	95	84	91

Air - Jupiter

91	84	95	89
86	98	83	92
85	90	88	96
97	87	93	82

Earth - Jupiter

89	92	96	82
95	83	88	93
84	98	90	87
91	86	85	97

Water - Jupiter

97	85	86	91
87	90	98	84
93	88	83	95
82	96	92	89

	Number	Angel Value (Arabic)	Angel Value (Hebrew)	Jinn Value (Arabic)	Jinn Value (Hebrew)
Usurper	82	41	51	123	113
Guide	98	57	67	139	129
Mystery	180	139	149	221	211
Adjuster	2872	2831	2841	2553	2543
Leader	8616	8575	8585	8297	8287
Regulator	11488	11447	11457	11169	11159
General Governor	22976	22935	22945	22657	22647
High Overseer	2251648	2251607	2251617	2251329	2251319

Fire - Mars

59	87	77	71	65
72	66	60	83	78
84	74	73	67	61
68	62	85	75	69
76	70	64	63	86

Air - Mars

76	68	84	72	59
70	62	74	66	87
64	85	73	60	77
63	75	67	83	71
86	69	61	78	65

Earth - Mars

86	63	64	70	76
69	75	85	62	68
61	67	73	74	84
78	83	60	66	72
65	71	77	87	59

Water - Mars

65	78	61	69	86
71	83	67	75	63
77	60	73	85	64
87	66	74	62	70
59	72	84	68	76

	Number	Angel Value (Arabic)	Angel Value (Hebrew)	Jinn Value (Arabic)	Jinn Value (Hebrew)
Usurper	59	18	28	100	90
Guide	87	46	56	128	118
Mystery	146	105	115	187	177
Adjuster	359	318	328	40	30
Leader	1077	1036	1046	758	748
Regulator	1436	1395	1405	1117	1107
General Governor	2872	2831	2841	2553	2543
High Overseer	249864	249823	249833	249545	249535

Occult Encyclopedia of Magic Squares

Fire - Sun

42	53	75	59	63	67
48	58	69	74	46	64
54	78	62	52	68	45
65	44	55	70	49	76
71	60	51	43	77	57
79	66	47	61	56	50

Air - Sun

50	56	61	47	66	79
57	77	43	51	60	71
76	49	70	55	44	65
45	68	52	62	78	54
64	46	74	69	58	48
67	63	59	75	53	42

Earth - Sun

79	71	65	54	48	42
66	60	44	78	58	53
47	51	55	62	69	75
61	43	70	52	74	59
56	77	49	68	46	63
50	57	76	45	64	67

Water - Sun

67	64	45	76	57	50
63	46	68	49	77	56
59	74	52	70	43	61
75	69	62	55	51	47
53	58	78	44	60	66
42	48	54	65	71	79

	Number	Angel Value (Arabic)	Angel Value (Hebrew)	Jinn Value (Arabic)	Jinn Value (Hebrew)
Usurper	42	1	11	83	73
Guide	79	38	48	120	110
Mystery	121	80	90	162	152
Adjuster	359	318	328	40	30
Leader	1077	1036	1046	758	748
Regulator	1436	1395	1405	1117	1107
General Governor	2872	2831	2841	2553	2543
High Overseer	226888	226847	226857	226569	226559

Occult Encyclopedia of Magic Squares

Fire - Venus

27	68	53	38	58	73	42
74	43	28	62	54	39	59
40	60	75	44	29	63	48
64	49	34	61	76	45	30
46	31	65	50	35	55	77
56	71	47	32	66	51	36
52	37	57	72	41	33	67

Air - Venus

67	33	41	72	57	37	52
36	51	66	32	47	71	56
77	55	35	50	65	31	46
30	45	76	61	34	49	64
48	63	29	44	75	60	40
59	39	54	62	28	43	74
42	73	58	38	53	68	27

Earth - Venus

52	56	46	64	40	74	27
37	71	31	49	60	43	68
57	47	65	34	75	28	53
72	32	50	61	44	62	38
41	66	35	76	29	54	58
33	51	55	45	63	39	73
67	36	77	30	48	59	42

Water - Venus

42	59	48	30	77	36	67
73	39	63	45	55	51	33
58	54	29	76	35	66	41
38	62	44	61	50	32	72
53	28	75	34	65	47	57
68	43	60	49	31	71	37
27	74	40	64	46	56	52

	Number	Angel Value (Arabic)	Angel Value (Hebrew)	Jinn Value (Arabic)	Jinn Value (Hebrew)
Usurper	27	346	356	68	58
Guide	77	36	46	118	108
Mystery	104	63	73	145	135
Adjuster	359	318	328	40	30
Leader	1077	1036	1046	758	748
Regulator	1436	1395	1405	1117	1107
General Governor	2872	2831	2841	2553	2543
High Overseer	221144	221103	221113	220825	220815

Occult Encyclopedia of Magic Squares

Fire - Mercury

13	29	77	58	47	63	44	28
21	37	66	50	55	74	36	20
64	48	27	43	30	14	57	76
75	56	19	35	38	22	49	65
42	26	45	61	79	60	15	31
34	18	53	72	68	52	23	39
59	78	32	16	25	41	62	46
51	67	40	24	17	33	73	54

Air - Mercury

54	73	33	17	24	40	67	51
46	62	41	25	16	32	78	59
39	23	52	68	72	53	18	34
31	15	60	79	61	45	26	42
65	49	22	38	35	19	56	75
76	57	14	30	43	27	48	64
20	36	74	55	50	66	37	21
28	44	63	47	58	77	29	13

Earth - Mercury

51	59	34	42	75	64	21	13
67	78	18	26	56	48	37	29
40	32	53	45	19	27	66	77
24	16	72	61	35	43	50	58
17	25	68	79	38	30	55	47
33	41	52	60	22	14	74	63
73	62	23	15	49	57	36	44
54	46	39	31	65	76	20	28

Water - Mercury

28	20	76	65	31	39	46	54
44	36	57	49	15	23	62	73
63	74	14	22	60	52	41	33
47	55	30	38	79	68	25	17
58	50	43	35	61	72	16	24
77	66	27	19	45	53	32	40
29	37	48	56	26	18	78	67
13	21	64	75	42	34	59	51

t

	Number	Angel Value (Arabic)	Angel Value (Hebrew)	Jinn Value (Arabic)	Jinn Value (Hebrew)
Usurper	13	332	342	54	44
Guide	79	38	48	120	110
Mystery	92	51	61	133	123
Adjuster	359	318	328	40	30
Leader	1077	1036	1046	758	748
Regulator	1436	1395	1405	1117	1107
General Governor	2872	2831	2841	2553	2543
High Overseer	226888	226847	226857	226569	226559

יה	ל	שׁ	עַ
69	301	33	12
32	13	68	302
299	71	14	31

ה	י	ל	שׁ	עַ
ל	שׁ	עַ	ה	י
עַ	ה	י	ל	שׁ
י	ל	שׁ	עַ	ה
שׁ	עַ	ה	י	ל

Fire - Jupiter

96	107	101	111
110	102	104	99
106	97	112	100
103	109	98	105

Air - Jupiter

105	98	109	103
100	112	97	106
99	104	102	110
111	101	107	96

Earth - Jupiter

103	106	110	96
109	97	102	107
98	112	104	101
105	100	99	111

Water - Jupiter

111	99	100	105
101	104	112	98
107	102	97	109
96	110	106	103

	Number	Angel Value (Arabic)	Angel Value (Hebrew)	Jinn Value (Arabic)	Jinn Value (Hebrew)
Usurper	96	55	65	137	127
Guide	112	71	81	153	143
Mystery	208	167	177	249	239
Adjuster	3320	3279	3289	3001	2991
Leader	9960	9919	9929	9641	9631
Regulator	13280	13239	13249	12961	12951
General Governor	26560	26519	26529	26241	26231
High Overseer	2974720	2974679	2974689	2974401	2974391

Occult Encyclopedia of Magic Squares

ire - Mars

71	95	89	83	77
84	78	72	91	90
92	86	85	79	73
80	74	93	87	81
88	82	76	75	94

Air - Mars

88	80	92	84	71
82	74	86	78	95
76	93	85	72	89
75	87	79	91	83
94	81	73	90	77

Earth - Mars

94	75	76	82	88
81	87	93	74	80
73	79	85	86	92
90	91	72	78	84
77	83	89	95	71

Water - Mars

77	90	73	81	94
83	91	79	87	75
89	72	85	93	76
95	78	86	74	82
71	84	92	80	88

	Number	Angel Value (Arabic)	Angel Value (Hebrew)	Jinn Value (Arabic)	Jinn Value (Hebrew)
Usurper	71	30	40	112	102
Guide	95	54	64	136	126
Mystery	166	125	135	207	197
Adjuster	415	374	384	96	86
Leader	1245	1204	1214	926	916
Regulator	1660	1619	1629	1341	1331
General Governor	3320	3279	3289	3001	2991
High Overseer	315400	315359	315369	315081	315071

Occult Encyclopedia of Magic Squares

Fire - Sun

51	62	86	68	72	76
57	67	78	85	55	73
63	89	71	61	77	54
74	53	64	79	58	87
80	69	60	52	88	66
90	75	56	70	65	59

Air - Sun

59	65	70	56	75	90
66	88	52	60	69	80
87	58	79	64	53	74
54	77	61	71	89	63
73	55	85	78	67	57
76	72	68	86	62	51

Earth - Sun

90	80	74	63	57	51
75	69	53	89	67	62
56	60	64	71	78	86
70	52	79	61	85	68
65	88	58	77	55	72
59	66	87	54	73	76

Water - Sun

76	73	54	87	66	59
72	55	77	58	88	65
68	85	61	79	52	70
86	78	71	64	60	56
62	67	89	53	69	75
51	57	63	74	80	90

	Number	Angel Value (Arabic)	Angel Value (Hebrew)	Jinn Value (Arabic)	Jinn Value (Hebrew)
Usurper	51	10	20	92	82
Guide	90	49	59	131	121
Mystery	141	100	110	182	172
Adjuster	415	374	384	96	86
Leader	1245	1204	1214	926	916
Regulator	1660	1619	1629	1341	1331
General Governor	3320	3279	3289	3001	2991
High Overseer	298800	298759	298769	298481	298471

Fire - Venus

35	76	61	46	66	81	50
82	51	36	70	62	47	67
48	68	83	52	37	71	56
72	57	42	69	84	53	38
54	39	73	58	43	63	85
64	79	55	40	74	59	44
60	45	65	80	49	41	75

Air - Venus

75	41	49	80	65	45	60
44	59	74	40	55	79	64
85	63	43	58	73	39	54
38	53	84	69	42	57	72
56	71	37	52	83	68	48
67	47	62	70	36	51	82
50	81	66	46	61	76	35

Earth - Venus

60	64	54	72	48	82	35
45	79	39	57	68	51	76
65	55	73	42	83	36	61
80	40	58	69	52	70	46
49	74	43	84	37	62	66
41	59	63	53	71	47	81
75	44	85	38	56	67	50

Water - Venus

50	67	56	38	85	44	75
81	47	71	53	63	59	41
66	62	37	84	43	74	49
46	70	52	69	58	40	80
61	36	83	42	73	55	65
76	51	68	57	39	79	45
35	82	48	72	54	64	60

	Number	Angel Value (Arabic)	Angel Value (Hebrew)	Jinn Value (Arabic)	Jinn Value (Hebrew)
Usurper	35	354	4	76	66
Guide	85	44	54	126	116
Mystery	120	79	89	161	151
Adjuster	415	374	384	96	86
Leader	1245	1204	1214	926	916
Regulator	1660	1619	1629	1341	1331
General Governor	3320	3279	3289	3001	2991
High Overseer	282200	282159	282169	281881	281871

Fire - Mercury

20	36	84	65	54	70	51	35
28	44	73	57	62	81	43	27
71	55	34	50	37	21	64	83
82	63	26	42	45	29	56	72
49	33	52	68	86	67	22	38
41	25	60	79	75	59	30	46
66	85	39	23	32	48	69	53
58	74	47	31	24	40	80	61

Earth - Mercury

58	66	41	49	82	71	28	20
74	85	25	33	63	55	44	36
47	39	60	52	26	34	73	84
31	23	79	68	42	50	57	65
24	32	75	86	45	37	62	54
40	48	59	67	29	21	81	70
80	69	30	22	56	64	43	51
61	53	46	38	72	83	27	35

Air - Mercury

61	80	40	24	31	47	74	58
53	69	48	32	23	39	85	66
46	30	59	75	79	60	25	41
38	22	67	86	68	52	33	49
72	56	29	45	42	26	63	82
83	64	21	37	50	34	55	71
27	43	81	62	57	73	44	28
35	51	70	54	65	84	36	20

Water - Mercury

35	27	83	72	38	46	53	61
51	43	64	56	22	30	69	80
70	81	21	29	67	59	48	40
54	62	37	45	86	75	32	24
65	57	50	42	68	79	23	31
84	73	34	26	52	60	39	47
36	44	55	63	33	25	85	74
20	28	71	82	49	41	66	58

	Number	Angel Value (Arabic)	Angel Value (Hebrew)	Jinn Value (Arabic)	Jinn Value (Hebrew)
Usurper	20	339	349	61	51
Guide	86	45	55	127	117
Mystery	106	65	75	147	137
Adjuster	415	374	384	96	86
Leader	1245	1204	1214	926	916
Regulator	1660	1619	1629	1341	1331
General Governor	3320	3279	3289	3001	2991
High Overseer	285520	285479	285489	285201	285191

Fire - Moon

50	63	25	34	87	18	54	70	14
10	53	75	30	46	62	17	39	83
79	22	38	74	6	58	67	29	42
77	9	52	61	32	45	82	16	41
37	81	21	57	73	8	44	66	28
24	49	65	20	33	86	13	56	69
23	36	80	7	59	72	27	43	68
64	26	48	85	19	35	71	12	55
51	76	11	47	60	31	40	84	15

Earth - Moon

14	83	42	41	28	69	68	55	15
70	39	29	16	66	56	43	12	84
54	17	67	82	44	13	27	71	40
18	62	58	45	8	86	72	35	31
87	46	6	32	73	33	59	19	60
34	30	74	61	57	20	7	85	47
25	75	38	52	21	65	80	48	11
63	53	22	9	81	49	36	26	76
50	10	79	77	37	24	23	64	51

Air - Moon

15	84	40	31	60	47	11	76	51
55	12	71	35	19	85	48	26	64
68	43	27	72	59	7	80	36	23
69	56	13	86	33	20	65	49	24
28	66	44	8	73	57	21	81	37
41	16	82	45	32	61	52	9	77
42	29	67	58	6	74	38	22	79
83	39	17	62	46	30	75	53	10
14	70	54	18	87	34	25	63	50

Water - Moon

51	64	23	24	37	77	79	10	50
76	26	36	49	81	9	22	53	63
11	48	80	65	21	52	38	75	25
47	85	7	20	57	61	74	30	34
60	19	59	33	73	32	6	46	87
31	35	72	86	8	45	58	62	18
40	71	27	13	44	82	67	17	54
84	12	43	56	66	16	29	39	70
15	55	68	69	28	41	42	83	14

	Number	Angel Value (Arabic)	Angel Value (Hebrew)	Jinn Value (Arabic)	Jinn Value (Hebrew)
Usurper	6	325	335	47	37
Guide	87	46	56	128	118
Mystery	93	52	62	134	124
Adjuster	415	374	384	96	86
Leader	1245	1204	1214	926	916
Regulator	1660	1619	1629	1341	1331
General Governor	3320	3279	3289	3001	2991
High Overseer	288840	288799	288809	288521	288511

ANGEL OF FIFTH QUINANCE: MIHAEL (86)

אל	ה	י	מ
39	11	8	28
7	29	38	12
9	41	30	6

ל	א	ה	י	מ
ה	י	מ	ל	א
מ	ל	א	ה	י
א	ה	י	מ	ל
י	מ	ל	א	ה

Numerical Squares See Page: 514

SATURN

SATURN: SHABBATHAI (713)

א	ת	ב	ש
299	3	403	8
402	9	298	4
1	301	10	401

י	א	ת	ב	ש
ת	ב	ש	י	א
ש	י	א	ת	ב
א	ת	ב	ש	י
ב	ש	י	א	ת

Fire - Jupiter

170	181	175	187
186	176	178	173
180	171	188	174
177	185	172	179

Air - Jupiter

179	172	185	177
174	188	171	180
173	178	176	186
187	175	181	170

Earth - Jupiter

177	180	186	170
185	171	176	181
172	188	178	175
179	174	173	187

Water - Jupiter

187	173	174	179
175	178	188	172
181	176	171	185
170	186	180	177

Occult Encyclopedia of Magic Squares

	Number	Angel Value (Arabic)	Angel Value (Hebrew)	Jinn Value (Arabic)	Jinn Value (Hebrew)
Usurper	170	129	139	211	201
Guide	188	147	157	229	219
Mystery	358	317	327	39	29
Adjuster	5704	5663	5673	5385	5375
Leader	17112	17071	17081	16793	16783
Regulator	22816	22775	22785	22497	22487
General Governor	45632	45591	45601	45313	45303
High Overseer	8578816	8578775	8578785	8578497	8578487

Fire - Mars

130	157	148	142	136
143	137	131	153	149
154	145	144	138	132
139	133	155	146	140
147	141	135	134	156

Air - Mars

147	139	154	143	130
141	133	145	137	157
135	155	144	131	148
134	146	138	153	142
156	140	132	149	136

Earth - Mars

156	134	135	141	147
140	146	155	133	139
132	138	144	145	154
149	153	131	137	143
136	142	148	157	130

Water - Mars

136	149	132	140	156
142	153	138	146	134
148	131	144	155	135
157	137	145	133	141
130	143	154	139	147

	Number	Angel Value (Arabic)	Angel Value (Hebrew)	Jinn Value (Arabic)	Jinn Value (Hebrew)
Usurper	130	89	99	171	161
Guide	157	116	126	198	188
Mystery	287	246	256	328	318
Adjuster	713	672	682	394	384
Leader	2139	2098	2108	1820	1810
Regulator	2852	2811	2821	2533	2523
General Governor	5704	5663	5673	5385	5375
High Overseer	895528	895487	895497	895209	895199

Occult Encyclopedia of Magic Squares

Fire - Sun

101	112	134	118	122	126
107	117	128	133	105	123
113	137	121	111	127	104
124	103	114	129	108	135
130	119	110	102	136	116
138	125	106	120	115	109

Air - Sun

109	115	120	106	125	138
116	136	102	110	119	130
135	108	129	114	103	124
104	127	111	121	137	113
123	105	133	128	117	107
126	122	118	134	112	101

Earth - Sun

138	130	124	113	107	101
125	119	103	137	117	112
106	110	114	121	128	134
120	102	129	111	133	118
115	136	108	127	105	122
109	116	135	104	123	126

Water - Sun

126	123	104	135	116	109
122	105	127	108	136	115
118	133	111	129	102	120
134	128	121	114	110	106
112	117	137	103	119	125
101	107	113	124	130	138

	Number	Angel Value (Arabic)	Angel Value (Hebrew)	Jinn Value (Arabic)	Jinn Value (Hebrew)
Usurper	101	60	70	142	132
Guide	138	97	107	179	169
Mystery	239	198	208	280	270
Adjuster	713	672	682	394	384
Leader	2139	2098	2108	1820	1810
Regulator	2852	2811	2821	2533	2523
General Governor	5704	5663	5673	5385	5375
High Overseer	787152	787111	787121	786833	786823

Fire - Venus

77	118	103	88	108	127	92
128	93	78	112	104	89	109
90	110	129	94	79	113	98
114	99	84	111	130	95	80
96	81	115	100	85	105	131
106	125	97	82	116	101	86
102	87	107	126	91	83	117

Occult Encyclopedia of Magic Squares

Earth - Venus

102	106	96	114	90	128	77
87	125	81	99	110	93	118
107	97	115	84	129	78	103
126	82	100	111	94	112	88
91	116	85	130	79	104	108
83	101	105	95	113	89	127
117	86	131	80	98	109	92

Air - Venus

117	83	91	126	107	87	102
86	101	116	82	97	125	106
131	105	85	100	115	81	96
80	95	130	111	84	99	114
98	113	79	94	129	110	90
109	89	104	112	78	93	128
92	127	108	88	103	118	77

Water - Venus

92	109	98	80	131	86	117
127	89	113	95	105	101	83
108	104	79	130	85	116	91
88	112	94	111	100	82	126
103	78	129	84	115	97	107
118	93	110	99	81	125	87
77	128	90	114	96	106	102

	Number	Angel Value (Arabic)	Angel Value (Hebrew)	Jinn Value (Arabic)	Jinn Value (Hebrew)
Usurper	77	36	46	118	108
Guide	131	90	100	172	162
Mystery	208	167	177	249	239
Adjuster	713	672	682	394	384
Leader	2139	2098	2108	1820	1810
Regulator	2852	2811	2821	2533	2523
General Governor	5704	5663	5673	5385	5375
High Overseer	747224	747183	747193	746905	746895

Occult Encyclopedia of Magic Squares

Fire - Mercury

57	73	123	102	91	107	88	72
65	81	110	94	99	120	80	64
108	92	71	87	74	58	101	122
121	100	63	79	82	66	93	109
86	70	89	105	125	104	59	75
78	62	97	118	112	96	67	83
103	124	76	60	69	85	106	90
95	111	84	68	61	77	119	98

Earth - Mercury

95	103	78	86	121	108	65	57
111	124	62	70	100	92	81	73
84	76	97	89	63	71	110	123
68	60	118	105	79	87	94	102
61	69	112	125	82	74	99	91
77	85	96	104	66	58	120	107
119	106	67	59	93	101	80	88
98	90	83	75	109	122	64	72

Air - Mercury

98	119	77	61	68	84	111	95
90	106	85	69	60	76	124	103
83	67	96	112	118	97	62	78
75	59	104	125	105	89	70	86
109	93	66	82	79	63	100	121
122	101	58	74	87	71	92	108
64	80	120	99	94	110	81	65
72	88	107	91	102	123	73	57

Water - Mercury

72	64	122	109	75	83	90	98
88	80	101	93	59	67	106	119
107	120	58	66	104	96	85	77
91	99	74	82	125	112	69	61
102	94	87	79	105	118	60	68
123	110	71	63	89	97	76	84
73	81	92	100	70	62	124	111
57	65	108	121	86	78	103	95

	Number	Angel Value (Arabic)	Angel Value (Hebrew)	Jinn Value (Arabic)	Jinn Value (Hebrew)
Usurper	57	16	26	98	88
Guide	125	84	94	166	156
Mystery	182	141	151	223	213
Adjuster	713	672	682	394	384
Leader	2139	2098	2108	1820	1810
Regulator	2852	2811	2821	2533	2523
General Governor	5704	5663	5673	5385	5375
High Overseer	713000	712959	712969	712681	712671

Fire - Moon

83	96	58	67	121	51	87	103	47
43	86	108	63	79	95	50	72	117
113	55	71	107	39	91	100	62	75
110	42	85	94	65	78	116	49	74
70	115	54	90	106	41	77	99	61
57	82	98	53	66	120	46	89	102
56	69	114	40	92	105	60	76	101
97	59	81	119	52	68	104	45	88
84	109	44	80	93	64	73	118	48

Earth - Moon

47	117	75	74	61	102	101	88	48
103	72	62	49	99	89	76	45	118
87	50	100	116	77	46	60	104	73
51	95	91	78	41	120	105	68	64
121	79	39	65	106	66	92	52	93
67	63	107	94	90	53	40	119	80
58	108	71	85	54	98	114	81	44
96	86	55	42	115	82	69	59	109
83	43	113	110	70	57	56	97	84

Occult Encyclopedia of Magic Squares

Air - Moon

48	118	73	64	93	80	44	109	84
88	45	104	68	52	119	81	59	97
101	76	60	105	92	40	114	69	56
102	89	46	120	66	53	98	82	57
61	99	77	41	106	90	54	115	70
74	49	116	78	65	94	85	42	110
75	62	100	91	39	107	71	55	113
117	72	50	95	79	63	108	86	43
47	103	87	51	121	67	58	96	83

Water - Moon

84	97	56	57	70	110	113	43	83
109	59	69	82	115	42	55	86	96
44	81	114	98	54	85	71	108	58
80	119	40	53	90	94	107	63	67
93	52	92	66	106	65	39	79	121
64	68	105	120	41	78	91	95	51
73	104	60	46	77	116	100	50	87
118	45	76	89	99	49	62	72	103
48	88	101	102	61	74	75	117	47

	Number	Angel Value (Arabic)	Angel Value (Hebrew)	Jinn Value (Arabic)	Jinn Value (Hebrew)
Usurper	39	358	8	80	70
Guide	121	80	90	162	152
Mystery	160	119	129	201	191
Adjuster	713	672	682	394	384
Leader	2139	2098	2108	1820	1810
Regulator	2852	2811	2821	2533	2523
General Governor	5704	5663	5673	5385	5375
High Overseer	690184	690143	690153	689865	689855

Fire - Saturn

21	39	46	84	75	121	68	60	92	107
32	96	89	80	123	105	23	65	51	49
47	52	76	122	106	91	40	28	69	82
53	78	120	108	41	87	95	36	25	70
66	119	110	45	56	79	83	93	38	24
73	30	31	98	86	62	58	48	103	124
85	67	27	34	100	55	43	104	127	71
99	88	63	22	33	50	101	126	74	57
109	42	54	61	29	37	125	72	90	94
128	102	97	59	64	26	77	81	44	35

Earth - Saturn

128	109	99	85	73	66	53	47	32	21
102	42	88	67	30	119	78	52	96	39
97	54	63	27	31	110	120	76	89	46
59	61	22	34	98	45	108	122	80	84
64	29	33	100	86	56	41	106	123	75
26	37	50	55	62	79	87	91	105	121
77	125	101	43	58	83	95	40	23	68
81	72	126	104	48	93	36	28	65	60
44	90	74	127	103	38	25	69	51	92
35	94	57	71	124	24	70	82	49	107

Air - Saturn

35	44	81	77	26	64	59	97	102	128
94	90	72	125	37	29	61	54	42	109
57	74	126	101	50	33	22	63	88	99
71	127	104	43	55	100	34	27	67	85
124	103	48	58	62	86	98	31	30	73
24	38	93	83	79	56	45	110	119	66
70	25	36	95	87	41	108	120	78	53
82	69	28	40	91	106	122	76	52	47
49	51	65	23	105	123	80	89	96	32
107	92	60	68	121	75	84	46	39	21

Water - Saturn

107	49	82	70	24	124	71	57	94	35
92	51	69	25	38	103	127	74	90	44
60	65	28	36	93	48	104	126	72	81
68	**23**	40	95	83	58	43	101	125	77
121	105	91	87	79	62	55	50	37	26
75	123	106	41	56	86	100	33	29	64
84	80	122	108	45	98	34	22	61	59
46	89	76	120	110	31	27	63	54	97
39	96	52	78	119	30	67	88	42	102
21	32	47	53	66	73	85	99	109	128

	Number	Angel Value (Arabic)	Angel Value (Hebrew)	Jinn Value (Arabic)	Jinn Value (Hebrew)
Usurper	21	340	350	62	52
Guide	128	87	97	169	159
Mystery	149	108	118	190	180
Adjuster	713	672	682	394	384
Leader	2139	2098	2108	1820	1810
Regulator	2852	2811	2821	2533	2523
General Governor	5704	5663	5673	5385	5375
High Overseer	730112	730071	730081	729793	729783

ARCHANGEL: TZAPHQIEL (311)

יאל	ק	פ	צ
89	81	103	38
102	39	88	82
79	91	40	101

ל	א	י	ק	פ	צ
פ	ק	ל	צ	י	א
י	צ	א	פ	ל	ק
צ	פ	ק	י	א	ל
ק	ל	פ	א	צ	י
א	י	צ	ל	ק	פ

Numerical Squares See Page: 636

ANGEL: CASSIEL (121)

אל	י	ם	כ
19	61	13	28
12	29	18	62
59	21	30	11

ל	א	י	ם	כ
י	ם	כ	ל	א
כ	ל	א	י	ם
א	י	ם	כ	ל
ם	כ	ל	א	י

Numerical Squares See Page: 216

INTELLIGENCE: AGIEL (45)

ל	א	י	אג
3	11	4	7
3	8	2	12
9	5	9	2

ל	א	י	ג	א
י	ג	א	ל	א
א	ל	א	י	ג
א	י	ג	א	ל
ג	א	ל	א	י

Fire - Jupiter

3	14	8	20
19	9	11	6
13	4	21	7
10	18	5	12

Air - Jupiter

12	5	18	10
7	21	4	13
6	11	9	19
20	8	14	3

Earth - Jupiter

10	13	19	3
18	4	9	14
5	21	11	8
12	7	6	20

Water - Jupiter

20	6	7	12
8	11	21	5
14	9	4	18
3	19	13	10

	Number	Angel Value (Arabic)	Angel Value (Hebrew)	Jinn Value (Arabic)	Jinn Value (Hebrew)
Usurper	3	322	332	44	34
Guide	21	340	350	62	52
Mystery	24	343	353	65	55
Adjuster	360	319	329	41	31
Leader	1080	1039	1049	761	751
Regulator	1440	1399	1409	1121	1111
General Governor	2880	2839	2849	2561	2551
High Overseer	60480	60439	60449	60161	60151

SPIRIT: ZAZEL (45)

Numerical Squares See Page: 663

OLYMPIC SPIRIT: ARATHRON (858)

Occult Encyclopedia of Magic Squares

Fire - Jupiter

207	218	212	221
220	213	215	210
217	208	222	211
214	219	209	216

Air - Jupiter

216	209	219	214
211	222	208	217
210	215	213	220
221	212	218	207

Earth - Jupiter

214	217	220	207
219	208	213	218
209	222	215	212
216	211	210	221

Water - Jupiter

221	210	211	216
212	215	222	209
218	213	208	219
207	220	217	214

	Number	Angel Value (Arabic)	Angel Value (Hebrew)	Jinn Value (Arabic)	Jinn Value (Hebrew)
Usurper	207	166	176	248	238
Guide	222	181	191	263	253
Mystery	429	388	398	110	100
Adjuster	6864	6823	6833	6545	6535
Leader	20592	20551	20561	20273	20263
Regulator	27456	27415	27425	27137	27127
General Governor	54912	54871	54881	54593	54583
High Overseer	12190464	12190423	12190433	12190145	12190135

Fire - Mars

159	186	177	171	165
172	166	160	182	178
183	174	173	167	161
168	162	184	175	169
176	170	164	163	185

Air - Mars

176	168	183	172	159
170	162	174	166	186
164	184	173	160	177
163	175	167	182	171
185	169	161	178	165

Earth - Mars

185	163	164	170	176
169	175	184	162	168
161	167	173	174	183
178	182	160	166	172
165	171	177	186	159

Water - Mars

165	178	161	169	185
171	182	167	175	163
177	160	173	184	164
186	166	174	162	170
159	172	183	168	176

Occult Encyclopedia of Magic Squares

	Number	Angel Value (Arabic)	Angel Value (Hebrew)	Jinn Value (Arabic)	Jinn Value (Hebrew)
Usurper	159	118	128	200	190
Guide	186	145	155	227	217
Mystery	345	304	314	26	16
Adjuster	858	817	827	539	529
Leader	2574	2533	2543	2255	2245
Regulator	3432	3391	3401	3113	3103
General Governor	6864	6823	6833	6545	6535
High Overseer	1276704	1276663	1276673	1276385	1276375

Fire - Sun

125	136	159	142	146	150
131	141	152	158	129	147
137	162	145	135	151	128
148	127	138	153	132	160
154	143	134	126	161	140
163	149	130	144	139	133

Air - Sun

133	139	144	130	149	163
140	161	126	134	143	154
160	132	153	138	127	148
128	151	135	145	162	137
147	129	158	152	141	131
150	146	142	159	136	125

Earth - Sun

163	154	148	137	131	125
149	143	127	162	141	136
130	134	138	145	152	159
144	126	153	135	158	142
139	161	132	151	129	146
133	140	160	128	147	150

Water - Sun

150	147	128	160	140	133
146	129	151	132	161	139
142	158	135	153	126	144
159	152	145	138	134	130
136	141	162	127	143	149
125	131	137	148	154	163

Occult Encyclopedia of Magic Squares

	Number	Angel Value (Arabic)	Angel Value (Hebrew)	Jinn Value (Arabic)	Jinn Value (Hebrew)
Usurper	125	84	94	166	156
Guide	163	122	132	204	194
Mystery	288	247	257	329	319
Adjuster	858	817	827	539	529
Leader	2574	2533	2543	2255	2245
Regulator	3432	3391	3401	3113	3103
General Governor	6864	6823	6833	6545	6535
High Overseer	1118832	1118791	1118801	1118513	1118503

Fire - Venus

98	139	124	109	129	146	113
147	114	99	133	125	110	130
111	131	148	115	100	134	119
135	120	105	132	149	116	101
117	102	136	121	106	126	150
127	144	118	103	137	122	107
123	108	128	145	112	104	138

Earth - Venus

123	127	117	135	111	147	98
108	144	102	120	131	114	139
128	118	136	105	148	99	124
145	103	121	132	115	133	109
112	137	106	149	100	125	129
104	122	126	116	134	110	146
138	107	150	101	119	130	113

Air - Venus

138	104	112	145	128	108	123
107	122	137	103	118	144	127
150	126	106	121	136	102	117
101	116	149	132	105	120	135
119	134	100	115	148	131	111
130	110	125	133	99	114	147
113	146	129	109	124	139	98

Occult Encyclopedia of Magic Squares

Water - Venus

113	130	119	101	150	107	138
146	110	134	116	126	122	104
129	125	100	149	106	137	112
109	133	115	132	121	103	145
124	99	148	105	136	118	128
139	114	131	120	102	144	108
98	147	111	135	117	127	123

	Number	Angel Value (Arabic)	Angel Value (Hebrew)	Jinn Value (Arabic)	Jinn Value (Hebrew)
Usurper	98	57	67	139	129
Guide	150	109	119	191	181
Mystery	248	207	217	289	279
Adjuster	858	817	827	539	529
Leader	2574	2533	2543	2255	2245
Regulator	3432	3391	3401	3113	3103
General Governor	6864	6823	6833	6545	6535
High Overseer	1029600	1029559	1029569	1029281	1029271

Fire - Mercury

75	91	142	120	109	125	106	90
83	99	128	112	117	139	98	82
126	110	89	105	92	76	119	141
140	118	81	97	100	84	111	127
104	88	107	123	144	122	77	93
96	80	115	137	130	114	85	101
121	143	94	78	87	103	124	108
113	129	102	86	79	95	138	116

Occult Encyclopedia of Magic Squares

Earth - Mercury

113	121	96	104	140	126	83	75
129	143	80	88	118	110	99	91
102	94	115	107	81	89	128	142
86	78	137	123	97	105	112	120
79	87	130	144	100	92	117	109
95	103	114	122	84	76	139	125
138	124	85	77	111	119	98	106
116	108	101	93	127	141	82	90

Air - Mercury

116	138	95	79	86	102	129	113
108	124	103	87	78	94	143	121
101	85	114	130	137	115	80	96
93	77	122	144	123	107	88	104
127	111	84	100	97	81	118	140
141	119	76	92	105	89	110	126
82	98	139	117	112	128	99	83
90	106	125	109	120	142	91	75

Water - Mercury

90	82	141	127	93	101	108	116
106	98	119	111	77	85	124	138
125	139	76	84	122	114	103	95
109	117	92	100	144	130	87	79
120	112	105	97	123	137	78	86
142	128	89	81	107	115	94	102
91	99	110	118	88	80	143	129
75	83	126	140	104	96	121	113

Occult Encyclopedia of Magic Squares

	Number	Angel Value (Arabic)	Angel Value (Hebrew)	Jinn Value (Arabic)	Jinn Value (Hebrew)
Usurper	75	34	44	116	106
Guide	144	103	113	185	175
Mystery	219	178	188	260	250
Adjuster	858	817	827	539	529
Leader	2574	2533	2543	2255	2245
Regulator	3432	3391	3401	3113	3103
General Governor	6864	6823	6833	6545	6535
High Overseer	988416	988375	988385	988097	988087

Fire - Moon

99	112	74	83	138	67	103	119	63
59	102	124	79	95	111	66	88	134
130	71	87	123	55	107	116	78	91
126	58	101	110	81	94	133	65	90
86	132	70	106	122	57	93	115	77
73	98	114	69	82	137	62	105	118
72	85	131	56	108	121	76	92	117
113	75	97	136	68	84	120	61	104
100	125	60	96	109	80	89	135	64

Earth - Moon

63	134	91	90	77	118	117	104	64
119	88	78	65	115	105	92	61	135
103	66	116	133	93	62	76	120	89
67	111	107	94	57	137	121	84	80
138	95	55	81	122	82	108	68	109
83	79	123	110	106	69	56	136	96
74	124	87	101	70	114	131	97	60
112	102	71	58	132	98	85	75	125
99	59	130	126	86	73	72	113	100

Occult Encyclopedia of Magic Squares

Air - Moon

64	135	89	80	109	96	60	125	100
104	61	120	84	68	136	97	75	113
117	92	76	121	108	56	131	85	72
118	105	62	137	82	69	114	98	73
77	115	93	57	122	106	70	132	86
90	65	133	94	81	110	101	58	126
91	78	116	107	55	123	87	71	130
134	88	66	111	95	79	124	102	59
63	119	103	67	138	83	74	112	99

Water - Moon

100	113	72	73	86	126	130	59	99
125	75	85	98	132	58	71	102	112
60	97	131	114	70	101	87	124	74
96	136	56	69	106	110	123	79	83
109	68	108	82	122	81	55	95	138
80	84	121	137	57	94	107	111	67
89	120	76	62	93	133	116	66	103
135	61	92	105	115	65	78	88	119
64	104	117	118	77	90	91	134	63

	Number	Angel Value (Arabic)	Angel Value (Hebrew)	Jinn Value (Arabic)	Jinn Value (Hebrew)
Usurper	55	14	24	96	86
Guide	138	97	107	179	169
Mystery	193	152	162	234	224
Adjuster	858	817	827	539	529
Leader	2574	2533	2543	2255	2245
Regulator	3432	3391	3401	3113	3103
General Governor	6864	6823	6833	6545	6535
High Overseer	947232	947191	947201	946913	946903

Occult Encyclopedia of Magic Squares

Fire - Saturn

36	54	61	99	90	131	83	75	107	122
47	111	104	95	133	120	38	80	66	64
62	67	91	132	121	106	55	43	84	97
68	93	130	123	56	102	110	51	40	85
81	129	125	60	71	94	98	108	53	39
88	45	46	113	101	77	73	63	118	134
100	82	42	49	115	70	58	119	137	86
114	103	78	37	48	65	116	136	89	72
124	57	69	76	44	52	135	87	105	109
138	117	112	74	79	41	92	96	59	50

Earth - Saturn

138	124	114	100	88	81	68	62	47	36
117	57	103	82	45	129	93	67	111	54
112	69	78	42	46	125	130	91	104	61
74	76	37	49	113	60	123	132	95	99
79	44	48	115	101	71	56	121	133	90
41	52	65	70	77	94	102	106	120	131
92	135	116	58	73	98	110	55	38	83
96	87	136	119	63	108	51	43	80	75
59	105	89	137	118	53	40	84	66	107
50	109	72	86	134	39	85	97	64	122

Air - Saturn

50	59	96	92	41	79	74	112	117	138
109	105	87	135	52	44	76	69	57	124
72	89	136	116	65	48	37	78	103	114
86	137	119	58	70	115	49	42	82	100
134	118	63	73	77	101	113	46	45	88
39	53	108	98	94	71	60	125	129	81
85	40	51	110	102	56	123	130	93	68
97	84	43	55	106	121	132	91	67	62
64	66	80	38	120	133	95	104	111	47
122	107	75	83	131	90	99	61	54	36

Occult Encyclopedia of Magic Squares

Water - Saturn

122	64	97	85	39	134	86	72	109	50
107	66	84	40	53	118	137	89	105	59
75	80	43	51	108	63	119	136	87	96
83	**38**	55	110	98	73	58	116	135	92
131	120	106	102	94	77	70	65	52	41
90	133	121	56	71	101	115	48	44	79
99	95	132	123	60	113	49	37	76	74
61	104	91	130	125	46	42	78	69	112
54	111	67	93	129	45	82	103	57	117
36	47	62	68	81	88	100	114	124	138

	Number	Angel Value (Arabic)	Angel Value (Hebrew)	Jinn Value (Arabic)	Jinn Value (Hebrew)
Usurper	36	355	5	77	67
Guide	138	97	107	179	169
Mystery	174	133	143	215	205
Adjuster	858	817	827	539	529
Leader	2574	2533	2543	2255	2245
Regulator	3432	3391	3401	3113	3103
General Governor	6864	6823	6833	6545	6535
High Overseer	947232	947191	947201	946913	946903

JUPITER

JUPITER: TZEDEK (194)

No Hebrew Squares Available

FIRE - JUPITER

41	52	46	55
54	47	49	44
51	42	56	45
48	53	43	50

Air - Jupiter

50	43	53	48
45	56	42	51
44	49	47	54
55	46	52	41

Earth - Jupiter

48	51	54	41
53	42	47	52
43	56	49	46
50	45	44	55

Water - Jupiter

55	44	45	50
46	49	56	43
52	47	42	53
41	54	51	48

Occult Encyclopedia of Magic Squares

	Number	Angel Value (Arabic)	Angel Value (Hebrew)	Jinn Value (Arabic)	Jinn Value (Hebrew)
Usurper	41	360	10	82	72
Guide	56	15	25	97	87
Mystery	97	56	66	138	128
Adjuster	1552	1511	1521	1233	1223
Leader	4656	4615	4625	4337	4327
Regulator	6208	6167	6177	5889	5879
General Governor	12416	12375	12385	12097	12087
High Overseer	695296	695255	695265	694977	694967

Fire - Mars

26	54	44	38	32
39	33	27	50	45
51	41	40	34	28
35	29	52	42	36
43	37	31	30	53

Air - Mars

43	35	51	39	26
37	29	41	33	54
31	52	40	27	44
30	42	34	50	38
53	36	28	45	32

Earth - Mars

53	30	31	37	43
36	42	52	29	35
28	34	40	41	51
45	50	27	33	39
32	38	44	54	26

Water - Mars

32	45	28	36	53
38	50	34	42	30
44	27	40	52	31
54	33	41	29	37
26	39	51	35	43

	Number	Angel Value (Arabic)	Angel Value (Hebrew)	Jinn Value (Arabic)	Jinn Value (Hebrew)
Usurper	26	345	355	67	57
Guide	54	13	23	95	85
Mystery	80	39	49	121	111
Adjuster	194	153	163	235	225
Leader	582	541	551	263	253
Regulator	776	735	745	457	447
General Governor	1552	1511	1521	1233	1223
High Overseer	83808	83767	83777	83489	83479

Occult Encyclopedia of Magic Squares

Fire - Sun

14	25	50	31	35	39
20	30	41	49	18	36
26	53	34	24	40	17
37	16	27	42	21	51
43	32	23	15	52	29
54	38	19	33	28	22

Air - Sun

22	28	33	19	38	54
29	52	15	23	32	43
51	21	42	27	16	37
17	40	24	34	53	26
36	18	49	41	30	20
39	35	31	50	25	14

Earth - Sun

54	43	37	26	20	14
38	32	16	53	30	25
19	23	27	34	41	50
33	15	42	24	49	31
28	52	21	40	18	35
22	29	51	17	36	39

Water - Sun

39	36	17	51	29	22
35	18	40	21	52	28
31	49	24	42	15	33
50	41	34	27	23	19
25	30	53	16	32	38
14	20	26	37	43	54

	Number	Angel Value (Arabic)	Angel Value (Hebrew)	Jinn Value (Arabic)	Jinn Value (Hebrew)
Usurper	14	333	343	55	45
Guide	54	13	23	95	85
Mystery	68	27	37	109	99
Adjuster	194	153	163	235	225
Leader	582	541	551	263	253
Regulator	776	735	745	457	447
General Governor	1552	1511	1521	1233	1223
High Overseer	83808	83767	83777	83489	83479

Fire - Venus

3	44	29	14	34	52	18
53	19	4	38	30	15	35
16	36	54	20	5	39	24
40	25	10	37	55	21	6
22	7	41	26	11	31	56
32	50	23	8	42	27	12
28	13	33	51	17	9	43

Earth - Venus

28	32	22	40	16	53	3
13	50	7	25	36	19	44
33	23	41	10	54	4	29
51	8	26	37	20	38	14
17	42	11	55	5	30	34
9	27	31	21	39	15	52
43	12	56	6	24	35	18

Air - Venus

43	9	17	51	33	13	28
12	27	42	8	23	50	32
56	31	11	26	41	7	22
6	21	55	37	10	25	40
24	39	5	20	54	36	16
35	15	30	38	4	19	53
18	52	34	14	29	44	3

Water - Venus

18	35	24	6	56	12	43
52	15	39	21	31	27	9
34	30	5	55	11	42	17
14	38	20	37	26	8	51
29	4	54	10	41	23	33
44	19	36	25	7	50	13
3	53	16	40	22	32	28

	Number	Angel Value (Arabic)	Angel Value (Hebrew)	Jinn Value (Arabic)	Jinn Value (Hebrew)
Usurper	3	322	332	44	34
Guide	56	15	25	97	87
Mystery	59	18	28	100	90
Adjuster	194	153	163	235	225
Leader	582	541	551	263	253
Regulator	776	735	745	457	447
General Governor	1552	1511	1521	1233	1223
High Overseer	86912	86871	86881	86593	86583

ARCHANGEL: TZADQIEL (235)

אל	ק	ד	צ
89	5	103	38
102	39	88	6
3	91	40	101

ל	א	י	ק	ד	צ
ד	ק	ל	צ	י	א
י	צ	א	ד	ל	ק
צ	ד	ק	י	א	ל
ק	ל	ד	א	צ	י
א	י	צ	ל	ק	ד

677

Occult Encyclopedia of Magic Squares

Fire - Jupiter

51	62	56	66
65	57	59	54
61	52	67	55
58	64	53	60

Air - Jupiter

60	53	64	58
55	67	52	61
54	59	57	65
66	56	62	51

Earth - Jupiter

58	61	65	51
64	52	57	62
53	67	59	56
60	55	54	66

Water - Jupiter

66	54	55	60
56	59	67	53
62	57	52	64
51	65	61	58

	Number	Angel Value (Arabic)	Angel Value (Hebrew)	Jinn Value (Arabic)	Jinn Value (Hebrew)
Usurper	51	10	20	92	82
Guide	67	26	36	108	98
Mystery	118	77	87	159	149
Adjuster	1880	1839	1849	1561	1551
Leader	5640	5599	5609	5321	5311
Regulator	7520	7479	7489	7201	7191
General Governor	15040	14999	15009	14721	14711
High Overseer	1007680	1007639	1007649	1007361	1007351

Fire - Mars

35	59	53	47	41
48	42	36	55	54
56	50	49	43	37
44	38	57	51	45
52	46	40	39	58

Air - Mars

52	44	56	48	35
46	38	50	42	59
40	57	49	36	53
39	51	43	55	47
58	45	37	54	41

Earth - Mars

58	39	40	46	52
45	51	57	38	44
37	43	49	50	56
54	55	36	42	48
41	47	53	59	35

Water - Mars

41	54	37	45	58
47	55	43	51	39
53	36	49	57	40
59	42	50	38	46
35	48	56	44	52

678

Occult Encyclopedia of Magic Squares

	Number	Angel Value (Arabic)	Angel Value (Hebrew)	Jinn Value (Arabic)	Jinn Value (Hebrew)
Usurper	35	354	4	76	66
Guide	59	18	28	100	90
Mystery	94	53	63	135	125
Adjuster	235	194	204	276	266
Leader	705	664	674	386	376
Regulator	940	899	909	621	611
General Governor	1880	1839	1849	1561	1551
High Overseer	110920	110879	110889	110601	110591

Fire - Sun

21	32	56	38	42	46
27	37	48	55	25	43
33	59	41	31	47	24
44	23	34	49	28	57
50	39	30	22	58	36
60	45	26	40	35	29

Air - Sun

29	35	40	26	45	60
36	58	22	30	39	50
57	28	49	34	23	44
24	47	31	41	59	33
43	25	55	48	37	27
46	42	38	56	32	21

Earth - Sun

60	50	44	33	27	21
45	39	23	59	37	32
26	30	34	41	48	56
40	22	49	31	55	38
35	58	28	47	25	42
29	36	57	24	43	46

Water - Sun

46	43	24	57	36	29
42	25	47	28	58	35
38	55	31	49	22	40
56	48	41	34	30	26
32	37	59	23	39	45
21	27	33	44	50	60

Occult Encyclopedia of Magic Squares

	Number	Angel Value (Arabic)	Angel Value (Hebrew)	Jinn Value (Arabic)	Jinn Value (Hebrew)
Usurper	21	340	350	62	52
Guide	60	19	29	101	91
Mystery	81	40	50	122	112
Adjuster	235	194	204	276	266
Leader	705	664	674	386	376
Regulator	940	899	909	621	611
General Governor	1880	1839	1849	1561	1551
High Overseer	112800	112759	112769	112481	112471

Fire - Venus

9	50	35	20	40	57	24
58	25	10	44	36	21	41
22	42	59	26	11	45	30
46	31	16	43	60	27	12
28	13	47	32	17	37	61
38	55	29	14	48	33	18
34	19	39	56	23	15	49

Air - Venus

49	15	23	56	39	19	34
18	33	48	14	29	55	38
61	37	17	32	47	13	28
12	27	60	43	16	31	46
30	45	11	26	59	42	22
41	21	36	44	10	25	58
24	57	40	20	35	50	9

Earth - Venus

34	38	28	46	22	58	9
19	55	13	31	42	25	50
39	29	47	16	59	10	35
56	14	32	43	26	44	20
23	48	17	60	11	36	40
15	33	37	27	45	21	57
49	18	61	12	30	41	24

Water - Venus

24	41	30	12	61	18	49
57	21	45	27	37	33	15
40	36	11	60	17	48	23
20	44	26	43	32	14	56
35	10	59	16	47	29	39
50	25	42	31	13	55	19
9	58	22	46	28	38	34

	Number	Angel Value (Arabic)	Angel Value (Hebrew)	Jinn Value (Arabic)	Jinn Value (Hebrew)
Usurper	9	328	338	50	40
Guide	61	20	30	102	92
Mystery	70	29	39	111	101
Adjuster	235	194	204	276	266
Leader	705	664	674	386	376
Regulator	940	899	909	621	611
General Governor	1880	1839	1849	1561	1551
High Overseer	114680	114639	114649	114361	114351

ANGEL: SACHIEL (109)

אל	י	ח	ס
59	9	13	28
12	29	58	10
7	61	30	11

ל	א	י	ח	ס
י	ח	ס	ל	א
ס	ל	א	י	ח
א	י	ח	ס	ל
ח	ס	ל	א	י

Fire - Jupiter

19	30	24	36
35	25	27	22
29	20	37	23
26	34	21	28

Air - Jupiter

28	21	34	26
23	37	20	29
22	27	25	35
36	24	30	19

Earth - Jupiter

26	29	35	19
34	20	25	30
21	37	27	24
28	23	22	36

Water - Jupiter

36	22	23	28
24	27	37	21
30	25	20	34
19	35	29	26

	Number	Angel Value (Arabic)	Angel Value (Hebrew)	Jinn Value (Arabic)	Jinn Value (Hebrew)
Usurper	19	338	348	60	50
Guide	37	356	6	78	68
Mystery	56	15	25	97	87
Adjuster	872	831	841	553	543
Leader	2616	2575	2585	2297	2287
Regulator	3488	3447	3457	3169	3159
General Governor	6976	6935	6945	6657	6647
High Overseer	258112	258071	258081	257793	257783

Fire - Mars

9	37	27	21	15
22	16	10	33	28
34	24	23	17	11
18	12	35	25	19
26	20	14	13	36

Air - Mars

26	18	34	22	9
20	12	24	16	37
14	35	23	10	27
13	25	17	33	21
36	19	11	28	15

Earth - Mars

36	13	14	20	26
19	25	35	12	18
11	17	23	24	34
28	33	10	16	22
15	21	27	37	9

Water - Mars

15	28	11	19	36
21	33	17	25	13
27	10	23	35	14
37	16	24	12	20
9	22	34	18	26

	Number	Angel Value (Arabic)	Angel Value (Hebrew)	Jinn Value (Arabic)	Jinn Value (Hebrew)
Usurper	9	328	338	50	40
Guide	37	356	6	78	68
Mystery	46	5	15	87	77
Adjuster	109	68	78	150	140
Leader	327	286	296	8	358
Regulator	436	395	405	117	107
General Governor	872	831	841	553	543
High Overseer	32264	32223	32233	31945	31935

INTELLIGENCE: IOPHIEL (136)

ל	א	י	ם	ה	י
ה	ם	ל	י	י	א
י	י	א	ה	ל	ם
י	ה	ם	י	א	ל
ם	ל	ה	א	י	י
א	י	י	ל	ם	ה

יאל	ם	ה	י
9	6	83	38
82	39	8	7
4	11	40	81

Fire - Jupiter

26	37	31	42
41	32	34	29
36	27	43	30
33	40	28	35

Air - Jupiter

35	28	40	33
30	43	27	36
29	34	32	41
42	31	37	26

Earth - Jupiter

33	36	41	26
40	27	32	37
28	43	34	31
35	30	29	42

Water - Jupiter

42	29	30	35
31	34	43	28
37	32	27	40
26	41	36	33

	Number	Angel Value (Arabic)	Angel Value (Hebrew)	Jinn Value (Arabic)	Jinn Value (Hebrew)
Usurper	26	345	355	67	57
Guide	43	2	12	84	74
Mystery	69	28	38	110	100
Adjuster	1088	1047	1057	769	759
Leader	3264	3223	3233	2945	2935
Regulator	4352	4311	4321	4033	4023
General Governor	8704	8663	8673	8385	8375
High Overseer	374272	374231	374241	373953	373943

Fire - Mars

15	40	33	27	21
28	22	16	36	34
37	30	29	23	17
24	18	38	31	25
32	26	20	19	39

Air - Mars

32	24	37	28	15
26	18	30	22	40
20	38	29	16	33
19	31	23	36	27
39	25	17	34	21

Earth - Mars

39	19	20	26	32
25	31	38	18	24
17	23	29	30	37
34	36	16	22	28
21	27	33	40	15

Water - Mars

21	34	17	25	39
27	36	23	31	19
33	16	29	38	20
40	22	30	18	26
15	28	37	24	32

	Number	Angel Value (Arabic)	Angel Value (Hebrew)	Jinn Value (Arabic)	Jinn Value (Hebrew)
Usurper	15	334	344	56	46
Guide	40	359	9	81	71
Mystery	55	14	24	96	86
Adjuster	136	95	105	177	167
Leader	408	367	377	89	79
Regulator	544	503	513	225	215
General Governor	1088	1047	1057	769	759
High Overseer	43520	43479	43489	43201	43191

Fire - Sun

5	16	37	22	26	30
11	21	32	36	9	27
17	40	25	15	31	8
28	7	18	33	12	38
34	23	14	6	39	20
41	29	10	24	19	13

Earth - Sun

41	34	28	17	11	5
29	23	7	40	21	16
10	14	18	25	32	37
24	6	33	15	36	22
19	39	12	31	9	26
13	20	38	8	27	30

Air - Sun

13	19	24	10	29	41
20	39	6	14	23	34
38	12	33	18	7	28
8	31	15	25	40	17
27	9	36	32	21	11
30	26	22	37	16	5

Water - Sun

30	27	8	38	20	13
26	9	31	12	39	19
22	36	15	33	6	24
37	32	25	18	14	10
16	21	40	7	23	29
5	11	17	28	34	41

	Number	Angel Value (Arabic)	Angel Value (Hebrew)	Jinn Value (Arabic)	Jinn Value (Hebrew)
Usurper	5	324	334	46	36
Guide	41	360	10	82	72
Mystery	46	5	15	87	77
Adjuster	136	95	105	177	167
Leader	408	367	377	89	79
Regulator	544	503	513	225	215
General Governor	1088	1047	1057	769	759
High Overseer	44608	44567	44577	44289	44279

SPIRIT: HISMAEL (136)

לא	מ	ס	ה
4	61	43	28
42	29	3	62
59	6	30	41

ל	א	מ	ס	ה
מ	ס	ה	ל	א
ה	ל	א	מ	ס
א	מ	ס	ה	ל
ס	ה	ל	א	מ

Numerical Squares See Page: 683

OLYMPIC SPIRIT: BETHOR (618)

ר	ו	ת	בי
11	401	9	197
8	198	10	402
399	13	199	7

ר	ו	ת	י	ב
ת	י	ב	ר	ו
ב	ר	ו	ת	י
ו	ת	י	ב	ר
י	ב	ר	ו	ת

Fire - Jupiter

147	158	152	161
160	153	155	150
157	148	162	151
154	159	149	156

Air - Jupiter

156	149	159	154
151	162	148	157
150	155	153	160
161	152	158	147

Earth - Jupiter

154	157	160	147
159	148	153	158
149	162	155	152
156	151	150	161

Water - Jupiter

161	150	151	156
152	155	162	149
158	153	148	159
147	160	157	154

	Number	Angel Value (Arabic)	Angel Value (Hebrew)	Jinn Value (Arabic)	Jinn Value (Hebrew)
Usurper	147	106	116	188	178
Guide	162	121	131	203	193
Mystery	309	268	278	350	340
Adjuster	4944	4903	4913	4625	4615
Leader	14832	14791	14801	14513	14503
Regulator	19776	19735	19745	19457	19447
General Governor	39552	39511	39521	39233	39223
High Overseer	6407424	6407383	6407393	6407105	6407095

Occult Encyclopedia of Magic Squares

Fire - Mars

111	138	129	123	117
124	118	112	134	130
135	126	125	119	113
120	114	136	127	121
128	122	116	115	137

Air - Mars

128	120	135	124	111
122	114	126	118	138
116	136	125	112	129
115	127	119	134	123
137	121	113	130	117

Earth - Mars

137	115	116	122	128
121	127	136	114	120
113	119	125	126	135
130	134	112	118	124
117	123	129	138	111

Water - Mars

117	130	113	121	137
123	134	119	127	115
129	112	125	136	116
138	118	126	114	122
111	124	135	120	128

	Number	Angel Value (Arabic)	Angel Value (Hebrew)	Jinn Value (Arabic)	Jinn Value (Hebrew)
Usurper	111	70	80	152	142
Guide	138	97	107	179	169
Mystery	249	208	218	290	280
Adjuster	618	577	587	299	289
Leader	1854	1813	1823	1535	1525
Regulator	2472	2431	2441	2153	2143
General Governor	4944	4903	4913	4625	4615
High Overseer	682272	682231	682241	681953	681943

Fire - Sun

85	96	119	102	106	110
91	101	112	118	89	107
97	122	105	95	111	88
108	87	98	113	92	120
114	103	94	86	121	100
123	109	90	104	99	93

Earth - Sun

123	114	108	97	91	85
109	103	87	122	101	96
90	94	98	105	112	119
104	86	113	95	118	102
99	121	92	111	89	106
93	100	120	88	107	110

Occult Encyclopedia of Magic Squares

Air - Sun

93	99	104	90	109	123
100	121	86	94	103	114
120	92	113	98	87	108
88	111	95	105	122	97
107	89	118	112	101	91
110	106	102	119	96	85

Water - Sun

110	107	88	120	100	93
106	89	111	92	121	99
102	118	95	113	86	104
119	112	105	98	94	90
96	101	122	87	103	109
85	91	97	108	114	123

	Number	Angel Value (Arabic)	Angel Value (Hebrew)	Jinn Value (Arabic)	Jinn Value (Hebrew)
Usurper	85	44	54	126	116
Guide	123	82	92	164	154
Mystery	208	167	177	249	239
Adjuster	618	577	587	299	289
Leader	1854	1813	1823	1535	1525
Regulator	2472	2431	2441	2153	2143
General Governor	4944	4903	4913	4625	4615
High Overseer	608112	608071	608081	607793	607783

Fire - Venus

64	105	90	75	95	110	79
111	80	65	99	91	76	96
77	97	112	81	66	100	85
101	86	71	98	113	82	67
83	68	102	87	72	92	114
93	108	84	69	103	88	73
89	74	94	109	78	70	104

Earth - Venus

89	93	83	101	77	111	64
74	108	68	86	97	80	105
94	84	102	71	112	65	90
109	69	87	98	81	99	75
78	103	72	113	66	91	95
70	88	92	82	100	76	110
104	73	114	67	85	96	79

Air - Venus

104	70	78	109	94	74	89
73	88	103	69	84	108	93
114	92	72	87	102	68	83
67	82	113	98	71	86	101
85	100	66	81	112	97	77
96	76	91	99	65	80	111
79	110	95	75	90	105	64

Water - Venus

79	96	85	67	114	73	104
110	76	100	82	92	88	70
95	91	66	113	72	103	78
75	99	81	98	87	69	109
90	65	112	71	102	84	94
105	80	97	86	68	108	74
64	111	77	101	83	93	89

	Number	Angel Value (Arabic)	Angel Value (Hebrew)	Jinn Value (Arabic)	Jinn Value (Hebrew)
Usurper	64	23	33	105	95
Guide	114	73	83	155	145
Mystery	178	137	147	219	209
Adjuster	618	577	587	299	289
Leader	1854	1813	1823	1535	1525
Regulator	2472	2431	2441	2153	2143
General Governor	4944	4903	4913	4625	4615
High Overseer	563616	563575	563585	563297	563287

Occult Encyclopedia of Magic Squares

Fire - Mercury

45	61	112	90	79	95	76	60
53	69	98	82	87	109	68	52
96	80	59	75	62	46	89	111
110	88	51	67	70	54	81	97
74	58	77	93	114	92	47	63
66	50	85	107	100	84	55	71
91	113	64	48	57	73	94	78
83	99	72	56	49	65	108	86

Earth - Mercury

83	91	66	74	110	96	53	45
99	113	50	58	88	80	69	61
72	64	85	77	51	59	98	112
56	48	107	93	67	75	82	90
49	57	100	114	70	62	87	79
65	73	84	92	54	46	109	95
108	94	55	47	81	89	68	76
86	78	71	63	97	111	52	60

Air - Mercury

86	108	65	49	56	72	99	83
78	94	73	57	48	64	113	91
71	55	84	100	107	85	50	66
63	47	92	114	93	77	58	74
97	81	54	70	67	51	88	110
111	89	46	62	75	59	80	96
52	68	109	87	82	98	69	53
60	76	95	79	90	112	61	45

Water - Mercury

60	52	111	97	63	71	78	86
76	68	89	81	47	55	94	108
95	109	46	54	92	84	73	65
79	87	62	70	114	100	57	49
90	82	75	67	93	107	48	56
112	98	59	51	77	85	64	72
61	69	80	88	58	50	113	99
45	53	96	110	74	66	91	83

	Number	Angel Value (Arabic)	Angel Value (Hebrew)	Jinn Value (Arabic)	Jinn Value (Hebrew)
Usurper	45	4	14	86	76
Guide	114	73	83	155	145
Mystery	159	118	128	200	190
Adjuster	618	577	587	299	289
Leader	1854	1813	1823	1535	1525
Regulator	2472	2431	2441	2153	2143
General Governor	4944	4903	4913	4625	4615
High Overseer	563616	563575	563585	563297	563287

Fire - Moon

72	85	47	56	114	40	76	92	36
32	75	97	52	68	84	39	61	110
106	44	60	96	28	80	89	51	64
99	31	74	83	54	67	109	38	63
59	108	43	79	95	30	66	88	50
46	71	87	42	55	113	35	78	91
45	58	107	29	81	94	49	65	90
86	48	70	112	41	57	93	34	77
73	98	33	69	82	53	62	111	37

Earth - Moon

36	110	64	63	50	91	90	77	37
92	61	51	38	88	78	65	34	111
76	39	89	109	66	35	49	93	62
40	84	80	67	30	113	94	57	53
114	68	28	54	95	55	81	41	82
56	52	96	83	79	42	29	112	69
47	97	60	74	43	87	107	70	33
85	75	44	31	108	71	58	48	98
72	32	106	99	59	46	45	86	73

Occult Encyclopedia of Magic Squares

Air - Moon

37	111	62	53	82	69	33	98	73
77	34	93	57	41	112	70	48	86
90	65	49	94	81	29	107	58	45
91	78	35	113	55	42	87	71	46
50	88	66	30	95	79	43	108	59
63	38	109	67	54	83	74	31	99
64	51	89	80	28	96	60	44	106
110	61	39	84	68	52	97	75	32
36	92	76	40	114	56	47	85	72

Water - Moon

73	86	45	46	59	99	106	32	72
98	48	58	71	108	31	44	75	85
33	70	107	87	43	74	60	97	47
69	112	29	42	79	83	96	52	56
82	41	81	55	95	54	28	68	114
53	57	94	113	30	67	80	84	40
62	93	49	35	66	109	89	39	76
111	34	65	78	88	38	51	61	92
37	77	90	91	50	63	64	110	36

	Number	Angel Value (Arabic)	Angel Value (Hebrew)	Jinn Value (Arabic)	Jinn Value (Hebrew)
Usurper	28	347	357	69	59
Guide	114	73	83	155	145
Mystery	142	101	111	183	173
Adjuster	618	577	587	299	289
Leader	1854	1813	1823	1535	1525
Regulator	2472	2431	2441	2153	2143
General Governor	4944	4903	4913	4625	4615
High Overseer	563616	563575	563585	563297	563287

Fire - Saturn

12	30	37	75	66	107	59	51	83	98
23	87	80	71	109	96	14	56	42	40
38	43	67	108	97	82	31	19	60	73
44	69	106	99	32	78	86	27	16	61
57	105	101	36	47	70	74	84	29	15
64	21	22	89	77	53	49	39	94	110
76	58	18	25	91	46	34	95	113	62
90	79	54	13	24	41	92	112	65	48
100	33	45	52	20	28	111	63	81	85
114	93	88	50	55	17	68	72	35	26

Earth - Saturn

114	100	90	76	64	57	44	38	23	12
93	33	79	58	21	105	69	43	87	30
88	45	54	18	22	101	106	67	80	37
50	52	13	25	89	36	99	108	71	75
55	20	24	91	77	47	32	97	109	66
17	28	41	46	53	70	78	82	96	107
68	111	92	34	49	74	86	31	14	59
72	63	112	95	39	84	27	19	56	51
35	81	65	113	94	29	16	60	42	83
26	85	48	62	110	15	61	73	40	98

Air - Saturn

26	35	72	68	17	55	50	88	93	114
85	81	63	111	28	20	52	45	33	100
48	65	112	92	41	24	13	54	79	90
62	113	95	34	46	91	25	18	58	76
110	94	39	49	53	77	89	22	21	64
15	29	84	74	70	47	36	101	105	57
61	16	27	86	78	32	99	106	69	44
73	60	19	31	82	97	108	67	43	38
40	42	56	14	96	109	71	80	87	23
98	83	51	59	107	66	75	37	30	12

Water - Saturn

98	40	73	61	15	110	62	48	85	26
83	42	60	16	29	94	113	65	81	35
51	56	19	27	84	39	95	112	63	72
59	**14**	31	86	74	49	34	92	111	68
107	96	82	78	70	53	46	41	28	17
66	109	97	32	47	77	91	24	20	55
75	71	108	99	36	89	25	13	52	50
37	80	67	106	101	22	18	54	45	88
30	87	43	69	105	21	58	79	33	93
12	23	38	44	57	64	76	90	100	114

	Number	Angel Value (Arabic)	Angel Value (Hebrew)	Jinn Value (Arabic)	Jinn Value (Hebrew)
Usurper	12	331	341	53	43
Guide	114	73	83	155	145
Mystery	126	85	95	167	157
Adjuster	618	577	587	299	289
Leader	1854	1813	1823	1535	1525
Regulator	2472	2431	2441	2153	2143
General Governor	4944	4903	4913	4625	4615
High Overseer	563616	563575	563585	563297	563287

MARS

MARS: MADIM (94)

מ	י	ד	מ
39	5	13	37
12	38	38	6
3	41	39	11

מ	י	ד	מ
מ	ד	י	מ
י	מ	מ	ד
ד	מ	מ	י

Fire - Jupiter

16	27	21	30
29	22	24	19
26	17	31	20
23	28	18	25

Air - Jupiter

25	18	28	23
20	31	17	26
19	24	22	29
30	21	27	16

Earth - Jupiter

23	26	29	16
28	17	22	27
18	31	24	21
25	20	19	30

Water - Jupiter

30	19	20	25
21	24	31	18
27	22	17	28
16	29	26	23

	Number	Angel Value (Arabic)	Angel Value (Hebrew)	Jinn Value (Arabic)	Jinn Value (Hebrew)
Usurper	16	335	345	57	47
Guide	31	350	360	72	62
Mystery	47	6	16	88	78
Adjuster	752	711	721	433	423
Leader	2256	2215	2225	1937	1927
Regulator	3008	2967	2977	2689	2679
General Governor	6016	5975	5985	5697	5687
High Overseer	186496	186455	186465	186177	186167

Fire - Mars

6	34	24	18	12
19	13	7	30	25
31	21	20	14	8
15	9	32	22	16
23	17	11	10	33

Air - Mars

23	15	31	19	6
17	9	21	13	34
11	32	20	7	24
10	22	14	30	18
33	16	8	25	12

Earth - Mars

33	10	11	17	23
16	22	32	9	15
8	14	20	21	31
25	30	7	13	19
12	18	24	34	6

Water - Mars

12	25	8	16	33
18	30	14	22	10
24	7	20	32	11
34	13	21	9	17
6	19	31	15	23

	Number	Angel Value (Arabic)	Angel Value (Hebrew)	Jinn Value (Arabic)	Jinn Value (Hebrew)
Usurper	6	325	335	47	37
Guide	34	353	3	75	65
Mystery	40	359	9	81	71
Adjuster	94	53	63	135	125
Leader	282	241	251	323	313
Regulator	376	335	345	57	47
General Governor	752	711	721	433	423
High Overseer	25568	25527	25537	25249	25239

ARCHANGEL: KAMAEL (91)

ל	א	מ	ב
19	41	4	27
3	28	18	42
39	21	29	2

ל	א	מ	ב
ב	מ	א	ל
א	ל	ב	מ
מ	ב	ל	א

Numerical Squares See Page: 401

ANGEL: ZAMAEL (78)

ל	א	מ	ז
6	41	4	27
3	28	5	42
39	8	29	2

ל	א	מ	ז
ז	מ	א	ל
א	ל	ז	מ
מ	ז	ל	א

Numerical Squares See Page: 91

INTELLIGENCE: GRAPHIEL (325)

יאל	פ	רא	ג
2	202	83	38
82	39	1	203
200	4	40	81

ל	א	י	פ	א	ר	ג
י	פ	א	ר	ג	ל	א
א	ר	ג	ל	א	י	פ
ג	ל	א	י	פ	א	ר
א	י	פ	א	ר	ג	ל
פ	א	ר	ג	ל	א	י
ר	ג	ל	א	י	פ	א

Numerical Squares See Page: 441

697

Spirit: Bartzabel (325)

אל	ב	צ	בר
201	91	5	28
4	29	200	92
89	203	30	3

Numerical Squares See Page: 441

Olympic Spirit: Phaleg (113)

Hebrew Squares Not Available

Fire - Jupiter

20	31	25	37
36	26	28	23
30	21	38	24
27	35	22	29

Air - Jupiter

29	22	35	27
24	38	21	30
23	28	26	36
37	25	31	20

Earth - Jupiter

27	30	36	20
35	21	26	31
22	38	28	25
29	24	23	37

Water - Jupiter

37	23	24	29
25	28	38	22
31	26	21	35
20	36	30	27

Occult Encyclopedia of Magic Squares

	Number	Angel Value (Arabic)	Angel Value (Hebrew)	Jinn Value (Arabic)	Jinn Value (Hebrew)
Usurper	20	339	349	61	51
Guide	38	357	7	79	69
Mystery	58	17	27	99	89
Adjuster	904	863	873	585	575
Leader	2712	2671	2681	2393	2383
Regulator	3616	3575	3585	3297	3287
General Governor	7232	7191	7201	6913	6903
High Overseer	274816	274775	274785	274497	274487

Fire - Mars

10	37	28	22	16
23	17	11	33	29
34	25	24	18	12
19	13	35	26	20
27	21	15	14	36

Air - Mars

27	19	34	23	10
21	13	25	17	37
15	35	24	11	28
14	26	18	33	22
36	20	12	29	16

Earth - Mars

36	14	15	21	27
20	26	35	13	19
12	18	24	25	34
29	33	11	17	23
16	22	28	37	10

Water - Mars

16	29	12	20	36
22	33	18	26	14
28	11	24	35	15
37	17	25	13	21
10	23	34	19	27

	Number	Angel Value (Arabic)	Angel Value (Hebrew)	Jinn Value (Arabic)	Jinn Value (Hebrew)
Usurper	10	329	339	51	41
Guide	37	356	6	78	68
Mystery	47	6	16	88	78
Adjuster	113	72	82	154	144
Leader	339	298	308	20	10
Regulator	452	411	421	133	123
General Governor	904	863	873	585	575
High Overseer	33448	33407	33417	33129	33119

Occult Encyclopedia of Magic Squares

Fire - Sun

1	12	34	18	22	26
7	17	28	33	5	23
13	37	21	11	27	4
24	3	14	29	8	35
30	19	10	2	36	16
38	25	6	20	15	9

Air - Sun

9	15	20	6	25	38
16	36	2	10	19	30
35	8	29	14	3	24
4	27	11	21	37	13
23	5	33	28	17	7
26	22	18	34	12	1

Earth - Sun

38	30	24	13	7	1
25	19	3	37	17	12
6	10	14	21	28	34
20	2	29	11	33	18
15	36	8	27	5	22
9	16	35	4	23	26

Water - Sun

26	23	4	35	16	9
22	5	27	8	36	15
18	33	11	29	2	20
34	28	21	14	10	6
12	17	37	3	19	25
1	7	13	24	30	38

	Number	Angel Value (Arabic)	Angel Value (Hebrew)	Jinn Value (Arabic)	Jinn Value (Hebrew)
Usurper	1	320	330	42	32
Guide	38	357	7	79	69
Mystery	39	358	8	80	70
Adjuster	113	72	82	154	144
Leader	339	298	308	20	10
Regulator	452	411	421	133	123
General Governor	904	863	873	585	575
High Overseer	34352	34311	34321	34033	34023

SUN

SUN: SHEMESH (640)

Hebrew Squares Not Available

Fire - Jupiter

152	163	157	168
167	158	160	155
162	153	169	156
159	166	154	161

Air - Jupiter

161	154	166	159
156	169	153	162
155	160	158	167
168	157	163	152

Earth - Jupiter

159	162	167	152
166	153	158	163
154	169	160	157
161	156	155	168

Water - Jupiter

168	155	156	161
157	160	169	154
163	158	153	166
152	167	162	159

	Number	Angel Value (Arabic)	Angel Value (Hebrew)	Jinn Value (Arabic)	Jinn Value (Hebrew)
Usurper	152	111	121	193	183
Guide	169	128	138	210	200
Mystery	321	280	290	2	352
Adjuster	5120	5079	5089	4801	4791
Leader	15360	15319	15329	15041	15031
Regulator	20480	20439	20449	20161	20151
General Governor	40960	40919	40929	40641	40631
High Overseer	6922240	6922199	6922209	6921921	6921911

Fire - Mars

116	140	134	128	122
129	123	117	136	135
137	131	130	124	118
125	119	138	132	126
133	127	121	120	139

Air - Mars

133	125	137	129	116
127	119	131	123	140
121	138	130	117	134
120	132	124	136	128
139	126	118	135	122

Earth - Mars

139	120	121	127	133
126	132	138	119	125
118	124	130	131	137
135	136	117	123	129
122	128	134	140	116

Water - Mars

122	135	118	126	139
128	136	124	132	120
134	117	130	138	121
140	123	131	119	127
116	129	137	125	133

	Number	Angel Value (Arabic)	Angel Value (Hebrew)	Jinn Value (Arabic)	Jinn Value (Hebrew)
Usurper	116	75	85	157	147
Guide	140	99	109	181	171
Mystery	256	215	225	297	287
Adjuster	640	599	609	321	311
Leader	1920	1879	1889	1601	1591
Regulator	2560	2519	2529	2241	2231
General Governor	5120	5079	5089	4801	4791
High Overseer	716800	716759	716769	716481	716471

Occult Encyclopedia of Magic Squares

Fire - Sun

89	100	121	106	110	114
95	105	116	120	93	111
101	124	109	99	115	92
112	91	102	117	96	122
118	107	98	90	123	104
125	113	94	108	103	97

Air - Sun

97	103	108	94	113	125
104	123	90	98	107	118
122	96	117	102	91	112
92	115	99	109	124	101
111	93	120	116	105	95
114	110	106	121	100	89

Earth - Sun

125	118	112	101	95	89
113	107	91	124	105	100
94	98	102	109	116	121
108	90	117	99	120	106
103	123	96	115	93	110
97	104	122	92	111	114

Water - Sun

114	111	92	122	104	97
110	93	115	96	123	103
106	120	99	117	90	108
121	116	109	102	98	94
100	105	124	91	107	113
89	95	101	112	118	125

	Number	Angel Value (Arabic)	Angel Value (Hebrew)	Jinn Value (Arabic)	Jinn Value (Hebrew)
Usurper	89	48	58	130	120
Guide	125	84	94	166	156
Mystery	214	173	183	255	245
Adjuster	640	599	609	321	311
Leader	1920	1879	1889	1601	1591
Regulator	2560	2519	2529	2241	2231
General Governor	5120	5079	5089	4801	4791
High Overseer	640000	639959	639969	639681	639671

Fire - Venus

67	108	93	78	98	114	82
115	83	68	102	94	79	99
80	100	116	84	69	103	88
104	89	74	101	117	85	70
86	71	105	90	75	95	118
96	112	87	72	106	91	76
92	77	97	113	81	73	107

Occult Encyclopedia of Magic Squares

Earth - Venus

92	96	86	104	80	115	67
77	112	71	89	100	83	108
97	87	105	74	116	68	93
113	72	90	101	84	102	78
81	106	75	117	69	94	98
73	91	95	85	103	79	114
107	76	118	70	88	99	82

Air - Venus

107	73	81	113	97	77	92
76	91	106	72	87	112	96
118	95	75	90	105	71	86
70	85	117	101	74	89	104
88	103	69	84	116	100	80
99	79	94	102	68	83	115
82	114	98	78	93	108	67

Water - Venus

82	99	88	70	118	76	107
114	79	103	85	95	91	73
98	94	69	117	75	106	81
78	102	84	101	90	72	113
93	68	116	74	105	87	97
108	83	100	89	71	112	77
67	115	80	104	86	96	92

	Number	Angel Value (Arabic)	Angel Value (Hebrew)	Jinn Value (Arabic)	Jinn Value (Hebrew)
Usurper	67	26	36	108	98
Guide	118	77	87	159	149
Mystery	185	144	154	226	216
Adjuster	640	599	609	321	311
Leader	1920	1879	1889	1601	1591
Regulator	2560	2519	2529	2241	2231
General Governor	5120	5079	5089	4801	4791
High Overseer	604160	604119	604129	603841	603831

Fire - Mercury

48	64	113	93	82	98	79	63
56	72	101	85	90	110	71	55
99	83	62	78	65	49	92	112
111	91	54	70	73	57	84	100
77	61	80	96	115	95	50	66
69	53	88	108	103	87	58	74
94	114	67	51	60	76	97	81
86	102	75	59	52	68	109	89

Earth - Mercury

86	94	69	77	111	99	56	48
102	114	53	61	91	83	72	64
75	67	88	80	54	62	101	113
59	51	108	96	70	78	85	93
52	60	103	115	73	65	90	82
68	76	87	95	57	49	110	98
109	97	58	50	84	92	71	79
89	81	74	66	100	112	55	63

Air - Mercury

89	109	68	52	59	75	102	86
81	97	76	60	51	67	114	94
74	58	87	103	108	88	53	69
66	50	95	115	96	80	61	77
100	84	57	73	70	54	91	111
112	92	49	65	78	62	83	99
55	71	110	90	85	101	72	56
63	79	98	82	93	113	64	48

Water - Mercury

63	55	112	100	66	74	81	89
79	71	92	84	50	58	97	109
98	110	49	57	95	87	76	68
82	90	65	73	115	103	60	52
93	85	78	70	96	108	51	59
113	101	62	54	80	88	67	75
64	72	83	91	61	53	114	102
48	56	99	111	77	69	94	86

	Number	Angel Value (Arabic)	Angel Value (Hebrew)	Jinn Value (Arabic)	Jinn Value (Hebrew)
Usurper	48	7	17	89	79
Guide	115	74	84	156	146
Mystery	163	122	132	204	194
Adjuster	640	599	609	321	311
Leader	1920	1879	1889	1601	1591
Regulator	2560	2519	2529	2241	2231
General Governor	5120	5079	5089	4801	4791
High Overseer	588800	588759	588769	588481	588471

Fire - Moon

75	88	50	59	112	43	79	95	39
35	78	100	55	71	87	42	64	108
104	47	63	99	31	83	92	54	67
102	34	77	86	57	70	107	41	66
62	106	46	82	98	33	69	91	53
49	74	90	45	58	111	38	81	94
48	61	105	32	84	97	52	68	93
89	51	73	110	44	60	96	37	80
76	101	36	72	85	56	65	109	40

Earth - Moon

39	108	67	66	53	94	93	80	40
95	64	54	41	91	81	68	37	109
79	42	92	107	69	38	52	96	65
43	87	83	70	33	111	97	60	56
112	71	31	57	98	58	84	44	85
59	55	99	86	82	45	32	110	72
50	100	63	77	46	90	105	73	36
88	78	47	34	106	74	61	51	101
75	35	104	102	62	49	48	89	76

Air - Moon

40	109	65	56	85	72	36	101	76
80	37	96	60	44	110	73	51	89
93	68	52	97	84	32	105	61	48
94	81	38	111	58	45	90	74	49
53	91	69	33	98	82	46	106	62
66	41	107	70	57	86	77	34	102
67	54	92	83	31	99	63	47	104
108	64	42	87	71	55	100	78	35
39	95	79	43	112	59	50	88	75

Water - Moon

76	89	48	49	62	102	104	35	75
101	51	61	74	106	34	47	78	88
36	73	105	90	46	77	63	100	50
72	110	32	45	82	86	99	55	59
85	44	84	58	98	57	31	71	112
56	60	97	111	33	70	83	87	43
65	96	52	38	69	107	92	42	79
109	37	68	81	91	41	54	64	95
40	80	93	94	53	66	67	108	39

	Number	Angel Value (Arabic)	Angel Value (Hebrew)	Jinn Value (Arabic)	Jinn Value (Hebrew)
Usurper	31	350	360	72	62
Guide	112	71	81	153	143
Mystery	143	102	112	184	174
Adjuster	640	599	609	321	311
Leader	1920	1879	1889	1601	1591
Regulator	2560	2519	2529	2241	2231
General Governor	5120	5079	5089	4801	4791
High Overseer	573440	573399	573409	573121	573111

Occult Encyclopedia of Magic Squares

Fire - Saturn

14	32	39	77	68	111	61	53	85	100
25	89	82	73	113	98	16	58	44	42
40	45	69	112	99	84	33	21	62	75
46	71	110	101	34	80	88	29	18	63
59	109	103	38	49	72	76	86	31	17
66	23	24	91	79	55	51	41	96	114
78	60	20	27	93	48	36	97	117	64
92	81	56	15	26	43	94	116	67	50
102	35	47	54	22	30	115	65	83	87
118	95	90	52	57	19	70	74	37	28

Earth - Saturn

118	102	92	78	66	59	46	40	25	14
95	35	81	60	23	109	71	45	89	32
90	47	56	20	24	103	110	69	82	39
52	54	15	27	91	38	101	112	73	77
57	22	26	93	79	49	34	99	113	68
19	30	43	48	55	72	80	84	98	111
70	115	94	36	51	76	88	33	16	61
74	65	116	97	41	86	29	21	58	53
37	83	67	117	96	31	18	62	44	85
28	87	50	64	114	17	63	75	42	100

Air - Saturn

28	37	74	70	19	57	52	90	95	118
87	83	65	115	30	22	54	47	35	102
50	67	116	94	43	26	15	56	81	92
64	117	97	36	48	93	27	20	60	78
114	96	41	51	55	79	91	24	23	66
17	31	86	76	72	49	38	103	109	59
63	18	29	88	80	34	101	110	71	46
75	62	21	33	84	99	112	69	45	40
42	44	58	16	98	113	73	82	89	25
100	85	53	61	111	68	77	39	32	14

Water - Saturn

100	42	75	63	17	114	64	50	87	28
85	44	62	18	31	96	117	67	83	37
53	58	21	29	86	41	97	116	65	74
61	**16**	33	88	76	51	36	94	115	70
111	98	84	80	72	55	48	43	30	19
68	113	99	34	49	79	93	26	22	57
77	73	112	101	38	91	27	15	54	52
39	82	69	110	103	24	20	56	47	90
32	89	45	71	109	23	60	81	35	95
14	25	40	46	59	66	78	92	102	118

	Number	Angel Value (Arabic)	Angel Value (Hebrew)	Jinn Value (Arabic)	Jinn Value (Hebrew)
Usurper	14	333	343	55	45
Guide	118	77	87	159	149
Mystery	132	91	101	173	163
Adjuster	640	599	609	321	311
Leader	1920	1879	1889	1601	1591
Regulator	2560	2519	2529	2241	2231
General Governor	5120	5079	5089	4801	4791
High Overseer	604160	604119	604129	603841	603831

ARCHANGEL: RAPHAEL (311)

ל	א	ם	ר
199	81	4	27
3	28	198	82
79	201	29	2

ל	א	ם	ר
ר	ם	א	ל
א	ל	ר	ם
ם	ר	ל	א

Numerical Squares See Page: 636

ANGEL: MICHAEL (101)

Hebrew Squares See Page: 600

Numerical Squares See Page: 247

INTELLIGENCE: NAKHIEL (111)

49	21	13	28
12	29	48	22
19	51	30	11

Fire - Jupiter

20	31	25	35
34	26	28	23
30	21	36	24
27	33	22	29

Air - Jupiter

29	22	33	27
24	36	21	30
23	28	26	34
35	25	31	20

Earth - Jupiter

27	30	34	20
33	21	26	31
22	36	28	25
29	24	23	35

Water - Jupiter

35	23	24	29
25	28	36	22
31	26	21	33
20	34	30	27

Occult Encyclopedia of Magic Squares

	Number	Angel Value (Arabic)	Angel Value (Hebrew)	Jinn Value (Arabic)	Jinn Value (Hebrew)
Usurper	20	339	349	61	51
Guide	36	355	5	77	67
Mystery	56	15	25	97	87
Adjuster	888	847	857	569	559
Leader	2664	2623	2633	2345	2335
Regulator	3552	3511	3521	3233	3223
General Governor	7104	7063	7073	6785	6775
High Overseer	255744	255703	255713	255425	255415

Fire - Mars

10	35	28	22	16
23	17	11	31	29
32	25	24	18	12
19	13	33	26	20
27	21	15	14	34

Air - Mars

27	19	32	23	10
21	13	25	17	35
15	33	24	11	28
14	26	18	31	22
34	20	12	29	16

Earth - Mars

34	14	15	21	27
20	26	33	13	19
12	18	24	25	32
29	31	11	17	23
16	22	28	35	10

Water - Mars

16	29	12	20	34
22	31	18	26	14
28	11	24	33	15
35	17	25	13	21
10	23	32	19	27

	Number	Angel Value (Arabic)	Angel Value (Hebrew)	Jinn Value (Arabic)	Jinn Value (Hebrew)
Usurper	10	329	339	51	41
Guide	35	354	4	76	66
Mystery	45	4	14	86	76
Adjuster	111	70	80	152	142
Leader	333	292	302	14	4
Regulator	444	403	413	125	115
General Governor	888	847	857	569	559
High Overseer	31080	31039	31049	30761	30751

Occult Encyclopedia of Magic Squares

Fire - Sun

1	12	32	18	22	26
7	17	28	31	5	23
13	35	21	11	27	4
24	3	14	29	8	33
30	19	10	2	34	16
36	25	6	20	15	9

Air - Sun

9	15	20	6	25	36
16	34	2	10	19	30
33	8	29	14	3	24
4	27	11	21	35	13
23	5	31	28	17	7
26	22	18	32	12	1

Earth - Sun

36	30	24	13	7	1
25	19	3	35	17	12
6	10	14	21	28	32
20	2	29	11	31	18
15	34	8	27	5	22
9	16	33	4	23	26

Water - Sun

26	23	4	33	16	9
22	5	27	8	34	15
18	31	11	29	2	20
32	28	21	14	10	6
12	17	35	3	19	25
1	7	13	24	30	36

	Number	Angel Value (Arabic)	Angel Value (Hebrew)	Jinn Value (Arabic)	Jinn Value (Hebrew)
Usurper	1	320	330	42	32
Guide	36	355	5	77	67
Mystery	37	356	6	78	68
Adjuster	111	70	80	152	142
Leader	333	292	302	14	4
Regulator	444	403	413	125	115
General Governor	888	847	857	569	559
High Overseer	31968	31927	31937	31649	31639

SPIRIT: SORATH (666)

ח	ר	ו	ס
59	7	203	397
202	398	58	8
5	61	399	201

ח	ר	ו	ס
ס	ו	ר	ח
ר	ח	ס	ו
ו	ס	ח	ר

Fire - Jupiter

159	170	164	173
172	165	167	162
169	160	174	163
166	171	161	168

Air - Jupiter

168	161	171	166
163	174	160	169
162	167	165	172
173	164	170	159

Earth - Jupiter

166	169	172	159
171	160	165	170
161	174	167	164
168	163	162	173

Water - Jupiter

173	162	163	168
164	167	174	161
170	165	160	171
159	172	169	166

	Number	Angel Value (Arabic)	Angel Value (Hebrew)	Jinn Value (Arabic)	Jinn Value (Hebrew)
Usurper	159	118	128	200	190
Guide	174	133	143	215	205
Mystery	333	292	302	14	4
Adjuster	5328	5287	5297	5009	4999
Leader	15984	15943	15953	15665	15655
Regulator	21312	21271	21281	20993	20983
General Governor	42624	42583	42593	42305	42295
High Overseer	7416576	7416535	7416545	7416257	7416247

Occult Encyclopedia of Magic Squares

Fire - Mars

121	146	139	133	127
134	128	122	142	140
143	136	135	129	123
130	124	144	137	131
138	132	126	125	145

Air - Mars

138	130	143	134	121
132	124	136	128	146
126	144	135	122	139
125	137	129	142	133
145	131	123	140	127

Earth - Mars

145	125	126	132	138
131	137	144	124	130
123	129	135	136	143
140	142	122	128	134
127	133	139	146	121

Water - Mars

127	140	123	131	145
133	142	129	137	125
139	122	135	144	126
146	128	136	124	132
121	134	143	130	138

	Number	Angel Value (Arabic)	Angel Value (Hebrew)	Jinn Value (Arabic)	Jinn Value (Hebrew)
Usurper	121	80	90	162	152
Guide	146	105	115	187	177
Mystery	267	226	236	308	298
Adjuster	666	625	635	347	337
Leader	1998	1957	1967	1679	1669
Regulator	2664	2623	2633	2345	2335
General Governor	5328	5287	5297	5009	4999
High Overseer	777888	777847	777857	777569	777559

Fire - Sun

93	104	127	110	114	118
99	109	120	126	97	115
105	130	113	103	119	96
116	95	106	121	100	128
122	111	102	94	129	108
131	117	98	112	107	101

Earth - Sun

131	122	116	105	99	93
117	111	95	130	109	104
98	102	106	113	120	127
112	94	121	103	126	110
107	129	100	119	97	114
101	108	128	96	115	118

Occult Encyclopedia of Magic Squares

Air - Sun

101	107	112	98	117	131
108	129	94	102	111	122
128	100	121	106	95	116
96	119	103	113	130	105
115	97	126	120	109	99
118	114	110	127	104	93

Water - Sun

118	115	96	128	108	101
114	97	119	100	129	107
110	126	103	121	94	112
127	120	113	106	102	98
104	109	130	95	111	117
93	99	105	116	122	131

	Number	Angel Value (Arabic)	Angel Value (Hebrew)	Jinn Value (Arabic)	Jinn Value (Hebrew)
Usurper	93	52	62	134	124
Guide	131	90	100	172	162
Mystery	224	183	193	265	255
Adjuster	666	625	635	347	337
Leader	1998	1957	1967	1679	1669
Regulator	2664	2623	2633	2345	2335
General Governor	5328	5287	5297	5009	4999
High Overseer	697968	697927	697937	697649	697639

Fire - Venus

71	112	97	82	102	116	86
117	87	72	106	98	83	103
84	104	118	88	73	107	92
108	93	78	105	119	89	74
90	75	109	94	79	99	120
100	114	91	76	110	95	80
96	81	101	115	85	77	111

Earth - Venus

96	100	90	108	84	117	71
81	114	75	93	104	87	112
101	91	109	78	118	72	97
115	76	94	105	88	106	82
85	110	79	119	73	98	102
77	95	99	89	107	83	116
111	80	120	74	92	103	86

Occult Encyclopedia of Magic Squares

Air - Venus

111	77	85	115	101	81	96
80	95	110	76	91	114	100
120	99	79	94	109	75	90
74	89	119	105	78	93	108
92	107	73	88	118	104	84
103	83	98	106	72	87	117
86	116	102	82	97	112	71

Water - Venus

86	103	92	74	120	80	111
116	83	107	89	99	95	77
102	98	73	119	79	110	85
82	106	88	105	94	76	115
97	72	118	78	109	91	101
112	87	104	93	75	114	81
71	117	84	108	90	100	96

	Number	Angel Value (Arabic)	Angel Value (Hebrew)	Jinn Value (Arabic)	Jinn Value (Hebrew)
Usurper	71	30	40	112	102
Guide	120	79	89	161	151
Mystery	191	150	160	232	222
Adjuster	666	625	635	347	337
Leader	1998	1957	1967	1679	1669
Regulator	2664	2623	2633	2345	2335
General Governor	5328	5287	5297	5009	4999
High Overseer	639360	639319	639329	639041	639031

Occult Encyclopedia of Magic Squares

Fire - Mercury

51	67	118	96	85	101	82	66
59	75	104	88	93	115	74	58
102	86	65	81	68	52	95	117
116	94	57	73	76	60	87	103
80	64	83	99	120	98	53	69
72	56	91	113	106	90	61	77
97	119	70	54	63	79	100	84
89	105	78	62	55	71	114	92

Earth - Mercury

89	97	72	80	116	102	59	51
105	119	56	64	94	86	75	67
78	70	91	83	57	65	104	118
62	54	113	99	73	81	88	96
55	63	106	120	76	68	93	85
71	79	90	98	60	52	115	101
114	100	61	53	87	95	74	82
92	84	77	69	103	117	58	66

Air - Mercury

92	114	71	55	62	78	105	89
84	100	79	63	54	70	119	97
77	61	90	106	113	91	56	72
69	53	98	120	99	83	64	80
103	87	60	76	73	57	94	116
117	95	52	68	81	65	86	102
58	74	115	93	88	104	75	59
66	82	101	85	96	118	67	51

Water - Mercury

66	58	117	103	69	77	84	92
82	74	95	87	53	61	100	114
101	115	52	60	98	90	79	71
85	93	68	76	120	106	63	55
96	88	81	73	99	113	54	62
118	104	65	57	83	91	70	78
67	75	86	94	64	56	119	105
51	59	102	116	80	72	97	89

Occult Encyclopedia of Magic Squares

	Number	Angel Value (Arabic)	Angel Value (Hebrew)	Jinn Value (Arabic)	Jinn Value (Hebrew)
Usurper	51	10	20	92	82
Guide	120	79	89	161	151
Mystery	171	130	140	212	202
Adjuster	666	625	635	347	337
Leader	1998	1957	1967	1679	1669
Regulator	2664	2623	2633	2345	2335
General Governor	5328	5287	5297	5009	4999
High Overseer	639360	639319	639329	639041	639031

Fire - Moon

78	91	53	62	114	46	82	98	42
38	81	103	58	74	90	45	67	110
106	50	66	102	34	86	95	57	70
105	37	80	89	60	73	109	44	69
65	108	49	85	101	36	72	94	56
52	77	93	48	61	113	41	84	97
51	64	107	35	87	100	55	71	96
92	54	76	112	47	63	99	40	83
79	104	39	75	88	59	68	111	43

Earth - Moon

42	110	70	69	56	97	96	83	43
98	67	57	44	94	84	71	40	111
82	45	95	109	72	41	55	99	68
46	90	86	73	36	113	100	63	59
114	74	34	60	101	61	87	47	88
62	58	102	89	85	48	35	112	75
53	103	66	80	49	93	107	76	39
91	81	50	37	108	77	64	54	104
78	38	106	105	65	52	51	92	79

Occult Encyclopedia of Magic Squares

Air - Moon

43	111	68	59	88	75	39	104	79
83	40	99	63	47	112	76	54	92
96	71	55	100	87	35	107	64	51
97	84	41	113	61	48	93	77	52
56	94	72	36	101	85	49	108	65
69	44	109	73	60	89	80	37	105
70	57	95	86	34	102	66	50	106
110	67	45	90	74	58	103	81	38
42	98	82	46	114	62	53	91	78

Water - Moon

79	92	51	52	65	105	106	38	78
104	54	64	77	108	37	50	81	91
39	76	107	93	49	80	66	103	53
75	112	35	48	85	89	102	58	62
88	47	87	61	101	60	34	74	114
59	63	100	113	36	73	86	90	46
68	99	55	41	72	109	95	45	82
111	40	71	84	94	44	57	67	98
43	83	96	97	56	69	70	110	42

	Number	Angel Value (Arabic)	Angel Value (Hebrew)	Jinn Value (Arabic)	Jinn Value (Hebrew)
Usurper	34	353	3	75	65
Guide	114	73	83	155	145
Mystery	148	107	117	189	179
Adjuster	666	625	635	347	337
Leader	1998	1957	1967	1679	1669
Regulator	2664	2623	2633	2345	2335
General Governor	5328	5287	5297	5009	4999
High Overseer	607392	607351	607361	607073	607063

Occult Encyclopedia of Magic Squares

Fire - Saturn

17	35	42	80	71	110	64	56	88	103
28	92	85	76	112	101	19	61	47	45
43	48	72	111	102	87	36	24	65	78
49	74	109	104	37	83	91	32	21	66
62	108	106	41	52	75	79	89	34	20
69	26	27	94	82	58	54	44	99	113
81	63	23	30	96	51	39	100	116	67
95	84	59	18	29	46	97	115	70	53
105	38	50	57	25	33	114	68	86	90
117	98	93	55	60	22	73	77	40	31

Earth - Saturn

117	105	95	81	69	62	49	43	28	17
98	38	84	63	26	108	74	48	92	35
93	50	59	23	27	106	109	72	85	42
55	57	18	30	94	41	104	111	76	80
60	25	29	96	82	52	37	102	112	71
22	33	46	51	58	75	83	87	101	110
73	114	97	39	54	79	91	36	19	64
77	68	115	100	44	89	32	24	61	56
40	86	70	116	99	34	21	65	47	88
31	90	53	67	113	20	66	78	45	103

Air - Saturn

31	40	77	73	22	60	55	93	98	117
90	86	68	114	33	25	57	50	38	105
53	70	115	97	46	29	18	59	84	95
67	116	100	39	51	96	30	23	63	81
113	99	44	54	58	82	94	27	26	69
20	34	89	79	75	52	41	106	108	62
66	21	32	91	83	37	104	109	74	49
78	65	24	36	87	102	111	72	48	43
45	47	61	19	101	112	76	85	92	28
103	88	56	64	110	71	80	42	35	17

Water - Saturn

103	45	78	66	20	113	67	53	90	31
88	47	65	21	34	99	116	70	86	40
56	61	24	32	89	44	100	115	68	77
64	**19**	36	91	79	54	39	97	114	73
110	101	87	83	75	58	51	46	33	22
71	112	102	37	52	82	96	29	25	60
80	76	111	104	41	94	30	18	57	55
42	85	72	109	106	27	23	59	50	93
35	92	48	74	108	26	63	84	38	98
17	28	43	49	62	69	81	95	105	117

	Number	Angel Value (Arabic)	Angel Value (Hebrew)	Jinn Value (Arabic)	Jinn Value (Hebrew)
Usurper	17	336	346	58	48
Guide	117	76	86	158	148
Mystery	134	93	103	175	165
Adjuster	666	625	635	347	337
Leader	1998	1957	1967	1679	1669
Regulator	2664	2623	2633	2345	2335
General Governor	5328	5287	5297	5009	4999
High Overseer	623376	623335	623345	623057	623047

OLYMPIC SPIRIT: OCH (15)

No Hebrew Squares Available

Numerical Squares See Page:

VENUS

VENUS: NOGAH (64)

ה	ג	ו	נ
49	7	6	2
5	3	48	8
5	51	4	4

ה	ג	ו	נ
נ	ו	ג	ה
ג	ה	נ	ו
ו	נ	ה	ג

Fire - Jupiter

8	19	13	24
23	14	16	11
18	9	25	12
15	22	10	17

Air - Jupiter

17	10	22	15
12	25	9	18
11	16	14	23
24	13	19	8

Earth - Jupiter

15	18	23	8
22	9	14	19
10	25	16	13
17	12	11	24

Water - Jupiter

24	11	12	17
13	16	25	10
19	14	9	22
8	23	18	15

	Number	Angel Value (Arabic)	Angel Value (Hebrew)	Jinn Value (Arabic)	Jinn Value (Hebrew)
Usurper	8	327	337	49	39
Guide	25	344	354	66	56
Mystery	33	352	2	74	64
Adjuster	512	471	481	193	183
Leader	1536	1495	1505	1217	1207
Regulator	2048	2007	2017	1729	1719
General Governor	4096	4055	4065	3777	3767
High Overseer	102400	102359	102369	102081	102071

ARCHANGEL: HANIEL (97)

לא	י	נ	הא
5	51	13	28
12	29	4	52
49	7	30	11

ל	א	י	נ	א	ה
א	נ	ל	ה	י	א
י	ה	א	א	ל	נ
ה	א	נ	י	א	ל
נ	ל	א	א	ה	י
א	י	ה	ל	נ	א

Fire - Jupiter

16	27	21	33
32	22	24	19
26	17	34	20
23	31	18	25

Air - Jupiter

25	18	31	23
20	34	17	26
19	24	22	32
33	21	27	16

Earth - Jupiter

23	26	32	16
31	17	22	27
18	34	24	21
25	20	19	33

Water - Jupiter

33	19	20	25
21	24	34	18
27	22	17	31
16	32	26	23

	Number	Angel Value (Arabic)	Angel Value (Hebrew)	Jinn Value (Arabic)	Jinn Value (Hebrew)
Usurper	16	335	345	57	47
Guide	34	353	3	75	65
Mystery	50	9	19	91	81
Adjuster	776	735	745	457	447
Leader	2328	2287	2297	2009	1999
Regulator	3104	3063	3073	2785	2775
General Governor	6208	6167	6177	5889	5879
High Overseer	211072	211031	211041	210753	210743

Fire - Mars

7	33	25	19	13
20	14	8	29	26
30	22	21	15	9
16	10	31	23	17
24	18	12	11	32

Air - Mars

24	16	30	20	7
18	10	22	14	33
12	31	21	8	25
11	23	15	29	19
32	17	9	26	13

Earth - Mars

32	11	12	18	24
17	23	31	10	16
9	15	21	22	30
26	29	8	14	20
13	19	25	33	7

Water - Mars

13	26	9	17	32
19	29	15	23	11
25	8	21	31	12
33	14	22	10	18
7	20	30	16	24

	Number	Angel Value (Arabic)	Angel Value (Hebrew)	Jinn Value (Arabic)	Jinn Value (Hebrew)
Usurper	7	326	336	48	38
Guide	33	352	2	74	64
Mystery	40	359	9	81	71
Adjuster	97	56	66	138	128
Leader	291	250	260	332	322
Regulator	388	347	357	69	59
General Governor	776	735	745	457	447
High Overseer	25608	25567	25577	25289	25279

ANGEL: ANAEL (82)

This square not possible

ל	א	נ	א
א	נ	א	ל
א	ל	א	נ
נ	א	ל	א

Fire - Jupiter

13	24	18	27
26	19	21	16
23	14	28	17
20	25	15	22

Air - Jupiter

22	15	25	20
17	28	14	23
16	21	19	26
27	18	24	13

Earth - Jupiter

20	23	26	13
25	14	19	24
15	28	21	18
22	17	16	27

Water - Jupiter

27	16	17	22
18	21	28	15
24	19	14	25
13	26	23	20

	Number	Angel Value (Arabic)	Angel Value (Hebrew)	Jinn Value (Arabic)	Jinn Value (Hebrew)
Usurper	13	332	342	54	44
Guide	28	347	357	69	59
Mystery	41	360	10	82	72
Adjuster	656	615	625	337	327
Leader	1968	1927	1937	1649	1639
Regulator	2624	2583	2593	2305	2295
General Governor	5248	5207	5217	4929	4919
High Overseer	146944	146903	146913	146625	146615

Fire - Mars

4	30	22	16	10
17	11	5	26	23
27	19	18	12	6
13	7	28	20	14
21	15	9	8	29

Air - Mars

21	13	27	17	4
15	7	19	11	30
9	28	18	5	22
8	20	12	26	16
29	14	6	23	10

Earth - Mars

29	8	9	15	21
14	20	28	7	13
6	12	18	19	27
23	26	5	11	17
10	16	22	30	4

Water - Mars

10	23	6	14	29
16	26	12	20	8
22	5	18	28	9
30	11	19	7	15
4	17	27	13	21

	Number	Angel Value (Arabic)	Angel Value (Hebrew)	Jinn Value (Arabic)	Jinn Value (Hebrew)
Usurper	4	323	333	45	35
Guide	30	349	359	71	61
Mystery	34	353	3	75	65
Adjuster	82	41	51	123	113
Leader	246	205	215	287	277
Regulator	328	287	297	9	359
General Governor	656	615	625	337	327
High Overseer	19680	19639	19649	19361	19351

INTELLIGENCE: HAGIEL (49)

אל	י	ג	ה
4	4	13	28
12	29	3	5
2	6	30	11

ל	א	י	ג	ה
י	ג	ה	ל	א
ה	ל	א	י	ג
א	י	ג	ה	ל
ג	ה	ל	א	י

Fire - Jupiter

4	15	9	21
20	10	12	7
14	5	22	8
11	19	6	13

Air - Jupiter

13	6	19	11
8	22	5	14
7	12	10	20
21	9	15	4

Earth - Jupiter

11	14	20	4
19	5	10	15
6	22	12	9
13	8	7	21

Water - Jupiter

21	7	8	13
9	12	22	6
15	10	5	19
4	20	14	11

	Number	Angel Value (Arabic)	Angel Value (Hebrew)	Jinn Value (Arabic)	Jinn Value (Hebrew)
Usurper	4	323	333	45	35
Guide	22	341	351	63	53
Mystery	26	345	355	67	57
Adjuster	392	351	361	73	63
Leader	1176	1135	1145	857	847
Regulator	1568	1527	1537	1249	1239
General Governor	3136	3095	3105	2817	2807
High Overseer	68992	68951	68961	68673	68663

SPIRIT: KEDEMEL (175)

ל	א	ם	ר	ק
ם	ר	ק	ל	א
ק	ל	א	ם	ר
א	ם	ר	ק	ל
ר	ק	ל	א	ם

אל	ם	ר	ק
99	5	43	28
42	29	98	6
3	101	30	41

Occult Encyclopedia of Magic Squares

Fire - Jupiter

36	47	41	51
50	42	44	39
46	37	52	40
43	49	38	45

Air - Jupiter

45	38	49	43
40	52	37	46
39	44	42	50
51	41	47	36

Earth - Jupiter

43	46	50	36
49	37	42	47
38	52	44	41
45	40	39	51

Water - Jupiter

51	39	40	45
41	44	52	38
47	42	37	49
36	50	46	43

	Number	Angel Value (Arabic)	Angel Value (Hebrew)	Jinn Value (Arabic)	Jinn Value (Hebrew)
Usurper	36	355	5	77	67
Guide	52	11	21	93	83
Mystery	88	47	57	129	119
Adjuster	1400	1359	1369	1081	1071
Leader	4200	4159	4169	3881	3871
Regulator	5600	5559	5569	5281	5271
General Governor	11200	11159	11169	10881	10871
High Overseer	582400	582359	582369	582081	582071

Fire - Mars

23	47	41	35	29
36	30	24	43	42
44	38	37	31	25
32	26	45	39	33
40	34	28	27	46

Air - Mars

40	32	44	36	23
34	26	38	30	47
28	45	37	24	41
27	39	31	43	35
46	33	25	42	29

Earth - Mars

46	27	28	34	40
33	39	45	26	32
25	31	37	38	44
42	43	24	30	36
29	35	41	47	23

Water - Mars

29	42	25	33	46
35	43	31	39	27
41	24	37	45	28
47	30	38	26	34
23	36	44	32	40

Occult Encyclopedia of Magic Squares

	Number	Angel Value (Arabic)	Angel Value (Hebrew)	Jinn Value (Arabic)	Jinn Value (Hebrew)
Usurper	23	342	352	64	54
Guide	47	6	16	88	78
Mystery	70	29	39	111	101
Adjuster	175	134	144	216	206
Leader	525	484	494	206	196
Regulator	700	659	669	381	371
General Governor	1400	1359	1369	1081	1071
High Overseer	65800	65759	65769	65481	65471

Fire - Sun

11	22	46	28	32	36
17	27	38	45	15	33
23	49	31	21	37	14
34	13	24	39	18	47
40	29	20	12	48	26
50	35	16	30	25	19

Air - Sun

19	25	30	16	35	50
26	48	12	20	29	40
47	18	39	24	13	34
14	37	21	31	49	23
33	15	45	38	27	17
36	32	28	46	22	11

Earth - Sun

50	40	34	23	17	11
35	29	13	49	27	22
16	20	24	31	38	46
30	12	39	21	45	28
25	48	18	37	15	32
19	26	47	14	33	36

Water - Sun

36	33	14	47	26	19
32	15	37	18	48	25
28	45	21	39	12	30
46	38	31	24	20	16
22	27	49	13	29	35
11	17	23	34	40	50

Occult Encyclopedia of Magic Squares

	Number	Angel Value (Arabic)	Angel Value (Hebrew)	Jinn Value (Arabic)	Jinn Value (Hebrew)
Usurper	11	330	340	52	42
Guide	50	9	19	91	81
Mystery	61	20	30	102	92
Adjuster	175	134	144	216	206
Leader	525	484	494	206	196
Regulator	700	659	669	381	371
General Governor	1400	1359	1369	1081	1071
High Overseer	70000	69959	69969	69681	69671

Fire - Venus

1	42	27	12	32	45	16
46	17	2	36	28	13	33
14	34	47	18	3	37	22
38	23	8	35	48	19	4
20	5	39	24	9	29	49
30	43	21	6	40	25	10
26	11	31	44	15	7	41

Air - Venus

41	7	15	44	31	11	26
10	25	40	6	21	43	30
49	29	9	24	39	5	20
4	19	48	35	8	23	38
22	37	3	18	47	34	14
33	13	28	36	2	17	46
16	45	32	12	27	42	1

Earth - Venus

26	30	20	38	14	46	1
11	43	5	23	34	17	42
31	21	39	8	47	2	27
44	6	24	35	18	36	12
15	40	9	48	3	28	32
7	25	29	19	37	13	45
41	10	49	4	22	33	16

Water - Venus

16	33	22	4	49	10	41
45	13	37	19	29	25	7
32	28	3	48	9	40	15
12	36	18	35	24	6	44
27	2	47	8	39	21	31
42	17	34	23	5	43	11
1	46	14	38	20	30	26

	Number	Angel Value (Arabic)	Angel Value (Hebrew)	Jinn Value (Arabic)	Jinn Value (Hebrew)
Usurper	1	320	330	42	32
Guide	49	8	18	90	80
Mystery	50	9	19	91	81
Adjuster	175	134	144	216	206
Leader	525	484	494	206	196
Regulator	700	659	669	381	371
General Governor	1400	1359	1369	1081	1071
High Overseer	68600	68559	68569	68281	68271

OLYMPIC SPIRIT: HAGITH (421)

ת	י	ק	ח
7	101	13	397
12	398	6	102
99	9	399	11

ת	י	ק	ח
ח	ק	י	ת
י	ת	ח	ק
ק	ח	ת	י

Numerical Squares See Page:

731

MERCURY

MERCURY: KOKAB (48)

ב	ב	ו	ב
21	8	18	1
18	3	19	8
7	17	5	19

ב	ב	ו	ב
ב	ו	ב	ב
ב	ב	ב	ו
ו	ב	ב	ב

Numerical Squares See Page:

ARCHANGEL: MICHAEL (101)

Hebrew Squares See Page:

Numerical Squares See Page:

ANGEL: RAPHAEL (311)

Numerical Squares See Page: 636

יאל	ר	י	ט
8	11	203	38
202	39	7	12
9	10	40	201

ל	א	י	ר	י	ט
י	ר	ל	ט	י	א
י	ט	א	י	ל	ר
ט	י	ר	י	א	ל
ר	ל	י	א	ט	י
א	י	ט	ל	ר	י

Fire - Jupiter

57	68	62	73
72	63	65	60
67	58	74	61
64	71	59	66

Air - Jupiter

66	59	71	64
61	74	58	67
60	65	63	72
73	62	68	57

Earth - Jupiter

64	67	72	57
71	58	63	68
59	74	65	62
66	61	60	73

Water - Jupiter

73	60	61	66
62	65	74	59
68	63	58	71
57	72	67	64

Occult Encyclopedia of Magic Squares

	Number	Angel Value (Arabic)	Angel Value (Hebrew)	Jinn Value (Arabic)	Jinn Value (Hebrew)
Usurper	57	16	26	98	88
Guide	74	33	43	115	105
Mystery	131	90	100	172	162
Adjuster	2080	2039	2049	1761	1751
Leader	6240	6199	6209	5921	5911
Regulator	8320	8279	8289	8001	7991
General Governor	16640	16599	16609	16321	16311
High Overseer	1231360	1231319	1231329	1231041	1231031

Fire - Mars

40	64	58	52	46
53	47	41	60	59
61	55	54	48	42
49	43	62	56	50
57	51	45	44	63

Air - Mars

57	49	61	53	40
51	43	55	47	64
45	62	54	41	58
44	56	48	60	52
63	50	42	59	46

Earth - Mars

63	44	45	51	57
50	56	62	43	49
42	48	54	55	61
59	60	41	47	53
46	52	58	64	40

Water - Mars

46	59	42	50	63
52	60	48	56	44
58	41	54	62	45
64	47	55	43	51
40	53	61	49	57

	Number	Angel Value (Arabic)	Angel Value (Hebrew)	Jinn Value (Arabic)	Jinn Value (Hebrew)
Usurper	40	359	9	81	71
Guide	64	23	33	105	95
Mystery	104	63	73	145	135
Adjuster	260	219	229	301	291
Leader	780	739	749	461	451
Regulator	1040	999	1009	721	711
General Governor	2080	2039	2049	1761	1751
High Overseer	133120	133079	133089	132801	132791

Occult Encyclopedia of Magic Squares

Fire - Sun

25	36	61	42	46	50
31	41	52	60	29	47
37	64	45	35	51	28
48	27	38	53	32	62
54	43	34	26	63	40
65	49	30	44	39	33

Air - Sun

33	39	44	30	49	65
40	63	26	34	43	54
62	32	53	38	27	48
28	51	35	45	64	37
47	29	60	52	41	31
50	46	42	61	36	25

Earth - Sun

65	54	48	37	31	25
49	43	27	64	41	36
30	34	38	45	52	61
44	26	53	35	60	42
39	63	32	51	29	46
33	40	62	28	47	50

Water - Sun

50	47	28	62	40	33
46	29	51	32	63	39
42	60	35	53	26	44
61	52	45	38	34	30
36	41	64	27	43	49
25	31	37	48	54	65

	Number	Angel Value (Arabic)	Angel Value (Hebrew)	Jinn Value (Arabic)	Jinn Value (Hebrew)
Usurper	25	344	354	66	56
Guide	65	24	34	106	96
Mystery	90	49	59	131	121
Adjuster	260	219	229	301	291
Leader	780	739	749	461	451
Regulator	1040	999	1009	721	711
General Governor	2080	2039	2049	1761	1751
High Overseer	135200	135159	135169	134881	134871

Fire - Venus

13	54	39	24	44	58	28
59	29	14	48	40	25	45
26	46	60	30	15	49	34
50	35	20	47	61	31	16
32	17	51	36	21	41	62
42	56	33	18	52	37	22
38	23	43	57	27	19	53

Occult Encyclopedia of Magic Squares

Earth - Venus

38	42	32	50	26	59	13
23	56	17	35	46	29	54
43	33	51	20	60	14	39
57	18	36	47	30	48	24
27	52	21	61	15	40	44
19	37	41	31	49	25	58
53	22	62	16	34	45	28

Air - Venus

53	19	27	57	43	23	38
22	37	52	18	33	56	42
62	41	21	36	51	17	32
16	31	61	47	20	35	50
34	49	15	30	60	46	26
45	25	40	48	14	29	59
28	58	44	24	39	54	13

Water - Venus

28	45	34	16	62	22	53
58	25	49	31	41	37	19
44	40	15	61	21	52	27
24	48	30	47	36	18	57
39	14	60	20	51	33	43
54	29	46	35	17	56	23

	Number	Angel Value (Arabic)	Angel Value (Hebrew)	Jinn Value (Arabic)	Jinn Value (Hebrew)
Usurper	13	332	342	54	44
Guide	62	21	31	103	93
Mystery	75	34	44	116	106
Adjuster	260	219	229	301	291
Leader	780	739	749	461	451
Regulator	1040	999	1009	721	711
General Governor	2080	2039	2049	1761	1751
High Overseer	128960	128919	128929	128641	128631

Fire - Mercury

1	17	62	46	35	51	32	16
9	25	54	38	43	59	24	8
52	36	15	31	18	2	45	61
60	44	7	23	26	10	37	53
30	14	33	49	64	48	3	19
22	6	41	57	56	40	11	27
47	63	20	4	13	29	50	34
39	55	28	12	5	21	58	42

Earth - Mercury

39	47	22	30	60	52	9	1
55	63	6	14	44	36	25	17
28	20	41	33	7	15	54	62
12	4	57	49	23	31	38	46
5	13	56	64	26	18	43	35
21	29	40	48	10	2	59	51
58	50	11	3	37	45	24	32
42	34	27	19	53	61	8	16

Air - Mercury

42	58	21	5	12	28	55	39
34	50	29	13	4	20	63	47
27	11	40	56	57	41	6	22
19	3	48	64	49	33	14	30
53	37	10	26	23	7	44	60
61	45	2	18	31	15	36	52
8	24	59	43	38	54	25	9
16	32	51	35	46	62	17	1

Water - Mercury

16	8	61	53	19	27	34	42
32	24	45	37	3	11	50	58
51	59	2	10	48	40	29	21
35	43	18	26	64	56	13	5
46	38	31	23	49	57	4	12
62	54	15	7	33	41	20	28
17	25	36	44	14	6	63	55
1	9	52	60	30	22	47	39

	Number	Angel Value (Arabic)	Angel Value (Hebrew)	Jinn Value (Arabic)	Jinn Value (Hebrew)
Usurper	1	320	330	42	32
Guide	64	23	33	105	95
Mystery	65	24	34	106	96
Adjuster	260	219	229	301	291
Leader	780	739	749	461	451
Regulator	1040	999	1009	721	711
General Governor	2080	2039	2049	1761	1751
High Overseer	133120	133079	133089	132801	132791

SPIRIT: TAPHTHARTHARATH (2080)

ת	ר	ה	ר	ה	פ	ת
ת	ר	ה	פ	ה	ה	ר
ת	פ	ה	ה	ר	ה	ר
ת	ה	ר	ה	ר	ה	פ
ר	ה	ר	ה	פ	ה	ת
ר	ה	פ	ה	ה	ר	ה
פ	ה	ה	ר	ה	ר	ת

תת	תר	תר	תם
479	601	603	397
602	398	478	602
599	481	399	601

Fire - Jupiter

512	523	517	528
527	518	520	515
522	513	529	516
519	526	514	521

Air - Jupiter

521	514	526	519
516	529	513	522
515	520	518	527
528	517	523	512

Earth - Jupiter

519	522	527	512
526	513	518	523
514	529	520	517
521	516	515	528

Water - Jupiter

528	515	516	521
517	520	529	514
523	518	513	526
512	527	522	519

Occult Encyclopedia of Magic Squares

	Number	Angel Value (Arabic)	Angel Value (Hebrew)	Jinn Value (Arabic)	Jinn Value (Hebrew)
Usurper	512	471	481	193	183
Guide	529	488	498	210	200
Mystery	1041	1000	1010	722	712
Adjuster	16640	16599	16609	16321	16311
Leader	49920	49879	49889	49601	49591
Regulator	66560	66519	66529	66241	66231
General Governor	133120	133079	133089	132801	132791
High Overseer	70420480	70420439	70420449	70420161	70420151

Fire - Mars

404	428	422	416	410
417	411	405	424	423
425	419	418	412	406
413	407	426	420	414
421	415	409	408	427

Air - Mars

421	413	425	417	404
415	407	419	411	428
409	426	418	405	422
408	420	412	424	416
427	414	406	423	410

Earth - Mars

427	408	409	415	421
414	420	426	407	413
406	412	418	419	425
423	424	405	411	417
410	416	422	428	404

Water - Mars

410	423	406	414	427
416	424	412	420	408
422	405	418	426	409
428	411	419	407	415
404	417	425	413	421

	Number	Angel Value (Arabic)	Angel Value (Hebrew)	Jinn Value (Arabic)	Jinn Value (Hebrew)
Usurper	404	363	373	85	75
Guide	428	387	397	109	99
Mystery	832	791	801	513	503
Adjuster	2080	2039	2049	1761	1751
Leader	6240	6199	6209	5921	5911
Regulator	8320	8279	8289	8001	7991
General Governor	16640	16599	16609	16321	16311
High Overseer	7121920	7121879	7121889	7121601	7121591

Fire - Sun

329	340	361	346	350	354
335	345	356	360	333	351
341	364	349	339	355	332
352	331	342	357	336	362
358	347	338	330	363	344
365	353	334	348	343	337

Air - Sun

337	343	348	334	353	365
344	363	330	338	347	358
362	336	357	342	331	352
332	355	339	349	364	341
351	333	360	356	345	335
354	350	346	361	340	329

Earth - Sun

365	358	352	341	335	329
353	347	331	364	345	340
334	338	342	349	356	361
348	330	357	339	360	346
343	363	336	355	333	350
337	344	362	332	351	354

Water - Sun

354	351	332	362	344	337
350	333	355	336	363	343
346	360	339	357	330	348
361	356	349	342	338	334
340	345	364	331	347	353
329	335	341	352	358	365

	Number	Angel Value (Arabic)	Angel Value (Hebrew)	Jinn Value (Arabic)	Jinn Value (Hebrew)
Usurper	329	288	298	10	360
Guide	365	324	334	46	36
Mystery	694	653	663	375	365
Adjuster	2080	2039	2049	1761	1751
Leader	6240	6199	6209	5921	5911
Regulator	8320	8279	8289	8001	7991
General Governor	16640	16599	16609	16321	16311
High Overseer	6073600	6073559	6073569	6073281	6073271

Fire - Venus

273	314	299	284	304	318	288
319	289	274	308	300	285	305
286	306	320	290	275	309	294
310	295	280	307	321	291	276
292	277	311	296	281	301	322
302	316	293	278	312	297	282
298	283	303	317	287	279	313

Occult Encyclopedia of Magic Squares

Earth - Venus

298	302	292	310	286	319	273
283	316	277	295	306	289	314
303	293	311	280	320	274	299
317	278	296	307	290	308	284
287	312	281	321	275	300	304
279	297	301	291	309	285	318
313	282	322	276	294	305	288

Air - Venus

313	279	287	317	303	283	298
282	297	312	278	293	316	302
322	301	281	296	311	277	292
276	291	321	307	280	295	310
294	309	275	290	320	306	286
305	285	300	308	274	289	319
288	318	304	284	299	314	273

Water - Venus

288	305	294	276	322	282	313
318	285	309	291	301	297	279
304	300	275	321	281	312	287
284	308	290	307	296	278	317
299	274	320	280	311	293	303
314	289	306	295	277	316	283
273	319	286	310	292	302	298

	Number	Angel Value (Arabic)	Angel Value (Hebrew)	Jinn Value (Arabic)	Jinn Value (Hebrew)
Usurper	273	232	242	314	304
Guide	322	281	291	3	353
Mystery	595	554	564	276	266
Adjuster	2080	2039	2049	1761	1751
Leader	6240	6199	6209	5921	5911
Regulator	8320	8279	8289	8001	7991
General Governor	16640	16599	16609	16321	16311
High Overseer	5358080	5358039	5358049	5357761	5357751

Occult Encyclopedia of Magic Squares

Fire - Mercury

228	244	293	273	262	278	259	243
236	252	281	265	270	290	251	235
279	263	242	258	245	229	272	292
291	271	234	250	253	237	264	280
257	241	260	276	295	275	230	246
249	233	268	288	283	267	238	254
274	294	247	231	240	256	277	261
266	282	255	239	232	248	289	269

Earth - Mercury

266	274	249	257	291	279	236	228
282	294	233	241	271	263	252	244
255	247	268	260	234	242	281	293
239	231	288	276	250	258	265	273
232	240	283	295	253	245	270	262
248	256	267	275	237	229	290	278
289	277	238	230	264	272	251	259
269	261	254	246	280	292	235	243

Air - Mercury

269	289	248	232	239	255	282	266
261	277	256	240	231	247	294	274
254	238	267	283	288	268	233	249
246	230	275	295	276	260	241	257
280	264	237	253	250	234	271	291
292	272	229	245	258	242	263	279
235	251	290	270	265	281	252	236
243	259	278	262	273	293	244	228

Water - Mercury

243	235	292	280	246	254	261	269
259	251	272	264	230	238	277	289
278	290	229	237	275	267	256	248
262	270	245	253	295	283	240	232
273	265	258	250	276	288	231	239
293	281	242	234	260	268	247	255
244	252	263	271	241	233	294	282
228	236	279	291	257	249	274	266

Occult Encyclopedia of Magic Squares

	Number	Angel Value (Arabic)	Angel Value (Hebrew)	Jinn Value (Arabic)	Jinn Value (Hebrew)
Usurper	228	187	197	269	259
Guide	295	254	264	336	326
Mystery	523	482	492	204	194
Adjuster	2080	2039	2049	1761	1751
Leader	6240	6199	6209	5921	5911
Regulator	8320	8279	8289	8001	7991
General Governor	16640	16599	16609	16321	16311
High Overseer	4908800	4908759	4908769	4908481	4908471

Fire - Moon

235	248	210	219	272	203	239	255	199
195	238	260	215	231	247	202	224	268
264	207	223	259	191	243	252	214	227
262	194	237	246	217	230	267	201	226
222	266	206	242	258	193	229	251	213
209	234	250	205	218	271	198	241	254
208	221	265	192	244	257	212	228	253
249	211	233	270	204	220	256	197	240
236	261	196	232	245	216	225	269	200

Earth - Moon

199	268	227	226	213	254	253	240	200
255	224	214	201	251	241	228	197	269
239	202	252	267	229	198	212	256	225
203	247	243	230	193	271	257	220	216
272	231	191	217	258	218	244	204	245
219	215	259	246	242	205	192	270	232
210	260	223	237	206	250	265	233	196
248	238	207	194	266	234	221	211	261
235	195	264	262	222	209	208	249	236

Air - Moon

200	269	225	216	245	232	196	261	236
240	197	256	220	204	270	233	211	249
253	228	212	257	244	192	265	221	208
254	241	198	271	218	205	250	234	209
213	251	229	193	258	242	206	266	222
226	201	267	230	217	246	237	194	262
227	214	252	243	191	259	223	207	264
268	224	202	247	231	215	260	238	195
199	255	239	203	272	219	210	248	235

Water - Moon

236	249	208	209	222	262	264	195	235
261	211	221	234	266	194	207	238	248
196	233	265	250	206	237	223	260	210
232	270	192	205	242	246	259	215	219
245	204	244	218	258	217	191	231	272
216	220	257	271	193	230	243	247	203
225	256	212	198	229	267	252	202	239
269	197	228	241	251	201	214	224	255
200	240	253	254	213	226	227	268	199

	Number	Angel Value (Arabic)	Angel Value (Hebrew)	Jinn Value (Arabic)	Jinn Value (Hebrew)
Usurper	191	150	160	232	222
Guide	272	231	241	313	303
Mystery	463	422	432	144	134
Adjuster	2080	2039	2049	1761	1751
Leader	6240	6199	6209	5921	5911
Regulator	8320	8279	8289	8001	7991
General Governor	16640	16599	16609	16321	16311
High Overseer	4526080	4526039	4526049	4525761	4525751

Fire - Saturn

158	176	183	221	212	255	205	197	229	244
169	233	226	217	257	242	160	202	188	186
184	189	213	256	243	228	177	165	206	219
190	215	254	245	178	224	232	173	162	207
203	253	247	182	193	216	220	230	175	161
210	167	168	235	223	199	195	185	240	258
222	204	164	171	237	192	180	241	261	208
236	225	200	159	170	187	238	260	211	194
246	179	191	198	166	174	259	209	227	231
262	239	234	196	201	163	214	218	181	172

Earth - Saturn

262	246	236	222	210	203	190	184	169	158
239	179	225	204	167	253	215	189	233	176
234	191	200	164	168	247	254	213	226	183
196	198	159	171	235	182	245	256	217	221
201	166	170	237	223	193	178	243	257	212
163	174	187	192	199	216	224	228	242	255
214	259	238	180	195	220	232	177	160	205
218	209	260	241	185	230	173	165	202	197
181	227	211	261	240	175	162	206	188	229
172	231	194	208	258	161	207	219	186	244

Air - Saturn

172	181	218	214	163	201	196	234	239	262
231	227	209	259	174	166	198	191	179	246
194	211	260	238	187	170	159	200	225	236
208	261	241	180	192	237	171	164	204	222
258	240	185	195	199	223	235	168	167	210
161	175	230	220	216	193	182	247	253	203
207	162	173	232	224	178	245	254	215	190
219	206	165	177	228	243	256	213	189	184
186	188	202	160	242	257	217	226	233	169
244	229	197	205	255	212	221	183	176	158

Water - Saturn

244	186	219	207	161	258	208	194	231	172
229	188	206	162	175	240	261	211	227	181
197	202	165	173	230	185	241	260	209	218
205	**160**	177	232	220	195	180	238	259	214
255	242	228	224	216	199	192	187	174	163
212	257	243	178	193	223	237	170	166	201
221	217	256	245	182	235	171	159	198	196
183	226	213	254	247	168	164	200	191	234
176	233	189	215	253	167	204	225	179	239
158	169	184	190	203	210	222	236	246	262

	Number	Angel Value (Arabic)	Angel Value (Hebrew)	Jinn Value (Arabic)	Jinn Value (Hebrew)
Usurper	158	117	127	199	189
Guide	262	221	231	303	293
Mystery	420	379	389	101	91
Adjuster	2080	2039	2049	1761	1751
Leader	6240	6199	6209	5921	5911
Regulator	8320	8279	8289	8001	7991
General Governor	16640	16599	16609	16321	16311
High Overseer	4359680	4359639	4359649	4359361	4359351

OLYMPIC SPIRIT: OPHIEL (128)

אל	י	פ	אן
6	81	13	28
12	29	5	82
79	8	30	11

ל	א	י	פ	ו	א
ו	פ	ל	א	י	א
י	א	א	ו	ל	פ
א	ו	פ	י	א	ל
פ	ל	ו	א	א	י
א	י	א	ל	פ	ו

Occult Encyclopedia of Magic Squares

Fire - Jupiter

24	35	29	40
39	30	32	27
34	25	41	28
31	38	26	33

Air - Jupiter

33	26	38	31
28	41	25	34
27	32	30	39
40	29	35	24

Earth - Jupiter

31	34	39	24
38	25	30	35
26	41	32	29
33	28	27	40

Water - Jupiter

40	27	28	33
29	32	41	26
35	30	25	38
24	39	34	31

	Number	Angel Value (Arabic)	Angel Value (Hebrew)	Jinn Value (Arabic)	Jinn Value (Hebrew)
Usurper	24	343	353	65	55
Guide	41	360	10	82	72
Mystery	65	24	34	106	96
Adjuster	1024	983	993	705	695
Leader	3072	3031	3041	2753	2743
Regulator	4096	4055	4065	3777	3767
General Governor	8192	8151	8161	7873	7863
High Overseer	335872	335831	335841	335553	335543

Fire - Mars

13	40	31	25	19
26	20	14	36	32
37	28	27	21	15
22	16	38	29	23
30	24	18	17	39

Air - Mars

30	22	37	26	13
24	16	28	20	40
18	38	27	14	31
17	29	21	36	25
39	23	15	32	19

Earth - Mars

39	17	18	24	30
23	29	38	16	22
15	21	27	28	37
32	36	14	20	26
19	25	31	40	13

Water - Mars

19	32	15	23	39
25	36	21	29	17
31	14	27	38	18
40	20	28	16	24
13	26	37	22	30

Occult Encyclopedia of Magic Squares

	Number	Angel Value (Arabic)	Angel Value (Hebrew)	Jinn Value (Arabic)	Jinn Value (Hebrew)
Usurper	13	332	342	54	44
Guide	40	359	9	81	71
Mystery	53	12	22	94	84
Adjuster	128	87	97	169	159
Leader	384	343	353	65	55
Regulator	512	471	481	193	183
General Governor	1024	983	993	705	695
High Overseer	40960	40919	40929	40641	40631

Fire - Sun

3	14	39	20	24	28
9	19	30	38	7	25
15	42	23	13	29	6
26	5	16	31	10	40
32	21	12	4	41	18
43	27	8	22	17	11

Air - Sun

11	17	22	8	27	43
18	41	4	12	21	32
40	10	31	16	5	26
6	29	13	23	42	15
25	7	38	30	19	9
28	24	20	39	14	3

Earth - Sun

43	32	26	15	9	3
27	21	5	42	19	14
8	12	16	23	30	39
22	4	31	13	38	20
17	41	10	29	7	24
11	18	40	6	25	28

Water - Sun

28	25	6	40	18	11
24	7	29	10	41	17
20	38	13	31	4	22
39	30	23	16	12	8
14	19	42	5	21	27
3	9	15	26	32	43

Occult Encyclopedia of Magic Squares

	Number	Angel Value (Arabic)	Angel Value (Hebrew)	Jinn Value (Arabic)	Jinn Value (Hebrew)
Usurper	3	322	332	44	34
Guide	43	2	12	84	74
Mystery	46	5	15	87	77
Adjuster	128	87	97	169	159
Leader	384	343	353	65	55
Regulator	512	471	481	193	183
General Governor	1024	983	993	705	695
High Overseer	44032	43991	44001	43713	43703

MOON

MOON: LEVANAH (87)

ה	נ	ב	ל
29	3	53	2
52	3	28	4
1	31	4	51

ה	נ	ב	ל
ל	ב	נ	ה
נ	ה	ל	ב
ב	ל	ה	נ

Numerical Squares See Page: 630

ARCHANGEL: GABRIEL (246)

יאל	ד	ב	ג
2	3	203	38
202	39	1	4
1	4	40	201

ל	א	י	ד	ב	ג
ב	ד	ל	ג	י	א
י	ג	א	ב	ל	ד
ג	ב	ד	י	א	ל
ד	ל	ב	א	ג	י
א	י	ג	ל	ר	ב

Numerical Squares See Page: 79

ANGEL: GABRIEL (246)

Hebrew Squares See Page: 750

Numerical Squares See Page: 79

INTELLIGENCE: MALKA BE-TARSHISHIM VE-AD BE-RUAH SHEHAKIM (3321)

שחלים	רוחות	ועד	בתרשישים	מלכא
ועד	בתרשישים	מלכא	שחלים	רוחות
מלכא	שחלים	רוחות	ועד	בתרשישים
רוחות	ועד	בתרשישים	מלכא	שחלים
בתרשישים	מלכא	שחלים	רוחות	ועד

שחלים	ועד רוחות	בתרשישים	מלכא
90	1583	703	945
702	946	89	1584
1581	92	947	701

Occult Encyclopedia of Magic Squares

Fire - Jupiter

822	833	827	839
838	828	830	825
832	823	840	826
829	837	824	831

Air - Jupiter

831	824	837	829
826	840	823	832
825	830	828	838
839	827	833	822

Earth - Jupiter

829	832	838	822
837	823	828	833
824	840	830	827
831	826	825	839

Water - Jupiter

839	825	826	831
827	830	840	824
833	828	823	837
822	838	832	829

	Number	Angel Value (Arabic)	Angel Value (Hebrew)	Jinn Value (Arabic)	Jinn Value (Hebrew)
Usurper	822	781	791	503	493
Guide	840	799	809	521	511
Mystery	1662	1621	1631	1343	1333
Adjuster	26568	26527	26537	26249	26239
Leader	79704	79663	79673	79385	79375
Regulator	106272	106231	106241	105953	105943
General Governor	212544	212503	212513	212225	212215
High Overseer	178536960	178536919	178536929	178536641	178536631

Fire - Mars

652	677	670	664	658
665	659	653	673	671
674	667	666	660	654
661	655	675	668	662
669	663	657	656	676

Air - Mars

669	661	674	665	652
663	655	667	659	677
657	675	666	653	670
656	668	660	673	664
676	662	654	671	658

Earth - Mars

676	656	657	663	669
662	668	675	655	661
654	660	666	667	674
671	673	653	659	665
658	664	670	677	652

Water - Mars

658	671	654	662	676
664	673	660	668	656
670	653	666	675	657
677	659	667	655	663
652	665	674	661	669

Occult Encyclopedia of Magic Squares

	Number	Angel Value (Arabic)	Angel Value (Hebrew)	Jinn Value (Arabic)	Jinn Value (Hebrew)
Usurper	652	611	621	333	323
Guide	677	636	646	358	348
Mystery	1329	1288	1298	1010	1000
Adjuster	3321	3280	3290	3002	2992
Leader	9963	9922	9932	9644	9634
Regulator	13284	13243	13253	12965	12955
General Governor	26568	26527	26537	26249	26239
High Overseer	17986536	17986495	17986505	17986217	17986207

Fire - Sun

536	547	567	553	557	561
542	552	563	566	540	558
548	570	556	546	562	539
559	538	549	564	543	568
565	554	545	537	569	551
571	560	541	555	550	544

Air - Sun

544	550	555	541	560	571
551	569	537	545	554	565
568	543	564	549	538	559
539	562	546	556	570	548
558	540	566	563	552	542
561	557	553	567	547	536

Earth - Sun

571	565	559	548	542	536
560	554	538	570	552	547
541	545	549	556	563	567
555	537	564	546	566	553
550	569	543	562	540	557
544	551	568	539	558	561

Water - Sun

561	558	539	568	551	544
557	540	562	543	569	550
553	566	546	564	537	555
567	563	556	549	545	541
547	552	570	538	554	560
536	542	548	559	565	571

	Number	Angel Value (Arabic)	Angel Value (Hebrew)	Jinn Value (Arabic)	Jinn Value (Hebrew)
Usurper	536	495	505	217	207
Guide	571	530	540	252	242
Mystery	1107	1066	1076	788	778
Adjuster	3321	3280	3290	3002	2992
Leader	9963	9922	9932	9644	9634
Regulator	13284	13243	13253	12965	12955
General Governor	26568	26527	26537	26249	26239
High Overseer	15170328	15170287	15170297	15170009	15169999

Fire - Venus

450	491	476	461	481	497	465
498	466	451	485	477	462	482
463	483	499	467	452	486	471
487	472	457	484	500	468	453
469	454	488	473	458	478	501
479	495	470	455	489	474	459
475	460	480	496	464	456	490

Earth - Venus

475	479	469	487	463	498	450
460	495	454	472	483	466	491
480	470	488	457	499	451	476
496	455	473	484	467	485	461
464	489	458	500	452	477	481
456	474	478	468	486	462	497
490	459	501	453	471	482	465

Air - Venus

490	456	464	496	480	460	475
459	474	489	455	470	495	479
501	478	458	473	488	454	469
453	468	500	484	457	472	487
471	486	452	467	499	483	463
482	462	477	485	451	466	498
465	497	481	461	476	491	450

Water - Venus

465	482	471	453	501	459	490
497	462	486	468	478	474	456
481	477	452	500	458	489	464
461	485	467	484	473	455	496
476	451	499	457	488	470	480
491	466	483	472	454	495	460
450	498	463	487	469	479	475

	Number	Angel Value (Arabic)	Angel Value (Hebrew)	Jinn Value (Arabic)	Jinn Value (Hebrew)
Usurper	450	409	419	131	121
Guide	501	460	470	182	172
Mystery	951	910	920	632	622
Adjuster	3321	3280	3290	3002	2992
Leader	9963	9922	9932	9644	9634
Regulator	13284	13243	13253	12965	12955
General Governor	26568	26527	26537	26249	26239
High Overseer	13310568	13310527	13310537	13310249	13310239

Fire - Mercury

383	399	449	428	417	433	414	398
391	407	436	420	425	446	406	390
434	418	397	413	400	384	427	448
447	426	389	405	408	392	419	435
412	396	415	431	451	430	385	401
404	388	423	444	438	422	393	409
429	450	402	386	395	411	432	416
421	437	410	394	387	403	445	424

Occult Encyclopedia of Magic Squares

Earth - Mercury

421	429	404	412	447	434	391	383
437	450	388	396	426	418	407	399
410	402	423	415	389	397	436	449
394	386	444	431	405	413	420	428
387	395	438	451	408	400	425	417
403	411	422	430	392	384	446	433
445	432	393	385	419	427	406	414
424	416	409	401	435	448	390	398

Air - Mercury

424	445	403	387	394	410	437	421
416	432	411	395	386	402	450	429
409	393	422	438	444	423	388	404
401	385	430	451	431	415	396	412
435	419	392	408	405	389	426	447
448	427	384	400	413	397	418	434
390	406	446	425	420	436	407	391
398	414	433	417	428	449	399	383

Water - Mercury

398	390	448	435	401	409	416	424
414	406	427	419	385	393	432	445
433	446	384	392	430	422	411	403
417	425	400	408	451	438	395	387
428	420	413	405	431	444	386	394
449	436	397	389	415	423	402	410
399	407	418	426	396	388	450	437
383	391	434	447	412	404	429	421

Occult Encyclopedia of Magic Squares

	Number	Angel Value (Arabic)	Angel Value (Hebrew)	Jinn Value (Arabic)	Jinn Value (Hebrew)
Usurper	383	342	352	64	54
Guide	451	410	420	132	122
Mystery	834	793	803	515	505
Adjuster	3321	3280	3290	3002	2992
Leader	9963	9922	9932	9644	9634
Regulator	13284	13243	13253	12965	12955
General Governor	26568	26527	26537	26249	26239
High Overseer	11982168	11982127	11982137	11981849	11981839

Fire - Moon

373	386	348	357	409	341	377	393	337
333	376	398	353	369	385	340	362	405
401	345	361	397	329	381	390	352	365
400	332	375	384	355	368	404	339	364
360	403	344	380	396	331	367	389	351
347	372	388	343	356	408	336	379	392
346	359	402	330	382	395	350	366	391
387	349	371	407	342	358	394	335	378
374	399	334	370	383	354	363	406	338

Earth - Moon

337	405	365	364	351	392	391	378	338
393	362	352	339	389	379	366	335	406
377	340	390	404	367	336	350	394	363
341	385	381	368	331	408	395	358	354
409	369	329	355	396	356	382	342	383
357	353	397	384	380	343	330	407	370
348	398	361	375	344	388	402	371	334
386	376	345	332	403	372	359	349	399
373	333	401	400	360	347	346	387	374

Occult Encyclopedia of Magic Squares

Air - Moon

338	406	363	354	383	370	334	399	374
378	335	394	358	342	407	371	349	387
391	366	350	395	382	330	402	359	346
392	379	336	408	356	343	388	372	347
351	389	367	331	396	380	344	403	360
364	339	404	368	355	384	375	332	400
365	352	390	381	329	397	361	345	401
405	362	340	385	369	353	398	376	333
337	393	377	341	409	357	348	386	373

Water - Moon

374	387	346	347	360	400	401	333	373
399	349	359	372	403	332	345	376	386
334	371	402	388	344	375	361	398	348
370	407	330	343	380	384	397	353	357
383	342	382	356	396	355	329	369	409
354	358	395	408	331	368	381	385	341
363	394	350	336	367	404	390	340	377
406	335	366	379	389	339	352	362	393
338	378	391	392	351	364	365	405	337

	Number	Angel Value (Arabic)	Angel Value (Hebrew)	Jinn Value (Arabic)	Jinn Value (Hebrew)
Usurper	329	288	298	10	360
Guide	409	368	378	90	80
Mystery	738	697	707	419	409
Adjuster	3321	3280	3290	3002	2992
Leader	9963	9922	9932	9644	9634
Regulator	13284	13243	13253	12965	12955
General Governor	26568	26527	26537	26249	26239
High Overseer	10866312	10866271	10866281	10865993	10865983

Fire - Saturn

282	300	307	345	336	380	329	321	353	368
293	357	350	341	382	366	284	326	312	310
308	313	337	381	367	352	301	289	330	343
314	339	379	369	302	348	356	297	286	331
327	378	371	306	317	340	344	354	299	285
334	291	292	359	347	323	319	309	364	383
346	328	288	295	361	316	304	365	386	332
360	349	324	283	294	311	362	385	335	318
370	303	315	322	290	298	384	333	351	355
387	363	358	320	325	287	338	342	305	296

Earth - Saturn

387	370	360	346	334	327	314	308	293	282
363	303	349	328	291	378	339	313	357	300
358	315	324	288	292	371	379	337	350	307
320	322	283	295	359	306	369	381	341	345
325	290	294	361	347	317	302	367	382	336
287	298	311	316	323	340	348	352	366	380
338	384	362	304	319	344	356	301	284	329
342	333	385	365	309	354	297	289	326	321
305	351	335	386	364	299	286	330	312	353
296	355	318	332	383	285	331	343	310	368

Air - Saturn

296	305	342	338	287	325	320	358	363	387
355	351	333	384	298	290	322	315	303	370
318	335	385	362	311	294	283	324	349	360
332	386	365	304	316	361	295	288	328	346
383	364	309	319	323	347	359	292	291	334
285	299	354	344	340	317	306	371	378	327
331	286	297	356	348	302	369	379	339	314
343	330	289	301	352	367	381	337	313	308
310	312	326	284	366	382	341	350	357	293
368	353	321	329	380	336	345	307	300	282

	Number	Angel Value (Arabic)	Angel Value (Hebrew)	Jinn Value (Arabic)	Jinn Value (Hebrew)
Usurper	282	241	251	323	313
Guide	387	346	356	68	58
Mystery	669	628	638	350	340
Adjuster	3321	3280	3290	3002	2992
Leader	9963	9922	9932	9644	9634
Regulator	13284	13243	13253	12965	12955
General Governor	26568	26527	26537	26249	26239
High Overseer	10281816	10281775	10281785	10281497	10281487

SPIRIT: CHASHMODAI (369)

י	דא	מו	חש
307	47	8	7
7	8	306	48
45	309	9	6

י	א	ד	ו	מ	ש	ח
ד	ו	מ	ש	ח	י	א
מ	ש	ח	י	א	ד	ו
ח	י	א	ד	ו	מ	ש
א	ד	ו	מ	ש	ח	י
ו	מ	ש	ח	י	א	ד
ש	ח	י	א	ד	ו	מ

Numerical Squares See Page: 169

OLYMPIC SPIRIT: PHUL (116)

Hebrew Squares Not Available

Numerical Squares See Page: 310